INDUSTRIAL IRELAND
1750-1930

AN ARCHAEOLOGY

For Stella
and in memory of my parents
Patrick Rynne (1930-1995) and Margaret Rynne, née Caldwell, (1930-1989)

INDUSTRIAL IRELAND
~ 1750 - 1930 ~
AN ARCHAEOLOGY

COLIN RYNNE

The Collins Press

PUBLISHED IN 2006 BY THE COLLINS PRESS

West Link Park
Doughcloyne
Wilton
Cork

British Library Cataloguing in Publication Data

Rynne, Colin
Industrial Ireland 1750-1930: an archaeology
    1. Industrial buildings - Ireland - History - 18th century
    2. Industrial buildings - Ireland - History - 19th century
    3. Industrial buildings - Ireland - History - 20th century
    4. Industrial archaeology - Ireland
    5. Ireland - Antiquities
    I. Title
    609.4'15'09034

ISBN-10: 1905172044
ISBN-13: 978-1905172047

Book design and typesetting: Anú Design, Tara
Font: Bembo 11.5 point
Printed in Malta

This publication has received support from the Heritage Council under the 2006 Publications Grant Scheme.
This publication has received support from The Department of the Environment, Heritage and Local Government.
This publication has received support from the Faculty of Arts, University College Cork, Publication Fund.

Contents

Preface and Acknowledgements

In Ireland upwards on 100,000 sites of industrial archaeological interest survive, varying in size from small rural lime kilns (probably the most common) to Ballincollig Gunpowder Mills, County Cork which, at 435 acres, is the largest industrial archaeological site in Ireland and the second largest of its type ever to have been constructed in Europe. Many of these sites are commonly found within incredibly rich and varied landscapes which, up to the advent of the 'Celtic tiger' economy, had survived without almost any human interference. This extremely fortunate state of affairs is, for the most part, a consequence of the general lack of industrial development in Ireland. However, while this has enabled a large number of important sites in Ireland to survive – even within the environs of the major towns and cities – these have remained hidden from view: there has long been a need for a general introduction to the industrial archaeology of Ireland.

The present survey is primarily intended for the general reader, but the content is also designed to cover the basic ground for a number of undergraduate courses which I have taught, since 2001, in the Department of Archaeology at University College Cork. As the archaeology of so many of Ireland's historic industries has been poorly documented, I have opted for a thematic, introductory, industry by industry approach. Each industry is dealt with in outline (processes, technology, markets, key surviving sites and so forth), and in this way the reader is introduced to the basic concepts underlying their context and chronology. I am also aware that a considerable amount of the primary and secondary source material for Irish industrial archaeology would be unfamiliar to potential readers of this book. From the outset, therefore, it was my clear intention that this account should be properly referenced and to this end I have endeavoured to provide an extensive and up-to-date bibliography of Irish industrial archaeology.

This book is divided into seventeen chapters, the first three of which examine industrial motive power, namely animal, wind, water and steam power and the early development of internal combustion engines, along with fossil fuels (coal and turf) in Ireland. Chapters 4-6 deal with the main extractive industries: iron and steel and building materials, such as stone, brick, lime and cement, and ceramics and glass. The archaeology of Ireland's principal manufacturing industries – textiles, food-processing, engineering, chemicals, along with miscellaneous industries such as tanning and papermaking – are evaluated in five chapters (7-11). The elements of Ireland's unique transport infrastructure – roads, bridges, canals, railways and ports and harbours – are described in Chapters 12-15. The final section chapters (16 and 17), deal with the main utility industries – water, gas and electricity – and the origins of Ireland's urban transport networks and telecommunications.

Many kind, accommodating and hospitable people have made the task of writing this book a light burden. May I begin – and I gladly break with tradition here – by thanking my wife, Stella Cherry, for her encouragement and support over the years: I am not exactly sure why partners are thanked last in book acknowledgements, especially when one considers that their help and guidance is the most important of all. A handful of friends and colleagues have, over the years, tirelessly responded to queries, provided vital information and insights on individual sites, and important illustrations for this book. Of these, I would particularly like to thank some remarkable individuals – Dr Fred Hamond, Flor Hurley, Paul Duffy, Dr Ron Cox and Mary Sleeman – whose help over the years has been invaluable. A number of specialist scholars in the field of industrial archaeology, Ruth Delany, Ewan Duffy, Dr David Gwyn, Dr John Morris and Dr Mike Nevell, all kindly agreed to read chapters of this book and their intervention, attention to detail and useful comments are warmly and gratefully acknowledged. Dr Neil Buttimer also read the entire book in manuscript and suggested many important changes. Any errors factual or otherwise are, however, my entire responsibility.

My thanks to my friends and colleagues in the Industrial Heritage Association of Ireland, Norman Campion, Billy Dunlop, Michael Lynch, Paul and Mary McMahon, Barry O'Reilly and Ken Pullin whose expert knowledge has enriched my own, and who provided excellent company on many of the Association's field trips. I am also indebted to a large number of others, both individuals and institutions, who have also provided information, illustrations and access to sites over the years: Billy and Judy Wigham, William Dick, Robert Guinness and Mike Hargreaves (Straffan Steam Museum), Dr Austin O'Sullivan, Dr Michael Conry, Paul Maguire (Party furnace), Dr Colman O'Mahony, Elena O'Brien, Ken Mawhinney, Brendan Kelleher, Chris Southgate, Richard and Mary Irwin, Anne Marie Lennon, Billy Williams, Dr Andy Bielenberg, Dr David Edwards and Ken Nicholls (Department of History, University College Cork), John Irwin (Department of Civil Engineering, University College Cork), Michael O'Brien (Cork City Council), Peter Foynes (Cork Butter Museum), Kieran Burke and John Mullins (Cork City Library), the staff of the Library, University College Cork, Amy and Chris Ramsden (Day Collection of photographs), the Society of Antiquaries of Ireland, the National Library of Ireland, the Ulster Museum, Birmingham City Libraries, Stella Cherry, Dan Breen and Douglas Walsh (Cork Public Museum), the late Jim Hurley, Mick and Judith Monk, Kieran McCarthy and Patsy Foley, the late Walter McGrath, Barry Kelleher (Barry Kelleher and Associates), Mike

Saville (Cork County Council), David Jones, Martin Watts, Dr David Dickson (Department of History, Trinity College, Dublin), Barry and Niamh Rynne, Josephine Gilsenan and Mrs Mary Owens.

Finally my sincere thanks to Karen Carty, of Anú Design. My thanks, also, to the Heritage Council, The Department of the Environment, Heritage and Local Government, and the Faculty of Arts University College Cork, for making generous subventions towards the cost of publishing this book.

COLIN RYNNE

April 2006

Introduction

Some persons despair of this country, because we have not coal or iron … I say that although we want coal in Ireland, and though it is not as accessible as in other countries, there is no reason why we should not have manufactures … We have cheap labour, we have an intelligent people, and, above all, gentlemen, you have amongst you the very thing which has enabled us to meet here today – you have capital.

(Address by John Francis Maguire
at launch of Cork and Macroom Railway, 24 May 1866)

(1) Industrial Ireland 1750-1930

In many ways an archetypal Irish economic nationalist, John Francis Maguire (1815-72), generally appears to have experienced difficulty in sounding a sombre note about the prospects for the native Irish economy. Maguire was the founder of the *Cork Examiner* newspaper and a prime mover in the creation of the Cork Gas Consumers' Company (which had successfully wrested control of the city gas supply in 1857, thus ending a monopoly exercised by the United General Gas Company of London) and of the Cork Spinning and Weaving Company (which had built the first modern flax spinning in Munster, in 1866). Of course, the sentiments articulated by him were shared by many, but while he at least could point to a good track record, others could not. Outside Ulster, indeed, similar sentiments, though passionately held, were seldom physically expressed. Sir Robert Kane had earlier extolled the advantages of Ireland in 1844, in his *Industrial Resources of Ireland* which remains, perhaps, the most optimistic (and most incorrect) assessment of the island's notional industrial strengths.

Contrary to the hopes and aspirations of many, and despite its immediate proximity to the cradle of European industrialisation, most of Ireland never became industrialised in either an English or a European sense. Consequently, in English industrial archaeology explanation begins with why industrialisation took place: in Ireland the issue is why it did not and, more to the point, who was to blame. 'Failure' is the key word in the economic history of Ireland, but while its resonances have been all-pervasive they have all too often hidden the successes.

The progress of truly large-scale industrialisation in Ireland in the nineteenth century exhibits a pronounced regional bias, with British levels of industrialisation being experienced mostly in the Ulster counties and towns of Armagh, Antrim, Down, Derry, Tyrone, Belfast, Carrickfergus and Belfast, and only rarely in towns such as Drogheda.[1] The province, in general, faced the same resource constraints as the rest of the island, yet it proved more adept at developing successful forms of regional specialisation within the economy of the United Kingdom. The growing of flax was well suited to this region of generally poor soils, but with a mild climate and small-scale cropping patterns. The low profitability of Ulster farms compelled local landlords to find other means of increasing their incomes, and to this end new tenants, with weaving skills, began to receive more favourable treatment. In the late seventeenth century, fine linens remained the only important good that an increasingly self-sufficient British economy still had to import. The tariffs on continental linens were consequently increased, while import duties on Irish and Scottish linens exported to Britain were removed in 1696.[2] A new merchant class emerged to co-ordinate the finishing and distribution of the cloth, and by this means goods produced in what was essentially a cottage industry found national and international markets. By the 1780s, up to one-fifth of the adult male population in Ulster was involved in linen weaving. In the early decades of the eighteenth century, important new techniques, which included the wash mill and beetling mill (see Chapter 8) had already been developed for the improvement of essential cloth finishing methods, some of which were already being adopted in Scotland in the 1730s.[3] The evolution of the Ulster linen industry, therefore, exhibits all the principal characteristics of proto-industrialisation and was eventually transformed into a factory-based industry. Linen manufacturers imitated the *modus operandi* of the Belfast cotton mills and, after the latter's decline, became the main textile industry in eastern Ulster during the 1820s and thereafter the largest of its type in the world.

In the rest of Ireland attempts at regional specialisation were less successful – often spectacularly so – and industrial development remained well below the European norm. In the period 1730-1775, the rapid development of the British Atlantic economy brought with it an increased demand for Irish agricultural produce, and the Irish economy, working to its strengths, adjusted to accommodate it. This specialisation brought about a general change from tillage to pasture and the provision trade began to enjoy considerable success in the ports of Dublin, Cork and Waterford.[4] From the 1760s onwards, Ireland was already developing some of the largest food-processing industries in Britain, but by 1800 foreign markets for Irish provisions had already begun to decline. Furthermore, as events were to prove, even the establishment of large industrial units within the immediate environs of the main ports generated too few spin-off effects to provide a firm base for future industrial development. At the end of the eighteenth century it was becoming clear that there was an over reliance on the provision trade, and more so in the aftermath of the Napoleonic Wars when the lucrative government con-tracts ended. The contraction of demand for Irish agricultural goods in the post-1815 era brought with it a depression, famine and insurrection in the Munster countryside. But the Irish economy never properly adjust-ed to the challenges and changing conditions it was to face in the nineteenth century.

The closing years of the eighteenth century saw Ireland's industrial development already beginning to fall behind that of England. With the notable exception of linen, brewing, distilling and shipbuilding, it was effectively in decline in the first half of the nineteenth century. In 1841, 28 per cent of Ireland's workforce was employed in manufacturing, while some 47 per cent worked in agriculture: in Britain the corresponding percentages were 41 and 22. Only in the eastern Ulster counties were these figures reversed.[5] The onset and aftermath of the Great Famine, during which one million Irish people are believed to have died, dealt the severest blow to any hopes there might have been for an industrial recovery. Emigration from Ireland after 1815 had been high by European standards, but between 1850 and 1914 upwards of four million people had left the island, a decline that continued in rural areas as recently as the 1990s.[6] In 2004 the population of Ireland reached four million: the highest figure since 1871.

(2) The Early Development of Industrial Archaeology

The historic process of industrialisation, as understood in most European countries, cannot be comfortably applied to Irish social and economic conditions. As in most of the UK, the archaeology of the period tradi-tionally described as the 'industrial revolution' has generally only been explored through the medium of indus-trial archaeology. More recent evaluations of the usefulness of this discipline, in view of its general tendency towards site-specific analysis and to ignore the non-industrial material culture of the period, have concluded that it has been more of a 'thematic' than a 'period' archaeology. However, more recent initiatives such as the Manchester methodology have sought to remedy this by more effectively drawing attention to the hundreds of other building forms and landscape features created during this period.

The first use of the term 'industrial archaeology', as it would commonly be understood today, was by Michael Rix in 1955.[7] As late as the early 1990s, its primary focus in both Britain and Ireland continued to centre on the physical remains of industrial processes, with little or no emphasis on the society that created them. This was in stark contrast to the American tradition of *historical archaeology* which, firmly rooted in anthropology, had long since moved beyond traditional archaeological concerns such as the collection of data and its classification. Archaeologists working within historical archaeology commonly employed concepts such as ethnicity, gender and kinship to create a more inclusive archaeology, in which marginalised or under-represented social groups could now legitimately form part of archaeological study.[8] Hitherto, archaeologists of the *processual* school had believed that they had 'objectively' recorded and interpreted the past, about which they attempted to formu-late general statements on human behavior. But by the 1980s, this approach had increasingly come under attack by what became known as *post-processual* archaeology, which began to criticise the processualists' lack of an anthropological perspective along with their failure to appreciate the active role of individuals in the creation of material culture. Post-processualists also placed a greater emphasis on meaning, disadvantaged social groups and on attempting to ascertain the 'lived experience of everyday life' in the past. At the same time archaeological theory became more politically explicit. This is tacitly accepted (although why is by no means satisfactorily explained) in modern archaeological thought, even though only a very narrow range of left-wing ideologies have thus far been generally employed. Indeed, the dominance of certain points of view in post-processual archaeology can occasionally leave one with the feeling that the expression 'theoretically informed' (when applied to archaeological interpretation) effectively means 'neo-Marxist' or 'feminist', or both.

Ideological considerations aside, post-processual archaeological thought has contributed immeasurably to the development of modern theoretical and methodological agendas in industrial archaeology. Palmer and Neaverson's *Industrial archaeology: principles and practice* (1998) provided an essential break with industrial archaeology's traditional core interests or 'my favourite steam engine' origins. Marilyn Palmer had earlier argued that industrial archaeology was 'a period study embracing the tangible evidence of social, economic and technological development in the period since industrialisation'.[9] More recent commentators, however, have challenged the idea that industrial archaeology is a period discipline within archaeology. Richard Newman has argued that it is 'a thematically based method of archaeological enquiry dealing with industrialisation, its remains and associated features'.[10] Of course, there is more to the material culture of industrialisation than simply industry and its 'associated features' and this is where the credentials of industrial archaeology as a period discipline had been suspect. It had, as Newman and others have pointed out, functioned as a thematic discipline, dealing only with the material culture and remains of industry: thus far its attempts to become a period discipline had been aspirational.

However, as we shall now see, the study of the archaeology of industrialisation has since moved on, beginning with Palmer and Neaverson's influential book, which has provided a modern, theoretical and methodological framework for the understanding of the archaeology of British industrialisation, both in terms of its impact on the landscape and the society from which it sprang.

Modern archaeology, then, seeks to understand its subject matter, material culture, in terms of the societies that created it. In the mid-1990s, John Walker and Michael Nevell of the University of Manchester Archaeological Unit, developed what has become known as the *Manchester methodology*, in an attempt to understand how an agrarian community at Tameside in Greater Manchester, became transformed into an industrial society. Walker and Nevell's approach to the study of industrial landscapes laid particular emphasis on material remains, but at the same time identified new, non-industrial monument types which made an appearance in this period. This was an industrial landscape in which all monuments of the period – everything from courthouses to shops – now formed part of archaeological study, but crucially, the Manchester methodology now sought to relate all these to the existing social structure.[11] The Manchester methodology could thus claim to offer a uniquely archaeological perspective on industrialisation. It has subsequently been applied to the Vale of Ffestiniog in north-west Wales and in Ireland, in a study of the Grand Canal towns of County Offaly.[12] And, while the Manchester methodology has thus far been applied to social and economic conditions that, in Ireland, only historically existed in the Ulster counties, its basic approach still proved invaluable in outlining a social archaeology for the Irish midlands.[13]

In Ireland, however, as opposed to most of western Europe, the archaeological study of industrial landscapes (principally because of unique economic conditions) has been concerned more with sporadic industrial activity than with long-term industrialisation. Indeed, this latter phenomenon was largely confined to the area around the Lagan Valley: and herein lies a problem with more contemporary views on the definitional parameters of industrial archaeology. In Ireland, industry was not the dominant economic activity well into the twentieth century. In real terms, Belfast was the only Victorian industrial city, the economic fabric of both Dublin and Cork being essentially commercial rather than industrial. Small pockets of dispersed industrial activity became established near the ports and larger towns such as Dundalk, with varying degrees of success, but overall this patchwork of industry can in no way be characterised as large-scale industrialisation. In Ireland, therefore, there was industrial scale production but little industrialisation, and thus Irish conditions poorly fit definitions that specify 'industrialisation' as a study parameter.

The problem thus arises of where should we locate industrial archaeology in general, and Irish industrial archaeology in particular. David Cranstone proposes that '"Industrial archaeology" remains torn between a period identity, and an identity as a study of industry regardless of period'. According to Cranstone, therefore, industrial archaeology's attempts to embrace 'period' status have clearly failed. He also argues that it sits more comfortably within the redefined parameters of 'historical archaeology' and that it can and should be re-integrated into post-medieval archaeological studies in general.[14] Perhaps it is premature to designate industrial archaeology as a subfield of historical archaeology, or even as a distinct chronological period within post-medieval archaeology. Moreover, its basic methodology and theoretical imperatives, as with historical archaeology in general, will tend to be fragmented and it is difficult to dissent from the view that there will never be a unified global perspective on any aspect of historical archaeology.[15] Yet it is, nonetheless, as Cranstone has pointed out, concerned with the study of large-scale industrial production (as opposed to industrialisation) and this, in its broadest sense, can be used to define the material remains of Ireland's historic industries.[16]

On the face of it, this is a difficult if not intractable problem. Post-medieval and industrial archaeology may only be beginning to develop in Ireland, but the problem also involves a lack of integration with that of similar studies in the UK, particularly for the archaeology of industrialisation. The attitude of UK professionals to such developments in a region that, up to just over 80 years ago formed an important part of their national territory, has not helped matters. During the period of British industrialisation Ireland was, of course, part of the United Kingdom, and well before the passing of the Act of Union her economy had already become closely integrated with that of Britain. In the seventeenth century, Ireland and her principal ports became the cornerstone of the English transatlantic provision trade. Furthermore, in the same period, Ireland's agricultural economy had become highly commercialised and increasingly geared to export. Not only was Ireland an important supplier of agricultural produce to Britain but also to many of her important colonies and, in particular, the West Indian plantations. Very much in the shadow of its neighbour, and with extremely limited mineral resources, Ireland

5

worked to her strengths. The island's mild and temperate marine climate was ideal for most forms of arable farming and, in particular, dairy farming. The burgeoning industrialisation of Britain became the main market both for Ireland's agricultural produce and agricultural processing industries. Industrialisation in Britain, therefore, had an important Irish dimension, which also included a two-way transfer of technology, a theme scarcely explored in British post-medieval archaeology. A fuller exploration of the physical boundaries of British industry requires immediate consideration by practitioners on both sides of the Irish Sea. Ireland's linen, shipbuilding, brewing and distilling industries were important sectors of 'British' industry up to 1922. Thereafter, they did not historically cease to be so. The limits of British industrialisation did not magically shrink within the geopolitical boundaries created by the Government of Ireland Act of 1922: British industrial archaeologists can no longer conveniently ignore developments in Ireland.[17] Even Northern Ireland, indeed, hardly features at all in any of the more recent general surveys of 'British' industrial archaeology, home to its largest shipyards and the world's largest linen industry.

(ii) The Development of Industrial Archaeology in Ireland[18]

In the late 1950s and early 1960s some of the earliest government-financed industrial archaeological surveys in the world were to be undertaken in County Down by the late Professor Rodney Green. Under the auspices of the Ancient Monuments Council of Northern Ireland, Green surveyed textile-processing sites of the linen industry, along with complexes associated with food-processing industries (brewing, distilling, grain milling and so forth) and aspects of the transport and communications of the area. The publication of the results of County Down survey in 1963 was the first of its type for any region of the UK or the Republic of Ireland.[19] Elsewhere in the UK, only in Scotland, where nineteenth-century industrial buildings began to feature in the Royal Commission of Ancient and Historic Monuments county inventories, compiled in the 1950s, had any comparable effort been made to focus attention on aspects of industrial heritage. Indeed, the Industrial Monuments Survey in England was only established by the Council for British Archaeology and the English Ministry of Public Buildings and Works in 1963, the year Rodney Green's survey appeared. Unfortunately, even the most recent account of the origins of the industrial archaeological survey has failed to recognise the truly pioneering work carried out by Green and, later, by McCutcheon in Ulster.[20]

In 1962 the Ancient Monuments Council appointed Dr Alan McCutcheon to carry out a more detailed survey of the industrial archaeology of the province. McCutcheon embarked upon a systematic industrial archaeological study of the six counties funded by the Northern Ireland Department of Finance, and the results of his fieldwork, undertaken between 1962 and 1968, complemented by an extensive documentary survey, were published as *The Industrial Archaeology of Northern Ireland* (1980). Although this was the first comprehensive, large-scale survey of its type in either Britain or Ireland, McCutcheon's published account is a somewhat erratic compilation, in that it covers only road infrastructure, canals and river navigations, railways, industrial energy, the linen industry and coalfields. A casual glance by the reader at the contents page of the present book will give a very good idea of what should have been included. The rest of the industrial archaeology of the province, indeed, is covered, very unsatisfactorily, in a series of black and white photographs at the very end of the book. McCutcheon's record of the industrial archaeology of Northern Ireland was, nonetheless, also a timely one. During the 1960s, when his work was underway, many of the North's traditional industries were closing down, whilst key linen mills in the Falls and Crumlin Road areas of Belfast were to be later destroyed during the 'troubles'. Documentary sources also played a critical role in the description and analysis of the industrial sites featured in his inventory, and McCutcheon must be credited as the first fieldworker to demonstrate their effectiveness in a large-scale survey.[21] In 1982 a research fellowship funded by the Historic Monuments and Buildings Branch (HMBB) of the Department of the Environment, Northern Ireland (DOENI), enabled Cormac Scally to transform the McCutcheon archive – more than 20,000 photographs, slides and glass-plate negatives, business records and architectural and engineering drawings – into an Industrial Archaeological Record (IAR) for the province.[22] McCutcheon had begun, but was unable to complete, a photographic survey of Belfast, and since the late 1960s when he had finished his fieldwork, a potentially difficult situation had arisen in which the city of Belfast and its environs had not been surveyed. Clearly such an inventory was required for planning purposes, and the HMBB, later the Environment and Heritage: Built Heritage (EHS:BH) agency of the DOENI, commissioned Dr Fred Hamond and Cormac Scally to produce an industrial archaeological record of the Greater Belfast region. Some 1,160 sites, dating from 1830 to 1930, were identified in a 180 sq km area during the course of fieldwork for the Greater Belfast Industrial Archaeology Survey (GBIAS), completed in 1988, and this has since been integrated into the province's IAR, now called the Industrial Heritage Record (IHR).[23] During the 1980s further extensive survey work has been carried out by EHS:BH throughout the province. These include a detailed study of Rathlin Island, off the north coast of Ulster, along with a series of thematic surveys of sites such as gasworks and canals. Other activities included a re-survey of around 500 or so sites which were singled out by McCutcheon, in his original fieldwork, as being among the most important in the six counties. In 1991 the Natural Heritage agency of the EHS also commissioned Hamond to undertake an industrial archeological survey within the Areas of Outstanding Natural Beauty (AONBs) in northern and eastern County Antrim.[24]

Inevitably, perhaps, given the AD 1700 cut-off date for the inclusion of archaeological sites deemed worthy of study and preservation in the early *National Monuments Acts*, the specific study of industrial monuments in the Republic of Ireland did not really get underway until the late 1960s and early 1970s. In reality, though, it was already flourishing, albeit under other names. The Irish Railway Record Society (IRRS), established in 1946, with active branches in the larger Irish cities and in London, has long been involved in the conservation and preservation of Ireland's railway heritage, and the establishment of an all-Ireland Steam Preservation Society has resulted in a series of ambitious restoration schemes. An abiding enthusiasm for Irish canals, coupled with a realisation of their enormous potential for amenity use and tourism, led to the establishment of the Inland Waterways Association of Ireland (IWAI), co-founded by Colonel Harry Rice and Vincent Delany in 1954.[25] The IWAI has been actively involved in canal conservation projects and scored a notable success in its campaign to save the Dublin section of the Royal Canal. The 1990s witnessed further important developments such as the re-generation of the Ballinamore and Ballyconnell Canal (now restored as the Shannon-Erne Waterway) and the creation of a cross border body called Waterways Ireland, in 2000 (see Chapter 13).

Unfortunately, the enthusiasm shown for railways and inland waterways in Ireland was slow to spread to other areas. In the early 1970s the Irish Society for Industrial Archaeology was established whose members (notably William Dick, Gavan Bowie and Ken Mawhinney) published a wide variety of short pieces on the more notable Irish sites in the magazine *Technology Ireland* (1969-) The latter were aimed at a general readership, and their expert insight, when wedded to an attractive magazine design, did much to focus attention on the country's industrial heritage. Yet by the end of the 1970s this society was defunct. A new organisation, the Society for Industrial Archaeology in Munster – a predominantly Cork-based body – was established in 1986. The latter also sprang from promising origins but eventually met with the same fate. However, in June 1996 a new society, the Industrial Heritage Association of Ireland (IHAI), with a 32 county membership concerned with the preservation and recording of the industrial heritage of Ireland, was established. Since its foundation the membership of this society has been actively involved in survey work, conservation and in influencing government policy on matters of relevance. Its most successful project to date, in conjunction with Fingal County Council, has been the restoration of the former Shackleton's Anna Liffey Mill near Lucan, County Dublin.

Successive governments in the Irish Republic have been slow to realise that industrial archaeology forms an important part of Ireland's historic landscape, a fact all too clearly illustrated by the exclusion of such sites from previous National Monuments legislation. Under the earlier acts archaeology officially ended in the year 1700, but under the 1987 Amendment to the *National Monuments Acts* the Office of Public Works (later Dúchas, the state heritage service) became empowered to use its discretion where post-1700 sites of national importance were involved. Under this new provision the proprietors of industrial archaeological sites deemed to be important now required planning permission in order either to alter or demolish such sites. In 1994 a further amendment to the *National Monuments Acts* enabled industrial archaeological sites to be added to the national record of monuments, and thus be afforded a measure of statutory protection.

On the face of it, the 1994 amendment would appear to have come a little too late. Fortunately the former inadequacies of the *National Monuments* legislation were in no small part countered by local government measures which, since the early 1960s, had been working in favour of Ireland's important historic industrial monuments. Under the 1963 *Local Government (Planning and Development) Act* local authorities in Ireland were required to draft development plans. Furthermore, any buildings which were deemed to be of artistic, architectural or historic interest by an authority could feature on a list of sites to be included in a development plan which were considered to be worthy of preservation. By 'listing' a building in this way, a local authority had the right to refuse planning permission for any alterations to it that were deemed unsuitable or which might interfere with its long-term survival. Since 2000, the *Local Government (Planning and Development) Act*, has obliged local authorities to list important historic buildings. Under the provisions of the act, they must now set up and maintain a *Record of Protected Structures* (RPS), in which they are to include buildings and structures of special architectural, historical, artistic, cultural, scientific or technical interest. The act also provides for the creation of *Architectural Conservation Areas* (ACAs), in which groups of important buildings and their setting can be afforded protection in local authority development plans. The *Architectural Heritage (National Inventory) Act* of 1999 empowered the Minister for Arts Heritage and the Gaeltacht and the Islands to recommend to Irish local authorities that certain historic buildings be included in their listing of protected structures. Structures listed by the National Inventory of Architectural Heritage as being of regional, national or international significance can now feature in these listings. In 2002, the control of the government departments responsible for built heritage was transferred to the Department of Environment, Heritage and Local Government (DOELG).[26] The *Heritage Act* of 1995, which established the Heritage Council as a statutory body, also made provision (Section 10 [4]) for the designation of structures in public ownership, as in the case of semi-state companies such as the Bord na Móna or the Electricity Supply Board, as heritage buildings.[27]

In the 1970s An Foras Forbartha (AFF) commissioned a series of county-based surveys of industrial monuments and sites in the Irish Republic, which were undertaken by Dr Gavan Bowie on its behalf. As early as 1971 a Conservation and Amenity Service (CAAS) was established by AFF. In the years 1973 to 1975, Gavan Bowie completed survey work (mostly of water-powered mills and bridges) in eight southern counties (Cavan, Clare, Donegal, Kerry, Kildare, Louth, Monaghan and north Tipperary) and was later followed by John Courlander who undertook fieldwork in a further ten over a three-year period. These included counties Carlow, north Cork, south Dublin, Longford, Mayo, Meath, Sligo, Waterford, Wexford and Wicklow. A further, more comprehensive survey, was conducted in County Kildare in 1986, by Fred Hamond for Kildare County Council. This latter was also initiated by CAAS and involved the examination of 650 sites, some 165 of which were to feature in Kildare's County Development Plan.[28]

It was not until the 1980s, however, with the initiation of the Office of Public Works-sponsored Archaeological Survey of County Cork, that the Irish government became officially involved in the systematic recording of industrial sites and monuments. The publication of the inventories compiled by the Cork Archaeological Survey by Dúchas, however, which include a selection of industrial archeological sites in County Cork, surveyed by Mary Sleeman, are an important development.[29] Similarly, the inclusion of selected industrial monuments (mostly windmills) in the *Archaeological inventory of County Wexford* (1996) is also to be welcomed. Further survey work has been undertaken in County Dublin (by Fingal County Council), in Dublin's Docklands and in the city of Cork and its immediate environs.[30] In 1985 Ireland signed the Grenada Convention on the protection of Europe's architectural heritage, but until such time as a comprehensive database of the many thousands of post-1700 AD sites had been prepared little could be done to protect them. Thus, in 1991, a pilot project was initiated in Carlow town by the then Office of Public Works, and so began the survey of an estimated one million buildings in the Irish Republic. This was to develop into the National Inventory of Architectural Heritage (NIAH), which is currently managed by the Department of the Environment, Heritage and Local Government. A number of introductory county surveys have been published to date, namely Carlow, Kerry,

Kildare, Fingal, Laois, Leitrim, Meath, Roscommon, South Dublin County, Waterford and Wicklow. All of the latter contain sites of industrial archaeological interest.[31]

Recent legislation regularising the maintenance of local authority archives, many of which are also repositories of important business documents, will also further advance research and survey work by facilitating access to, and by preserving, important documentary materials relating to Ireland's industrial heritage. The establishment of the Centre for Civil Engineering Heritage Trinity College, Dublin and the Technological Heritage Archive in University College, Galway, are further important developments, as is the publication of an excellent guide to the archives of the Irish Board of Works.[32] The Mining Heritage Trust of Ireland (formerly the Mining History Society of Ireland) was established in 1996 to cater for a growing interest in the development of Irish mines and their history. In 2004 it completed important conservation works on a rare man engine house at Allihies, County Cork (see Chapter 5) and is currently undertaking (2004-6) similar works on the Bunmahon/ Tankardstown mining complex in County Waterford, where it plans to provide interpretive facilities. The Society has recently reprinted Grenville Cole's important monograph (1922) on mineral resources in Ireland and, since 2001, regularly produces an excellent journal.[33]

The conservation of the island's industrial heritage has proceeded apace in more recent years. The National Trust in Northern Ireland has been active in restoring industrial archaeological sites such as Wellbrook Beetling Mill, County Tyrone, Florence Court Sawmill, County Down, Castle Ward Corn Mill, County Down and Patterson's Spade Mill, County Down.[34] Local interest groups and local authorities have also made important contributions to preserving the industrial heritage of Northern Ireland, as in the case of Annalong Corn Mill in County Down and Moneypenny's Lock in County Armagh. The Department of the Environment (Northern Ireland) has played a significant role in listing and scheduling industrial archaeological sites within the six counties. Indeed, in both jurisdictions, important industrial archaeological sites such as Ballycopeland Windmill in County Down and the Newmills complex in County Donegal have been taken into state care, while the Irish and British governments have co-operated on the development of the Erne-Shannon waterway. The large-scale promotion of heritage tourism in the Irish Republic, fuelled by European Reconstruction and Development funding during the 1980s, enabled a number of important sites to be restored and made accessible to the public.[35] Again, the implementation of many such schemes like the Blennerville Windmill in County Kerry, Ballincollig Gunpowder Mills in County Cork, the windmills and watermill at Skerries, County Dublin and the Cork Corporation Waterworks, could not have come about without the active involvement of local authorities, private interest groups and state-sponsored bodies such as FÁS.[36]

Past Problems and Current Perceptions

Industrial archaeological sites have presented very special problems to planning authorities and to state agencies entrusted with the care and maintenance of historic buildings and landscapes. At a very basic level, this may involve the sheer size of some industrial enterprises, or the perceived degree of 'redundancy' of a particular building type when adapting it for modern use is being considered. Yet there is also a marked bias towards buildings which, for whatever reason, are considered to be more aesthetically pleasing and thus more worthy of retention than others which are deemed not to be. If an industrial building meets this rather basic and clearly superficial criterion of value then it may well be considered worthy of retention. At best, a limited number of sites will survive under this notion, but at worst this rather superficial register of value will not be applied to the original machinery. Most industrial structures dating to the early decades of the present century, indeed, are not buildings in a strict architectural sense. It is therefore well-nigh impossible to apply values and criteria taken from art/architectural history to certain industrial structures. The basic policy options in regard to preservation, it is clear, should involve more than superficial visual qualities.[37]

The application of the term 'derelict' to describe industrial buildings and landscapes by planning authorities will often be as good as a green light to a developer to demolish and redevelop. That other historic landscapes may be equally so in the sense that, while they are of undisputed historical value they are unlikely to be 'used' for anything else, appears to matter little. Dereliction denotes fundamental untidiness, ugliness and, of course, ultimate worthlessness while in the 'derelict' state. The common response is to tidy up the 'mess'.[38] In recent years the tendency to 'clean up' historic industrial areas, through either well-intentioned but over-designed re-adaptation or complete re-development, has been all too evident. Buildings which have survived as ruins, for example, are a case in point. Thus, a roofless, floorless warehouse, on an urban riverfront, will only in the most exceptional circumstances be allowed to escape re-development, whereas interference with the remains of a medieval building in a similar location will generally not be tolerated. The medieval building may have no great architectural merit nor be able to lay claims to association with an important historic personage or event. Its age, however, will almost certainly guarantee its protection. Therefore, as a building's value is often seen as being proportionate to its age (regardless of the frequency with which such building types occur elsewhere or even within a particular locality), 'derelict' industrial buildings dating to the last 200 years have traditionally been unprotected. The perception that a building's historical value is directly related to its age is a deep-rooted one. Thus while surviving eighteenth-century cotton mills in the Republic of Ireland are extremely rare it is much more likely that a preservation order would be placed on a nondescript tower house than on a cotton mill.

The idea of 'dereliction' as commonly applied to industrial buildings and landscapes definitely requires reappraisal. Apart from the connotations outlined above, dereliction has also been viewed as a component of the 'nuisance value' of redundant industrial buildings. Buildings which have been abandoned after fire or cumulative neglect, particularly in run-down urban areas, can present a danger to the public, either through imminency of collapse, as a health hazard or simply because they attract the homeless or vandals. In these and in similar circumstances a requirement that such buildings be retained would be viewed as a severe development constraint. Regardless of the historic or technological importance of the buildings concerned, it is unlikely that either the buildings would be conserved *in situ* or that, at the very least, an alternative use for them would be sought.

The sites of former extractive industries such as quarries and mines can prove to be particularly troublesome. The most common problems are pollution, erosion, underground structural collapse and subsidence and general health and safety hazards resulting from the use of many extractive sites as unofficial rubbish tips and landfill sites.[39] Moreover, the recording and conservation of these sites is extremely problematical. They can often cover several acres, while features such as mineshafts and tunnels may not be accessible to surveyors. Indeed, even if a mine or quarry is considered worthy of conservation, how does one go about it? Surface features such as engine houses, dressing floors and workers' accommodation may be an obvious focus of attention, but how does one define the extent of the underground features? Even when industrial archaeological sites and landscapes are readily acknowledged as important in themselves, or at least on a par with archaeological sites of earlier periods, basic considerations such as recording and conservation can represent huge financial burdens. Cork County Council has already directed considerable resources towards the development of Ballincollig Gunpowder Mills, the largest industrial archaeological site in Ireland. The resources involved, while considerable have, nonetheless, been expended largely over the years 1986-1993. If, for example, a similar complex, spatially extensive and diverse site were to require immediate recording prior to demolition or adaptation for modern use, the resources necessary for such an investigation to proceed within a short period of time would be difficult to come by. In the first instance a prospective developer would view a requirement that such an investigation was necessary as a negative constraint, and would have a similar view about a stipulation that certain features of existing buildings (or indeed that the buildings themselves) be retained.

The adaptive re-use of industrial buildings is more likely to occur than to archaeological sites of earlier periods. This should be, and often is, a welcome development in that it allows many industrial buildings a new lease of life. Adaptive re-use can often ensure their survival by justifying their continued existence, to the extent that a building or complex of buildings can, as it were, earn their keep by accommodating alternative functions. There are, however, no general guidelines governing such developments with regard to certain key areas. The de-commissioning of public utilities and components of the public transport system, for example, can present special problems. To begin with, many of the de-commissioned elements such as waterworks, electricity generating stations, railway stations and so forth, will themselves be of industrial archaeological interest. Water distribution networks will generally be controlled by either municipal or county authorities, but there are no policy guidelines on their recording, conservation or re-adaptation, although the recent conservation and opening to the public of the former Cork Corporation Waterworks, by Cork City Council, has provided an excellent model for future projects. Yet, Iarnród Éireann and the Irish Defence Forces are not statutorily obliged to manage the heritage of sites of industrial archaeological interest either in their ownership or under their control. The Electricity Supply Board (ESB), however, has recently led the way by publishing an inventory of site of industrial archaeological importance in its ownership.

As with archaeological sites of most periods, historic industrial buildings and landscapes have survived basically through inertia. Even buildings in a ruinous state have continued to exist simply because of the expense involved in demolishing them. Others, however, are extant because their original use is still valid, as in the case of many railway stations, or because an alternative employment has been found for them. Some buildings, indeed, can have been re-used several times for different industrial purposes. At any stage during a building's history accretive adaptations are likely to have occurred, and it is these adaptations which define the building's function over certain periods of time. These adaptations can vary greatly. They can be purely structural, as in the case of the addition of an extra storey, an annex or fireproof flooring. Motive power and plant can also change through time either through modernisation or a complete changeover to another manufacturing process. In the latter case, internal changes to the building may be much more in evidence, but in all instances changes to a building's form and function will determine the extent to which it will survive the next period of technological modernisation or economic change. A building or complex whose form has become too specialised is unlikely to be re-used when its original purpose has become obsolete, and in consequence its chances of survival would, in normal circumstances, be considerably reduced. But in Ireland de-industrialisation in many areas during the nineteenth century and subsequent economic underdevelopment has created a relatively high survival rate for many different varieties of archaeological site. Many important Irish industrial archaeological sites have also benefited from this circumstance, and have survived in recent times without protective legislation.

In the absence of statutory protection for industrial archaeological sites, and with the 1987 and 1994 amendments to the *National Monuments Acts* yet to prove their efficacy in this regard, a building must still demonstrate that it can be adapted for modern use to ensure its continued survival. In normal circumstances this will have an important bearing on planning decisions. However, the extent to which the planning authorities will be prepared to force developers to re-adapt existing buildings rather than to demolish and build anew is another matter. Regardless of its state of preservation, a prospective developer may be reluctant to re-adapt an historic building when the option to demolish is available, if he can demonstrate that the building is manifestly unsuitable for the future intended purposes. A stipulation to have an archaeological record (generally unspecified) made of the building before demolition is often the only avenue open to the planning authorities, unless the Department of Environment and Local Government (DOELG) takes firm action.

The conservation problem is further compounded by the fact that certain types of industrial archaeological site can be impossible to satisfactorily adapt to new uses. Indeed, the most common options availed of – modern light industry, offices and domestic dwellings – are themselves quite limited. In the main, these options tend to favour small industrial buildings, although in Ireland larger complexes such as defunct nineteenth-century textile mills and distilleries tend to be re-used as industrial estates. Coercion in regard to the re-use of old buildings is necessary to a certain degree, but encouragement should also be given to developers, home buyers and the like to make re-use an economically attractive option.

Regardless of the state of preservation in which an historic building's fabric has survived, original machinery remaining *in situ* can cause serious problems for its re-use. In the case of traditional water-powered flour mills, for example, where a simple two- or three-storey mill is considered for re-use as a domestic dwelling, the retention of the machinery would practically rule out any such conversion. From a conservation viewpoint, the retention of the machinery is critical to enable the building to maintain its historic integrity; indeed, the argument should be made that with the removal of the machinery the building loses its context. In other words, it effectively ceases to be a mill. If the machinery had long since been removed and the building re-used for another purpose, then its removal can be legitimately considered to be an accretive adaptation of the site. However, if the machinery survives it should be retained as it is in every way as much a fixture of the site as the buildings housing it. Up until very recently the contents of buildings, owing to a legal loophole, were not protected by a listing order, but new legislation is set to remedy this.

Like all historic buildings, those associated with industrial archaeological sites also require extensive research to provide a detailed outline of their development through time, as well as extensive recording of the surviving fabric in order to facilitate conservation and repair work. Rarely, however, is such research undertaken for industrial archaeological structures, as traditionally they have not been seen as important as sites of other periods. For conservation and repair work on most historic buildings before AD 1700 the consent of the DOELG is necessary. There are, however, no firm statutory guidelines on how such works should be undertaken, and at the present showing the Republic of Ireland has no equivalent of the UK's Planning Policy Guideline note 15 (PPG 15).

1

Animal, Wind and Water Power

The extent of Ireland's available sources of industrial energy and, in particular, the all-too-obvious paucity of mineral fuels such as coal for raising steam, have traditionally been viewed as a debilitating physical constraint on the island's capacity to industrialise. We shall explore these and related themes in later chapters but, in the pre-steam era, the availability of appropriate and sustainable energy sources for Ireland's developing industries was never really lacking. Ireland was certainly not disadvantaged with regard to any of the forms of energy to be considered in the present chapter. Indeed, the island proved to be an innovative force with regard to the development of water-powered prime movers within the former United Kingdom. As we shall see, this is clearly demonstrated by the archaeological record. The largest single concentration of windmills in these islands is in County Down, while the first modern water turbines in either Britain or Ireland were manufactured and used on this island. In the pre-heat engine phase of Ireland's economic development, industrial energy cannot, therefore, be realistically considered as a resource constraint. Of course, no one could really argue that the lack of native coal ever discouraged the use of steam engines in Ireland. When an economically attractive opportunity presented itself to Irish industrialists, they appear to have had little difficulty either with acquiring steam-driven prime movers or with importing fuel to power them (see Chapter 2). But, as we shall see, they were also sufficiently flexible to adapt new means of increasing the productive capacity of traditional sources of industrial energy.

1.1 *Reconstructed nineteenth-century horse whim at Glengowla lead and silver mines, Oughterard, County Galway.*

Animal Power

The employment of animals for traction and for working machinery played an important part in the early development of Irish agriculture and industry. In certain industries, indeed, early attempts at mechanisation relied heavily on the use of horses. Within the confines of a small urban brewery or distillery, or at a remote mining site, animal-powered machinery offered the only practical means of powering machinery in the absence of a usable source of water power. Even the early industrial development of Ireland's textile industries did, to a certain extent, involve animal-powered plant. In many urban breweries and distilleries established during the eighteenth century, access to a source of water power was not an important concern, as all of the essential plant could be worked by horse-powered machinery. Man-powered machinery – principally windlasses used in early ships' patent slips and in dredging operations, early fire-fighting apparatus, cranes and prison treadmills – was also used in Ireland during the eighteenth and nineteenth centuries.

There are basically two types of horse-powered machine which may be defined, as in water-powered wheels, by the plane in which they rotate. The first involve *vertical* wheels, in which the animal walks on treads on the interior face of the wheel (*treadwheels*), or wheels with treads set on the exterior face of a wheel's circumference (*treadmills*) operated by men. In either case, the motion of the wheel is communicated to a horizontal axle. With the exception, perhaps, of dog-powered roasting spits, which are recorded from County Clare in the 1870s, animal treadwheels appear to have been rare in Ireland.[1] The second variety of animal-powered wheel rotates in a *horizontal* plane, where the animal moves in a circle to turn a wheel set on a central pivot. Horizontal animal-powered wheels may be further subdivided in accordance with how the motion of the wheel is transferred to the machine:

(i) *Direct:* where the motion of the wheel is directly transferred to the implement or device, of which there are two main types; *roller crushers*, in which the horse pulls a circular stone set on edge (*edge-runner*) around a specially prepared platform or trough to crush seeds, break flax, etc; and rope-winding machines (*horse gins* or *whims*), where a circular winding drum pivotting on a central, vertical shaft is set in motion by a horse or team of horses moving in a circle.

(ii) *Indirect:* where the motion of the wheel is transferred to the machine by means of an intermediate gearwheel. The two main varieties of indirectly driven animal-powered wheels are the *horse wheel*, usually a large diameter wooden gearwheel which pivots on a vertical shaft. The wheel is set above the level of the horse's head, and the horse or horses are harnessed to the spokes of the wheel. The second type of indirectly driven wheel, which has been called a horse engine, is a nineteenth-century development. This is usually a cast-iron low-level gear, to which the horse or horse team is harnessed above the gear ring. Such wheels were generally used for agricultural purposes, and as the gear was set at a low level, the horses often had to step over the drive shaft emanating from the gear ring as they made their rotation.[2]

By the first half of the nineteenth century, horse-powered machinery was extensively used in Irish extractive industries. Mining, quarrying and industries involved in the preparation of building materials, such as brick making, made full use of horse-powered machinery. Pumps powered by horses for mine drainage, ventilation fans and winches for raising ore were all employed, occasionally in conjunction with water-powered plant. The horse *gin* or *whim* continued to be used in many mining districts even after steam-powered plant was introduced. In its most basic form, the gin or whim was operated by a single horse or a team of horses, working in shifts, to turn a large wooden drum, around which a winding rope had been coiled. The drum pivoted on a stout wooden pole and was often supported by a wooden framework. A shaft connected to this arrangement was tethered to the working horses, who walked around it in a circle to rotate the drum. On average, a horse gin could raise loads out of a mine shaft at a rate of about 80 ft (24.3 m) per minute.[3]

Our information about the operation of these horse-powered machines is almost entirely culled from documentary sources. It is, however, abundantly clear that horse-powered machinery was at work, during various periods, at all of the principal Irish mines and quarries. At the Castlecomer Collieries in County Kilkenny, for

1.2 *Pugmill at Carley's pottery, County Wexford in the 1940s.*

example, no fewer that six horse engines were used for pumping water in 1802, whilst in the 1830s, coal was raised to surface at the Annagher Colliery, near Stewartstown, on the Tyrone coalfield by horse gins.[4] The Curraghbally slate quarry in County Tipperary used six horse gins to raise stone from a deep quarry floor in the 1840s.[5] No fewer than three horse gins were erected at the Allihies copper mines, in west Cork, during 1820, whilst gins were also used in conjunction with water-powered plant at the Lackamore and Hollyford copper mines in County Tipperary in the 1850s.[6] As late as 1921, a horse gin was still at work at the Lickfinn Colliery on the Slieveardagh coalfield in County Tipperary, raising coal trucks.[7] Furthermore, horse gins were also employed on Ducart's tub boat canal (see Chapter 13) at each plane to haul craft out of the upper pound.[8] There are no known surviving instances of the latter in Ireland, but an example has recently been reconstructed at the Glengowla Lead Mines in County Galway (figure 1.1).

Throughout the nineteenth century, and into the early decades of the last century, horse-powered machinery was used on nearly all of Ireland's numerous brick fields, in processes associated with the preparation of brick clay, as at Lissue, County Antrim, and Florencecourt near Enniskillen, County Fermanagh.[9] Horse-powered wheels were employed to power the machinery used in the preparation of potters' clay, as at Youghal, County Cork, and Carley's Bridge, County Wexford (figure 1.2) and later in the grinding of alabaster in nineteenth-century Cork city.[10]

Animal-powered plant also featured in the early mechanisation of Ireland's textile, brewing and distilling industries. Horse-powered cotton machinery had been installed in George Allman's mill at Bandon, County Cork, by the early 1780s, whilst a woollen manufacturer in Cork city had set up horse-powered machinery in 1795.[11] In the late eighteenth century, horse-powered cotton spinning mills had also been installed at Enniskillen and in the Belfast area. By the early 1800s, Belfast had become the centre of the Irish cotton industry, and at least six of the cotton mills established in the general area by 1812 were powered by horses.[12] The use of horse-powered plant in Ireland's premier food-processing industries, brewing and distilling, particularly in those established in urban centres towards the end of the 1700s, was critical to their development in the period before the advent of steam power. In Cork city, the main centre of the Irish brewing and distilling industries at the end of the eighteenth century, horse wheels were used to power nearly all the machinery in its main breweries and in some of its distilleries. Up to 1818, all the machinery in Beamish and Crawford's brewery, set up in 1792, was worked by horses, and even after steam power had been installed, horse wheels were still used to work water pumps until the early 1830s.[13] Horse-powered machinery for grinding malt, as in Beamish and Crawford's brewery, was also used in Guinness' Brewery at James' Gate in Dublin. Guinness' horse wheel was replaced by a steam engine in 1809, as was the horse wheel employed at Madder's Brewery on James' Street, Dublin, in the same year.[14] The horse wheels in the Watercourse Distillery in Cork city and at Walker's Brewery in Fermoy, County Cork, were both replaced in 1811 and 1814 respectively.[15] At Tuam, County Galway, horse-powered machinery was still at work in the local brewery in 1850.[16]

Wooden horse wheels were also employed in pumping water for domestic use. In 1837, a horse wheel served as a back-up for water-powered pumping plant, which supplied water to a large cavalry barracks at Ballincollig, County Cork, from a mill-race at Ballincollig Gunpowder Mills.[17] It also seems likely that a pile-driving machine in Dublin Bay during the early eighteenth century had been powered by a horse wheel. In 1716, a pile-driving engine was brought over from Holland to drive piles along the South Bull in Dublin Bay, and a similar engine was made in the Dublin area in 1717 for this same purpose. It would appear, from contemporary European practice, that these machines are likely to have been actuated by teams of horses.[18]

Up to quite recent times, edge-runner stones were in use in Counties Donegal, Tyrone and Derry for flax breaking.[19] Horse mills were also attested at Irish bleach greens during the eighteenth and early nineteenth centuries. In 1750, Robert French bought one for his bleach green at Monivea, County Galway, whilst a two-horse mill for grinding kelp is recorded at a bleach green at Glasheen, near Cork city, in 1802.[20] A number of the stones used were shod with iron bands around their circumference to prevent splitting, as is noted in the case of a large two-horse kelp grinding mill in Cork city in 1840. As late as the mid-nineteenth century, the bark-crushing mills of many Irish tanneries took the form of horse-powered edge-runner stones. In these mills, it was usual for one side of the stone to be bevelled, to work on the bark, while the horse walk was normally enclosed in a large circular or sub-rectangular shed. Water-power was also used to crush bark, but in city-based tanneries, horse-powered machinery was generally replaced by portable steam engines.[21] Smaller versions of horse-powered edge-runner stones were also extensively employed for breaking *culm*, the coal dust or slack associated with Irish coal workings. The stones were used to crush the culm to form 'balls', which were used as a kind of compressed fuel for domestic purposes (figure 1.3 see Chapter 3).[22]

Human muscle power was a plentiful and cheap commodity in pre-Famine Ireland. Its cheapness did, to a large extent, inhibit the introduction of labour-saving devices into Irish agriculture. Typical Irish farms were quite small (30-40 acres), and a combination of small landholdings and inexpensive labour encouraged the widespread survival of spade cultivation. Only shortly before the Great Famine, and in its immediate aftermath, did mechanisation become a viable option (see Chapter 7). The earliest horse-powered threshing machines used in Ireland were introduced in the late eighteenth century, which were powered by wooden horse wheels, the earliest-known Irish example of which, on present evidence, being installed at the Latouche Estate, County Laois in 1794 (figure 1.4), followed by that at Kircassock, near Magheralin, County Down, in either 1797 or 1799.[23] By around 1800, further examples are recorded from Counties Cavan, Louth and Dublin. As both the machinery and the horse wheel would have been made of timber, it was necessary to enclose these in covered buildings to protect them from the elements. In order to afford some ventilation for the horses working the wheel, the high,

1.3 *Reconstruction of County Kilkenny culm crusher. Courtesy of Dr Michael Conry.*

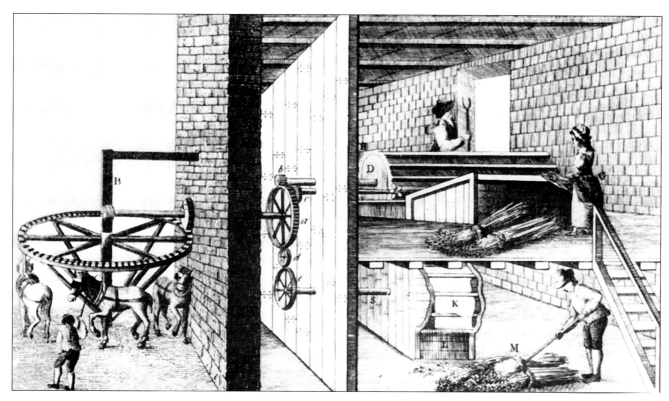

1.4 *Latouche estate horse-powered threshing mill (above);* **1.5** *Horsewheel, Holywood County Wicklow (left).*

steeply-pitched, conical or pyramidal roofs were often supported on piers. This arrangement left a series of vertical ventilation holes and afforded some comfort to the working horses, which were employed in teams of two to six. A fine example of one of these early horse engine houses, dating to the 1800s, has survived at Broom-mount, near Moira, County Armagh, which has a timbered conical roof, finished with tarred felt. Openings under the eaves of the roof in the house's enclosing wall provided ventilation.[24] A later horse engine house, of the 1840s, octagonal in plan, but with a slated conical roof, can also be seen at the Suir Mills, near Cahir, County Tipperary. The sole surviving Irish example of a wooden horse gear (used for churning butter) is at a farm at Holywood in the Glen of Imaal, County Wicklow (figure 1.5).[25] Horses and donkeys were also used for powering milk churns from the late eighteenth century onwards, a practice widely attested throughout County Kilkenny.

In the early 1830s, a number of iron foundries around the country were supplying horse-powered threshing machines to an expanding market, as in Dublin, by Courtney and Stephens of Blackhall Place, Keenan's of Fishamble Street and Chambers of Downpatrick, who were all manufacturing agricultural machinery. As early as 1832, Perrott's Hive Iron Foundry at Cork was manufacturing threshing machines for the Munster market. The Dublin, Cork and Ulster manufacturers were later joined by Pierce of Wexford in 1837, and a number of other important producers such as Kennedy's of Coleraine (who installed the first of some 2,000 of its threshing machines in Ulster in 1842), Grendon's of Drogheda, Lucas of Newry and Henry Sheridan of Dublin.[26] The products of these foundries were a series of compact, cast-iron horse engines, where the drive was taken from the top of the wheel rather than at the bottom of the drive shaft, as in the traditional wooden horse wheel. The use of cast metal added to the durability of the mechanism, and it no longer became necessary to construct an elaborate engine shed to protect it from the weather.[27] By 1875, it was estimated that some 10,000 horse engines for threshing machinery were at work in Ireland. The sites of horse-powered threshing machines are marked on the first editions of the Ordnance Survey, and one such example, at Young Grove House, near Lisgoold in County Cork, (*c.* 1842), survives as a raised, circular earthen platform.[28] Horse and donkey engines were also used for churning milk and sawing wood, and the remains of these and of threshing engines and their emplacements are still relatively common throughout the Irish countryside.[29]

Man-powered treadmills were also employed in Ireland between the early 1830s and the mid-1850s, although their operators – invariably prison inmates – did not work them voluntarily. Both Cork City Gaol and Galway County Gaol had man-powered treadmills at work in the early 1830s.[30] The Galway treadmill was used to power a turning and polishing machine, along with a stone saw mill used for cutting Galway black marble. The idea was copied from the use of similar treadmills in English gaols, and elsewhere in Ireland, Kilmainham and Mountjoy prisons followed suit. In 1848, Richard Perrott, of the Hive Iron Foundry in Cork, installed one of his 'Registered Capstan Mills', a large capstan wheel made to his own design, in Cork County Gaol. This device was designed to keep upwards of 100 people engaged in the laborious work of turning the arms of the capstan, which powered millstones and a water pump. Perrott managed to sell his invention to the Irish Poor Law Commissioners, who had similar devices installed in the workhouses in Cork city, Midleton, County Cork, and Athlone, County Westmeath. The self-evident inhumanity of their continued use, however, persuaded the Poor Law Commissioners to abandon them in 1855.[31]

Capstans and windlasses were principally used for lifting heavy loads at all industrial sites, from mines to city quaysides where, in the main, human muscle power was employed. By the late 1820s, patent slips had been constructed at Dublin, Waterford and Cork, for ship repairs and construction. The carriages which were employed to haul the ships up the slipway were all originally operated using man-powered winches.[32] Windlasses were also used in early dredging operations. *Spoon dredging* was employed in Dublin Bay during the eighteenth century, the 'spoon' piece (actually a cast-iron ring with a net attached to it) being dragged along the bottom by means of a windlass operated by a small team of men.[33] Before the introduction of steam power all cranes, indeed, were manually operated, and continued to be so for most purposes long afterwards. Hand-operated swivelling derrick cranes, with geared ratchets, were a universal feature of Ireland's canal, river and port quaysides (see Chapters 13, 14 and 15), while during the early railway age in Ireland, rail-mounted derrick cranes were commonly employed in the construction of railway bridges and viaducts. In 1854, for example, Mallet's Dublin foundry built a hand-operated travelling crane for work on the Boyne Viaduct at Drogheda.[34] Manually-operated pumps, dating from the last century, are still commonly used throughout rural Ireland. In many small country towns, up until the widespread construction of public water supply networks towards the end of the nineteenth century, these pumps would often be the only means of water supply for most purposes. Wooden, hand-operated pumps were the mainstay of many Irish tanneries throughout the nineteenth century, and it is often forgotten that early fire-fighting equipment relied heavily on manually operated machinery.[35] Robert Mallet's iron foundry in Dublin built three large 36 man-power fire engines in 1841, which were still in use some 40 years later. Indeed, when Dublin Corporation set up a paid fire brigade in 1862, it had four manual fire engines in its possession.

Wind Power

The earliest recorded wind-powered mill in Ireland was at Kilscanlan, near Old Ross, County Wexford, which was at work in A.D. 1281.[36] This is generally thought to have been a *post mill*, a number of which are known to have been in existence in the seventeenth century outside a number of Irish walled towns. In post mills, the actual mill building is rotated about a central wooden pivot in order that the wind sails can face into prevailing wind. The entire structure could be turned through 360 degrees by means of a *tail pole*, which enabled the miller to adjust the position of his sails to accommodate changes in wind direction by the simple expedient of rotating the entire mill building. The mill machinery was contained within a wooden framework, and the entire structure was usually erected on high ground, often on a specially prepared mound, adjacent to a township. A number of possible later or early post-medieval windmill mounds have been identified at Diamor, Bartramstown, Derrypatrick, Hurdlestown and Agher, in County Meath.[37] There are no surviving examples of post mills in Ireland, but their former existence can also be confirmed from early maps. Pictorial representations in seventeenth-century cartography suggest that the Irish examples closely mirrored contemporary English post mills, as on Thomas Phillips' plans of Charlemont, County Armagh, and of Derry in the 1680s, whilst the *Pacata Hibernia* map of Youghal, County Cork, from around the same period, depicts one outside the town walls.[38] On present evidence, it would appear that post mills were no longer built in Ireland after the seventeenth century.

The earliest depiction of the type of windmill that was to become relatively common in Ireland's main grain-producing counties on the eastern seaboard is shown on a map of 1591 from Waterford harbour.[39] This shows a *tower mill* – so called because the mill machinery is contained within a typically cylindrical, masonry tower – at Templetown on the Hook peninsula in County Wexford. In the early decades of the seventeenth century, these mills begin to appear in the Irish midlands, where they are first mentioned in the early 1630s at Warren, County Roscommon, and at Knock, County Longford.[40] In the tower mill, the building is a fixed entity, and the moving portion containing the sails and the drive shaft (or *windshaft*) is carried in a rotating *cap* section set on top of the tower. A tail pole with a tiller wheel at its lower end was connected to the cap portion, a movement of the pole in any direction enabling the miller to turn the cap and thence the sails into the prevailing wind. At Rindoon, County Roscommon, the stump of a possible seventeenth-century tower mill survives on what may well be a medieval post windmill mound.[41] The continuity of use of windmill sites, indeed, can be demonstrated at two County Wexford locations, Bargy, which is listed in the Civil Survey of the 1650s, and Bing, which is shown on the Down Survey maps for the area.[42]

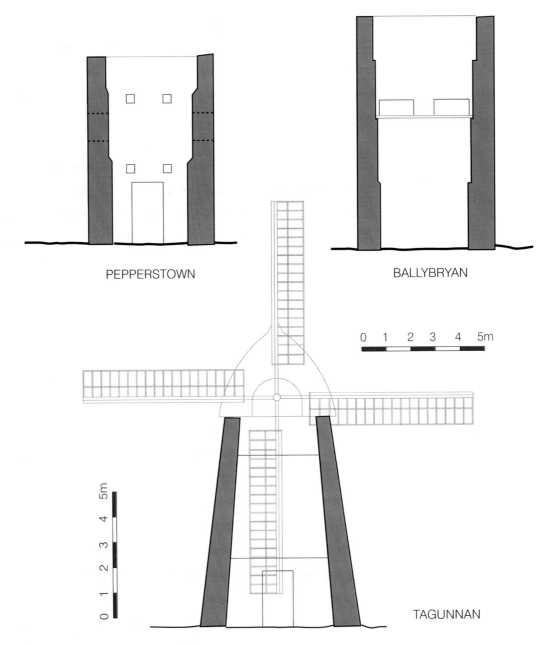

PEPPERSTOWN

BALLYBRYAN

0 1 2 3 4 5m

TAGUNNAN

5m 4 3 2 1 0

1.6 *Windmill stumps (after Bowie 1978): Pepperstown, County Louth, Ballybryan, County Down, Tagunnan, County Wexford.*

The automatic fantail, developed in England by Edmund Lee in 1745, enabled the cap section to swivel automatically into wind, but this device was virtually unknown in Ireland. Automatic fantails, as recorded at the windmill at the Conlig and Whitespots lead mines or on the surviving Ballycopeland windmill, both in County Down, are, in fact, quite rare in Ireland where, even in the multi-storey mills, a manually operated endless chain drive was used to rotate the cap section.[43] The design of early Irish tower mills owes much to contemporary British practices, particularly to those characteristic of the western seaboard of Britain. A small number of surviving windmill structures – five in County Down and one in County Dublin – also have vaulted extensions (similar to those found in southern Scottish tower mills) to provide extra storage space, while there is even an example in the west at Noggra, near Cooranroo, County Galway, that would also appear to have been influenced by this design. The tower mills built before about 1770 in Ireland tend to be cylindrical, three-or four-storey rubblestone structures, around 3-4 m in internal diameter and about 6-7.5 m high, developing just enough power from their sails to work two pairs of millstones. At ground floor level, there are generally opposing doors, in order that at least one would not be blocked off by rotating sails when the mill was in operation (figure 1.6).[44] A good example of this type of mill at Elphin, County Roscommon, built by Edward Synge, Bishop of Elphin, about 1750, has recently been restored to working order. Almost invariably, this type of mill survives as a shell, but as in nearly all Irish windmills of this period, its gearing would have been of wood, while its movable cap portion would have had a wooden roof covered with thatch. However, a small tower mill at Tacumshin, County Wexford, complete with tail pole and thatched cap and with many of the features of the early eighteenth-century examples, attests to the survival and durability of traditional millwrighting practices. In fact, it was built in 1846 by a millwright called James Moran, who had been an apprentice in a Rotterdam mill, and operated as a windmill until *c.* 1908.[45] Tacumshin windmill also has the distinction of being the first industrial archaeo-logical monument to be taken into state care in the Republic of Ireland.

The period after 1770 and ending around the close of the Napoleonic Wars, during which the cultivation of cereals in Ireland became a very profitable activity, witnessed a spate of windmill construction on the island. The windmills associated with this expansion in cereal cultivation were larger and more powerful. Although the smaller, cylindrical tower mills continued to be built into the 1800s, these were primarily attuned to local needs, but the newer mills produced for much larger markets and were designed for increased output. By the early 1800s, tower mills of tapered profile (rather like a truncated cone, to make them more structurally sound), around 5-8 m in diameter and about 10 m high were becoming much more common. Many had four to five floors, the upper floors housing the milling plant and the rest being used for storage. The increased height of these mills enabled larger sails to be used, and the consequent increase in motive power made it possible for up to four sets of millstones to be employed. The difference in power ratio created by a relatively small increase in height is quite remarkable: a 30 ft (9.14 m) high windmill has twice the power of a 20 ft (6.09 m) high example. As the sails no longer extended to the ground, a wooden staging, built at first-floor level, was now provided to enable the miller to adjust the sails, and at the multi-storey tower mill at Dundalk, County Louth, the external joist sockets that would have supported such a stage are still in evidence (figure 1.7).[46]

The additional height was also necessary for windmills located in urban areas, where tall buildings could adversely affect the flow of the wind. At 118.5 ft (34.29 m) in height, the Thomas Street windmill in Dublin, which now forms part of the Guinness Brewery complex, is the tallest surviving tower mill in either Britain or Ireland. Built throughout with locally made brick it now, as more recent research has indicated, appears to have been built in the period 1790-1810 (and was certainly defunct by 1830), its upper section being refurbished about 1810 (figure 1.8).[47] Windmill Lane, in Dublin, takes its name from a five-storey example, which former-ly stood on Sir John Rogerson's Quay.[48] A number of largely similar mills were built around the same time at Armagh, Balrath, Blennerville, Derry, Dundalk, Lifford and Warrenpoint. Of these, two multi-storey examples,

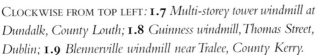

CLOCKWISE FROM TOP LEFT: **1.7** *Multi-storey tower windmill at Dundalk, County Louth;* **1.8** *Guinness windmill, Thomas Street, Dublin;* **1.9** *Blennerville windmill near Tralee, County Kerry.*

each built *c.* 1800, at Ballycopeland, County Down, and Blennerville, near Tralee, County Kerry, built by Sir John Blennerhassett, have been restored to working order (figure 1.9). The Ballycopeland mill, however, in terms of the design of its sails, is rather atypical, not only of Irish windmills but of windmills in general (figure 1.10).

Some 250 windmills are shown on the first editions of the Ordnance Survey, compiled between the 1830s and 1842 (figure 1.11). The vast majority are in County Down, mostly on the Ards and Lecale peninsulas (which alone accounted for over 100 of this total in 1834), and in County Wexford. The concentration of windmills on the Ards peninsula was the densest in either Britain or Ireland in *c.* 1800. A number of factors

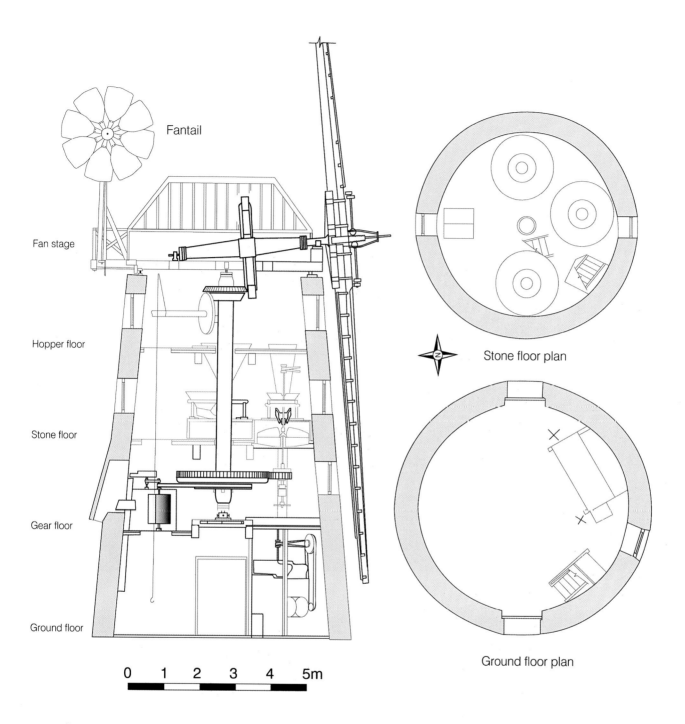

Fantail

Fan stage

Hopper floor

Stone floor

Gear floor

Ground floor

0 1 2 3 4 5m

Stone floor plan

Ground floor plan

I.10 *Ballycopeland windmill, County Down (after Green 1963).*

were responsible for this eastern distribution. To begin with, both counties were important cereal producers, thanks to favourable climatic conditions and proximity to large centres of population. However, as the catchment areas of many of the rivers on the east coast were somewhat restricted, both regions experienced difficulty in expanding their milling capacity based on water power. Such expansion was crucial if these areas were to capitalise on the increased demand for cereals in the period 1770–1815, but, fortunately, wind speeds along the eastern

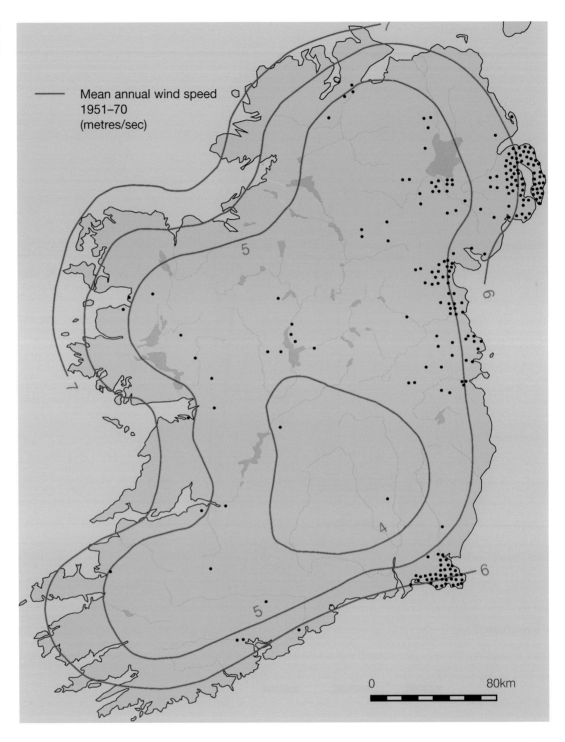

1.11 *Distribution of Irish windmills (after Hamond 1997).*

Mean annual wind speed
1951–70
(metres/sec)

0   80km

coastal strip of Ireland favoured the construction of windmills. In many cases, windmills were used as a supplement to water mills, particularly those whose watercourses tended to dry up during the summer months.[49]

Thus far we have considered the use of windpower to actuate milling plant, but traditional wind-powered prime movers also found a limited use in pumping water and in flax scutching on the Ards and Islandmagee peninsulas in Ulster. The remains of wind-powered flax scutching mills are still in evidence on the Ards peninsula in County Down, at Ballywalter and Kearney.[50] There is, indeed, at least one recorded instance of a tower windmill being built specifically for pumping water, for cotton processing at Prosperous, County Kildare, in 1783, at a cost of £100.[51] Traditional windmills were also used for threshing in Ulster and for draining quarries. During the early 1800s, a windmill was used to drain water from a calp limestone quarry at Rathgar, County Dublin, whilst in the 1840s, a windmill (originally used a grain mill) was employed to power ore-dressing machinery at the Conlig and Whitespots lead mines in County Down, until the mine's closure in 1865.[52]

Although wind power as an energy source had all but died out by the second half of the nineteenth century, the introduction of wind engines, mainly for pumping water but also for electricity generation, gave wind power in Ireland a new lease of life. In its essentials, the wind engine was an annular metal wheel, with curved metal vanes, set vertically on top of a steel pylon. A crank on the wheel's drive shaft drove a pump rod, which was directed down through the support pylon to work a pump set into a borehole for water. Many examples of similar devices are still at work on remote farms all over the world, but only a few are still used in Ireland. Most of the Irish examples such as the 'Climax' wind engine at Bellinteer House, near Navan, County Meath, were imported from England. At the Rock of Kilmainham, outside Mountmellick, County Laois, a Climax wind engine was employed to pump water to evaporation pans used in the processing of rock salt from Carrickfergus, County Antrim.[53]

A wind engine of J.W. Titt's design was used to drain slobland in north County Derry in c. 1910, while at Clogher, County Tyrone, and on the West Clare Railway, wind engines were put to work to pump water for locomotives' boilers. Less well known are the instances of public supplies being created through the use of wind-powered pumps, in parts of Dalkey, County Dublin, from 1886 to c. 1900 and in some areas of western County Galway from the 1920s to the early 1950s (see Chapter 16). Wind engines, as one would expect, were also installed for draining quarries and clay pits, as at Dundalk brickworks in the early 1900s and at the brickworks near Hollymount House in the Shrule district of County Laois.[54]

From the first editions of the Ordnance Survey, it is clear that many Irish windmills were already disused by the early 1830s. Indeed, in direct contrast to Britain, where the wind-powered corn mill continued to undergo technical improvement throughout the nineteenth century and, significantly, continued to be widely used, in Ireland, the opposite was the case.[55] An important factor was the contraction in demand for milled cereals at the end of the Napoleonic Wars in 1815. But the increasing concentration of the milling industry in Ireland's ports, processing imported grain in newly-erected steam-powered mills, forced both smaller water and wind-powered grain mills into decline. Wherever practicable, water power was preferred to wind power. Wind power, unlike water power, could not be stored and was notoriously difficult to control, whereas water could be held in mill ponds and regulated by means of sluices or inlet control gates. Furthermore, only by altering the area of the canvas spread on the individual sails could the speed of the windmill be regulated, while in windmills without automatic fantails the cap had to be turned into the wind. Of the 116 wind-powered devices at work in Ireland in 1912, the vast majority appear to have been wind engines, with only one traditional windmill – Ballycopeland, County Down – still at work. Ballycopeland is thought to be the last windmill to be worked in Ireland, closing in 1915.[56] In the last century, from about the

1920s onwards, the vast majority of Irish wind engines were replaced by various forms of internal combustion engines and electrically driven motors, particularly where the pumping of water for ordinary domestic use was concerned.

Water Power

Water power was the backbone of Irish industry for the greater part of the eighteenth and nineteenth centuries. It alone provided some respite from the physical restraints the island's lack of suitable mineral fuels for industrial use placed on its ability to industrialise. Irish millwrights and engineers played a crucial role in the adoption and development of new water-powered prime movers, whilst Irish industrialists demonstrated an alacrity rarely matched by their English contemporaries in their efforts to maximise the resources nature had placed at their disposal. Even in the nineteenth century, steam power in many Irish industries was a supplement to rather than a replacement for water-powered prime movers. In 1870, water power accounted for almost one-fourth of Ireland's recorded industrial horsepower at 9,879 hp (this figure was one-twentieth in Britain), with the Irish textile industry responsible for just over 83 per cent of Irish total water power in 1870.

The early history of water power in Ireland is clearly one of the most remarkable in post-Roman Europe. Ireland, apart from possessing the largest number of archaeological sites of European early-medieval water-powered mills, has thus far produced the earliest evidence for the craft of millwrighting or mill erection. The *saer muilinn*, or millwright of the early medieval Irish language documentary sources, is the earliest reference we have to the existence of specialist craftsman anywhere in medieval Europe engaged in the construction of water mills. Many examples of their work have come to light in Ireland, and all of these exhibit a high degree of skill in carpentry.[57]

To date, an incomparable corpus of early water-powered mill sites in Ireland has been scientifically dated, either by dendrochronology (tree-ring dating) or radio-carbon dating, to the period from the early seventh to the thirteenth centuries A.D. There are, indeed, more dated pre-tenth-century water-powered mill sites in County Cork alone than there are in the rest of Europe. There can be little doubt that water-powered mills and their associated features – mill dams, races and ponds – were a common feature of the early medieval Irish landscape. The vast majority of these water mills, as both the documentary and archaeological sources clearly indicate, were *horizontal-wheeled* mills.[58] In the horizontal-wheeled mill, the water-wheel has a vertical drive shaft and the wheel rotates in a horizontal plane. To work the mill, a small fast-flowing stream was impounded by the simple expedient of constructing a dam of earth, stones or clay to create a small reservoir or millpond (*lind*), from which a shallow feeder channel or mill-race (*taídiu*) was led to the millhouse. Incoming water was directed into a hollowed-out wooden chute, internally splayed so as to develop a concentrated water jet, which was then discharged against the dished paddles of the water-wheel. The motion of the water-wheel was directly communicated to the upper, rotating millstone – no gearing was necessary as in the vertical water-mill – and one revolution of the water-wheel produced a corresponding revolution of the upper millstone. On High Island, off the coast of County Galway, the remains of such a mill built for an adjacent early medieval monastery, complete

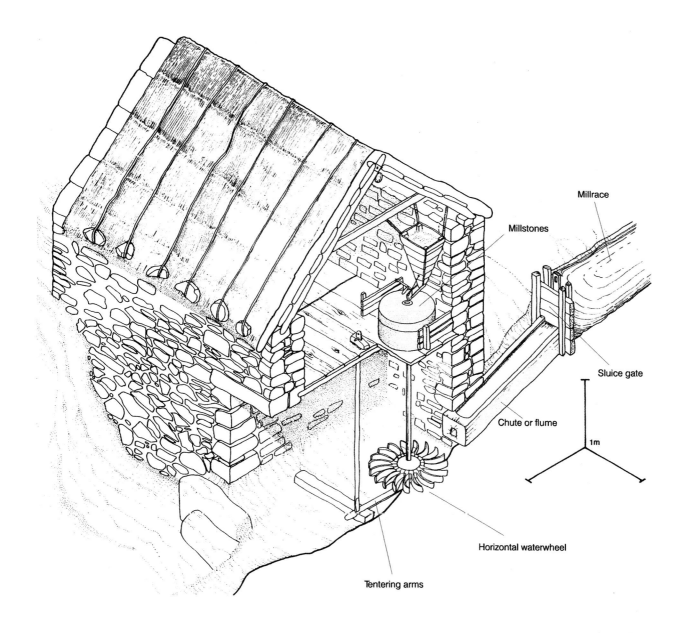

1.12 *Reconstruction of ninth-century horizontal watermill on High Island, off the coast of County Galway.*

with its millponds, mill-races and mill building, have survived in what is an almost completely unspoilt early medieval landscape (figure 1.12). This is the oldest surviving monastic water mill in Europe.[59]

The early medieval Irish water-wheels which have come to light, such as those from Nendrum, County Down (*c.* AD 617), Cloontycarthy, County Cork (*c.* AD 833), or Moycraig, County Antrim, are the earliest known examples of a type of horizontal water-wheel characteristic of Mediterranean Europe in more recent times. The Irish examples attest to the durability of this water-wheel design, which is found in a wide arc stretching from Ireland to the foothills of the Carpathian Mountains in modern-day Romania.[60] The Nendrum site has also produced the earliest documented use of horizontal water-wheels using flat-vaned paddle, a type found

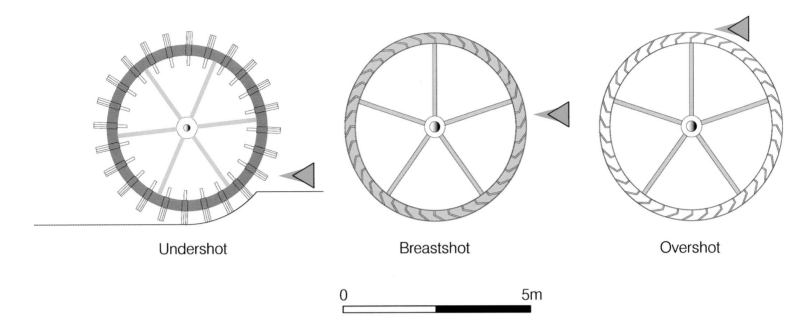

Undershot   Breastshot   Overshot

0   5m

1.13 *Water-wheel types*

throughout northern Europe and in eastern Asia.[61] Ireland has also produced the earliest known examples of horizontal water mills which employed two chutes or mill flumes. The earliest instance was investigated at Little Island in Cork harbour, being dated to AD 630, and, at the time of writing, at least six examples of this type of mill are known in Ireland. Similar mills were used throughout Europe and Asia up until very recent times.

The horizontal-wheeled mill survived in Counties Down and Sligo until about the end of the seventeenth century, and in Counties Galway, Mayo and Roscommon to the twentieth century. However, while these are clearly survivals of an early medieval milling tradition – as late as the 1930s a modernised version of the Old Irish word for sluice gate (*comla*) was still being used in horizontal-wheeled mills in Connemara – the surviving examples of horizontal water-wheels in Ireland are debased versions of their early medieval ancestors. In the remainder of the island, however, it appears that horizontal water-wheels had long since gone out of use by the middle of the seventeenth century. Surviving examples of horizontal-wheeled grain mills can still be seen at Gannon's Mill, Meeltraun, County Roscommon, Flatley's Mill, Cullentra and Bunadober (near Ballinrobe), County Mayo – the only example currently in state care – and Killaguile, County Galway.

The use of the *vertical water-wheel* in Ireland is at least as early as the horizontal water-wheel. The vertical water-wheel, as it name suggests, rotates in the vertical plane on a horizontal axle. But unlike the horizontal water-wheel, the motion of its axle cannot be directly transferred to the mechanism it is to set in motion. Some form of intermediate power transmission (in early mills usually gear wheels set at right angles to each other) was always necessary. Vertical water-wheels are normally characterised by the means by which the incoming water is delivered onto either paddles or buckets set on their periphery. One of the most basic types, the *undershot* water-wheel, in which the water strikes the water-wheel near the lower part of its circumference, had been employed at Little Island, County Cork, in *c.* AD 630.[62] A further early medieval site at which an undershot water-wheel was used has been investigated at Morett, County Laois (*c.* AD 710); and the earliest identifiable components of an Irish vertical water-wheel have been recovered from Ardcloyne, County Cork and dendro-dated to *c.* AD 787.[63] The vertical water-wheel came to replace the horizontal water-wheel in grain mills throughout Ireland, and after the twelfth century AD was adopted to power other industrial processes. Up to the introduction of the water turbine (which is itself a lineal descendant of the horizontal water-wheel), the vertical water-wheel was the most important water-powered prime mover used in Irish industry.

There are five basic varieties of vertical water-wheel, most of which were employed in Ireland during the last 250 years (figure 1.13), which are as follows:

(1) *stream:* here the water-wheel was immersed directly in a stream or river, and the water in watercourse directly struck open paddles at the lowest part of the wheel's circumference. This variety of wheel is commonly depicted in seventeenth-century illustrations of Irish villages and towns, but appears to have generally been replaced by either undershot or breastshot water-wheels by the end of the eighteenth century.

(2) *undershot:* here the water-wheel is suspended over an artificial channel and the incoming water is carefully guided, by means of wooden or stone-lined troughs, onto paddles at a point slightly above the lower part of the water-wheel's circumference. These wheels were generally employed in low-lying areas, where the fall of water was negligible, such as large rivers or tidal estuaries, or in mills built on bridges in urban areas. Good examples are in evidence at Tuam, County Galway and Kells, County Kilkenny (figure 1.14), whilst the finest surviving example of an undershot water-wheel in an Irish bridge mill has been preserved in Bridge Mills in Galway city. Both stream and undershot water-wheels use the *kinetic energy* of falling water, where the impellant force of the water striking their paddles sets them in motion. This is the least mechanically efficient means of directing water on to a water-wheel and is generally thought to be only around 35 per cent efficient. However, in 1823, the French engineer Jean Victor Poncelet (1788–1867) substantially modified the traditional undershot water-wheel by replacing its flat paddles with curved vanes and providing an angled sluice or inlet control gate, which allowed the incoming water as close to the vanes as possible. Poncelet's improved design successfully married the principal advantages of the traditional undershot water-wheel (low construction and maintenance costs) to the demands of increased mechanical efficiency. The use of curved vanes and the enhanced sluice arrangement enabled incoming water to enter the vanes without impact and to exit with little or no velocity. Greater efficiencies equivalent to those obtained with overshot water-wheels, from relatively low falls, were now possible with this type of wheel. A Poncelet-type water-wheel was introduced into Ireland in the early 1830s and came to be widely adopted at mill sites where

33

traditional undershot water-wheels had formerly utilised low falls. Kilbeggan Distillery, County Westmeath, Athgarvan mills and Morristown Lattin, County Kildare, and Glanworth Woollen Mills and Fermoy flour mills in County Cork retain fine examples of such water-wheels with cast-iron frames and curved wooden vanes, all of which were in use up until quite recently. In the main, Poncelet-type wheels are relatively common in the Munster region, particularly on rivers on low falls, and throughout the midlands. In the Ulster counties, nonetheless, they are somewhat less common. The traditional undershot water-wheel, however, survived on Ireland's north-western seaboard well into the nineteenth century, in County Galway, and in adjacent counties such as Roscommon and Leitrim.

(3) Breastshot: The more efficient varieties of vertical water-wheel used the *potential energy* of falling water, where the weight of the water, directed into enclosed buckets on the periphery of the water-wheel, set it in motion. There were three basic types of breastshot water-wheel, (a) *low breast shot*, which received water from a point below the level of the axle, (b) *breast shot*, where the water was received about midway up the circumference of the water-wheel and (c) *high breast shot*, where the water entered the buckets at a point above the axle. These varieties became popular in Ireland towards the end of the eighteenth century, and by the early decades of the nineteenth century, breast wheels were beginning to outnumber other types of water-wheel in many parts of the country. Breast wheels could provide efficiencies of between 55-66 per cent on falls of 6-15 ft (1.82-4.57 m), and, before Poncelet wheels became available, there was a tendency to replace undershot wheels with low breast shot wheels when possible. Generally speaking, the high breast shot water-wheel was used at upriver locations where the fall of water would normally compensate for any insufficiency of water flow. Breast shot and low breast shot wheels, on the other hand, are normally to be found at downstream sites. The 'classic' Irish breast shot wheel is, perhaps, best exemplified by that at the Newmills Flax Mill, County Donegal, which is fed by a long wooden launder (feeder chute) mounted on trestles.[64] Good examples of high breast shot wheels survive throughout Ireland, notably the composite wheel at Castlebridge maltings, county Wexford, fed by a masonry aqueduct and an elaborate cast-iron launder, and the remarkable, all-wooden examples, of clasp-arm construction, within the Monard and Coolowen ironworks complex in County Cork. Two excellently preserved high breast wheels, which form part of the former Coalisland, County Tyrone, spade mill (figure 1.15, see Chapter 10) are on display in the Ulster Folk and Transport Museum at Cultra, County Down.

(4) Overshot: In the overshot water-wheel, the water is delivered into buckets at the top of the wheel. Of all the traditional varieties of water-wheel, this was the most effective, being capable of providing, from the same volume and fall of water, almost twice as much power as an undershot

CLOCKWISE FROM TOP LEFT: **1.14** *Under shot water-wheel at Kells, County Kilkenny;* **1.15** *Breast shot waterwheels from Coalisland spademill, County Tyrone, on display at the Ulster Folk and Transport Museum, Cultra, County Down;* **1.16** *All-iron suspension waterwheel of* c. 1860 *at Bealick Mills near Macroom, County Cork.*

wheel. It was generally used in upstream locations with falls of roughly 15-50 ft (4.57-15.24 m). These also came to be replaced by wider varieties of breast shot water-wheels during the nineteenth century in Ireland, particularly when the power requirements of most industries began to expand. The 80 ft (24.38 m) diameter overshot water-wheel erected at McDonnell's paper mill, at Saggart, County Dublin, appears to have been the largest water-wheel ever built in these islands.[65] However, none of the larger examples of this type, described in nineteenth-century sources, has survived and, curiously enough, there are few extant examples of most varieties of overshot water-wheel in existence here today. There are probably two main reasons for this. The substitution of overshot wheels for high breast shot models is likely to have been more widespread than has previously been imagined, while it is possible, also, that with the advent of water turbines, the installation of larger and more powerful overshot types was dispensed with. At the Monard and Coolowen Ironworks, County Cork, three overshot water-wheels of early twentieth-century date each with a diameter of 3.19 m, complete with cast-iron frameworks (but with wooden elbow buckets), survive *in situ*.

(5) *Pitch back:* One of the disadvantages of the overshot water-wheel *vis á vis* the high breast shot water-wheel was its inability to cope with backwatering, a phenomenon which occurred when water leaving the water-wheel was impeded by partial flooding. In such circumstances, partial flooding tended to impede the rotation of the wheel. However, if the water-wheel could be made to rotate in the same direction as the water flow, a much more creditable performance could be expected from it if backwatering occurred. The English engineer, John Smeaton (1724–92) developed the *pitch back* water-wheel, on which water was delivered onto a point on top of the water-wheel in such a way as to alter its direction of rotation from clockwise to counter-clockwise, and thus increase its ability to handle backwater. This variety of water-wheel was never widely adopted in Ireland, and, in most cases, high breast shot water-wheels came to be employed where high falls were exploited. A mixed *pitch back* and breast shot water-wheel has been restored at Killarn, between Dundonald and Newtownards, County Down.

Until the second half of the eighteenth century, all Irish water-wheels were made entirely of wood. However, by the 1770s, some Irish foundries were already manufacturing cast-iron water-wheel axles for export, and it seems reasonable to assume that some of these were being used in Ireland around this time. The transition from wood to metal water-wheels was, nonetheless, a relatively slow process. Around 1820, what were termed 'compound' overshot water-wheels, which were composite water-wheels generally consisting of cast-iron axles, with plate iron buckets supported by timber arms, were already being used here. Mallet's foundry in Dublin and Steele and Hopkins foundry in Cork were already producing large numbers of these water-wheels for Counties Dublin and Wicklow and the greater Munster area, respectively. Indeed, as late as 1863, it was reported that all-metal water-wheels were still considered to be too costly by Irish mill owners.[66] The first all-metal water-wheel erected in Ireland is believed to be that installed at Dyan Mills, Caledon, County Tyrone in 1829 (reputedly by William Fairbairn of Manchester) for the Earl of Caledon.

In Ireland, the increased difficulty in importing timber during the period of the Napoleonic Wars provided an extra fillip for the substitution of wood by cast and wrought iron.[67] Beginning with the substitution of oak axles with cast-iron ones, and following up with cast-iron wheel rims and, ultimately, cast-iron transmission, English engineers such as John Smeaton, John Rennie, Thomas Hewes and William Fairbairn revolutionised mill construction. The latter three had all undertaken mill work in Ireland in the early decades of the nineteenth century, and there can be little doubt that their ideas were copied by Irish foundries, a number of which, in any case, employed English millwrights and foremen. From the late eighteenth century onwards, the establishment of larger factories and mills in Ireland required water-wheels of greater power. Yet while the diameter and width of Irish water-wheels were increasing, further refinements were also being made to their design.

In the early 1800s, Thomas C. Hewes (1768-1832) of Manchester was developing what was to become known as the *suspension water-wheel*. Before the introduction of this type, the motion of the water-wheel was transmitted to the gear wheels via its wooden axle. The stresses involved required that the axle be of stout construction, made of a single balk of timber or of a number of large timbers strapped and bolted together. The *compass arms* or struts supporting the external rim of the water-wheel, or the framework of *clasp arms* introduced in the eighteenth century for the same purpose, also added to the weight of the water-wheel and thus increased the pressure on the axle. However, in the suspension water-wheel, power transmission from the wheel was transmitted from its rim. As the principal driving wheel or *segment* was now affixed, in sections, to the outer rim of the water-wheel, there was no longer a need for either a large axle or a heavy frame. It now became possible for the diameter of the axle and the cross-sectional area of the arms to be greatly reduced. Heavy wooden axles could be replaced with slender cast-iron ones, with internal wrought-iron suspension rods providing support for the framework of the wheel. In *c.* 1802, Thomas Hewes erected the earliest-known Irish example of a suspension water-wheel at Overton Cotton Mills, near Bandon, County Cork. This was 40 ft (12.19 m) and 5 ft (1.52 m) wide and, while most of it was made of metal, the soleing and the buckets were of wood.[68] On present evidence, this would appear to be the first example of such a water-wheel ever built, and fortunately, its original shaft has been retained *in situ*.

In the late 1820s, William Fairbairn (a former employee of Thomas Hewes) developed *ventilated buckets*, a further refinement to the new, all-iron water-wheel, which greatly improved the way in which individual buckets handled the entrance and exit of water.[69] Fairbairn played an important role in the dissemination of the suspension water-wheel in Britain and Ireland. During the 1840s and 1850s, an increasing number of these water-wheels were installed in Ireland, either supplied by Fairbairn himself or copied by Irish iron foundries. An important example was installed by Fairbairn at Millford Mills, County Carlow, in the 1830s, which was 22 ft (6.7 m) in diameter and developed 120 hp, but the only surviving instance of a Fairbairn-built, high breast shot water-wheel is that installed at Midleton Distillery, County Cork, in 1852, which is only one of two in either Britain or Ireland.[70] Around the same time, foundries throughout Ireland were already producing similar wheels for factories and mills. Good examples of Irish-made suspension wheels dating from the 1850s survive at Croom Mills, County Limerick, where two suspension water-wheels, one by the Vulcan Foundry of Cork dating from the 1840s and a second by Perrott's of Cork (early 1850s), can be seen. The earlier of two survives *in situ* at Lyons flour mill on the River Maigue, near Croom bridge, the second, from Manistear, near Croom, has been re-erected and restored to working order in the Croom Mills Heritage Centre. Other examples of note include two manufactured by McSwiney's Foundry at Cork at Bruree Mills, County Limerick (1850s), and at Bealick Mills, County Cork (*c.* 1860) (figure 1.16).

Within the larger mills and factories, the buildings housing the machinery increased in height to accommodate newly mechanised processes and extra manufacturing capacity. However, traditional water-wheel sizes,

I.17 *Reconstructed cog and rung gearing at, Mullycovet mill, County Fermanagh.*

which were still quite common in the early 1830s, could rarely produce more than 30 hp. Multi-storey mills, however, required anything up to 140 hp, and for this to be supplied by a single prime mover, much larger water-wheels were required. In 1834-8, the average diameter of the water-wheels employed in the flax-spinning mills of Counties Antrim and Down were already between 29 and 35 ft (8.83-10.66 m).[71] From this period onwards, the diameter and power of water-wheels gradually began to increase at new Irish industrial sites, from metal mines to linen mills, where almost every conceivable industrial process was beginning to be mechanised. Power transmission from the water-wheel became increasingly more complex, particularly in large multi-storey buildings, while from about the 1840s onwards, the installation of back-up steam engines required that the drive from the water-wheel be immediately transferrable to the flywheel of a steam engine.

Early power transmission systems for water-wheels consisted entirely of wooden components. In *cog and rung* gearing, a wooden, toothed gear wheel set on the water-wheel's axle communicated its motion to a *lantern pinion*, set at right angles to it, usually to power an upper millstone via an upright shaft. Close-grained woods like elm and crab apple were often used by the traditional mill carpenter or millwright for the gear teeth. This type of gearing was used throughout Ireland well into the nineteenth century, usually in small country oat and meal mills. Indeed, a number of examples have survived up to recent times in southern County Fermanagh and in County Cavan. At Mullycovet, County Fermanagh, remnants of an 8.5 ft (2.59 m) diameter wooden pit wheel, recovered during the archaeological excavation of an eighteenth/nineteenth-century grain mill, have been replicated and installed in a fully restored mill (figure 1.17), while a small mill near Virginia, County Cavan retained its complement of wooden gearing up to recently.[72] However, before the introduction of spur gearing, multiple gear linkages, in which several devices could be powered from a single prime mover, were not possible. Thus, where more than one set of millstones or a number industrial processes were involved, it was necessary to power each with a separate water-wheel. This led to the development of 'double mills', where often two water-wheels operated under a single roof, powering either a single pair of millstones each or entirely different processes. Waters Mills in the Blackpool suburb of Cork is referred to as such in 1755, while a rare nineteenth-century survival of such an arrangement has been investigated at the Black Mills at Roscrea, County Tipperary, where two overshot water-wheels operated side by side, powering single sets of millstones.[73]

In Ireland, probably from the late 1780s (and certainly from the early 1790s onwards), the wooden trundle wheel was being replaced by a cast-iron bevel gear or *pit wheel*, which meshed with a further bevelled gear or *wallower* set at right angles to it.[74] The use of a spur gear set on top of the wallower's upright shaft enabled a series of devices to be powered via auxiliary shafting, an advance that would appear to be closely associated with the development of multi-storey flour mills in later eighteenth-century Ireland. Where the individual storeys of a large mill or factory complex were involved, a long horizontal shaft (*line shaft*) enabled machines to be powered from a large water-wheel set some distance away. The use of line shafting, however, only really became technically possible with the introduction of the suspension water-wheel, and would not have been common in Ireland until at least the 1830s onwards. Geared transmission was extensively used for everything from simple grain mills to large textile mills. But for a number of mechanised industrial processes, such as those involved in the finishing of textiles, like linen and wool, the dressing of ores, metal-working bellows and spade and shovel manufacture, the *cam* was the principal means of power transmission. A series of radial cams set in a wheel affixed to the water-wheel's axle was generally used to set a vertical stamp hammer (see Chapter 5), a trip hammer, a forge bellows (see Chapter 10), fulling stocks and beetling engines (see Chapter 8) in motion.

Great care and skill was generally exercised in providing a regular supply of water for a mill. The construction of dams, artificial channels (*mill-races* or *leats*) and storage reservoirs (*millponds*) not only required sound planning but often involved considerable expense. The most basic type of mill system utilised the stream water-wheel, which could be set directly over a natural watercourse, although when this did occur, the wheel would generally be at the mercy of flood water. However, in most cases, an artificial channel (the *head race*) was used to direct water from a natural watercourse such as a river or stream, either onto the floats of undershot water-wheels or into the buckets of breast shot or overshot water-wheels. The water leaving the water-wheel was then directed back into the natural watercourse downstream of the mill by means of a further artificial channel called the *tail race*. An excellent, eighteenth-century account survives for the construction of a mill-race at the Wellbrook bleach green at Cookstown, County Tyrone, where its owner, Hugh Faulkner, confidently expected that it could be completed by 33 men digging for eight days.[75]

By siting a water-wheel near a natural waterfall or rapids, the length of the head race could be shortened considerably. Such locations were thus greatly favoured by millwrights, but if, as in the case of lowland rivers, the available fall of water was low, a head race channel of several kilometres was often required to compensate for this, as at Plassy Mills, near Limerick (now in the grounds of the University of Limerick), built in 1824, where a mill-race over one mile long is led over land with a very slight gradient (figure 1.18). The sides of mill-races were often revetted with masonry to counteract erosion, whilst the base of the channel was commonly sealed with puddled clay (i.e., clay which had been washed and worked into a plastic consistency) to prevent leakage. Both the head race and tail race channels were normally excavated, often deeply, into bedrock to maintain the fall of water required to lead the water from its source to the mill works. Not infrequently, the mill-race could also follow the contours of a hillside to ensure that the fall was adequately maintained. However, in certain instances, one side (or both) of the mill-race had to be formed with embankments to carry it over a low-lying and/or marshy area. An early example of such a mill-race, which was in existence in the 1780s, survives at Riverstown Distillery, near Glanmire in County Cork. The main section of this channel is a cut feature, which follows the contours of adjacent hillsides for virtually a mile from its source, before taking an almost 90-degree turn to pass under a roadway. The remaining section, approximately 180 m in length, is an elaborately constructed embanked mill-race, the inner side of which is formed, on its southern edge, by the outer face of a hillside, the outer edge of the mill-race being formed by two stepped earth and clay embankments, one built on top of the other. The embanked section ends in a millpond, formed by high embankments on each side, that on the northern side being up to 8 m in height. A large section of the mill-race at Plassy mills, County Limerick, is also formed by an artificial embankment on one side.

The most elaborate system of mill-races to survive in Ireland is at the Ballincollig Gunpowder Mills, County Cork (see Chapter 11). This is one of the largest hydro-power sites of any type in Europe where, in its initial phase of construction (*c.* 1794-1809), over 9 km of mill-races (which also served as canals for transportation purposes) were laid out to power up to 30 water-powered installations. During the early 1830s, some 12 miles of mill channels were constructed to convey water to a 40 ft (12.19 m) overshot water-wheel powering drainage pumps and other machinery at the Knockmahon copper mines in County Waterford. The water exiting from the large diameter water-wheel was then led, in succession, to three further water-wheels of 30 ft (9.1 m), 15 ft (4.57 m) and 12 ft (3.65 m) in diameter (see Chapter 5). Mining complexes, indeed, which were often sited in upland areas, required elaborate mill-races.[76] The Lackamore copper mine, County Tipperary, was equipped with over five miles of mill-races in 1841, while a two-mile-long mill-race was also built to service the stamping mill at the Coosheen copper mine in west Cork in 1848.[77]

The flow of water in the channel at the entry to it or immediately before its discharge on to the water-wheel was controlled by sliding vertical control gates, called sluices. On the main head race channel, the sluice gates were normally placed at a point near or on the juncture of the main inlet with a weir. By this means, the entry of water into the head race could be carefully controlled, particularly during the winter months when floods were a common hazard, not only to the lands traversed by the mill-race, but to the integrity of the mill-race

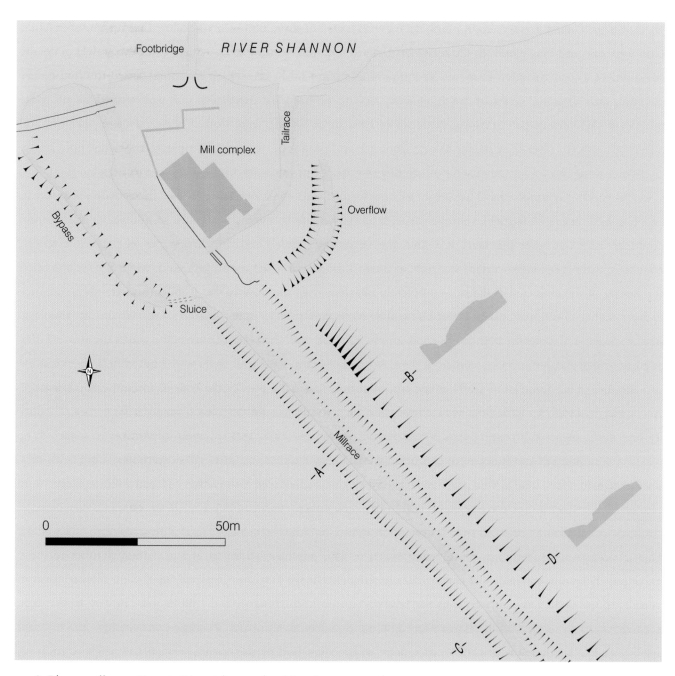

1.18 *Plassy mill-race, County Limerick, completed in 1824.*

itself. The sluice gates could also, if required, be used to drain the mill-race for maintenance and repairs. At smaller mill sites, a bypass or overflow sluice, set in the wall of the head race channel close to the mill building, was commonly provided as a ready means of shutting off excess flow to the water-wheel and directing water back into the river.

Depending upon the power requirements of the mill unit, the width of the head race channel could vary considerably, but the greater the power input the greater the corresponding width required for the inlet sluices, as at Sion Mills, County Tyrone, which has one of the widest sets of sluice gates surviving in Ireland. The revetment walls of large sluice inlets were commonly faced with large cut stone blocks, as at Ballincollig Gunpowder Mills, County Cork, and Plassy mills in County Limerick, to counteract erosion. The sluice gates themselves generally consisted of a stout wooden framework, comprising a large sill beam, which extended across the bed of the channel, into which a series of anything from one to perhaps six externally grooved vertical beams were morticed. The vertical gate sections, made up of horizontal boards, were slotted between these uprights, and raised upwards (or closed) by means of cast-iron rack and pinion gears, manually operated with a simple crank.

Weirs were also commonly used both to divert water from rivers into mill-races and to increase the fall of water available for a mill site. The height of the weir caused the river level to rise immediately behind it, enabling mill-races set a higher level than the river bed to be supplied with river water. In this way, greater control could be exercised over the level at which the incoming water could be directed onto the water-wheel, enabling (at the very least) certain varieties of breast shot wheel to be employed. And, while the weir assisted the raising of the river bed, it did not completely interfere with the flow of water (but was certainly a nuisance to boat traffic) in the river, excess water being allowed to flow over its upper section or sill. By the late medieval period, substantial weirs for both fishing and supplying water mills had been constructed across the River Liffey at Islandbridge and across both channels of the River Lee at Cork. Early mill weirs were built with timber or stone or a mixture of both, and were nearly always laid diagonally across the flow of the river to minimise flood damage. According to Hugh Faulkner, the weir constructed on a local river for his bleach green at Wellbrook, County Tyrone, in the eighteenth century, took six days '110 men and 20 horses and 15 gallons of whiskey to make'.[78]

In the eighteenth and nineteenth centuries, weirs constructed across wide rivers were now built with substantial rubble cores, held within a timber framework externally faced with either pitched rubble or cut stone blocks. The excavation of the late eighteenth/early nineteenth-century Fennessy's Weir, on the River Nore at Archersgrove, Kilkenny, revealed that its core of limestone boulders, externally faced with a pitching of boulders, had no prepared foundation or plinth with which to gain purchase on the river bed.[79] Indeed, other recently excavated Kilkenny city weirs of similar date, at Green's Bridge and the Ormond Weir, were formed around vertical roundwood stakes, driven into the riverbed, around which earth and rubble cores or clay banks were packed.[80] Certain sections of the River Nore in County Kilkenny also have 'V'-shaped weirs, where the inverted apex of the 'V' section was formed in the centre of the river, and by this means service, the needs of mills on opposing banks, as at Thomastown, County Kilkenny. By the closing decades of the nineteenth century, considerable technical skill and resources were being expended in the construction of mill weirs. At the Monard and Coolowen Ironworks, near Cork, where a series of overflow weirs dating to the late 1780s survive *in situ*, the outer face of each weir consists of a series of stepped and splayed masonry plinths. In each case, these are used as a means of impounding water in narrow mill ponds, over which water in excess of certain levels (and which might create flooding) was allowed to flow over its crest or upper edge. The height of the water in the main ponds could also have been increased, as desired, by laying boards on edge along the sill of the weir. For the most part, however, traditional mill weirs functioned (in part at least) as gravity dams, where it was the weight of the material incorporated within the weir which created a resistance to the flow of water in a river, enabling it to act as an impounding element. Mill weirs built on the arch dam principle, where the external face of the weir is concave in form and curved outwards from the centre, were much rarer. This configuration resembles an arch laid on its side, and enabled the weir to assume the considerably improved load-bearing properties of an arch (see Chapter 12). A well preserved and relatively early example of this phenomenon was constructed at Cloon, near Gort, County Galway, in 1849. Cloon Weir, which formed part of drainage works on the Annagh River, is a cut stone structure, 79 ft (24.07 m) long along its curve, over 19 ft (5.79 m) high and 10.5 ft (3.20 m) wide at its base. The river bed leading up to it was, in addition, paved with cut stone to ameliorate its discharge flow and to protect its upper edges.[81] Towards the end of the nineteenth century, concrete was also beginning to be incorporated into the construction of mill weirs, as at Cork Corporation Waterworks weir in 1888.[82]

In situations where either water tended to be scarce or the available flow of water was limited, artificial reservoirs or millponds were formed to store the water. A supply of water was usually built up in the pond overnight for use during the day. The bed of the pond was normally sealed with puddled clay to prevent leakage, while the sides of the pond were often faced with stone walling to counteract erosion. The inlets and outlets to millponds were generally controlled by sluices, primarily as a means of controlling the level of water in the pond but also as a defence against flooding. Millponds were prone to silting and the growth of vegetation (which could damage the lining of the pond) and required regular maintenance. Where the outlet from the pond was via a weir, silting was a common problem, and it was often necessary to have a means of draining the pond to effect repairs, usually by means of a drainage channel controlled by a sluice. Ponds varied in size from about one to several acres, depending on local conditions. When steam engines were introduced as supplementary power sources, the pond or ponds frequently doubled up as a supply for the boilers. At the Monard and Coolowen Ironworks, near Cork, a series of millponds were ingeniously constructed in a series of narrow, sandstone gorges in a glacial valley on the headwaters of the Blarney River in the 1780s. These latter were constructed at three different levels, the water in the upper pond being used by a succession of mills, each served by separate millponds. Water exiting from the upper mill passed into a pond immediately below it, and, in this way, four separate mills could be worked during various parts of the day: the upper mill in the early morning and the lowest mill in the afternoon.[83] For the most part, the pond basin tended to be excavated by hand, although it was by no means uncommon, if circumstances demanded, to form this by raising earthen embankments, as the Riverstown Distillery, County Cork and the Black Mills in Roscrea, County Tipperary.

On High Island off the Galway coast an early medieval millpond, used to power a small horizontal-wheeled grain mill for the island's monastery, survives relatively undisturbed. This appears to have been a naturally formed lake which the monks modified to serve as a storage reservoir for their mill.[84] Almost 1,000 years later, a similar solution was adopted by early Victorian engineers in a scheme to regulate the waters of the Upper River Bann. The Manchester engineer, William Fairbairn, was approached by mill owners in this locality in 1836 to design a scheme whereby the flood waters of the Upper Bann could be stored for hydro-power purposes. Fairbairn and his future son-in-law, J.F. Bateman (who was later to act as a consultant to many Irish local corporations on the construction and maintenance of waterworks (see Chapter 16), set about this task by modifying a natural lake, Lough Island Reavy, into a gigantic millpond (figure 1.19). Bateman designed and supervised the construction of four large embankments. These modifications increased the depth of the lake to 35 ft (10.7m), and when surplus water was led into the lake from the nearby River Muddock, Lough Island Reavy increased in size from 92.5 acres (37.5 ha) to 253 acres (101.2 ha). A second lake, Corbet Lough, was similarly modified, in this instance to 74.5 acres (30.2 ha), with a depth of 18 ft (5.5 m).[85]

Changes in water levels effected by the tides around Ireland's coastline were also exploited by water mills from at least the seventh century AD onwards. Through the use of millponds filled by the incoming tides, *tide mills* had a regular, seasonally uninterrupted source of water with which a mill could be operated during the ebb tide. The entire process was then repeated, the pond being filled on the flow tide. The world's earliest recorded tide mills, dated by dendrochronology to *c.* AD 617, have recently been excavated at Nendrum on Strangford Lough, while two further water-mills at Little Island, County Cork, have been dendro-dated to *c.* AD 630.[86] Tide mills are also known to have been used at Basra on the Persian Gulf in the tenth century AD, but, elsewhere, documentary references to their use in Europe are somewhat later. However, there are no further recorded instances of their use in Ireland until the sixteenth century. There were two tide mill sites at Dunbrody and Tintern in County Wexford, each of which was associated with Cistercian monasteries in the 1540s.[87] Indeed, part of the dam for the Dunbrody mill still survives as a causeway, although its associated pond has been filled in and reclaimed.[88] Further tide mill sites can be documented at Portmarnock and Malahide, County Dublin, and the Red Abbey Mill on the south channel of the River Lee at Cork in the 1650s, while in the later seventeenth century, there is clear-cut evidence for the existence of a tidal millpond for Gilbert Mabbot's Mill in Dublin.[89] At Ballycanvan Big, County Waterford, the remains of a tide mill site (mentioned in the Civil Survey of *c.* 1650), which include some probable seventeenth-century mill buildings, and a tidally filled, stone revetted millpond of *c.* 2 acres, still survive.[90] A small section of an eighteenth-century tide mill on Strangford Lough is extant in the fabric of a later, nineteenth-century fresh water mill at Castle Ward, County Down.

The remainder of surviving Irish examples of tide mills date to the nineteenth century. From these, it is clear that there was an obvious preference for small tidal inlets, across which a dam could be constructed to form a tidal pond of anything between 10 and 30 acres. Tidal millponds were usually equipped with wooden sluice gates which would open automatically with the pressure of the incoming tide. Once the reservoir was full, the pressure of the water in it would close the flap-like control gates, and retain the water in the pond when the tide receded. The tidal range – the difference in level between the ebb an flow tides – varied over a fourteen-and-a-half-day cycle, and over six-monthly periods during each year. For the most part, it was possible to operate a water-wheel for anything up to three hours before and three hours after low water. In the vast majority of cases, owing to the low falls available, undershot water-wheels were used. At the Saltwater tide mill at Finnabrogue, County Down, built in 1824, a 3.8 m diameter undershot water-wheel was employed in recent times.[91] Two further nineteenth-century tide mill sites survive in County Galway at Corranroo Bay, Aughinish, built by the de Basterau family in 1804 and at Hynes, Oranmore Bay, which was still in operation as late as 1938.[92] Substantial remains of the drystone embankment, used to form the mill pond for the Cooranroo tide mill, survive *in situ*.

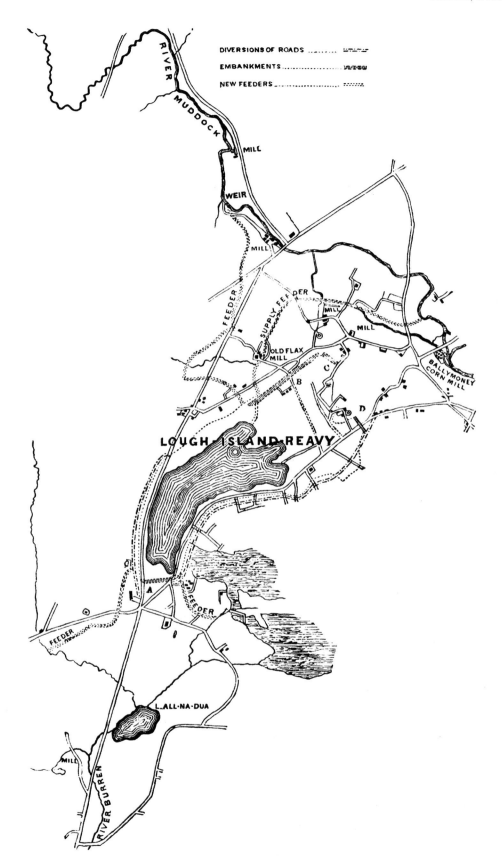

DIVERSIONS OF ROADS

EMBANKMENTS

NEW FEEDERS

RIVER MUDDOCK

MILL

WEIR

MILL

FEEDER

SUPPLY FEEDER

MILL

MILL

OLD FLAX MILL

BALLYMONEY CORN MILL

B

C

D

LOUGH ISLAND REAVY

A

FEEDER

FEEDER

FEEDER

L. ALL-NA-DUA

MILL

RIVER BURREN

1.19 *Lough Island Reavy in 1841, from Fairbairn 1871.*

The Water Turbine

Despite the many improvements made to the design of vertical water-wheels from the late eighteenth century onwards, the mechanical energy generated by them (regardless of the available water supply) could only be increased by constructing wheels of larger diameters. However, while wheels of *c.* 50–70 ft (15.24–21.33 m) diameter were constructed in Ireland, the locations at which they might be used were extremely limited. At existing mill sites, where power requirements had increased, the employment of large diameter water-wheels was very often simply impossible owing to the exigencies placed upon them by its available water supply. In many cases, particularly in urban areas where existing watercourses were already seriously congested at the end of the eighteenth century, the only alternative was to acquire steam-driven prime movers to facilitate further expansion or, indeed, to establish new industrial sites. The development of the water turbine presented enormous opportunities for many Irish industrialists, particularly those involved in branches of linen manufacture. Here was an excellent opportunity both to capitalise on existing water resources and to reduce an increasing reliance on steam-powered plant. Irish industrialists and millwrights were, for the most part, quick to grasp the significance of this new technology.

All water turbines, past and present, fall into two categories which are loosely based on the principles which govern their motion. In the early period of their development, the term 'horizontal water-wheel' was applied to all turbines to distinguish them from the vertical water-wheels then in common use, but as designs improved and methods of water delivery were modified, the terms *impulse* and *reaction* were introduced to differentiate between turbines utilising one or other of the two basic types of fluid energy. Impulse turbines utilise fluid energy in its kinetic form, where the potential energy of the water in the reservoir is converted into kinetic energy as it falls towards the turbine. A conduit or pipe, called a *penstock*, developed a jet of water which was discharged against the vanes of the turbine. In reaction turbines, on the other hand, the vanes of the turbine are completely submerged when it is in operation, and no water jet is formed. Only part of the potential (pressure) energy of the water is converted into kinetic energy as the water passes *through* the turbine.

On an island with limited coal resources, the continued development of existing sources of water power became a technological imperative for Irish industrialists. Imported coal added to the cost base of Irish industry, and so all means were explored to make the most of existing hydro-power sites. In this regard the water turbine offered considerable advantages over the various types of vertical water-wheel. By the late 1840s, water turbines could produce efficiencies equal to and often higher than the most developed vertical water-wheels, utilising falls of less than one foot (0.3 m) to upwards of hundreds of feet. The equivalent range for vertical water-wheels was about 2–50 ft (0.6–15.24 m) and, whereas the vertical water-wheel could not operate efficiently when flooded, the water turbine could continue to work effectively when entirely submerged.[93] The vertical axle of the water turbine rotated at much higher speeds than any variety of vertical water-wheel, which in practice meant that less gearing was needed to step up the speed of the axle required to power industrial machinery. Furthermore, and perhaps most important of all from the point of view of the Irish mill owner, water turbines were much more compact and could deliver more power per unit of size than a conventional water-wheel. In vertical water-wheels, incoming water was only applied to one bucket or vane at a time, whereas in the water turbine, the entire surface came into contact with the water flow. This latter contrast, coupled with the fact that water turbines also developed considerably higher axial speeds, meant in practice that the water turbine could be much smaller than a vertical water-wheel capable of producing the same power output.

The earliest-known turbine operating on the reaction principle in Ireland was at work at Brague, County Down, in 1834.[94] This appears to have been a type of *Barker's mill*, whose basic mode of operation is very similar to the whirling lawn sprayers of our own era. This same principle was incorporated into the *Scotch turbine*, developed by the Glasgow engineer, James Whitelaw, in 1839. Whitelaw's turbine operated by forming the arms of Barker's rotating jets into an 'S'-shaped spiral, with the addition of a special speed-regulating device. Scotch turbines were in use at Ballylinny and Mallush, County Antrim, in 1860, and, most notably, at Collooney, County Sligo, around the same time, where the rotating arms were enclosed in a cast-iron box. The Collooney turbine was made by Randolph of Glasgow, and was used to power fourteen pairs of millstones.[95]

The main design elements of the water turbines used in Britain and Ireland were developed in France, though engineers in Britain, Ireland and the United States made substantial improvements to the pre-existing designs and greatly extended their range. The contribution of Irish engineers was not inconsiderable, the main impetus being provided by Sir Robert Kane, who first brought the work of the French engineer Benöit Fourneyron (1802-67) to an Irish audience in the 1840s. Fourneyron's design was to greatly influence turbine development throughout the nineteenth-century industrialised world. In Fourneyron's turbine, incoming water was admitted into the centre of the turbine. A series of centrally positioned, fixed guide vanes then directed the water, simultaneously, onto the curved blades of a rotating outer wheel (the *runner*). The outward movement of the water leaving the turbine exerted pressure on these curved blades, the motion of which was transferred to the turbine's drive shaft.[96]

Sir Robert Kane's account of contemporary developments in turbine design was to have a lasting effect on three Ulstermen: William Kirk, who owned several flax-spinning and line-bleaching works, Samuel Gardner (owner of the Armagh Foundry), and a millwright called William Cullen. Kirk and Gardner appeared to have formed an association which culminated in the installation of a Fourneyron-type turbine at one of Kirk's mills in 1850. At least one of these men had actually travelled to France between 1844 and 1848 to meet with Fourneyron with a view to manufacturing his patent in Ireland. However, Fourneyron had other ideas, and William Cullen, in a separate venture to manufacture the design in Ireland, found the Frenchman less than co-operative. Cullen resorted to industrial espionage and, after visiting a number of sites in France where Fourneyron's turbines had been installed, he acquired enough information on them to build a working model of one on his return to Ireland. Later, in association with Robert MacAdam of the Soho Foundry in Belfast, a Fourneyron-type turbine, built to Cullen's specifications, was installed in Barklie's bleach mill at Mullaghmore, County Antrim, in 1850.[97] At least one contemporary Ulster engineer, James Thomson (1822-92), however, was not content with the mere dissemination of Fourneyron's ideas. As early as 1846, Thomson had developed what he termed a 'vortex turbine' which, in terms of its design characteristics, effectively superseded existing turbines. Thomson's design used adjustable guide vanes, which were to become incorporated into many later turbine designs, and, whereas the water passing through Fourneyron-type turbines did so outwardly, in the vortex turbine the opposite was the case, the water flowing inwards from the periphery. The first vortex turbine was built in Glasgow and was later installed in a linen beetling mill at Dunadry, County Antrim, in 1852, and the first to be installed in England was at James Copper's paper mill, at Cowan Head, near Kendal in Cumbria, England.[98]

Between 1850 and 1896, MacAdam's Foundry in Belfast built Fourneyron-type turbines (figure 1.20). Many of these were used in the Ulster linen industry, and the latter's influence in the south of Ireland led to their adoption in processes associated with flax-related industries in County Cork in the early 1850s, one of the first counties outside Ulster were such trends can be discerned.[99] The earliest surviving reaction turbine, built on the Fourneyron model in either Britain or Ireland would appear to be that installed at 'The Old Bobbin Mill', Force Forge, Satterthwaite, in Cumbria around 1850, in all likelihood by an Ulster foundry such as MacAdam's or Gardner and Company of Armagh.[100] In 1858, Cork Corporation Waterworks became the first in either Britain or Ireland to use water turbines, built by MacAdam of Belfast on the Fourneyron model, to power pumping machinery.[101] An early example of a MacAdam turbine, dating to the mid-1850s, survives *in situ* at Green's flour mill, Cavan, and has recently been restored to full working order.

During the 1850s, Mallet's foundry in Dublin was also manufacturing and installing turbines (probably of the Fourneyron type), beginning with a flax-scutching

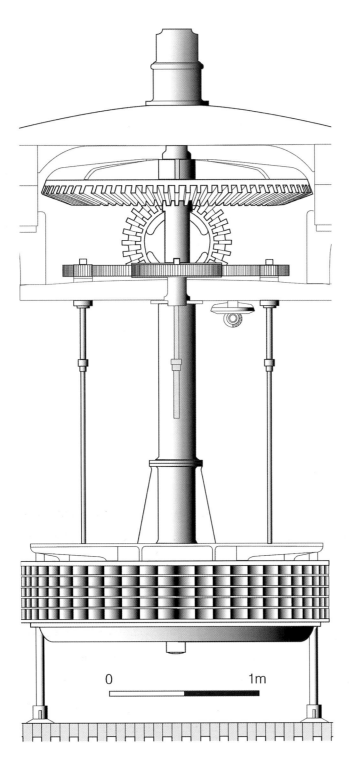

1.20 *Fourneyron turbine, c. 1860, based on pen and ink wash drawing in Ulster Museum (after McCutcheon 1980).*

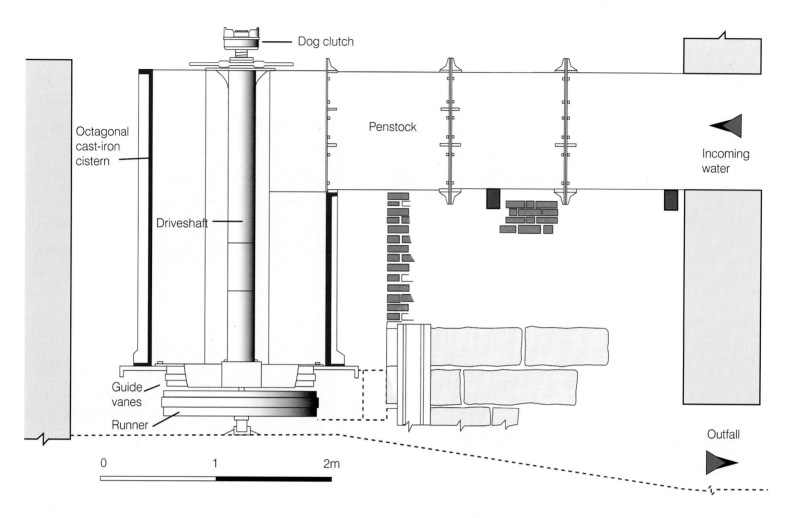

1.21 *Jonval turbine, manufactured at the Hive Iron Foundry, Cork, in 1855, for the sawmill at Ballincollig Gunpowder Mills, County Cork. This is the earliest example of its type to have survived,* in situ, *in Ireland.*

mill on the River Inny near Ballymahon.[102] However, whilst Fourneyron turbines accounted for the majority of those in use in Ireland before 1860, other designs had already been adopted by certain Irish foundries. Perrott's Hive Iron Foundry in Cork, for example, built and installed a Jonval-type turbine for a sawmill at Ballincollig Gunpowder Mills in County Cork around 1855 (figure 1.21). The Ballincollig turbine could generate 16 hp from a fall of 8 ft (2.43 m), over twice that of any of the breast shot water-wheels used elsewhere in the same complex. Kennedy's of Coleraine manufactured their 'Empress' turbines (based on American designs) between 1879 and 1921, installing 70 of these mostly in northern and western Ireland.[103] By the early 1870s, either Irish-manufactured or imported English or American water turbines were replacing vertical water-wheels at many Irish water-powered industrial sites, to power a wide variety of industrial processes. In 1889, for example, the main prime movers employed at the Ardfinnan Woollen Mills, County Tipperary, and Ashgrove Woollen Mills, at Kenmare, County Kerry, were, respectively, an Alcott turbine and an American Turbine.[104]

A surprising number of nineteenth- and early twentieth-century water turbines still survive *in situ* around the Irish countryside. Apart from the Irish-manufactured turbines dating to the second half of the nineteenth century at Green's Mills and Ballincollig Gunpowder Mills, an entire battery of turbines installed at Cork Corporation Waterworks between 1888 and 1916 were still in commission until 1993. The two Fourneyron-type turbines installed in 1858 were replaced by two imported 'New American' turbines which were brought into commission in 1890 (370 hp in total), to which a further two examples were added in 1901. All four of these turbines were reconditioned in the period 1912-16, and a fifth was added in 1916. Until 1993, when the facility was decommissioned, these turbines continued to pump about 10 per cent of Cork city's daily needs to storage reservoirs on an adjacent hillside (see Chapter 16). Since 2002, two of these turbines are being used to generate electricity which is supplied to the present Cork City Council. At Shackleton's Anna Liffia Mills near Lucan, County Dublin, one late nineteenth-century and two early twentieth-century turbines (all in potential working order) survive *in situ*. The earliest of these is a Francis-type Alcott turbine of 45 hp, which was installed in 1884 to power roller milling plant (see Chapter 9), followed by a Jonval-type, of 70 hp, manufactured by the Swiss firm of Escher Weiss of 1901-02. A further Francis-type turbine of 12 hp, by Gilbert Gilkes and Gordon of Kendal, was installed to a power-generating plan for the mills in 1905.

The Hydraulic Ram

Before closing this section on industrial energy, we should pause, briefly, to consider a device that has been much neglected in the literature on the development of water power in Ireland, despite its admirable simplicity and high degree of ingenuity. In its essentials, the *hydraulic ram* was a water pump which operated without an independent power source. Falling water was led to a constricted passage in which the water flow was suddenly arrested. The sudden increase in pressure resulting from this stoppage was used to force a small volume of water up to a greater height. In 1797, Joseph de Montgolfier (1740-1810) designed and built the first successful hydraulic ram.[105] The earliest-known Irish example was manufactured by Robert Mallet Snr in 1828 for the archiepiscopal residence at Clogher, County Tyrone, which was also used to supply water to the town of Clogher itself. Robert Mallet Jnr built a hydraulic ram at Westland Row railway station, Dublin, to pump water for railway locomotives, while a similar device was later installed to supply the adjacent railway works at Grand Canal Street.[106] Hydraulic rams required next to no maintenance, apart from the periodic replacement of valves. During the nineteenth century, they were installed at large country houses, on farms and by local authorities as a cheap means of ensuring a pumped water supply. Electrically-driven pumps became common in the wake of rural electrification, and the use of hydraulic rams went into decline. At the Botanic Gardens in Dublin, a ram manufactured by Maguire and Gatchell of Dublin was in use for pumping water up to the mid-1960s, when it was replaced by an oil engine.[107] Another fine example survives at Florencecourt, County Fermanagh.

2

Steam and Internal Combustion Engines

For the most part, the development and adoption of the steam-powered prime movers in Ireland, in the eighteenth and nineteenth centuries, is very similar to that of the rest of the former United Kingdom. There are a number of reasons for this, not least of which was Ireland's immediate geographical proximity to Britain's industrial heartland and its own incipient (but for many Irish regions, unsuccessful) industrialisation, briefly experienced at the end of the eighteenth century and in the early decades of the nineteenth. Yet, regardless of the degree of success in such endeavours, it soon became apparent that Ireland's larger units of industrial production could only expand and, most importantly of all, continue to do so, through the adoption of steam-powered prime movers. Even moderately sized mills and factories, with excellent waterpower resources, were obliged to acquire what effectively became 'back-up' engines to carry them over the summer months, when river levels ran low. But all such advances came at a relatively high cost. Ireland's native coal resources were pitifully small and poorly served by transit facilities, even during the railway age (see Chapter 3), while the boilers of imported British manufactured steam engines were, as one might expect, designed for use with British coal, which had to be imported to ensure their efficient operation. Ireland's ability to benefit almost instantly from early technological advances in Britain, and her effective world monopoly of Boulton and Watt's steam patents, thus involved the significant burden of importing British coal to sustain industrial growth.

2.1 *A Newcomen engine at Griff, Warwickshire, from J.T. Desaguiliers,* A Course of Experimental Philosophy, *(1744).*

Industrial steam engines are generally referred to as *stationary* steam engines, to distinguish them from loco-motive engines, i.e., those used for tractive purposes although, as in the rest of the former United Kingdom, the first working steam engines used in Ireland were employed in pumping out deep mines. In the period *c.* 1792–*c.* 1815, the majority of the as yet small numbers of steam engines at work in Irish industry were manufactured by Matthew Boulton and James Watt's Soho Foundry in Birmingham. Apart from Boulton and Watt's expertise, this was primarily because they controlled important steam engine patents, while in the period before 1815, Irish foundries were only beginning to emerge as important entities in their own right (see Chapter 10). Nonetheless, as early as 1802, a steam engine, of indeterminate type, was being made up in Lagan Foundry in Belfast, while Robinson's of Dublin, in 1816, became the first Irish foundry to manufacture a steam engine for a Cork distillery.[1]

The increasingly complex and diverse nature of steam engines and plant led to the growth of foundries specialising in their manufacture and, in the second half of the nineteenth century, most engines used in Ireland were purchased from specialist English firms. Coates, Combe and Barbour, and Rowan's foundries in Belfast became the principal specialist Irish firms, although the larger provincial foundries such as Perrott's and McSwiney's of Cork also made engines to order for local needs when the occasion arose. Nonetheless, the dominance of the Belfast foundries is reflected in the small surviving corpus of Irish-built engines, many of which were manufactured by Belfast firms.[2]

Just over half of the Boulton and Watt engines sold to Irish manufacturers in the years 1792-1815 were involved in aspects of important food-processing industries, principally, distilling, brewing and milling.[3] In the years leading up to and including the Napoleonic Wars, these were, of course, important sectors of the Irish provisions trade, where only through the acquisition of steam-powered prime movers could the larger units of these industries hope both to augment and sustain levels of production. In many other industries, however, available water power could, at least for the present, maintain existing levels of production. As late as 1834-8, only four steam engines were in operation amongst some 150 linen finishing enterprises in Counties Antrim, Armagh and Down, and in 1854-5, most of the bleach works in the Ulster counties still employed water-powered machinery.[4] In other sectors of the Northern textile industries where one might expect significant growth, such as flax spinning, however, the evidence clearly indicates the contrary. The first steam plant used in Ulster flax-spinning was not installed until 1825 and, while in the years 1826-38 upwards on eighteen engines were erected in the Belfast area, from the 733 hp of the energy generated by cotton and flax spinning mills in the region in 1834, 547 hp was created by water-powered prime movers. In 1842, many Ulster spinning mills still relied on water power.[5] Elsewhere in Ireland, the introduction of steam plant was, for the most part, a relatively slow process. In the capital, the adoption of steam plant increased in use by just over 57 per cent in period 1839-43, and the corresponding figure for Cork for roughly the same time span was slightly more than 41 per cent.[6] In 1870, from a total of 40,892 hp in Irish industry, 31,013 hp, or just over 75 per cent of recorded horsepower was generated by steam.

(1) The development of the stationary steam engine in Ireland

(a) c. 1740-1815

The earliest recorded use of a steam engine in Ireland was at Doonane, County Laois, on the Kilkenny coalfield in 1740. Little is known about the Doonane engine except that it is likely to have been an atmospheric engine of the Newcomen type.[7] In the engine designed by Thomas Newcomen (1663-1729), a vertical cylinder

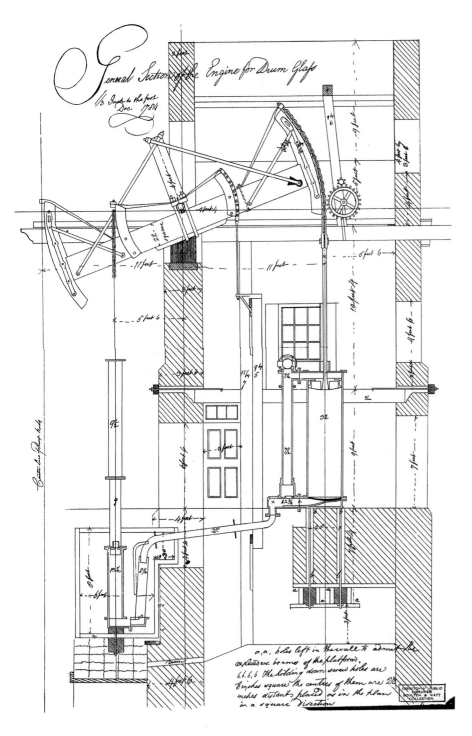

General Section of the Engine for Drum Glass

1/3 Inch to the foot
Dec. 1784

a,a, holes left in the wall to admit the
cylinder beams of the platform.
6.6.6.6 The holding down screw holes are
8 inches square the centres of them are 2
inches distant placed as in the plan
in a square direction

2.2 *The Boulton and Watt beam pumping engine at*
Drumglass, County Tyrone installed between 1784-6.

was fed with steam from a boiler positioned immediately beneath it. A piston in the cylinder was connected by a chain to the working beam, and, when low-pressure steam (generally just above atmospheric pressure) was admitted into the cylinder, the weight of the pump rods on the opposite side of the working beam raised the piston upwards (figure 2.1). By injecting cold water into the cylinder, the steam was rapidly condensed. The sudden change in atmospheric pressure drove the piston downwards, pulling with it the chains attached to the beam, and, in the same process, raising the pump rods at its opposite end. The completion of this cycle is called the working *stroke* but, in the Newcomen engine, the necessity of heating and cooling the cylinder during this cycle involved large quantities of coal.[8] With the possible exception of a textile mill engine in Belfast, the Doonane colliery pumping engine appears to have been the only Newcomen engine ever used in Ireland. Elsewhere in Ireland, indeed, excessive fuel consumption demands may well have precluded their widespread use.

In the second half of the eighteenth century, a number of important improvements in steam engine design, principally by James Watt (1736-1819), greatly expanded the range of early steam engines. In 1769, Watt patented his *separate condenser*, which he developed from his discovery that, by keeping the engine cylinder continually hot (instead of cooling it at every stroke), the engine could be run much more efficiently. The steam was now condensed in a cast-iron box (the *condenser*) beneath the cylinder, which obviated the need for reheating the cylinder. Watt's second major contribution was the application of the double-acting principle to the engine's cylinder. In early Newcomen and Watt engines, the steam acted on one side of the piston only. But by allowing the steam to act on both sides of the piston, alternately, it was now possible to derive twice the power from the same size of cylinder. By this means, Watt was able to develop the first double-acting steam engines, a principle which he patented in 1782. Around this time, Boulton and Watt's Soho Foundry in Birmingham supplied a single-acting, beam pumping engine to replace the original Newcomen engine at the Doonane Colliery in the period 1782-3.[9] A few years later, in 1784-6, a second Boulton and Watt engine of this type was installed at a coal mine at Drumglass, between Coalisland and Dungannon. Both the Doonane and the Drumglass engines were equipped with separate condensers (figure 2.2).[10] The first double-acting beam engine supplied to Ireland by Boulton and Watt was that used at Arigna, County Roscommon, to power a blast furnace in the 1790s (see Chapter 4).[11]

In terms of power transmission, the rocking, reciprocating motion of the engine's beam was originally suited only to working pumping machinery. In the period 1783-99, several cotton mills in the Manchester region used a combination of steam and water power to operate textile machinery. These are generally termed *water-returning engines*, where the drive from a conventional vertical water-wheel was used to power the machinery, with a steam-powered pump being employed to return the water exiting from the water-wheel to its feeder cistern. In this way, the steam-powered plant enabled the water flowing through the mill system to be continuously recycled. There is, apparently, only one recorded instance of the use of a water-returning engine in Ireland, at Stevenson's cotton mill at Springhill, Belfast, in 1791. In the Manchester area, both Newcomen engines and Savery steam pumps were used in water-returning systems, but it is not known which variety was used in the Springhill mill.[12] The Savery steam pump was the first successful steam-powered pump. The creation of a vacuum in a closed vessel, by rapidly condensing steam supplied to it from a boiler, enabled water to be raised up a suction pipe. Although this device could only raise water to moderate heights, it was admirably suited for employment in water-returning systems. It was also much cheaper to buy than the early Boulton and Watt engines, but its high fuel consumption eventually compelled mill owners to invest in the former.[13] In an Irish context, it is likely that a Newcomen engine would be a much more attractive option. Moreover, the Springhill water-returning engine, although probably influenced by contemporary practices in Manchester cotton mills, was installed at a time when the first Boulton and Watt engines capable of directly powering industrial machinery were beginning to be imported into Ireland.

The development of *rotative* steam engines in the 1780s, in which the motion of the beam could be adapted for rotary motion, enabled engines to drive almost any type of machinery. A 15 hp Boulton and Watt rotative engine, bought in Glasgow, transported to and eventually installed in James Wallace's cotton mill at Lisburn, County Antrim, in 1789-90, was the first rotative engine used in Ireland.[14] In 1791, a second rotative engine was at work in an iron foundry at Old Church Street in Dublin and, by 1800, at least five others were in operation in Dublin and Cork. These latter appear to have been pirated versions of Boulton and Watt engines built by Irish foundries.[15] In early Boulton and Watt rotative engines, the reciprocating motion of the beam could be translated into the rotary motion required for driving machinery in two ways. A crank and flywheel combination connected to the working beam, patented by James Pickard in 1780 (much to Watt's annoyance), led to the creation of Watt's ingenious 'sun and planet' gear, developed by Boulton and Watt's Soho Foundry in Birmingham to get around Pickard's patent. Both of these means of power transmission were in use in Ireland by about 1800. The sun and planet gear consisted of two cog wheels held in mesh by a link, one of which was attached to the beam's connecting rod and the other to the flywheel. The motion of this type of gearing enabled the shaft to rotate at twice the speed of the engine, which proved to be extremely effective in textile mills where line shafting was used. Furthermore, as the speed of the flywheel was twice the speed of the engine it could be made more lightweight. The first example of a Boulton and Watt engine with a sun and planet gear in Ireland was bought by the Grand Canal Company in 1792, and was a 3 hp model originally made for the Birmingham Canal Company. This was one of the two sun and planet engines known to have been employed in Ireland, the other is the only known example to have been supplied directly to Ireland. This was installed in Isaac Morgan's flour mill near George's Quay in Cork in 1800. It was later dismantled after a fire in 1802 and brought to Dublin for use in Roe's Distillery in 1811.[16]

In the years 1796-98, the first recorded examples of *compound* engines were erected at the Coolbawn and Curragh collieries on the Wandesforde Estates in County Kilkenny.[17] Up to this time, all the beam pumping and rotative engines at work here had a single cylinder which would have used low-pressure steam. The principle of compounding, which involved two cylinders (and later improved boilers) enabled high-pressure steam to be used, first in a *high-pressure cylinder* and then in a larger, *low-pressure cylinder*, in which the steam continued to expand and to perform useful work on the same beam. The two Coolbawn Colliery engines (called *Pollough* and *Curragh*) were installed by Irish engineer Michael Fenton, who had earlier, as colliery engineer at Doonane, County Laois, superintended the Boulton and Watt beam pumping engine there. However, it is not known which system of compounding these engines was employed, although it was probably either Jonathan Hornblower's system developed in the period 1781-82, or Adam Heslop's of 1790-91. Both systems infringed Watt's patents, and only small numbers of each appear to have been built. Hornblower's system, while it did employ double cylinders, was not very efficient, and could not lay any legitimate claim to significant fuel savings over single cylinder engines. Heslop's, on the other hand, which he patented in 1790, used a cylinder worked on Watt's principle to push the working beam, and one worked on Newcomen's principle, positioned at the opposite end of the beam, to pull it.[18]

In Ireland and Britain early beam engines were heavily reliant on the structures housing them for both support and shelter, the working beam often resting on one of the end walls or on an intermediate supporting wall. These are generally called *house-built* engines, after the early practice (continued with Cornish pumping engines) of building beam engines as an integral feature of the engine house. There are only two surviving engines of this type in Ireland. The earliest extant instance is a 25 hp, single cylinder beam engine dating to the 1830s, at Caledon Woollen Mills, County Tyrone. The associated multi-storey woollen mill was demolished in recent years but the former woollen factory was originally used as a flour mill, which was fitted out by William Fairbairn in the 1820s. Fairbairn's association with the site raises the possibility that this engine was supplied by him, but whatever the case may be, the Caledon beam engine appears to have been modified in 1882 for the operation

2.3 *The Millhouse engine, originally installed in Jameson's distillery, Bow Street, Dublin, in 1884 by Victor Coates of Belfast, as exhibited in School of Engineering building on the Belfield campus of University College, Dublin.*

of the former woollen mill.[19] The second surviving house-built engine is the Millhouse engine, installed in Jameson's Distillery, Bow Street, Dublin, in 1884 by Victor Coates of Belfast (figure 2.3). It by no means clear why such an antiquated design was employed at this late date, but one explanation is that the boilers associated with the original engine on the site had insufficient power for a more modern engine design.[20] A more likely explanation is the highly conservative nature of the distilling industry. Moreover, it is clear that the Millhouse engine replaced, and closely corresponded to, an earlier Boulton and Watt model of 1804. This had originally been bought to pump fresh water to the city's north side by Dublin Corporation, but was later sold and installed in Jameson's Distillery in 1808.[21] The expansion gear for the Coates engine, operated by a porter type governor,

2.4 *Beam engine originally installed, second hand, c. 1866-77, at Midleton Distillery, County Cork, now on display as a working exhibit at the Steam Museum at Straffan, County Kildare (above);* **2.5** *Small, single-column beam engine, reputedly bought by William Smithwick in 1847 at the Manchester Exhibition and installed in the St Francis Abbey Brewery, Kilkenny, where it was worked up until about 1930 (right). Now maintained as working exhibit at the Steam Museum at Straffan, County Kildare.*

is of note. This gear was designed and patented by Alexander Craig, a County Down engineer, in 1876. In 1987-89, the Millhouse engine was removed to the Belfield campus of University College, Dublin, where it has been attractively incorporated into the new School of Engineering building as a working exhibit, now powered by an electric motor.

Boulton and Watt, however, developed *independent* beam engines, which enabled beam engines to operate in conditions that did not require a large masonry engine house. An engine bed consisting of large masonry blocks was now built to support a framework of anything from one to six cast-iron columns, which was used to carry the weight of the beam. In the period 1800-14, Boulton and Watt supplied five independent beam engines to Irish industrialists, two of which (including Guinness' first steam engine) had six-column frameworks.[22] Four of these independent engines were built for breweries, three in Dublin (1809-10) and one for Walker's Brewery in Fermoy, County Cork (1814). The fifth engine, installed in the Watercourse Distillery in Cork in 1811, was of the *side lever* variety.[23] In the side lever independent engine, the beam is set *below* the cylinder. By pivoting the beam at a low level, significant savings in headroom could be achieved, and the design was widely used in early paddle steamers up until the mid-nineteenth century.

The best-preserved example of a six-column independent beam engine in Ireland is on display, *in situ*, at Midleton Distillery, County Cork. This was built by Peele and Williams of Manchester, and was installed in 1835.[24] A second engine of similar construction, from the same site, and dating from around the same period, has been dismantled and removed to the Steam Museum at Straffan, County Kildare, where it has been installed as a working exhibit (figure 2.4). It now seems likely that this engine (probably manufactured locally by a reliable local foundry like Perrott's or McSwineys of Cork) was acquired second-hand and installed in the distillery in the period *c.* 1866-77.[25] Also maintained in the Straffan collections is a small, single-column beam engine, reputedly bought by William Smithwick in 1847 at the Manchester Exhibition and installed in the St Francis Abbey Brewery, Kilkenny, where it was worked up until about 1930 (figure 2.5).

A variant form of independent engine, the '*A*'-*framed engine*, employed a working principle in which the engine acted directly upon the crankshaft. In this and in later *direct acting* engines, the motion of the

2.6 *An A-framed engine from Allman and Dowden's Brewery at Bandon, County Cork, dating from the 1830s, restored to full working order at the Steam Museum at Straffan, County Kildare.*

piston could be transferred directly to the crankshaft without the interposition of the beam. In 'A'-frame engines, the flywheel and the crankshaft were mounted on two 'A'-shaped trestles or frames, the cylinder being set directly upon a base plate. This was an early form of *vertical engine*, in which an *overhead crankshaft* (i.e., positioned above the cylinder) was employed. The earliest recorded Irish example of an 'A'-framed engine was built by the Neath Abbey Iron Company in 1817 for a Mr Shaw of Dublin.[26] An A-framed engine from Allman and Dowden's Brewery at Bandon, County Cork, which dates to the late 1830s, has recently been restored to full working order at the Straffan Steam Museum (figure 2.6).

Boulton and Watt continued to supply engines to Irish customers in the period 1800-14. The largest engine they built for an Irish industrial unit was the 40 hp beam engine for Walker's Distillery, at Crosse's Green, Cork (*c.* 1800).[27] Their principal customers continued to be involved in either the textile or food-processing industries, but other interesting uses were found for their engines, such as the 6 hp example bought for grinding mortar at the Howth Harbour works (1810) and the 20 hp engine used in the construction of the Dublin Custom House Docks in 1815.[28] A pumping engine was also supplied to the Ross Island Mine near Killarney, County Kerry, in 1807 (see Chapter 5).

(b) *c.* 1815-1910

As has been seen, foundries in Dublin and Cork were already producing pirated versions of Boulton and Watt engines before the end of the eighteenth century. After the expiry of Watt's patents in 1800, an increasing number of foundries, mainly in Dublin, Cork and Belfast, began to construct engines for the Irish market. However, very little technical information on the engines involved has thus far come to light, although there were some notable technical successes. One year after the first Irish-built steamship, the *City of Cork*, left the stocks at Cork harbour, the first Irish-made marine steam engines were built by James Atkinson at Thomas A. Barnes' Hive Iron Works, Cork, in 1816, for the *Waterloo*, the first wholly Irish-built paddle steamer. This was probably a side-lever model based on those supplied for the *City of Cork* by Boulton and Watt in 1815 (see Chapter 10). In 1820, the Lagan Foundry of Coates and Young in Belfast manufactured the 70 hp engines for the paddle steamer, *Belfast*, whilst the first marine steam engines by a Dublin foundry were built at the Ringsend Foundry in 1829 for the *Marchioness Wellesley* (see Chapter 10).

The next important development in steam engine design was the introduction of high-pressure steam. Early boiler designs were unable to withstand high-pressures, and in early Watt engines, the risk of boiler explosions generally prevented steam pressures greater than a few pounds above the atmosphere from being employed. Yet high-pressure steam did have significant advantages. By using steam pressure alone, the engine stroke of a typical beam engine could be dispensed with, as it would be no longer necessary to condense the steam in the cylinder to achieve the desired effect. The development of improved boilers by engineers such as the Cornishman, Richard Trevithick (1771-1833) in the early years of the nineteenth century, facilitated the advent of *non-condensing* engines. Trevithick's 'Cornish boiler' enabled steam engines to become more compact and portable, characteristics which Trevithick exploited to adapt high-pressure steam engines to power-wheeled vehicles, and thus produce the first steam locomotive engines. Portable high-pressure engines based on Trevithick's were made in Dublin by Popplewell's Foundry in the Liberties until about 1820, the earliest recorded instance of their manufacture and probable use in Ireland.[29]

Trevithick's Cornish boiler was first used in Great Britain in 1812 and effectively enabled the development of the Cornish beam engine, the most important prime mover in the British and Irish mining industries during the nineteenth century. Around the same period Trevithick was developing the *Cornish cycle* associated with this distinctive pumping engine. In the Cornish engine, high-pressure steam was admitted into the engine's cylinder to initiate the first part of the stroke. However, a steam valve was employed to shut off the steam so that the remainder of the stroke could be made by its expansive properties. As in Watt's single-acting engines, the steam acted on top of the piston. Yet in this instance, both the expansive energy of the steam and the vacuum created by its condensation were used to make the working stroke. By using the steam expansively, significant fuel savings were possible, whilst sufficient levels of steam were maintained within the cylinder to permit a smoother action of the piston. This arrangement was ideally suited for beam pumping engines. The Cornish engine was the ultimate house-built engine, its enormous beam extending out from the reinforced end (or *bob*) wall of the engine house, which gave protection from the elements for the engine's mechanism. The outer end of the working beam and the upper sections of the pump rods were outside the bob wall.[30] In deep mines, the pump rods often extended hundreds of feet downwards into the mineshaft. Most of the timber used for pump rods in Irish mines was either Oregon or Danzig pine, made up in 18 in (0.457 m) square sections, the entire pump rod linkage often weighing up to 30 tons.[31]

The Cornish engine was in use in Ireland from at least the early 1820s onwards. However, the largely English complement of mine captains and skilled personnel, brought over to Ireland by contemporary mining companies, preferred to have their engines made in Britain by reputable firms such as Harvey's of Hayle in Cornwall or the Neath Abbey Iron Co. in Wales (see Chapter 5). The vast majority of Irish foundries, indeed, appear never to have manufactured Cornish engines, perhaps for this very reason. By at least 1813, James Atkinson at the Hive Iron Works in Cork appears to have been manufacturing mine pumping engines.[32] Indeed, while the Ringsend Foundry in Dublin did manufacture Cornish boilers for the Dublin Atmospheric Railway in 1844, the only Cornish pumping engine of note to be manufactured by an Irish foundry during the nineteenth century was a 90 hp model built by MacAdam's of Belfast for Cork Corporation Waterworks in 1858.[33] Nonetheless, imported Cornish engines were widely used for mine drainage at Irish mining sites throughout the nineteenth century. In 1815, the Neath Abbey Iron Company in Wales supplied a beam pumping engine to a mining company at Allihies, County Cork. It is by no means clear precisely what kind of engine was involved here, but the engine with the 36 in diameter cylinder supplied by Harvey and Company of Hayle, Cornwall, to Dooneen Copper Mine in the Allihies area in 1824 would, on present evidence, appear to be the first Cornish engine used in Ireland.[34]

Beam engines continued to be used in Ireland into the last century, although in nearly all cases these had been modified to enable the use of high-pressure steam. The principle of compounding, as we have already seen, was employed in at least two Irish pumping engines in the early 1800s. It was not until the introduction

2.7 *The No. 1 (1878) brewhouse engine (one of two McNaughted compound beam engines) built by Turnbull, Grant and Jack of the Canal Basin Foundry, Glasgow, for Power's Distillery, John's Lane, Dublin (now the National College of Art and Design).*

of the Woolf compound engine, however, that this principle became more widely adapted by engine manufacturers. As has been seen, Jonathan Hornblower's method of compounding was not very successful, and it was not until after 1804, with the introduction of Arthur Woolf's (1766-1837) improved system of compounding, that the principle of progressively expanding steam, using two cylinders, was successfully incorporated into engine design. Woolf's main contribution was in using the correct size ratios between the two cylinders. In Woolf's system, high-pressure steam admitted into the smaller, *high-pressure* cylinder, was permitted to expand to around three times its entry volume. The steam was then exhausted at a lower pressure into a second, larger (*low-pressure*) cylinder, where it was allowed again to expand to about three times its entry volume. The efficiency of this system was such that economies of up to 50 per cent were possible over Boulton and Watt low-pressure engines.[35] In the 1870s, the compounding principle was carried to three expansions by the addition of a third cylinder in *triple-expansion* engines.

Arthur Woolf's association with the Neath Abbey Iron Company in the early decades of the nineteenth century led to the construction of a number of Woolf compound engines for customers in England and Wales. It is even possible that the beam pumping engine supplied to the Allihies Mining Company from Neath in 1815 was of this type. Indeed, it is likely that a number of Woolf compounds were used in Ireland in the first half of the nineteenth century. However, low-pressure rotative beam engines would have been the norm in most Irish mills and factories until the second half of the nineteenth century. By the late 1840s, a great many water-powered industrial sites in Ireland would have installed auxiliary steam engines to obviate any insufficiency of water supply over the dryer, summer months. Most of these engines were of the rotative beam type, but by the late 1850s, many are likely to have been modified for the use of high-pressure steam on McNaught's system. In 1845 William

McNaught (1818-91) patented a method of compounding existing low-pressure, single-cylinder engines by the addition of a small high-pressure cylinder. The second cylinder was positioned on the crank side of the beam, and the existing cylinder was used for low-pressure steam. These modifications not only added to the increased power and economy of the engine but also spared the expense of acquiring a larger engine. Subsequently, new engines were supplied as McNaughted engines. The only two such McNaughted compound beam engines to survive *in situ* in Ireland are the No. 1 (1878) and the No. 2 (1886) brewhouse engines, both of which were built by Turnbull, Grant and Jack of the Canal Basin Foundry, Glasgow, for Power's Distillery, John's Lane, Dublin (now the College of Art and Design). Both of these are fine examples of their type, with Watt-type governors controlling a valve gear patented by John Turnbull in 1878 (figure 2.7).[36] These latter, along with another Turnbull, Grant and Jack example at Kilbeggan Distillery, are the only engines built by this foundry now in existence.

On present evidence, compound engines were certainly in wider use in Ireland by the late 1850s, and the larger flour mills, situated in the immediate hinterland of the island's ports, appear to have been amongst the first Irish industries to acquire them. These mills were often seriously disadvantaged relative to the newer, exclusively steam-powered mills built on the quaysides of Ireland's major ports. The acquisition of the most up-to-date steam plant was thus the only way in which they could hope to compete. At Thomas Dawson's flour mill at Millfield near Cork, for example, a 30 hp single cylinder engine was working in 1849. This was replaced in the early 1850s by a compound engine. Around the same time, the steam mill at Douglas, on the eastern out-skirts of Cork, was also working a compound engine. But by the late 1850s, *horizontal engines* were beginning to be introduced to Ireland. The compound engine in the Millfield flour mill, indeed, was being worked in conjunction with a 25 hp horizontal engine in 1857, whilst at least two further flour mills in Cork were operating horizontal engines in 1861.[37] For mill owners, horizontal engines had many advantages, the most important of which was the saving of space. Early independent beam engines had certainly freed mill and factory owners from the expense of large engine houses. However, in the horizontal engine, the beam could be dispensed with entirely, and from the outset these engines were direct-acting. The cylinder was laid horizon-tally, but there was initially a reluctance to use horizontal cylinders as it was believed that non-vertical cylinders would wear unevenly. Trevithick was the first to challenge this orthodoxy, producing the first stationary steam engine with a horizontal cylinder in 1802. Engines of this type, with horizontal cylinders, were being built in Popplewell's Foundry in the Dublin Liberties (presumably for an Irish market) before 1820.[38] The engine still required a solid bedding, but the compactness of single-cylinder horizontal engines enabled them to be conveniently tucked into the corner of the ground floor of a mill building. Although horizontal engines were in use in Ireland at a relatively early period, they appear not to have become common until the 1860s, by which period compound forms were in use in Irish linen mills. The most basic form of compound horizontal engine was the *single-tandem compound*, an arrangement in which the high-pressure and low-pressure cylinders were positioned one behind the other, driving one crank. The cylinders could also be set side by side (*cross-compound*), where each cylinder acted upon its own crank. A further arrangement called *twin-tandem*

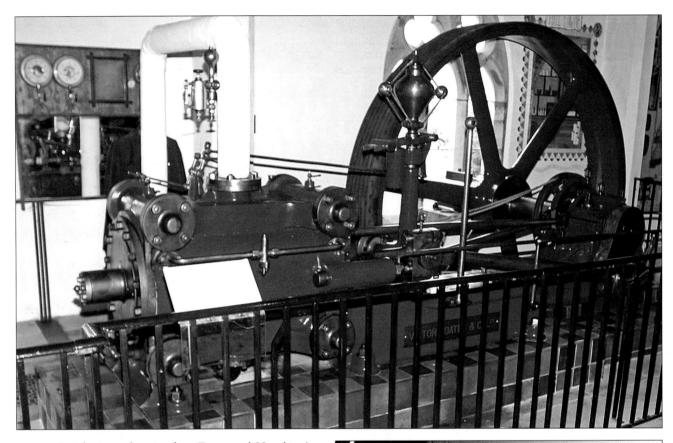

2.8 A horizontal engine from Frazer and Haughton's former bleach works at Cullybackey, near Ballymena, County Antrim (above). It was originally built by Victor Coates of Belfast in 1900, and was later installed at Cullbackey in 1903 where it worked up until 1976. It is now a working exihibit at the Steam Museum, Straffan, County Kildare; **2.9** *Tandem-compound horizontal engine built at Coates' Lagan Foundry in Belfast in 1899, which worked up until 1979 (right). It was originally installed in a Belfast mill but was moved to a linen mill at Tullymore Etra, Benburb, County Tyrone in 1938, now the Benburb Valley Heritage Centre.*

compound, involving two single-tandem compounds operating side by side, in which each tandem arrangement worked its own crank, was also employed. The increasing power requirements of textile mills in particular led to the construction of large, multi-cylinder compound horizontal engines, which developed thousands of horse power.

All the surviving examples of horizontal engines

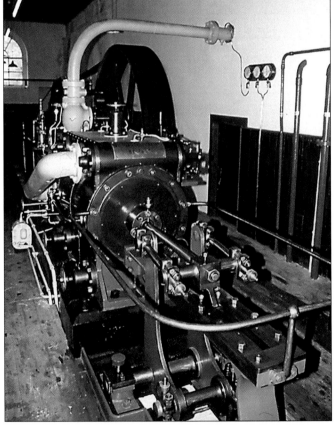

in Ireland date to the second half of the nineteenth century. The horizontal engine at Daly's Tullamore Distillery, County Offaly, has a valve gear which could belong to the 1840s but might still, nonetheless, date to the 1880s.[39] The 45–55 bhp horizontal engine built by John Rowan and Sons of Belfast in 1876 for Ulster Woollen Mills, Crumlin, County Antrim, is the only example of its type to survive.[40] At Belfast Corporation No.1 pumping works, Duncrue Street, Belfast, two horizontal non-condensing engines by W.H. Allen of Bedford, installed in the 1880s to pump storm water from sewers, survive *in situ*, whilst at the Cook's Lane Maltings of Guinness' Brewery in Dublin is to be found the only extant example of a single-cylinder, horizontal non-condensing engine made by a southern Irish foundry.[41] The Guinness engine was manufactured by William Spence of Cook Street, Dublin, in *c.* 1896. The Steam Museum at Straffan has a horizontal engine from Frazer and Haughton's former bleach works at Cullybackey, near Ballymena, County Antrim. It was originally built by Victor Coates of Belfast in 1900, and was later installed at Cullybackey in 1903 where it worked up until 1976 (figure 2.8).

At a former linen mill (now the Benburb Valley Heritage Centre) at Tullymore Etra, Benburb, County Tyrone, one of two tandem-compound horizontal engines (originally installed in Belfast but moved to Benburb in 1938) to survive in Ireland is displayed as a working exhibit (figure 2.9). The engine was built at Coates' Lagan Foundry in Belfast in 1899 and was worked up until 1979.[42] The second example, manufactured by Combe Barbour of Belfast, in 1910, is in the former Coalisland Weaving Company's mill at Coalisland, County Tyrone.[43] Surviving examples of horizontal cross-compound engines are equally rare. Locke's Distillery, at Kilbeggan, County Westmeath, retains *in situ* a horizontal cross-compound condensing engine, erected in 1887 by Canal Basin Foundry, Port Dundas, Glasgow, whilst at Belfast's No. 1 Pumping Station at Duncrue Street, Belfast, further examples by Victor Coates of Belfast, installed in the 1880s to drive sewerage pumping machinery, also survive.[44]

By the mid-1860s, there is evidence that *Corliss engines* were being used in Irish textile mills. The American engineer, George Henry Corliss (1817-88), developed a quick-acting valve gear which facilitated greater economy of use in steam engines in which they were employed. The Corliss valve was introduced into Britain in 1863, and in that same year, a variant on the Corliss valve was patented by William Inglis (1835-90). Inglis and his associate, John Frederick Spencer, were largely responsible for the adoption of Corliss engines in Britain. Inglis became involved with the Bolton firm of Hick and Hargreaves in the mid-1860s, and used Spencer's release mechanism (patented in 1865) and his own double-ported slide or Corliss valve in many of the engines made by him for Hick and Hargreaves.[45] In 1866, an Inglis-Corliss engine with 40 nominal horse power and a Spencer-Corliss valve gear, made by Hick and Hargreaves, was supplied to Wallis and Pollock's spinning mill at Donnybrook, near Cork.[46] This is the earliest recorded use of such an engine in Ireland. The only surviving Irish example of an Inglis and Spencer 'Improved Corliss Engine', by Hick and Hargreaves of Bolton, is a 300 hp model installed in a power loom factory at Edenderry, Banbridge, County Down in 1909, which was used for electricity generation.

In the 1870s, the principle of two steam expansions in compounded engines was expanded to three with the addition of a third cylinder to create the *triple-expansion engine*. The desired effect was achieved by adding

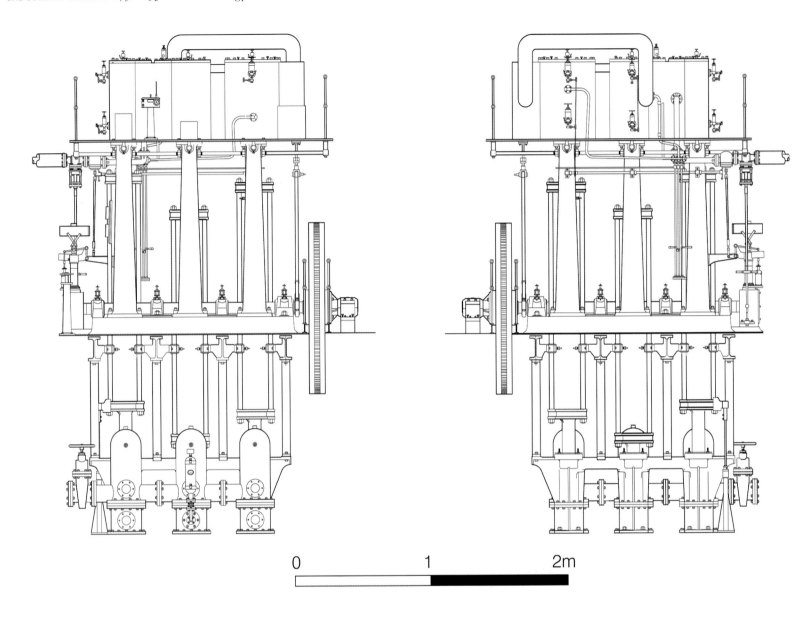

2.10 *Elevations of engine no. 229, an inverted, vertical triple expansion engine built by the Belfast firm of Combe and Barbour in 1905, and installed between 1905–07, at the Cork Corporation Waterworks.*

an intermediate pressure cylinder between the high- and low-pressure cylinders. This working principle was widely applied to direct-acting *vertical engines*, whose main advantage was that they required considerably less floor space than compound horizontal engines of equivalent power. In the early 1850s, James Nasmyth (1808–90) produced the first *inverted vertical engine* in which the crankshaft was positioned beneath the cylinder, as opposed to the overhead position typical of conventional vertical engines. Vertical and inverted vertical engines were widely adopted as marine engines in the late nineteenth century, and in Great Britain were generally employed in public utilities, such as water pumping stations and sewerage plants, to replace beam engines. Although, in comparative terms, large water-pumping stations were a rare feature of Irish nineteenth-century municipal water supply schemes, the existing Cornish pumping engine at Cork Corporation Waterworks was replaced by three inverted triple-expansion engines built by the Belfast firm of Combe and Barbour in 1905, and installed between 1905-07 (figures 2.10 and 2.11).[47] A further Belfast firm, Victor Coates and Co. Ltd, also manufactured triple and quadruple (four steam expansion) engines, examples of which include a 1,000 hp inverted triple expansion engine, built for Omrod, Hardcastle Ltd's Flash Street Mill in Bolton, Lancashire, in 1900, and a 4,000 hp vertical triple-expansion engine, built for the Newcastle-upon-Tyne Electric Tramways Company in 1904.[48] The principle of compounding was also adapted for vertical engines, where the cylinders (positioned side by side) were linked to one crankshaft. A large vertical compound condensing engine of 400 bhp,

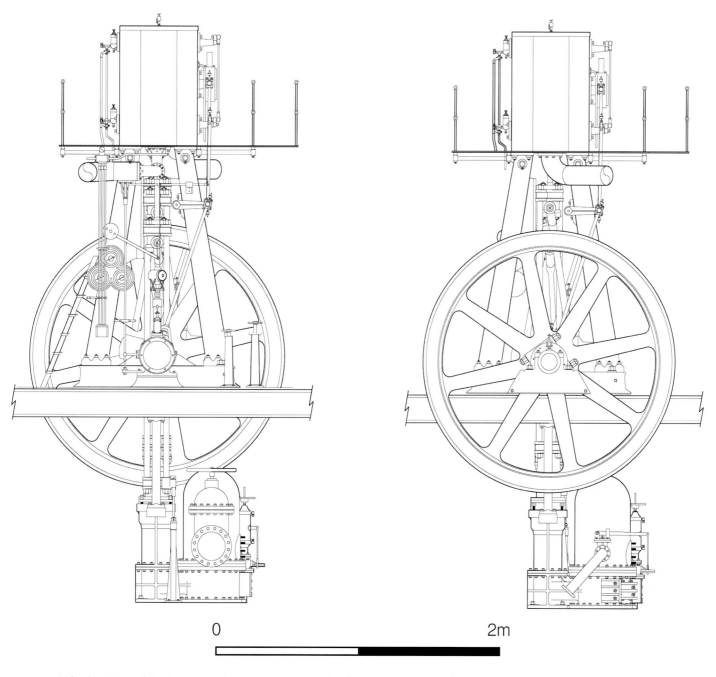

0   2m

2.11 *Side elevations of Cork waterworks engine 230. See also figure 2.10.*

built by Victor Coates and Co. Ltd of Belfast in 1898 for the Falls Flax Spinning Co. of Cupar Street, Belfast, is on display in the Ulster Museum.

The advent of electricity generation in Ireland in the early 1880s for powering electric tramways and public lighting was initially accommodated by generators powered by water turbines (see Chapters 16 and 17) and slow-speed steam engines. However, as early generators needed to turn at high speeds to produce a suitable current, and as existing steam engines worked at much slower speeds, the drive from the engine to the generator had to be speeded up through the use of belting. This, in turn, required larger buildings to accommodate the transmission system, whilst the generator itself needed special foundations. The fact that the engine was not directly coupled to the generator also involved a loss of power in the transfer of the engine's power to the generator. High-speed engines were thus developed to get around the problems created by early generators, whilst electrical engineers also began to develop generators which required slower rotational speeds in the late 1880s, which could be coupled directly to the engine.

The high-speed, single-acting, compound vertical engine patented by the English engineer, Peter William Willans (1851-92) in 1884-5, in which the distribution of the steam in the engine was controlled by centrally placed piston valves, was a commonly employed design in early British electricity generating stations. A Willans high-speed vertical compound engine was installed in Guinness' Brewery in the 1880s for powering a dynamo; the parts of the engine still survive and were until recently on display in the Guinness Hopstore. A further engine of this type, originally built for John Power and Sons Distillery in Dublin in the 1890s, is on display in Midleton Distillery, County Cork, with its original generator set.[49] There is, however, no evidence that they were used in early Irish generating stations employed for street lighting. Nonetheless, by the 1890s, generators worked by steam engines were at work in electricity generation stations in Ireland's larger cities like Dublin, Belfast and Cork. At Dublin's Fleet Street Power Station, opened in 1892, the engines drove the generators through belting, but at Cork's first electricity generating station, opened in 1898 at Albert Road, the three McIntosh and Seymour tandem-compound condensing engines were directly coupled to the generators. In the late nineteenth and early twentieth centuries, the first high-speed engines manufactured by the Birmingham firm of Bellis and Morcom were supplied to Ireland. The chief draughtsman at Bellis and Morcom, Albert Charles Pain, patented a system of forced lubrication in 1890, in which a pump forced oil onto the engine's main bearings, which effectively made the engine self-lubricating. Forced lubrication enabled the engine, which was now completely enclosed, to operate uninterrupted at high speeds for long periods, with minimal wear and tear.[50] At William Clarke and Sons works, Upperlands, County Derry, three enclosed high-speed engines by Bellis and Morcom, and one by Howden of Glasgow, each coupled to DC generators and installed in 1910-11, survive *in situ*; all were still at work in the 1970s. The Howden engine is the only known surviving example in Ulster.[51] The basic Bellis and Morcom design was eventually made more economical by the use of the triple expansion principle. Three Bellis and Morcom triple-expansion engines were installed in the Albert Road generating station in Cork in 1919 to replace the original tandem-compound engines.[52] Smaller high-speed engines were widely used in Ireland for electricity generation in factories, hospitals and laundries, where the steam could also be used for heating or for other industrial purposes. At Frazer and Haughton's works at Cullybacky, County Antrim, one of two engines still in regular use in the 1970s for electricity generation was a high-speed enclosed engine by W.H. Allen of Bedford of 375 hp, installed in 1903.[53]

In the late 1880s, Murphy's Lady's Well Brewery in Cork had installed a Parsons *steam turbine* for electricity generation which is, on present evidence, one of the earliest recorded uses of a Parsons steam turbine in Ireland. The Parsons steam turbine was developed by Sir Charles Parsons (1854-1931), sixth son of William the third Earl of Rosse, of Birr Castle, County Offaly.[54] In Parsons' design, steam was used to set a turbine in motion rather than exert pressure on a piston, as in a conventional steam engine. Early models proved to have a heavy steam consumption, which was quickly rectified, but, from the outset, Parsons' turbine could demonstrate considerable advantages over conventional reciprocating engines. To begin with, the necessity of directing oil to lubricate the pistons in reciprocating engines involved the lubricants mixing with the steam and consequential, but nonetheless unavoidable, losses of oil. This did not happen in the operation of steam turbines and considerable savings in maintenance were effected. Furthermore, the elaborate foundations or engine bed required for reciprocating engines, by which means the tremendous vibrations created by their operation were transmitted to the ground, could be dispensed with in steam turbines which were, even with their generator sets, considerably lighter and more compact.[55] The original patent was acquired in 1884 and, by 1889, around 250 had been manufactured and sold. Charles Parsons went on to found what was to eventually become N.E.I. Parsons of Newcastle.[56] The Parsons model, which, like all steam turbines, ran at high speeds, was ideally suited to electricity generation and was available in a non-condensing form by 1891. By the early 1890s, Parsons' turbines capable of large power outputs were already beginning to match the efficiency of large reciprocating steam engines, which they were destined to succeed in power generating plants where heat engines were employed.[57]

In 1896, Guinness' Brewery in Dublin was operating a Parsons' turbine where, in 1900, it became the first to re-use high-pressure steam which, in the operation of steam turbine, could be passed on for use in other industrial processes. As we have seen, the steam passing through a turbine does not mix with lubricants and, in the environment of a brewery or other food-processing facility, this was extremely advantageous, as it could be used, for example, for heating liquids. In Guinness' Brewery, exhaust steam from the Parsons' turbine was re-used to heat brewery vats.[58] In the early decades of the twentieth century, rival forms of steam turbine were beginning to appear in Ireland. In 1917, a 1,500 kw geared Curtis steam turbine was installed at the Albert Road generating station in Cork. In its essentials, the 'velocity compounding' steam turbine developed by Charles Gordon Curtis (1850-1953) was an impulse turbine, whereas the Parsons turbine worked on the reaction principle.[59]

(2) Features associated with steam engines

(a) Engine Houses

While surviving steam plant in Ireland is, comparatively speaking, somewhat rare, the structures built to house them are by no means uncommon, although early engine houses are, and none from the eighteenth century

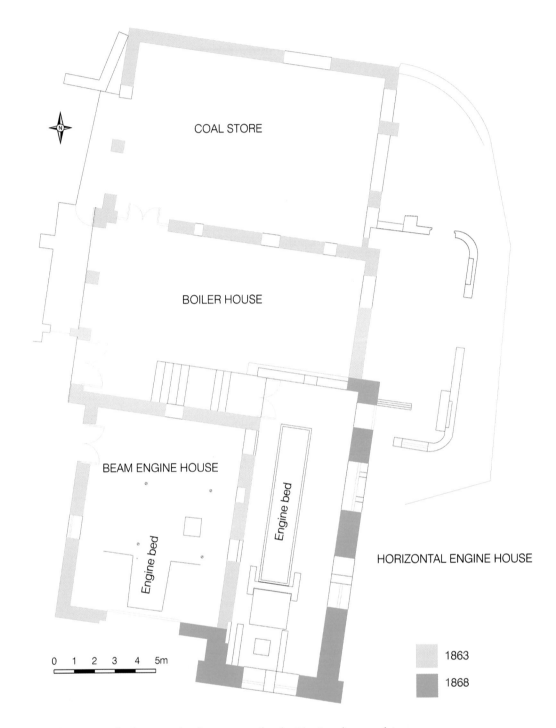

COAL STORE

BOILER HOUSE

BEAM ENGINE HOUSE

Engine bed

Engine bed

HORIZONTAL ENGINE HOUSE

0 1 2 3 4 5m

1863

1868

2.12 *Cork Corporation Waterworks beam engine houses, completed 1863-6 and restored in 2004-5.*

are known to have survived. The earliest extant example is a structure for a house-built engine at Beamish and Crawford's Cork Porter Brewery at Cork in 1818, a formal building of ashlar limestone. However, while this latter engine contains none of its original engine house fittings, there are two house-built engine houses, associated with Jonathan Pim's former cotton mill in St Catherine's Parish, Dublin, probably dating to the late 1830s, that retain, *in situ*, fluted transverse beams. One of these is a large inverted 'T'-sectioned cast-iron beam

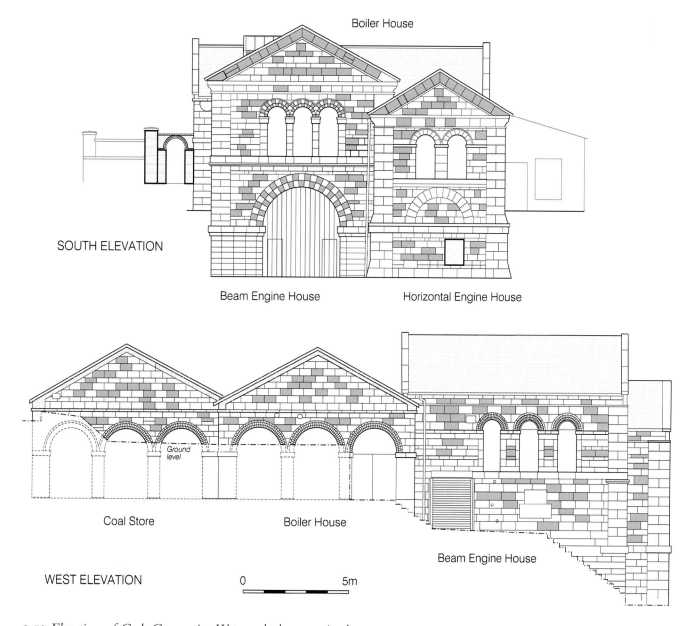

Boiler House

SOUTH ELEVATION

Beam Engine House   Horizontal Engine House

Ground level

Coal Store   Boiler House

Beam Engine House

WEST ELEVATION   0   5m

2.13 *Elevations of Cork Corporation Waterworks beam engine houses.*

with a classical engine entablature on its outer face, upon whose lower face are two square sockets which are externally formed into moulded pediments. Into these latter would have been inserted two vertical columns for the engine frame, the beam itself originally being used to support the engine's working beam.

A firm foundation was always provided for the engine, and this generally took the form of a deep bed of coursed, ashlar masonry on to which the engine frame was bolted. Good examples of these engine beds survive in the former Power's Distillery engine houses on Thomas Street, Dublin, and in the Cork Corporation Waterworks beam engine houses which date to 1863-6. Most of the early nineteenth-century engine houses, however, seem generally to have been demolished when newer engines were installed. The Cork Corporation Waterworks complex, on the Lee Road in Cork, retains the best-preserved examples of nineteenth- and early

71

twentieth-century engine houses in Ireland. These include an entire range of auxiliary beam and horizontal engine houses, along with associated boiler houses and coal stores, dating to the period 1863-1907 (figures 2.12 and 2.13). Also contained within this complex is the only complete set of inverted vertical triple-expansion engines, housings and associated plant in Ireland, dating to the period 1904-7 (figure 2.14). The Lee Road triple-expansion engine house also retains, *in situ*, its own English manufactured gantry crane, installed by Combe Barbour of Belfast in 1926.

A number of Cornish engine houses have survived at the sites of Irish mineral mines in Counties Cork, Tipperary, Clare, Waterford and Wicklow, where a number of the earliest surviving examples belong to the 1830s (see Chapters 3 and 5). The advent of independent engines and horizontal engines meant that smaller engine houses could be built, but the introduction of tandem-compound engines brought with it the necessity of lengthening the engine bed and the engine house. Nonetheless, tall engine houses continued to be built, particularly in Irish linen mills, even though these generally employed compound engines from the 1860s onwards. A number of well-preserved engine houses associated with linen mills and weaving factories can still be seen in the

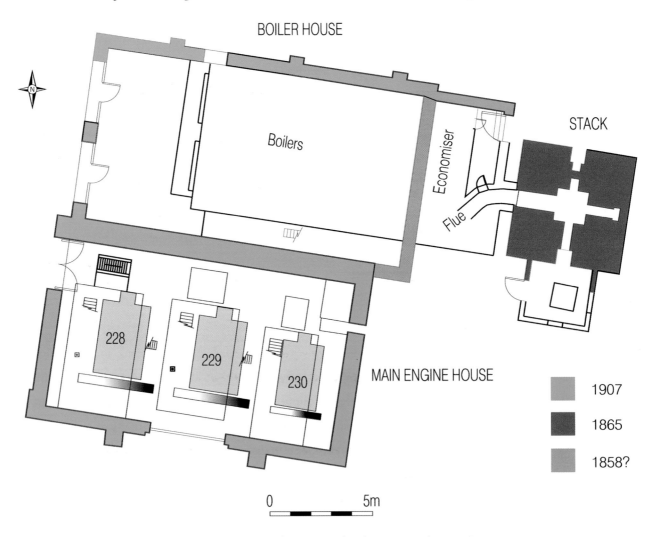

2.14 *Cork Corporation Waterworks pumping engine houses, completed 1904-7, and restored in 2004-5.*

greater Belfast area. Many of those erected after 1860 are brick built, with elaborate Venetian-arched windows. Their interiors are often panelled with classical entablatures, to complement similar designs cast on the metal parts of the engine's frame, as in the engine house at the Edenderry flax spinning mill on the Crumlin Road in Belfast.

(b) Boilers and Boiler Houses

The earliest-known steam engine used in Ireland at Doonane, County Laois, is likely to have employed a *haystack boiler*. This was basically a copper cylinder with a concave base and domed top, very similar to the coppers used by brewers for boiling wort with sugar and hops. Haystack boilers were normally contained within a brick base rather than in a covered building: none survive in Ireland. With the introduction of Boulton and Watt engines, this design was replaced with the *wagon boiler*. Such boilers are shown on the earliest surviving drawings of Boulton and Watt engines supplied to Ireland, where the boiler retains the distinctive cross section of the haystack type but is now elongated and often rectangular in plan. The wagon boiler was also equipped with a flue that runs along the entire length of the boiler, which increased the heating surface. The development

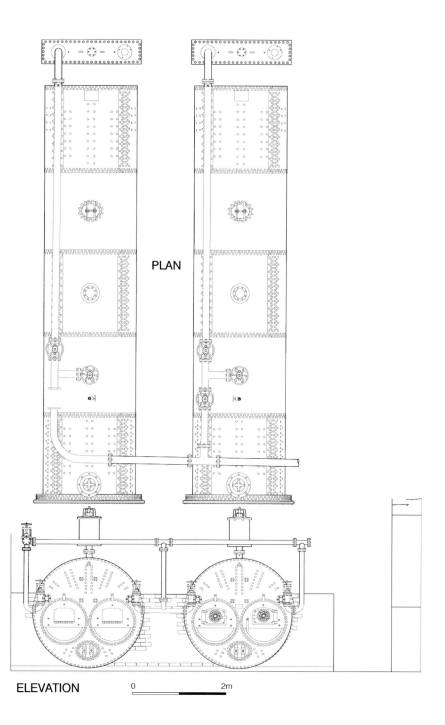

PLAN

ELEVATION

0   2m

2.15 *Plan and elevation of Lancashire boilers at Cork Corporation Waterworks, built by Victor Coates of Belfast in 1904.*

2.16 *Lancashire boilers at Cork Corporation Waterworks (above). See also figure 2.15 which shows a line drawing of this feature;* **2.17** *72-tube Green's Economiser at Cork Corporation Waterworks, installed in 1904 (right). This is the only example in Ireland to be retained* in situ.

of the Cornish and Lancashire boilers, which enabled both the use of higher steam pressures and increased fuel economy, led to the eventual abandonment of the wagon boiler. In the Cornish boiler, steam pressures of around 50 psi became possible, whilst the *Lancashire boiler*, which was similar to the Cornish type except that it employed two fire tubes, was easier to clean out. The Lancashire boiler, patented by William Fairbairn and John Hetherington in 1844, had the additional advantage of a larger grate area; it became the most commonly used type in Ireland during the second half of the nineteenth century. The best-preserved Irish boiler house retaining all its original fittings, which includes two Lancashire boilers, manufactured by Victor Coates of Belfast in 1904, is at Cork Corporation Waterworks (figures 2.15 and 2.16).[60] Six large Lancashire boilers by Hick and Hargreaves of Bolton, built in 1907 for the Edenderry flax spinning mill on the Crumlin Road, also survive *in situ*. In the closing decades of the nineteenth century, *water-tube boilers*, such as that patented by George Herman Babcock (1832-93) and Stephen Wilcox (1830-93) in America in 1867, were introduced into Ireland. In water tube boilers, an inclined battery of straight tubes, through which water circulated, absorbed the heat from hot gases circulating around the tubes. The bank of tubes provided an increased heating surface which allowed steam to be raised more quickly than in Lancashire boilers, whilst the tubes themselves were both easier to clean and capable of withstanding higher steam pressures. Babcock and Wilcox boilers were employed in the Fleet Street Power Station in Dublin in 1892 and in the Cork Generating Station at Albert Road in 1898 (see Chapter 16).

Regardless of whether or not the boiler house was a separate structure, certain features were virtually standard. In many instances, the roof was provided with a louvred vent running the entire length of the ridge to reduce condensation, or with cast-iron water tanks to hold feed water for the boilers. It was also common for the front wall of the boiler house to have a series of arches, the number of which usually corresponded to the number of boilers accommodated within it. The arches allowed the boilers to be installed and coal to be brought into the boiler house in barrows or bogeys. In textile mills, it was also common for an extra floor to be positioned above the boilers to facilitate drying.

(c) Economisers

From the late 1840s onwards, Edward Green of Wakefield's patent *economiser* enabled industrialists throughout Britain to make significant savings on fuel costs. In Green's economiser, the boilers' feed water was heated by the exhaust gases leaving the boiler furnaces. A series of metal pipes, fed with boiler feed water, were set into the flues leading from the furnaces to the chimney. The water in these pipes was heated by the exhaust gases from the boiler furnaces before these exited up the chimney, and in this way the cost of producing steam could be reduced by up to around 20 per cent. The build-up of soot on the exterior of the economiser tubes was counteracted by a special scraper mechanism. Economisers became common throughout Ireland in the second half of the nineteenth century, but very few have survived. The only example in Ireland to be retained *in situ* is the 72 tube Green's Economiser at Cork Corporation Waterworks, installed in 1904 (figure 2.17).[61]

(d) Chimneys

The most dominant feature of many nineteenth-century industrial sites, the mill chimney or *stack*, was designed both to disperse the exhaust fumes from the boiler furnaces whilst also helping to create a draught for the furnaces themselves. Early chimneys tended to be square-sectioned, built with either cut or rubble stone, with quoins being employed at the corners to emphasise their verticalilty, but these could later be polygonal or circular in plan for decorative effect. Brick became the most common building material used in their construction in the second half of the nineteenth century, when engine sizes became bigger and the height of chimneys was increased to accommodate them. In early engines, chimneys tended to be small, although at least one Irish example, at Stein and Browne's Distillery at Limerick, was 115 ft (*c.* 35 m) high in 1822. The Cork Waterworks stack, completed in 1865, is the most elaborate of its type to survive in Ireland. It is built on a cut stone plinth, surmounted by alternating string courses of cut limestone and sandstone blocks. It is square-sectioned and is 44 m high from the base to the capping, and 5.49 m wide. The main section of the stack gently tapers upwards from the base and is formed of seven brick panels separated by cut limestone string courses with stressed, cut limestone quoins (figure 2.18).

(3) The Internal Combustion Engine

In the internal combustion engine, a mixture of air and fuel (gas, oil or petrol) is ignited and exploded within a closed cylinder. The piston in the cylinder is then driven by the force of the explosion to the opposite end of the cylinder, and the resulting movement is used to turn a crankshaft. The first successful internal combustion engine, which used piped, town gas as fuel, was developed by the Paris-based Belgian engineer, Jean Joseph Etienne Lenoir, in 1860.[62] In 1869, the Earl of Rosse did, indeed, own a 'steam carriage' powered by a Lenoir coal gas engine, which was responsible for the death of the naturalist, Mary Ward, in the same year – the first recorded motor-car fatality in these islands.[63] Internal combustion engines operate on a four-phase cycle, commonly called the *Otto cycle* (or constant volume cycle), developed by the German engineer, Nicholaus August Otto (1832-91) in his *Otto Silent Engine* of 1876. In the Otto four stroke cycle the basic sequence involves two revolutions of the engine for every power stroke, which is then repeated. The four strokes which make up the cycle are the *suction* of the air-gas mixture into the cylinder, its *compression* during the inward stroke, *ignition* followed by expansion and the *exhaust* of the burnt gases on the fourth stroke. In 1880, a two-stroke version was developed, which effectively eliminated the suction and exhaust strokes, and in such engines, the working sequence involved one working stroke for each revolution of the engine.[64]

In Otto's engine, the compression of the air-gas mixture before ignition led to increased power output and efficiency. And, while the early reliance of such engines on town gas limited their use to sites with access to a piped gas supply, even in their early stages of development, gas engines held a number of important advantages over steam. Gas engines were capable of higher thermal efficiencies than engines fed by steam boilers. They could be started up instantly and, as they did not require boilers, they were at once cheaper to instal and took up less space than steam plant. Furthermore, engines run on piped gas supplies created no ashes or smoke nuisance. From the 1880s onwards, the increased availability of *producer gas* units freed gas engines from their reliance on the more expensive town gas networks. In Ireland, producer gas was generally made from low-grade, home-produced fuel such as peat and graded anthracite, cheaper to manufacture than town gas, but which was invariably made from imported coal. In the producer unit, gas was manufactured in a vertical steel cylinder internally lined with firebrick. The turf or anthracite was fed into a charging bell at the top of cylinder, which fed the fuel into the cylinder without allowing any gas to escape. Before being fed to the engine, the gas was passed through a *scrubber*, which removed impurities such as tar.[65] Producer gas was also known as *suction gas*, after the motion of the engine's piston which created a draught sufficient to draw air into the system.

2.18 *Elevation of chimney at Cork Corporation Waterworks, completed in 1865.*

2.19 *Gas producer plant of 1902, recommended by Crossley's of Manchester for Kilkenny anthracite*

One of the earliest recorded uses of Otto gas engines and gas-producer plant in Ireland dates to 1885-7, when a gas producer plant was installed on Tory Island off the Donegal coast to produce gas for a lighthouse and to power two Otto gas engines required for operating fog horns. In 1888, the large railway engineering works at Inchicore Dublin also had two large gas producers. Many of the gas engines used in Ireland in the late nineteenth and early twentieth centuries were manufactured by Crossley Brothers. In 1876, they had acquired sole rights to Otto's silent gas engine, and, by 1876 Frank and William Crossley were already producing these at their Manchester works. In the early 1900s, anthracite from the Kilkenny coalfield began to be washed and screened for producer gas plants used with Crossley gas engines (figure 2.19).[66] By the end of the nineteenth century, gas engines capable of power outputs equivalent to the larger steam engines were being built, and some of up to 400 hp were already beginning to be installed in the larger Irish towns. They were also used as back-up engines as at the Galway hydro-electric station, where a gas engine was on stand-by in 1902.[67] The makers claimed that they were five times more economical than steam engines, but regardless of such claims, they proved well suited for rural or remote locations. They were also eminently more adaptable to conditions of intermittent working. Peat was also used for producer gas units, the most noteworthy example being the system adapted by the Hamilton Robb weaving factory at Portadown between 1911 and 1920. Hamilton Robb harvested peat by traditional methods from a bog on the shores of Lough Neagh, which was transported to their factory along the River Bann by barges pulled by tugs. At the factory, the peat was transferred from the barges to the producers by means of a conveyor. The producer plant supplied gas to two engines of 120 bhp each and an engine of 150 bhp, an arrangement which cut Hamilton Robb's fuel costs by about one-half (figure 2.20).[68]

In the 1880s, oil and petrol engines were developed in which atomised oil or petroleum in air was ignited in the engine's cylinder, by means of either a spark or a hot tube. Petrol engines were developed principally through the independent efforts of the German engineers, Gottlieb Daimler and Karl Benz, in the years 1884-5. These engines also utilised the Otto cycle, and Benz's spark ignition system is the model for those employed today. The use of liquid fuels further increased both the versatility and mobility of internal combustion engines. By the early 1900s, Crossley Brothers were supplying oil engines for powering pumps, laundries, dynamos and

2.20 *Hamilton Robb gas producer plant at Portadown in c. 1915.*

creameries throughout Ireland, which could use common lamp oil (available in most small towns and villages) as fuel.[69] As early as 1885, Benz had fitted his petrol engine to a three-wheeled carriage, initiating a new era of motorised transport in which the fuel could be carried on the vehicle's tank for both convenience and increased mobility. However, the use of self-propelled vehicles employing either steam or petrol engines on the roads of both Britain and Ireland towards the end of the nineteenth century was severely curbed by existing legislation. The first petrol engine imported into Ireland, by Frederick Richard Simms in 1891, seems to have been a means of getting around the problems caused by existing legislation with regard to fully assembled motor cars. Indeed, the first motor car used in Ireland, in 1895, appears to be a Benz model driven by a visitor, Henry Hewetson, who was followed by Dr John Colohan with his the 4.5 hp Benz. Colohan became the first documented Irish motorist in around 1896.[70] By 1912, Irish industrial prime movers included 85 gas engines, 92 petrol engines and 565 oil engines, along with 800 steam engines, 650 water-wheels and 116 windmills (mostly wind engines).[71]

3

Fossil Fuels

At the close of the seventeenth century, by Sir William Petty's estimate, some 40,000 tons of English coal were being imported into Ireland annually, by which time, he noted, coal was 'the general and uniform fuel' of the inhabitants of Dublin.[1] By the middle of the eighteenth century, imported coal was such an important commodity in the ports of both Dublin and Cork that the civic authorities in each city were forced to act to prevent speculators from monopolising the import trade. Legislation was also enacted to restrict the sale of coal to public coal yards in the 1760s, in order to ensure that coal was both equitably distributed and sold at fair prices.[2] From the mid-seventeenth century onwards, the Whitehaven collieries in Cumberland were the principal source of Dublin's imported coal, although during the eighteenth century, coal from Swansea and from Scotland was also beginning to be brought on a regular basis into other Irish ports. From the outset, these supplies were, in relative terms, quite cheap, and an increased reliance on imported coal for domestic use appears not to have unduly troubled contemporaries. By 1750, 98,000 tons were imported, increasing to 399,000 tons in 1800 and 717,000 in 1825-8 where, as early as 1818, some 40 per cent of the total was already being consumed in Dublin. By the 1860s, some 2.5 million tons were being imported for both domestic and industrial purposes.[3]

Apart from domestic space heating, imported coal was, of course, also increasingly used for industrial processes and for raising steam while native coal, as we shall presently see, was not only under used but generally found fewer markets beyond the immediate localities where it was mined. But whereas Irish coal was, relative to the rest of the former United Kingdom, a scarce commodity, the truly vast native resources of peat (or *turf* as it is universally known in Ireland) found few uses in Irish industry well into the early years of the twentieth century.

3.1 *The coalfields of Ireland.*

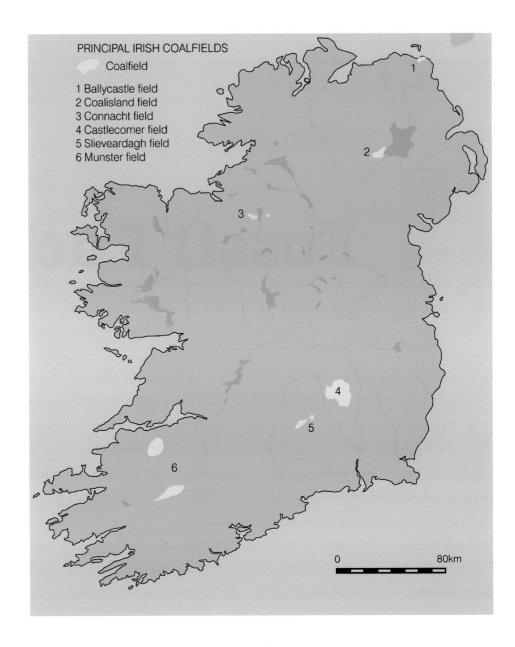

PRINCIPAL IRISH COALFIELDS

Coalfield

1 Ballycastle field
2 Coalisland field
3 Connacht field
4 Castlecomer field
5 Slieveardagh field
6 Munster field

0   80km

(1) Coal

The coal deposits exploited in Ireland up until very recent times are, in general terms, similar to those of England, Scotland and Wales (figure 3.1). But whereas the coal measures of Britain were left relatively undisturbed by subsequent geological movements, those of Ireland were seriously eroded. Only in parts of Counties Antrim, Derry and Tyrone, where the coal deposits had been protected by a subsequent lava flow, were these processes largely prevented. Indeed, such was the extent of this erosion that the surviving Irish coal measures could in no way compare in extent with those of Britain. Ireland's relatively meagre coal deposits were, in addition, further disturbed by geological events. In the Munster coalfields, deposits of coal which had originally formed as horizontal strata were subsequently forced upwards to form contorted vertical seams. These latter proved difficult and expensive to work and, because of this, they were never extensively mined. By the closing decade of the eighteenth century, contemporaries were already skeptical about the island's future self sufficiency in coal resources. In 1790 the French consul, Charles Etienne Coquebert de Montbret, took a keen interest in Ireland's coal-mining industry and even allowed himself to be winched down into the deep shaft of the Doonane mine, on the Castlecomer field.[4] His comments on the contemporary Irish coal industry, recorded in his diary, are worth quoting at length:

> *Mr Bolton* [sic. Matthew Boulton of the Boulton and Watt steam engine partnership, see Chapter 2] *of Bermingham* [sic.] *came to Ireland to examine all the places containing coal. He thought it would be possible to set up a successful business in many of them and for that purpose he was prepared to provide five-sixths of the capital. But nobody offered to take up the remainder. He did not find the Lough Allen mines, being too shallow, were likely to prove very productive. Nor does he ever believe it will ever be possible, by means of a canal, to sell this coal as cheaply in Dublin as that brought from England.*

The main coal deposits worked in Ireland during the last 250 years may be grouped into three main regions:

(a) The *Anthracite area*: this includes the *Leinster Coalfield* (mostly in County Kilkenny around the Castlecomer plateau), the *Slieveardagh Coalfield* (mostly in County Tipperary) and the *Munster Coalfield* (to the south of the Shannon estuary). These coalfields are similar to those of west Wales. As a fuel, anthracite has a high percentage of carbon, a high calorific content, and burns slowly with relatively little smoke or ash. It was used extensively for lime burning throughout Ireland when locally available and also, because of the lack of smoke given off by it, for malting.

(b) The *Bituminous* area: Ireland's three exposed coalfields, the *Connacht Coalfield*, the *Coalisland Coalfield* and the *Annaghone Coalfield*, correspond, in terms of their geology, with the Scottish coalfields in Lothian, Fife, Lanarkshire and Ayrshire. Most of the mining activity on the Connacht field was confined to the Arigna block to the west of Lough Allen in County Leitrim, where the seams had suffered little disturbance and were almost horizontal. The coal of the Connacht field was, however, semi-anthracitic in character. On the Coalisland field, mining tended to concentrate in eastern County Tyrone. Bituminous coal, which burns freely with a long flame, was generally used for steam engines and for manufacturing town gas, although most of the coal used for these purposes in Ireland was imported from Britain. Indeed, most coal used as domestic fuel in Ireland's major cities and towns was imported British bituminous coal.

(c) The *Lower Carboniferous* area: This area contains only one exposed coalfield, the Ballycastle field in County Antrim. Most of the seams are bituminous, but some anthracitic coal is also present. In general terms, the Ballycastle coalfield, while bedded at a lower level than the other Irish coal seams, is similar to the limestone coal measures of the Mull of Kintyre in Scotland.[5]

The Development of Coal Mining in Ireland *c.* 1680-1922

The origins of small-scale commercial mining in Ireland probably date to the late seventeenth century.[6] In the Castlecomer area, coal deposits may have been mined as early as the 1680s, and by the years 1717-18, at least 40 small pits had been sunk on the Castlecomer field.[7] On the Tyrone coalfield, the seams at Drumglass, which appear to have been discovered in 1692, had at least four collieries at Drumglass, Creenagh, Gortnaskea and Brachaville at work in 1729.[8] In County Tipperary, the main coal bearing area, situated in a plateau of the Slieveardagh Hills, may also have been worked from the seventeenth century onwards, and was certainly being mined from about 1730. Most of this activity was centred on the Killenaule Collieries, which were the principal suppliers to the County Tipperary towns of Cahir, Cashel, Thurles, Fethard and Littleton in 1814.[9] The development of the Ballycastle collieries in County Antrim began in the 1720s, against the backdrop of an Irish government prize of £1,000 for anyone who could supply 500 tons of Irish coal to Dublin. Two enterprising Dublin merchants, Richard and William Maguire, obtained the mining rights to the Ballycastle-Fairhead district from the Earl of Antrim in 1720 and went on to claim the bounty. However, mining in the Ballycastle area went into decline soon afterwards, but was revived by Hugh Boyd in the 1730s.[10] The development of the Munster coalfield was somewhat slower, with the opening of a colliery at Dromagh near Kanturk, County Cork, in the 1740s.[11] On the Connacht coalfield, the main or 'three foot seam' of the Arigna valley was first discovered in 1765 on the Leitrim-Roscommon border and, while mining activity was centred around Arigna, County Roscommon, pits were also opened in County Sligo.

Coal mining at the Ballycastle collieries went into decline after Hugh Boyd's death in 1767, but by the mid-1800s, most of the collieries in the area had been worked out. Inland collieries were, however, opened at Murlough Bay in 1905.[12] In the 1840s, the most extensive collieries on the Munster field were situated in the Duhallow area of County Cork and, although the most important colliery at Dromagh was initially closed as early as 1861, it re-opened some years later before closing for the last time in 1882.[13] Mining on the Tyrone coalfields peaked in the 1850s but, by the 1870s, only about seven pits were being worked (figure 3.2). Samuel Kelly's Annagher Colliery near Coalisland, which operated in the years 1924-6, was an ambitious attempt to revive coal mining in the area, but proved to be a costly failure.[14] The Slieveardagh field employed upwards on 1,000 men in the 1840s. However, by the late 1880s, only a number of small pits were being operated in the Killenaule area of south-west Tipperary.[15] By 1919, mining was at a low ebb on the Slievardagh fields, although the mines were re-opened by the Irish government during the Second World War.

In 1866 there were some 73 collieries in Ireland, 31 of which were located in Leinster and 29 in Munster.[16] Irish coal production declined steadily in the nineteenth century, from 148,750 tons in 1854 to 92,400 tons in 1914, while the demand for industry met, as we have seen, by importing British coal, significantly increased. The Irish

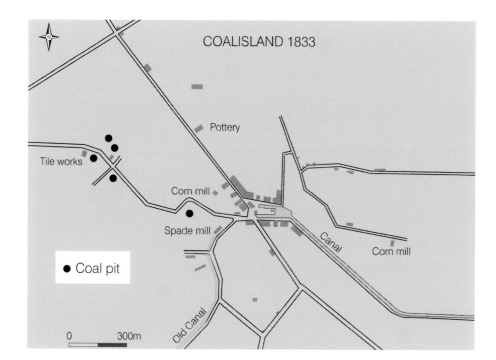

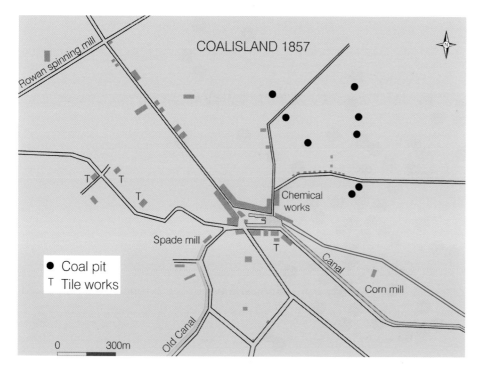

3.2 *Coalisland, County Tyrone, coal mining and the industrial development of the town of Coalisland (after Dillon 1968).*

output was but a tiny fraction of that of Britain. At its apogee, in 1913, the British industry as a whole produced some 287 million tons of coal and employed 1,100,000; in 1918, the Irish industry produced less than 1 per cent of the British total and employed 893 people above and below ground.[17] As we shall see later, Irish coal was generally used for lime burning, malting and the kiln drying of grain in general, for brick making and as a domestic fuel. It was rarely employed for raising steam, so much so, indeed, that recorded instances of such occurrences in the nineteenth and early twentieth centuries were considered noteworthy by contemporaries.

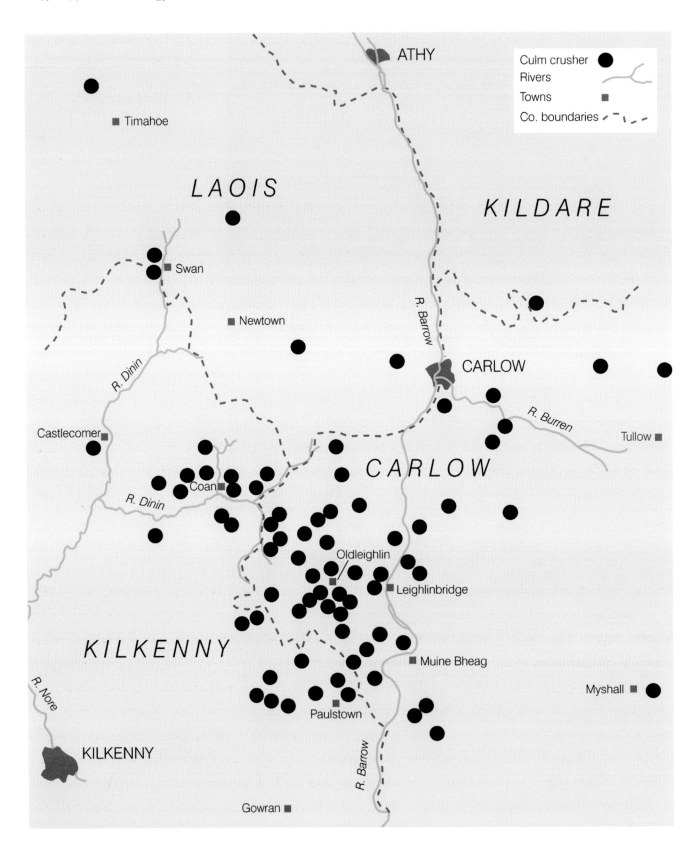

3.3 *Distribution of culm crushers in Counties Carlow, Kildare, Kilkenny and Laois (after Conry 1999).*

During the 1880s, coal from Arigna was used in the Midland and Great Western Railway's Shannon steamers, whose boilers were specially modified for this purpose, and in the locomotives of the Cavan and Leitrim Railway at the turn of the twentieth century.[18] If one were to add the small number of steam engines known to have been employed on Ireland's coalfields to this list, assuming, that is, that their boilers had been adopted for locally produced coal (though this is by no means clear), then one could conservatively estimate that less than 1 per cent of the coal mined in Ireland since the first steam engine was introduced in the 1740s was used to raise steam.

Around a number of Irish coalfields, particularly within the environs of Castlecomer and Arigna, *culm* or anthracitic slack, was mixed with clay and tempered underfoot by either humans or horses to manufacture *culm balls* or *bombs* for use as domestic fuel. However, within a narrowly defined geographical area on the Leinster coalfield, *culm crushers*, consisting of large edge-runner stones of either granite of limestone up to 1.34 m in diameter, were also employed for this purpose. The stones were attached to a central iron pivot, around which they were turned, by a horse, on a circular, prepared stone pavement, upon which the clay and culm mixture had been spread. Upwards of 50 of these culm crushers were set up in the period dating from the 1850s to the 1920s (figure 3.3), their overall geographical distribution being confined to Counties Carlow, Kilkenny, Laois and Kildare, with a noticeable concentration in Old Leighlin and Coon (where good quality limestone and granite were more readily available for the manufacture of edge runner stones).[19] These were also frequently used to grind limestone and to mix mortar, while the trampling motion of horses employed to turn animal-powered machines for churning butter, within the same geographical area in which culm crushers were erected, was also put to good use to temper the culm.[20]

The Archaeology of Coal Mining in Ireland

Ireland's coal-mining landscapes are much less spectacular than their European counterparts and, indeed, than those associated with Irish non-ferrous metal mining (see Chapter 5). One is immediately struck at the small, even tentative, scale of Irish coal mining and also, on an island where the lack of subsequent industrial development has generally enabled facets of early industries to survive, the extent to which their cumulative landscape impacts have been so quickly erased. At the time of writing, Ireland has no commercial coal mining. This activity had barely been sustained on the Arigna, Castlecomer and Slieveardagh fields into the second half of the twentieth century, with one of the largest Irish collieries at Deerpark, on the Castlecomer field in County Kilkenny, closing as early as 1969.[21] The main colliery at Ballingarry on the Slieveardagh field was initially closed in 1971, to be re-opened in 1979 for a number of years, but nowadays, Ireland's coal deposits are worked only by individuals, generally for private, domestic use.[22]

Early coal mining in Ireland, as elsewhere in Europe, took the form of opencast or surface working, where coal could be dug from outcrops on or near the surface. *Bell pits*, so called because the shallow undercutting at their bases gave them a distinctive bell-shaped cross section, were then resorted to so as to exploit deeper seams,

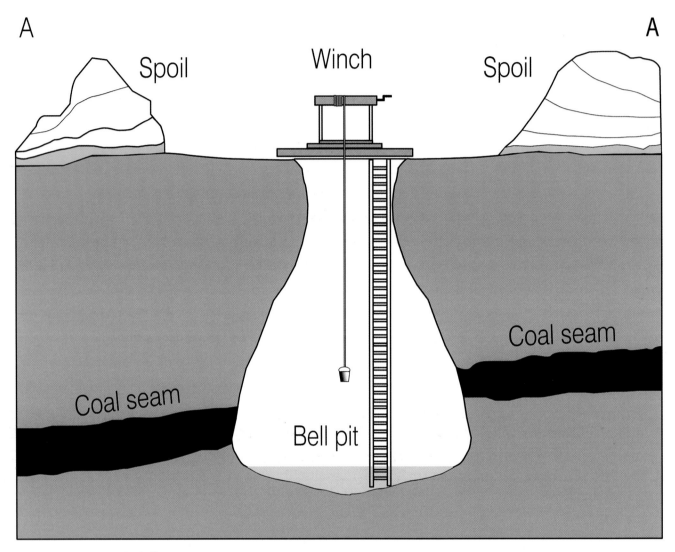

3.4 *Reconstruction of a bell pit.*

but when these pierced the water table they had often to be abandoned because of flooding (figure 3.4). When one of these shallow workings was abandoned, another would be opened a short distance from it in order not to miss the seam, and in this way the landscape became pock marked with abandoned workings as mining activity was transferred from one localised area to another. This mining technique was, however, uneconomic and ultimately wasteful of coal. The working life of pits was very short, and deeper mines could only be worked with the aid of water-powered pumping machinery. The use of inclined drainage adits was possible where the seams were higher than ground level, when water could be led away from the workings. However, drainage adits and early power-activated pumps (animal- or water-powered) also had their limitations, and the sinking of deep shafts to exploit more productive seams only became possible with the use of steam-powered plant.

Bad management was a universal complaint of contemporaries about Irish coal mines.[23] As in all Irish mining operations, the problem was generally solved by importing British expertise. Lady Ormonde employed a manager from Hull in Yorkshire to organise her Castlecomer collieries in 1802, whilst other colliery owners began to introduce supervisors from the Durham coalfields from the mid-1820s onwards.[24] Many of these English colliery managers came from the north-eastern coalfields of England, where a large number of coal pits were to be found on a rough axis formed by Durham, Chester le Street and Newcastle-upon-Tyne. Indeed, such was the extent of their influence that the main seam worked on the Castlecomer field in the nineteenth century came to be known as the Jarrow seam.

The excavation of bell pits was gradually replaced by deeper shafts with horizontal headings progressing outwards from the base of the shaft. The miners left stout pillars of coal in between these headings to provide support for the roof, a technique called *pillar and stall*, which seems to have been introduced directly from the Durham coalfields (figure 3.5). Pillars could often be six yards square, as on the Tyrone coalfield, or 180 by 90 cm at intervals as recorded on the Leinster field.[25] Pillar and stall working was employed on the Ballycastle, County Antrim collieries in the 1720s and on the East Tyrone coalfield in the 1780s. Curiously enough, the *long wall* method, in which coal was extracted from a continuous coal face rather than from individual headings, and where the roof was supported with stone walls instead of pillars of coal, appears to have been widely used on the Tipperary, Munster and Connacht fields during the eighteenth century. This technique, which was later to prove ideal for mechanical methods of coal extraction, only became widespread on British coalfields by the middle of the nineteenth century. In Ireland, the long wall method was also attempted at one of the Tyrone

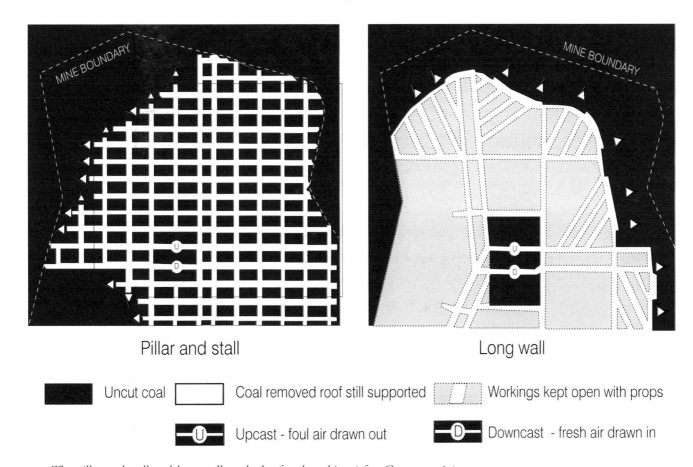

Pillar and stall   Long wall

■ Uncut coal   □ Coal removed roof still supported   ▨ Workings kept open with props

—Ⓤ— Upcast - foul air drawn out   —Ⓓ— Downcast - fresh air drawn in

3.5 *The pillar and stall and long wall methods of coal working (after Cossons 1987).*

coalfield pits, but ultimately failed because of a shortage of rock for supporting the roof.[26] However, on the Connacht coalfield where, unlike most Irish coal deposits, the seams were almost horizontal, this technique proved easy to adopt, and the Rover Colliery on the Arigna field is known to have been worked by this method early in the twentieth century.[27]

Poor management continued in many areas in the 1840s, and as late as the 1870s on the Tyrone field, the mining techniques were still primitive, with coal being roughly cut out in a way that impaired its quality. After being cut from the seam, it was shovelled into a sledge called a *hurry*, and brought to the pit mouth where, after a second shovelling into barrels, it was carried to the surface, by now reduced to slack mixed with fire clay and stone. The miners often worked in pairs and progressed along the seam, coal being raised to the surface in wooden or iron *kibbles* (a dome-shaped receptacle containing 3cwt) powered by manually operated winches.[28] The coal was then sorted by workers on the surface. In 1812, in the Ballycastle collieries, gunpowder was used for progressing, where a three-man team of cutter, bearer and trammer could produce 1 ton of coal per day.[29] Well into the twentieth century, Castlecomer miners were still hauling coal sledges underground by means of a chain attached to a girdle, tied around a man's body.[30] All lighting within the mines was provided by candles (12-15 lbs per day being consumed in County Kilkenny mines in 1812), which also served as a means of gauging the quality of the air and for measuring the time elapsed for shifts.[31] Even after candles had been replaced by oil (and later electric lamps) during the course of the nineteenth century, Rathborne's candle factory in Dublin was still supplying candles for indicating the duration of shifts in County Kilkenny coal mines as late as 1949.[32]

The introduction of English specialists to the Castlecomer field in the 1820s and the subsequent sinking of deeper mineshafts has already been briefly alluded to. Elsewhere in Ireland, a similar trend can be discerned in the same period with the development of coal mines on the Slieveardagh field by the Mining Company of Ireland, from 1825 onwards, and at Tullynaha, County Roscommon (on the Connacht coalfield) associated with the Arigna ironworks in the period 1825-30.[33] Even on difficult sections of the Munster field, deeper pits began to be sunk, and bore holes made in the 1950s established that the original shafts were dug to surprising depths, the main Dromagh shaft, for example, being worked to a depth of 210 ft (64 m).[34] On the east Tyrone field, many pits were sunk on or near a seam outcrop, although shafts were not generally more than 150ft (45.72 m) deep, but at the Annagher Colliery, near Coalisland, during the period 1924-26, brick-lined shafts were sunk to what were, in Irish coal-mining terms, unprecedented depths of 1,072 ft (326.74 m) (figure 3.6). Unfavourable geological conditions did, however, make the seams uneconomic to work. This latter pit was, in its day, one of the most modern in these islands, being modelled on the Haig Pit of the Whitehaven Colliery Company of Cumberland. With the sole exception of this latter site, however, Irish coal workings never approached the depths recorded at Irish nineteenth-century metal mines (see Chapter 5).

The increased depth of coal shafts, however, brought with it new challenges. Proper drainage was a perennial problem for all Irish coal mines during the eighteenth and early nineteenth centuries. As early as 1740, a Newcomen beam pumping engine was at work at the Doonane colliery on the Leinster field (see Chapter 2). From this date onwards, various engines were in use for pumping purposes on this field which were occasionally employed in conjunction with horse-powered pumps, as at the Coolbawn Colliery in 1802.[35] Water-powered pumping machinery was also in operation on Irish coalfields. Hugh Boyd erected a water-wheel at Ballycastle, County Antrim, in 1749 to drain his Saltworks pit, whilst at Coalisland, County Tyrone, a 40 ft (12.19 m) diameter wheel was powered by a mile-long leat (which even included an aqueduct), installed at a pit at Drumglass some time before 1752.[36] Water-powered pumps were also used on the Munster field, as recorded at Castlecor near Kanturk, County Cork, where Edward Deane used a large water-wheel to power water pumps for coal workings in 1810.[37] Conditions on the east Tyrone field, indeed, occasionally allowed the construction of drainage adits.

As has been seen (see Chapter 2), a steam-powered pumping plant was already in operation on the Castlecomer and Coalisland fields during the eighteenth century. On the other Irish coalfields, this development almost invariably corresponds with the sinking of deeper shafts in the 1820s, in accordance with contemporary English mining practice, where coal was now being extracted from lower seams, and the wasteful practice of digging shallow pits, in close proximity to each other, is beginning to be replaced in accordance with the principles of modern commercial mining. The use of steam plant, indeed, not only enabled deeper shafts to be sunk, but effectively allowed workings which had earlier been abandoned to be re-opened. Charles Langley of Coalbrook, Killenaule, County Tipperary, had, by 1814, installed what appears to have been one of the first steam-powered pumping engines on the Slieveardagh field.[38] The Irish Mining Company erected a pumping engine at its

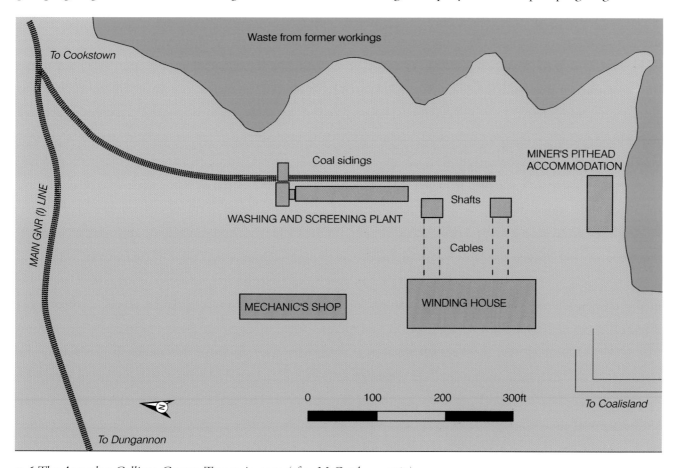

3.6 *The Annagher Colliery, County Tyrone, in 1924 (after McCutcheon 1980).*

Tullynaha, County Roscommon, pit in 1825, and was followed by the Mining Company of Ireland (MCI) in 1826, who set up a pumping engine at its Mardyke Colliery on the Slieveardagh field.[39] According to Samuel Lewis in 1837, eight pumping engines were in operation among the 34 working pits on the Slieveardagh field, compared to a recorded total of six on the Castlecomer field in the period 1827-38.[40] However, unlike Irish metal mines, where the vast majority of steam engines were of the Cornish type (see Chapter 2 and Chapter 5), this was by no means always the case at Irish collieries.[41] In archaeological terms, and in comparison to the engines employed at Ireland's metal mines, little is currently known about the types of engines operated at Irish collieries during the second half of the nineteenth century. Clearly the best surviving examples of the structures associated with Irish colliery engines are on the Slieveardagh field. At Knocknalonga, there are the remains of a small rotative engine house, while at Earlshill, there is circular stack and an enclosed rotative engine house. The only surviving Cornish pumping engine house associated with an Irish coal mine is that at the Mardyke Colliery, which was built by William West in 1841 and originally housed a 55-inch cylinder engine.[42]

Drainage was not the only problem created by the sinking of deeper shafts. It became increasingly difficult to circulate air within the mine workings and thereby ventilate them and, from the outset, artificial and often very primitive means of ventilation were devised. As the pit became deeper, early forms of ventilation often consisted of an air shaft built next to the main working shaft, into which fresh air was directed by means of draught boards that encouraged, simultaneously, the downflow of fresh air on one side of the air shaft and the exit of foul air on the other. In the nineteenth century, on the Castlecomer field, air conditioning was provided by burning coal at the base of the shaft to create an air current, but as inadequate roof support and poor ventilation was the norm up until the end of the century, mining could only be carried out by sinking many air shafts, more commonly referred to as *pollacks*. In the second half of the nineteenth century, tall chimney ventilators were also constructed, the most impressive surviving structure being the 98 ft (29.87 m) high 'steeple of copper' ventilation shaft on the Slieveardagh field, completed in 1863.[43] In the Castlecomer district, a single, nineteenth-century ventilation shaft survives at Hollypark.[44] The first steam-powered rotary fans employed for ventilating Irish coal mines appear to have been used at the Jarrow Colliery at the end of the nineteenth century.[45]

With regard to almost every aspect of Irish mining in the eighteenth and nineteenth centuries, technology transfer was very much a one-way exchange from contemporary Britain. But there is one area in which the innovative ideas of an Irish mining engineer made an enormous contribution, not only to mine ventilation but in the proper, scientific sampling of exploratory cores. Some time before 1804, James Ryan (*c.* 1770-1849) invented a boring machine that enabled, for the first time, accurate stratigraphic data to be extracted from cores and, at the same time, provide ventilation for mines. Ryan had been employed as a 'mineral surveyor' by the Canal Company of Ireland (GCI) since 1800, during which time, and up to the first reference to his invention in 1804, he appears to have been working on its development. He was later appointed engineer to the Undertakers of the GCI, who were so clearly impressed with its results that they provided financial assistance for him to take out a patent. The Company's interest was, however, by no means paternalistic. In order to build up trade on the canal, they had leased collieries at Doonane, County Laois, in 1803, a venture in which Ryan's patent would give them a clear edge in the area of prospection.[46] Nonetheless, despite favourable notices from the scientific community, Ryan's invention was viewed with suspicion by many English mine owners, who saw it as slower and more expensive than traditional methods of ventilating mines. Even the vastly improved quality of the data collected in Ryan's device was viewed as an irrelevance and, worse still, an unnecessary expense. There was also, it is clear, some anti-Irish prejudice involved. Fortunately, not all mine owners were oblivious to the benefits of Ryan's invention, particularly those of the South Staffordshire region, where it was used successfully to vent mine gases. Its overall contribution to mine safety was also greatly appreciated by the miners who had experienced its benefits, to whom he was fondly known as 'Count Sulphur'.[47] Ryan, who was also a passionate advocate for his cause and for improved mine safety, has the distinction of setting up Britain's first purpose-built mining school in 1819-31, at Middletown Hill, Montgomeryshire, in Wales.[48]

Well into the nineteenth century, coal was brought to the surface by horse-powered gins or whims (see Chapter 1) on nearly all the Irish coalfields, particularly in the East Tyrone region. In 1854, the Mardyke, Earlshill, Coalbrook and Bolantlea pits on the Slieveardagh field, run by the MCI, all employed horse whims to raise coal to the surface.[49] Steam-powered head gear for raising coal or miners was a rarity on Irish coalfields until the late nineteenth century, and did not become relatively common until the early decades of the last century (figure 3.7). The short working life of Irish pits (often up to one year) was perhaps the main reason for this, for while it was possible to employ a steam pumping engine to drain a number of pits, the provision of a steam winding engine for individual pits simply proved to be too expensive. Neither, it is clear, was much money invested in providing improved means by which coal could be moved around inside the mine. As we have seen, primitive sledges were used for this purpose up to quite recent times, but from the 1830s onwards, wrought-iron rails were beginning to be employed in some collieries, most notably in the Arigna mines and in the Annagher mine, on the Tyrone field, which was being managed by Richard Griffith during this period.[50] Wheeled bogies or rail trucks made of wood were much more common on Irish coalfields in the second half of the nineteenth century, but were by no means universally employed (figure 3.8). Wooden tramways and trucks were still in use in the Rossmore Colliery on the Castlecomer field in the 1920s.[51] For a limited period in 1910-25, pit ponies were employed for underground hauling in the Rock and Vera mines at Castlecomer, which had applied to the Durham region of north-east England for replacements in 1915 (figure 3.9).[52] None of the pits worked in Ireland, as late as 1920, had any mechanical coal-cutting, sorting, or breaking machinery. Indeed, the Wolfhill colliery was the only one to have installed washing and power plant by this period.[53]

The surface transportation of coal has a direct bearing on the early development of railways in Ireland, which is dealt with more fully in Chapter 14, but in order that we might more fully appreciate why this industry remained so underdeveloped in Ireland, we must first briefly consider the failure to develop efficient means of distribution. In the main, Irish coal deposits were too small to admit large-scale capitalisation (figure 3.10). Poor transit facilities were, in particular, a general malaise of the Irish coal mining industry, where transport costs often reduced the use of coal to a 20-30 mile radius of pits, although on the Tyrone coalfield existing supplies were quickly used up by expanding local industries.[54] But such instances (where the tangible benefits of a localised

CLOCKWISE FROM TOP:
3.7 *The Wolfhill Colliery, County Laois c. 1915;* **3.8** *Coalminers outside pit entrance at Arigna, County Roscommon, c. 1915, with wooden trucks in foreground;* **3.9** *Entrance to one of the Rockmine pits, County Kilkenny, opened in 1924. Compare with fig. 3.8.*

canal network for the development of collieries are immediately apparent) are rare in Ireland, and the arrival of the railway in the nineteenth century brought few improvements for the industry.

As shall be seen in Chapter 13, the origins of Ireland's network of inland navigations and canals were closely linked to the exploitation of coal deposits. This was, however, by no means always a positive development. While the construction of the Grand Canal enabled some of the coal from the Castlecomer field to reach larger markets (as did the River Barrow), these same trade routes also enabled the transit of cheaper, imported coal from Swansea to reach inland markets. Coal from the Arigna collieries, however, was sent in large quantities to Dublin and Limerick via the Shannon and midlands canal networks during the 1880s, whenever English coal tended to become too expensive. David Aher, the engineer to the Castlecomer collieries, had, as early as 1807, begun to alleviate the transportation difficulties of getting coal overland through the Castlecomer plateau's high passes by laying out new lines of road to towns such as Kilkenny, Carlow and Athy.[55]

Even the development of Ireland's rail network did little to rectify matters. In 1853, the opening of the Killarney Junction Railway linking Killarney with Mallow and, ultimately, with the Dublin-Cork section of the Great Southern and Western Railway, brought a national rail link within two miles of the Dromagh Collieries. The Mining Company of Ireland's Duhallow Colliery was adjacent to the Rathcoole siding of the Killarney line in 1882 but, despite the accessibility of such an important national rail link, the development of the Kanturk coalfield never expanded to serve a truly national market. Up to 1919, indeed, with the notable exception of the Coalisland field through which ran the Great Northern Railway and Lagan Navigation (which had its terminus at Coalisland), all Ireland's collieries had no rail transit facilities.[56] In early 1921, the Commission of Inquiry into the Resources of Ireland could report, without any amazement, that the Slieveardagh field still had no rail link. Thus the general inadequacy of the transport networks serving Irish coalfields often meant that many native supplies of coal were effectively landlocked, well into the twentieth century, while the inveterate instability of the industry itself even led to the cutting off of transport links built for them. Thus, in 1930, the line from the Wolfhill Colliery on the Castlecomer field was terminated, along with most of the Arigna Valley line.[57]

As in other Irish mining operations, collieries often became the focus for mining communities, and small mining settlements were established on all the main Irish coalfields. Those associated with the Castlecomer region, where

3.10 *The Arigna mine in c. 1902.*

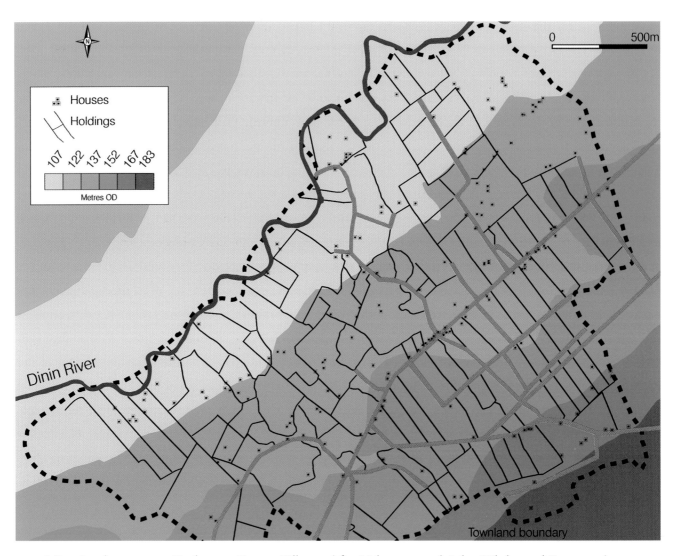

3.11 *Miners' settlements near Castlecomer, County Kilkenny (after Nolan 1979 and Aalen, Whelan and Stout 1997).*

organised 'estate'-controlled mines were already in existence on the Wandesforde estates in the period 1716–17, were to be characterised by concentration of basic rural cabins for the ordinary miners or colliers and more substantial higher-status houses for mine managers – a pattern which was to be repeated elsewhere in most Irish mining areas, whether associated with collieries or metalliferous ores in the eighteenth and nineteenth centuries. By the middle of the 1700s, colliers on the Wandesforde estates were to become tenants of the estate and to work for payment in kind (usually for culm), content to do so in the knowledge that security of tenure was a mutually convenient trade-off for their mining skills (figure 3.11).[58] Some non estate-run mines, however, on the Castlecomer and Slievardagh fields, opted for more purpose-built settlements, although these were somewhat rarer and tend to be a feature associated with the early decades of the nineteenth century. The Grand Canal Company established the colliery village of Newtown in early years of the nineteenth century, while in 1826, the Mining Company of Ireland erected 33 miners houses at Mardyke in the parish of Killenaule on the Slievardagh field in County Tipperary.[59] For the most part, newcomers were commonly subsumed into existing settlements near Ireland's coalfields. In County Tipperary, new settlements, developed by local landlords and their main tenants, with names such as New Birmingham, reflected the confidence of the age, though the optimism shown by these and by later commentators such as Sir Robert Kane in the 1840s proved to be groundless.[60] However, in 1920, the chronic lack of accommodation for miners and their families at Castlecomer and Wolfhill, was considered to have a negative impact on the development of the industry.[61]

(2) Turf

Peat, more commonly called turf in Ireland, is a *biogenic* deposit, that is, one formed by living organisms. It is created under waterlogged conditions, when debris from plants are deposited at a faster rate than natural processes can decompose or break them down. The rate of peat bog growth is quite slow, generally in the region of 10–100 cm every 1,000 years, but over several millennia, substantial bogs have grown to cover a relatively large portion of the Irish landscape. Just over 16 per cent or 1.34 million hectares of Ireland is covered by peat bogs, most of which are to be found in the midlands and in the west, a percentage which in Europe is only surpassed by that of Finland (figure 3.12).[62] It appears that some 800,000 acres of turf have been cut away between 1814 and 1907, and it has been estimated that by 1946, when Bord na Móna was founded, upwards of half the raised bogs recorded in the Irish midlands in 1814 had already been removed by turf cutters.[63]

Indeed, up until the late 1940s, mechanised peat cutting had only played a very small part in commericial development of Ireland's bogs. Turf was traditionally cut using a slane (Irish *sleaghán*) a specialised form of spade, and stacked for drying completely by hand, processes which are still widely practiced all over Ireland. Unlike

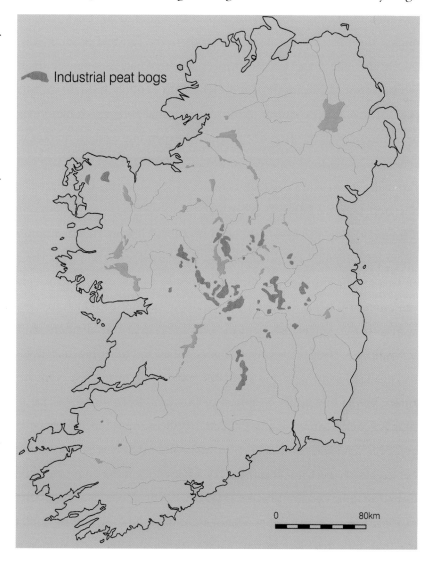

3.12 *Distribution of Irish industrial bogs (after Hammond 1979).*

97

other fossil fuels, its extraction from the bog was almost exclusively a seasonal activity, the turf being harvested like a crop. The upper metre or so of the bog contains *white turf*, which comprises the remains of sphagnum mosses, and immediately beneath this is what is generally termed *brown peat* which, while still containing a lot of sphagnum and other plants, is largely made up of the woody remains of heather. The lowest part of the bog contained black turf, which comprised the remains of the plants that had grown in the fenlands upon which the bog had formed. When dried in the wind and sun, black turf became very hard and brittle, and unlike brown and white turf which retained their basic sod form after drying, tended to break up more easily when transported. It was, nonetheless, the longest-burning fuel harvested on Irish bogs, and charcoal made from it was used by Irish blacksmiths in working wrought iron up to about the middle of the nineteenth century. On the majority of Irish bogs, it was possible to cut turf into sods, but on certain bogs in Counties Cavan, Leitrim, Down and Sligo, where conditions prevented this, *mud turf* was made. In the manufacture of mud turf, the peat was first macerated (i.e., broken up) and occasionally mixed with water. It was then spread out to facilitate drying and cut into roughly 1 ft (0.30 m) squares around 18 inches thick. This process was still in evidence in County Louth during the 1980s on the Ardee Bog, where the finished product was transported on cots to Ardee.[64]

By the end of the seventeenth century, turf had become the main fuel used in most rural Irish households, whilst population growth in the eighteenth century brought an increasing reliance on its use by urban Irish populations. The extension of the Grand Canal as far as Monasterevin, County Kildare, in 1786, opened up the peat resources of the Bog of Allen to an expanding Dublin market where, by the early nineteenth century, the canal was being used to transport around 30,000 tons of turf from the Bog of Allen to Dublin on a yearly basis. From about 1825 onwards, Stein and Browne's Distillery in Limerick was being successfully supplied, via the River Shannon, from the Mona Bog between O'Brien's Bridge and Castleconnell. The transport of the 5,000 tons or so of turf produced annually was facilitated by a canal linking the Shannon with the bog.[65] The extensive turf-cutting operation provided employment to a large workforce, and after the closure of the Limerick distillery in 1842, all this hand-won turf was then sold locally. As late as 1921, throughout Ireland as a whole, about six million tons were still being cut each year as domestic fuel, of which just over one-third was used in Connacht.[66]

From the nineteenth century onwards, there was an increasing awareness of the industrial potential of Ireland's bogs, both as important sources of fuel and other raw materials. Many schemes were initiated to mechanise the production of peat, but until the early years of the last century, nearly all these proved to be short-lived affairs, waylaid by either technical or financial difficulties. In 1844, at Cappoge (Cappagh) in the Bog of Allen near Kilcock, County Kildare, Charles Williams developed a process for manufacturing fuel from wet peat by pressure. Williams also began to manufacture peat charcoal for smelting ores, raising steam and other purposes, but his efforts were not commercially successful and the enterprise failed after a few years.[67] An English company, using Gwynne's patent process, established a briquette factory at Sliabh Each near Cahirciveen, County Kerry, in 1851. The enterprise appears not to have lasted long, but examples of its compressed peat were displayed at the Irish Industrial Exhibition of 1853. Although long since abandoned, the remains of a 10 m high tower and the foundations of some of the original buildings still survive on the site.[68]

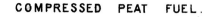

COMPRESSED PEAT FUEL.
Plate 35.
River Barrow
Canal formerly used
Lower Drain
Railway up Bog
Upper Drain
Drying Kilns
Engine house
New Peat Store
Gas Works
Foundry
Offices
Old Store
Railway to Canal Wharf
Primitive Bog
A
B
C
Fig. 1. General Plan of Derrylea Peat Works.
Scale 1/6000th
0
500
1000
1500
2000 Feet

COMPRESSED PEAT FUEL.
Plate 36.
Travelling Girder for dragging the Harrows over the Bog.
Fig. 2. Side Elevation.
D
Fig. 3. Plan.
Engine
Scale 1/480th
0
50
100
150
200
250
Feet 300
Fig. 4. Elevation of Girder at centre.
Scale 1/120th
Fig. 5. End Elevation.

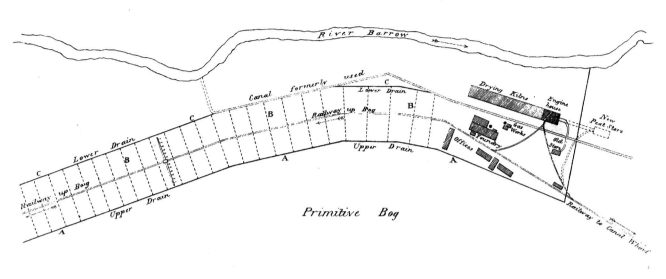

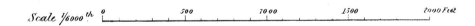

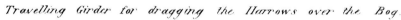

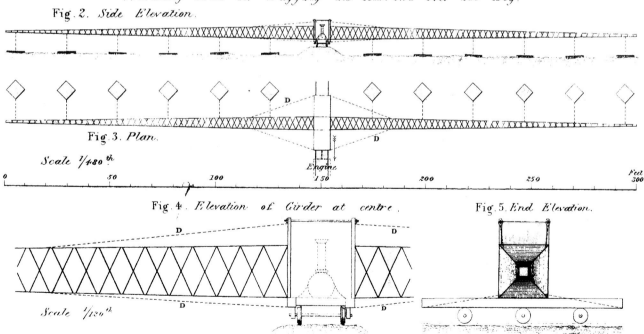

3.13 *Hodgson's peat briquette works at Derrylea, near Monasterevin, County Kildare, in 1865.*

In 1855, the Irish Peat Company employed Gwynne's Dry Press Process at Kilberry near Athy, County Kildare, to manufacture peat briquettes. In Gwynne's process, air-dried turf was subjected to further artificial drying to considerably lessen its moisture content, before being reduced to a powder. This was then steam-heated in cylinders and then compressed, the end product being almost as dense as coal. Once again, this enterprise was unsuccessful, largely due to technical difficulties. A Gwynne press had been operated by Charles Hodgson at Galway in 1854, who encountered the same problems as the Irish Peat Company. Hodgson, however, went on to develop the first successful peat briquette press in 1858. The German engineer, Carl Exter, had patented a similar machine some months earlier, but Hodgson's was more sophisticated and its basic design is incorporated in modern briquette presses. Indeed, John Gwynne, whose process had been tried by Hodgson, appears to have been in contact with both Exter and Hodgson.[69] In 1860, Hodgson established his remarkable, though short-lived, briquette works at Derrylea, near Monasterevin, County Kildare (figure 3.13). Hodgson had discovered that, by harrowing the surface of a bog, large amounts of powdered peat up to four times dryer than freshly-cut sods, could be acquired. At Derrylea, a small steam locomotive on rails carried a 300 ft (91. 44 m) long girder, from which were suspended a series of zig-zag harrows. The surface of the bog was repeatedly harrowed in dry weather to further reduce the moisture content of the powder, which was then transported by a narrow gauge railway to the briquette works.[70] Derrylea, with its works village, became the precursor of the Bord na Móna villages of the second half of the twentieth century.

Industrial Uses of Turf

With the exception of David Sherlock's works at Rahan (1885-1925) and General McQuaid's moss peat works at Umeras, County Kildare (1890-1940), all the peat enterprises established in Ireland during the second half of the nineteenth century were commercial failures. For the most part, there appears to have been no lack of initiative on the part of individuals, but both the British government and the early post-1922 Irish administrations which succeeded it showed neither the confidence nor co-ordination to develop Ireland's bogs.

From contemporary European experience, there could be little doubt as to the potential of peat as industrial fuel. During the nineteenth century, turf was used for raising steam in a number of coal-poor regions of Britain such as Devon and Cornwall, and also in the Netherlands, where the boiler grates which had been designed for coal were modified for the combustion of peat fuel. During the 1840s, a pumping engine at the Derrynoos lead mine, County Armagh, was fuelled with black turf not, it appears, with any conspicuous success, although two Westmeath woollen mills do appear to have operated successfully powered by turf-fuelled steam engines in 1865.[71] Nonetheless, the calorific value of turf won by traditional methods is *c.* 3,300 kcal/kg, which is about half that of coal but significantly more than wood. Theoretically, then, with modifications to the boilers, the use of peat could produce significant savings in the operation of steam plant. However, the construction of an experimental peat-fuelled boiler in the Dublin Steam Packet Company's Liverpool yard during the 1830s highlighted the fact that only turf won in dry seasons could be profitably put to use for raising steam. Yet this did not prevent Charles Wye Williams of the Dublin Steam Packet Company from experimenting with peat as fuel, in the company's first transatlantic steamer, the *Royal William*, in 1838. Williams was also instrumental in the conversion of the Inland Navigation Company's steamers on the River Shannon to turf fuel in the 1840s, which led to savings of about one-third on the company's fuel bills.[72] Other initiatives and experiments undertaken in Ireland, however, during the second half of the nineteenth century, met with little success. In the early 1860s, peat was used in the blowing and forge engines at the Creevelea Iron Works in County Leitrim, while in 1874, Alexander McDonnell manufactured mechanically won turf at Mountrath, County Laois, and Monasterevin, County Kildare, for use as fuel in locomotive engines and at least one stationary steam engine. The Creevelea enterprise lasted until about 1872, but McDonnell quickly found that his own enterprise would be economically unviable.[73]

Indeed, Irish industrialists seem to have had few grounds for supposing that Ireland's vast supplies of peat would or could meet their expanding energy needs. Turf was certainly expensive to transport and was more easily damaged in transit.[74] Furthermore, as more recent research has indicated, turf was not as cheap as one might expect. Industrialists in both Limerick and Galway clearly preferred to pass on the opportunity to use supplies of local, hand-won turf and pay extra for imported coal.[75] It was not until the early decades of the twentieth century that peat was successfully used as a fuel in steam and gas engines in Ireland. Hamilton Robb's gas producer plant at Portadown in the period 1911–20 has already been cited (see Chapter 2). But this latter initiative, along with other innovative schemes, such as the generation of electricity using turf-fuelled steam engines, between 1906 and 1922 at the Marconi transatlantic cable station near Clifden, County Galway, were the exceptions rather than the rule. Yet while a private act of parliament had been passed as early as 1901 to facilitate the setting up of a peat-fired electricity generating station in the Leinster basin (which came to nothing), Ireland's first such installation, at Clonsast, near Portarlington, was not commissioned until 1950 by the Electricity Supply Board. This latter was demolished in April 1996, despite the pleas of conservationists. Four smaller peat fuelled stations built along the western seaboard of the Irish Republic, at Cahirciveen, County Kerry, Miltown Malbay, County Clare, Screebe, County Galway and Gweedore, County Donegal, were subsequently closed.[76]

The use of turf charcoal for smelting and other metallurgical processes developed in Europe from at least the seventeenth century onwards. Irish blacksmiths in rural areas, especially in the northern counties, generally used charcoal made from black turf at their forges, until cheaper coal became more widely available with the extension of the railway network. The absence of phosphorous in the peat made it well suited to iron working, and tools and other iron goods manufactured with it certainly enjoyed a high reputation in rural communities.[77] Yet, with two notable exceptions, the use of peat charcoal was not developed to anywhere near the same extent in Ireland's metallurgical industries as it was on the continent. In 1751, Robert Rainey was awarded a grant of £300 from the Irish House of Commons to develop his ironworks near Lough Neagh which, he claimed, used only peat charcoal in the conversion of pig iron into wrought iron.[78] This was clearly a significant development, given that, up to this time, Irish iron works used only wood charcoal and also, as we shall see in Chapter 4, because they could not develop along the same lines as their English counterparts. However, it was not until

3.14 *Charcoal retort employed at the Irish Amelioration Society's peat charcoal works at Derrymullen, near Robertstown, County Kildare, as depicted in* Illustrated London News, *September 1850.*

1838, when Charles Wye Williams patented a process for manufacturing peat charcoal at his Cappagh works, that we find any evidence of a renewed interest in its manufacture for smelting.[79] Indeed, it was not until the early 1860s that iron smelting using peat charcoal, on any large scale, was carried out in Ireland at the Creevelea Iron Works in County Leitrim. Between 1850 and 1857, the Irish Amelioration Society manufactured peat charcoal at Derrymullen, near Robertstown, County Kildare, most of whose production was to be intended for export, but the anticipated demand for its product never materialised (figure 3.14).[80]

Unlike coal and petroleum, peat, owing to its more recent origin, retained a number of physical properties which made it a surprisingly rich source of chemicals. The tar resulting from the production of peat gas could be broken down to manufacture a wide range of by-products, including petroleum and lubricating oil, creosote, calcium acetate (used in the manufacture of acetic acid and acetone), paraffin wax and methyl alcohol (used as fuel and in the manufacture of varnish and dyes). In 1849, a Welsh chemist called Rees Reece set up the Irish Peat Company at Kilberry near Athy, County Kildare, to manufacture peat gas and tar, along with the wide range of by-products associated with them. This was the first manufactory of its type in the world, but it succumbed to financial difficulties within ten years or so of its establishment.[81] A further peat-based chemical industry, in which ammonium sulphate for use in fertilisers was extracted from turf, was set up at Carnlough, County Antrim, in the early 1900s. Mountain peat identified in the townlands of Harphall and Lemnlary near Carnlough was identified as being particularly rich in the variety of peat from which ammonia could be extracted. In 1903, an aerial ropeway on 24 trestles was built to carry peat down the mountainside in large buckets to the processing works. The peat was burnt with sulphuric acid in large, lead-lined retorts to create sulphate of ammonia. However, by early 1908, the ammonia content of the available peat resources was dimin-

ishing, and the works had to effectively close down. Most of the plant was sold off in *c.* 1915, and the ropeway was dismantled and re-erected at a Cumberland coal mine.[82]

In 1890, a more successful peat-based industry – the manufacture of moss peat – was begun in Ireland by Kieran Farrelly at Turraun (figure 3.15). Moss peat was an excellent bedding material for stables. It had almost no smell, was easier to store than straw owing to its lack of bulk, and possessed up to four times the

3.15 *Moss peat works at Turraun, County Offaly in* c. *1915 (top);* **3.16** *Turf cutting at Maghery peat works, County Tyrone, in* c. *1915.*

3.17 *Rahan peat works, County Offaly, c. 1915.*

absorptive capacity of straw. Furthermore, as the moss peat could absorb more ammonia, it produced a manure of a higher nitrogen content. A successful moss peat enterprise, based on the demand from British cavalry barracks, was established at Umeras, County Kildare, in 1890, which continued in production up to 1940. Other moss peat factories were established around Ireland, most notably at Inchichore and Ringsend in the Dublin area, Maghery, County Tyrone (figure 3.16), Ferbane and Rahan, County Offaly (figure 3.17) and Portglenone, County Derry, from the early 1900s.[83] One of the more conspicuously successful moss peat works was established by John Purser Griffith in 1924. Griffith was a tireless advocate of the industrial development of Ireland's peatlands under both the British and early Free State governments, and, in 1924 he embarked, at his own expense, upon an ambitious scheme to develop two bogs at Ticknaun near Edenderry and Turraun near Ballycumber, County Offaly. In 1924, he set up the Leinster Carbonising Company at Turraun where, using German machinery adapted to local conditions, he successfully produced sod peat. This enterprise was a qualified success and was eventually bought by the Free State government's Turf Development Board (the forerunner of Bord na Móna) in 1935.[84] Another innovative but short-lived enterprise which used Irish peat as a raw material was the Callender Paper Company. Between 1900-03, it manufactured brown wrapping paper made from a mixture of peat fibre and paper pulp, at Celbridge, County Kildare.[85]

4

Iron and Steel

In the seventeenth century, English speculators had established iron smelters and processing works throughout Ireland in areas with seemingly unlimited stands of timber, smelting a mixture of native and imported ores in charcoal-fired blast furnaces.[1] But an industry established on these lines could only last as long as the forests that it consumed, and by 1778, there were only two charcoal-fuelled furnaces operating in Ireland, at Enniscorthy, County Wexford, and Mountrath, County Laois.[2] The industrial revolution in iron and steel manufacture in England based on the substitution of coal for charcoal as fuel did not take place in Ireland. As we have seen, Irish coal resources were meagre and more difficult to work, but the industrialisation of a native industry not only required substantial deposits of coal but also that similar quantities of usable iron ores be available within close proximity to it. Irish locations at which this was possible were extremely rare: only in two localities – Arigna, County Roscommon, and Creevelea, County Leitrim – could large-scale iron working be realistically attempted during the nineteenth century. Thus, from the late eighteenth century onwards, iron manufacture in Ireland began to be concentrated in Irish ports, where ores, bar iron and fuel could be imported easily.

All the ferrous metals in common use during the last 200 years – wrought-iron, cast-iron and steel – are alloys of iron and carbon, whose individual properties are determined by the amount of carbon present. *Wrought iron*, which has a melting point of $1535°$ C, is almost pure iron, containing only a small amount of carbon (not more than 0.15 per cent). It is a soft, ductile material (i.e., could be drawn into wire), which could be re-worked by a smith if re-heated, but could not be hardened or tempered. It was originally smelted directly from the ore and later by the indirect process in Ireland from the seventeenth century onwards – when refined from cast-iron. Wrought-iron is, in addition, stronger in tension but weaker in compression than cast-iron.

Cast-iron is the product of the blast furnace, and has a lower melting point than wrought-iron (1150-$1200°$ C), owing to higher percentage of carbon present, around 3-4 per cent. Its crystalline structure makes it brittle,

4.1 *Iron ore deposits in Ireland (after Scott 1991).*

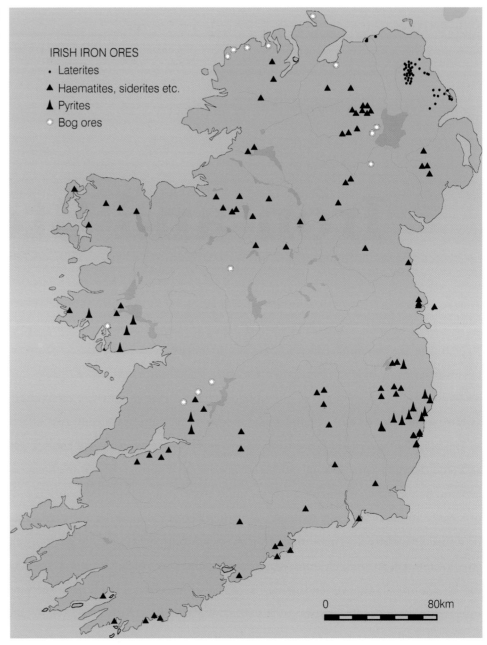

IRISH IRON ORES
· Laterites
▲ Haematites, siderites etc.
▲ Pyrites
○ Bog ores

0   80km

and it cannot be re-worked by a smith unless it is refined into wrought iron. It can, however, be cast into an infinite number of complex shapes, enabling its use instead of wood for machine components and as a building material. It is strong in compression but only about one-third as strong in tension as wrought iron. The carbon content of *steel* varies between 0.5 and 1.7 per cent, the amount varying in accordance with type of steel required. Higher-carbon steels, such as those used in lathe tools, contained 1.4 per cent carbon, whilst mild steel (which began to replace cast-iron for most purposes) contains about 0.25 per cent carbon. It is both strong in tension and compression, which gives it a practical edge over cast-iron, which is weak in tension. Steel could be hardened by a smith if rapidly cooled by quenching at the forge, which made it indispensable for all edged weapons and, of course, all craftmen's tools that required a sharp edge.

(1) Native ores and iron mining in Ireland

Many native Irish ores had a high phosphorous content which made them unsuitable, not only for the manufacture of steel but also for making good-quality wrought iron. Nonetheless, four main types of iron ore were regularly mined in Ireland in the period dating from the early seventeenth century until the end of the nineteenth century (figure 4.1):

(i) *Bog ores:* These comprise hydrated ferric or iron oxide, which are formed from iron-rich water under the kind of conditions found in either peat bogs or lake beds. The cycle of their deposition occurs over decades: in some cases, it is possible to harvest the ore every 30 or so years. The ease with which such ores could be reduced in primitive smelters made them a prime target for iron workers from the earliest times. They were extensively worked in Ireland during the medieval period, and in the succeeding early modern period, the term 'bogge myne' was used in contemporary written accounts to describe them. In more recent times, bog ores were mined in Counties Donegal and Leitrim, and at Mountrath, County Laois, for use in gas purification.[3]

(ii) *Siderites:* In Ireland, these are generally found in carboniferous coal measures, where they occur as large nodules in bands formed in between the coal seams. Siderites are made up of iron carbonate (Fe_2Co_3), of which large outcrops occurring in the area around Lough Allen, County Leitrim, gave rise to the name *Sliabh an Iarainn* ('Iron Mountain').[4]

(iii) *Bedded haematites and limonites:* Comparatively speaking, these ores are rare in Ireland, being found at Deehommed, County Down, and at Lissan and Kildress near Cookstown, County Tyrone, where they were smelted during the seventeenth century. Haematite was also mined at an important site at Dysert, County Laois, from the seventeenth century until 1730.[5] Both ores are forms of ferric oxide and contain only small amounts of phosphorus, which increased their utility for iron making. Their distribution in Great Britain is confined to south Wales, the Forest of Dean (which includes western Gloucestershire, eastern Monmouthshire and southern Herefordshire) and Cumbria, from which they were exported to Ireland from the seventeenth century onwards.

(iv) *Laterite ores:* Laterisation is a process during which ore beds were moved upwards (in Ulster, in layers of basalt) in a chemical process caused by weathering. In Ireland, the ore present is haematite, which became laterised over a wide area of County Antrim and extending into County Derry. These are also known as *interbasaltic* ores, upwards of 228, 000 tons of which were raised in north-east Ireland in 1880.[6]

From the late sixteenth century onwards, iron ores were mined all over Ireland, but during the nineteenth and in the early decades of the twentieth centuries, most of the Irish-produced ores were raised in the Ulster counties, particularly Antrim, Tyrone and Donegal. Very little is currently known about how iron ore was mined in Ireland during the seventeenth and eighteenth centuries. Bog ores were simply stripped away from bog, but opencast workings and bell pits are most likely to have been used to extract other varieties of iron ore. Shallow pits about 6 ft (1.82 m) deep are reported by Gerard Boate at Dysert, County Laois, in 1652, but at least one mine Ballyregan, in County Cork, had a shaft 60 ft (18.28 m) deep which was drained by a mechanical pump. The latter mine had also been exploited by the Earl of Cork, Richard Boyle, from about 1615 onwards, and was among the deepest in either Britain or Ireland during the seventeenth century.[7] Opencast or basset work was also practiced both in County Laois and in mid-Antrim. However, when it became necessary to tunnel into the Antrim basalt, the seams of ore allowed self-draining horizontal adits to be used, whilst timbering could be kept to a minimum because of uniform basalt overlay. In the Glenravel mines, both long wall and pillar and stall workings are recorded from the late 1860s, where horizontal adits were also cut in a 'H'-plan to augment air circulation.[8] At Ballycastle, County Antrim, iron was systematically mined from the 1800s onwards but, in the 1860s, the main focus of activity shifted to Glenravel Valley and mid-County Antrim, whose ores were shipped to Britain. Over 400 workings have been noted in County Antrim and, while most of these have been sealed off, many spoil heaps are still visible.[9] In 1915, the total Irish production of iron ore (all from County Antrim), was 39,326 tons and, by the 1920s, the only locations at which iron ore was being mined in Ireland were in north-eastern County Antrim.[10] Elsewhere in Ireland, during the nineteenth century, only a handful of sites are known to have produced iron ores for export, notably two sites in Counties Donegal and Derry from which ore was exported through the port of Ballyshannon for use in gas purification, Drumslig, County Waterford (1850-60), and Gortinee on the River Shannon, south-east of Drumsna (1860-80).[11]

For general convenience and to minimise transportation costs, ore mines are likely to have been close to furnaces during the seventeenth and eighteenth centuries.[12] In this period, it was common for the ore to be carried on horseback into the forested areas where the early charcoal-fired furnaces were situated. Iron ore raised near Tuamgraney, County Clare, is believed to have been transported by boat to furnaces in the region, whilst at the Blackstones furnace in County Kerry in 1709, ore was brought by both boat and horseback.[13] Tramways were constructed at the Arigna ironworks in the 1820s, and later on, mineral railways were used to transport ore from the Glenravel and Tristan mines in county Antrim. The first narrow-gauge line in Ireland was in fact built to accommodate the movement of iron from the Glenariff mines in County Antrim to the coast. An aerial ropeway was even built by the Antrim Wire Tramway Co. in 1872 to link the Glenravel, Evishcrow and Largan ore mines with Red Bay Pier in County Antrim.[14]

From about the mid-seventeenth century, English, Scottish and Welsh ores were imported to be mixed with native ores.[15] Cinders from English blast furnaces – the residues of iron-rich slags resulting from earlier blasts, which were used to reduce the amount of ore needed for smelting, yet still produce a hard iron – were also imported from the Forest of Dean for use in a number of Wicklow and Wexford ironworks. High quality or *tough pig iron* could only be manufactured from non-phosphoric ores which, as we have seen, were rare in Ireland. In England, these ores were mined in the Forest of Dean and the Cumberland/North Lancashire areas. Low-quality ores, containing a high phosphorus content, were only suitable for the making of *cold short* iron (iron which was brittle when cold, and thus unsuitable for making steel), which was generally used in the manufacture of nails. Very few Irish ironmasters successfully negotiated the import of English ores and cinders. Sir William Petty, for example, had difficulty in importing regular supplies of English ores. The ironworks at Enniscorthy, County Wexford, one the few conspicuously successful seventeenth-century enterprises, did actually manage to import regular supplies of ore and cinders from the Forest of Dean.[16]

All the ores raised in Ireland required some preliminary treatment prior to smelting. Bog ores were roasted to remove water, breaking up into small porous lumps which were ideally suited to primitive furnaces. Carbonate ores and siderites, indeed, also needed to be roasted to make them more porous and to remove carbon dioxide, as did those containing sulphur, such as haematites. Roasting could be undertaken by making heaps of the ore on the ground, in stalls or, where fuel was expensive, in special kilns, as at the Arigna ironworks in County Roscommon in the 1820s, although lime kilns could also be used.

(2) Industrial Ironworking in Ireland: the Seventeenth-Century Background

In the rest of the former United Kingdom, charcoal-fired blast furnaces continued to operate in parts of Scotland and Wales well into the nineteenth (and in some instances into the twentieth) century, long after iron had begun to be smelted using coal.[17] The last Irish iron charcoal-fired furnace was put out in 1798, principally because the activities of ironmasters in the previous century had been undertaken without any thought being given to proper woodland management. The extensive virgin forest of Ireland had been a prime target for seventeenth-century English settlers, many of whom had hoped to make quick profits from their extensive new Irish plantations. Charcoal for ironworking, as some earlier commentators had argued, was much cheaper in Ireland and offered (or so it seemed) excellent opportunities for rapid enrichment.[18] However, the cost of English charcoal *vis-à-vis* that of Ireland, while ostensibly more expensive, did not necessarily offset the cost of operating in this country, to which both English ores and skilled labour also had to be imported. It is, perhaps, too simplistic to argue that cheaper Irish charcoal necessarily encouraged English investment in Irish ironworks which were, with few exceptions, unprofitable. Moreover, as has long been known, the English charcoal-fired blast furnace industry was never threatened by a shortage of fuel.[19] The only documented and ultimately abortive attempt by English ironmasters to transfer their operations to Ireland, from the Sussex Weald to Sir Walter Raleigh's estates in east Cork, in the late sixteenth century, was by Herbert Pelham and George Goring in 1596. Their contemporaries, it is clear, were unconcerned about future charcoal shortages.[20]

As early as 1589, Robert Payne had typically exaggerated Ireland's natural advantages in relation to the development of ironworking, after investigating the site for a projected ironworks (never completed) at Kilnameaky, County Cork, as also did Gerard Boate (1605-50) in his *Ireland's Natural History*, published posthumously in 1652,

4.2 *Distribution of Irish ironworks, c. 1593-1798 (after McCracken 1971).*

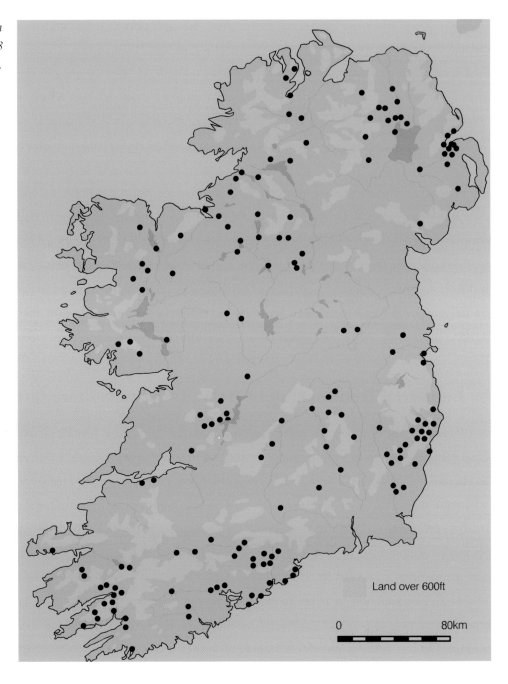

Land over 600ft

0   80km

compiled with a view to attracting English settlers to Ireland.[21] However, the profits from the various Irish ventures were greatly exaggerated by Boate: for the most part, these were largely confined to the period up to 1630. Richard Boyle, the First Earl of Cork's, ironworks were, indeed, only profitable in the years 1626-31, when wartime demand accounted for most of this, but the return on his investment was modest in terms of the capital outlay involved in setting up his iron works. His considerable wealth, which was assumed by contemporaries to originate from his ironworks, did in fact stem from his land dealings.[22] There was in any case a very small domestic market for Irish iron, which faced increasing competition from higher-quality iron made in Sweden, England and Spain.

On present evidence, the earliest Irish blast furnaces appear to have been established on Sir Walter Raleigh's estates in County Cork in the 1590s. Raleigh had probably already set up ironworks by the early 1590s, while Sir Thomas Norreys had actually leased land from Raleigh for this express purpose in 1593, establishing a furnace at Mogeely in the same year.[23] This latter is the first documented site in Ireland, and was still in existence in 1606.[24] All told, some 154 Irish blast furnaces have been identified from documentary sources which, when compared to the number of documented English sites at work after 1660, a total of 174, is a relatively high figure (figure 4.2).[25] For the most part, however, Irish charcoal-fired ironworks were seventeenth-century or later, while the concentration of ironworking activity at any given time in either Britain or Ireland does not bare close comparison. It is generally agreed that most of the early seventeenth-century Irish works were destroyed in the 1641 rebellion and, after this period, the resurgence of the Irish industry was slow.[26] In 1672, Sir William Petty, in his *Political Anatomy of Ireland*, claimed that there were only ten blast furnaces and slightly more than twenty forges and bloomeries operating in Ireland, a rather low figure when compared with 71 blast furnaces in England and Wales in the period 1670-9.[27]

The more notable seventeenth-century ironworks were established in south Munster, which included Richard Boyle's, who had acquired Sir Walter Raleigh's Youghal estates in 1604. Boyle established blast furnaces at Kilmackoe (1608), Lismore (1615), Cappoquin (1615), Lisfinny (1620) and Araglin (1625), all in County Waterford.[28] Early ironworks at Dundaniel at County Cork had also been set up in 1612, on the confluence of the Brinny and Bandon rivers.[29] Access to a navigable waterway such as the River Blackwater was an important locational consideration for the seventeenth-century industry in Waterford, while post-Restoration ironworks such as Kenmare and Enniscorthy required direct access to the sea, as imported English ores were necessary for a successful operation. So also was the acquisition of skilled ironworkers, which was always a problem for the prospective Irish-based ironmaster during the seventeenth century. Their scarcity in England necessitated high wages to encourage them to work in Ireland, where one's rivals tended to poach them with even higher offers. In this fashion, Sir William Petty acquired skilled workers from other ironmasters and even borrowed the agent from the successful Enniscorthy works to provide guidance on the siting of his furnace and forges at Kenmare.[30] Irish-based ironmasters tended to create colonies of foreign workers to run their ironworks. Some 2,500 foreign workers (mostly English and Dutch) were employed by Sir Charles Coote at his ironworks in Counties Cavan, Leitrim and Roscommon.[31] William Petty's Kenmare ironworks was run by a colony of about 800 English ironworkers, whilst a number of English families were brought to Enniscorthy after the Restoration.[32] Belgians from Liège were also involved in the operation of a furnace at Ballinakill, County Laois, and Walloons were employed by Richard Crowley, a partner of Boyle, at Tuamgraney, County Clare.[33] Even Irish workers were temporarily employed by Coote at Mountrath in 1654 as a stop-gap measure until English workers could be obtained. These settlements of ironworkers, including worker accommodation and plots of farming land, could involve anything from 200-400 acres of land.[34] Considerable resources were, therefore, invested in the development of Irish ironworks, not least of which involved the transplanting of English and European technical expertise to the wooded fastnesses of Ireland. Trifling matters such as the long-term ecological effects of rapid deforestation on the future economic development of the industry even though the contemporary English iron industry could only survive through rigorous and disciplined woodland management – were seldom allowed to enter into the calculations of Irish-based ironmasters. The main causes of the failure of Ireland's charcoal-fired ironworks in the eighteenth century, therefore, can be traced to the profligacy of the adventurers of the previous century with an important natural resource.

(3) The Technology of the Blast Furnace in Ireland, *c.* 1620-1798

From the earliest times up until the late sixteenth century, wrought iron in Ireland was produced in one step in a *bloomery* by smelting the iron directly from its ores. This is generally referred to as the *direct process*, to distinguish it from the *indirect process* whereby cast-iron is produced in a blast furnace and later refined to make wrought iron. In primitive furnaces, where temperatures reached about 800° C, a spongy mixture of metal and slag was formed, which was then hammered on an anvil both to consolidate the iron and remove as much slag as possible. The bloom, after being worked at the forge, was then ready for immediate use. As in the later indirect process, charcoal was used as fuel. Nonetheless, in the direct process, as much as 70 per cent of the metal was discarded with the slag which was profligate of the ore, although, during the medieval period, it became possible to increase the amounts of semi-molten slag by raising the temperature in the furnace to around 1,150° C. A large proportion of the slag could now be tapped off in the furnace during the smelting process, and the amount of slag which had to be hammered out from the bloom greatly reduced. The introduction of water-powered bellows and hammers greatly assisted these processes and led to an increase in iron production. The blast furnace, as has been seen, was probably introduced into Ireland towards the end of the sixteenth century. As in the bloomery furnaces, charcoal was used as the fuel, but in the blast furnace, the iron is reduced to a liquid state by employing a continuous blast of air from water-powered bellows, to produce temperatures of at least 1,540° C. Limestone was employed as a flux to combine with the impurities in the furnace and to assist in the formation of slag, which floated above the molten metal where it could be easily tapped off. The molten metal was then run off into a sand bed where it was either cast into pigs or into moulds. The sand bed had a central runnel (the *sow*), with smaller oblong side channels led off at right angles (*pigs*): the passing resemblance of this arrangement to a sow suckling pigs gave rise to the term 'pig iron' (figure 4.3). By decarburising (i.e., divesting it of its high carbon content), cast-iron could also be refined into wrought iron by being processed in a finery forge. The principal advantages of this method were that large quantities of cheap metal could be produced at a time, which was particularly important for large casting such as cannon.[35]

In the manufacture of charcoal, the timber (usually hardwoods such as oak) was cut and stripped of its bark to facilitate the escape of moisture. It was then formed into circular stacks, which were subsequently covered with turves and earth to form a beehive shape. The stack was provided with a number of inlet flues at its base and one outlet flue at the top. Once ignited, the skilled collier or charcoal burner tended it for about five days and nights, during which the wood was slowly burnt to form charcoal. The charcoal burners normally slept in

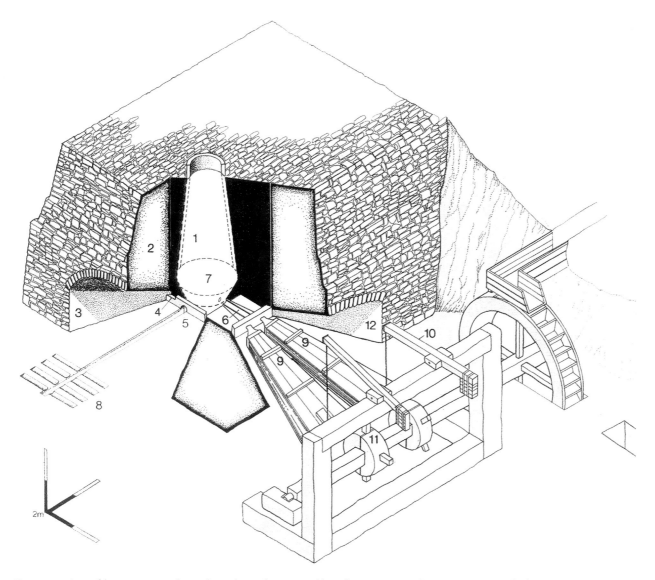

4.3 *Reconstruction of late seventeenth- early eighteenth-century blast furnace at Araglin, County Waterford.*

improvised shelters near the stacks, emerging to control the draughts by means of hurdle work windshields or by opening or closing off draught-holes at the base of the stacks. At Lugduff, County Wicklow, along the northern and southern sides of the Upper Lake at Glendalough, the remains of around 75 or so oval platforms, 9 by 6 m in extent, appear to be those of charcoal-burning platforms, associated with seventeenth- and eighteenth-century iron working in the area. A second series of platforms, in the same general area, also contain at least two raised areas which could well be the remains of charcoal-burners' huts.[36]

The timber for fuel was measured in *cords*, which were generally 12 ft (3.65 m) long and 4 ft (1.21 m) in diameter, of which twenty were required to process one ton of bar iron. At Boyle's ironworks at Lismore in 1600-17, some three tons of charcoal were needed to produce one ton of bar iron; similar amounts were used in the Forest of Dean in the 1640s.[37] Contemporary accounts refer to woodcutters and colliers along with the *wood reeve*, who supervised the felling and coaling of the timber. Given that two tons of iron required up to

113

one acre of woodland, the effect of a single smelting season (usually about four months) on mature forests can be readily appreciated. With Irish furnaces producing anything from 120-400 tons of iron each season, this would have clearly involved the destruction of 80-200 acres of woodland in the vicinity of a single ironworks. Basic forms of woodland management such as *coppicing* only appear to have been practiced in County Wicklow.[38] Coppicing involved cutting a tree above its bole, and allowing up to twenty poles to grow from the stump to a height of about 15 ft (4.57 m). Roughly 8,000 or so poles could be obtained from one acre of woodland managed in this way, which was renewed in a fourteen to sixteen year rotation.[39] In Ireland, therefore, what was potentially a renewable resource became rapidly denuded and, as early as 1622, an occupant of the English Pale, Richard Hudsor, was already expressing serious concern at the all-too-obvious lack of proper woodland management.[40] The level of uncontrolled felling was such that, by the 1630s, the cost of Irish charcoal was already increasing.

(4) The Archaeology of the Charcoal-Fired Blast Furnace in Ireland

To date around eight blast furnaces of late seventeenth/eighteenth-century date are known to have survived in Ireland, mostly in the Munster counties of Clare, Cork, Kerry and Waterford. These include Araglin, County Waterford, Derrycunihy and Muckross, County Kerry, and Dunboy, County Cork. In addition, three other sites are known to survive, in good condition, at Whitegate and Raheen (Tuamgraney) in County Clare and at Partry, County Mayo (figure 4.4).[41] The foundations of a further County Cork blast furnace have also recently been excavated at Adrigole on the Beara peninsula, while the partial remains of the former early seventeenth-century East India Company furnace at Dundaniel, County Cork, also survive.[42] Other sites, it is clear, will also come to light throughout Ireland. It is worthy of note that upwards of 28 or so sites survive in England, Scotland and Wales, despite the fact that charcoal-fired blast furnaces were in use for longer there, while many English furnaces were also converted for use with coke.[43]

In Ireland, blast furnace sites were nearly always located within forested areas, close to a useable source of waterpower, or on sites at which the ore and the fuel could be transported by boat. The availability of a reliable source of waterpower was, indeed, a critical locational factor. At Araglin, County Waterford, a mill-race was drawn from the adjacent Araglin River to power what appears to have been an overshot water-wheel, while at Adrigole, County Cork, the remains of a silted-up mill-race were investigated.[44] The Derrycunihy and Muckross furnaces, by way of contrast, were situated almost directly on fast-flowing rivers. At Derrycunihy, indeed, the furnace had been deliberately sited below a small waterfall on the adjacent Galway river, which cleverly utilised a steep fall to power what was probably a breastshot water-wheel. The surface remains of an elevated mill channel are still in evidence on the riverside section of the furnace, where the water-wheel would have originally been positioned. At Muckross, the elevation of the surviving furnace stack clearly indicates that a raised mill-race was also employed to direct water from a point upstream from the adjacent river.[45] The Partry furnace in County Mayo, however, originally diverted water from the Cloon river, some 100 m or so away from the furnace site.

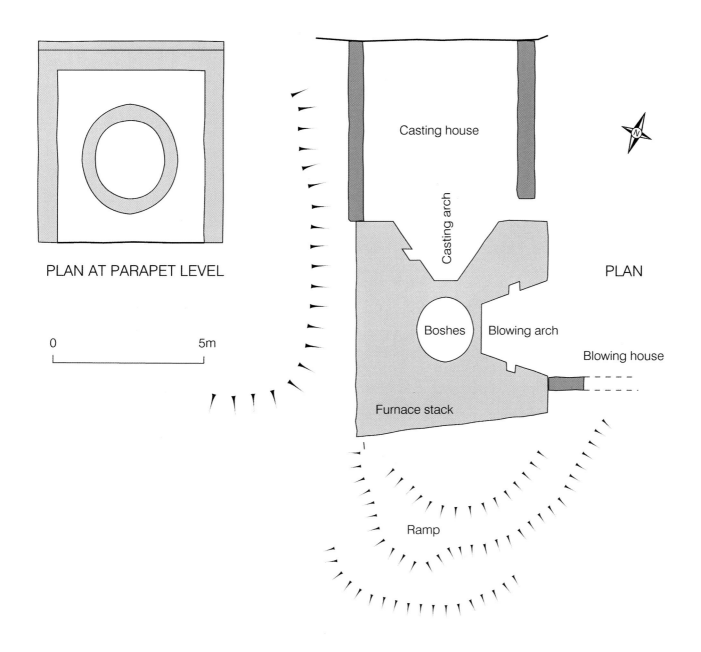

PLAN AT PARAPET LEVEL

0   5m

Casting house

Casting arch

PLAN

Boshes   Blowing arch

Blowing house

Furnace stack

Ramp

4.4 *Ground plan of Partry blast furnace, County Mayo.*

The Irish blast furnace almost invariably took the form of a stone tower, externally and internally tapered upwards from the base, and was constructed with coursed rubble (in south Munster commonly of sandstone) masonry, with a sturdy rubble core. The Araglin furnace was 4.76 m high, and around 7.8 m square at the base; that at Muckross about 4.7 m high and some 7.52 m square, and the Partry furnace around 7 m square. In 1652, Gerard Boate described the Irish furnace as 'being of the height of a pike and a half or more' (i.e., 4–5 m) and four square in figure'. One furnace, indeed, at Drumshanbo, County Leitrim, was reported as being 18–20 ft (5.48–6.09 m) high and 3 ft (0.91 m) square in the interior, while others at Dromod, County Cavan, and Killeskin Glen, County Laois, are also reported as having been 'square'.[46] By way of contrast, early English furnaces were

4.5 *Partry blast furnace, County Mayo.*

5.2 to 6.5 m square in plan.[47] At Araglin, Muckross and Partry, the inward taper of the furnace stack tended to commence at a point just above the springing line of the casting arch, but at Araglin, this taper was formed in stepped facets, features that also seem to have been in evidence at the Derrycunihy furnace.[48] The analogy with a malt kiln made by Boate in 1652, where the base tapered upwards towards the top, is readily understood by reference to the upstanding remains at Araglin, Muckross and Partry, and from an early illustration of Derrycunihy (figure 4.5 and 4.6). These former three sites, despite the geographical distance between them, display a remarkable similarity in terms of their basic constructional details, and there can be little doubt that they are the product of a post-Restoration furnace building tradition in Ireland. In England, Scotland and Wales, by way of contrast, such furnaces were often finished externally with ashlar masonry, one of many basic physical differences between surviving British and Irish furnaces which will described below.

The Araglin, Muckross and Partry furnaces also display putlog holes immediately above the casting arch, which were used either to position external timber frames, to counteract the stresses caused by the weight of the molten metal contained within the main shaft of the furnace, or on a lean-to structure for covering the casting area. The external shoring framework is recorded for sixteenth-century English furnaces, but has not been noted on later eighteenth-century British examples.[49] Furthermore, both the Araglin and Muckross furnaces were also provided with small stone buttresses. At Muckross, this took the form of a small 'flying buttress', built up against the south-west corner of the stack, while at Araglin a simpler, small buttress had been erected against the north wall of the furnace. Similar features are also in evidence on Fisher's 1789 print of the Derrycunihy furnace, while there is at least one documented English example of this practice at an eighteenth-century cementation steel furnace at Derwentcote, County Durham.[50]

The exterior walls of the furnace stack provided insulation for the smelting process, while the egg-shaped profile of its interior assisted the passage of the molten iron and slag through the body of the furnace to the *boshes* (the flared section at the lower end of the furnace). This carefully shaped internal profile helped to prevent the molten contents from sticking to the side walls of the furnace. On two adjacent sides of the furnace, large arches were formed, the side or *blowing* arch, accommodating the bellows tuyère (an iron nozzle which directed the air blast from the bellows into the base of the furnace), and the *casting* or tapping arch, from which the molten metal was run off into the casting or *pig bed*. The lining of the hearth was made with refractory sandstone and would have been replaced, along with that of the boshes, at the end of a smelting campaign. The mixture of ores, cinders, charcoal and limestone (the *charge*) would have been fed into the upper section of the shaft, the furnace either being provided with a charging ramp or built into a hillside to facilitate this. The smelting process could

4.6 *Blast furnace at Derrycunihy, County Kerry. Print by Fisher of 1789.*

4.7 *Boshes of Party blast furnace, County Mayo (left);* **4.8** *Casting arch on Muckross blast furnace, County Kerry (right).*

take as long as twelve hours, with two half-ton batches being produced within 24 hours at a single furnace.[51]

Only one Irish site, Partry, County Mayo, is known to have retained a large section of its boshes (figure 4.7), although the surviving lower section of the Derrycunihy furnace has exposed traces of part of its boshes, adjacent to the surviving section of its blowing arch. The shadow of the boshes of the Muckross furnace can be seen in the slag residues which have adhered to the interior of the stack, in evidence on all four interior walls. In addition, the north-western and north-eastern corners of the interior of the Muckross stack (figure 4.8) retain, *in situ*, roughly-dressed corbels which would have provided support for the base of the boshes.[52] In British furnaces, from the late seventeenth century onwards, the boshes began to be lined with refractory brick, but to date there is currently no clear-cut evidence in Ireland for this practice.[53]

Very little is as yet known about the types of hearths associated with these furnaces, an important feature which required rebuilding after every blowing campaign, and in a number of instances in Ireland, special hearthstones (usually a durable sandstone) were imported.[54] At the Enniscorthy furnace, for example, which was completed in 1658 and which, in all likelihood, was probably built by a furnace builder from the Forest of Dean, special stones for the construction of the hearth were imported from the Forest of Dean region of England.[55] There is also an indenture of 1635, which details a grant from the Earl of Londonderry to Richard Blacknell of Macroom, County Cork, who, amongst other rights, was given 'liberty' to quarry 'hearthstones' for his newly-acquired ironworks in Counties Kilkenny and Laois.[56] Indeed, at most Irish ironworks, it seems likely that these would have been quarried locally, as in the case of the Blackstones furnace in County Kerry, where the hearthstones, according to Samuel Molyneux in 1709, were quarried at Glenbehy. Molyneux also noted that good hearthstones could last up to six months and that 'The making up of a new hearth is allways a charge to them, but more or less as they find a proper stone near or further from the works'.[57] At the Irish blast-furnace sites described thus far, a single furnace hearth would have been involved. However, by 1618 Richard Boyle had a double furnace at Cappoquin, County Waterford, where a double hearth is likely to have been used to accommodate the casting of larger pieces of ordnance such as demi-cannon.[58] Demi-cannon could weigh up to three tons, and the double hearth enabled larger items such as this to be cast in one piece. Nonetheless, it was not until at least 1625 that cannon were cast at Cappoquin.[59]

At surviving Irish blast furnaces, the casting arch is a very distinctive feature. This was generally the larger of two arches set into the outer walls of the furnace, good examples of which have survived at Muckross, County Kerry, and Partry, County Mayo (figure 4.10). This feature enabled molten metal to be tapped from the furnace and led to a sand bed immediately outside the arch in which, if basic pig iron or simple castings were required, furrows were formed in the sand. At Muckross and Araglin, the main arches were segmental in form with undressed sandstone voussoirs that at Partry is semi-circular, with a roughly-cut keystone. The Muckross casting

4.9 *Casting arch, Partry blast furnace, County Mayo.*

arch was 4.47 m wide and 1.85 m high on its exterior face, that at Araglin was 4.25 m wide on the external elevation. The most curious feature of both the casting and blowing arches of the Muckross, Araglin and Partry furnaces is that they are all formed into curved vaults, which are expertly splayed both inwards and downwards towards the base of the hearth. This feature is noticeably absent from the surviving sites in England, Scotland and Wales, all of which are, in any case, eighteenth century. Nearly all the latter have cast-iron lintels, while the casting and blowing arches tend to be much more angular, as at the Bonawe (1752) and Cracleckan (1753) furnaces in Argyll in Scotland, the Dyfi furnace, Cardiganshire, Wales (1755), and Rockley, Yorkshire (*c.* 1700).[60] Indeed, only three British sites, at Duddon (built in 1737-8) and Nibthwaite (1735-6), in the Furness region of northern England, and Glenkinglass, Argyll, are known to have had vaulted blowing and castings arches.[61] Curiously enough, the Glenkinglass furnace was built by Irish adventurers in about 1722, in a partnership that included Captain Arthur Galbraith of Dublin, a tanner called Roger Murphy of Enniskillen, County Fermanagh, Charles Armstrong of Mount Armstrong, County Kildare, and William Kettlewell of Thomastown, County Meath.[62] Yet while the Duddon and Nibthwaite blast furnaces have vaulted arches very similar to those recorded in Ireland, their general morphology has more in common with the Bonawe, Craclecken and Dyfi furnaces. The practice of employing cast-iron lintels in furnace arches is recorded in Sussex as early as 1542, yet there is, nonetheless, no evidence for vaulted stone furnace arches in the areas of England where we might expect to find the inspiration for the surviving Irish examples, such as the Sussex Weald or the Forest of Dean.[63]

In Boate's account of 1652, it is clearly implied that the casting floor was enclosed within a 'barn' structure. In Britain, the provision of either a timber or stone casting house, built up against the casting arch, appears to have been almost universal.[64] As has already been briefly alluded to above, putlog holes were in evidence above the extrados, or upper edge, of the casting arches at Araglin and Muckross, while at Partry, these were accompanied by a ledge. Given the need for a covered area for the casting bed, it seems likely that these accommodated a lean-to structure with either a wooden or a slate roof. The remains of mould fragments used to cast smaller items such as cauldrons, pots and firebacks, described in seventeenth- and eighteenth-century Irish sources, have yet to be found, but doubtless these will turn up in future excavations. Moreover, the Irish seventeenth-century furnaces at which cannon were cast, such as Ballinakill, County Laois, almost certainly employed casting pits lined with either wood or stone, similar to those excavated in England at Batsford, Sussex and Dyfi in Wales.[65]

The furnace bellows, as we have seen, would have been driven by a water-wheel. Cams or lugs set onto the water-wheel's axle would have depressed directly upon the bellows bottom boards, which would have been hinged to expel the air. As in Britain, no seventeenth- or eighteenth-century bellows have survived, nor are there any contemporary Irish illustrations of these. The Earl of Londonderry's indenture of 1635, referred to above, mentions bellows and bellows leather which were, of course, vital to the operation and maintenance of the furnace.[66] Boate describes 'two vast pair of bellows, the which resting upon the main peeces of timber, and with their pipes into one of the sides of the furnace, are perpetually kept in motion by the means of the great wheel …', which suggests that the bellows rested upon a wooden frame. Connected to the extremities of the bellows, and extending into the hearth via the casting arch, was an iron tuyère or nozzle. At Partry and Araglin, the bellows opening consisted of a segmental arch with sandstone voussoirs, which was vaulted in the manner already described for the casting or tapping arch (figure 4.10). At Araglin, the bellows arch is 4.07 m wide, and is splayed inwards and downwards towards the tuyère aperture where it is 1.79 m wide. The bellows arch at Muckross has an internal aperture which facilitated the tuyère, a flat-headed or 'soldier' arch, formed with undressed sandstone voussoirs, some 1.75 m wide. In the centre of this opening, a tuyère hole, consisting of two inwardly sloped stones, survives *in situ*.[67] This latter is not dissimilar to that recorded at the Glenkinglass furnace in Scotland, already mentioned, and is only the second example to have been identified in either Britain or Ireland. Finally, given the importance of the pair of bellows and perishability of its leather components, it would have been expedient to protect these from the elements. Bellows houses have been recorded at English and Scottish furnace sites, but thus far, only one likely example at Araglin, County Waterford, where a low wall at one corner of the furnace appears to have been associated with such a feature, has been identified in Ireland.[68] Nevertheless, it seems highly probable that the bellows would have been protected by either a stone-walled or earthfast structure, to provide shelter from the elements at all the Irish sites.

At English sites, the practice of providing some means of drainage for the furnace is well-documented, but thus far, this has yet to be archaeologically attested at Irish sites.[69] In Samuel Molyneux's account of 1709, however, reference is made to 'a passage or gutter to carry off the water which gathers under all at H [ie, under the hearth]'.[70] Nonetheless, it seems clear that the siting of the Muckross, Araglin, Derrycunihy and Partry sites took this into account. The Muckross and Derrycunihy furnaces, for example, were built adjacent to river banks, which would have readily accommodated run-off, while the Araglin and Partry sites were built on inclines.

Access to the furnace mouth for charging (i.e., filling the boshes with ore, 'cinders', charcoal and lime) would normally have been facilitated by a ramp or incline built at the rear. Of the Irish examples described thus far, only the Araglin furnace has a clearly defined charging ramp, which is some 6 m wide at its greatest extent. It is built into a spur in the adjacent hillside, and has traces of a revetment wall on its northern face. Large pieces of slag have been discovered on the slope of this revetment, and it seems very likely that waste from the furnace was used, on a long-term basis, to build up the ramp. The Derrycunihy furnace was built into the slope of a river bank, which facilitated access to the mouth of the furnace from the rear, while at Muckross, there is a raised mound a few metres to the north of the casting arch. This latter feature, however, is more likely to form part of another associated structure or even a slag dump, as it is

4.10 *Bellows arch, Araglin blast furnace, County Waterford.*

most unlikely that a charging ramp would have been built over the casting arch. Indeed, the south-facing eleva-tion of the furnace (i.e., that directly opposite the casting arch) has a horizontal groove into which a wooden ramp may have originally been emplaced for gaining access to the furnace mouth. Samuel Molyneux's account of the Blackstones furnace refers to '… many fillers, who from a loft above keep the Furnace continually sup-plyed with fresh materials and whose business it is breake the mine with hand hammers and to charge the Furnace at first'.[71] The 'loft' suggests some kind of superstructure over the furnace which facilitated charging, but it could also refer to the charging ramp. From seventeenth-century accounts, it appears that as much as three tons of ore were required to make one ton of pig iron. The blast furnace at the Enniscorthy ironworks, which was ready to blow in 1658, required ¾ ton of ore and 2¼ ton of imported cinders to make one ton of pig iron. It was also provided with a lime kiln (for producing flux), a special dwelling for the founder and a coal yard for storing charcoal. This furnace made up to 400 tons of iron a year, much larger than other Irish works. Richard Boyle's, for example, produced 160 tons, while Petty's Kenmare operation yielded 120 tons, fig-ures equivalent to a middle-sized English works.[72]

An essential component of Irish ironworks was the means by which the pig iron could be refined into wrought or bar iron, which was called the *finery* forge. In the finery forge, the pig iron was re-melted using water-powered bellows in a charcoal-fired hearth, a process that effectively burnt out the excess carbon in the unrefined pig iron, to reduce its carbon content to that of wrought-iron. In this process, a bloom of iron was formed along with large quantities of slag which, in the next process, was removed from the bloom using a water-powered tilt hammer. The bloom was then returned to the finery where it was re-heated and any remaining impurities expelled. The iron, thus formed, was then reheated and hammered into an *ancony*, a long bar with a knob at each end, by means of a water-powered hammer.[73] At early English sites, a second forge, called a *chafery*, was used for this purpose, but there is currently no evidence for its use in Ireland in the seventeenth and eighteenth centuries. A hammer head from an Irish seventeenth-century forge at Garrison, County Fermanagh, which was burned in 1641, is preserved in the collections of the Ulster Folk and Transport Museum at Cultra, County Down.[74] Normally, these forges would be employed to refine cast-iron produced in Irish blast furnaces but there is, however, at least one recorded seventeenth-century example, at Carnew, County Wicklow, that is known to have processed sow iron produced in the Bristol region.[75]

To date, only one possible water-powered finery forge, of likely early eighteenth-century date, has been identified in south Munster. This survives immediately to the west of the casting arch of the Araglin blast furnace, described above (figure 4.11). The forge building is a two-storey structure, built with sandstone rubble but which, save for the east gable, survives mostly at foundation level.[76] According to one near-contemporary account, a new ironworks was built here in around 1741 for the manufacture of bar iron and it seems likely that the building dates to this period.[77] Sir William Petty reports there were at least twenty forges at work country-wide in 1672. Finery forges appear to have been normally situated away from the blast furnace in local towns and villages, but in Samuel Molyneux's account, of 1709, of the Blackstones Bridge furnace in Glencar (1670-1754), County Kerry, it is implied that the finery (as at Araglin) could also be located close by.[78] In 1608, Richard

Boyle brought over a refiner and hammerman to Ireland, and later established finery forges at Moycollop, Kilmackoe and Lisfinny in the Blackwater valley of County Waterford.[79] As early as the 1560s, a Colonel Roberts had established an ironworks at Enniscorthy, County Wexford, which manufactured sword blades, while the Idrough ironworks on the Castlecomer plateaux had forges and scythe mills in 1640s.[80] Two forges associated with what appears to have been the same Enniscorthy ironworks in 1650s, one of which was situated at Camolin, had forge hammers and anvils which were imported from Sussex Weald.[81] Other specialist installations such as *slitting mills* were introduced into Ireland in the early decades of the seventeenth century. In the slitting mill, red-hot iron sheets were cut into rods or bars by passing the sheet through water-powered rollers, which cut and shaped them to a desired cross-section. On present evidence, the earliest recorded example was in operation at Boyle's works in County Waterford by 1629.[82]

4.11 *Forge building of* c. 1740, at Araglin, county Waterford.

Yet as late as the 1780s, there were still only eight slitting and rolling mills in the entire country.[83]

In general, smelting continued in most areas of Ireland as long as there were woods available for charcoal making, and the island, which was densely forested in 1600, was reduced to being a net imported of timber by 1711.[84] Yet despite the depletion of Irish woodlands in the first half of the seventeenth century, by 1670 Ireland still retained some very good quality woodlands, although these were in what we would consider to be inaccessible locations.[85] Sir William Petty's ironworks at Glaneroughty (of which only scattered slag dumps survive) near Kenmare, County Kerry, began work in 1667, but by the 1670s, the forests had been depleted and his smelting operations were compelled to move to Killarney where wood for charcoal manufacture was still readily available.[86] This latter ironworks, at Muckross, remained in operation until around 1753.[87] According to Charles Smith, in 1756, the workmen at the Blackstones ironworks, County Kerry, 'were obliged to stop smelting for want of charcoal' and that, he noted, 'the greater part of the hills, and mountains, hereabouts, were formerly covered with trees, which have been destroyed by the Ironworks'.[88] In County Waterford, it appears that the entire smelting industry became concentrated around the Moycollop valley at Araglin, where Boyle had established two furnaces in 1625. In 1760, the Araglin works was still in operation, manufacturing bar iron, pots, dishes, fish kettles, griddle backs for grates, stoves for sugar boilers, smoothing irons, pans for soap boilers, bleachers and dyers. The works were to be let in 1767 by the Shee family.[89] Nonetheless, charcoal-fired blast furnaces continued to operate in Ireland until the end of the eighteenth century. Arthur Young noted that there were only four charcoal-fired furnaces at work in 1785, which included those at Mountrath, County Laois and Enniscorthy, County Wexford, the latter operating until 1792. The last recorded Irish example to use wood charcoal appears to have been that at Dromod, County Cavan, which ceased to function in 1798.

From the foregoing, it is clear that a number of blast furnaces in Counties Waterford, Kerry and Mayo bear a striking resemblance to each other, but little to many of the surviving British sites. Given, then, the proximity of the British industry and its vital early role in providing both skilled personnel and essential ores for the incipient Irish industry, what, if any, was its influence on the design of the Irish blast furnace? There are two key points

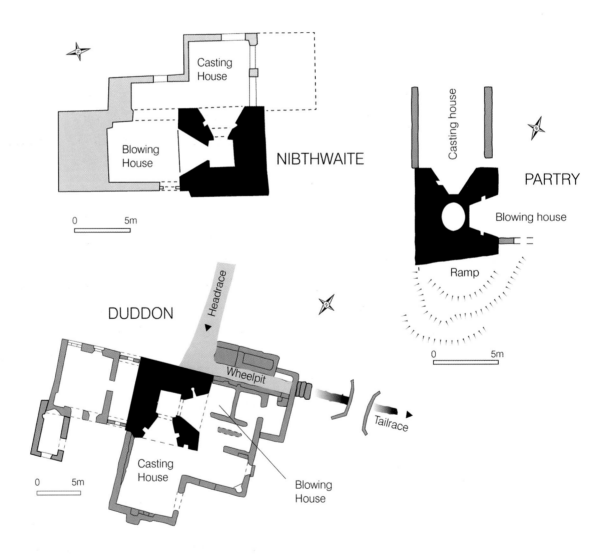

4.12 *Ground plans of blast furnaces at Duddon and Nibthwaite in Cumbria, (after Scott 2000) and Partry. County Mayo.*

of divergence in terms of the design of the surviving Irish and early British furnaces. To begin with, the British examples generally have ashlar masonry on the exterior of the stack, while the openings for the tapping and blowing arches are lintelled, whereas the Irish furnaces are constructed with rubblestone masonry and the arches are vaulted. As we have seen, only three of the north-British sites have evidence for rubble vaulted casting and blowing arches, and one of these, Glenkinglass, has an important Irish connection (figure 4.12). Furthermore, the surviving British examples and the Araglin, Muckross and Partry furnaces are all known to have been operating early in the eighteenth century: this is exactly the same period when skilled Irish manpower and charcoal were being exported to the Barrow in Furness region.[90] The possibility that early eighteenth-century Irish ironworks influenced furnace design in contemporary northern Britain is tantalising, but we should not forget that the Irish works were themselves influenced by earlier English practices. There can be little doubt that the blast furnace, as it existed in Ireland in the seventeenth and eighteenth centuries, was a technological implant. However, if the vast majority of surviving Irish examples have no close parallels in areas such as the Forest of Dean and the Sussex Weald (and we should not forget that the Scottish furnaces are also quite different), regions with which the Irish industry had close ties from the seventeenth century onwards, do the Irish furnaces represent a survival of an earlier phase of the British furnace building tradition and, if so, where do they come from? On present evidence, almost all Britain's furnaces have lintelled arches, features which are also known to have existed at sixteenth century sites in the Sussex Weald. Nevertheless, there are, to date, no British furnaces with vaulted arches earlier than the eighteenth century, and those which have them, particularly the Scottish example, can be argued to have been influenced by Irish practices.

However, even if one concludes that furnaces at Araglin, Muckross, Derrycunihy and Partry were built in the early eighteenth century, if for no other reason than they are known to have been in operation, what then were their exemplars? Clearly, the Irish furnaces have nothing in common with the surviving southern British examples, all of which are eighteenth century. Thus, if we assume that the Irish examples do have British exemplars, then one can only presume that these no longer exist and, indeed, there are no standing examples of seventeenth-century English furnaces with complete tapping and blowing arches. If, then, the Irish furnaces are a variant of a British original – and there is evidence that English furnace builders were brought over to Ireland, as at the Enniscorthy works in 1658 – then they must surely precede the surviving examples in Britain. It seems likely, therefore, that the Araglin, Derrycunihy, Muckross and Partry instances could date to the late seventeenth century, or at the latest to the early decades of the eighteenth.[91]

(5) Coal-Fired Blast Furnaces in Ireland *c.* 1788-1896

One of the key turning points in British eighteenth-century industrialisation was the successful substitution of coke for charcoal as the fuel employed in blast furnaces, first undertaken by Abraham Darby at Coalbrookdale, Shropshire, in 1709.[92] This latter was, in many ways, a technological imperative for the British iron industry. For British ironmasters, owing to the conversion (and consequent removal) of large tracts of woodland to pasture,

4.13 *Arigna ironworks in the 1850s, from Dalton 1856.*

found themselves not only with a rapidly dwindling fuel resource but with an increasing reliance on Swedish-manufactured wrought iron. Yet with Darby's discovery, the British industry could now relocate to regions where both coal and ironstone occurred in significant quantities. Such considerations, of course, bore little relevance to, and could do little to ameliorate, Irish fuel shortages. Coal, as we have seen, was a much scarcer commodity in Ireland. Rarer still, as we shall now see, were locations at which coke-fired furnaces could be set up.

In 1788, almost 80 years after Abraham Darby's breakthrough, the O'Reilly brothers became the first Irish ironmasters to smelt iron using coal as fuel at Arigna, County Roscommon. The local Arigna river was dammed to provide a head for their water-powered plant, which included an overshot water-wheel for working the blast furnace bellows.[93] From the early 1790s onward, a Boulton and Watt double-acting beam engine (the first of its type to be used in Ireland, see Chapter 2), was installed to supplement the water-wheel and to provide a blast for the furnace. The furnace, as described in 1830, was 44 ft (13.41 m) high and 17 ft (5.18 m) in the bosh. Both castings and bar iron from Arigna were sold in Dublin up to around 1808, but by 1817 the works seems to have been operating sporadically. A new company revamped the works in the period 1825-30, employing English engineers, smiths and masons, as well as setting up a new blowing engine, and a roasting kiln for the local ores.[94]

Iron was smelted between 1825-30, until the furnace became accidentally blocked, a disaster which appears to have brought about the closure of the works (figure 4.13). The site had great potential in other spheres, with excellent fireclay for making bricks for the furnace available from a local source. This clay had been used by the O'Reillys and La Touches (who had operated the works between 1824-25). Some six local collieries provided coal for the works, one of which, at Aughabehy, was linked to the works by a tramway just over three miles long. In the period 1825-30, around 200 people were employed in the Arigna ironworks and its associated collieries.[95] Unfortunately, very little of this site survives – the furnace and associated buildings have been completely demolished – while the earliest pictorial representation is a highly stylised reconstruction of how the ironworks would originally have looked while in operation, from around the middle of the nineteenth century. The earliest-known photograph of the ruins of the Arigna ironworks, dating from the late 1890s, does, however, show an extensive range of buildings with a tall, tapering furnace stack.

In the second half of the nineteenth century, a further attempt to establish a coke-fired ironworks was made at a remote site at Creevelea, near Drumkeerin, County Leitrim. A charcoal-fired furnace had operated in the locality as late as 1768, but the Scottish company which established the new works were mainly interested in the local coal measures and the availability of ores. Operations were begun in 1852, with two large blast furnaces and a smaller furnace, along with roasting kilns for the ore and coking kilns for the manufacture of coke. One of the larger furnaces was powered by a 100 hp engine.[96] The owner also built tramways and workers' houses, but after two years he appears to have become bankrupt. Potts of Dublin later rented the site and attempted to smelt iron using peat charcoal, but gave up their efforts to do so in 1858-9.[97] At least one cannon cast at Creevelea is reputed to have been used in the Crimean War, whilst iron manufactured on the site was also employed in some of the marine engines made by Coates and Young of Belfast.[98] A hollow, cast-iron shaft was also manufactured for the remarkable 40 ft (12.19 m) diameter scoop wheel installed by Courtney and Stephens of Dublin at the Drinagh pumping station on the Wexford slobs in the 1850s.[99] The Creevelea works were closed in the mid-1850s owing to problems caused by the distance of the collieries from the site, but appear to have been active again by the 1860s. In 1861, peat compressed using Buckland's patent apparatus was being used to make charcoal for the furnaces, with a novel conveyor belt 1½ miles long being employed to transport the peat from Gowlaun Mountain. During this period, the works were managed by George Murrall, who had been involved in the Staffordshire and South Wales iron industries.[100] As has been seen in Chapter 3, experiments in charring peat for use as fuel in blast furnaces had been attempted in Ireland as early as the 1750s. Indeed, Nicholas Crommelin had built a peat-fired smelter on the banks of Skerry Water, County Antrim, in the 1840s. The furnace, which still survives, is made of basalt, and is just over 18 ft (5.48 m) square and *c.* 20 ft (6.09 m) high:

4.14 *Creevelea blast furnace in 1903.*

it was a dismal failure, its builders neglecting to provide a proper blowing engine.[101] Murrall's experiments, however, showed some potential, but while the finished product was of superlative quality, the process proved to be uneconomic. It was soon abandoned, with smelting operations resuming with coke fuel by the mid-1860s. The Creevelea works were again idle by 1872 because of the falling price of iron. Further activity on the site was initiated in 1894, but it failed again in 1896.[102] A photograph of the site, taken a few years after its closure, shows a tall engine house, a square stack and a circular blast furnace, finished externally with ashlar masonry (figure 4.13). This formerly extensive complex was largely demolished by blasting during the Second World War, but the large furnace base of *c.* 1862, complete with a semi-circular casting arch, survives *in situ*.[103]

The large-scale production of steel using the Bessemer process did not take place in Ireland until 1939, with the construction of a steel mill on the 35-acre Haulbowline Island in Cork Harbour. Indeed, not even the global pre-eminence of the Belfast shipbuilding industry could encourage Belfast firms to establish such a plant in Ireland, and Harland and Wolff preferred to buy the Clydeside steel firm of Colville's to meet its needs. Colville's became their principal supplier in 1919, and continued to do so up to the mid-1920s. The Haulbowline site was an extraordinary choice of location for a steel works, with local job creation being the primary consideration. For the greater part of its working life, all communication was made by boat, the first land connection by bridge, via Rocky Island, was not built until 1966.[104] The steel mill was closed for the last time in 2001.

5

Non-Ferrous Metals and Minerals

Despite the relatively meagre extent of Ireland's mineral resources, both in terms of coal and metals, mining activity in Ireland during the nineteenth century continued apace. While on the one hand Ireland's natural resources could in no way be compared with those of England or Wales, on occasion, some of its mineral resources became the focus of keen British interest. The barytes mines of west Cork and the iron pyrites mines of County Wicklow, were, at key periods, the most important producers in the former United Kingdom, while the only workable deposits of bauxite in either Britain or Ireland were to be found in County Antrim. However, while there was mining activity in almost every Irish county during the nineteenth century, the vast majority were, in economic terms, marginal activities, undertaken when market conditions for particular minerals were buoyant.

Richard Griffith's *Catalogue* of mines and mineral occurrence in Ireland of 1854 – which was by no means comprehensive – enumerates up to 277 non-ferrous metal mines that were either then in operation or had formerly been worked.[1] English Board of Trade records for the period 1858-1920 also provide important information on the extent of interest in developing Irish metal mines. No fewer than 86 companies (some of which were in existence for less than six months) had non-ferrous metal mining interests in Ireland.[2] Yet, as late as 1824, almost all such activity in Ireland has been small-scale, sporadic, under-capitalised and financed without the relative cushion of wider public investment. Indeed, not until the mining boom of 1824-5 did large public companies such as the Mining Company of Ireland begin to become established.[3] In the period 1780-4 only three Irish mines are known to have exported copper and lead and, by 1800, this figure had barely increased at

5.1 *Eighteenth- and nineteenth-century Irish copper mines. These were often located in demanding locations.*

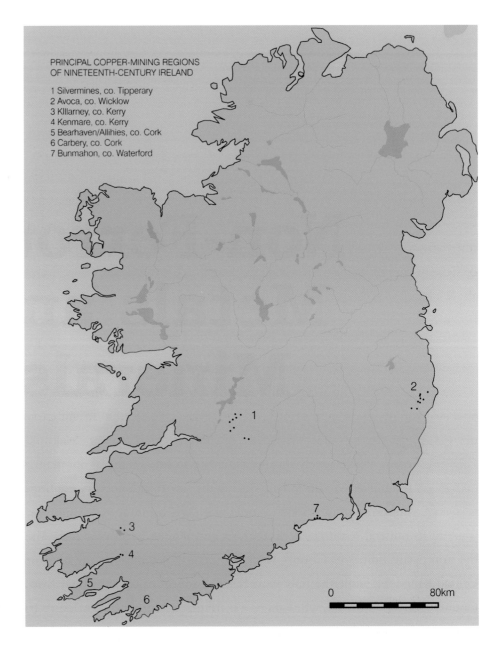

PRINCIPAL COPPER-MINING REGIONS
OF NINETEENTH-CENTURY IRELAND

1 Silvermines, co. Tipperary
2 Avoca, co. Wicklow
3 Kíllarney, co. Kerry
4 Kenmare, co. Kerry
5 Bearhaven/Allihies, co. Cork
6 Carbery, co. Cork
7 Bunmahon, co. Waterford

0   80km

all.[4] Throughout the nineteenth century, Irish non-ferrous metal mining operated on the periphery of the economy, both physically and financially. With the notable exception of Dublin and its environs, these mines were nearly always situated in remote areas where all the resources required to exploit them, human or otherwise, had to be established in what were often demanding locations (figure 5.1).

(1) The Archaeology of Non-Ferrous Metal Mining in Ireland *c.* 1750-1922

From the later medieval period onwards, the expertise marshalled to exploit Ireland's metal mines has been garnered from either England or the continent.[5] Throughout the nineteenth century in Ireland, skilled labour was imported from the Cornish mines, where mine 'captains', generally experienced mining engineers, acted as general overseers and mine managers for Irish mine owners. This technological hegemony brought specialists from all of Britain's main mining regions, and both Cornish and Welsh miners were at one time employed in Irish copper mines. The veins of ore or *lodes* were located in outcrops or through the excavation of *costean* or exploratory pits. Not surprisingly, most of the technical terms used in nineteenth-century Irish metal mines are derived from Cornish practice. Once identified, potentially profitable lodes were first worked by bell pits and then by horizontal *adits* or tunnels driven through the hillside. The adit was normally sloped downwards from the surface to facilitate drainage from the surface workings. During the nineteenth century, the adit was usually connected by means of a vertical access shaft to the surface. Beneath the adits, lodes were worked from a series of working tunnels or galleries, called *levels*, which were excavated at intervals of about 10-12 fathoms (one fathom = 6 ft or 1.82 m) along the lode. Miners blasted the rock with black gunpowder, creating a series of steps or *stopes*, enabling the ore to be removed horizontally, layer by layer.[6] The excavation of the ore from above by inserting the gunpowder charge in the roof was called *overhead stopeing*, which was generally the easiest method, as gravity assisted the removal of the ore. *Underhand stopeing*, however, which involved laying the charge on the floor and the extraction of the ore from below, was also practiced.[7] The black powder was normally stored in isolated magazines called 'powder houses', the best examples of which have survived at the west Cork mines. These include a double shell structure at Allihies Mountain Mine, which is rectangular in plan and has a vaulted roof. Circular powder magazines survive at the Dhurode and Crookhaven mines, the former having decorative, mock battlements.[8] A further example, at the Glengowla lead mines in County Galway, has recently been restored.

By the early years of the nineteenth century, Irish metal mines were becoming progressively deeper which increased drainage problems and made life more arduous for miners. The Cronebane mine in the Avoca complex, County Wicklow, was already being worked to 390 ft (118.87 m) in 1809, whilst at Knockmahon, County Waterford, one copper mine was worked to almost 1,300 ft (396.24 m) by 1847.[9] In deep mines, the descent was made by wooden ladders up to 24 ft (7.31 m) long, and at the copper mines at Allihies, where miners went down 300 fathoms or more, this process involved a double journey which could take up to two hours. At the Mountain Mine in the west Cork Allihies complex a man-lifting engine or 'man engine', the first and only example of its kind ever to be built in Ireland, was erected *c.* 1862. The man engine, of Cornish design, of which only 21 examples are known to have built worldwide, consisted of two vertical rods set side by side, extending to the base of the mineshaft, onto which a series of wooden platforms were fixed at regular intervals. As the rods were moved up and down by steam power, alternately, a man standing on one of these platforms could be lifted to the surface in 12 ft (3.65 m) hoists with every stroke of the engine by simply stepping onto a platform on the adjacent rod.[10] The Mountain Mine man engine was reputedly installed by the Cornish engineer, Michael Loam, who was been responsible for the earliest recorded example to have been used in a Cornish mine, in 1842. During its working life, the Allihies man engine seems likely to have operated to depths of up to 1, 494ft (455.37 m), and continued in use up to the closure and abandonment of the mine in 1882 (figure 5.2).[11] It was very recently the focus of an ambitious conservation scheme, managed by the Mining Heritage

5.2 *The 'man engine' house at Allihies, County Cork, completed c. 1862, after extensive conservation works by Mining Heritage Trust of Ireland in 2004 (top);* **5.3** *The Ross Island pumping engine, erected 1807-8 (below).*

Trust of Ireland and completed in 2004. By the late 1870s, work in Ireland's deep copper mines was becoming uneconomic, and the Dooneenmore and Kealogue (in 1875) mines in west Cork, along with the deep Knockmahon mine in County Waterford (in 1878), were abandoned.[12]

Mine drainage presented one of the main engineering problems for Irish mining companies during the eighteenth and nineteenth centuries. Man-powered pumps were still used in the Ballymurtagh copper mines in the late eighteenth and early nineteenth centuries but, more often than not, either water- or steam-powered pumping machinery was employed.[13] Work at the Knockeen copper and lead mine at Silvermines, County Tipperary, was abandoned in 1803 owing to an insufficiency of water (during a dry summer) to power a water-wheel employed to drive the drainage pumps.[14] Between 1825-27, water-powered pumping machinery was at work at Castlemaine lead and silver mine, County Kerry, whilst the Knockmahon mines in County Waterford made elaborate provision for similar plant in the early 1830s.[15] At Knockmahon, some 12 miles of mill-races were constructed to service the four water-wheels employed there during this period, which included a 40 ft (12.19 m) diameter wheel that proved sufficient to power all the plant in operation at the complex as late as 1832 (see also Chapter 1).[16] Indeed, some very large diameter water-wheels were in use for pumping at Irish metal mines in the first half of the nineteenth century, as at the Keeldrum lead mine in County Donegal in late 1820s, where a 50 ft (15.24 m) diameter example was at work. Water-wheels were also in use for this purpose at the Hollyford copper mines, County Tipperary, where a 34 ft (10.36 m) example was employed to work pumping machinery,

24 hours a day, during the 1840s.[17] A 50 ft diameter example used for pumping is reported at Shallee East in the Silvermines complex during the 1850s.[18] At the Ross Island mines, near Killarney, County Kerry, a series of coffer dams totalling some 445 m in extent, were constructed in the period 1804-10 to prevent the flooding of the mine workings by the adjacent lake. In the years 1825-7, the Hibernian Mining Company rebuilt sections of this (which had originally drained an area of 1.8 ha) in stone, parts of which are still exposed along the southern and western shorelines of the lake.[19]

Early forms of reciprocating beam engines for mine drainage, as has been seen, were introduced into Ireland by the middle of the eighteenth century, but water-powered plant was by no means ever wholly replaced, and remained in use for ore-processing machinery in most mining regions. To be sure, at the Luganure mines in County Wicklow, such was the sufficiency of water for industrial energy that steam-powered plant was never installed. The first recorded example of a steam-powered pumping engine at an Irish metal mine was at Ross Island, near Killarney, County Kerry, where a 21 hp beam engine (fuelled with coal shipped from Swansea) was installed in 1807, but was later removed and erected at the Caminche copper mine in County Cork in 1829 (figure 5.3).[20] For the most part, however, close ties between Cornwall, Wales and Irish metal-mining districts ensured that Cornish pumping engines made by reputable Cornish foundries, such as Harvey's of Hale (from 1823) or the Neath Abbey Ironworks in Wales (from 1815), were imported into Ireland.[21]

Nothing is, perhaps, more iconographic of nineteenth-century Irish metal-mining landscapes than surviving Cornish engine houses and their tapering stacks which were, in most cases, almost exact copies of their English counterparts. More than two-thirds of the surviving Cornish engine houses in Ireland are located in the Munster counties, although in Ulster and Leinster the remains of engines are more commonly marked by surviving stacks.[22] In Leinster, some four of the original thirteen Cornish engine houses erected in the Avoca region survive, along with a solitary example at Barrystown in County Wexford.[23] The last surviving Cornish engine house in Ulster, at the Conlig and Whitespots mines in County Down, collapsed in the 1970s.[24] Williams' engine house in Avoca (named after the Williams Brothers of Perranarwortal in Cornwall) and built, c. 1860, by the Perran Foundry of Cornwall, is the largest extant Cornish engine house in Ireland. It had an enormous 60-inch diameter cylinder and two chimneys along with a curious back-to-front arrangement of its condenser.[25] Further good surviving examples of Cornish pumping engine houses at Irish metal mines include Kealogue ('Puxley's engine', built by the Perran foundry in 1845 with a 52-inch cylinder) in the Allihies mining region and at Tankardstown, County Waterford (figures 5.4 and 5.5).[26] As in the case of winding engines, no Irish mine pumping engine survives, principally because engines were frequently sold on to other Irish mines or to English mines after a site was worked out or abandoned.

Within the mine, transport of material was generally by means of trucks or bogies pulled on wooden tramways along the adits, as was the case at the Allihies mines from the 1820s onwards. At many eighteenth- and early nineteenth-century mines, hand-operated capstans and horse whims (figure 5.6, see also Chapter 1) were commonly used to raise ore out of the mine in *kibbles* (originally large wooden and, later bell-shaped cast-iron, buckets). The Ross Island mine, for example, had a horse whim in operation in the period 1754-8.[27] However,

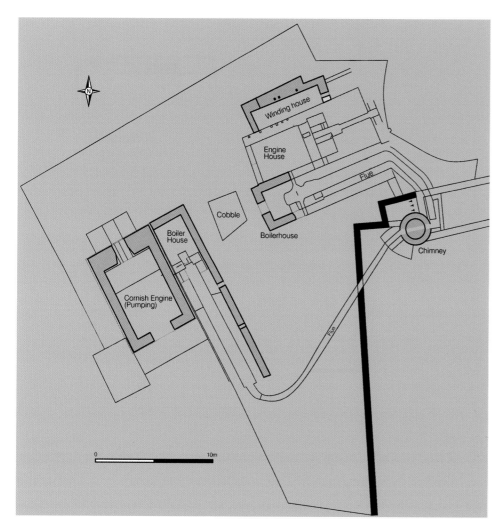

Labels in figure: N, Winding house, Engine House, Flue, Cobble, Boiler House, Boilerhouse, Chimney, Cornish Engine (Pumping), Flue, Flue, 0 10m

OPPOSITE PAGE: **5.4** *Cornish engine house of the 1850s at Tankardstown copper mines, County Waterford.*
LEFT: **5.5** *Plan of Tankardstown engine houses, County Waterford.*

as the workings became deeper, the deployment of either water- or steam-powered lifting gear was unavoidable, as at the Mountain and Caminche copper mines in 1834, when horse whims were replaced by steam-powered winding engines.[28] Water-powered whims were employed at Luganure throughout its operational use, at Knockmahon up to 1832 and at Lackamore up to the early 1850s.[29] By the second half of the nineteenth century, however, most Irish mine winding engines were steam powered (figure 5.7). Winding or whim engines operated on the rotative beam engine principle (either single- or double-acting), and were fitted with a flywheel to communicate rotary motion to a winding drum. Their housing structures are generally smaller than those that accommodated pumping engines as at the Knockmahon mines and at Cronebane, County Wicklow, and other mining sites throughout Ireland. There is, indeed, at least one recorded example of a whim engine at the Mountain Mine, Allihies, that was installed some 28 fathoms below the surface.[30]

Once brought to the surface, wheelbarrows or tramways were used to transport the ore to the dressing floors. In certain instances, inclined planes, where ore was hauled up a steep slope on rails by means of a winch powered by a stationary steam engine, were in operation, as at the Gortavallig mine, in County Cork, traces of which are still in evidence.[31] The processes involved in concentrating the ores of copper and lead were very

135

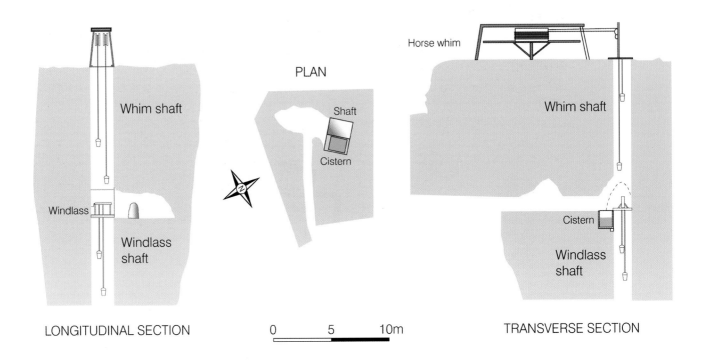

5.6 *Plan and section of Wheel Church mine, County Kildare, in 1826 (after contemporary sketch by M. Healey in Cowman 2002).*

similar but, owing to their high density, lead ores were often easier to prepare for smelting than those of other metals. Beneficiation, the processes involved in washing and dressing metallic ores, was designed to separate the ore from the gangue or waste material. On the surface, the larger material was broken down with a long-handled *spalling* hammer. This prepared the material for the next stage of concentration where it was further reduced to pea-size pieces with a flat-faced *bucking* hammer. In Ireland, this laborious work was nearly always undertaken by women and young girls on specially prepared dressing floors.[32] The remains of these are still in evidence at a number of Irish sites, which include the Mountain Mine complex in County Cork and the Wicklow Gap lead mines.[33]

As early as 1552, a water-powered stamp mill for crushing lead ores (the earliest recorded of its type in Ireland) had been erected by German mining adventurers at Ross, County Wexford. A not entirely dissimilar technology was still being employed at the early nineteenth-century Irish metal mines, where crushing mills employing vertical stamps with cast-iron hammer heads, lifted by a cam on the water-wheel's axle, were becoming increasingly common in Ireland's copper and lead mines. Water-powered stamp (and later roller crusher) mills were generally more common at Irish metal mines than those actuated by steam power. In 1819, two water-powered stamp mills were installed at the Caminche copper mine in west Cork, the remains of which still survive, whilst similar machinery was at work at a further County Cork copper mine at Cappagh in the 1820s, at Knockmahon, County Waterford, in 1832 and Hollyford, County Tipperary, in 1858.[34] In 1828, an eighteenth-century windmill, which survives, *in situ*, at the Conlig and Whitespots lead mines, was refurbished to power

5.7 *General view of Tankardstown, County Waterford, showing Cornish pumping engine house (left), stack (centre) and winding engine house (right) before conservation.*

stamp mills.[35] Water-powered roller crushing mills were operated at the Knockmahon mines in 1838, at the Allihies mines in County Cork and at the Lackamore mines in County Tipperary by the mid-1850s.[36] The best preserved water-powered nineteenth-century crusher houses are at the Baravore mines at Glenmalure, County Wicklow, where the oldest of the two surviving examples, which dates to *c.* 1859, has a wheel pit and the remains of sockets in the mill's north wall, into which were inserted the levers that compressed the ore crusher rollers (figure 5.8).[37] Good extant examples of water-powered crusher houses have also survived at Glendasan, County Wicklow, and Clement's Mine, near Maum, County Galway.[38] The development and adaptation of steam plant for these processes was, however, somewhat slower, although steam-powered grinding machinery had been installed at Puxley's west Cork mines in 1830-1, at Ballyhickey, County Clare, in 1834, at Ballygowan in the Silvermines complex (1854, the engine house of which is extant) and at Ballycorus, County Dublin, in 1857.[39] Indeed, the expense of importing coal for the west Cork grinding engines (some 1,100 tons per-year in the mid-1870s) led to their abandonment and a return to water-powered crushing plant.[40]

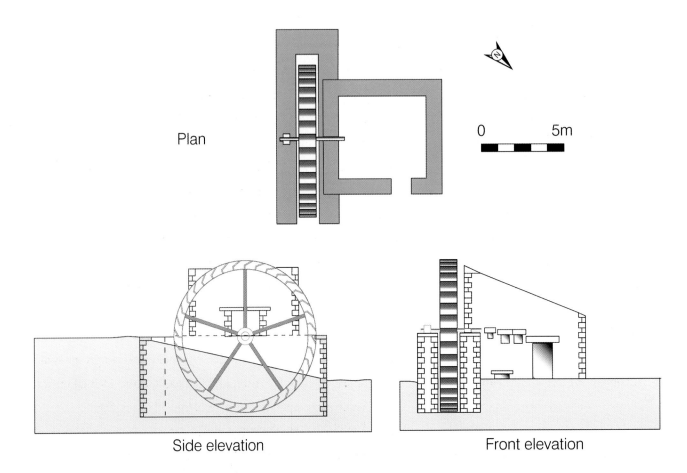

Plan

0   5m

Side elevation

Front elevation

5.8 *Reconstruction of 'Old' crusher house at Baravore, Glenmalure, County Wicklow, c. 1859 (after Chester and Burns 2001).*

The ores were further concentrated by *jigging* or sieving the material in water, a process which was mechanised at certain County Cork and County Waterford copper mines by the early 1840s, and at the Lackamore and Hollyford mines, County Tipperary, by water power in the 1850s. The final stage of concentration was called *buddling*. In its essentials, the buddle was an ore-cleaning device which used a continuous trickle of water to encourage the metallic ore and its accompanying waste materials to separate in accordance with their densities. In their most basic form, buddles were inclined and wooden troughs constructed near the mine workings, to which a watercourse was directed to facilitate their use. As the water poured down the buddle, waste material lighter than the ore tended to be washed away. The ore itself also tended to settle differentially, with the heavier pieces of metallic ore settling at the top end of the buddle floor, the lighter pieces coming to rest at the lower end. By the middle of the nineteenth century, horse- or water-powered *circular* or *round buddles* were introduced. These could have either concave or convex floors, which were equipped with rotating paddles powered by either horse or water-powered rotating sweeps which agitated the crushed ore. Convex buddles received the ore slurry at the centre where the heavier material collected, while concave buddles were fed at the edge.[41] Two round buddles, powered by a water-wheel, are listed in an inventory of the Lackamore coppermines, County Tipperary, in 1859.[42] The remains of buddling operations are in evidence at Glendasan, County Wicklow, where a number of circular emplacements that would originally have accommodated round buddles, survive *in situ*, while other traces of such activities remain at a number of the west Cork mines.[43]

Apart from the pumping machinery and ore-dressing plant, further buildings were also necessary for accommodating the needs of the various ancillary trades required within the mine complex. Most mines would have needed saw pits, forges (underground forges were even used in some of the Allihies mines), carpenters' and millwrights' shops, storage sheds and offices, all of which are commonly listed in mine inventories. For the most part, however, ancillary mine buildings are often poorly preserved at Irish metal mining sites. The largest extant mine building associated with any Irish nineteenth-century metal mine is at the Tassan lead mines in County Monaghan, a three-phase structure whose earliest section dates from 1854-5 (figure 5.9). Also surviving here, *in situ*, is a late nineteenth-century cast-iron horse whim which appears to have provided motive power for the machinery in a carpenter's shop.[44] Other surviving buildings of note include the likely workshop complex at Baravore, County Wicklow, and a blacksmith's workshop (now restored) at the Glengowla mines, County Galway.[45] Storage reservoirs supplying the needs of water-powered plant, beneficiation processes and also for the boilers of steam plant had to be constructed in upland areas, often in demanding locations. Impressive and elaborate water supply systems were created in upland regions with high heads, an excellent example of which survives above the Mountain Mine in the Allihies complex, and also at Coosheen, Cappagh, Brow Head, Dhurode and Gortavallig (built on a cliff top) in West Carbery, together with Baravore in County Wicklow.[46]

With the exception of one abortive attempt to smelt copper ores in Ireland in the late eighteenth century, thereafter, all copper ores mined here were shipped by schooner to Wales for smelting. Ore raised at the Allihies mines was loaded on to ships in Ballydonegan Bay, to be shipped either directly to Swansea or temporarily stored

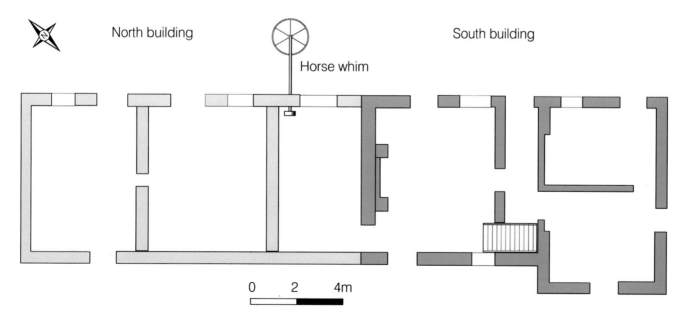

5.9 *Tassan mine buildings, County Monaghan. The earliest section of these buildings dates to 1854-5 (after Morris, Lally and Cowman 2002).*

5.10 *Remains of the cutting of horse-drawn mineral tramway at Tankardstown, County Waterford. The tramway transported ore from the mines at Tankardstown (see figure 5.7) to the village of Bunmahon where it was processed.*

in company facilities at Dunboy. The remains of the latter, which include copper and timber stores, have survived, while many of the west Carbery mines such as Ballycummisk, Cappagh and Coosheen also had associated wharfage.[47] At the Wicklow mines, ore had to be transported 16 miles by road to the port of Wicklow, although the owner of the Ballygahan mine, Henry Hodgson, opened a horse-drawn mineral tramway which carried ore from the mine to the quayside at Arklow. The embankments for this tramway, and a single tramway arch, which carried it over a local road, still survive at Ballygahan (see Chapter 14).[48] Ore from the Ballyhickey and Kilbreckan lead and silver mines in County Clare was also transported a short distance by road to the estuary of the river Fergus (a tributary of the Shannon) for shipment to Wales. Horse tramways were built by the Mining Company of Ireland around 1870 to service the Knockmahon copper mines, the cutting for which can still be traced on the ground (figure 5.10).

The social archaeology of Ireland's industrial metal mining landscapes is physically expressed in the mining settlements at which, by the middle of the nineteenth century, sizeable communities had been created. Up to 2,000 miners and surface workers were employed in the County Wicklow mines in the 1840s, 1,100 at the Waterford mines around the same period, and *c.* 1,200–1,500 in the west Cork mines by the 1850s.[49] For mining companies, two main factors influenced their direct (if largely minimalist) intervention in the provision of living quarters for their workforce: the need to attract the right type of mining operatives, and the fact that the isolation of many mining sites simply compelled them to provide accommodation, along with other basic facilities such as churches, for incipient mining communities. The best surviving example of such structures are associated with the village of Allihies, in the Berehaven mining complex, County Cork. During the nineteenth century, a large mining village grew up here, but immediately next to this, the mining company built a separate 'Cornish village', with two-storey dwellings to accommodate the company's English engineers, mining specialists and their families. English miners also erected a small Protestant church here in around 1845.[50] In many instances, however, underground and surface workers, employed from the locality, lived in appalling conditions

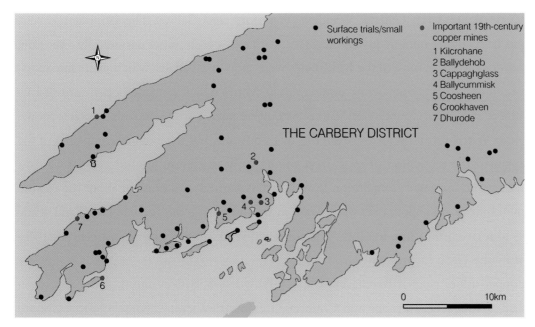

5.11 *The west Carbery mines (after O'Brien 1994).*

in one-roomed *botháin* (a *bothán* being a singled-roomed labourers' dwelling) with their families. The Mining Company of Ireland was amongst a small number of employers who built houses for its workers, beginning in 1836-41, at Knockmahon, County Waterford, a number of which have survived.[51] On the Sheep's Head peninsula, in west Carbery, a row of ten miners' cottages, built by the Southern and Western Mining Company in 1846 for the Gortavallig mines, are also extant. Several good company houses were also constructed for senior personnel at the Hollyford mines in the first half of the nineteenth century, but only a scarcity of miners at Ballymurtagh, County Wicklow, encouraged the Wicklow Copper Mining Company to build miners' houses in the 1870s.[52] Social status and practicality commonly decreed that larger and more comfortable two-storey dwellings be built in close proximity to the mine workings, for the mine captains or the company's agents, such as those surviving at the Cappagh mine in the west Carbery district, at Glandore, also in County Cork, at Annaglogh, County Monaghan, or even the mine agent's cottage (now restored) at the Glengowla mines in County Galway.[53] The Puxley family mansion, Dunboy Castle near Castletownbere, originally built in the early eighteenth century and extended in 1821 and, later still, in 1867, at enormous expense, by Henry Puxley, does, of course, represent the pinnacle of social status in nineteenth-century Irish mining communities.[54]

(2) Copper

Ireland has produced some of the oldest copper mines in Europe, the largest concentration of which has been identified on Mount Gabriel on the Mizen peninsula in western County Cork. Some 30 workings here have been dated by radio-carbon dating to *c.* 1700-1500 BC, but, at the time of writing, the earliest evidence for copper mining in Ireland has been discovered at Ross Island near Killarney, County Kerry, dating to 2400-2000 BC.[55] Yet it is not until the early eighteenth century that principal copper ore bodies here began to be systematically

141

exploited, in Counties Cork (figure 5.11), Leitrim, Wicklow, Waterford, and Galway. The Napoleonic Wars occasioned an expansion in Irish copper mining during the 1800s, with seven Irish mines periodically exporting ore to Swansea during 1806-12. However, most of the Irish mines were short-lived affairs, which maintained production for anything between one to five years before closing down. Mines which remained open for relatively long periods of time, such as at Allihies, County Cork (1812-1884), were rare by Irish standards. Sporadic workings were opened in Counties Waterford and Wicklow from the 1820s onwards, but the 'bubble' companies of the early 1850s disastrously impaired the reputation of most Irish mining ventures. From around 1855 onwards, a gradual decline in metal prices and increased competition from North American ores brought about the closure of many Irish copper mines. Indeed, no copper ores were raised in Ireland during the years 1892-96, and while there were some attempts to revive production in Cork, Waterford and Wicklow early in the last century, these were effectively killed off by the Great Depression.

The principal Irish copper mines were at Berehaven/Allihies, Ballydehob, Ballycummisk and Cappagh in County Cork; Ballymurtagh, Cronebane, Tigroney and Connoree in County Wicklow; Knockmahon, County Waterford and Ross Island and Kenmare/Ardtully, County Kerry. Copper mines were also worked at Silvermines, County Tipperary, and in Counties Armagh, Leitrim, Galway and Mayo. However, although their combined output exceeded that of Ireland's lead and silvermines, the smelting of copper ores in Ireland during the eighteenth century proved to be a costly failure. In the 1780s, the Hibernian Mining Company built five conical kilns for calcining ores on the seashore at Arklow along with a smelter. But as coal could only be landed during the summer months, output was greatly reduced. Thereafter, all Irish copper ores were shipped directly to the Swansea region of Wales for smelting.

(3) Lead and Silver

Of the non-ferrous metals to be smelted in Ireland during the last 200 years, only lead was smelted on a continuous basis, copper smelting at Arklow being short-lived. Whereas copper ores in Ireland are more often associated with Old Red Sandstone areas, ores of lead and zinc often occur in carboniferous limestone regions. Galena was the most common ore of lead found in Ireland, and nearly all galena mined here was *argentiferous* or silver bearing. In consequence, lead was often mined because silver could be extracted from it. This was particularly true of the pre-industrial period, where lead and silver mines were opened to obtain this precious metal for specie or coinage. Lead was a remarkably versatile metal. It was commonly used for water and gas service pipes, for roofing (from an early period), for shot, guttering and in the manufacture of sulphuric acid. Alloyed with tin, it formed pewter, which was extensively employed for tablewares in the eighteenth and nineteenth centuries until superseded by cheaper earthenwares.[56]

Within the last 200 years or so, lead workings became widely distributed throughout Ireland. Medieval and post-medieval mining has already been noted for the Silvermines area of County Tipperary and for County Wexford. In 1745, a small amount of lead was being raised in one of the copper mines at Bunmahon, County

Waterford. During the second half of the eighteenth century, seven main mines, including Shallee East and West and Ballygowan South, were being worked in the Silvermines district, and at Ringabella near Cork harbour as early as the 1750s.[57] The greater Dublin area is unique in Ireland for the number of lead-mining ventures within the environs of a large urban centre, which include a large number of eighteenth-century mines (amongst others) at Robbs Walls, Malahide (*c.* 1740), Castleknock (1745), Dolphin's Barn (*c.* 1756-70), Clontarf (1756- *c.* 1770) and Kilmainham (1767-9).[58] Elsewhere in Leinster, in the nineteenth century, lead mines were opened in County Wicklow at Glendalough, Luganure and Glenmalure, and at Barrystown, County Wexford.[59] In the Ulster Counties, the principal lead mines were concentrated in Counties Monaghan and Armagh, around Ballybeg, Clontibret, Keady-Crossmaglen and Castleblayney, along with Glentogher, County Donegal, and Conlig and Whitespots, County Down.[60] The Clonlig and Whitespots mines were owned by George William Dumbell in 1840s, who later went on to set up the Laxey Mining Company in the Isle of Man.[61] In Munster, as has been seen, lead ores were extensively worked in Counties Tipperary, Waterford, Cork and Clare, and in Connacht in the counties of Galway, Mayo and Sligo. At the time of writing, the only Irish nineteenth-century non-ferrous metal mines open to the public are the Glengowla silver and lead mines, near Oughterard, County Galway (figure 5.12). The latter operated from 1851 to 1865, the ore being brought by carts to a specially constructed pier on Lough Corrib near Oughterard. An interesting collection of mining tools was recovered during the clearing of the mineshaft, which includes one of the original wooden ladders, currently on display in the mine itself (figure 5.13).

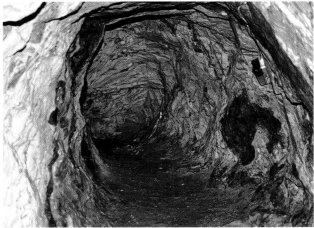

5.12 *Shaft at the Glengowla lead and silver mines, Oughterard, County Galway (top). These mines were operated between 1851 and 1861;* **5.13** *Original miner's ladder on display in the shaft at Glengowla lead and silver mines, Oughterard, County Galway (below).*

Lead Smelting

The earliest lead smelters used in Ireland were probably *bole hearths*, in which a primitive hearth was built within a stone-walled enclosure on an exposed site open to the prevailing winds. Large pieces of lead ore were simply layered with brushwood and timber, which were ignited. As lead has a low melting point of 327° C, smelting readily took place, the molten lead running off into a stone mould constructed at the side of the hearth.[62] Samuel Molyneux describes a bole hearth at work at Silvermines in 1709, where 'The blue and brown oar [is thrown into] a great wood fire, from whence the ore runs out at the bottom'.[63] There is, indeed, an oblique reference to the survival of primitive bole hearths, using turf as fuel, operating at Glenmalure around the turn of the nineteenth century.[64] During the sixteenth century in Britain, a two-stage smelting process was developed to compensate for the poor rate of extraction from the bole hearth. Slags from these were now re-smelted using charcoal as fuel in a bellows smelter. A water-powered smelter was erected at Ross, County Wexford, in 1552, in association with a German venture, where an inventory of the miners' equipment suggests that a wood-fired, bellows-operated smelter was actually in use.[65] The next clear reference to what was obviously a water-powered smelter is by Gerard Boate who, in 1652, refers to smelters, refining houses and mills as being within half a mile of the mines at Silvermines.[66] This same works was briefly described and illustrated by Thomas Dineley in 1681, where the smelter was operated by 'a large water wheele by whose motion a Great Forge bellows is lifted and blown'.[67]

In *c.* 1689-90, a new form of smelter, the *reverberatory furnace*, developed by John Hodges, appears to have been introduced into Ireland.[68] This latter is an interesting development, as these furnaces seem not to have been employed in important English production centres in Derbyshire or the Pennines region until the 1740s.[69] In the reverberatory furnace (or *cupola*), the ore to be smelted was kept away from the direct heat of the coal fire in a separate chamber. The heat from the fire was, instead, drawn into the melting chamber and reflected down onto the ore by means of a firebrick roof. The fuel was thus isolated from the ore, which reduced contamination by sulphur. A tall chimney or stack was now employed (instead of a bellows) to provide a draught for the furnace. Samuel Molyneux, in 1709, provides a description of a 'great sort of reverbarating furnace, as they call it. The fire, which is wood, lyes at one part, the lead oar at another part of the furnace, so placed that by the draught of the chimney the flame is drawn to it', in operation at Silvermines, which is clearly a furnace that had been used on the site since the 1680s.[70] In the late 1720s, William Barker of the London Lead Company, built a coal-fired reverberatory furnace, on Edmund Wright's patent (a design developed in the 1690s and now controlled by the London company) at Silvermines, the first of its type used in Ireland.[71] In 1724, a lead refiner at Killarney, Edward Key, was manufacturing bricks to line his smelting furnace, which appears to have been used to process ores from either the Killarney or Kenmare districts of County Kerry.[72]

Only a small number of lead smelters are known to have been built in Ireland during the eighteenth and nineteenth centuries, namely Dolphin's Barn (1760s) and Clontarf (1818-24) in County Dublin, Cornamucklagh South, near Ballybay, County Monaghan (*c.* 1800), three water-powered smelters operating at the Glendalough mines around 1809 and where, according to a contemporary account, some 10 cwt of lead was smelted on a daily basis with coal shipped in from Wicklow, and at Ballycorus, County Dublin.[73] In 1824, the Mining Company of Ireland took over the lead mines at Glendalough, and thereafter, all of its smelting operations were carried on at Ballycorus, where new smelting and rolling machinery was installed in 1828. The Ballycorus smelter was in operation in 1824 and was described as an 'air [reverberatory] furnace' in 1828.[74] According to Sir Robert Kane, in 1845, the bed of the Ballycorus furnace was dished so that molten lead would trickle down the sides to the centre, from which it was run off into moulds to form pigs. Most of the lead ores processed at Ballycorus in this period were mined at the MCI mines in Counties Donegal and Wicklow (ore from Keeldrum, County Donegal, being sent to the Ballycorus as early as 1826), along with ores from the Caime mine in County Wexford.[75] However, while mining in Ballycorus area seems to have ended by the 1860s, the smelting works remained open smelting ore from Wicklow. In 1880s, it became no longer profitable to use Irish ores, and the smelter was employed up to 1913 in processing ores mined at the Great Laxey complex in the Isle of Man.[76] The surviving sections of the smelting works at Ballycorus include a part of the building that housed the furnace, along with purification tanks, stores, the weighbridge house at the works' entrance, company-built worker's cottage (in local granite) and a manager's house.[77] Elsewhere in Ireland, lead ores from Conlig and Whitespots, County Down, and Kilbreckan and Ballyhickey, County Clare, was shipped for smelting to the River Dee.

Silver was the only desirable impurity of the lead smelting process, and this was refined from the lead in a process called *cupellation*, during which the lead was reheated in a shallow hearth (the *cupel*) to 1000-1100° C. An air blast was used to oxidise the lead to litharge (PbO) or lead oxide, in which the base metals were absorbed: the silver was not oxidised, and could be collected at the bottom of the cupel.[78] At Silvermines in 1772, it was claimed that every ton of lead could produce 80 oz of silver, whilst ore from Kilbreckan, County Clare, was producing 120 oz of silver to the ton in 1843.[79] Litharge was an important by-product of the cupellation process, and was widely used in Ireland in the manufacture of flint glass. It was also converted into red lead (Pb_3O_4) which was employed in the manufacture of paints and varnishes.

During the late 1770s, it was observed that sizeable quantities of lead could be extracted from the vapours emitted from the reverberatory furnaces, if these vapours were provided with an opportunity to settle. Long horizontal masonry flues were thus developed to encourage these vapours to precipitate slowly along their course, into which partitions were built both to increase the surface area on which these airborne lead particles could precipitate, and to extend further the time in which vapours could settle. The flues were often several hundred feet in length, and in order to disperse the poisonous vapours emitted from them, tall chimneys were built at the end of the flue to minimise pollution. The flue and chimney at Ballycorus, County Dublin, are the only examples ever to have been built in Ireland, where the draught from the furnace was drawn off through a horizontal granite masonry flue (with a brick-arched roof), some 1,500 metres long, with an inspection/access door set along its entire length, to exhaust through a tall, granite-built chimney, which still stands (figures 5.14 and 5.15). Both the chimney and the horizontal flue were constructed in 1836 to replace an earlier, smaller unit.[80]

In 1843, sheet lead, pipe litharge and shot were being manufactured at Ballycorus. A shot tower was built

5.14 *The Ballycorus flue, Ballycorus, County Dublin, completed c. 1836, a granite masonry structure (with a brick-arched roof), some 1,500 metres long (left);* **5.15** *The Ballycorus chimney, a granite masonry structure completed c. 1836 (right).*

here in 1829, which appears to be the first and perhaps the only recorded instance of such a tower in Ireland. These towers were constructed for the manufacture of lead shot for firearms and could be up to 150 ft (45.72 m) high. At the top of the tower, an alloy of molten lead and arsenic was poured through a perforated zinc tray. While falling through the air for a distance of at least 100 ft (30. 48 m), the lead globules formed spheres (and thus the perfect shape for shot) before being caught in a water bath at the bottom of the tower. A section of one of the original shot towers had been restored, while a second, no longer extant, example was described in 1912 as 'a handsome, substantial structure, having a spiral stairs within, terminating in an artistic iron verandah on the outside, nearly 100 ft from the ground'.[81]

(3) Barytes

Barytes or barium sulphate ($BaSO_4$), which is often found in association with lead and copper sulphide deposits in Ireland, began to be used as a filler in the second half of the nineteenth century in many materials such as linoleum, rubber and paper. In Ireland, barytes was mined at Gleniff and Tormore, County Sligo, Carrickartagh, County Monaghan, Glenmalure, County Wicklow, and a number of locations in county Armagh.[82] But the undisputed centre of Irish barytes mining and, indeed, of the former United Kingdom, were the mines of the Bantry district of County Cork. On present evidence, the earliest mining activity for barytes appears to have been at Derreenalomane, near Durrus, County Cork, in the 1840s, where some 2,500 tons were being raised in 1851, compared to a combined output of just over 800 tons for the other three localities in the United Kingdom producing barytes in the same period.[83] However, by the end of the 1850s, the output of the Bantry mines was eventually superceded by the barytes mines of Derbyshire. Nonetheless, the decline of copper mining in west Cork in the 1870s shifted mining interest to the extraction of barytes.[84]

At Derreenalomane, County Cork, the material was washed and then dried in a revolving furnace, after which it was crushed between steel rollers and then milled. The milling involved the passage of the rolled material through a steel mill and then grinding with French burr stones (see Chapter 7) to produce barytes flour. The flour was subsequently packed into bags, which were carried to an island jetty in Dunmanus Bay by an aerial ropeway 1.25 miles long for shipment to London, Liverpool and Glasgow.[85] At Dunnamark, near Schull, County Cork, an 8-bay, 3-storey barytes crushing plant, used to process barytes from the nearby Mount Gabriel mines in the late nineteenth century, has recently been converted to a boathouse. A second west Cork barytes mill survives at the falls of Dunnamark at the head of Bantry Bay.

(5) Sulphur

The main forms of iron pyrites (FeS_2, iron disulphide or 'fools gold') and copper pyrites ($CuFe S_2$) were important sources of sulphur. Sulphur was used in the manufacture of sulphuric acid, a crucial component in the making of dyes, bleaching powders and metal refining. Sulphur itself was also, of course, one of the principal constituents of black gunpowder. However, in Ireland's Avoca mineral belt, iron pyrites was commonly extracted with copper ores, and in the earlier years of the nineteenth century, sulphur was refined from copper pyrites at the Cronebane mine. For the greater part of the nineteenth century, most of the sulphur imported into Great Britain was mined in Sicily. However, when the government of Naples leased the mines to a French company, the price of sulphur was substantially increased in 1840, and the attention of English manufacturers shifted to the vale of Avoca as an alternative source. From 1840 onwards, large quantities of iron pyrites were shipped from Arklow and Wicklow to England for the manufacture of sulphuric acid and, between 1857-69, 85 per cent of the total of all iron pyrites raised in the United Kingdom originated in the vale of Avoca.[86] Most of the iron pyrites in the Wicklow area were mined at Connary, Cronebane, Tigroney, Ballygahan and Ballymurtagh, many of which locations, as we have already seen, were also important copper producing sites. Many pyrites mines in the Avoca district were abandoned in the 1880s as demand declined, but during the years 1914-18, the Cronebane Mining Co. of Avoca began to raise pyrites for the new sulphuric acid plants established in the towns of Arklow and Wicklow (see Chapter 11). During the Second World War, a shortage of sulphur led an Irish state company to recommence pyrites mining during the period 1942-47.

(6) Bauxite

Hydrated oxide of aluminium, or bauxite, is the principal source of aluminium. In Great Britain, native supplies were, for a long period, obtainable only in Counties Antrim and Derry. The silica content of Irish bauxite generally confined its use to the manufacture of aluminium sulphate, which was required for the making of bleach and paper manufacture. From the 1880s onwards, several former iron ore mines in County Antrim began to extract bauxite.[87] The mines involved included the Antrim Iron Company's workings at Essathohan (which was the last bauxite mine to close in 1933) and former iron mines such as Spitals Drift, Cargan, Evishacrow and Parkmore.

Around 1900, the British Aluminium Company established a processing plant at Larne, at which small amounts of County Antrim bauxite was processed into alumina or aluminium oxide; most of the bauxite, however, was imported from other countries. The Antrim alumina was exported to Scotland where pure aluminium was extracted electrolytically.[88]

(7) Zinc

The principal ores of zinc, zinc carbonate (or calamine) and zinc sulphide (blende or sphalerite), became important in the mid-nineteenth century when zinc began to be used in galvanising, where iron was either electro-plated with zinc or simply dipped in molten zinc to protect it from atmospheric corrosion. Zinc extraction was closely associated with lead mining as at Abbeytown, County Sligo, Glengowla, County Galway, Connary, County Wicklow, and Milltown, County Clare.[89] Calamine and blende were mined at Silvermines (in association with copper and lead) during the years 1859-74, and from 1866 until 1872, zinc began to be processed there by burning it to form zinc oxide. However, this venture, which began with the construction of no fewer than eleven furnaces when a mere handful would have sufficed, quickly proved uneconomic, as the market for its product had been small from the outset.[90] Overall, in relative terms, the amounts raised in Ireland were quite small, the total extracted during the period 1856-1915 being about one-twentieth that of England.[91]

6
Building Materials (Stone, Lime, Brick, Cement), Ceramics and Glass

Ireland's native industries in the period 1750-1930, as we have seen, were almost wholly reliant on imported coal, while important base metals such as copper, even though their ores were extensively mined here up to the closing decades of the nineteenth century, were also imported from other regions of the former United Kingdom. Seldom, it is clear, were native industries requiring either fossil fuels or ferrous and non-ferrous metals ever in a position to strike a balance between the exploitation of locally sourced and imported raw materials. However, there were other Irish extractive industries which were, at various times, able to accommodate all the island's industrial and domestic needs. Several thousand quarries, of varying sizes, provided the raw materials for the building industry, such as stone, brick and cement, while others met the needs of industries producing important commodities such as ceramics and glass. There were also, as we shall see, a number of important technical developments associated with many of these industries.

(1) Stone

From the medieval period in Ireland onwards, building stones, owing to the cost of transportation, have been quarried locally, and in this way the buildings of Ireland's cities and towns are in many ways a reflection of their

149

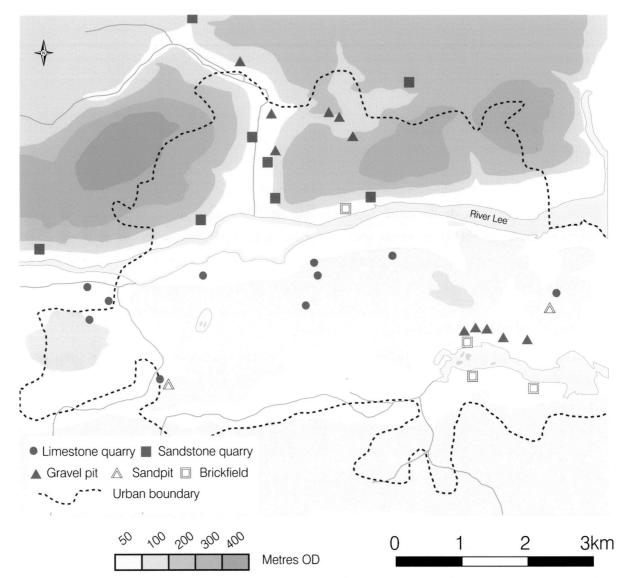

6.1 *Principal eighteenth- and nineteenth-century stone quarries within the environs of Cork city. These, along with other building materials such as brick clay and gravel were generally sourced as close as possible to Irish urban centres to minimise transport costs.*

local geology. This same pattern of exploitation was current during the eighteenth and early nineteenth centuries, when almost all the structures in Ireland's main urban areas were constructed with locally quarried stone. Other important features such as bridges and quaysides were also built with stone sourced with a narrow radius of the construction site, and, to accommodate this demand, many new quarries were opened around Ireland's major cities. However, access to a navigable waterway also enabled stone to be transported not only over considerable distances inland but to destinations across the Irish Sea. The seventeenth-century Catholic prelate, David Rothe, reported that Kilkenny quarries actually exported their products overseas, partial confirmation of which can be inferred from the order of black Kilkenny marble by Inigo Jones, the Master of the King's Works, for the newly designed steps of St Paul's Cathedral in London in 1637, and by the use of Galway black 'marble' by Sir Christopher Wren in the staircases of Kensington Palace.[1] As will be seen, Irish building stone continued to be exported to other regions of the former United Kingdom during the eighteenth and nineteenth centuries.

In the larger towns like Dublin, Belfast and Cork, from around the second half of the eighteenth century, local corporations embarked on ambitious schemes to pave urban streets. In Dublin, for example, from 1717 onwards, a series of measures were enacted for the paving of the capital's streets, culminating in a 1774 Act which created the Commissioners for the Paving of the Streets of Dublin.[2] The establishment of ballast offices in Ireland's principal ports during the eighteenth century also increased demand (see Chapter 15), as did the road maintenance and building schemes of Ireland's Grand Juries (see Chapter 12). Nonetheless, large quantities of Portland Stone were imported into Ireland during the eighteenth century. The fashion for using this high-quality limestone (which was ideally suited for ornamental work) quarried on the Isle of Portland in Dorset had begun with Christopher Wren, who employed it to effect in the rebuilding of London after the Great Fire of 1666. Portland stone was used in the reconstruction of St Paul's Cathedral and in the construction of Somerset House (1771-81) in London.[3] In Ireland, it was employed in prestigious buildings such as the houses of the aristocracy, where it became an outward symbol of great wealth. Enormous amounts were absorbed in the construction of Gandon's Custom House in the 1780s, but from the 1740s, granite from County Dublin was already beginning to supplant it.[4] An artificial stone with a smooth, creamy texture and finish resembling terracotta, known as Coade stone, after its manufacturers, G. and E. Coade of Lambeth, London, became popular in Ireland towards the end of the eighteenth century. Notable Irish uses of Coade stone include the reliefs designed by James Gandon for the Rotunda Lying-In Hospital, on Parnell Street, Dublin (1786), H.A. Baker's Rutland memorial fountain in Merrion Square, Dublin (1791), and the Bermingham family mausoleum in Athenry Friary, County Galway (1790). It was well-suited for decoration as it could be cast into statues, chimney pieces panels and friezes, but its manufacture effectively ceased when the firm closed in about 1840.[5] During the nineteenth century, coloured sandstones from England and Scotland were also imported into Ireland and used for decorative effect in buildings.

In the main, stone was selected for its working properties, generally its hardness, colour and its reaction to tools (which greatly influenced the way in which it was worked by craftsmen). Many sedimentary rocks such as limestone and most varieties of sandstone have horizontal or *bedding lines* running through them (similar to the grain in wood). At the quarry face, these provided natural lines of breakage along which large blocks of stone could be freed from rock outcrops, by means of wedges and chisels.[6] Indeed, when the finished stone was laid in a building, it was important that the stone mason ensured that its grain was laid running in the same direction as it was in the quarry, and in this way, the stone would be more resistant to weathering.

For the most part, Irish quarries were opened on an *ad hoc* basis to minimise transport costs for a special building project in an isolated area, away from good communications, or simply because large amounts of stone were needed for a project which could not be met from existing sources. There were two basic types of quarry, those which supplied *dimension* or *freestone* (i.e., good-quality stone, which could be freely cut in any direction and could be cut to any size) and *rubblestone*, this latter variety being used for walling and as a road-building material.[7] Quarries open on a continuous basis tended to supply the general needs of the building industry, although some quarries, such as those involved in millstone manufacture, met specialist requirements. The individual qualities of the various types of stone could vary considerably from quarry to quarry, and even within the same quarry. During the later eighteenth and nineteenth centuries, new quarries were opened near large towns, while existing ones expanded to take advantage of favourable building trends (figure 6.1). The abandonment of a quarry, more often than not, was a function of diminishing returns, brought on by the increasing depth of the workings, reduced demand, and a lack of space for the removal of waste rock and flooding.

In deeper quarries, flooding tended to be a serious problem when the workings pierced the water table and, wherever possible, excess water was usually siphoned out or manually operated pumps were employed, as at the Greyabbey slate quarries, County Down, in the late 1820s and 1830s.[8] Water-powered drainage pumps were in use at the Glenpatrick slate quarries, near Kilsheelan, County Waterford by 1830, and the Victoria Slate Quarries near Ahenny, County Tipperary, during the nineteenth century.[9]

Wind-powered pumps were employed in a calp limestone quarry at Rathgar, County Dublin, in the early 1800s (see Chapter 1), while a further limestone quarry at Drinagh South, County Wexford, is known to have been drained by a wind-powered pump erected within a former wind-powered grain mill during the second half of the nineteenth century.[10] By the mid-nineteenth century, steam-pumping plant had to been introduced at a small number of the larger slate quarries, as at the Killaloe (where the engine house survives) and the Victoria Quarries in County Tipperary and the Glentown Quarry, County Donegal.[11]

In early periods, suitable rock outcrops were removed laboriously by the use of wedges to split the rock, and up to quite recent times, half-round iron bars (the *feathers*) were inserted into a crevice in the rock face, and a wedge (the *plug*), driven between them to cleave the rock apart.[12] Blasting with gunpowder became relatively common in Ireland by the end of the eighteenth century.[13] In order to prevent the rock from being completely shattered, the quarrymen would prepare a charge hole with a drill, into which the gunpowder charge and fuse could be inserted. After the charge had been set and ignited, the large lumps of stone freed from the rock face were then broken up by the quarrymen into more manageable sizes. During the nineteenth century, the quarrymen set out a line of punched-out holes across the face of the stone blocks, into which the wedges were inserted in sequence. When the wedges were hammered into position, the block of stone tended to break along the cleavage line created by them, the process being repeated until such time as the desired size was achieved. The stone was then lifted out of the quarry, either by sledges pulled by horses, by crane or by tramway, and removed to stockpiles near the stone cutters' working areas (figure 6.2). The stonecutters were also known as *bankermasons* after the stone benches at which they worked.[14] At the Newcastle, County Down, granite quarries stone cutters used portable shelters called *shoddy huts* or *sett boxes* when dressing sets in exposed areas.[15] These were highly skilled stone workers, whose job it was to cut and finish the rough stone to the desired shape, using a series of moulds. When elaborate pieces such as window tracery were involved, the various pieces making up the window were carefully laid out at the quarry, to ensure an adequate fit before their transportation to the building site. Nearly all Irish quarries and, in particular, those situated close to major towns, produced architectural pieces such as cornices, lintels, steps, coping stones for walls and pier caps. Kerbing, flagging and sets

6.2 *The Parnell Granite Quarry, County Wicklow c. 1915, with horse-drawn tramline.*

were also manufactured in large quantities for the municipal authorities of Ireland's larger urban centres. Indeed, in the larger cities like Dublin, Belfast and Cork, it was common for corporations to employ their own stonecutters to make sets and kerbs for their paving departments.

Permanent or portable forges were used at most quarries to enable quarry workers to re-edge tools. At the larger quarries, ancillary buildings for storage and specialist buildings such as gunpowder magazines were also provided, as was stabling for horses used to operate whims and to pull wagons. Large nineteenth-century timber-framed cranes, employed for lifting large blocks of stone, are still in evidence at the Ballynockan granite quarries in County Wicklow, one of which was manufactured by Grendon's ironworks of Drogheda in 1873.[16] Aerial rope-ways, introduced by Welsh slate quarrying specialists, are known to have been used in the Killaloe slate quarries, near Portroe, in County Tipperary. An illustration of 1845 shows the operation of *skylines* in this quarry, whereby a rope stretched across the top of the open quarry was used to hang a vertical rope by means of an eye (figure 6.3). One end of the rope was attached to a horse whim, whose winding drum trailed the rope along the bottom of the workings to lift blocks of slate and to allow these to be wound in at the other end.[17]

The mechanisation of stone cutting begins surprisingly early in Ireland, principally through the efforts of

153

6.3 *'Skylines' at Killaloe slate quarry, near Portroe, County Tipperary (right). From Wilkinson 1845;*
6.4 *Water-powered marble cutting and polishing mill constructed on the River Shannon at Killaloe, County Clare, in 1832, by Charles Wye Williams, the founder of the Dublin Steam Packet Company (below).*

William Colles (1702-70), a Kilkenny quarry owner, alderman and uncle of the architect Christopher Colles (1738-1816), one of Davis Ducart's assistants on the construction of the Limerick Custom House.[18] In the early years of the eighteenth century, Colles experimented with a water-powered stone-dressing machine, whose success encouraged him to take a lease out on a quarry to the south-east of Kilkenny town.[19] In 1730, he developed a machine for boring stone water pipes, which he supplied to Cork and Dublin, and by 1732, his Kilkenny quarry had as many as ten water-powered stone-cutting saws and a machine for grinding Kilkenny 'marble' with sand.[20] In 1802, the saws were powered by a 10 ft (3.04 m) diameter water-wheel, one end of which was attached to a crank which set the saw frames in motion, each saw being capable of making a cut 10 inches deep in a single day. The other extremity of the water-wheel's axle was apparently attached to a frame of five stone polishers.[21] Exposed sections of this quarry, along with the ruins of the stone-sawing mills, still survive near Kilkenny town, where the River Nore runs through a ravine near the quarry faces, creating uniquely favourable conditions for water-powered stone processing. Colles' initiative significantly pre-dates English developments, the closest chronological parallel being marble polishing mills at Derby, which were created some time before 1802.[22]

In 1832 Charles Wye Williams, the founder of the Dublin Steam Ship Company (see Chapter 2) had a water-powered marble cutting and polishing mill constructed on the River Shannon at Killaloe, County Clare (figure 6.4). The mill was involved in the manufacture of sawn and polished marble items such as mantle pieces, monuments and dairy slabs, its machinery powered by a 16 ft (4.87 m) diameter water-wheel. At the peak of its activity, the mill employed up to 100 men, but was converted to a woollen mill in 1867, later operating as a grain mill until 1890. Substantial remains of the site, now used as a depot by the ESB, still survive.[23] The slate yard at Knightstown on Valentia Island, completed in 1839, was the second largest ever built in the former United Kingdom. Its squaring house was equipped with the earliest-known steam-powered slate saws in the 1830s: the earliest evidence for similar practices in Wales (which possessed the world's largest slate quarries) dates to 1842. Indeed, as early as 1851, the Valentia slate yard could lay claim to having the largest circular slate saws in the world.[24] In 1888, John Miller and Company of Galway was operating water-powered planing and cutting machinery to process Connemara black marble from Angliham, County Galway.[25] The introduction of steam-powered mechanised stone saws and polishers enabled these processes to be carried out on the site, but these were generally only undertaken at the larger, isolated quarries such as on Valentia Island. In any case, even after cutting, both sand polishing or some form of hand finishing were generally necessary for all architectural features, undertaken in the quarry or in specialist stone yards. In the main, it was cheaper to conduct polishing and other finishing processes at a location where coal for raising steam could be readily imported, rather than bringing the coal to the quarry itself. From about 1830 onwards, granite from quarries at Castlewellan, County Down, was brought to John Robinson and Sons' polishing works on Queen's Quay in Belfast.[26] During second half of the nineteenth century, polished granite was also manufactured at the Bessbrook Granite Company, County Armagh, at Carnsore, County Wexford, and Arklow, County Wicklow.[27]

In 1816, George Halpin (*d.* 1854), inspector of works to Dublin Ballast Board, was ordered to construct 'metal railed ways', through the quarries at Bullock and Sandycove, to accommodate the transportation of large stones. A number of Irish stone quarries were served by plateways as early as the 1820s, as on Valentia Island, and the granite quarries at Dalkey and Glasthule during the construction of Kingstown (Dún Laoghaire) harbour. Indeed, the first rail line to be incorporated in Ulster in 1832 was a horse-drawn tramway built to connect a quarry on the south side of Cavehill outside Belfast with quaysides on Belfast Lough, which opened in 1840 (see Chapter 14).[28] In the second half of the nineteenth century, other industrial railways were built to facilitate the transportation of stone from the quarry to stone processing plants. The marble quarries at Angliham, County Galway, were linked by a railway to the marble works at Galway, four miles distant, by 1863, whilst the Drinagh limestone quarries on Wexford harbour, were connected with the cement works there, around by 1883, by means of a 3 ft 7 in gauge railway. Limestone from the extensive quarries near Carnlough, County Antrim, was brought by a 4 ft 8 in line to the harbour there, a second quarry opened in around 1890 was served by a 3 ft 6 in gauge line which operated up until 1922. Inclined planes were by no means common being found only at the larger Irish quarries such as the Valentia slate quarry, at Newcastle and Scrabo, County Down and in a number of County Antrim quarries.

Stone quarries, unlike metal mines, were less likely either to require or employ an imported workforce, although specialist workers from Wales were relatively common in Irish slate quarries. In consequence, quarry owners felt it unnecessary to provide workers' housing. However, managers' houses have survived at larger quarries, such as that on Valentia Island, while at Ballyknockan, County Wicklow, a small village of stoneworkers grew up near the famous granite quarries of the same name. A number of finely detailed workers' cottages are still very much in evidence here, as is a fine two-storey quarry manager's house of *c.* 1900, the only really formal building in the village itself.[29] Workers are also known to have migrated from the Wicklow quarries to work the Mourne granite in the Bessbrook and Newry quarries.[30]

Limestone

Outcrops of carboniferous limestone in Ireland cover around three times the area of similar deposits in England, Scotland and Wales and, with the exception of Wicklow, and a number of the Ulster counties, good-quality carboniferous limestone was generally available throughout Ireland.[31] Calp limestone underlies most of the city of Dublin and was used in the construction of Gandon's Custom House, the Parliament House (1729, the present Bank of Ireland) and the General Post Office (1814), although these buildings were faced with either Leinster granite or Portland stone. The limestone quarried within the environs of Cork city, on the other hand, was of much higher quality and was extensively used for public buildings such as the Court House (1835) and the Cork Savings Bank (1842) and St Fin Barre's Cathedral (1865-79). In 1892, the Carrigmore quarries, on the Mahon peninsula to the east of Cork, covered a total area of some 120 acres, and were the largest limestone quarries in Ireland. The limestone of the Carrigacrump quarries near Cloyne, County Cork, which, while retaining the same basic properties as Carrigmore stone ('Beaumount Dove'), could also be raised in large blocks; it was preferred in certain instances for steam engine beds. A good example of the latter is Wallis and Pollock's Douglas flax spinning mill, whose engine beds incorporate both Carrigacrump limestone and stone from Foynes, County Limerick, which was also incorporated into the reservoirs of the Cork Corporation Waterworks in 1858.[32] During the nineteenth and early twentieth centuries, extensive limestone quarries were worked in the neighbourhood of Carnlough, County Antrim, which were linked by a mineral railway to Carnlough harbour, from which the stone was exported. A *whiting* mill was established nearby to crush the limestone into a fine powder, which was used as a filler in commodities as diverse as flour, paint and tooth-paste.[33] The Gortin and Creggan workings – each with enormous quarry faces – can still be seen above the town at Carnlough from the Antrim coast road to the south. The limestone quarries at Drinagh, County Wexford, which had traditionally provided building stone and lime, became associated with Ireland's first Portland cement works established there in 1871.

The lime kiln, in which limestone was calcined for a wide variety of uses, is Ireland's most numerous and widely distributed industrial monument. The primary use of lime was agricultural, where it was employed as an alkali to neutralise acidic soils, but it was also a key raw material for many industries. In a process called cal-cining, the calcium carbonate in the limestone is subjected to high temperatures to form calcium oxide or *quicklime*. This was then slaked in pits with water, with which it acted exothermically to form hydrated or *slaked* lime. A further chemical reaction with carbon dioxide and moisture in the atmosphere, which caused it to *recarbonate* (i.e., revert to calcium carbonate), enabled it to be used as a cement (*lime putty*) when mixed with sand. The resulting mortar does not 'go off' in the conventional sense but continues to harden in a hydraulic set when exposed to the air over a number of years. Up to the 1820s, lime-based mortar was the only bond-ing material available for most purposes. The type of quicklime used as fertiliser, on the other hand, while gen-erally unslaked into a fine powder, could be incorporated into the soil in any number of different ways. Lime was also used as a flux in blast furnaces, in the purification of town gas, in the production of bleaching pow-der and of soda from common salt, and in de-hairing hides in the tanning process. Hydraulic limes, which are derived from limestones that contain compounds such as calcium aluminate (which are insoluble in water), were also quarried and burnt in Ireland. These were used to manufacture limes that would harden under water, and thus were ideal for civil engineering works such as bridges and docks. At Benburb, County Tyrone, for example, a local compact blue limestone was used to make hydraulic limes which were employed in the construction of the Ulster Canal in the years 1825-42 (see Chapter 13), while a quarry at Gilloge Lock, near Limerick city, produced hydraulic limes used in the building of city's new wet dock in 1853 (see Chapter 15).[34]

Two basic varieties of traditional lime kiln have been used in Ireland over the past 250 years. The first and earliest of these was the *intermittent* kiln, in which the body of the kiln was charged, fired and allowed to cool off before being emptied, after which it was re-charged for the next firing campaign. These were generally *flare* kilns, in which the fuel and the limestone charge were separated within the main body of the kiln by a crude arch or dome constructed with limestone blocks (figure 6.5). In this way, the fuel and the unslaked lime did not come into contact, giving an ash-free and purer product. The second type of kiln is the *continuous* type, with a *mixed feed* of fuel and limestone, which were continuously fed into and burnt in the kiln bowl, with quicklime drawn off at the base. With the spread of improved agricultural techniques in the second half of the

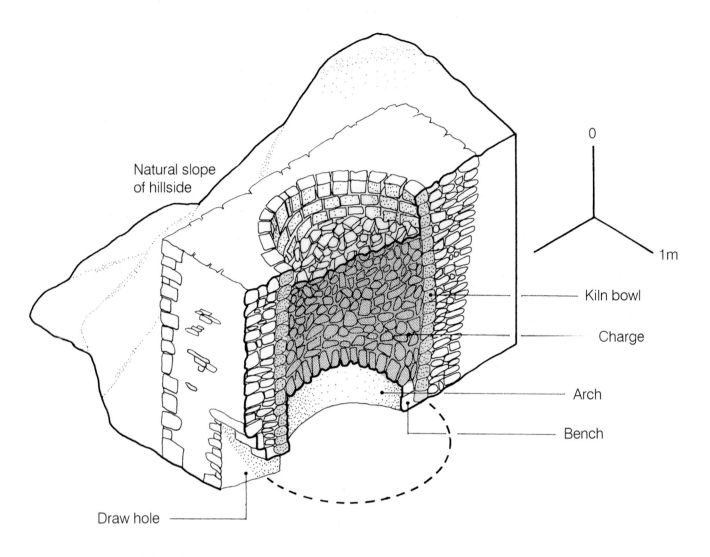

Natural slope
of hillside

0

1m

Kiln bowl

Charge

Arch

Bench

Draw hole

6.5 *Reconstruction of flare kiln.*

eighteenth century (see Chapter 7), the increased demand for quicklime as fertiliser led to the construction of larg-er continuous draw kilns.[35]

The vast majority of the lime kilns surviving in Irish rural areas are continuous draw kilns, which tend to be rubblestone structures, around 4-8 m wide and about 5-8 m high, with a square or rectangular (and occa-sionally circular) ground plan (figure 6.6). The central body of the kiln has either a stone or brick-lined *pot* around 2 m in diameter, in which the layers of fuel and limestone were burnt. As in blast furnaces, the sides of the pot are gently curved, to prevent the charge from settling or sticking to the sides. Immediately above the draw hole, at the base of the kiln, a poke hole was often provided through which the kiln workers could insert a stick to assist in the burning process by dislodging ash. The draw hole was set into an arched or lintelled recess, high enough to admit at least two men standing up, or even a horse and cart.[36] In small country kilns, this recess would often be supported by a simple lintel, but in the larger, more developed kilns, elaborate arches with cut-stone voussoirs were common. A lean-to structure was often built into the face of the kiln to protect the freshly burnt lime raked out at the base from the rain.

The kiln funnel was charged with stone and fuel (either culm or peat, or even furze), which was lighted from the recess at the base.[37] Kilns in rural areas were operated *intermittently*, where the firing campaign (during which the lime burner added more fuel and stone over a period of up to 48 hours, and temperatures of between 900-1,200° C were reached within the kiln) was usually tied into the agricultural cycle.[38] Lime for the building industry or for other industrial purposes, however, was generally produced on a continuous basis. In Irish

6.6 *Double lime kiln at Castlelyons, County Cork.*

coastal towns and ports, it was a common practice for the heat rising out of the kiln to be used for refining salt. In what were called salt and lime works (see Chapter 11), which originated in the mid-eighteenth century, salt pans were positioned over lime kilns, whose rising heat was used to boil the water in the pans. In this way, expensive imported coal could be employed to undertake two important industrial processes. At Muddy Hill lime and salt works, near Mallow, County Cork, the remains of what is likely to have been a salt pan, in the form of a corroded iron lining, survive on top of a battery of two lime kilns built into a rock face.[39]

Lime kilns were commonly located in quarries, at the roadside or at coastal locations to facilitate transport. Many were either built into a slope or were provided with a ramp to assist the charging process. A not uncommon occurrence in Ireland was for lime kilns to be built into the enclosing banks of early medieval ringforts, where the bank was used as a charging ramp. A good example of this phenomenon has been investigated at Lisduggan North, near Kanturk, County Cork, where it appears that originally the top of the kiln was level with the ringfort's bank.[40] Batteries of kilns - where two or more kilns were built side by side – were also relatively common in larger quarries or at coastal sites, where at least one kiln could be kept burning while another was cleaned out. At coastal sites, coal could be shipped in and the quicklime taken out by sea. The larger, more elaborate, kilns, such as that at Proleek, near Dundalk, County Louth, were often provided with a parapet, occasionally castellated for decorative effect. Many of the latter were also commonly associated with the larger landed estates.

In *c.* 1800, Count Rumford, founder of the Royal Institution, designed and built an improved form of kiln near Dublin, in which the basic principle of the flare kiln, where, as we have seen, the fuel is not mixed with the unslaked lime, was combined with a continuous feed.[41] This latter type appears not to have been adopted elsewhere in Ireland, and it is not until the second half of the nineteenth century that newer forms of kilning technology were introduced. In 1866, Robert Murland of Castle Espie, near Comber in County Down, built one of the first Hoffman kilns (normally associated with the firing of brick) in the former United Kingdom that is known to have been used both to calcine lime and burn brick. The introduction of the Hoffmann kiln for lime burning enabled industrial-scale production of quicklime to be undertaken: each of the 24 Castle Espie kiln chambers could hold 100 tons of limestone, facilitating a weekly output of upwards of 600 tons of lime.[42] The kiln (sections of which still survive) was designed by engineer Charles Bagnell, who went on to design further lime burning Hoffmann kilns for the Boston Lime Company, at the Grand Canal Docks in Dublin in the late 1860s, and for the Munster Brick and Lime Company near, Clonmel, County Tipperary, in 1873. The use of these kilns was a significant advance on traditional continuous kilns because of savings of 60–80 per cent on fuel costs and the fact that limestone no longer had to be broken down to small pieces in order to be properly fired.[43] However, their operation was very labour-intensive, and after the First World War, this tended to make them less economical to run, especially for lime burning, while the introduction of rotary kilns, which required less labour and in which it was easier to control the temperature and air flow, led to rapid decline in their use, except for brick making. Towards the end of the nineteenth century, bottle-type kilns were also employed for lime burning in Ireland at Carnlough, County Antrim.[44]

Granite

Aside from its often eye-catching and consistent colouring, the principal properties of granite are its toughness and resistance to weathering, while at the same time being capable of taking a polish and being worked with abrasives. The granite of Counties Dublin and Wicklow was to the architecture of Dublin what limestone was to the towns of Cork and Limerick. From Blackrock, County Dublin, eastwards, the southern areas of Dublin Bay were underlain with granite, and quarries at Blackrock, Bullock, Sandycove and Dalkey supplied large amounts of the stone for civil engineering works in the greater Dublin area. From around the middle of the eighteenth century onwards, the streets of Dublin were flagged with granite from quarries at Blessington and Ballyknockan, County Wicklow and some areas of County Dublin. Granite from the Ballybrew quarries in County Dublin was employed in the construction of Kingsbridge Station in Dublin, Golden Hill granite (near Blessington, County Wicklow) was used to build Russborough House, while Leinster granite was exported in large blocks for use in the Thames Embankment.[45]

Mourne granite was also extensively quarried in Counties Armagh and Down around Bessbrook and Newry, and was favoured for use in architectural and monumental work throughout the nineteenth century. In the 1880s, the Bessbrook Granite Company in County Armagh quarried no fewer than five different qualities of granite, its No. 2 quality enjoying widespread use as setts by many English tramway companies such as those of Wigan, Bristol, Chester, Southport, Edinburgh, and, similarly, by corporations in Liverpool, Preston and Huddersfield.[46] The hard-wearing granite of Castlewellan, County Down, was also exported to England, where it was employed in London pavements and in the construction of the Thames Embankment. Sir J.N. Douglas, engineer to the Corporation of Trinity House, London, chose it for the reconstruction of the Bishop Rock Lighthouse in the Scilly Isles, yet its highest accolade was the British War Office's preference for its use in construction of the embrasures of artillery batteries.[47] Galway granite was also exported, with notable uses in the new post office at South Kensington in London and for the base of the Fontenoy Memorial in Belgium.[48]

Sandstone

Although currently employed principally as aggregate, sandstone ('brownstone') was also widely quarried and used throughout Ireland as building stone. Within the city of Cork and its immediate environs, local red sandstone was attractively combined with local limestone to create a polychrome style. Alternate courses of red sandstone and limestone created a pleasing effect in some buildings; however, even in formal buildings where the principal facing stone was sandstone, limestone was nearly always used for quoins, window and door dressings in Cork. 'Flaherty's' or the Brickfield Quarry on the eastern outskirts of the city was the principal source of sandstone in Cork up until the early 1860s, and its output was used in a number of important buildings such as the North Cathedral and St Peter and Paul's Church and Convent.[49] In south Leinster and throughout Munster, sandstone flags, such as the famous Shankill flags of County Kilkenny, were also in demand for flooring and road construction. These had the advantage of being raised from the quarry, in flag form, in sizes of anything from 12 to 14 ft (3.65-4.26 m) square, and were widely employed for flooring in industrial buildings such as warehouses and grain stores.[50] According to Kinahan, in the late 1880s, the best quality sandstone to be quarried in Ireland came from County Tyrone, around which time the distinctive sandstones of Scrabo and Dundonald were still used in the buildings of neighbouring Belfast.[51]

Apart from more obvious uses such as in architecture and road construction, sandstone was also employed in millstone manufacture. Conglomerate sandstones were generally preferred for this purpose, and at Ballyhack, County Wexford, there is evidence for millstone quarrying from at least the 1680s. Indeed, at both Ballyhack, which overlooks the estuary of the rivers Barrow, Nore and Suir, and Templetown, some seven miles to the south east, prepared rock platforms from which millstone rough-outs have been cut, along with unfinished millstones, are still in evidence.[52] Extensive remains of similar quarrying activity survive on Ballyhoura Hill in County Cork, which include several unfinished millstones. In the period from *c.* 1790, up to the late 1820s, a millstone quarry at Dunmore, County Galway, supplied a number of mills in that county, including those of Galway city, while in 1836, a Mrs Walker was operating a number of millstone quarries in County Donegal which are reported to have exported up to 40 pairs of stones a year to destinations such as Liverpool and America.[53] County Donegal sandstone was also in use for the manufacture of flax crushers (see Chapters 1 and 8), but these were superseded by flax breaking machinery, while one quarry at Lettercrann supplied stones to the Belleek pottery in County Fermanagh for the grinding of the materials used to make liquid slip.[54] Further important millstone quarries were worked at Carnmore, County Monaghan, and Drumdowney, County Kilkenny. According to Kinahan in 1889, however, 'this trade … seems to be altogether a thing of the past, as nowhere, as far as we can learn, is it now followed'.[55]

Slate

In addition to being almost chemically inert, compact and non-porous, slate can readily be split into thin or thick sheets, properties that led to its widespread use as a roofing, flooring and cladding material.[56] Irish slates, however, unlike their Welsh counterparts, were generally only of average quality for use as roofing material, but were, nonetheless, well suited for heavier items such as flooring slabs and architectural pieces like lintels and chimneys. The main Irish quarries were established on Valentia Island off the County Kerry coast, in County Tipperary at Curraghbally (the 'Killaloe' quarries) and the Victoria Quarries, the Ormond Quarries in County Kilkenny, the Drinagh and Benduff quarries in County Cork, the Kilcavan quarries in county Wexford, and the Glentown quarries in County Donegal.[57]

Large-scale commercial working began on Valentia Island in 1816, although smaller operations had been undertaken during the late eighteenth century. The quarrying techniques used at Valentia can be broadly paralleled with those employed at Blaenau Ffestiniog and Corris in Wales, where the slate was extracted from what was, to all intents and purposes, an underground quarry (figure 6.7). However, the large gantry crane used at the Valentia quarries in the 1850s, where it was installed at the entrance to the underground openings to load heavy blocks onto tramway waggons, appears to have been unique to Valentia. Only about 5 per cent of the rock detached from the face was suitable for processing. Hammers and broad chisels were used to manufacture roofing slates, but the production of large slabs required mechanised saws in order to cut the blocks to the required size and to create the neat, squared edges required for architectural and ornamental work (figure 6.8).[58] Valentia slate was quite commonly used in the construction of a number of important English Victorian railway stations, including Waterloo, Charing Cross, Blackfriars, Rugby and Leicester. It was also employed to roof the British Houses of Parliament at Westminster.[59] There are extensive remains of the quarries on the island, which include those of the squaring house of 1839 (figure 6.9).

The Curraghbally quarries near Portroe, County Tipperary, were opened in 1826 by the Mining Company of Ireland, and at their greatest extent, the pit was some 200 ft (60.96 m) deep. Up to 700 men and boys were employed in the 1830s (Valentia Island and the Benduff and Froe quarries each employed 100-150 at their peak) producing up 10,000 tons each year.[60] Immediate access to the Shannon allowed this quarry to develop commercially on a large scale, unlike many other Irish quarries, which were generally isolated from centres of demand.[61] Welsh expertise was widely used in Irish slate quarries. The Hibernian Mining Company employed a Welsh overseer at the Valentia quarry in 1827, while around the same time, Welsh experts were brought in to create a quarrying industry at Benduff, which opened in 1830.[62] The slate quarries at Clashnasmut, County Tipperary, and Kilcavan, County Wexford (figure 6.10) quarries had, in addition, either Welsh foremen or quarry managers, and such was the extent of Welsh involvement at Curraghbally during the nineteenth century that it even had its own Welsh-speaking community.[63]

In the 1880s, Kinahan described the *modus operandi* of most Irish slate quarries as 'surface grubbing' or 'primitive' and reported that were no proper management of the waste, which was allowed to choke the mouth of the working, a development that, in his view, had enabled imported Welsh slate to dominate the market.[64] Yet imported Welsh slate had always overshadowed the native product, especially in the urban markets. A decade later, however, there was a building boom in Belfast and Dublin, when almost 5,300 new houses were constructed in Belfast alone in 1895-6, with a similar number being built in Dublin during the same period. All

6.7 *Entrance to the Valentia slate quarry on Valentia Island, County Kerry (left);* **6.8** *Reconstructed ground plan of Valentia squaring house (after Gwyn 1991), below.*

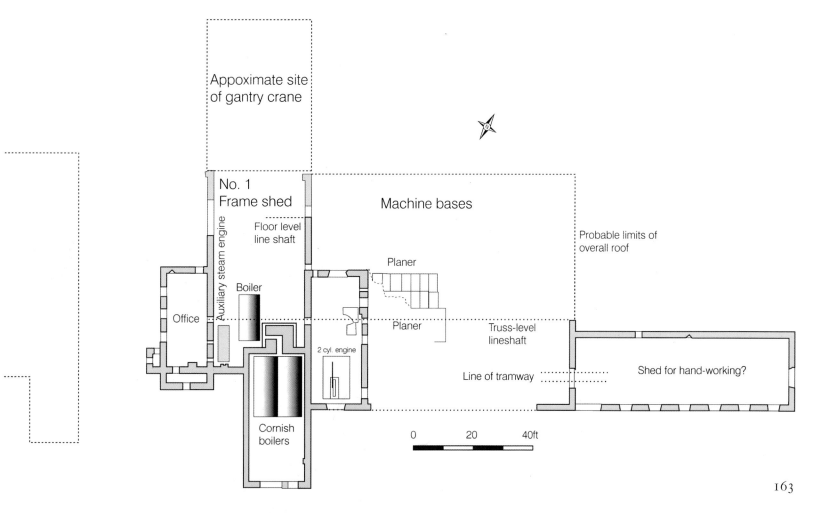

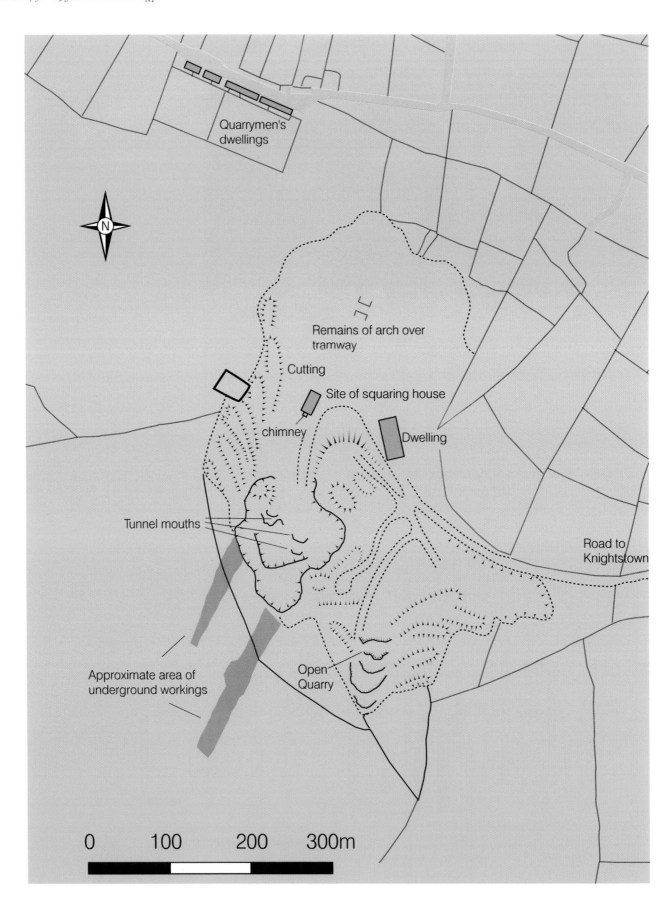

Quarrymen's
dwellings

N

Remains of arch over
tramway

Cutting

Site of squaring house

chimney

Dwelling

Tunnel mouths

Road to
Knightstown

Approximate area of
underground workings

Open
Quarry

0   100   200   300m

6.9 *General plan of Valentia slate quarry (after Gwyn 1991) (opposite);* **6.10** *The Kilcavan slate quarry, County Wexford in the 1930s.*

were roofed with slate from North Wales, but in 1896-7, a long-running industrial dispute at the Penryhn quarry led to a temporary interruption of supply, a gap that was, for a short period, filled by imported American slate.[65] In the years immediately following Independence, there was pressure on the new Irish government to decrease its reliance on imported building materials in general which, for a brief period, created a boom for Irish slate quarries. By 1923, the Killaloe and Benduff quarries were busily occupied producing slates for Dublin's housing schemes. Indeed, even when the Benduff slates were deemed to be of an unusable quality, Dublin Corporation opted for Welsh rather than English slates.[66]

Irish 'Marbles'

In Ireland, certain varieties of coloured stones, and even limestones which could be polished, were commonly referred to as 'marbles'. The principal Irish 'marbles' were the Connemara 'greens', the Cork 'reds' and the Galway and Kilkenny black marble, all of which were widely used for ornamental purposes. While not real marbles in the sense of being metamorphosed limestones, when used for decoration, the effect was close enough. Cork 'reds' from Little Island, County Cork, were used in the Liverpool and Manchester exchanges and in St John's College, Cambridge, whilst both Little Island and Fermoy 'reds' were also used in St Fin Barre's Cathedral in Cork.[67] Black marble quarried at Angliham, County Galway, was exported to London, Liverpool, Bristol, Glasgow and America.[68] At the time of writing, only the Connemara and Kilkenny marbles are still quarried, all the Cork red marble quarries, indeed, having been closed since the beginning of the twentieth century.

(2) Brick Making

In Ireland, the manufacture and use of brick in architectural work is somewhat anomalous in that, unlike the rest of Europe, it appears to have been wholly a post-medieval phenomenon. Decades of fieldwork in later medieval archaeology in Ireland have failed to record a single instance of the use of brick before the sixteenth century, even amongst the Anglo-Norman and later immigrant populations. The earliest written record we possess for the manufacture of brick is by German miners in County Wexford, in 1551-2, while the first archaeologically documented uses of it are in sixteenth-century buildings such as the Ormond manor house at Carrick-on-Suir, County Tipperary, Carrickfergus Castle, County Antrim, and Bunratty Castle, County Clare.[69]

In the latter part of the sixteenth and for most of the seventeenth century, the use of brick in Ireland was closely associated with high-status buildings such as country houses, but towards the end of the seventeenth century, it was also beginning to be employed, in a limited way, in vernacular housing in parts of Ulster.[70] Some 5,500 Belfast bricks were exported to London for the inner brick cupola of the dome of St Paul's Cathedral in London, while in 1706, 300,000 bricks manufactured in the Belfast area are known to have been sent to Dublin.[71] By the beginning of the eighteenth century, town houses built of brick became common in Dublin, Cork and other coastal centres, where both locally manufactured and imported brick was employed. In Dublin and Cork, large quantities of brick were shipped in from England, Holland, Flanders and France, to meet the demand of urban growth in the 1770s. In Cork, indeed, Dutch brick was commonly brought in as ship's ballast.[72]

As early as the 1690s, there were 'brick Kills' at Clontarf, County Dublin, and by the early eighteenth century, the clay of the Sandymount area was being used for building in the area around Merrion Square. Such was the extent of this activity that a small community of brick workers evolved in an area originally known as Scald Hill, and later as Bricktown or Brickfieldtown in the 1760s.[73] The extent of brick making operations in Dublin and Cork in the second half of the eighteenth century was such that the smoke from the firing clamps had become a public nuisance. In Dublin, clamp kilns were prohibited within 'one mile of the public lamps' in 1766, whilst clamps on the northern bank of the north channel of the River Lee at Cork were banned in 1778 within two miles of the Cork Exchange.[74]

Brick 'clay' is often found around river estuaries, which had the added advantage of facilitating the transport of bulky cargoes of finished brick. Indeed, during the construction of the Grand Canal, the drainage of certain boglands in the midlands also exposed brick clays, which were widely exploited in County Kildare, where the canal itself secured easy access for the finished product to the Dublin market.[75] Even the smallest brick fields established during the period *c.* 1750-1830 would generally cover a few acres, as at Lissue Brickfield near Lisburn, County Antrim.[76] At the Arney Brickfields, County Fermanagh, the top soil was first stripped and removed, to enable a clayhole 2-3 m wide and *c.* 1.5 m deep to be dug by labourers.[77] On the Gillen, County Offaly, brick fields the clay pit (called a 'mine'), was about 4 yds wide and about 100 yds long, and provided enough material for a season's work. At Gillen, as on most brick fields, indeed, the clay was normally dug out in the first four months of year to allow it to weather.[78] Brick making was generally a seasonal activity on the smaller Irish brick fields, where brick makers could be casual workers or even farmers, the main period of production being around April to September. Even at the larger brickworks established near Ireland's principal cities, the clay was still dug out by hand. Many of these were established on relatively large acreages of brick clay, such as the Ballinphellic brickworks in County Cork, which was set within 45 acres of clay soil owned by the company, and the Annadale Brick Company's works at Belfast, set on 50 acres of clay soil. In the latter case, the land not immediately quarried by the company was farmed out to supply grazing for the company's horses.[79] At large brickworks outside major urban centres, workers' housing was sometimes provided, as at Ballinphellic, County Cork, in late 1890s, and remains of the late nineteenth-century workers' housing at the Belvelly works on Great Island in Cork harbour still survive.[80]

After being dug out of the clay pit, the brick clay was left for a few days to sour. Stones were then picked out of it by hand, and traditionally, the clay was worked to the right consistency for moulding, by watering it and trampling it underfoot. This process, called *tempering*, was still undertaken in this way on the Glenmore Brickyards of County Kilkenny in the late nineteenth century.[81] At larger brickyards, this process began to be replaced by the *pug mill*, in which the mud was mechanically macerated into a plastic consistency. This mill was normally powered by a horse, jennet or mule, and consisted of an inverted metal cone

6.11 *Pug mill at Kilmagner pottery works, near Youghal, County Cork.*

with a series of knives set into a vertical axle for chopping and mixing the clay. A good example of a pug mill survived, up to quite recently, at the Kilmagner brick field (*c.* 1820-70) near Youghal, County Cork (figure 6.11).[82]

After its preliminary processing, a *wheeler* would barrow the clay won by the traditional method to the moulding table where the *moulder* (usually the owner of the brick field) spread the brick in wooden moulds shod with iron. Under Pearce's Act of 1729, brick fields were obliged to manufacture brick to more or less standard sizes, but despite this, there were some slight variations throughout the island. Brick sizes in the Munster counties, for example, vary between 8-9 in x 4 x 2-3 in. From the moulding bench, an *off-bearer* (usually a young boy) carried the brick mould to a drying ground where it was emptied out of the mould and left to harden. After a preliminary drying in the air, the bricks were arranged in *hacks*, long rows consisting of small stacks five bricks high and one brick wide.

In many parts of Ireland from the seventeenth to early twentieth century, bricks were traditionally fired in a *clamp kiln*, a rectangular arrangement consisting of alternate courses of bricks (figure 6.12). The construction of the clamp, which on the smaller brick fields was usually undertaken by the owner, could take up to two weeks, and involved the building of a series of pillars with unfired brick, which were gradually formed into a series of 8-12 arches. The arches, which were at right angles to the long axis of the clamp, served as fire settings, into which either coal, culm or turf were placed and ignited. At Gillen, County Offaly, the completed clamp kiln was the in the region of 25 yds square by 10 ft (3.04 m) high. On the Glenmore Brickfields and at Gillen, the clamp was allowed to burn for about five days, being constantly tended, and at Clonown brick field, near Athlone, County Westmeath, the clamp stokers were provided with a one-legged stool to discourage them from nodding off.[83] With a bulky product such as brick, transport was an important consideration, and at estuarine locations, the clamp site was carefully chosen, not only to facilitate access to water transport by barge or lighter, but also

6.12 *The construction of a clamp kiln, as shown in* L'art du tuilier et du briquetier *('The art of the tilemaker and brickmaker') compiled and published by the French Academy of Science in 1763.*

to ensure that it was always well-drained. A possible seventeenth-century clamp kiln has recently been excavated in woodland to the south east of Portumna Castle, County Galway, which had regularly spaced fire settings, while at Ballynora, County Cork, three eighteenth- or nineteenth-century clamp kilns (in which the position of the fire settings was indicated by charcoal spreads) have also recently been investigated.[84] Clamp kiln sites, similar to that at Portumna, have also been excavated at Conigar and Dollas Upper, County Limerick and Garraun, County Clare, the latter site situated on the banks of the River Shannon.[85]

Towards the middle of the nineteenth century, many of the basic processes involved in brick manufacture were already becoming mechanised. Beginning with pug mills, additional machinery for preparing the brick clay, such as grinding rollers and presses for the manufacture of higher-quality 'facing' brick, came to be installed in larger and more specialised works throughout Ireland, where brick manufacture was no longer a casual, seasonal process. Traditional wooden moulds were dispensed with and new, mechanical means of forming the bricks were introduced, while vast improvements in the firing process were made possible by the introduction of new kilns. By the 1880s, machine-made bricks were manufactured throughout Ireland, and the Bridgewater bricks imported from England were beginning to be replaced by native products. Bricks made in Belfast and at Kingscourt, County Cavan, were becoming widely used in the Dublin building trade. In the 1870s, Belfast was experiencing a building boom which, in no small part, was facilitated by the availability of cheap high-quality brick. In the last 30 years of the nineteenth century, the city's housing stock quadrupled, and between 1880 and 1900 some 50,000 new houses were built. By 1900, Belfast had 30 brickyards within its immediate environs, including the largest in Ireland, H. and J. Martin's on the Ormeau Road. Bricks were, by this period, already being produced in Belfast at half the price of those in Dublin.

Nearly all the machinery in the modern brickworks was powered by steam, where the various installations were now positioned around the buildings housing the steam plant, within an extensive area containing brick clays. Sophisticated means were also provided for the movement of materials within the works as at Kingscourt, County Cavan, in 1903, and at Dardistown near Julianstown, County Meath, where funicular railways were built to transport clay from the pits to the brickworks.[86] Aerial ropeways were also commonly employed for this purpose, as at the Durrow Brick and Tile Company's works at Durrow, County Laois.[87]

Bricks formed in wooden moulds and fired in clamp kilns, especially those made from non-refractory clays, tended to be poorly fired and variable both in size and colour. These are generally referred to as *commons*, and when used for building purposes, they had either to be rendered or covered with an external stone cladding. *Facing* bricks, on the other hand, were generally weatherproof, and could be used externally without rendering.[88] In the second half of the nineteenth century, two new mechanical processes were introduced for moulding bricks, the first of which, the *wire-cut process*, was widely employed in the larger Irish brickworks, as at Kingscourt, County Cavan. Bricks formed in this manner were extruded through a metal die and then cut off to the required size by wires, while they also commonly had holes cut into them to reduce their weight and to make them easier to handle. In the *stiff-plastic process*, the brick clays are first crushed, ground and mixed mechanically to form a stiff paste. This latter is then pressed into the required shape and size in a brick press, which generally produced a

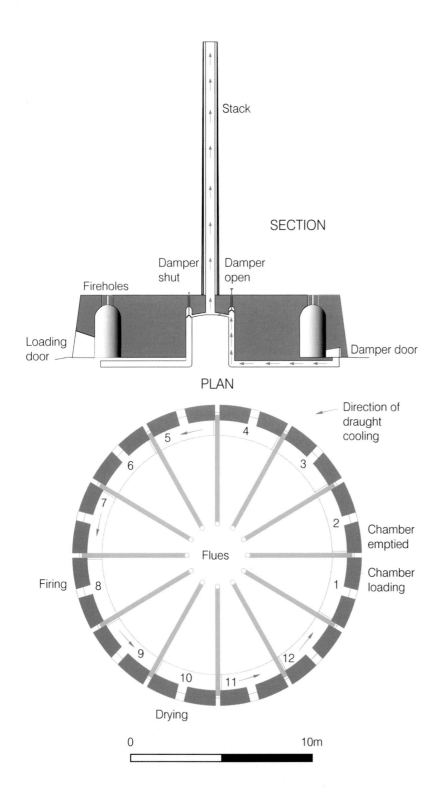

SECTION

Stack

Fireholes

Damper shut

Damper open

Loading door

Damper door

PLAN

Direction of draught cooling

5

4

6

3

7

2

Chamber emptied

Flues

Chamber loading

Firing

8

1

9

12

10

11

Drying

0

10m

6.13 *Schematic plan and section through circular Hoffman kiln (after Brunskill 1990).*

smooth brick with true corners and edges.[89] By 1903, this was the exclusive process at the Annadale works near Belfast, were some five brick presses were employed.[90]

Clamp kilns were almost universal on Irish brick fields in the mid-nineteenth century, but by the early 1850s, more permanent kiln structures were beginning to be built. There are two basic varieties of brick kiln – *intermittent* and *continuous* – which are further categorised in accordance with the way in which they were fired as either *up-draught* or *down-draught*.[91] Brick-built up-draught kilns used coal as the fuel, which was often fed into grates at the base of the kiln, as at the Florencecourt Tile and Pottery Works, near Enniskillen, County Fermanagh, in the 1850s. This kiln appears to have been a roofed structure in which the fuel was ignited under the floor, the heat passing upwards through the kiln and exiting through apertures in the roof.[92] Down-draught kilns, on the other hand (which could also be intermittent, i.e., re-charged after every firing), allowed more close control of the firing process (see below). Intermittent, up-draught *beehive kilns*, which are circular in plan and have low-domed, bee-hived shaped roofs, were also introduced into Ireland in the nineteenth century. These were in use at Coalisland, County Tyrone, and Youghal, County Cork, in the late nineteenth century, and up to the late twentieth century in County Laois and at Slane, County Meath.[93]

The Hoffman kiln, in which both brick drying and firing became a series of uninterrupted processes, was the first *continuous* brick kiln to be widely used in Ireland. Friedrich Hoffman, a German engineer, had acquired an English patent for his kiln in 1859, and by the mid-1860s, they were being built for lime and brick burning in Britain and Ireland. The early forms of this kiln were circular in plan, but rectangular types were later introduced, although both are termed 'annular', as the limestone or the raw bricks were fired in an *annulus* or continuous chamber (figure 6.13).[94] The annular chamber itself was divided into between twelve to 24 chambers by movable partitions, the bricks being set within these with the fumes dispersed through a central chimney. Coal was almost exclusively used as the fuel, which was fed into a series of fuel holes in the roof of the kiln. The individual chambers were filled, their contents dried, fired, cooled off and finally emptied in turn, the heat from the bricks being cooled was then employed to dry the freshly set bricks. The largest Hoffman kiln to have been built in Ireland, in the late nineteenth century, was at the Annadale Brick Company on the Ormeau Road in Belfast. This covered two acres and had 24 chambers, with a capacity of 50,000 bricks.[95] Outside Belfast, Hoffman kilns varied in size from about ten chambers, as at Dundalk brickworks in the late 1890s, and the fourteen-chamber kiln at Ballinphellic, County Cork, of *c.* 1897.[96] The best surviving example of a Hoffman brick kiln in Ireland is the rectangular kiln at Youghal Brickworks, County Cork, built in 1894, a brick-built structure, 34.4 m x 18.3 m, with twelve chambers (figure 6.14). A small section of the Dundalk kiln also survives and has been incorporated into a more recent building.

Terracotta, a ceramic material, made from weathered clay mixed with grog (previously fired clay ground into a powder), began to be manufactured by a small number of the larger Irish brick and tile works (most

6.14 *The Youghal brickworks in 1902. The chimney and a large section of the Hoffman kiln of 1894 survive* in situ.

notably Kingscourt, Ballinphellic and Arklow) towards the end of the nineteenth century.[97] Either glazed or unglazed, and moulded into cornices, urns, chimney pots and so forth, it became popular for use as facing material and for more ornate architectural detailing in Irish towns, particularly in conjunction with brickwork. The Kingscourt works in County Cavan manufactured brick and terracotta for all of the former War Office contracts in Ireland, supplying the British army barracks at Portobello (Cathal Brugha) Barracks, Island Bridge (Collins), along with the Jacob's Factory on Peter Street, all in Dublin.[98]

The underdevelopment of internal communications in Ireland, in the pre-railway era, had an important bearing on the location of many brick fields. Brick was a bulky cargo, and the cheapest way to transport it was by water. For this reason, many of the brick fields established in Ireland during the late eighteenth and early nineteenth centuries were situated on or near rivers, estuaries or canals. All the brick fields in the locality of Gillen, County Offaly, and many in County Kildare, were sited near the Grand Canal. Brick field owners near ports very often owned small fleets of lighters and mud boats, as at Derry and Cork. At Ballinphellic, county Cork, an aerial ropeway was built to connect the works to Ballinhassig railway station on the Cork and Bandon line in 1902, at about one-third of the cost of a narrow gauge railway.[99] Indeed, several brickyards around Belfast and at least one at Carrickfergus had small horse-drawn tramways. As recently as 1948, the Courtown Brick and Tile Company, near Courtown Harbour in County Wexford, had a 1 ft 8 in gauge horse tramway which connected the company's quarry with its works.

(3) Cement and Concrete

Up to the 1930s in Ireland, the traditional mixture of lime putty and sand had been the principal bonding agent in all building works using either stone or brick. As has been seen, this type of mortar hardened over a long period of time as the lime putty and sand mixture reformed into calcium carbonate. The use of cement, however, where the limestone was fired with silica-rich clay, greatly speeded up the setting process. Cement-based mortar had the advantage of setting within hours rather than in years, setting occurring throughout its matrix and not from the exterior surface inwards as was the case with lime-based mortar. John Smeaton had developed an underwater cement for use in Eddystone lighthouse in 1756, whilst James Parker's 'Roman cement' had been patented in 1796. Parker's cement was made from *septaria*, a natural cement rock, and was used in stucco (usually exterior plasterwork), which became popular at the end of the eighteenth century. Roman cements were manufactured in Cork by at least 1840, when Wilson and Company, of South Friary Lane, were importing lump alabaster and preparing plaster of Paris in their horse-powered mills. Wilson's cements were used both in the preparation of stucco and in the manufacture of composite millstones.[100]

Parker's cement was eventually superseded by early forms of Portland cement, originally patented by Joseph Aspdin in 1824. Isaac Johnson's development of a new manufacturing process for Portland cement in 1844 enabled mass concrete to be widely used as a building material. Concrete is a mixture of Portland cement, sand and stone aggregate and, when used in the foundations of buildings in mass form, it helps to counteract compressive stresses. The use of formwork – wooden or steel shutters formed into moulds – enabled it to be cast into a wide variety of shapes, whilst it would also set underwater. The Irish engineer, Sir John Macneill, took out a patent for concrete roads as early as 1827 in England, but it is not until 1842, with Robert Mallet's use of 'concrete' in the foundations of masonry abutments in a swivel bridge on the Newry Navigation, that we find an explicit reference to its use in Ireland.[101] However, the binding agent here is likely to have been unslaked lime, the term concrete being loosely applied, as late as the mid-1840s, in Great Southern and Western (GS & WR) specifications for railway bridges, where concrete 'shall consist of good coarse gravel, perfectly free of loam or clay, and unslaked lime'.[102]

Mass concrete was employed in the foundations of the original Great Southern and Western Railway (GS & WR) terminus at Cork, designed by Sir John Benson and completed in 1858. Benson also used concrete in the construction of the new reservoirs for Cork Corporation Waterworks, completed in 1858-60, in the piers of St Patrick's Bridge in 1860, and in the roadway on the new North Gate Bridge in Cork completed in 1863.[103] In 1858, Malcomson's shipyard in Waterford came up with an innovative employment of concrete as an anti-corrosive measure in the hulls of iron ships, a practice later followed by Harland and Wolff in 1859-60.[104] As early as 1863, Bindon Blood Stoney was experimenting with masonry and concrete in Dublin port civil engineering work, and later used 350 tonnes concrete blocks to construct the North Wall extension in the 1870s.[105] Concrete was also in use in the decking of St Vincent's footbridge on the north channel of the River Lee at Cork, and to fill the steel caissons supporting it, in 1878, and in the construction of the new weir at Cork Corporation Waterworks completed in 1888.[106]

However, like stone, concrete is weak in compression, and so to counteract tensile stresses, wrought iron, and later steel rods, were added to reinforce it. In 1854, William Boutland Wilkinson acquired a patent for reinforced concrete beams, which he manufactured from colliery ropes made from steel wire. In the 1880s, Samuel Hill was using a form of reinforced (*ferro*) concrete in the construction of buildings at the Penrose Quay railway terminus in Cork. Indeed, in 1885, the GS & WR company had already erected coal stores at Knocklong station in County Tipperary with a thin mass concrete, cylindrical shell roof.[107] At the Goodbody's jute spinning mill in Clara, County Offaly, in 1884, the tallest concrete construction to be erected in Ireland up to that time – a 150 ft (45.72 m) high concrete-built chimney reinforced with sections of disused spinning frames – was completed.[108] But it was not until the closing years of the nineteenth century that reinforced (ferro) concrete came into its own through the work of the Frenchman Francois Hennebique, a former stonemason who became a successful building contractor. From the early 1890s onwards, Hennebique began to take out patents for ferro concrete, which he used in reinforced concrete beams, columns and floor panels. Louis Gustav Mouchel was appointed as the agent for the Hennebique system in Britain in 1897, and Weaver's Flour Mill in Swansea, completed in 1898, became Mouchel's first construction project in Britain using the Hennebique system. In Ireland, J. and R. Thompson of Roden Street, Belfast and Fairview, Dublin became Hennebique's licensee, and the Monarch Laundry in Belfast, completed in 1906 is, on present evidence, the earliest use of this system in Ireland. The Suir Bridge at Waterford which opened in 1913, and was later replaced by the present lifting bridge in the

6.15 *The Magheramorne cement works, County Antrim, c. 1915.*

mid-1980s, was also designed by Mouchel and constructed using the Hennebique system. In 1903, Julius Kahn, an American engineer, patented a reinforcing bar, which led to the development of the Kahn system of reinforced concrete. Kahn established the Trussed Concrete Steel Co., which granted the British license to the Trussed Steel Co. of Westminster. The earliest-known example of the use of the Kahn system in Ireland appears to be the King's Bridge on the Lagan embankment, which was opened to traffic in 1912.

The use of concrete as a building material in domestic architecture was a somewhat slower development, the home of the O'Conor Don at Clonalis, County Roscommon (which has unrendered mass concrete walls), built in 1878-80, being amongst the earliest examples.[109] The two-storey houses designed by the Irish architect, William A. Scott (1871-1921), for the model village at Greenvale, County Kilkenny, in 1906, were also concrete built.[110] But by the early decades of the twentieth century, the employment of mass and reinforced concrete, along with concrete building blocks, had become commonplace, to the extent that increasing unemployment of both stonemasons and bricklayers in the Irish building trade was raised in Dáil Éireann in the 1930s.[111]

The first successful Portland cement works in Ireland were established in the Drinagh limestone quarries on the southern outskirts of Wexford in 1871. The manufacturers claimed that after seven days, Drinagh cement could withstand tensile strengths of around 400 lbs psi. The Drinagh works came to supply a large section of the Irish market during its working life (1871-1925), and established a successful export trade with England, dispatching its cement out through the port of Wexford. In 1888, the extensive works, which included crushing, grinding, sifting and calcining plant, were powered by 250 hp engines built by Victor Coates and Company. The 110 ft (33.52 m) concrete chimney at the works, which was built around the late 1880s, was the second to be so constructed in Ireland.[112] At Independence, there were only two cement factories in Ireland, Drinagh and the British Portland Cement Co.'s works at Magheramorne, County Antrim (figure 6.15), whose combined output was insufficient to meet the demand of the Irish building industry.

(4) Pottery

In Britain and Ireland during the seventeenth century, sub-medieval coarse wares continued to be made in many areas, but towards the end of the century, some potters were already beginning to produce fine wares. Of these, *delftware*, which originated in an attempt by Dutch potters to imitate Chinese porcelain (whose secret of manufacture was as yet unknown to European potters), was to become the most commonly used household ware in England. Manufacturers of delftware now coated earthenware pots with an opaque, tin enamel which, while making the pot impermeable, also produced a background upon which decoration could be painted.[113] The resulting ceramic forms had the clean, porcelain-like look of china, but could be produced at considerably less cost.[114] During the late seventeenth century, the clay from the Carrickfergus area, and the availability of timber for fueling kilns, led to the establishment of delftware potteries in Belfast. Indeed, the earliest documented example of delftware pottery in Ireland is at Belfast in 1695. Carrickfergus clay was also extensively used in the delftware potteries of the Irish Sea area, but elsewhere in Ireland, the development of the industry was somewhat slower. By the close of the seventeenth century, delftware potteries had been established at Lambeth in London, Bristol, Liverpool and Belfast. In the eighteenth century, the ports of Bristol, Liverpool, Glasgow and Dublin became the principal manufacturing centres.[115]

Delftware was more or less continuously manufactured in Ireland from 1697 to 1771, during which time potteries were either established or attempted at Belfast, Dublin, Rostrevor, Youghal and possibly also at Limerick, but these were, for the most part, short-lived affairs. However, while these all utilised native clay, foreign expertise was required to work it. From *c.* 1735, at least one pottery manufacturing fine ware was at work on Dublin's North Strand. This was the 'White Pothouse', whose proprietor, John Chambers, had built a kiln and had brought potters to work for him from 'abroad'. Further delftware potteries were set up at Rostrevor in the period *c.* 1739-42 and possibly also at Youghal: no fewer than five delftware potteries were operating in the Dublin area between 1747 and 1751.[116]

However, by this period, the Irish delftware industry was already in decline, and in an effort to reverse this trend, the Dublin Society offered a premium for the establishment of a fine ware pottery which would imitate Delft, Rouen and Burgundy wares.[117] The premium was taken up by Captain Henry Delamain, who in 1752 took over the White Pothouse and commenced manufacture in 1753. Delamain erected kilns and warehouses and employed 40 families (which included a number of English workmen) in his pottery. No fewer than nine pottery kilns were operated by Delamain and, in addition to his water-powered colour-grinding mills at

Palmerstown, County Dublin, Delamain erected what appears to be the first flint grinding mill in Ireland.[118] Ground flint (silica) was crushed in circular vats (*flint pans*), powered by either animal or water power, the ground flint being incorporated into the main body of the pot as a whitener. Delamain also conducted pioneering experiments with coal-fired kilns. Up to this time, it had only been possible to fire tin-glazed delftware using wood as a fuel, but Delamain's success using coal can be gauged from the fact that Liverpool potteries were anxious to employ the services of William Stringfellow, Delamain's pottery manager.

The establishment of delftware potteries marks the beginning of industrial-scale pottery manufacture in Ireland. Bottle kilns, mechanised ancillary processes such as flint and colour-grinding mills, and the standardisation of ceramic pieces, were introduced into Ireland for the first time. The pottery kiln was now enclosed in a tall bottle-shaped building, which helped to protect it from the elements. The direct heat of the kiln furnace was separated from the area holding the pots, the heat being reflected down onto special containers holding the pots, called *saggars*, by the dome of the kiln. Saggars were boxes made from heat-resistant clay, into which the soft unfired pots were placed to protect them from the direct heat and smoke of the kiln furnace. The saggars could be sealed with a lid, but more often than not, they were stacked on top of one another within the kiln.

In 1709, the first hard porcelain manufactured in Europe (Dresdenware) was produced at Meissen near Dresden in Germany, where Freidrich Bottger had experimented with the use of *kaolin* (China clay). During the 1760s potters in France and England finally discovered how to manufacture hard porcelain by using kaolin. In 1746, a Plymouth chemist called John Cookworthy discovered large deposits of kaolin in Cornwall, and went on to manufacture the first hard paste porcelain in Britain, using kaolin and ground flint, in 1768. From the eighteenth century onwards, these deposits were extensively exploited, but it was not until the 1850s that similar deposits were discovered in Ireland. Nonetheless, as early as 1755, unsuccessful attempts were being made at Thomas Wyse's pottery at Waterford and by Jonathan Chamberleyne of Little Killiane, Wexford, to manufacture porcelain, although the Little Killiane site does, however, have what may be one of the earliest surviving eighteenth-century pottery buildings in Ireland.[119] The efforts of Irishmen in England, however, proved much more successful. A Dublin artist called Thomas Frye (1710-62), in addition to being among the first to take out a patent in England for the manufacture of porcelain, was the first to utilise calcined ox bone ashes as an ingredient in porcelain manufacture. Frye's former teacher, John Brooks of Cork Hill, Dublin, also made an important contribution to the evolution of porcelain manufacture in England. Brooks developed a new technique whereby decoration could be cheaply and uniformly applied to pottery. He had attempted to patent the idea in both Dublin and Birmingham in 1751, but made little headway until he became manager of the Battersea enamel factory in 1753.[120]

In 1853, both kaolin and *feldspar* (which was added to kaolin and fired to temperatures of 1,100 to 1450° C to produce transluscent porcelain) were discovered on the Bloomfield estate near Belleek, County Fermanagh. A pottery was established at Belleek in 1858 to take advantage of this natural bounty, originally producing glazed earthenware, whilst feldspar was also quarried and ground for export. Under the direction of Robert Williams Armstrong, new techniques for the manufacture of stoneware mortars were developed, while experiments with porcelain bodies were also undertaken.[121] A Fairbairn suspension water-wheel powered the pottery's pug mills, feldspar grinding pans, lathes and turning plates. Two bottle kilns were in operation in 1866 when the pottery's main buildings were finally completed to a design by Armstrong. In addition to the readily available supplies of kaolin and feldspar, both flint, which was used in the manufacture of stonewares, and shale for making saggars could also be procured locally. Only *ball clay*, which was used in the manufacture of coarse wares and as a stiffener in porcelain, had to be imported from either south Devon or Dorset.[122]

In 1863, the pottery brought over skilled Parian China makers from England, building special accommodation for them at Rathmore Terrace ('English Row') in Belleek. Parian ware gets its name from the Greek island on which white marble was quarried for Greek statuary work, the pale lustre of the ware being compared to that of Greek statues. English potters from Stoke-on-Trent made the first fine ware at the pottery in 1863, and a number of them had been employed at W.H. Goss' pottery in England, bringing with them Goss' techniques of producing egg-shell porcelain.

In its essentials, Belleek Parian ware was made by pouring liquid clay (*slip*) into plaster of Paris moulds: only the distinctive Belleek baskets and flowers, which were hand-made by skilled craftsmen, are not made in this way. Unfired or *green* pottery was then placed in a bottle kiln, the fired pottery being called *biscuit*, the term normally applied to pottery that has been fired only once. The biscuit ware was then checked for flaws and, if satisfactory, it was dipped in glaze and removed to the kiln for a *glass firing*, which baked the enamel onto the body of the pot. The final decoration of paint and gilt was then applied by highly skilled craftsmen, which was fixed to the body of the ware by firing in an enamel kiln.[123] Since the end of the Second World War, only Parian ware has been made at Belleek. In 1946, the original bottle kilns were replaced by modern ones and the pottery continues in production to this day. This latter pottery has proved to be the most enduring enterprise of its kind in Ireland.

In their efforts to produce higher quality earthenware and stonewares, English craftsmen in the Staffordshire potteries developed, in the first half of the eighteenth century, what became known as *creamwares*.[124] Whereas delftware strove to assume the appearance of china through the application of a thick white glaze, in creamwares, the actual body of the pot was fired to a pure-white colour. As such, only a thin transparent glaze needed to be applied to the exterior of the fabric, producing a ware both thinner and lighter than delftware, in addition to being more resistant to heat and damage from everyday wear and tear.[125] Josiah Wedgwood (1730-95) mass-produced creamware ceramics in the second half of the eighteenth century, and his 'Queensware', so-called after the patronage of Queen Charlotte, enjoyed considerable popularity in Britain. Wedgwood's marketing techniques also ensured that, by the 1780s, his products quickly replaced other fine wares used in Britain and Ireland, and large quantities of them were sold in Ireland through a Dublin retail outlet.[126]

With the exception of the Downshire pottery in Belfast, Irish attempts to manufacture creamwares during the eighteenth century met with little success. Potteries were set up at Doneraile, County Cork, in the 1750s and in 1771, the former delftware pottery at the World's End in Dublin was converted into a creamware manufactory. The Dublin pottery employed craftsmen from Staffordshire in the production of moulded, cream-coloured

Kiln entrance

Electric cable

Fire box 1

Fire box 2

Kiln wall

Edge of concrete road

0   1m

Original cobbles   Original brick floor   Kiln brick

Fused brick, mortar and charcoal in red and grey clay   Victorian brick

6.16 *Plan of the excavation of eighteenth-century bottle kiln, on the site of the Downshire pottery at Ballymacarett, near Belfast (after Francis 2001).*

ware, very typical of the Staffordshire potteries. However, it was out of business by 1774, in all likelihood because of the success of Wedgwood's marketing drive in Ireland during the 1770s.[127] In *c.* 1790-91, Thomas Greg and partners of Belfast began to manufacture creamwares in the Downshire pottery, on the bank of the River Lagan at Ballymacarett near Belfast, as part of an ambitious scheme to develop glass and fine ware factories in tandem. Greg also built what was then the only operational flint-grinding mill in Ireland, but the pottery ceased production in *c.* 1806. The site retains at least two Scrabo sandstone buildings associated with pottery, the only examples of their type to have survived in Ireland, one of which appears to have housed the main pottery and decorating rooms. A 75 metre-long stretch of eighteenth-century quayside, originally built for the pottery and glass works, also survives. Excavations on the site during the 1990s revealed the foundations of one of the original Staffordshire-type bottle kilns, which had an outer *hovel*, or masonry cone about 36 ft (10.97 m) in diameter, and an inner kiln some 15 ft (4.57 m) in diameter (figure 6.16).[128]

The manufacture of lead-glazed wheel-thrown earthenware in Ireland – the so-called country pottery – belongs largely to the pre-industrial phase of the Irish pottery industry, when the potter quarried his own clay and supplied a local market. Around 1654, the Carley brothers of Cornwall established a pottery west of Enniscorthy, County Wexford, on a site which now bears their name, Carley's Bridge. A present-day pottery in the area still uses clay from the original 7-acre site. During the same period a further County Wexford pottery was set up at Little Killiane. In Youghal in eastern County Cork, local potters were exploiting the clays in the area as early as 1652.[129] Little is currently known about the seventeenth- and eighteenth-century physical arrangements of Irish earthenware potteries, but recently a likely mid-1700s example was excavated at Tuam, County Galway. This latter was keyhole shaped in form, with an oven section 1.7 m in diameter, with a flue almost 2 m in length. The walls of the kiln were constructed with red brick and the wares associated with it were straight sided and probably used as measures.[130]

Irish earthenware potteries generally produced pots, dishes, earthenware and drain pipes. Their *modus operandi* was broadly similar to English potteries in the Irish Sea area, and, from the outset, the Irish potteries were established in regions with excellent local clays. English expertise filtered through to all areas, even Youghal, whose traditional designs still used medieval shapes as late as the 1930s. In Ulster, a number of small, family-owned potteries were established during the nineteenth and early twentieth centuries. Approximately twenty or so potteries were at work in Ulster during the nineteenth century, and the area around Coalisland became the focus of the local earthenware industry. The potters' clay was dug by hand and was transported by cart to the potteries where it was stored in heaps over the winter months to produce *soured* clay, which was then macerated in a pug mill. The potter's throwing wheel required two operators, a potter to shape the pot and an assistant to turn a crank which powered the throwing wheel, many of which were still used until the early decades of the twentieth century. The ware was then fired in bottle kilns, which were fuelled with locally harvested turf. The Coalisland potteries eventually lost out to new, more durable materials such as plastic, which almost completely replaced ceramics formerly in use for drainage pipes and the like, and the last surviving pottery closed in 1960.[131]

In 1853, J. Deering of Midleton, County Cork, displayed items made from clay quarried at Rostellan on Cork harbour at the Cork Exhibition, which had been experimentally fired in Staffordshire. However, it was not until the early 1900s that the Department of Agriculture and Technical Instruction for Ireland began to draw attention to these silica-rich deposits by arranging for a Cork contractor to quarry a sample of it. Some of this clay was shipped to England and, in 1902, a set of fine China made from Rostellan silica clay was commissioned and displayed. Yet despite the success of these experiments, the Rostellan deposits were not commercially quarried until the 1920s. The Ford tractor works (see Chapter 10)) provided a useful local market, and quantities were also exported to England. The Rostellan mine, however, proved to be short-lived, closing in 1928, but similar clay deposits at Cloyne, County Cork, continued to be quarried up until the early 1960s, and were shipped to British potteries via the small harbour of Ballinacurra near Midleton, County Cork. When most Irish potteries were in decline in the 1920s, a daring new venture was initiated at Carrigaline, County Cork, in 1928, which began by manufacturing teapots and flower pots from local clay. Yet this clay was unsuitable for the production of fine tableware, and as part of the company's expansion plans, the River Owenabue at Carrigaline was modified in the 1930s to enable ships carrying English white clay to discharge their cargoes at Carrigaline. In the 1960s, the Carrigaline pottery opened new markets in England the United States and Canada, but fell victim to the economic depression of the 1970s, closing in 1979.[132]

Some of the better preserved sites of Irish nineteenth-century potteries survive near Youghal in County Cork. At Curraghboy, near Youghal, there is a late nineteenth-century, three storey pottery building which encloses a bottle kiln. The bottle kiln is brick built with an internal diameter of 3.9 m and the base of the kiln has seven arched furnace holes. There is also a similar site at Muckridge of about the same period, which contains the remains of a bottle kiln 3.8 m in internal diameter with eight furnace holes. Remains of a further pottery, dating from the mid-nineteenth century, are also in evidence at Kilmagner, near Youghal, on the banks of the Tourig river (figure 6.17).[133]

The increased popularity of tobacco smoking led to the introduction of clay tobacco pipes into Ireland – their use, indeed, is recorded well into the twentieth century – and very quickly to the establishment of clay pipe factories here.[134] As early as the 1640s, clay pipes were being produced in Waterford, and by the end of the seventeenth century, many of Ireland's larger towns had followed suit. During the eighteenth century, a Scotsman called Buckley laid the foundations for an important local clay pipe industry at Knockcroghery, County Roscommon. During the early years, enough local clay was at hand to satisfy the demands of the industry, but in the nineteenth century, it became necessary to import clay from England and Wales. In the 1830s, upwards of 1,000 gross of clay pipes were produced weekly there by some 24 journeymen moulders, and by 1890, William Curley's factory at Knockcroghery was producing around 57,600 pipes per week.[135] The growing

6.17 *Nineteenth-century bottle kiln at Kilmagner pottery, near Youghal, County Cork.*

popularity of cigarettes, however, reduced the demand for clay pipes, although the demise of the Knockcroghery industry was brought about when the village was burned down by British forces in 1921.

There are no surviving clay pipe works in Ireland, but within the last two decades, a number of eighteenth-century pipe kilns have been excavated in Waterford and at least one multi-flue nineteenth-century example in Limerick.[136] The two main Waterford city kilns, at Olaf Street and Cooke Lane/Peter Street, appear to have been of the up-draught type, and these, along with a possible third site at High Street, all produced evidence that a *muffle* (i.e., a feature similar to a saggar, in that it protected the pipes from the direct heat of the furnace, save that it was a fixed entity, built into the furnace) had been employed. The layout of the Olaf Street kiln was conventional in outline, but that of Cooke Lane/Peter Street was somewhat larger, being around 5 m long. In each case, however, muffle wall fragments were found (figure 6.18).[137]

The city of Cork was another important centre of clay pipe manufacture. During the nineteenth century, some of six clay pipe manufactories were at work there, with a notable concentration in Adelaide Street. The clay used in these works was formerly brought into Cork from Clare, but later in the nineteenth century, all the clay was imported from England. In 1903, the raw clay was purchased in 28 1b blocks, which were first kiln-dried and then mechanically pulverised, before being reduced to a powder which was then steeped in large vats. The clay was subsequently taken out and beaten before being lumped into a stiff dough. A visitor to John Fitzgerald's Clay Pipe Factory on Adelaide Street in 1903 was informed that saggars were used to hold the pipes in the firing kiln. The clay was also imported from Devon and Cornwall, the principal source for many English works. The pipes were fired in a brick-lined kiln for eight to nine hours and the finished product was exported to New York, London, Liverpool and to most of Wales, especially Newport, Tredegar and Cardiff.[138]

(5) Glass works

In recent years the study of the post-medieval glass industry in Ireland has received a welcome boost through the discovery of the only upstanding late sixteenth- to early seventeenth-century glass furnace, in the appropriately-named townland of Glasshouse, near Shinrone, County Offaly (figure 6.19).[139] The Irish industry experienced mixed fortunes thereafter, however, and it was not until the eighteenth century, when excise duties on glass produced in England and the absence of restrictions on Ireland's ability to export home-produced glass provided great incentives to prospective Irish glass manufacturers, that industrial-scale production began in earnest. By the end of the eighteenth century, glass houses had been established in Dublin, Waterford, Drumrea (County Tyrone), Belfast, Cork, Newry and Ballycastle, five of which (Cork, Waterford, Belfast, Dublin and Newry) were set up after 1780. The most distinctive feature of Irish eighteenth- and nineteenth-century glass-works are the brick-built cones, the purpose of which was to provide an up-draught for their circular, centrally positioned, glass furnaces, and also to provide cover for the glass workers. The earliest recorded example in Europe was built in Dublin by Philip Roche in 1694, which has prompted speculation as to the ultimate origin of these cones.[140] The influential *Receuil des Planches …* compiled by Diderot and D'Alembert and published between

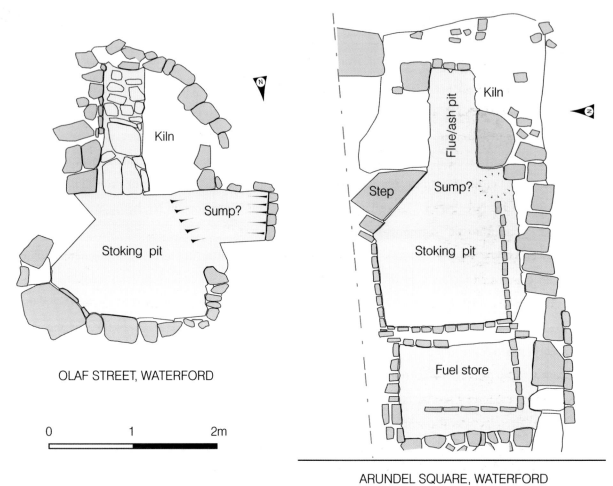

OLAF STREET, WATERFORD

0   1   2m

ARUNDEL SQUARE, WATERFORD

BROAD STREET, LIMERICK

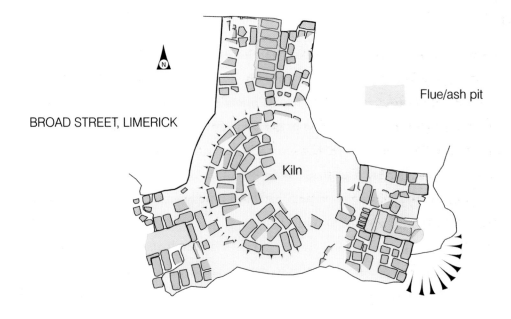

Flue/ash pit

6.18 *Excavated clay pipe kilns from Waterford and Limerick (after Peacey 1996).*

6.19 *Late sixteenth- to early seventeenth-century glass furnace, at Glasshouse, near Shinrone, County Offaly.*

1762–71, illustrates a glass cone typical of those used in Britain and Ireland with the caption '*Verrerie Anglaise*', which would appear to rule out a European origin.[141]

The furnace grate received air from an elaborate system of flues and ash tunnels which ran beneath the floor of the cone. The upper section of the furnace would accommodate up to ten of the clay pots in which the glass was melted, and an aperture in the furnace wall immediately above each pot (the *working hole*) enabled the glass-worker to extract the molten glass. Unfortunately, with the exception of the foundation of a cone at Ballycastle, County Antrim, none of the Irish examples have survived, and there are, indeed, only five examples extant in Britain. The largest example known to have been built in Ireland was erected at Belfast in 1784 as part of the entrepreneurial initiative created by Greg, in association with the Downshire Pottery. This was believed to have been around 120–150 ft (36.57–45.72 m) high, and was demolished as recently as 1938 after storm damage.[142] At Ballycastle, the remains of a glass cone built by Hugh Boyd in 1755 but demolished in the 1870s were excavated in 1974. The internal diameter of the cone was 18 m – one of the largest ever built in these islands – and the

6.20 *The preserved glassworks cone base at Ballycastle, County Antrim. The cone was erected by Hugh Boyd in 1755 and taken down in the 1870s.*

excavation revealed a large section of the central fire grate. The base of the cone (which has been partially preserved) also had arcading, a series of recesses in which the glass blowers would have worked, and a common feature of English and Irish glassworks (figure 6.20).[143] The glass cone at the Cork Glass House Company's works at Hanover Street in Cork, erected *c.* 1782, was brick built, had a maximum external diameter of approximately 54 ft (16.45 m) at the base, and was about 80 ft (24.38 m) high. It was demolished in 1915, but from a nineteenth-century ground plan, it is clear that it had six recesses at the base to accommodate glassworkers (figure 6.21).[144]

The sand used in the manufacture of Irish flint glass appears to have been imported from one of the principal English sources on the Isle of Wight or from Lynn in Norfolk, which have a low iron content, whilst that used for bottle glass was quarried locally. Dublin glasshouses, for example, procured sand for making flint glass from the North Bull, while Cork glassworks appear to have obtained theirs from Youghal, County Cork, and Tramore, County Waterford. Lead, saltpetre, potash and manganese, four of the five ingredients used in the manufacture of flint glass, were also imported from England, although potash was also imported from Quebec.[145] The ingredients of the particular type of glass to be manufactured were first weighed, and, after careful mixing, were calcined by partial fusion (*fritting*) in an oven, which helped to remove impurities. *Cullet* or broken glass was then added to assist the melting process, the batch or mixed ingredients being then shovelled into the pots. After fabrication, the glass pieces were slowly drawn through a long gallery called a *lehr* or *annealing* arch, in which they were allowed to cool gradually. Particular care was exercised in the manufacture of the glass clay pots, as the high temperatures to which they were exposed in the furnaces could lead to cracking, whilst the material used in their manufacture also had to be able to resist the solvent action of the molten glass. The most widely used refractory clay employed in the manufacture of these pots came from the Stourbridge region of the English West Midlands.

The four main types of glass produced in Ireland in the eighteenth and early nineteenth centuries were bottle, crown, plate and flint glass. *Bottle glass* was manufactured with cheap, easily obtainable materials, and could be made with locally acquired sand. *Flint glass* was made with silica sand with a very low iron content, along with lead oxide, potash (or pearlash), saltpetre and manganese. Flint or lead glasses (English Crystal) have a high refractive index, and are admirably suited both to hand manufacture and secondary working by cutters and engravers. *Window* or *crown* glass (which was made in Dublin as early as 1726) was formed by blowing,

6.21 *Sketch of Hanover Street Cork glass cone by William Roe (1838). The brick-built cone was erected in c. 1782 and taken down in 1915.*

heating and rolling the molten glass on a polished metal surface. The globe of molten glass formed by these actions was ultimately spun around on the end of an iron rod, which threw the molten glass out centrifugally to form a flat disc.[146] Pieces of crown glass were recovered from the remains of the Ballycastle glass cone. *Plate glass*, on the other hand, which was manufactured by casting molten glass, was generally made of much finer ingredients than those employed in window glass. It was normally made thicker than window glass in order that it could be ground and polished. Most plate glass was generally silvered for use as mirrors, although it was sometimes used for coach windows.

Glass-making expertise was provided by English craftsmen from Newcastle-upon-Tyne. Stourbridge and Bristol whilst the Waterloo Glass Co. employed at least one Stourbridge glassworker who had arrived in Cork via Dublin. In the English glass industry of the same period, ready access to cheap coal was one of the most important factors governing its location. A typical glass cone could consume up to 24 tons of coal per week, the quantity of which increased substantially when steam power began to be used to power glass-cutting machinery. The Cork Glass House Company installed a steam engine in 1813 for driving a glass-cutting plant, and was followed by the two later Cork glasshouses, the Waterloo Glass Company and the South Terrace works, which was equipped with a steam engine capable of actuating 40 glass cutting wheels.[147] The Penrose glassworks in Waterford

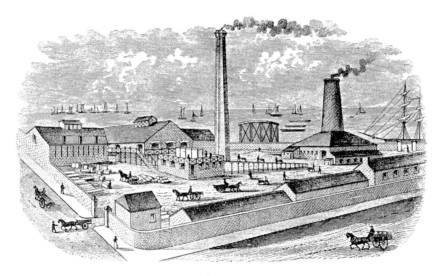

6.22 *The Ringsend Bottle Works, from Stratten and Stratten 1892.*

also employed a small 7 hp engine to power some of its machinery.[148] The reliance on imported coal from south Wales and other imported materials meant that most glassworks were established on sites adjacent to water transport. In Cork, for example, all three glasshouses were established on sites with direct access to the South Channel of the River Lee.

From 1825 onwards, the Irish glass industry was in terminal decline, and by 1852 only two glassworks survived, one in Dublin and one in Belfast. The only facet of the industry to survive up to recent times, indeed, was the industrial manufacture of bottle glass. The main glass bottle manufactory was at Ringsend (figure 6.22), near Dublin (which only closed down in 2002), but by 1870, there were at least five firms involved in their manufacture in the Dublin area, and eight by 1895. The principal raw material was recycled glass, and large amounts of coal were also involved. Technological change from the traditional 'coal tank' method to the Siemens gas system (which was much more fuel efficient, while at the same time producing a vastly improved product) was slow in the Dublin industry, even though demand was on the increase (particularly from the brewing and distilling industries), and local supplies could not always be guaranteed.[149] In 1920, there were only five bottle works in Ireland, four in Dublin and a single example in Belfast.[150]

7

Farming and Fishing

Although agriculture produced many of the raw materials for Ireland's internationally important textile and food-processing industries (see Chapters 8 and 9), very few Irish farms during the eighteenth and nineteenth centuries could be considered industrial archaeological entities in their own right. The vast majority of Irish farms did, in fact, operate at just above subsistence level. In 1841, over 40 per cent of Irish landholdings were 1-10 acres in extent, while over 70 per cent of holdings in all the counties of Connacht and Ulster, including Louth and Longford, were under 30 acres. Only 7,200 farm units in the Griffith Valuation in 1850 had a valuation in excess of £100.[1] Furthermore, it was not until the closing decades of the nineteenth century that Irish farms began to become owner occupied. As late as 1870, as little as 3 per cent of Irish farms were owned by their occupants, yet by 1908, this percentage was 46 per cent, and by 1914, 60 per cent of Irish farmers owned their holdings.[2] And, while a considerable amount of land reclamation was undertaken in the period 1780-1844, in 1841, some 6.3 million acres (around 30 per cent of Ireland's total surface area of 20.8 million statute acres) was still uncultivated.[3] Not surprisingly, then, there was no 'agricultural revolution' in Ireland, while mechanisation only began to gain momentum after the Great Famine of the 1840s when labour became more expensive.

Nonetheless, Ireland was a highly commercialised agricultural economy in the nineteenth century, producing not only enough food to feed its rural population but also for export. Before the Famine, agricultural productivity, owing to the labour-intensive nature of Irish agriculture, was paradoxically higher than that of the post-1850 period. Spade cultivation produced a finer tilth than the plough, while the availability of cheap spadesmen militated against the widespread adoption of agricultural machinery (see Chapter 10). Moreover, Irish crops were also manually hoed and weeded, which itself increased productivity, and on the eve of the Famine over two million acres of potatoes were cultivated on the island.[4] But in the aftermath of the Famine, the fall in population

7.1 *Water-powered threshing mill at Castle Ward estate, County Down.*

brought about a marked decline in the importance of arable farming, with a parallel rise in the demand for dairy products and meat.[5] It has been argued that the agricultural depression of 1859-64 represents a watershed in Ireland's agrarian economy, as it created an agriculture based largely on cattle.[6] Ireland's hay acreage effectively doubled in the period 1850 to 1910, from some 1.2 million acres to over 2.4 million, while by 1910 livestock made up some 84 per cent of agricultural output.[7] In addition, the productivity of Irish people working on the land, which was only 47 per cent of that of their English counterparts in 1871, had risen to 80 per cent by 1914.[8]

Technological change in Irish agriculture was a painfully slow process, and while many traditional practices continued to survive throughout the country well into the nineteenth century, this was often because they were better suited to existing conditions and resources.[9] As early as 1731, the Dublin Society was founded to initiate change in Irish agriculture, becoming the Royal Dublin Society (RDS) in 1820 when George IV ('farmer George') agreed to become its patron. The RDS was tireless in its efforts to improve Irish agriculture, and produced the remarkable series of County Statistical Surveys in the first two decades of the nineteenth century.[10] In 1826, an agricultural school was established at Templemoyle, County Derry, which, by 1850, was also training students from

England and Scotland, and in 1838, a 'model' farm was set up at Glasnevin near Dublin. Other agricultural improvement societies were established throughout the nineteenth century, but their essential functions were taken over by the Department of Agriculture and Technical Instruction in the early 1900s.[11]

Ireland's high rainfall and poor natural drainage were the fundamental natural environmental problems facing agricultural improvement. Considerable investment was clearly needed in land drainage and reclamation and, while quite a lot of this was undertaken in the period 1780-1845, large-scale reclamation projects, such as that initiated to drain extensive areas of the slobs around Wexford town, were rare in nineteenth-century Ireland.[12] There was, however, a general improvement in the quantity and quality of fertilisers used on Irish farms. Traditional manures like marl, seaweed and lime began to be supplemented with imported fertilisers such as Peruvian guano in the later nineteenth century, a development encouraged by the Irish co-operative movement.

A gradual improvement in farm implements began to take place shortly before the Famine, before which it had been generally recognised that Scottish 'swing ploughs' (i.e., wheel-less ploughs) could be used profitably on Irish tillage farms. Irish iron foundries (see Chapter 10) responded to this challenge by producing sizeable numbers of swing ploughs, which were still commonly employed throughout Ireland well into the twentieth century.[13] Other innovations included the slightly more widespread introduction and increased use of seed drills in the 1860s, and that of reaping and mowing machines around the same time. Animal-powered machines were first used in Irish agriculture in the final decade of the eighteenth century (see Chapter 1), and had become relatively common during the 1800s. Water-powered threshing mills were also beginning to appear early in the nineteenth century, but were never a widespread phenomenon in Ireland; indeed, they were rare even in the principal cereal growing counties. Only one example, on the Castle Ward estate in County Down (figure 7.1 recently restored), has survived with its full complement of machinery, and in the 1830s, the largest concentration of these mills in Ireland was in County Antrim, where six water-powered threshing mills were built between 1835 and 1839.[14] Nor, for that matter, did the use of steam-powered threshing machines become widespread on the larger farms until the 1860s.[15] But, as early as 1853, an English company, Garrett's of Suffolk, had exhibited a steam-powered thresher in Dublin. Garrett's went on to test a steam thresher at Adare, County Limerick in 1858, and thereafter these were to become a common feature of Irish grain harvests.[16] The first English steam plough was in use in 1836, but it was only through the introduction of lighter traction engines that this technology became viable. A steam plough could do more work in an hour than a single horse could do in a day, and although one was displayed at the RDS' Spring Show in 1864 these were rarely used in Ireland.[17] From the 1850s, 'muck spreaders' began to appear here, and their success in Irish conditions can be gauged by the fact that some 1,800 were in use throughout the island in 1912. The 'tumbling paddy', a horse-drawn hay-rake developed in America, became a firm favourite amongst Irish farmers towards the end of the nineteenth century, and was still commonly used as late as the early 1960s.[18]

The advent of the internal combustion engine tractor to Irish agriculture may have begun shortly before 1904, but the earliest firm evidence for the use of the English manufacturer's 'Universal' tractor in Ireland is at Barkerstown, County Wicklow, and Athy, County Kildare, in 1914. After 1914, International Mogul and Titan tractors became the most popular models in Ireland, before the introduction of Henry Ford's model, the Fordson, the first European-manufactured examples of which left a Cork production line in 1919 (see Chapter 10).[19] The Irish market for tractors, however, was originally very small, and by 1917, only around 70 of these machines were in use, although the Fordson (figure 7.2) tractor proved to be immensely popular with farmers. By 1928, at least 800 tractors had been bought by farmers in Ireland, rising to 2,000 on the eve of the Second World War.[20] One Irishman, Harry Ferguson, actually revolutionised the design of the tractor between 1917 and 1936 by introducing a three-point linkage system, which enabled the driver to control the agricultural machinery pulled behind the tractor and to drive at the same time, Ferguson actually went on to open a training school on the Powerscourt Estate for tractor drivers and mechanics.[21]

(2) Creameries and Dairy-Related Industries

The increased adoption of the potato in rural Irish diets from the late seventeenth century onwards enabled large amounts of butter manufactured throughout the dairying regions of Munster to be increasingly sent to market. By the 1730s, the port of Cork had become the centre of Ireland's export trade in butter based, largely on English and Dutch colonial demand. However, by the second half of the eighteenth century, the burgeoning industrial population of Britain was becoming the main target market for Irish butter exporters, whose principal centre was the city of Cork. Here, in 1769, was established what was to become, by the turn of the nineteenth century, the largest butter market in the world. In its essentials, the Munster butter trade was a domestic industry, in which the butter was manufactured by hand in the farmhouse dairy, packed in 56 lb wooden barrels bound with sally hoops, and dispatched by road to highly organised markets in Cork, Limerick and Waterford.[22] Mechanised churns, powered by water-wheels, are known to have been used in a limited way by the end of the eighteenth century, but, for the most part, almost all Irish butter was made by hand up to the closing decades of the nineteenth century.[23]

The development of centrifugal separators in the 1870s by de Laval and others in Denmark and Germany enabled the manufacture of butter to move from the farmhouse to the factory.[24] In Ireland, the first de Laval separator was exhibited in a display of butter and butter making held in the Corn Market in Cork in June 1879. The basic working principle of the mechanical separator involved rotating the milk in a container at extremely high speeds, in which the butter fat and buttermilk were more efficiently separated in accordance with their densities. De Laval's model turned at 2,000-4,000 rpm and was capable of separating the cream of 30 gallons of milk in 50 minutes: a process which had traditionally taken about two days could now be accomplished in minutes.[25] The first separators to be used in Ireland were hand operated, and early models such as the 'Alexandra', the 'Peterson' and the 'Laval', not being equipped with internal rotating disks, had a somewhat limited capacity. Not until 1889 did separators with both a higher capacity and disks become available in Ireland, but, from the early 1880s, high-capacity separators were already beginning to be mechanised.[26]

7.2 *A Fordson tractor, from an advertisement in Coakley 1919.*

Indeed, even the early de Laval models required a regular power supply and, for this reason, water turbines and steam engines were the preferred prime movers. Moreover, until such time as power-activated separators became available, in the period 1879-80, the creation of milk-receiving creameries was not practicable. The first such creamery in Ireland, established at Hospital, County Limerick in 1884, was powered by a 10 hp steam engine.[27] However, by 1889, water-powered creameries were in existence elsewhere in Munster, at Askeaton Dairy Factory, Askeaton, County Limerick (in which Petersen's separators were actuated by a water turbine), and at the Ruskeen Dairy Factory at Charleville, County Cork.[28]

From the outset, Irish creameries were housed in single-storey, functional buildings, constructed with a variety of materials, ranging from rubblestone to corrugated iron. Typically, these are rectilinear, that at Hospital was 75 by 60 ft (21.33 m by 18.28 m) in extent, and was provided with a deep well.[29] To accommodate the delivery of milk churns by horse cart, a high platform was constructed at one end of the building (usually, but not always, at the

7.3 *Power activated churn in Drumcollogher creamery, County Limerick (left);* **7.4** *Callan creamery County Kilkenny, established in 1905 (above).*

gable end), and from here, the churns were lifted by hand into the creamery. A milk measuring pan was also provided (later with a spring balance) to record the milk intake of individual farmers. Towards the end of the nineteenth century, the milk began to be pre-heated in a Danish flash heater, before admission to the churn. The flash heater was used to pasteurise it, but this latter process only began to become widespread in Ireland after the First World War.[30]

The churns employed in the early creameries were of two varieties: rotating barrel churns similar to the hand-operated variety, but of much larger capacity, and vertical stationary churns, in which the cream was agitated by means of internal revolving beaters. Upon completion of the churning process, the resultant butter grains were placed on a rotary butter worker, which worked them into a regular consistency. All the machinery – separators, churns and butter workers – was connected either to a small vertical steam engine and vertical boiler (usually separated from the dairy machinery by a flimsy partition), water turbine, gas or oil engine, by means of line shafting and pulleys.[31] Ireland's first co-operative creamery, at Drumcollogher, County Limerick, established in 1889, was restored to working order to coincide with its centenary in 1989 (figure 7.3). There, a small 6-9 hp engine (originally in the Castletown creamery in County Limerick) powers Alfa-Laval separators, barrel churns built by the Dairy Engineering Company of Ireland and a butter worker. All the transmission, some of which has been retained *in situ*, was originally installed by Carson's Foundry of Dublin. In Ireland, the co-operative movement, led by Sir Horace Plunkett and strongly advocated by Fr Finlay and others, fostered the development of local creameries. And, whereas in 1896 only 72 of Ireland's 279 creameries were co-operative ventures, by 1916, the vast majority were co-operatively run (figure 7.4 and 7.5). By 1926, there were some 580 creameries in the new Irish Free State, the most typical of which processed the milk of about 800-1,200 cows.[32]

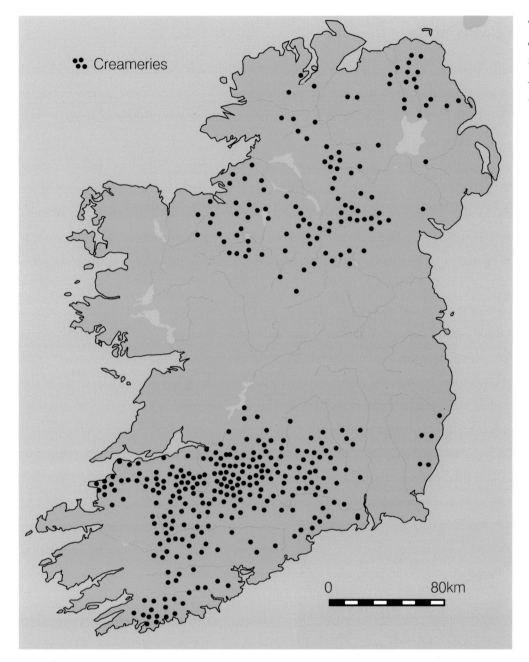

Creameries

7.5 *Distribution of co-operative creameries in Ireland in 1910 (after Aalen, Whelan and Stout 1997).*

Ireland's railway networks, for the most part, could guarantee fresh milk to the main urban centres on a daily basis, but in Dublin it became common for dairy herds to be kept in fields within a 6-7 mile radius of the city. Indeed, during the winter months, the cows were kept in yards in Dublin itself, where they were foddered with hay, spent grains from breweries and Indian meal. Some 250 dairy yards were at work in Dublin in 1893, many of which formed the basis of a city-wide milk retailing basis, although the yards began to disappear as supplies were obtained from further afield to meet expanding demand.[33] One of the last of these city yards was Rafter's Dairy on New Street in the Liberties area, which had a cobblestone yard for over 150 cows. Cowsheds were also provided, along with haylofts, an icehouse for storing milk and a 20-gallon steam-powered churn, which survived *in situ* to the late 1980s.[34]

(3) Water-Powered Grain Mills

Large numbers of small water-powered grain mills operated throughout Ireland during the eighteenth and nineteenth centuries and, in some instances, well into the twentieth century. In essence, these were vernacular structures, which were created to serve the needs of rural communities, but in terms of their technology and *modus operandi*, they were often a throwback to the later medieval period. As late as the 1840s, the vast majority of country mills in County Cavan had only one pair of millstones, a pattern largely discernible in contemporary western and midland Irish counties such as Offaly, Leitrim, Longford, Galway, Mayo and Sligo. Even in key grain-producing counties like Down, a high proportion of the rural mills in this period had a single set of millstones. At Mullycovet, County Fermanagh, a fine example of such a mill, along with parts of its original 8½ ft (2.59 m) diameter wooden cog and rung gearing (see Chapter 1), was excavated and subsequently restored to working order.[35] Malachy Canning's mill at Gorvagh, County Leitrim, restored in the 1970s, also has a single set of millstones, and had wooden gearing as late as 1917.[36]

In a number of regions, the medieval custom of *multure* (Latin, *multura*), or 'suit to the mill', whereby tenants on an estate were legally compelled to bring all their cereals to the lord's mill to be ground, continued well into the eighteenth century. Under this system, the miller charged a toll for this service (usually ¹⁄₁₆ or ¹⁄₂₀ of the meal or flour ground in the mill), and effectively the private ownership of water mills or rotary querns was outlawed. Eighteenth-century tenants of the Abercorn estates in County Tyrone and on the Downshire states in County Down, for example, were required to respect this custom, while Abercorn tenants were also obliged to provide labour service for scouring the millponds and races, in much the same way as manorial tenants were also under a similar obligation at Coole and Britway, in County Cork, in 1365.[37]

The extremely limited productive capacity of these rural mills can be inferred from their small water-wheels (usually 12–13 ft, 3.65–3.96 m in diameter), the absence of cleaning and dressing machinery for meal and flour, and the number of millstones: a single set early in the nineteenth century but increasing to two or even three pairs later on. Wooden gearing was also the norm until the early decades of the nineteenth century, after which the introduction of cast-iron gearing enabled a second pair of stones to be powered by a single water-wheel (figure 7.6 and 7.7). The millhouse was generally a simple, two-storey building (figure 7.8) which, despite the

7.6 *Undershot corn mill at Kells, County Kilkenny. Originally this would have powered a single set of millstones.*

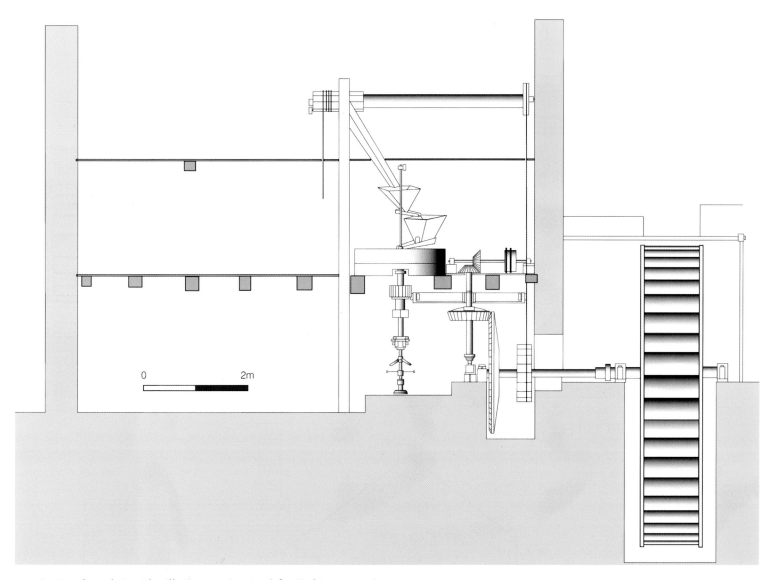

0   2m

7.7 *Section through Straid mill, County Antrim (after Robinson 2000).*

threat of rodent infestation, was still commonly roofed with thatch in the first half of the nineteenth century. At first-floor level (the *stone floor*), the millstones were housed in a wooden tun, above which was suspended a timber *hopper*, an automatic grain feed device from which a continuous trickle of grain was fed into the *eye* or opening of the upper, rotating millstone (figure 7.9). The lower millstone, or *bedstone*, was always stationary, and through its central perforation, the main drive shaft extended to connect with a steel cross-shaped power take-off device called a *rynd* bar. This latter fitted into sockets cut into the lower face of upper millstone (or *runnerstone*), and by this means set it in motion. However, the movement of the rynd bar was also communicated to a wooden chute (the *shoe*), attached to the base of the hopper, which was agitated by a device connected to the upper face of the rynd, called a *damsel*. Thus, when the mill was in motion, the rotating damsel touched the shoe, and by this means created a constant feed from the hopper to the millstones.

The roof of the mill was invariably an open, floored space which served as loft storage for grain, and was

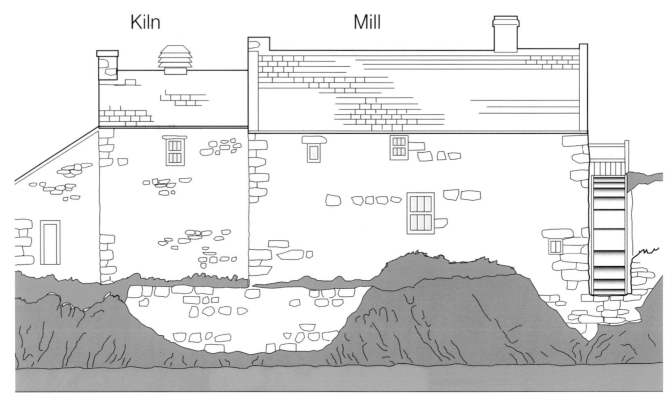

Kiln   Mill

HARBOUR ELEVATION

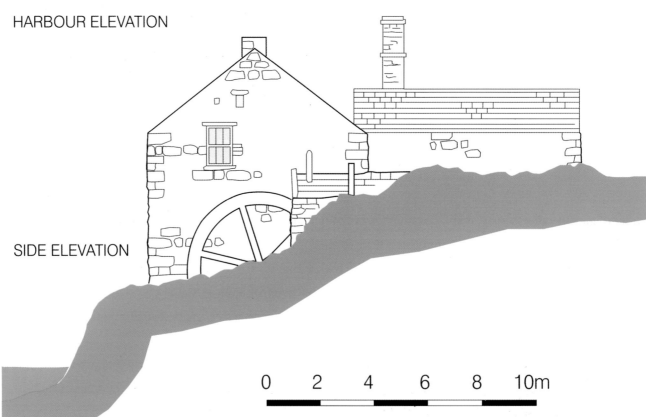

SIDE ELEVATION

0   2   4   6   8   10m

7.8 *Annalong mill, County Down a two-storey mill with attached drying kiln (after McCutcheon 1980), restored to working order by Newry and Mourne District Council in the early 1980s.*

7.9 *Interior of Castle Ward estate mill, showing gearing and two sets of millstones (left);* **7.10** *Restored winnowing fan in Castle Ward estate mill (right).*

later provided with a sack pulley, powered by a further drive from the water-wheel, as at Browne's Mills and the Garrylough mill in County Wexford.[38] The lower floor, however, in addition to housing the main mill gearing, was also used for weighing and bagging the flour or meal. Spur gearing enabled two millstone sets to be activated by a great spur wheel (which replaced the pinion in the traditional mill drive), and this wheel meshed with two or three smaller *stone nuts*, or cast-iron pinion wheels, each of which drove a single pair of stones. The earliest surviving example of this type of arrangement, dating to the late 1820s, is at the Dyan mill, County Tyrone. The introduction of a second set of stones effectively doubled the grinding capacity of a mill, where one pair of millstones could now be used for *shelling*, a process in which the oats or wheat, after cleaning and drying, were first passed through a pair of *shellers* or *shelling stones*, and set at a distance equivalent to the width of one grain apart, to remove the husks. In contemporary nineteenth-century accounts, these are commonly referred to as 'Irish' stones, being generally cut from conglomerate sandstone, but without the elaborately dressed working surfaces of grinding stones.

Shelling stones were usually manufactured in sizes of 3 ft 6 in- 5 ft (1.16 –1.52 m) in diameter. The *groats* or cereal berries and the husks were then passed through a sieve to remove dust, and the husks (*shells*) were then blown off by a mechanical winnowing fan (figure 7.10). From the 1850s onwards, mechanical bucket elevators were employed to lift the shelled oats to the upper mill floor that housed the grinding stones and, having passed through these, the resultant meal was then dressed with mechanically agitated sieves and fans to produce oatmeal.[39] Throughout the nineteenth century, *French* or *French burr* stones were extensively used for grinding wheaten flour in Ireland. The stone itself, which is quartz-like and had superior grinding surfaces, was quarried at La Ferte-sous-Jouarre and Bergerac near Paris. The millstones produced from it are called *composite* stones, as the stones themselves are normally manufactured from dressed blocks of the stone set in plaster within an iron hoop, in sizes up to 5 ft (1.52 m) in diameter. Unlike the grinding surfaces of shelling stones, these were

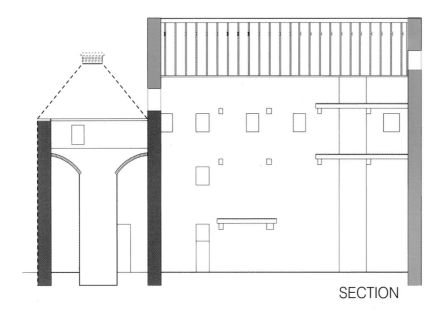

SECTION

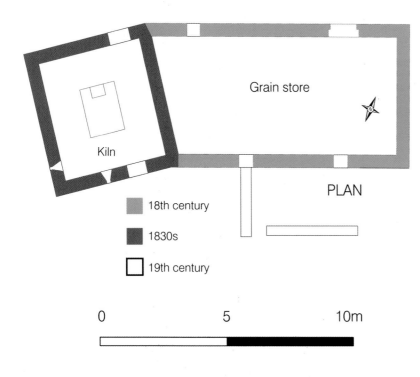

Grain store

Kiln

PLAN

■ 18th century

■ 1830s

□ 19th century

0   5   10m

dressed with diagonal *lands* and *furrows*, which creat-ed a scissor-like action for cutting open the cereal berries. All the available evidence suggests that French burr stones were either imported directly into Ireland from France or via English millstone manufactories such as Kay and Hilton of Liverpool.[40]

We have already alluded to the kiln drying of grain before milling, an essential practice in the relatively damp climate of Ireland, where any home-produced grain had to be kiln-dried to reduce its moisture content to facilitate milling. This was particularly important where oats was concerned, as the removal of the husks became more difficult if they were not rendered sufficiently brittle by kiln drying. In the western half of the country, traditional keyhole kilns, which have clear, later medieval antecedents, contin-ued in use into the early twentieth century, in associa-tion with horizontal-wheeled mills.[41] However, with the advent of merchant milling in Ireland in the 1760s (see Chapter 9), a more advanced variety of kiln, generally known as the flat-headed kiln, began to be adopted in Ireland by rural millers. In the *flat-headed kiln*, the miller had, at once, increased capacity and better control over the kilning process. A central furnace with a fire grate replaced the long stone-lined flue of the keyhole kiln, and the heat was now directed upwards to a drying floor, consisting of either perfo-rated metal plates or ceramic 'Worcester' kiln tiles, via a stone or brick vault.[42] In most cases, the kiln would have been built up against one wall of the mill building (or as at Ballysodare, County Sligo, figure 7.11), against an adjacent grain store, with access to the stone floor via a first-floor doorway, although in windmills (as, for example, at Tagunnan, County Wexford), the kiln was invariably an independent structure.[43] Later nineteenth-century kilns were equipped with pyramidal hoods

7.11 *Kilnhouse and grainstore, Ballysodare, County Sligo.*

capped with ridge ventilators, a practice widely adopted for malting kilns (see Chapter 9). The valuation surveys of the 1840s also occasionally refer to 'kilnsman's houses', as at Mullroddan, County Tyrone, which may have involved some form of temporary accommodation for an employee hired specifically for tending the kiln night and day.[44]

In many areas, turf was used as fuel for the kiln furnace, but in eastern counties, both culm and anthracite were available.[45] For the most part, however, the capacity of the kiln

7.12 *Nineteenth-century kiln house at Castle Ward estate, County Down.*

floor was limited, although some examples, as at Mallardstown, near Callan, County Kilkenny, could process up to 30 barrels of oats at a go, using culm, within a period of 36 hours.[46] Well preserved examples of flat-headed kilns in Ireland have become increasingly rare, but good examples with Worcester tile drying floors can still be seen at Browne's Mills, near Old Ross (figure 7.12), and at Garrylough Mill, both in County Wexford.[47] Kilns with pierced iron drying floors, are also known, and examples have been restored in the late 1990s at Craanford Mill, near Gorey, County Wexford, Newmills, County Donegal, and at Mullycovet Mill, County Fermanagh.

From the middle of the nineteenth century onwards, rural mills tended to increase in size (usually vertically by the addition of an extra storey) and to have mechanically driven bucket elevators for moving grain and meal from one location within the mill to another, as at Tuam mills, County Galway, Straid Mills, County Antrim, Annalong, County Down, and Garrylough, County Wexford.[48] By this period, two sets of millstones had become the norm, and mills with a single pair tended only to survive in relatively isolated areas. Nonetheless, mills with two to three pairs of stones were increasingly forced to compete with water- and steam-powered mills in the larger country towns, and by the turn of the twentieth century, the traditional rural watermill was becoming rarer. The important services and local knowledge of individual grain crops, garnered by the miller over a long period of time, were gradually forgotten. Only he knew how long a particular farmer's grain should be kept in the kiln, based on his knowledge of the local landscape and the types of climatic variation generally experienced within that locality. And so the country miller's craft tended also to die off with the closure of local mills. Millers' and mill managers' houses are also a common survival throughout the Irish countryside, as at Kilroe, County Galway, and Glanmire mills, County Cork, and are often substantial two- and three-storey dwellings.

(4) The Fishing Industry

From the medieval period onwards, both Irish and foreign fishing fleets had enjoyed the unrivalled bounty of Ireland's unique location, relative to the rich fishing grounds of the North East Atlantic and the Irish sea. On the one hand, proximity of the narrow continental shelf off the east coast required only a short journey for Irish fishing vessels to catch deep-water species such as ling and hake while, on the other, fish that tended to feed in the shallower coastal waters, like cod and haddock, could also be caught off the Irish coast. Two principal varieties of fish were exploited by Irish fishermen: *demersal*, or bottom-feeding fish (cod, hake, haddock and the white and flat fishes) and *pelagic*, or surface swimming and shoal-forming fish, such as herring and mackerel. The advantage of the former variety was that the species of fish involved tended to remain in the same general area even when spawning, and thus provided a localised resource. Pelagic fish, on the other hand, formed enormous shoals in the same general areas off the Irish coast, at specific times, thus facilitating commercially important catches by Irish and foreign fleets.[49]

Prior to the second half of the eighteenth century, Ireland's fisheries were developed with private capital, by magnates such as Richard Boyle, the earl of Cork (who developed the south Munster fisheries in the 1620s), the earl of Stafford on the Mayo coast and Sir William Petty, who set up fisheries in Kenmare Bay and Dursey Island.[50] The remains of seventeenth-century fish *palaces*, in which pilchards were pressed and cured, have survived on the west Cork coast at locations such as Sherkin Island.[51] Fish palaces, indeed, continued to operate well into the eighteenth century, Bishop Pococke of Ossory noting the existence of 'places for curing fish, commonly call'd fish palaces' in 1758.[52] While at Scilly Point near Kinsale, County Cork, 'a compleat Fishing-palace with Linnys and sheds for pressing fish' was advertised for sale in 1761.[53] Private schemes to develop fisheries in Ireland in the eighteenth century were invariably unsuccessful. In the 1780s, William Burton Conyngham began to develop sections of his estate in County Donegal as a first step in the establishment of a north west fishery. The local island of Inismacadurn was renamed Rutland Island, and in the period 1785-7, it was provided with docks and quays, and later with a small shipyard, workers' housing, a salthouse and storehouses. By 1787, some £40,000 had been spent on this venture, an ambitious but costly failure.[54] Substantial remains of the settlement survive, including some of the storehouses, the quays and some two-storey workers' housing.

Nonetheless, by the early eighteenth century, the Irish fishing industry was already in a serious decline, and it was not until 1763 that the Irish parliament was prepared to offer a subsidy on fish exports. The RDS also provided assistance in 1766 by offering premiums for the creation of coastal fisheries, but by 1810, there were still a mere 21 fish curing stations on the entire island, and in 1831, all government bounties for the industry were abandoned.[55] No government aid for the industry became available again until the 1890s, and in the meantime, the absence of proper port facilities provided no encouragement for Irish fishermen to invest in larger vessels. Moreover, fishing remained a part-time occupation which generated only a small number of shore jobs. In the period 1861-5, almost 46,000 men operated some 10,713 fishing craft; between 1876 and 1890, the number of fishermen had decreased by more than half.[56]

Improved harbour facilities and increased capitalisation within the industry were seriously lacking, and again progress throughout most of the century was slow. In the 1880s, Kilkeel harbour was provided with a new wharf, a jetty and boat building and maintenance facilities, while its basin was also deepened to accommodate the expansion of the herring fishery.[57] Around the same period, Kinsale, County Cork, one of the most important

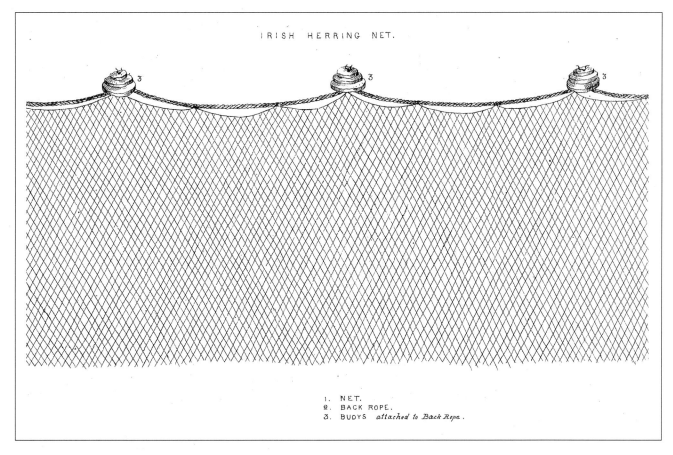

IRISH HERRING NET.

1. NET.
2. BACK ROPE.
3. BUOYS *attached to Back Rope.*

7.13 *Drift net as shown by W. Brabazon in* The deep sea and coast fisheries of Ireland with suggestions for the working of a fishing company. (Dublin 1848).

centres of the Irish spring mackerel fishery in 1870 (but which had no proper quays in the 1870s), became equipped with a boat building yard, along with a net factory later in the same decade, which employed machinery manufactured in the Isle of Man.[58]

Herring and mackerel were both caught in drift nets, the former being a summer industry on the east coast, the latter a spring activity on the south coast. Drift nets are suspended from floats and 'drift' below the surface to catch herring and mackerel; those used for mackerel, however, were made from a coarser and bigger mesh (figure 7.13).[59] By the end of the nineteenth century, nets could be anything from a mile to one and a half miles long, and were, in this period, beginning to be hauled in by steam capstans. Mackerel arrived off the south coast twice a year, the first season commencing in the spring around 17 March, but ending before the April storms. But whereas the spring mackerel season generally involved larger fishing vessels, that conducted in the autumn, because of the tendency of the shoals to lie in nearer to the shore, was carried out in rowing boats using *seine* nets.[60] In its essentials, seine netting involved two boats, which were used to skilfully manipulate a purse-like net around a shoal of fish. On the south coast, seine nets were up to 120 yards long and 30 ft deep, manufactured from small-mesh cotton, and once the fish were encircled, the net, which could weigh up to one ton when wet, could be closed shut by pulling a rope.[61] By this means, enormous amounts of fish could be taken at one

7.14 *West cove pier, County Kerry, in 1902.*

time, but by September these were replaced by gill (i.e., mesh) nets, which could be either drifted or anchored out at dusk.[62] During the mid-nineteenth century, a new form of seine netting was developed in Denmark for the North Sea fishing grounds, which began to be adopted in the Irish fisheries in the early years of the twentieth century. Danish seine nets were a cheap and effective means of catching white fish, and are first officially recorded in Irish waters as being carried by the experimental motor vessel, *Ovoca*, in 1907.[63]

Technological change in the types of fishing craft used in the Irish fishing grounds, given the general under-developed nature of the industry, was inevitably slow. In the late 1820s, the main Irish fishing vessel associated with the Kinsale grounds was the traditional *hooker*, a deckless boat with one forward mast for a mainsail. Seldom would such craft exceed 20 tons burthen, but from the early 1830s onwards, these were expected to compete with a new type of vessel developed in the Isle of Man, as a response to the introduction of Cornish *luggers*. Indeed, the lugger, which was not only faster, but could also sail closer to the wind, had proved to be a serious competitor in the Irish fishing grounds. The Manx fishing boat, although called a lugger by Irish and Isle of Man fishermen, was essentially a cross between a single-masted *smack* and the two-masted Cornish lugger, and became the fishing vessel of choice among both Irish and Manx herring fishermen by the 1860s.[64] The latter craft were, in turn, replaced by Cornish luggers between 1869 and the mid-1890s. This was as a direct result of the development of the Kinsale mackerel fishery by Robert Cronin of the Isle of Man, from 1862 onwards, initially using Manx luggers.[65] However, the arrival of Cornish luggers to fish off Kinsale was sufficient to demonstrate their manifest superiority over other fishing vessels of the period. As mackerel were caught up to 70 miles off the coast – journeys of only 12-25 miles were required to reach the herring grounds – and as this species of fish tend to deteriorate rapidly, it was essential that the catch was landed without delay to fetch a good market price. The success of the Cornish boats in this regard led to the adoption of the lugger by Irish fishermen on the south coast, while in the period 1870-96, pre-existing fishing vessel types in the Annalong and Kilkeel area of County Down were replaced by Cornish luggers and Manx boats based on this design.[66]

Yet despite the relative importance of the Irish sea fisheries, steam-powered craft were not generally adopted. By 1889, there were only three steam trawlers and five steam yachts operating in Ireland's commercial fisheries. Poor infrastructural development for sea-going fishing craft was a common problem throughout Irish ports (figure 7.14), a circumstance exacerbated by the small domestic market for fish within Ireland. Moreover, Ireland's herring fisheries, which had the potential for large-scale investment, were in the depths of a depression in the 1880s.[67]

Although drift netting was the principal means of catching fish off the coast of Ireland, trawling for bottom feeding fish had also been reasonably common from the eighteenth century onwards. Up to the 1860s, the pole trawl, which consisted of a bay and wings, distended by poles projecting from either side of a traditional fishing vessel, such as a hooker (a spread of up to 50 ft or 15.24 m on a large craft), was the main type of trawler gear employed in Irish waters. However, after 1860, otter boards, which enabled a much wider spread to the net, were introduced. The main trawling area centred on the relatively sheltered area of the Irish Sea, and the trawlers operated out of the ports of Dublin, Kingstown, County Down and Dingle. Towards the end of the nineteenth century, steam trawlers were brought into service all year round to meet the increased demand for fresh fish.[68]

After capture, the fish had to be processed as quickly as conditions allowed, either by being immediately dispatched in ice to a fresh fish market, or by *curing* in salt. From 1869 onwards, steamers were used to transport mackerel packed in ice (nearly all of which was imported from Norway) to English ports such as Milford Haven, from which they were distributed inland by rail. Curing was generally carried out on tables set on the open quayside by young women, a procedure in which the fish was split, gutted and thoroughly washed in fresh water. This latter process was essential, as all the blood had to be completely washed out or the fish would quickly decay. The availability of fresh water, indeed, was an important consideration in the siting of a curing station. Both sides of the fish were then rubbed in salt, after which it was laid in a barrel and covered with a pickle consisting of salt and water.[69]

Technological considerations aside, the training of young fishermen and experimental enquiry into improved practices received little attention in Ireland until the closing decades of the nineteenth century. Training schools were set up at Killybegs, County Donegal, and Baltimore, County Cork, but of these only the latter survived for any appreciable time. The Industrial Training School at Baltimore was established under the auspices of Baroness Burdett Coutts (1814-1906), who set up a fund in 1880 that eventually led to the opening of fishing school in 1887, managed by Fr Charles Davis. Baltimore had by this period succeeded Kinsale as the main fishing port on the Cork coast, after the shoals of fish began to concentrate closer to Baltimore, which became more convenient for landing the catches. In 1887, a survey by the fisheries inspectorate found that fish curing in Ireland had experienced no appreciable development, a need to which the Baltimore training school was able immediately to respond by the construction of a purpose-built curing house for its students.[70] The development of the Baltimore fishing industry was further boosted in 1893 with the opening of an extension line of the Cork, Bandon and South Coast Railway to Baltimore, funded under the Light Railways Act of 1889.[71] The establishment of the Baltimore industrial school also corresponded with the Royal Dublin Society-sponsored surveys of Ireland's fishing grounds of the 1890s. These latter were carried out by the steam yachts *Fingal* (1890) and *Harlequin* (1891), and were later followed by the setting up of a marine research laboratory. The Fisheries Branch of the Department of Agriculture and Technical Instruction also contributed to the development of Ireland's fisheries by providing the first fisheries protection vessel, *Helga* (figure 7.15).[72]

7.15 *The* Helga *in 1902.*

8

Textiles

By the end of the seventeenth century, the province of Ulster was already beginning to become the centre of a burgeoning Irish linen trade, where a combination of factors absent from the rest of the island were to lay the foundations of a proto-industrial economy. The phenomenal eighteenth-century growth of the Irish industry, however, relied heavily on the increasing demand from England for relatively inexpensive linen. Ulster weavers enjoyed cheaper living conditions and a tariff-free relationship with their principal market in England, and were, in consequence, able to produce plain linens much more cheaply than their competitors. Furthermore, landlords in Ulster (who were later followed by their counterparts in Connacht and Munster) were also prepared to provide incentives for their tenants to accrue additional income from linen manufacture. In 1711, the parliaments in both London and Dublin provided an additional fillip to the Irish linen industry by establishing the Irish Linen Board, which enjoyed some success in fostering the creation of the industry outside Ulster. Up to its demise in 1828, the Irish Linen Board provided grants for the setting up of bleach greens and for the dissemination of new technology and processes throughout Ireland.[1] Both flax and wool were, until the second half of the nineteenth century, almost wholly home-produced items. The vast majority of the flax acreage grown in Ireland in 1814 was in Ulster (72,263), with only just under 7,000 acres in Munster, over half of which was grown in County Cork. By 1863, the total acreage was 251,000, but by 1910 this had declined to just 45,000 acres, by which time almost 85 per cent of the flax used in the Irish linen industry was now imported from Russia, Holland and Belgium.[2] The greater bulk of Ireland's wool, on the other hand, came from Connacht, and was gradually replaced by imported New Zealand and Australian wool from the second half of the nineteenth century onwards.

The quantity of Irish linen exported grew from 0.3 million yards of cloth in 1700 to 18.7 million yards in 1780, and the success of the Ulster linen industry encouraged landlords in north Connacht and south Munster

8.1 *Distribution of flax scutching mills in Ireland in 1860 (after Smyth 1988).*

Scutch mills

0 80km

to invest in the establishment of linen manufacture. County Cork landlords such as Sir Richard Cox at Dunmanway (1735) and Thomas Adderley at Inishannon, and the County Galway landlord, Robert French, of Monivea, were already involved in such enterprises in the first half of the eighteenth century. Thomas Adderley, indeed, encouraged Ulster weavers to settle at Inishannon and provided workers' housing. The growth of the Cork industry was such that landlord-sponsored textile villages were already in existence at Blarney, Doneraile, Clonakilty, Macroom and at other locations before the 1770s. However, such activity outside Ulster remained heavily reliant on northern personnel, and in the aftermath of the Napoleonic Wars, the industry in Cork and

Drogheda was all but wiped out. The development of the Irish linen industry towards the end of the eighteenth century was temporarily arrested by the rise of the cotton industry, but the latter's demise in the 1820s allowed linen to take advantage of the new techniques pioneered in cotton mills. The industry was revived in the south during the 1850s, and by the 1860s, the northern mills were enjoying an expansionary period during which Irish linen temporarily replaced cottons, whose manufacture was interrupted by the American Civil War. By 1873, the Ulster linen industry was the largest in the world, but was already in decline. This latter trend continued after the First World War, when outside Ulster there was only one spinning mill in operation, at Millfield near Cork in the 1920s.

During the Anglo-Norman period, large flocks of sheep were established in Ireland and raw wool began to be exported to Flanders for processing, and an export trade in Irish woollen cloth followed soon after. From its medieval origins, the domestic manufacture of woollen cloth, where the yarn was spun on a traditional spinning wheel by the women of the household and woven on a hand loom by the man of the house, spread throughout Ireland. At the turn of the twentieth century, home-spun cloth was still being made from the wool of mountain sheep in Counties Donegal, Mayo, Galway and Kerry. By the mid-1770s, as Arthur Young noted, the carding and combing of half of the Irish wool production was carried out in County Cork, but the growth of Ireland's woollen industry was ultimately to be stymied by discriminating English legislation and was not to attain the level of industrial concentration experienced by the Ulster linen industry.[3] At the end of the nineteenth century, the province of Munster contained the greater part of the Irish woollen industry. In 1889, there were 82 woollen mills in Ireland, 38 of which were in Munster; 25 of these were in County Cork.

The early mechanisation of Ireland's textile industries is broadly analogous to that of Great Britain, from which it drew both its technical expertise and technology. Likewise, many of the industrial processes involved in the manufacture of textiles were shared between the various industries, as was also, to a certain extent, the layout of factory premises. The processes involved in the manufacture of the various types of cloth can be grouped together into four stages: preparation, spinning, weaving and finishing. Each of the latter will now be considered in relation to Ireland's linen, wool and cotton industries, before moving on to an outline of the development of the multi-storey textile mill in Ireland.

(1) Preparing the fibres for spinning

In the manufacture of woollen, linen and cotton cloth, the raw fibres required some processing preparatory to spinning. After harvesting, flax was soaked in water for about two weeks in *retting dams* or *flax ponds*, a process which loosened the useful part of the plant from the *shous*, the waste or non-usable portion. The retted flax was then removed by hand using a *scutching blade* and later, from the eighteenth century onwards, in water-powered *scutching mills*, where the flax fibre was separated from the shous by the action of rapidly rotating wooden scutching blades.[4] The water-powered flax-scutching mill was already widely distributed in the Ulster counties by the end of the eighteenth century (figure 8.1). In 1795, the Linen Board introduced a premium of £300

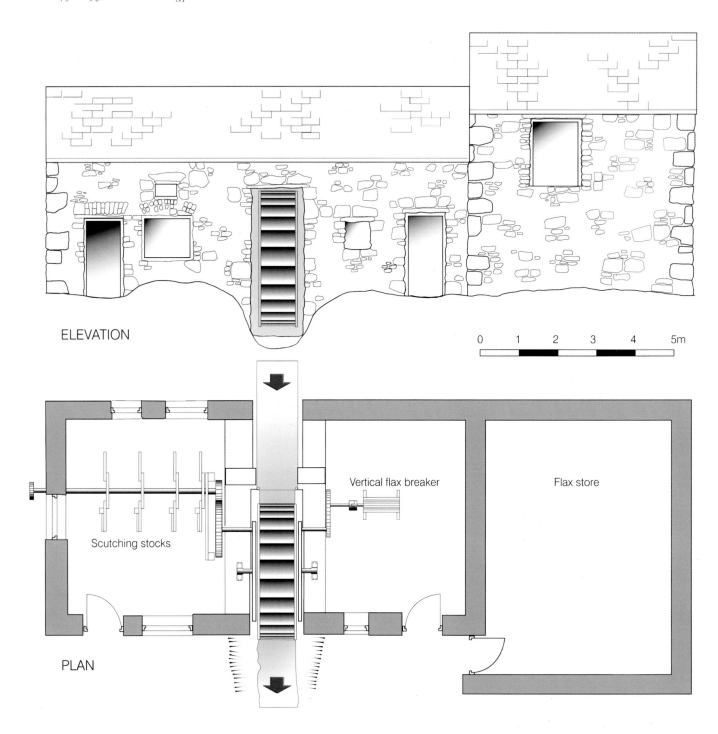

ELEVATION

PLAN

Scutching stocks

Vertical flax breaker

Flax store

0 1 2 3 4 5m

8.2 *Elevation and plan of scutch mill at Grillagh Bridge, near Upperlands, County Derry (after McCutcheon 1980).*

towards the construction of scutch mills, and by the 1830s, after its dissolution, some 500 scutching mills were in existence in the north-eastern counties of Ulster, increasing to 700 in 1852. Outside Ulster, however, scutching mills were relatively uncommon. In County Cork, one of the main flax growing areas in the south, there were only four scutching mills within the county – half of the total for the entire province of Munster in 1860.[5] At Moorefields, County Wexford, a scutching mill with a 6 ft (1.82 m) diameter water-wheel was built as early as about 1730, but in a county with no real linen tradition, it was certainly a distant memory by the middle of the nineteenth century.[6] The scutching mill in Ireland, therefore, was largely an Ulster phenomenon.

Flax scutching in Ulster was generally undertaken in the countryside. The scutched flax, which made up approximately 10 per cent of the entire plant, could, when divested of its waste, be transported more economically to the spinning mill. However, in the south of Ireland, the scarcity of scutch mills and the absence of proper flax markets effectively stymied attempts to encourage flax growing in the 1850s, and not until the 1860s was this situation partially rectified. Indeed, at the Cork Spinning and Weaving Co. Ltd. spinning mill at Millfield, near Cork, which relied mostly on imported flax, scutching was undertaken at the mill where the scutching stocks were powered by the mill's steam engine. Even when water-powered scutch mills were constructed in rural areas of County Cork, the skills involved were normally imported from Ulster. In 1848, for example, George Robinson engaged Belfast workmen to supervise the construction of his flax-scutching mill at Drimoleague, while in 1853, Edward Smyth of Newry built a scutching mill, powered by a water turbine, near Ballineen.[7]

In a typical Ulster scutching mill, a breastshot water-wheel powered break rollers and the scutching blades (figure 8.2). The outer skin of the plant was first broken in order that it could be stripped off in the scutching process. Edge runner stones, turned in a circle by a horse, were originally used in north-east Ulster to break the outer skin – a practice which survived until early in the twentieth century in Counties Donegal, Tyrone and Derry.[8] One such stone 'for rolling flax', 4 ft 6 in (1.37 m) in diameter and 11 ins thick (c. 0.28 m), was recorded by the Valuation Surveyors in the townland of Tamlaght in the late 1840s.[9] At Sion Mills, County Tyrone, a good surviving example of such a stone has been mounted as an external exhibit. Of course, these stones were too large to be used within early scutching mills, but in the 1850s, MacAdam brothers foundry of Belfast developed a mechanical flax breaker in which the flax stems were broken by fluted rollers. The area between each set of scutching blades was divided, by wooden partitions, into *berths*, the number of which varied from four upwards. A scutching mill from Gorticashel Upper, near Gortin, County Tyrone, has been removed to the Ulster Folk and Transport Museum at Cultra, while a combined corn and flax scutching mill has been restored to working order at Silcock's Mills, County Down, and at Newmills, County Donegal.

Native Irish wool was only suitable for items such as blankets and coarser woollen cloths, and from the second half of the nineteenth century, there was an increasing reliance on Australian and New Zealand raw wool, from which finer cloths were manufactured. Raw wool was first carefully sorted, after which it was washed to remove grease and dirt. The early stages of the preparation of cotton involved the blending of a number of raw bales to ensure consistency in the quality of the yarn, while it was also necessary to disentangle it before cleaning.[10] Both wool and cotton fibres then had to be *willeyed*, initially by hand and later on willeying machines, which further beat and separated the fibres, gently teasing them out preparatory to carding. However, if a patterned woollen cloth was required, the next preparatory stage after washing involved the dying of the wool, a practice called *stock-dying*. For woollen cloth and cotton, the final preparatory stage involved the creation of slivers, in which the fibres were straightened out. The latter process had originally been carried out by hand, but from the 1770s onwards, carding machines, in which the fibres were teased out by wire rollers to form loose threads

8.3 *Carding machinery at New Mills, County Cork.*

or *slivers* suitable for spinning, were generally available (figure 8.3).[11] Nicholas Grimshaw of Lancashire, who had originally established a colour printing works for cotton, linen and calico near Belfast by 1756, appears to have introduced a water-driven carding machine from the Lancashire area to Greencastle by the late 1770s. In 1778, Robert Joy of Belfast was conducting experiments with Grimshaw's carder.[12]

In the closing decades of the eighteenth century, the spread of new machinery used in the preparation of textile fibres continued apace. In 1795, Thomas Kemp in Cork was claiming that he was the first Irish manufacturer to introduce 'woollen machinery into this country', using, amongst other innovations, a *scribbler* (a form of carder employed in the woollen industry), a carding machine and a 35 spindle *slubbing billy* (a machine used in the preparatory stages of woollen cloth, to produce semi-spun slivers for use on jennies), all of which was actuated by horse machinery. Some Dublin woollen manufacturers, indeed, had already begun to use carding machinery from *c.* 1793 onwards.[13]

There are two basic types of cloth manufactured from wool, *woollen* cloth and *worsted* cloth, the home-produced wool of Ireland being essentially of the latter type.[14] Woollen cloth was manufactured with short fibre or short staple wool, the fibres of which had to be carded prior to spinning. Worsted cloth manufacture, on the other hand, involved the use of long staple wool, which had to separated from the short staple wool in a process called *combing*. In this latter process, heated combs were used to form slivers from the long woollen fibres, which were wound into a ball prior to being drawn and spun. Combing, however, was not successfully mechanised until the 1840s. Flax also involved long (*line*) and short (*tow*) fibres, each of which also required separate treatments prior to spinning. Tow was carded, but line had to be hackled, that is, drawn through combs, first by machine and then by hand (a highly skilled process) in a sorting shop. The tow was spun into coarser yarns, the line being reserved for finer ones.[15]

(2) Spinning

In its essentials, spinning involves a continuous process in which the fibres were drawn out and then twisted together to give strength to the finished yarn. Throughout the eighteenth century, and well into the nineteenth, the treadle-operated spinning wheel was used to spin linen, woollen and cotton yarn. By about 1800, most of the spinning wheels used in Ireland employed a flyer, by means of which the two formerly separate processes of spinning (draft and twist) and the winding on to the bobbin could now be undertaken simultaneously.[16]

8.4 *Spinning Jenny, from Baines 1835. This was the first multi-spindle spinning machine, first used in Ireland in the 1770s.*

However, while this was adequate for the needs of a small-scale domestic industry, the expansion in textile production required faster methods, which resulted in the development of multi-spindle devices.

The earliest machine successfully to use more than one spindle was James Hargreaves' *spinning jenny* of c. 1767, which was initially developed for speeding up the manufacture of cotton yarn (figure 8.4). This latter was manually operated, but in 1769, Richard Arkwright patented his water frame (operated on the principle of roller drawing, where four pairs of rollers, all of equal diameter, were used to draw out cotton fibres). The water frame could, in fact, be powered by animals or water, but its action was initially unsuited to the spinning of woollen yarn. From the 1780s onwards, however, it became possible to mechanically spin woollen worsteds. Samuel Crompton's *mule* – so-called because it combined the essentials of the jenny and the water frame – was revealed to the Lancashire cotton industry in 1779. Beginning initially with the capacity to spin 48 yarns, by the end of the century, these machines could spin up to 150, and by the early 1800s could accommodate 400 spindles. On Crompton's mule, the drafting rollers were emplaced on a stationary frame, but the revolving spindles were set on a moving carriage, which drew out the yarn as the twist was being imparted to it. In the 1820s, Richard Roberts patented a completely automatic self-acting mule, which could be powered by water or steam. Nonetheless, its operation still required skilled personnel as its principal elements could all be independently adjusted to produce different varieties of yarn. The throstle frame, which was essentially an improved version of the water frame, but which worked at a faster speed, was used in the Irish cotton spinning mills in the 1820s and was a one-time rival to the mule, but while the mule continued to be employed in the Irish woollen industry well into the twentieth century, the throstle was largely obsolete by the 1880s.

In Ireland, spinning jennies were first used on an experimental basis in a Belfast workhouse in 1777, and by the 1780s they were becoming widely employed in the recently established Dublin industry. The Irish Linen Board also grant-aided the introduction of spinning jennies as a fillip to the expanding Irish cotton industry.[17] In 1781, the Sadlier brothers, the largest cotton manufacturers in the south of Ireland, installed carding machinery and jennies (with a total of 1,606 spindles in 1783) in a warehouse at Lawton's Quay in Cork, while Baron Hamilton set up jenny shops at Balbriggan in south County Dublin around 1782.[18] The demand for spinning machinery in Ireland was such that in the period 1781-84, a former cabinet maker called James Kerchoffer established a machine-making factory in Dublin which supplied some 361 spinning jennies to Irish cotton manufacturers.[19] Indeed, a Yorkshire machine maker, based in Lisburn, was supplying cotton mills in the Belfast area some time before 1812, although by the 1820s, Irish cotton mill owners, north and south, were being supplied by Manchester machine makers.[20] During the 1780s and 1790s, the spread of textile spinning machinery in the Irish cotton and woollen industries continued: in Belfast, the number of spinning jennies rose from 25 in 1782 to 229 in 1791, whilst by the 1790s, these were quite common in the Cork woollen industry.[21]

Animal-powered cotton machinery was used by Robert Brooke at Prosperous, County Kildare, in 1782, and around the same time in a small cotton spinning mill at Enniskillen and in two Belfast manufactories.[22] In Allman's cotton mill in Bandon, County Cork, a horse wheel powered a 40-spindle slubbing billy, seven jennies (with 432 spindles) and two carding machines in 1783.[23] The first recorded cotton spinning mill in Ireland likely to have been powered by water appears to have been that of Joy, McCabe and McCracken, set up in 1778 in Belfast, which was followed by Henry Crosbie in either 1782 or 1783 (water-powered carding spinning and twisting) at Finglas near Dublin city. In 1789, James Wallace's cotton-spinning mill at Lisburn, County Antrim, was the first steam-powered textile mill in Ireland, using a 15 hp Boulton and Watt rotative engine which Wallace had imported from Scotland.[24] The steam-engine employed to drive mill machinery in a Manchester cotton mill, the Piccadilly Mill on Ashburn Street, was not at work until 1790.[25] By the first decade of the nineteenth century, Belfast had the largest concentration of steam-powered cotton mills in Ireland, with some fifteen at work in the period 1801-11.[26] The mechanisation of wool spinning was a later development, as the water frame could not be used for spinning worsted yarn until around 1784. However, in Ireland, there is little evidence to suggest that mechanised wool spinning had been introduced before the late 1790s in the Dublin area, while the first such installation in the Cork region, at Riverstown near Cork, was built some time before 1814. In 1815, the Mahony brothers brought over a specialist from the Yorkshire woollen industry to set up a steam-powered worsted factory near Cork, and by the 1820s had converted a former cotton mill at Blarney for the mechanical spinning of woollen and worsted yarns.[27] Yet water power continued to be important in the textile industry as a whole, where the size of water-wheels increased to meet the demands of new machinery and expanding output. As early as 1802, the Overton cotton mill near Bandon, County Cork had a 40 ft (12.19 m) diameter suspension water-wheel (see Chapter 1). James Murland's linen spinning mill at Annesborough, County Down, built in 1828, had two water-wheels, one 52 ft (15.84 m) in diameter, the other 50 ft (15.24 m), whilst Edmund Grimshaw's Mossley flax spinning mill, County Down had a 60 ft (18.28 m) diameter water-wheel, some 6 ft (1.82 m) wide, in *c.* 1835.[28]

The mechanisation of both woollen and flax spinning in Ireland took place around the same. Since the late 1790s, flax could now be spun by machine, thanks to the efforts of John Marshall of Leeds, and the dry spinning of flax then became a practical proposition.[29] But as the coarse yarn spun in this fashion was viewed as a future competitor with Irish yarn in the British market, the Irish Linen Board began to take steps to encourage the adoption of mechanical spinning frames in Ireland.[30] Thus, in 1796, the Board came to an agreement with W.H. Stevenson of Edinburgh for the erection of a water-powered spinning mill in Ireland. This latter scheme was not brought to fruition, but the Board did, nonetheless, arrange to have horse-powered spindles installed in the Dublin Linen Hall in 1797. By this date, however, Julius Besnard of the Douglas sailcloth manufactory, near Cork, was already in the process of building a water-powered spinning mill at Douglas and later, in 1801, he was able to persuade the Board to grant him the machinery that Stevenson had installed in Dublin.[31] From the outset, the Douglas mill experienced mechanical difficulties, but Besnard was able to commence production in 1801 by using a spinning frame built by John Drabble of Leeds (a former employee of John Marshall) and machinery based on that introduced into Ireland by Stevenson.[32] The next water-powered spinning mills was built by Samuel Crookshank at Rademon, County Down, in 1805, but, as we shall now see, water-powered flax spinning almost entirely collapsed in the wake of the Napoleonic Wars.[33]

While dry-spun linen yarn could only be used for coarse cloth, it was ideally suited to the mass-production of sailcloth. The subsequent development of the Douglas linen industry near Cork can be linked to the Napoleonic Wars, and to the increased demand for sailcloth and other goods manufactured from coarse, machine-spun yarn. The importance of its output was duly recognised and, in 1805, Lord Dundonald brought a millwright over with him to Ireland to make adjustments to the plant at Douglas and at other Irish installations. In 1806, Peter and John Besnard established a larger mill in nearby Ravensdale, with locally made machinery, which by 1809 was operating with 1,214 spindles. Barnes and Atkinson of Cork had been responsible for some of the machinery erected in the original late eighteenth-century Douglas spinning mill, shortly before 1807, and it is likely that either they or Drabble manufactured and erected the machinery for the Ravensdale mill.[34]

From around 1815 onwards, the demand for the type of linen products manufactured from dry-spun flax declined in the aftermath of the Napoleonic War. However, James Kay's process for the wet spinning of linen yarn enabled finer yarns to be produced by machinery, and brought about a decline in the domestic linen industry. In Kay's process, the flax fibre was passed through a trough of hot water, by which means the binding gums in the fibre could be dissolved, and this enabled finer yarns to be drawn off than had been possible in the dry spinning process. This was a crucial technological development for the Irish linen industry, enabling as it did the large-scale industrialisation along the lines of the cotton industry. Kay came to Dublin in 1825 to discuss the use of his patent in Ireland with the Linen Board, and following on from this, the Board sponsored experiments at Nicholson's mill at Bessbrook, County Armagh, and at Crosthwaite's mill in Dublin.

The first water-powered mills to use wet-spinning machinery were at work at Chapelizod near Dublin and Mount Caulfield near Newry, County Down, in 1826. No fewer than ten large wet spinning mills were built in Ulster by 1833; in 1838, 64 were in operation throughout Ireland. One of the best-preserved mills of the 1820s is James Murland's mill at Annesborough, near Castlewellan, County Down, which was long thought to be the earliest of its kind in Ireland.

(3) Weaving

A web of cloth consists of vertical threads called the *warp*, which are crossed over by horizontal threads called *weft*. On the traditional Irish loom, the weaver had first to *tackle* the loom by winding the warp threads around the beam roller, where the threads thus wound were closely spaced together and parallel to one another. Owing to the friction created by the loom when in operation, it was necessary for the warp threads to be more resilient than the weft, while the warp threads themselves were also held in tension on the loom frame. Arkwright's water frame was the first cotton-spinning machine capable of producing yarn which could be used for warps.[35] The warp threads were then pulled over and under a pair of *lease rods* (which kept the threads parallel), and thence through the eyes of the *heddles*, which lifted and lowered the warp threads to match the pattern of weaving. The warp threads are then pulled through the teeth of the comb called the *reed* (which served to keep the warp threads spaced evenly and in position), and were subsequently tied onto the cloth beam. The tackling or setting up of the loom was a highly skilled but time-consuming business, and could take up to a week.[36] It was also essential that the loom shop was kept cool and damp to minimise the risk of the individual threads drying out; repairs to broken threads were extremely tedious. As a further precaution against rising temperatures, the floors of the loom shop were always earthen.

In 1733, John Kay patented his *flying shuttle*, a device which speeded up weaving by enabling the weaver to propel the *shuttle*, a boat-shaped holder which carried the weft thread across the loom, by tugging a string. Using this simple, inexpensive device, a weaver could complete his task in about half the time, while the width of the cloth was no longer restricted to the distance he could actually stretch his arm across the loom to throw the shuttle. The upsurge in cloth production created an increase in the demand for yarn, which brought about the first spinning machines. The introduction of the flying shuttle into Ireland is traditionally attributed to the Moravian colony at Gracehill, near Ballymena, County Antrim, for line weaving, the innovation later being transferred to the Belfast cotton industry by Robert Joy, of the firm of Joy, McCabe and McCracken in 1788.[37] Incredibly, the flying shuttle was not used by the Donegal wool weavers until the 1880s.[38]

At the outset, the Irish cotton weaver, unlike the linen weaver who was nominally independent, was an employee of the merchant who provided him with machine spun yarn. In the north-east of the country, by around 1840, the cotton hand loom weavers occupied small cottages, about 17 to 24 ft (5.18-7.31 m) long, by 13-15 ft (3.96-4.57 m) wide. These were divided, very simply, into two rooms, one serving as a kitchen and the other as a loom shop. The majority of these dwellings had mud walls, but some were stone walled; all had mud floors (figure 8.5). Fenestration was minimal, as these were essentially poor people, but the exclusion of direct sunlight was also good for the yarn. The framework of the individual looms was supported by wooden posts driven into the earthen floor. A complete loom, which would be made by local specialist carpenters (reed making was also regarded as a specialised task), could cost between £2 and £3 by 1840, by which period the shop would have been lit artificially using oil lamps and large tin reflectors suspended on the loom.[39] In parts of north Armagh and west Down, extensions were even added to houses to accommodate looms. During the closing decades of the eighteenth century, traditional two-bay houses had a third bay added in which three to four looms would have been set up. The additional space required to accommodate these meant that the extension had to be built wider than the original house. But when new houses were built in the late eighteenth and early nineteenth century, however, the unit width of 17 ft (5.18 m) – the extent to which the new bays added to existing houses were widened to accommodate extra looms – became widely adopted.[40]

The provision of houses for weavers in the early linen villages was almost a standard practice, as seems also to have been the case in settlements established for cotton manufacture in the 1780s. In 1776, Arthur Young noted that at Blarney, near Cork, in the linen village established by Sir John Jefferies, 25 houses for weavers' families, with four looms in each, had been provided by Jefferies.[41] In Cork, the Sadlier brothers either built or rented out houses for their weavers in 1781, and in the city itself, there were some 2,000 looms for cotton at work by 1800. In Bandon, County Cork, some 2,000 cotton weavers were at work in 1820, where the majority of houses in side streets of the town had looms at work. Shannon Street alone had 300 looms, while one road leaving the town had weavers' houses for half a mile.[42]

By 1838, cotton manufacture in Ulster was confined to the city of Belfast and its environs, when there were

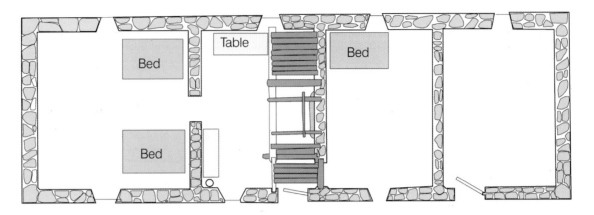

DERRYTRESK, County Tyrone

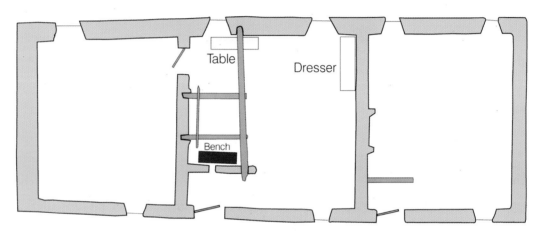

DERRYTRASNA, County Armagh

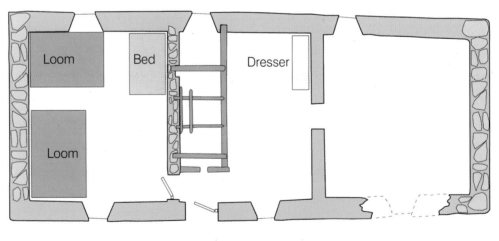

DERRYTAGH, County Armagh

8.5 *Ulster cotton weavers' cottages (after McCourt 1962).*

still around 12,000-15,000 weavers working within a ten-mile radius of it. Hand loom weaving, indeed, survived in the cotton industry up to the 1860s, but even where power looms were beginning to be become widely adopted, the weaving of linen on hand looms (although it did decline rapidly in second half of the nineteenth century) did not die off overnight. Higher-quality cloths still needed to be woven on hand looms, whilst power looms were not yet able to weave patterned damasks. As such, the use of hand looms for fine cloths survived into the twentieth century.[43] Hand looms for woollens were also widespread in County Donegal well into the twentieth century.[44]

The mechanisation of the loom proved to be a slow process. In 1785, the Rev Edmund Cartwright patented a power loom in England, and it may well be that the Samuel Strean of County Derry who claimed to have invented a water-powered power loom in 1788 was influenced by this development. As early as 1812, however, and up until 1814, Robert Honner was operating water-powered looms at Cork. This is the first recorded use of power looms in Ireland, and it seems likely that this development was influenced by the wartime expansion of the sailcloth industry as well as by Honner's probable contact with the Limehouse Spinning Mill in London, which was using power looms for weaving linen around the same time. But, ultimately, Honner's attempt to introduce such machinery proved to be unsuccessful, owing to the rapid contraction in the industry after 1814. The earliest firm evidence for the use of power looms in the Belfast cotton industry is associated with Mulholland's mill, some time before 1820, with a second cotton mill nearby employing power looms in 1821.[45] The Malcomson's cotton mill was operating with 360 power looms in 1837, which is the first recorded use of such plant in the industry outside Belfast.[46] In 1825, ten power looms for linen were erected by F. and A. Davison in County Monaghan, the first of their type to be used in the Ulster linen industry.[47]

Early power looms, it is clear, could only weave coarse linen cloths, but by the middle of the nineteenth century, linen manufacturers were facing stark new choices. The famine of the mid-1840s had created a scarcity of skilled weavers, which had in turn forced wages up. Belfast linen manufacturers were, in consequence, now compelled to seek mechanical alternatives. In the late 1840s, British firms were beginning to adapt their power looms to manufacture fine linens. But the diffusion of these new power looms to and within Ireland proved to be slow: only two Belfast firms were using power looms in 1850, and as late as 1862, just 3,000 power looms were at work around Belfast.[48] In the year 1850, there were a mere 50 power looms at work in the entire Ulster linen industry; by 1871, the total was 14,074.[49] However, by the late 1860s, the number of power looms used for linen in Ireland exceeded that of England, and was close to the number of Scottish looms. Elsewhere in Ireland, however, the introduction of new power looms for linen was much slower, the first recorded instance in Cork, since 1814, being *c.* 1866.[50] The introduction of the power loom to the Irish woollen industry, on the other hand, was broadly contemporary with the linen industry. On present evidence, Mahony's at Blarney, County Cork, were the first to use power looms in Ireland for wool, having purchased them at the Great Exhibition in London in 1852.[51] From the late 1850s onwards, however, they became more frequent, and other mills established subsequently, such as the Athlone Woollen Mills, built in 1859, appear to have used them from the outset.[52]

8.6 *The grassing of linen on a bleach field near William Barbour and Sons Thread Factory at Lisburn, County Antrim, from* The Pictorial World, *14 February 1889.*

(4) Finishing Processes

The basic processes involved in finishing textiles made from vegetable fibres such as linen and cotton comprised bleaching, dyeing and printing. In the eighteenth century the bleaching of brown linen cloth and cotton was a laborious and time-consuming process. The cloth was first steeped in a *keeve* (*kieve*) filled with cold water for a period of up to nine hours and then spread out on the ground (*grassed*) for up to four days, during which time it was sprinkled with water to keep it wet. In 1782, Thomas Harpur at Leixlip, County Kildare, invented a 'watering engine' for 'watering linens and cottons in the bleach', a horse-powered machine which enabled linen to be watered without laying it on grass. Its use appears to have been extremely localised, there being no other references to it in use elsewhere.[53]

The next stage, in which the cloth was *bucked*, involved the boiling of the cloth in an alkaline solution called *lye*, which was made with potash made from wood ash. Bucking was undertaken for twelve hours and was repeated every ten hours between each bucking. The cloth, at this stage in the process, was once again grassed, in this instance for two days. It was then steeped in buttermilk *sour*, weighed down with heavy objects and after being allowed to ferment in mild acid or sour. All these processes were repeated until such time as the cloth had been whitened. The grassing of the linen and cotton was undertaken out of doors and because of this was largely weather-dependent (figure 8.6). Until chemically manufactured bleaches became available, bleaching could only be conducted from early spring up until the beginning of the autumn and often took up to half a year. However, by the early 1760s, chemical bleaches were beginning to be manufactured in Ireland, and, by the close of the century a large number of factories producing Tennant's bleaching powder had been established in Ulster (see Chapter 11).

Bleach greens, both for linen and cotton, were established mainly throughout Ulster, but also within the environs of all the principal manufacturing centres, such as Cork and Dublin, throughout the eighteenth century. However, bleach greens for linen in Drogheda and Cork tended to be fewer and smaller than those established around the Lagan Valley. Large finishing works outside Ulster, indeed, such as Blarney in Cork, were quite rare: smaller bleach yards which bleached yarn only were more typical of the Drogheda and Cork industries. Regardless of size, a bleach green required a constant supply of clean water and an extensive area over which long webs of cloth could be spread. Watch huts for security were also provided at Ulster bleach greens, good examples of which have survived at Tullylish, near Banbridge, County Down. The largest bleachworks in west Belfast, the Glenbank Bleach Works, covered several acres and included a number of large stone-lined reservoirs for water storage, large volumes of which were used in the bleaching processes.

In Ulster bleach yards, after the final grassing, the cloth was removed to a *wash mill* for cleaning. In Ireland, the wash mill dates from around 1725, and it appears to have been modelled on fulling stocks. The wash mill emulated the beating action of fulling stock by pounding the cloth in water-filled troughs, fresh water being continually fed into the stocks and allowed to exit, along with impurities, via drainage holes at the base of the stocks. They are quite rare outside Ulster and remained in use in rural areas of Ulster until about 1950.

After washing, the linen web was passed through water-powered *beetling engines*, which imparted a sheen to the finished cloth, by allowing a series of vertical pounders or *beetles* made of beech to fall upon the cloth (figure 8.7).

8.7 *Beetling engine at Benburb, County Tyrone. For mill building see Fig. 8.8.*

8.8 *Beetling mill at Benburb, County Tyrone, now part of Benburb Valley Heritage Centre (above);*
8.9 *Steam calender in Coalisland spinning mill, County Tyrone (right).*

In the typical beetling mill, the beetling engines are positioned on the ground floor, the first floor (equipped with louvred vents) serving as a drying loft in which the damp cloth could hang to dry while being protected from direct sunlight (figure 8.8). The beetling mill, owing to the noise made by the pounding of the beetles (which could be in continuous 24-hour operation for anything up to a week), was built away from the other buildings in the bleach yard. The beetling engine also appears to be an Irish invention, and the first recorded instance of its use occurs at Drum Bridge on the River Lagan near Belfast in 1725. The National Trust in Northern Ireland has restored a fine eighteenth-century example at Wellbrook, near Cookstown, County Tyrone.[54] Linen cloth could also later be finished by *calendering*, a process which involved rolling the cloth between cylinders, to produce a sheen. Steam calenders were in widespread use in Ulster bleach yards during the second half of the nineteenth century; a good example has been preserved at the Coalisland spinning mill, County Tyrone (figure 8.9). However, large bleach works such as William Thorley's at Poullacurry near Glanmire, County Cork, established in about 1863, at which both steam calenders and beetling engines for finishing linen were employed, are quite rare outside Ulster.[55]

Both linen and cotton were also printed using either wooden blocks or rotating copper cylinders. During the eighteenth century, the Dublin Society offered premiums for improvements to textile printing processes in Ireland, while the Linen Board was also providing financial assistance for a printing works at Ballsbridge as early as 1727.[56] Most of the early printing works would have employed wooden blocks but, in the early 1750s, a printing works at Drumcondra claimed to be the first in Ireland to use copper plates for printing linen.[57] Some 70 printers on linen and cotton, along with fifteen cotton and calico printers, are thought to have operated in eighteenth-century Ireland, which include Leixlip, County Kildare, Ballsbridge, Dublin, Belfast, Stratford-on-Slaney, County Wicklow, Blarney and Glasheen, County Cork, and Mosney, County Meath.[58] Although cotton cloth was finished by bleaching in much the same way as white linen, by exposure to the air and through immersion in alkaline leys, it was frequently printed using blocks or machinery, or by calico printing, which was essentially a form of localised dyeing. The printing works themselves proved expensive to create, and many did not survive into the nineteenth century. Indeed, in some instances, English technicians and machinery had to be imported, as at Richardstown, County Louth, in 1766 and at Glasheen, near Cork, in the 1790s, which further increased establishment costs.[59]

The finishing processes for woollen and worsted cloths were different, not only to those employed for linen and cotton but to each other. For woollen cloth a preliminary scouring was required in an alkaline solution (either fullers' earth or urine), which was pounded in water-powered fulling stocks. This absorbed any grease, oil or dirt which had lodged in the cloth when it was woven, whilst simultaneously thickening the fabric. The cloth was then fulled, that is, continually pounded in a soapy solution by wooden fulling stocks, which imparted a felted finish. *Fulling* or *tuck* mills were in use in Ireland from the Anglo-Norman period onwards, but the vast majority of the surviving sites date to the eighteenth and early nineteenth centuries.[60] In certain instances, tenants were required to use manorial tuck mills, and this restriction was still present in County Kildare leases in the second half of the eighteenth century.[61] The term 'Tuck mill' (which is also common in the English west country) is the one most frequently used for such mills in Ireland, where their creation and employment is closely linked with the domestic woollen industry. Little is known about the internal arrangements of these mills in Ireland, and only one example of a fulling stock, on present evidence, is known to have survived in County Galway. In most cases, however, an undershot or, occasionally, a low breastshot water-wheel, would have driven a wooden drive shaft complete with iron-shod cams. The two sets of rotating cams would have pushed down the outer faces of a single pair of fulling stocks (which swung on a pendulum motion), each stock falling into either a single or separate wooden trough containing a web of cloth immersed in an alkaline or soapy solution. The troughs themselves would have been quite small, one example recorded by the Valuation Surveyors at Doonmacreena, County Leitrim in the late 1840s being 4 ft (1.21 m) long and 2 ft (0.60 m) wide.[62] In the vast majority of instances, the fulling machinery would be housed in the same building as a corn mill, often powered by a separate water-wheel though occasionally sharing the same water-wheel as the grinding machinery. The Irish tuck mill was already in decline by the 1840s, and with the advent of larger spinning mills in the early 1850s, it almost completely disappeared. The scouring and fulling processes were now incorporated into a factory complex, where rotary scouring and milling (i.e., fulling) machinery replaced the traditional fulling stocks.

After fulling, the woollen cloth was then *tentered*, a process during which the fabric was stretched under tension in the open air, on wooden racks, and later dried. The Celbridge woollen mills, County Kildare, had two tenter fields in 1831, as would all early woollen mills, a practice which continued, in certain instances, into the twentieth century.[63] A mechanical means of tentering was introduced during the second half of the nine-teenth century, but in Ireland this was only used in the larger woollen mills, as at St Patricks's Mills in Douglas village, near Cork, in 1883.[64] In the manufacture of woollen cloth, the object was to disguise the weave under a smooth nap, to which end the short fibres of the cloth were raised and then sheared, i.e., cut to the required even finish. Until the 1790s, this latter process in Ireland was carried out by hand, but in 1793, Marcus Lynch's mill at Midleton, County Cork, was already employing machines for raising the nap and shearing.[65] In worsted cloth manufacture, although the cloth was both scoured and sheared, it was the cloth's pattern which was important, and the desired effect was to expose the weave. The raising of the nap could thus be dispensed with.

During the early development of the linen trade in Ulster, the linen drapers, who bought brown linen from weavers and then processed it into white linen at their bleach greens, faced the problem of awaiting repayment while the cloth was being sold on to the London market. However, finance was available from Dublin-based factors, and in the period 1721-23, the Linen Board built the island's first white Linen Hall to accommodate such transactions in Dublin.[66] Up to the 1780s, white linen was brought by cart to Dublin, but disputes between the Linen Board and northern linen drapers led to the establishment of white linen halls at Newry in 1783 and at Belfast in 1785. By this period, however, the northern drapers were sufficiently wealthy to deal with the English market on their own account, and so the white linen halls in Ulster and Dublin were now largely redundant.[67] White linen halls were also created at Drogheda in 1770 and at Cork around the same time, but very few have survived, as at Newry (fragments only, although it originally covered six acres) and Castlebar, County Mayo.[68]

(5) The Development of the Spinning Mill in Ireland c. 1782-1840

Up to the 1780s in Ireland, the various preparing, spinning, weaving and finishing processes involved in textile manufacture were often undertaken at different installations. Indeed, before the adoption of the power loom in the cotton and linen industries, the manufacture of cloth could still involve three separate production units, the spinning mill, the weaver's house and the bleach green.

The integration of these processes at a single site had already taken place at Douglas, near Cork, in 1750, but appears not to have been attempted again until the early 1780s. From the outset, cotton manufacturers such as Brooke at Prosperous, County Kildare, between 1782 and 1786, and the Sadlier brothers at Glasheen and Riverstown near Cork in 1781-1801, had attempted to integrate all of the main processes.[69] Although both were financial failures (Brooke because of poor location and Sadliers because of an economic depression of 1800-1), the principle that such integration was possible had been established. Marcus Lynch was the first to integrate the processes used in woollen manufacture at Midleton, County Cork, in 1793, but again his efforts were short lived.[70] A similar large-scale venture was initiated in 1810 by Nolan and Shaw at the Merino factory in County Kilkenny (which was combined with a flock of Merino sheep), some remains of which still survive.[71] In the linen industry, the first main wave of integrated ventures was initiated in the first decade of the nineteenth century, mostly in county Cork. In 1806, Edward Shanahan built a linen spinning mill, beetling machinery, a wash mill and bleach green at Tower Bridge, near Blarney, County Cork, which was followed by similar works at Navan, County Meath, and Bessbrook and New Holland, County Armagh.[72] The introduction of the power loom into the Irish linen industry after 1850 led to the establishment of spinning and weaving factories, although, for the most part, the finishing processes were carried out at separate sites. In the vast majority of Irish woollen mills built after 1860, however, all the main processes were integrated.

The increasing demands which early industrial structures in Britain and Ireland placed on the repertoire of the vernacular building tradition grew from the need to accommodate a wider range of industrial machinery. In textile industries, as new mechanical means were developed for all of the individual preparation and spinning processes, it became no longer practical to link all of the machinery to a single power source within the same building, without the addition of extra storeys. The embryonic spinning mill, therefore, housed a series of integrated mechanical processes, generally powered by the same prime mover by means of vertical shafting.

The first purpose-built, multi-storey industrial buildings in Ireland that could facilitate power transmission from a water-wheel to each storey were the *bolting* or flour mills, which began to appear around the middle of the eighteenth century (see Chapter 9). In the pre-steam age, these were very much the prototype for multi-storey textile mills in Ireland, and it is clear that early cotton and flax spinning mills were constructed along similar lines, using local materials. Such mills, up to the introduction of iron frames, were usually laid out on a rectangular ground plan and did not exceed widths of about 9 m, which was around the maximum that unsupported roof trusses could span.[73] The roof and the timber floors relied on the mill's enclosing walls for support and, when it became necessary to widen the spans between the load-bearing walls, intermediate timber stanchions were introduced to provide support for the floor joists along the length of the building.[74] Internal lighting was assisted by rows of regularly spaced windows on each floor.

Purpose-built late eighteenth- and early nineteenth-century Irish textile mills tend to be four to five storeys high. The earliest multi-storey Irish textile mills were built in the latter part of the eighteenth century to house cotton spinning machinery, such as that at Balbriggan, County Dublin, completed in 1782 by Baron Hamilton, and Deaves' five storey cotton mill near Blarney, built in 1787.[75] In 1793, Marcus Lynch was building a six-storey woollen mill at Midleton, County Cork, the largest of its type to have hitherto been erected in Ireland.[76] By and large, the early Irish spinning mills mirror contemporary English building practice, which is to be expected, given the influx of English workers in the 1780s. And, at least one English millwright from the heart of the Manchester cotton industry, Thomas Cheek Hewes, is known to have executed work in Ireland. Hewes fitted out a Belfast mill in 1790 and subsequently built three cotton mills here, a five-storey example at Overton near Bandon in 1802, which he added to in 1810, and two others at unidentified locations in the period 1822-4.[77]

8.10 *Overton cotton mill, near Bandon, County Cork, original wing completed in c. 1802. This is the only surviving Irish cotton mill known to have been designed by Thomas Hewes of Manchester.*

The size of the early Irish cotton mills, while exhibiting considerable variation, does nonetheless fall within recognisable limits. Thomas Deaves' cotton mill near Blarney was 110 ft (33.52 m) by 28 ft (8.53 m) in 1787.[78] Allman's mill at Overton (134 ft long by 34 ft or 40.84 m by 10.36 m) at its greatest extent (*c.* 1810), was only slightly larger (figure 8.10),[79] while John Vance's five-storey cotton spinning mill at Woodburn near Carrickfergus, County Antrim, built in 1804 and later converted to flax spinning, was 110 ft by 40 ft (33.52 m by 12.19 m) as was Hannay and MacWilliams' cotton mill (built 1806) at Bangor, County Down.[80] Laurence Atkinson's Celbridge woollen mills of 1805 (also converted to flax spinning) were of similar proportions (figure 8.11).[81] The increase in width in Irish cotton spinning mills, noticeable after *c.* 1800, can be attributed to the introduction of throstle frames and early mules (installed in the Overton mill in 1802), which required wider buildings. By the mid-1830s, newly built flax-spinning mills in the Belfast region do not appear to have been appreciably larger; Bells and Calvert's flax spinning mill built in 1828 at Whitehouse, County Antrim, was three storeys high and 136 ft by 21 ft (41.45 m by 6.4 m) in extent.[82] Indeed, Robert Howe's four-storey cotton mill at Ballynure, County Antrim, completed in 1822, was 82 ft by 30ft (24.99 m by 9.14 m); while James Grimshaw's four-storey flax spinning mill at Whitehouse, County Antrim (1832) was 90 ft by 25 ft (27.43 m by 7.62 m).[83]

There can be little doubt that the increased width of mill buildings was facilitated by the introduction of cast-iron supporting columns, which were beginning to replace timber stanchions as intermediate floor supports. The technique has been used in England since the 1790s, but its adoption and development and, indeed, the early structural use of cast-iron in Ireland, is currently not fully understood.[84] In the period 1816-22, a series of multi-storey British Navy victualling warehouses were constructed on Haulbowline Island in Cork harbour. These latter were built with an early form of cast-iron framing, similar to that employed in contemporary English textile mills, although the internal floors of the Haulbowline stores were constructed with timber. On present evidence, therefore, the earliest recorded iron-framed building in Ireland is John Rennie's tobacco warehouse ('Stack A') constructed at the Custom House Docks, Dublin in 1821-2, (see Chapter 15). However, it seems likely that cast-iron columns were beginning to be incorporated into Irish cotton spinning mills during the early decades of the nineteenth century. Malcomson's cotton spinning mill at Portlaw, County Waterford, became one of the earliest examples of the use of this technique in Ireland when, in 1825, the memel pine floors of the southern end of the six-storey mill were supported with hollow 8-inch diameter cast-iron columns (figure 8.12).[85] The use of cast-iron members also served as an elementary form of fireproofing. The risk of fire in such buildings was, indeed, acute. Early multi-storey textile mills were lit with candles and oil, as at Celbridge in 1805, whilst oil dripping from machinery was also prone to catch fire.[86] Thus, at the Overton cotton mill in 1802, the wooden floors were sheathed with iron, while at the Athlumney flax spinning mill in County Meath, completed in 1806, the floors were of metal and the doors sheathed with iron.[87]

8.11 *Laurence Atkinson's Celbridge woollen mills, County Kildare, of 1805.*

8.12 *Malcomson's cotton mill at Portlaw, County Waterford, built in 1837.*

On present evidence, it would appear that by the 1830s, internal iron framing, in which the internal loading of the building was largely transferred from the external walls to a fireproof, free-standing cast-iron frame, was beginning to be employed in Irish textile mills. The principle had first been used by Charles Bage at a flax mill in Ditherington, Surrrey in 1796, and was further developed in the early years of the nineteenth century.[88] It was a standard feature of Irish linen mills constructed in the second half of the nineteenth century, where each of the internal floors of the mill was laid upon a matrix of brick, segmental *jack arches*, which were supported upon tiers of cast-iron girders. Jack-arched floors were the principal means by which textile mills of this period were rendered fireproof, and in some instances individual floors were also finished with fire clay tiles. The girders, in nearly all multi-storied textile mills of this period, are connected by wrought-iron tie rods, and are supported along the central long axis of each floor on cast-iron columns. The columns were nearly always cast with brackets to carry lineshafting, which transmitted power from the mill's prime mover to individual machines. However, such floors, while fireproof, could not withstand heavy loading, although the spinning frames were relatively light and, when in operation, created little vibration. One of the earliest documented examples of this type of internal frame in Ireland is in the northern section of Malcomson's cotton mill at Portlaw, built in 1837. The floors comprise a series of brick jack arches, which rest into both the main walls and along the centre of the building in saddle-back cast-iron beams. A bed of lime mortar was laid immediately over the brick arches, into which 2-inch thick flagstones were set to form the mill floors.[89] Ireland's larger textile mills would have had large metal workshops, but the Portlaw mill was unique in Ireland in having its own iron foundry, which even manufactured 20-ft diameter cast-iron water-wheel for it.[90] The Lansdowne Flax-Spinning Mill at Limerick, constructed between 1851-3, for the flour milling magnates J. N. Russell & Sons, has the oldest cast-iron framing and brick jack arches to survive in such a mill in the Republic of Ireland (figure 8.13).[91] The cast-iron columns were supplied by Rowan and Sons York Street Foundry of Belfast, and are date-stamped 1851.

As early as 1809, Laurence Atkinson was contemplating the use of gas lighting in his Celbridge woollen mills.[92] There is no evidence that he ever did so, and, in fact, the earliest recorded use of a private gas supply in Ireland is at Waterford in 1815 (see Chapter 16), but this was a precocious step as the first ever textile mill to be lit by gas was Lodge's mill at Sowerby Bridge in Yorkshire, in 1805.[93] In about 1826, Malcomson's mill six-storey cotton mill at Portlaw was lit by gas, supplied by their own gasworks. The latter also provided tar, which was used to seal the layers of unbleached calico employed as a roofing material, and the gasworks itself was later used to meet the needs of the town of Portlaw.[94] Similarly, the Grimshaws had installed gas plant for their works at Whitehouse Upper, County Antrim in 1835, which also supplied the local village at their own expense and also, surprisingly, the adjacent cotton mill of Bell and Calvert. James Murland's linen spinning mill, at

8.13 *'Jack arches' in former Lansdowne Flax Spinning Mill, Limerick, built between 1851-3.*

Annesborough, County Antrim, was also gas lit around the same time.[95] From the late 1820s onwards, nearly all the larger Irish textile mills would have been supplied by their own gas plant or by a town network.

(6) The Development of the Flax Spinning Mill, *c.* 1840-1900

The earliest Irish flax spinning mills, as we have noted, were established in Counties Cork and Down. Yet these were not always purpose-built structures. Indeed, the Rademon mill, the first in Ulster, was originally a multi-storey corn mill in which spinning frames had been installed.[96] A small number of other mills were also built in Counties Donegal, Armagh, Dublin, Cork and Meath before 1810. At Athlumney on the River Boyne in County Meath, John Blundell of Lancashire built a six-storey flax spinning mill on the Boyne Navigation in 1806 at a cost of £20,000. The river was used both to power the mill's machinery (which included a scutch mill) and as a cheap and convenient means of transport.[97] Surviving examples of early, purpose-built flax spinning mills, as at Ramelton, County Donegal, are quite rare, although the main building of Denis Connor's Springville sailcloth factory of *c.* 1807, at Cahergal on the outskirts of Cork, still survives. It was later converted to a flour mill and its mill-race, which passes through the centre of the building, is still extant.[98] Some 22 flax-spinning mills were operating in Ireland in 1839, and by 1835, 60 mills were at work, employing 17, 088 workers, mostly women.[99]

Up to the 1850s, flax spinning mills in Ireland were built with local stone, a good example of which is the Brookfield Flax Spinning Mill on the Crumlin Road in Belfast, which retains a flax store constructed with basalt masonry of about 1830. By this period, however, brick was increasingly used for window dressings and doorways. The Lansdowne Flax Spinning mill at Limerick, built with local limestone in the early 1850s, is one of the last flax spinning mills in Ireland to be so constructed (figure 8.14). From the 1860s onwards, Irish flax spinning mills from Belfast to Cork tend to be brick built, and the basic design and *modus operandi* of all of the Irish mills was closely modelled on Belfast practices.

In 1828, the influential Belfast cotton spinners, the Mulhollands, changed their cotton mill in Henry Street, Belfast, over to flax spinning after it had been destroyed by fire.

8.14 *The Lansdowne Flax Spinning Mill, Limerick, built between 1851-3 for J.N. Russell and Sons.*

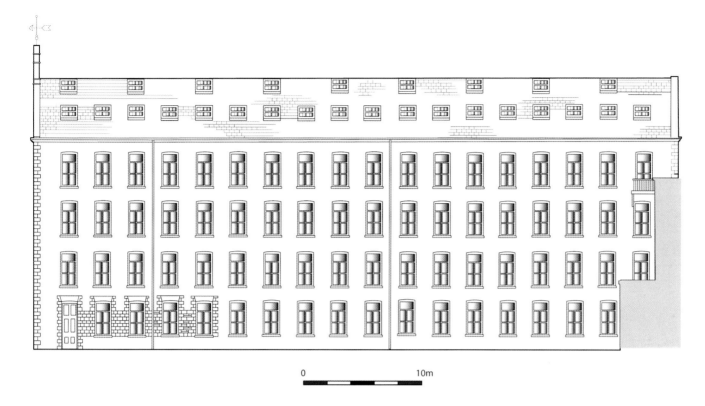

8.15 *Elevation of Andrews flax spinning mill at Comber, County Down (after McCutcheon 1980).*

That such a mill could be burnt down strongly suggests that it had wooden flooring, and raises the question of how common iron framing was in Belfast cotton mills by this period. Nonetheless, the mill's change of function took full advantage of the prevailing market conditions, which favoured flax spinning, and for the first time, flax spinning machinery was powered by steam in Ireland. Other Belfast cotton mill owners quickly followed suit.

Irish flax spinning mills built in the second half of the nineteenth century generally consist of a four- to seven-storey block (five storeys is the most common) with a rectangular ground plan (figure 8.15). The main spinning mill block often formed part of a courtyard, flanked by ancillary buildings such as hackling sheds, offices and stores. Many mills, such as the Brookfield Mill in Belfast, had a stone gate lodge, with a weighbridge for weighing the contents of incoming vehicles. Internal lighting in the main block was supplied by the mill's own gas plant which, as we have seen, became increasingly common in many of the larger Irish textile mills from about the 1820s onwards. Depending upon whether both spinning and weaving were undertaken on the same site, mill complexes could cover several acres. The Edenderry Spinning Mill on the Crumlin Road, for example, completed *c.* 1863, covers about three acres (1.2 ha.), whilst the Ewart's spinning and weaving complex directly opposite it, at its greatest extents, covered approximately 17 acres or *c.* 6.8 ha. Mills frequently also owned off-site buildings such as warehouses, in which either imported raw materials or finished yarn or cloth could be stored. The mill owners did, of course, also provide workers' housing (see Chapter 17)), but schools, churches, libraries and shops were also commonly built at the proprietor's expense. The mill complex was thus an extended entity which encompassed both the workplace and the everyday lives of the employees.

8.16 *Sion Mills, near Strabane, County Tyrone.*

Although steam-powered mills were already in existence in Belfast by the late 1820s, many of the mills in west Belfast were located there because of proximity to mountain streams such as the Ballysillan and Legoniel rivers. Despite the installation of steam engines in the majority of the Belfast spinning mills, those located in the Ballysillan and Legoniel areas continued to rely largely on waterpower. Water turbines were installed in the Wolfhill, Mountain and Ballysillan spinning mills, and the Glenbank Bleach Works, and even William Ewart's enormous spinning and weaving mill on the Crumlin Road had a turbine installed in 1886. At the Mountain Spinning Mill in Legoniel, which formed part of the Ewart empire, a 45 hp Gilkes turbine was installed in 1891, later to be replaced by a further Gilkes turbine in 1923, which survives *in situ*. Of course, other large spinning mills outside Belfast, such as Sion Mills, near Strabane, sited on the River Mourne (figure 8.16), and Dunbar and McMaster's at Gilford, County Down (figure 8.17), were deliberately sited near a good source of waterpower.

The vast majority of the linen-spinning mills built after 1860 were powered by steam engines. In purpose-built steam-powered spinning mills, the engine house could be positioned either at the gable end of the main mill block or at right angles to it. A good example of the former survives at the Edenderry mill, and of the latter

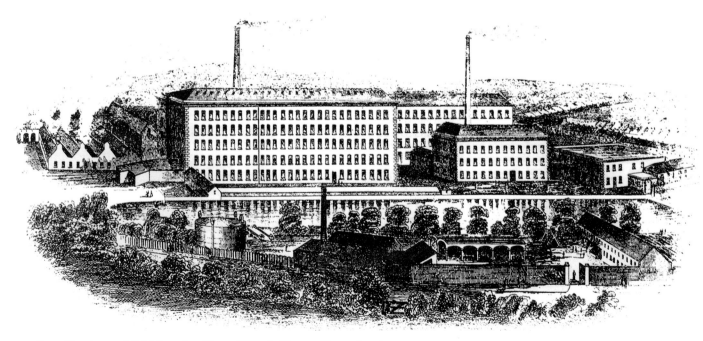

8.17 *Dunbar and McMaster's mills at Gilford, County Down in 1891.*

up to very recently at the Cork Spinning and Weaving Company's mill at Millfield, near Cork, completed in 1866. However, the Millfield engine house was built to accommodate a rope drive.[100] Rope driving – the single most important Irish contribution to the development of the factory – was first developed and used in Belfast by James Combe of the Falls Foundry in 1863, and its use in the Millfield spinning mill would appear to be one of the earliest examples outside Belfast.[101] The transmission arrangement involved a series of heavy cotton ropes which fitted into grooves formed on the engine's flywheel. Individual ropes powered line shafting on each of the mill's floors, the ropes themselves being accommodated in a vertical chamber called a *rope-race*, set at one end of the mill building. In terms of mill design, the adoption of rope-driving eventually led to engine houses, as at Millfield and at the Ballysillan mill in west Belfast, being built alongside the mill building.[102] Power transmission by rope driving was a tremendous improvement on that traditionally supplied by water-wheels, which involved large power losses, and enabled more efficient power transmission over greater distances.

In a typical spinning mill, the flax was prepared for spinning on the ground and first floors, before passing upwards to the second and third floors, which housed the wet spinning rooms. The spray from the spindles left the spinning room floors permanently wet, and the female spinners went barefoot and wore long leather aprons for protection. The wet spinning rooms were thus provided with metal drains running along the inner edge of the main walls, while the floors were also cambered to allow moisture and condensate falling from the spinning frames to be collected. Large cast-iron tanks, with a capacity of over 2,000 gallons, were often built into the roofs of spinning mills, the water of which was used to fill the troughs of the spinning frames. Intercommunication between the individual mill floors required additional refinements where fireproofing was concerned. Masonry stair towers, projecting from the gable of the main block and containing stone spiral staircases, as at Hilden and the Lansdowne Spinning Mill at Limerick, were present in some early flax mills. In later mills, however, a stone stairwell was built up against one of the gable walls, often with a cast-iron staircase set internally at the other end of the building, as at the Edenderry mill on the Crumlin Road in Belfast. The doors facilitating access to individual floors from the landings were also fireproofed.

The terms 'mill' and 'factory' in an Irish context were applied, respectively, to buildings used for spinning and weaving, although in many cases both activities were integrated and accommodated within a single complex. As early as 1750, a factory-type system had evolved at the Douglas sailcloth factory near Cork, where about 100 looms were at work under the one roof. This appears to be the first vertically integrated unit of its type in Ireland, which also included the various processes involved in preparing the flax for spinning, along with many of the finishing processes.[103]

As we have seen, the power loom was being widely adopted in the Ulster linen industry by the 1860s, where steam power had become the mainstay of the new weaving factories built around Belfast during this period. In the weaving factory, the looms were housed in a stone-built, single-storey shed, top-lit (that is, where natural light was channelled in through the roof) with a north facing aspect and a 'saw edge' profile roof. The shed-like, single-storey construction was necessary to enable the buildings to cope with the weight and vibration of the looms (figure 8.18). Indeed, the provision of good lighting was also essential for weaving, as shadows

8.18 *Power looms in weaving shed in York Street Flax Co. Ltd's mill, Belfast in early twentieth century.*

could hide faults in the weave. As weaving sheds could only be extended laterally to accommodate more power looms, in the larger works, such as Ewart's weaving factory on the Crumlin Road (demolished in 1998), the sheds could be spread over several acres. These complexes were also well ventilated, and in the vast majority of the Belfast weaving factories, louvred vents or extractor fans were installed on the gables of individual sheds. A complete weaving factory of about 1870, with its original power looms ranging in date from about 1890 to the 1940s, has been preserved at the Benburb Heritage Centre in County Tyrone.

(7) The Development of the Woollen Mill Complex *c.* 1850-1900

Multi-storey woollen spinning mills in Ireland were a rarity up to the middle of the nineteenth century, and six-storey mills, such as that built by Marcus Lynch in 1793, would have been exceptional. Spinning mills were, in any case, by no means common in Ireland by this period. There were only eleven in 1850, but by 1890, this figure had risen to 83, most of which were in Munster and with a sizeable concentration in County Cork.[104] Nonetheless, even with new sites established after 1860, there was considerable variation in their design and construction. Indeed, small two-storey spinning and carding mills, such as Glanworth, County Cork (*c.* 1855), and the Clare Bridge Mills, Newport, County Tipperary (established in 1838), in which carding, dyeing, napping and milling was still 'done for the public' (and where all of the freizes, blankets and serges continued to be woven on hand looms), could still co-exist with nationally important woollen mills like Blarney.[105]

Half of the sixteen or so woollen mills established in Counties Cork, Tipperary and Waterford after 1860 were powered by water alone in 1889, three of which (Ardfinnan, County Tipperary, Ashgrove Woollen Mills, Kenmare, and Beaufort in County Kerry) employed water turbines. Only three of the mills at work in 1889 were wholly steam-powered, two of which were in Cork, the remainder using both water and steam power.[106] Large woollen mills such as Blarney and Athlone were clearly the exception rather than the rule.

The variety of woollen mill designs in Ireland was primarily a question of scale. The Araglin (1884) and Dunmanway (1864) mills, in County Cork, the Kilrush mills, County Clare (1884) or the Lisbellaw, County Fermanagh, mills (built 1872-3) were relatively small factories, yet were far more typical, in terms of scale and productive capacity, of Irish woollen mills in general.[107] In most cases, the main spinning mill was only two to three storeys high. Ardfinnan Woollen Mills, County Tipperary, originally established by Mulcahy Redmond and Co. in 1869, but which, after being destroyed by fire in 1881, were rebuilt in 1882 as a range of two-storey buildings.[108] St Patrick's Mills in Douglas village, near Cork, completed in 1883 to a design by the Glasgow architect,

Richard Murray, were the last purpose-built woollen spinning and weaving mills to be built in County Cork. Yet the complex, consisting of three main blocks, of which the engine house occupied the central position, flanked, on each side, by the preparing, carding and spinning rooms in one block and the weaving and finishing shops in the other, was mainly constructed with cut limestone, the large-scale use of brick being confined to the gable ends to facilitate future additions.[109] St Patrick's Mills was the second largest of its type in County Cork but, while its spinning capacity was about one-third of that of the Blarney Mills, it operated more power looms than the latter.[110] Thus this complex was, in relative terms, quite a large one, but, although constructed in the early 1880s, the designer eschewed not only the use of multi-storey construction but also of brick as the main building material. The Convoy, County Donegal, mill, completed in 1884, while brick built was essentially a two-storey complex. Woollen mills erected in the first decade of the twentieth century, such as at Greenvale, Kilkenny, and Foxford, County Mayo and Convoy, County Donegal, also exhibit no uniform design.[111]

O'Mahony's Woollen Mills at Blarney were the largest in Ireland for the greater part of the nineteenth and twentieth centuries. In 1824, Martin Mahony moved his Cork city-based woollen manufacturing business to a converted eighteenth-century cotton mill, adjacent to Blarney village. Mahony's quickly expanded operations on the site, and by the end of the 1840s were operating 5,638 spindles. As we have seen, they were the first to introduce power looms into Ireland for woollens, and by the 1860s had the largest integrated mill of its type in Ireland. By 1889, the mills were powered by three steam engines and three water turbines, with a combined power of 550 hp.[112] The mills were largely destroyed by fire in 1869, but were rebuilt and expanded in 1870, yet in the process were not fireproofed: the surviving three-storey spinning mill of 1870 has wooden floors supported

8.19 *The Athlone woollen mills in 1891. The mills were originally established in 1859 in a former brewery complex.*

by cast-iron columns.[113] In fact, the only Irish woollen mills to be housed in fireproofed buildings were those established in converted flax-spinning mills such as Morrogh's woollen mill, at Donnybrook, near Cork, in 1885, and the Belfast Wool Spinning and Tweed Co. at Durham Street, Belfast, in 1886.[114] As in most of the larger Irish woollen mills, at Blarney, the spinning and carding machinery were installed in separate buildings. The Athlone Woollen Mills Company's complex, set up within a former brewery complex on the banks of the Shannon at Athlone, County Westmeath, was also extensive (figure 8.19). Established in 1859, the mills, which comprised a series of three-storey spinning mills, two-storey carding mills and weaving sheds, were spread over about three acres by the early 1890s, with machinery driven by a 250 hp horizontal engine and a 50 hp water turbine.[115]

9

Food-Processing Industries

During the eighteenth and nineteenth centuries, the rapid expansion of Ireland's principal historic food-processing industries – brewing, grain milling and distilling – often belied the general lack of growth in other sectors of the island's economy. Of the latter, flour and meal milling were the most widely dispersed, whereas brewing and distilling tended to be urban based to supply their main consumers. Distribution patterns aside, the phenomenal growth of Ireland's breweries, distilleries and grain mills, at a very early stage in their development, required that the structures intended to house them be redesigned, not only to facilitate increased capacity but also to accommodate their greater energy needs. In a very real sense, for eighteenth-century Irish flour mills, the only way was up: these were to become the first industrial structures to accommodate multi-storey power transmission. There is, in most associated industries of this period, a clear correspondence between scale (i.e., output) and technological innovation, the innovatory aspects generally arising from the need to adapt existing production methods to increased output. The brewing and distilling industries were the first in Ireland in which steam engines were widely adopted (see Chapter 2), while the world's first practical patent stills were developed in the Irish distilling industry. Yet, although in overall terms industrial concentration in Ireland was negligible, certain food processing industries expanded to become internationally significant manufacturing units. In its day, Jebb's mill at Slane was the largest in Europe, and Guinness's James' Gate Brewery had become the largest in the world by the end of the nineteenth century. There were, of course, other important food processing industries such as bacon curing and baking, but this chapter will concentrate on the larger industries that, in essence, processed cereal grains.

(1) Malting

Malted barley is one of the main ingredients of both beer and whiskey. The process by which it is manufactured essentially involves a partial germination of barley grains, to encourage enzymes in the grain to convert some of their starch into sugar. The degree to which this germination was allowed to proceed was carefully controlled, and was arrested at a critical point in order to conserve the amount of saccharine in the sprouting grain. At the brewery and the distillery, the sugar was then chemically transformed into alcohol in the fermentation process. In the traditional floor maltings, four basic processes were involved in the manufacture of malted barley – *steeping, couching, flooring* and *kiln-drying* - two of which were closely monitored by excise officials.

Up to the introduction of the steam thresher, barley was left to stand and mature after harvesting in order to encourage it to sweat and give off excess moisture. The widespread use of steam threshers in the second half of the nineteenth century, however, meant that this natural maturation process was no longer carried out. It therefore became necessary to undertake a preliminary kiln-drying of the grain, at a steady temperature of around 100° F over a 12-24 hour period, before the malting process could proceed.[1] The kiln-dried barley was then immersed in a stone (and later cast-iron) cistern called a *steep*, in which it was thoroughly soaked under controlled conditions. In the steep, seeds and other extraneous matter tended to float to the surface where they could be skimmed off, while the heavier cereal grains sank to the bottom. The floating debris was carefully removed, as failure to do so could result in the payment of extra excise duty (which was based on volume) and, worse still, the germination process would be impaired.[2] After a period of 54-60 hours, the water was drawn off, although not before being inspected a number of times by an excise officer. The swollen barley was then *couched* in a wooden-framed receptacle called a *couch* or *couch frame*, the size and construction of which were controlled by excise regulations, in which it was heaped to absorb some heat to help encourage germination when it was spread on the malting floors to grow. It was allowed to lie here for about 24 hours, and the swollen grains were then removed to one of the floors in the malt house, to be spread in layers of about 12 in thickness (figure 9.1).[3]

The flooring process was largely weather-dependent, taking around eight to ten days, during which germination was encouraged, with the maltster turning the sprouting grains (now termed *green malt*) regularly with a large wooden shovel, in order to regulate the temperature and to prevent the shoots from becoming entangled.[4] A temperature of around 50-58° F was needed, and, in addition to turning the grain and varying its depth on the floor, the maltster also had skilfully adjusted the amount of air allowed in from the windows.[5] He then

9.1 *Interior of one of the Guinness brewery maltings at James' Gate in 1902.*

determined at which point germination should be arrested, whereupon the grain was removed to a kiln where the introduction of strong heat, over a period of up to three days, reduced its moisture content to a level compatible with safe storage and prevented further germination taking place.[6] The malt was then stored in air-sealed bins, in which it was allowed to mature for a number of weeks.[7]

During the eighteenth century, a large number of small maltings were in operation throughout Ireland, with some 2,216 at work in 1785. By 1835, this had been reduced to 388, the majority of which were now controlled by breweries and distilleries but which were, nonetheless, manufacturing about double that of the smaller but more numerous eighteenth-century malt houses.[8] Dublin breweries such as Guinness bought malt from independent concerns all over Ireland, but in Cork and in smaller county towns, brewers generally preferred to have all their malting facilities within the brewery complex. For the most part, this presented few difficulties for small-scale eighteenth-century breweries, where animal-powered malt-milling plant could be relied upon to meet its power requirements. However, by the early 1790s, the expansion of city-based breweries required larger quantities of malt. Guinness simply engaged more suppliers, but its main rival in Ireland, Beamish and Crawford, chose to purchase additional malting capacity and, by the end of the 1830s, was in control of eight Cork city malt houses. In the early 1860s, the number of malt houses controlled by Beamish and Crawford had been reduced to five, and from about 1888 onwards, their malting operations became concentrated in the Lee Maltings and in the Morrison's Island Maltings.[9] Guinness, on the other hand, made some of their own malt, but also purchased large amounts from the Ballinacurra maltings, near Midleton in County Cork.

In Ireland, maltings were commonly associated with breweries and distilleries, but they were also stand-alone concerns. The maltings complex normally consisted of a multi-storey block, with closely spaced rows of small windows and wooden shutters. These are usually flanked at one end by a kiln (figure 9.2). The latter will normally have a pyramid-shaped head (e.g., Tullamore, County Offaly), with a metal cap or *hood*, through which heat and gases can escape. Rectangular kilns, however, were also relatively common in Ireland, where a ridge ventilator replaced the cap of the pyramidal kiln, as at Ballinacurra, County Cork. Inside the kiln, the lower section would be equipped with a cast-iron furnace grate, which would be stoked with anthracite and occasionally with turf. The heat generated by the kiln would be fed into brick arched vault, which directed it upwards to the kiln floor. The floor itself could be formed by either a series of regularly spaced cast-iron bars, laid across the rim of the kiln head and flanged to receive perforated ceramic (*Worcester*) tiles or by a series of perforated metal plates. In either case, the perforations were small enough to retain individual grains, but large and plentiful enough to admit heat evenly through the kiln floor. The periodic and tedious task of cleaning out grain which had lodged in these perforations was allotted to small boys. As we shall see, the grain-drying kilns associated with oat and flour mills were very similar, although those used for malting were invariably much larger. Indeed, some of the larger kilns in Dublin and Cork breweries and distilleries were three-storey structures, the first and second storeys of which served as drying floors.

The malt house had to accommodate a number of functions including storage of barley (usually adjacent to the steeps) and malt, steeps for soaking the barley, floors for growing and drying kilns. In Ireland, eighteenth-century

237

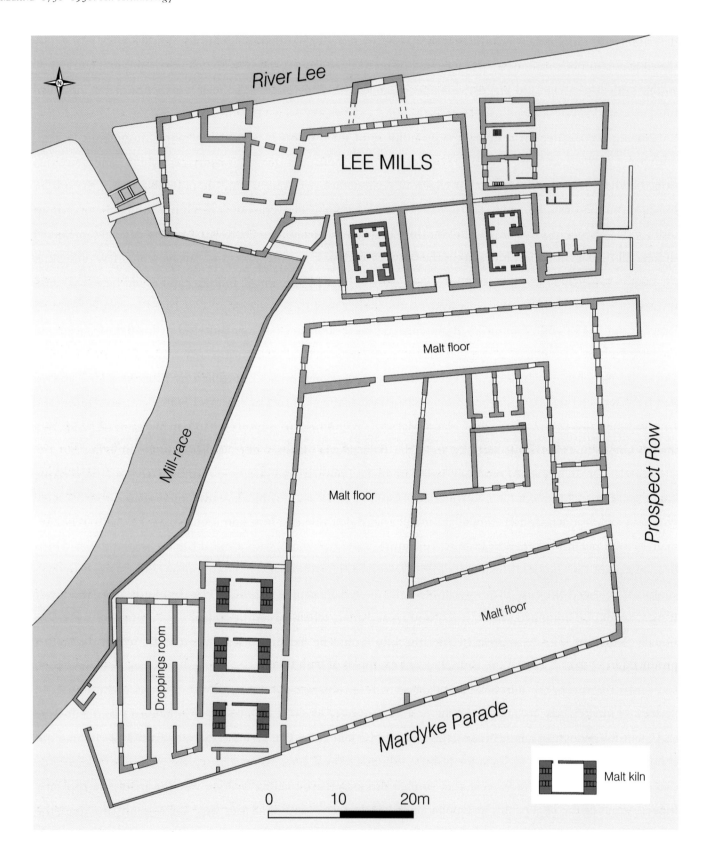

9.2 *The Lee Maltings, Cork, in 1890, established within a former flour mill and an adjacent brewery complex, by Beamish and Crawford.*

malt houses generally consist of a rectangular two- or three-storey block, with a hipped roof and a single kiln at one end. This configuration survived well into the twentieth century in smaller maltings and in malt houses associated with breweries and distilleries. By the middle of the nineteenth century, however, three or four blocks were combined to form what may be termed 'courtyard' maltings, as at Cowperthwaites maltings in Cork and the Muine Bheag maltings, County Carlow, where the rationale was to facilitate access for wheeled vehicles.

Internally, the maltings could accommodate from two to six wooden floors, with compressed floor-to-ceiling heights, which were supported midway either by wooden stanchions or cast-iron columns. Large cast-iron tie plates, to which wrought-iron tensioning rods would be attached (in order to counteract the internal stresses created by the weight of the grain on the individual floors) will also be in evidence on the external elevations of the maltings. Tie plates, indeed, are also found on kilns.

The steeps were positioned on either the ground floor or, later on, in a vertical wooden framework in one corner of the building, with individual floors being serviced by their own steep. These were later replaced by iron-framed structures, which supported cast-iron plates bolted together in sections to form cisterns. The former River Lee Porter Brewery complex had three cast-iron steeps by the mid-1860s, each steep positioned within a cast-iron framework made by Perrott's Hive Iron Foundry, which survived *in situ* until its removal by University College Cork, in June 1991. In the latter complex, wooden-framed wagons on iron bogeys, running on wooden rails, were used to transport malt to the steeps.[10] Water and steam power were later employed to operate bucket elevators and archimedian screws, which enabled malt to be transported from floor to floor. For the most part, however, mechanisation was confined to maltings contained within breweries and distilleries, although some large independent maltings, as at Castlebridge, County Wexford, employed water-powered plant. Malt houses without mechanised lifting apparatus were nearly always confined to three storeys, given the difficulties involved in moving the malt from floor to floor.

Eighteenth- and nineteenth-century malt house buildings are still relatively common throughout Ireland, the largest concentration of buildings of both centuries surviving in County Cork. The Cork area was one of the principal malt-producing regions of Ireland for the greater part of the nineteenth century. Some 18 per cent of the entire national output of malt was manufactured in Cork malt houses in 1829, almost four times that produced in Dublin.[11] Two of the earliest extant examples of Irish floor maltings can be seen on Rutland Street, Cork, one of which was in existence since at least 1753. This was acquired by Beamish and Crawford in 1813, and, by 1860, had a thirteen-bay malt floor and two kilns, one of which is a late eighteenth-century structure built of local slob brick. A second large maltings, dating from the 1790s, survives on the opposite side of Rutland Street. In the 1880s, Beamish and Crawford converted a multi-storey flour mill, the Lee Mills, into one of the largest floor maltings in Ireland. This adjoined one of its existing malting concerns in the former River Lee Porter Brewery which, by 1866, operated three substantial kilns. Three kilns survive within the Lee Maltings complex, the largest being constructed in or around 1903, and the other two date from about 1867. In 1889, Murphy's porter brewery at Lady's Well, Cork, built a large five-storey maltings on their premises, designed by the local architect, T. Hynes. The ground floor of the building was fireproofed with jack arches, and the latter,

239

along with the first floor, was used for grain storage, with the upper three storeys serving as malt floors. The steep was situated at the northern end of the building, whilst the sweating and malting kiln at the southern extremity of the building was equipped with an elaborate furnace. The bucket elevators within the malt house, by means of which malt was transferred between the floors, were powered by a horizontal engine by Roby's of Lincoln.[12]

At Castlebridge, County Wexford, a small village village on the confluence of the rivers Sow and Castlebridge, seven miles north of Wexford town, an extensive series of mills, grain stores and maltings were developed by entrepreneurs seeking to avoid paying bridge tolls in Wexford town.[13] In 1804 the first of the corn stores was built by Nicholas Dixon and, up to 1865, corn milling was the principal activity at Castlebridge, but thereafter malting dominated.[14] The mills and maltings were later provided with a direct link to the River Slaney in 1810, when Castlebridge and the river became linked by a canal. The early nineteenth-century maltings at Castlebridge, and the maltings at Athgarvan, County Kildare, are the two best surviving examples of water-powered maltings in Ireland. As the principal outlet for one Ireland's premier grain-growing regions, Wexford town had some 210 malt houses in 1796, with 100 small ships carrying malt to Dublin, and by 1831, was manufacturing 80,000 barrels of malt per year for Dublin's brewing and distilling industries.[15] Indeed, as early as 1796 Enniscorthy, County Wexford, already had as many as 23 registered malt houses, whose output was exported to Dublin via the River Slaney.[16] Good examples of nineteenth-century maltings can still be seen at King Street in Wexford town and at Enniscorthy.[17]

In the 1790s, the Scottish-born, Fermoy, County Cork based entrepreneur, John Anderson, built a malt house at Charleston, on Ballinacurra bay in Cork harbour, and thereby initiated what was to become one of the largest malt manufacturing and grain distribution centres in Ireland.[18] The original Charleston maltings of *c.* 1791, which formed the nucleus of a much larger malting complex developed between 1897 and 1924, still survives. Early in the nineteenth century, a second malt house was erected by John Halloran, directly across the bay in Ballinacurra townland. The Ballinacurra malt house was four storeys high, 50 m by 8.6 m in extent, with a total floor space in the main block of some 1290 m².[19] A third malt house was later established by the Bennett family at Kearney's Cross in Ballinacurra village which, until 2005, was the only working floor maltings in the country.

Tullamore, County Offaly, was also an important former malt-producing centre during the nineteenth century where three large maltings were in operation, supplying local distilleries and a national market via the Grand Canal. The best-preserved multi-storey example, which dates to the early 1850s, is on Harbour Street, directly opposite Tullamore's Grand Canal Harbour. Other fine examples of a floor maltings can be seen at Muine Bheag (1868), County Carlow, Birr, County Offaly, and Stradbally, County Laois.[20]

One of the greatest difficulties associated with the traditional floor maltings was the amount of space needed for growing malt, and that additional flooring capacity came at a cost whenever it became necessary to expand operations. But there were also other problems. Controlling the environment of the malting floor was extremely difficult, which increased the danger that overheating could damage or even destroy the malt. Moreover, when the malt lay in the couch frame, how exactly did one provide proper ventilation to ensure that sufficient oxygen was present to encourage the growing process? The first attempts to move away from the flooring process were made in the second half of the nineteenth century, in a series of patents which proposed mechanical means to control the environment of the malt. A number of patents were secured in the 1850s and 1860s in Europe and the USA, but the first practical system of what became known as *pneumatic* maltings was developed by Galland in France, and was patented in the United Kingdom by H.B. Barlow in 1874. In Galland's pneumatic process, the barley was first steeped in a sheet-iron vessel with a perforated bottom, which retained the barley once the water had been drained off. A ventilator fan immediately beneath the false bottom then created a partial vacuum, which drew down air that had been chilled in a special cooling tower through the germinating barley. By these means it was now possible to exercise considerable control over the environment of the growing malt, but while Galland attempted to put his ideas into practice at Maréville in France in 1873, it appears not to have been successful. Despite its obvious potential, Galland's system was ignored by European maltsters, and it was left to two County Tipperary brewers, Arthur Perry and Robinson Gale Perry, to put it into practice successfully.[21] The Perry brothers had already considered the problem themselves, and had secured patents in malting and kiln drying: clearly, Galland's system appeared to answer most of their existing problems. In 1876, they converted a flour mill on the Brosna river, about three miles north of Roscrea, County Tipperary, which provided plenty of clear water for their air-cooling tower. Extreme air cooling was never required at Perry's pneumatic maltings, as the Irish climate seldom created extreme weather conditions. In modern maltings the pneumatic process is widely employed, largely through the use of a drum, in which the malt is turned mechanically.[22]

(2) Brewing

Irish breweries are synonymous with porter, but ale, including weak table beer or small beer, was also produced by a number of Irish breweries. Indeed, Ireland's largest nineteenth-century porter breweries, Guinness in Dublin and Beamish and Crawford in Cork, had each produced either ales or beers at one time, though Guinness discontinued the manufacture of ales after 1799.[23] Nonetheless, the vast majority of Irish breweries established in the eighteenth and nineteenth centuries, such as the Anchor Brewery, Usher Street (1740), the Ardee Street Brewery, the Mountjoy Brewery (1852), in Dublin, and most of the Cork breweries, produced porter only.[24] The Castlebellingham Brewery, County Louth, which brewed only ale up till the middle of the nineteenth century, Smithwick's St Francis Abbey Brewery in Kilkenny[25] (founded in 1710 and the oldest Irish brewery in continuous use), the Enniscorthy Brewery, County Wexford, Arnott's Brewery in Cork and Caffrey's Brewery in Belfast, which produced either ale or beer along with porter over a long period of time are, comparatively speaking, rare in Ireland. In 1831, Ireland had 215 breweries, a figure which had shrunk considerably by the end of the nineteenth century, by which time Guinness's Brewery was the largest in the world, producing 20 per cent of the total output of the former United Kingdom and around two-thirds of all the beer manufactured in Ireland.[26] Many of the larger county towns had breweries, but most of these tended to be in important barley-growing districts along the east and south-east coast and in the midlands. There was only one brewery in Connacht by the end of the nineteenth century, while in Ulster (where the number of breweries had declined from 25 in 1850 to five in 1902), only three survived in 1920, Downe's in Enniskillen and McConnell's and Caffrey's in Belfast. Significantly, the Belfast breweries were relatively new, being set up at the end of the nineteenth century.[27]

The Brewing Process

By the end of the eighteenth century porter, a dark beer originating in England, had become the main product of most Irish breweries.[28] It has, rather confusingly, been known by many names, such as 'stout', 'stout ale', 'stout porter' or simply 'porter', but was easily distinguishable from either ale or beer by its darker colour. Porter was highly hopped but, while it was stronger than most beers, it was somewhat weaker than ales. It also had a creamy head which lasted much longer than that of other beers, its characteristically darker colour resulting from the use of heavily roasted malt. For the industrial brewer, however, its most important characteristic was that it improved in the cask, and its capacity to be stored directly facilitated mass production and industrial-scale breweries.

The type of malted barley preferred by porter brewers was generally drier than that used in the manufacture of ale. At the brewery, it was first lightly screened in rotating mesh drums and then bruised between millstones (and later between roller mills) to form grist. The malt-processing plant was often housed in a multi-storey building called the *malt loft*, with the malt-screening machinery positioned directly over the malt mills. The bruised malt or *grist* was then immersed in water in a *masher*, a vessel with internally mounted revolving arms which mixed the grist and water in a cylinder outside the mash tun. Patent mashers were introduced into Irish breweries in the second half of the nineteenth century, by which time the necessity of carefully mixing malt and hot water prior to its immersion in the mash tun was fully understood.

In the next process, a false-bottomed vessel, called a *mash tun*, was filled with the contents of the masher, and a series of revolving arms within the mash tun assisted the infusion of the grist and water (figure 9.3). The suspension of the grist in the mash tun facilitated the release of the enzyme *diastase*, which had been cultivated in the malting process, thereby transforming the starch in the malt into maltose. The resulting sludgy mixture, the *goods*, was then allowed to stand for about two hours at a controlled temperature. After mashing – a process common to both brewing and distilling – had been completed, the residue from the bruised malt, now termed *spent grains*, were collected on the false bottom of the mash tun.[29] The spent grains – an important by-product of ale breweries and whiskey distilleries – were generally sold as cattle feed. Up to the middle of the nineteenth century, many breweries produced *small* or *table beer* by mashing the grist for a second time, to manufacture a cheaper but much weaker beer which was bought by poorer people. The introduction of *sparging*, however, eliminated the need for re-mashing the grist.

The liquid drawn off from the mash tun was a sweet liquid called *worts*, which at this stage in the process would have a light head. When the average strength of the wort was stronger than that required by the brewer, a process called sparging was undertaken, in which the mash tun was mechanically sprinkled with hot water

9.3 *Mash tuns in Guinness's James' Gate brewery in Dublin during the 1920s;* **9.4** *Fermenting vats in McArdle's Dundalk brewery in 1902.*

to reduce the strength of the wort.[30] After mashing and sparging, the worts were conveyed to a large, domed copper vessel called a *copper*, in which the liquor was boiled for a couple of hours with dried hops and sugar. Sugar added to the colour, flavour and body of the beer, while the boiling of the hops imparted the characteristic bitterness to the porter or beer. The duration of the boiling time also determined the strength of beer, and arrested further enzyme activity.[31] After boiling, the worts were then conveyed into a vessel called a *hop back*, a false-bottomed receptacle which collected the spent hops and allowed the now clear liquor to pass into the coolers. It was important to cool the wort quickly in order that fermentation could begin, and until mechanical means of refrigeration became available, the summer months still presented problems for breweries.

Early coolers generally consisted of shallow wooden vessels, which were usually erected in the top floor of the brewery, above the mashing loft, where a ridge ventilator enabled the coolers to take full advantage of cold currents of air, particularly in the winter months. The best surviving Irish example of such a roof feature is in Beamish and Crawford's brewery at Cork.

Once the worts were allowed to cool they were then conveyed to a fermenting vat, where excise officers measured its specific gravity in order to calculate the amount of duty owed by the brewery (figure 9.4). Fermentation was then induced by the addition of yeast, which converted maltose into alcohol and produced carbon dioxide. During fermentation, the yeast reproduced itself about five times, and had to be continually skimmed off. The yeast thus acquired was formed into solid cakes, the surplus of which was commonly sold to distilleries. The brewer would check the specific gravity of the liquor (the level of which fell as the wort was converted into alcohol) to determine the progress of the fermentation, which could take up to eight days depending on the type of beer involved. After fermentation had proceeded to a satisfactory degree, the porter brewer would run the beer straight to the vats in order that it could be naturally conditioned through secondary fermentation when casked. This gave the beer a creamy head and induced natural carbonation (the formation of carbon dioxide) which prevented it from becoming flat. The final process, called *fining*, involved the addition of finings, a gelatinous substance made from the swim bladder of a sturgeon, which cleaned the beer by dragging particles of sediment to the bottom of the cask.[32]

The Development of the Irish Porter Brewery Complex

(i) *c.* 1790-1865

The main locational considerations for Ireland's larger mid- to late eighteenth-century breweries were immediate access to an urban population, a barley supply and, preferably, some form of water transport for the supply of bulky raw materials such as barley, hops, and coal for their coppers and kilns (and later their steam engines). In the main, eighteenth-century breweries and distilleries, particularly those established in built-up areas, employed horse-powered machinery and were actually able to begin their initial phases of large-scale industrial production without being tied down to a site which could be serviced by a hydraulic head. Thus, from the outset, breweries could comfortably occupy prime urban locations, unlike water-powered grain mills and many other mechanised industrial units which had to await the introduction of rotative steam engines.

As enormous volumes of water were used in the brewing processes, the maintenance of the water quality and quantity for breweries was extremely important, especially as the type of water used determined the finished product.[33] Porter, for example, required soft water but, regardless of type, the supply had to be free from contamination. Thus, in most Irish breweries, the water supply was originally provided by either artesian wells or rainwater cisterns, which in certain instances was supplemented by piped municipal supplies from the mid-nineteenth century onwards. A similar pattern, indeed, can be observed during the second half of the nineteenth century in English breweries, which were beginning to draw large supplies from water companies.[34] At least three artesian wells had been sunk in Beamish and Crawford's brewery before 1858, while Thomas Murphy's Clonmel brewery had two artesian wells, one of which was 70 ft (21.33 m) deep in the late 1880s.[35] The Drogheda brewery even went as far as boring through 400 ft (121.92 m) of rock to tap a prized spring.[36] For the greater part of its operational history, Guinness extracted water from the Grand Canal (later from filter beds at the fifth lock), and, by 1870 was consuming over 300,000 gallons per day, but even this did not meet its needs. Thus, in 1870, the brewery began to take water from Dublin Corporation's Vartry supply (see Chapter 16), which it used for as boiler feed water and for general cleaning purposes.[37]

By the second half of the eighteenth century, brewing in Ireland was becoming concentrated in larger units of production, but in many instances the larger breweries still had few specialised buildings. Arthur Guinness's Brewery at St James' Gate, Dublin, established in 1759, which was favourably sited near the pipe wall of the city watercourse, had two malt houses, a malt mill, a stable for twelve horses and what appears to have been a small brewhouse.[38] Beamish and Crawford's Cork Porter Brewery, established in 1792, had as its nucleus a brewery and maltings in Cremer's Square, converted by Aylmer Allen in 1782.[39] However, as the market for porter increased towards the end of the eighteenth century, the brewery buildings of both Beamish and Crawford and

Guinness expanded by acquiring adjacent buildings, plots of land and even whole streets. Brewery buildings such as grain stores, malt houses, coal storage sheds, brew houses (which accommodated the mash tuns, coppers and fermentation vats), cart sheds and workshops for ancillary trades, began to expand along street frontages, subsuming parallel laneways and streets along with entire blocks of buildings. Alternately, the existing buildings could be expanded upwards, and this, along with the horizontal expansion of Irish breweries, can be broadly paralleled with that of London brewers in the late eighteenth century.[40] Indeed, experienced operatives from London breweries were employed in a number of Cork porter breweries by the closing decades of the eighteenth century, and this both improved quality and had some influence on brewery architecture. Furthermore, there is also some evidence that British millwrights were designing water-wheels and transmission systems for Irish breweries. In 1811, Henry Walker, a wealthy brewery owner at Fermoy, County Cork, commissioned the noted Scottish engineer, John Rennie (1761-1821), to improve his brewery's motive power and to design and execute the necessary millwork.[41]

Purpose-built eighteenth-century breweries such as the River Lee Porter Brewery, constructed between 1796 and 1797, and Beamish and Crawford, appear to have been largely confined to Cork.[42] In the former, the three-storey brewery buildings are built around a quadrilateral courtyard, with most of the plant being housed in the west wing. The brewery also appears to have operated water-powered machinery, which seems likely to have been employed in the preparation of malt.[43] However, the use of water power in an urban brewery was exceptional, as almost all the other urban breweries in Cork and Dublin employed horse wheels. Indeed, the use of animal power for grinding malt and pumping water was itself a constraint on the expansion of a brewery which, given the locations of most urban breweries, could only be achieved by introducing steam engines. By 1800, John Sweetman's brewery on Francis Street, Dublin, was being powered by a steam engine, the earliest recorded use of such an engine in an Irish brewery.[44] Sweetman's brewery was established in 1798 at the enormous cost of £20,000, and it seems likely that this engine was its first steam-powered prime mover.[45] In 1809, Guinness of Dublin became the second Irish brewery to install a beam engine, while in Cork, Beamish and Crawford followed suit in 1818 (see Chapter 1), though neither brewery showed the precocity of certain Irish distilleries in this regard.[46]

Although Irish porter breweries such as Beamish and Crawford and Guinness were similar in size to many of the London breweries by the turn of the nineteenth century, their industrial architecture was quite different. In surviving mid-eighteenth-century brewery buildings, such as Lane's (1758), Drinan's brewery (c. 1760) and Cowperthwaite's (c. 1780) in Cork, it is clear that the individual buildings are mostly constructed around a courtyard. Of course, the latter may not have been typical of Irish urban breweries in general, but Cork was in this period one of the main centres of the Irish brewing industry and, by the end of the century, was home to Ireland's largest brewery. Nonetheless, the River Lee Porter Brewery, although built in the closing years of the 1790s, was still essentially a larger version of the earlier Cork city courtyarded breweries. However, it did have a wide, steeply pitched hipped slate roof – a characteristic shared with both Beamish and Crawford's brewery and those used on the London brewhouses of the 1790s. Yet, like Beamish and Crawford and the other earlier city breweries, it does not have the distinctive large semi-circular arched louvred windows of English brew-houses of the same period.[47] The early layout of Beamish and Crawford's brewery, on the other hand, does bear some resemblance to Whitbread's Chiswell Street Brewery in London, in that the buildings housing the malt mills, mash tuns, coppers and fermenting vats are constructed side by side to accommodate both power transmission and the movement of liquids by gravity.

By the middle of the nineteenth century, Irish urban breweries could cover up to five acres in extent, but up to the mid-1860s, brewery development remained largely a piecemeal affair. Thomas Murphy's brewery in Clonmel (originally established at Nelson Street in 1798), which was entirely rebuilt in the 1830s after a fire of 1829, is unique in this regard in that it is a rare Irish purpose-built brewery of the period.[48] It is also the only Irish brewery of the first half of the nineteenth century to have any architectural pretensions. The Nelson Street brewery, which was directly adjacent to Clonmel's New Quay on the River Suir, comprised a large, central, six-storey block with a castellated parapet.[49]

Nonetheless, smaller courtyarded breweries, such as Watergate Brewery (1843) in Bandon, County Cork, continued to be built, while new breweries could still be established in converted buildings.[50] Even the new Lady's Well Brewery in Cork, completed in 1857, the largest of the newer nineteenth-century Irish breweries, was established within a mid-eighteenth-century complex of buildings, the former Cork Foundling Hospital, whose main courtyarded block was converted into a brewery. The main body of the new buildings consisted of a multi-storey tower brewery constructed in the north-west corner of the former hospital, and a series of porter cellars to the south. The three-storey blocks of the hospital buildings were converted to malting floors. All these works were, however, supervised by a London brewer called Gresham Wiles, who had been brought over by the new company expressly for this purpose.[51] Wiles's involvement in the design of the Murphy's installation is the only known foreign intervention in the design of an Irish brewery in the nineteenth century where, as we shall shortly see, this was almost entirely the preserve of the breweries' own engineers.

(ii) 1865-1900

The demand for beer and porter in both Britain and Ireland by the early 1860s was such that breweries were presented with incredible opportunities for both expansion and modernisation. Beamish and Crawford's Cork Porter Brewery, which had steadily expanded since the late 1830s, was entirely refurbished in the period 1865-8, during which some £100,000 was invested in modernisation.[52] At least one wholly new brewery, the Ulster Brewery on Sandy Row, was built in Belfast in 1869 to a design by the Belfast architect Alex McAllister.[53] This is the only known example of an architect-designed brewery in Ireland, and is also the only Irish example to be built in the classical style. Surprisingly, despite its unrivalled importance in the Irish brewing industry, the large-scale modernisation of Guinness's St James' Gate Brewery came somewhat later. By 1860 the brewery was spread over about four acres on the south side of James' Street and Thomas Street but was almost doubled in size in 1873 when the company bought a large plot of land between James' Street and the River Liffey to the north.[54] Guinness proceeded to build a malt house on this site which, at 172 ft by 44 ft (54.42 m by 13.41 m) was the longest in the former United Kingdom.[55] Not until 1876, however, was a decision made to construct an entirely new brewery. Work on the latter, at Victoria Quay, was begun in 1877 and completed in 1879 under an extraordinary and innovative building campaign. Construction work was carried out between the hours of 6am in the morning and continued until 10pm at night with the aid of electric arc lights, powered by two Siemens dynamos – the first recorded industrial use of electric lighting in Ireland.[56] At the turn of the century, Guinness's Brewery covered over 50 acres and was the largest brewing concern in the world.[57]

By the 1880s, the St James' Gate Brewery occupied three different levels. The first, or upper, level was some 60 ft (18.28 m) above that adjacent to the river quayside, and included the old and new breweries, the fermenting rooms, the vat houses, the stables and the malt and hop stores. The second, or middle level accommodated the maltings, the grain stores and a vat house, while the third, or lower level on Victoria Quay consisted of the principal brewery workshops (cooperages and carpentry), cask-washing sheds and the main loading areas for river traffic and the adjacent Kingsbridge terminus of the Great Southern and Western Railway.[58] Each of the three levels was linked by an ingenious 22 in narrow-gauge railway, via a spiral tunnel, which enabled the specially designed locomotives and their wagons to ascend or descend to each level. The railway was the brainchild of the brewery's chief engineer, Samuel Geoghegan (1845-1928), who had also supervised the construction of the new brewery. He designed the railway locomotive and had a prototype built in England in 1882; a further eighteen were subsequently manufactured by William Spence's Cork Street Foundry between 1887 and 1921, which were in service up to 1947.[59] Indeed, Geoghegan was largely responsible for the brewery's nineteenth-century expansion, and established its international reputation for technical innovation. At his behest, the Irish engineer, Robert Worthington, designed the innovative Robert Street Store for the brewery, completed in 1884; which in its day had the tallest load-bearing brick walls in the world.[60] The brewery was also responsible for the introduction of skyscraper building technology into Ireland, when its engineer, A.H. Hignett, designed the brewery's eight-storey, steel-framed, Market Street Store (1900-2).[61]

All of Ireland's larger breweries and distilleries maintained cooperages, in which considerable numbers of coopers were employed in the manufacture and repair of casks. Cooperage yards were often extensive, as huge stocks of timber and finished casks required large open spaces for storage. In the 1860s, the Dublin iron founder and scientist, Robert Mallet, designed steam-powered cask-washing machinery for Guinness (the first used in Ireland), and later devised a machine for numbering the casks using the pentagraph principle.[62] The wooden cask remained the most important receptacle for beer well into the twentieth century but, by the end of the nineteenth century, most Irish breweries were operating mechanised bottling plants. Considerable attention was also paid to the transportation of the beer, and all of the large breweries maintained large stables and supported associated trades like wheel, cart and harness repair. In 1902, no fewer than 120 drays of stout left the St James' Gate Brewery every day, and Guinness kept 153 horses to pull its 160 drays and floats (two, and four-wheeled, low slung carts for transporting casks). As early as 1897, the brewery was already experimenting with steam carts, but abandoned the idea in favour of motor trucks. It also owned nine steam-powered river barges which facilitated transport of coal and other raw materials via the River Liffey from the port of Dublin (figure 9.5).[63]

9.5 *Guinness barges on River Liffey in 1902.*

A surprising amount of nineteenth-century brewing plant has survived in Ireland, but only Beamish and Crawford's brewery retains a sizeable amount of its original machinery *in situ*. The surviving St James' Gate machinery has mostly been removed to the Guinness Hop Store, the brewery's on-site heritage centre. This includes mash tuns, skimming tanks, a vertical high-speed steam engine (see Chapter 2) and malt roller mills, along with an excellent selection of coopers' tools. Beamish and Crawford's three-storey malt-milling loft is unique in Ireland in that it still retains its entire range of late nineteenth- early twentieth-century screening and milling plant. The upper floor of the tower contains the separator screens and the substance extractor/separator, by the English firm of Nalder and Nalder, which was used to extract unwanted grains and foreign matter, such as stones, from the malt before it was fed into the roller-milling apparatus. Immediately beneath the latter are three sets of roller mills, which were installed around 1902. The brewery also contains two cone-headed coppers (capacity 1,560 gallons each) by Llewellyns and James of Castle Green, Bristol, complete with their enormous brick furnaces, which were installed some time before 1884. Most of the impressive cast-iron superstructure of the main mashing loft dates to the period 1870-83, and the loft itself contains a single surviving mash tun by Robert Morton and Company of Burton on Trent of 1896.

(3) Distilling

Ireland had no fewer than 1,228 distilleries in 1780, but an act of 1779, which attempted to limit the evasion of payment of spirit, had reduced overall numbers to 246. The net result of this was to concentrate production in larger units, a development which was further assisted by an act of 1791, which decreed that all new stills had to have a capacity of 500 gallons or more.[64] During the eighteenth century, distillation was by no means wholly confined to the production of whiskey, for whiskey distillers in Ireland were also often involved in rectifying and compounding. These latter activities involved smaller pot stills, which were used to manufacture spirits of wine (a purified strong spirit used for scientific and industrial purposes) from raw spirit, along with drinks flavoured with ingredients such as coriander seed and aniseed.[65] Not until the early decades of the nineteenth century was a legal distinction made between the rectifier and the compounder but, from 1828, the distinction was no longer recognised. However, by 1805, whiskey distillation, rectifying and compounding had each become separate activities.[66] The Irish distilling industry, up to the 1830s, relied principally on the home market, but the harmonisation of excise rates with the rest of the UK (which effectively involved a sharp rise in the price of spirits in Ireland) led to a gradual decline in the production and consumption of spirits in Ireland. In consequence, the number of Irish distilleries was reduced in a five-year period between 1857-62, from 37 to 27.[67]

The Distilling Process

Traditionally, whiskey in Ireland has been distilled from malted barley mixed with a certain amount of raw barley and other cereals such as oats and later maize. In it essentials, whiskey distillation involves brewing beer and then distilling a spirit from it, the basic brewing processes being common to both industries. The cereal grains were first reduced to grist between millstones (and later in roller mills), and were then mixed with the ground malt in a mash tun. However, whereas the introduction of sparging ended re-mashing in breweries, in the whiskey distillery, the grains in the mash tun were continually re-mashed to extract as much saccharine matter as possible. Furthermore, while the brewer endeavoured to retain the aroma of his hops and malt, and to convert only a certain amount of the sugar in the wort to alcohol, the aim of the distiller was the exact opposite.

Whiskey distillation essentially involves the separation of alcohol from fermented wort, or *wash* as it is called by the distiller. As alcohol has a lower boiling point than water, it is given off first, and in the still the wash is converted into a vapour which is subsequently condensed into a liquid and collected in a vessel called a *receiver*. In Ireland, two basic varieties

9.6 *Pot stills in Power's Distillery, John's Lane, Dublin (now the National College of Art and Design).*

249

of still were used in whiskey distilleries, the *pot still* (by far the most common) and the *patent* or *continuous still*, which was predominantly employed in Ulster. The pot still is a flat-bottomed copper vessel, from the head of which extends a spiral copper tub called the *worm* (figure 9.6). The greater extent of the worm is coiled around the inside of an adjacent wooden vessel filled with water, known as the *worm tub*, which acted as a condenser. The spirit collected at this stage was by no means pure, and it was necessary to refine it in a series of three successive re-distillations. The first of these was called the *low wines*, which passed on to the *low wine receiver* and from thence to the *low wines still*, where it was re-distilled. The resulting distillate was then passed on to the *feints receivers*, and the purest of the feints was then conveyed to a third still from which it emerged as whiskey.[68]

The development of the patent still, in which Irish distillers played a pioneering role, arose out of a desire to reduce the amount of fuel needed to perform the various distillations associated with the pot still process. In the latter, a strong spirit could only be obtained from repeatedly distilling individual batches, which was wasteful of fuel and required that the stills be re-charged after each distillation. The desired object of early inventors, therefore, was to achieve distillation from wash to spirit in a single continuous process. Nineteenth-century Irish distillers such as M. Stein of the Clonmel Distillery, Joseph Shee of the Green Distillery, and Sir Anthony Perrier of the Spring Lane Distillery in Cork, were amongst the first in Europe to effect significant improvements to traditional distilling apparatus. Joseph Shee's process directly addressed the fuel consumption problem of the traditional pot still by employing a succession of four connected pot stills. The lowest still was heated by a fire, the steam from which passed upwards to the second still immediately above it, and thence to the third and fourth stills, each positioned at successively higher levels. As the wash entered the fourth and highest still, it flowed against the steam down to the first still, the rising vapours absorbing alcohol, which was condensed and tapped off from the fourth still. The entire arrangement was kept going by vapours from the exhausted wash from the first still.[69] However, while Shee's process did reduce fuel consumption, it was not technically a continuous one.

In 1822, Sir Anthony Perrier patented the first continuous still of Irish design, one of the earliest to be developed in Europe. In Perrier's still, the wash was allowed to flow over a heated surface equipped with baffles. Steam was then blown through it, the steam lifting the spirit-laden vapours.[70] However, both of the Cork innovations appear to have been used only in the inventors' own distilleries. But a significant step in the development of the patent still in Ireland was made some time before 1831, when a Saintmarc patent still was installed in the Millfield Distillery on the outskirts of Cork. Jean-Jacques Saintmarc's still, developed in the first decade of the nineteenth century, was the first practical continuous still, and consisted of a fire-heated pot still equipped with rectifying chambers in which pure spirit could be produced continuously. The concept was introduced into England by Saintmarc, a former veterinary surgeon, in 1823, and in 1825, he obtained a patent for it. From here, he appears to have sold a modified version for distilling wash to one of the owners of the Millfield Distillery, probably by the late 1820s but, although it was capable of producing more than a conventional pot still – the Millfield still could manufacture 180,000 gallons of whiskey in a season – it is only known to have been used in three Irish distilleries.[71] The Millfield Distillery still is the earliest recorded example used in Ireland, and a second example was at work in Belfast in 1834.[72]

The Saintmarc still and the Irish attempts of the early 1820s to solve the same basic problems of the tradition-al pot still were short lived, but the ultimate solution was soon to be arrived at by another Irishman. In 1830, Aeneas Coffey (1780-1852), a former inspector-general of excise in Ireland, patented a continuous still which was to become widely adopted in Irish and Scottish distilleries.[73]

In the Coffey still, the distilling process is continuous, cold wash being continuously fed into the still from which it is discharged as spirit. Coffey's still was the first successful heat exchanger. It consists of a pair of fractionating columns, one of which, the analyser, stripped the wash of spirit, and a second column, called the *rectifier*, which con-solidates and purifies the spirit. Within the still, the outgoing hot vapour is allowed to come into contact with the incoming wash awaiting distillation, the greater part of the heat from the hot vapour, by this means, being exchanged before it was conveyed to the condenser. A very strong spirit of upwards of 95 per cent alcohol could be obtained using this process, with significant fuel savings, although the main casualty was taste.[74] The latter could, nonetheless, be considerably improved upon through blending with pot still whiskeys, and the cost of the finished product was still cheaper than pot still whiskey. Nonetheless, in Ireland, only the larger distilleries which catered for expanding urban markets tended to convert to patent still production but, even then, most Irish distillers regarded patent still whiskey as an inferior product and proved reluctant to adopt it, even in the face of increased competition from patent distillers with lower cost bases.[75] In consequence, there were only eight patent stills in Ireland in 1833, one of the earliest of which was installed by Aeneas Coffey himself in the Abbey Street Distillery in Derry in 1833.[76] A further Coffey still was set up in the Watercourse Distillery in 1833, worked by a steam boiler, with which it was possible to distill 3,000 gallons of wash every hour.[77]

The Development of the Distillery Complex *c.* 1780-1900

As was the case with Ireland's brewers, whiskey distillers favoured urban locations in barley-producing regions. However, from the mid-eighteenth century on, distillers, even in large urban areas, showed a clear preference for water-powered sites. In Cork, which had become an important distilling centre by the end of the 1700s, all the principal sites, including the North Mall Distillery (1779), the Millfield Distillery (1783), St Dominick's Distillery (1789), the Watercourse Distillery (1794) the Dodge's Glen Distillery (*c.* 1803) and the Green Distillery (*c.* 1828), employed some form of water-powered machinery. Only in Dublin does it appear that the availability of water power was not a primary locational consideration for eighteenth-century distillers, as is evidenced by the Thomas Street Distillery (1757), the John's Lane Distillery (1771) and the Marrowbone Lane Distillery (1779). However, while this may well have been the case for the early Dublin distilleries, it clearly was not the case for sites established near the city in the later nineteenth century. Indeed, almost all the sites established in Ireland's county towns, such as Kilbeggan, County Westmeath (1757), Birr, County Offaly (1805), and Bandon, County Cork (1825), originally used water-powered plant.

As has been seen, whiskey distilling involves some of the same basic processes as brewing and, as such, whiskey distilleries also required a plentiful supply of water. In Dublin, the John's Lane Distillery took most of its water from Dublin Corporation's Vartry reservoir by the late 1880s, whereas the Thomas Street and

9.7 *The Thomas Street Distillery, Dublin, from Barnard 1887.*

Marrowbone Lane distilleries acquired theirs both from Vartry and the Grand Canal. The Phoenix Park Distillery (1878) drew water via a pipeline from the upper reaches of the River Liffey, while the Jones Lane site employed a one-mile-long pipe to lead water from the Royal Canal. The Bow Street Distillery appears to have been almost unique in Dublin in its reliance on two deep wells on site, although the Jones Lane site also had a 100 ft (30.48 m) deep well. In Cork, distillers used a conjunction of wells and water drawn from the River Lee and its north-side tributaries for a time, and later the municipal supply. The water supply for distilleries in the county towns was almost invariably drawn from local rivers, as at Kilbeggan from the River Brosna.[78] By the second half of the nineteenth century, many distilleries had large cast-iron water tanks installed on their roofs, for storage purposes. The Jones Road Distillery had an almost entirely flat roof to accommodate such storage cisterns.

The physical development of Ireland's distilleries can be broadly paralleled with that of the larger breweries, but, in many cases, the distillery premises would occupy a much larger surface area than that of most breweries. The North Mall Distillery in Cork covered over 23 acres, whilst some of the Dublin distilleries, such as Thomas Street (figure 9.7, 17 acres) and Marrowbone Lane (14 acres), were also quite large. For the most part, this was because the distillery would have also accommodated additional plant for distillation, while it would commonly require considerable storage space for whiskey maturing in the cask. A number of distilleries were deliberately built into sloping ground to facilitate the movement of liquids by gravity, as at the Watercourse Road Distillery and North Mall Distilleries in Cork, the Bishop's Water Distillery, Wexford (1827), and Allman's Distillery at Bandon, County Cork, completed in 1826.[79] Yet, while individual layouts varied considerably, even the medium-sized Irish distilleries tended to be from around six to ten acres in extent. From the second half of the eighteenth century on, distilleries generally have long ranges of buildings, set side by side, but, unlike contemporary breweries, large and capacious grain stores were constructed from the outset. The grain stores at the Watercourse Road Distillery, completed in 1794, consisted of two long, narrow, gabled four-storey buildings built with sandstone quarried from the adjacent hillside, whilst the malt house to the north of erected *c.* 1793 was probably the largest in any Irish distillery of the period.[80] Moreover, even when the buildings were well spread out, as in the Millfield Distillery (1783) and the Dodge's Glen Distillery (1803) on the outskirts of Cork, there was a clear preference for long, narrow, multi-storey buildings. The best surviving example of a grain store of the period is R. and J. Wallace's distillery at Birr, County Offaly, which was built in 1805, part of which has recently been converted as a dwelling. Wallace's grain store is three storeys high, and has a slated hipped roof similar to those of the surviving eighteenth-century buildings in Beamish and Crawford and River Lee Porter breweries in Cork.

By the middle of the 1800s Irish distilleries had built some of the largest multi-storey buildings then in existence on the island. John Jameson's Bow Street Distillery was spread over two streets and consisted of long ranges of four- and five-storey buldings: multi-storey grain stores, maltings, large kilns, mashing houses, malt mills, brewhouses, vat rooms, pot still houses and cooperages. One of its corn lofts was 225 ft by 48 ft (68.58 m by 14.63 m), while one malt kiln, heated by four furnaces, was 60 ft by 48 ft (18.28 m by 14.63 m). John's Lane Distillery, rebuilt after 1871, had a five-storey grain store 192 ft long and 100 ft wide (58.54 m by 30.48 m), in which hydraulic hoists, the first likely to have been employed in an Irish distillery, were used to lift grain from the adjacent courtyard.[81] The Thomas Street Distillery had one storage warehouse which was 360 ft (109.72 m) long, while its mash house contained the two largest mash tuns (each with a capacity of 100,000 gallons) in the former United Kingdom. The most extensive distillery maltings in Ireland were built at the Bandon Distillery, County Cork. The Bandon maltings were 168 ft long by 42 ft wide (51.2 m by 121.8 m), with floor heights of 8 ft (2.43 m), and was the second largest (after Guinness) in either Britain or Ireland.[82]

The pot stills were always housed in a separate tall building, with a wide span roof, which was necessary to accommodate the worm heads. The still house at the John's Lane Distillery was 68 ft by 66 ft (20.72 m) and 57 ft (17.37 m) high, while that at Jones Road was 60 ft (18.28 m) high and had a cast-iron superstructure, with double galleries.[83] In all cases the worm tubs were positioned immediately outside the still house, and were generally raised on stilts consisting of either stone pillars or cast-iron columns, in order to be level with the head of the pot still. At the Marrowbone Lane Distillery, the pot still house had open vents at the eaves to enable the head of the worm pipes to extend outside the building into the worm tubs which were set on cast-iron stilts. Positioning the worm tubs in the open air did, of course, also assist condensing of the vapours from the pot still.

In the late eighteenth century, large pot stills were generally manufactured in England, as the copper-smithing skills were not yet available here. The Watercourse Distillery in Cork, for example, purchased two large capacity stills, condensers and worms from by Edgar Curtis of Bristol in 1793. However, in the nineteenth century, at least one Irish company, Miller's of Dublin, specialised in the manufacture of pot stills, and supplied them to the Bow Street, Kilbeggan and Limerick distilleries. Irish distilleries also maintained the same range of ancillary trades as breweries (cooperages, stabling and the like), and were amongst the earliest Irish industrial installations to have fire engines on site, as was the case at the Limerick and Dundalk distilleries in the 1880s. An excellent example of an early twentieth-century fire engine is on display at Midleton Distillery, County Cork.

In the vast majority of Irish distilleries, the plant was powered by a combination of water and steam-powered prime movers, while in a number of instances, such as in the distilleries at Bandon, Phoenix Park, and Tullamore, along with the Nun's Island Distillery in Galway, only water-powered plant was in operation in the 1880s. Given the expense of importing coal water power, as in the case of other nineteenth-century Irish industries, was the preferred option when available, and it is interesting to note that at Jones Road, the last Irish distillery to be built in the nineteenth century, a Leffel turbine was installed in the 1870s. By the end of the eighteenth century, distillers in Cork and Dublin were already concerned about the constraints which the continued use of both animal- and water-powered machinery placed upon their ability to expand their operations. Two Irish distilleries, St Dominick's in Cork and Marrowbone Lane in Dublin, were using 'pirated' versions of Boulton and Watt engines by 1800, although as early as 1799, Thomas Walker and Company had formally approached Boulton and Watt about the installation of a steam engine at its St Dominick's Distillery.[84] Some time between 1800 and 1805, a new 40 hp Boulton and Watt double-acting beam crank engine was installed in this distillery. The latter was the first engine of its type to be installed in Ireland, and in its day was the most powerful Boulton and Watt engine in any Irish industrial complex.[85] Cork distillers, indeed, led the way in the adoption of steam engines in the industry, with two other distilleries in the city at North Mall (1808) and Watercourse Road (1811-12) installing Boulton and Watt engines.[86] By the middle of the 1800s most Irish distilleries operated with steam-powered plant and, by the end of that century, the skyline of almost every Irish distillery was broken by large smokestacks.

A large number of distillery buildings have survived throughout Ireland, although only two original sites, Midleton, County Cork and Bushmills, County Antrim, remain in use as whiskey distilleries. The two best-preserved examples are Midleton and Kilbeggan, County Westmeath, each of which has a sizeable proportion of its nineteenth-century plant, while the Thomas Street Distillery (now incorporated into the National College of Art and Design) retains its two nineteenth-century steam engines *in situ* (see Chapter 2). At Kilbeggan, the Poncelet-type water-wheel, built by Mallet's of Dublin, and a horizontal cross-compound condensing engine, installed in 1887 by Canal Basin Foundry, Port Dundas, Glasgow, have each been restored to full working order. Kilbeggan also has the most complete set of original working plant of any Irish distillery, which includes its fermenting vats (figure 9.8), a proofing vat, a set of three throw pumps (the only examples to survive *in situ* in Ireland) a large cast-iron mash tun by McLaghlan and Co. of Paisley (installed in 1892, figure 9.9) and three sets of millstones by Hilton and Hay of Liverpool for making grist from malt (1890s).[87] The millstones are the only

9.8 *Wooden fermenting vats in the Kilbeggan distillery, County Westmeath (above left);* **9.9** *Cast-iron mash tun by McLaghlan and Co. of Paisley, installed in 1892, in the Kilbeggan distillery, County Westmeath (above right);* **9.10** *Mildleton Distillery, County Cork, established in 1824 (left).*

surviving water-powered malt milling stones to survive in any Irish brewery or distillery.

Midleton Distillery, County Cork, was established by James Murphy in 1825 in Marcus Lynch's former woollen mill of 1793 (figure 9.10, see Chapter 8). The surviving range of buildings dates from the 1830s onwards and includes three malting kilns, and it is dominated by a six-storey grain store of *c.* 1830. In the latter, each floor could hold up to 250 tons (total weight 1,500 tons), and a series of buttresses had to be used to shore one side of the building against an adjacent one. The original wooden floors have been preserved, which makes it the most complete surviving distillery grain store in Ireland. A late nineteenth-century brew house, complete with steel mash tuns and vats, has recently been opened to the public as part of the distillery tour. The late eighteenth-century woollen mill was converted for use as a malt mill and mash house, powered by both water and steam. Its extant 22 ft (6.70 m) diameter water-wheel is by William Fairbairn of Manchester and was installed

255

in 1852, when it was used in conjunction with two steam engines, one of which, a six-column independent beam engine by Peele and Williams of Manchester installed in 1835, has been retained *in situ*. The Midleton distillery also boasts the largest pot still in the world, a wash still with a capacity of 31,648 gallons, installed in 1826, which required 4.06 tonnes of coal every 24 hours. The two more recent feints and low wine stills associated with the latter, built by D. Miller of Dublin in 1949, are preserved in an adjacent still house.

Much less has, unfortunately, survived in Dublin distilleries. Of these, the John's Lane Distillery, on Thomas Street, retains a reasonable amount of the original buildings, including its offices (fronting Thomas Street), its main grain store and engine houses. As has been seen in Chapter 2, two important steam engines are retained *in situ* on the site, but in terms of the industrial archaeology of distilling, three of the original pot stills have survived, although in the open air without the protection of their still house. Across the River Liffey, the surviving sections of the Bow Street Distillery have recently been adapted for modern commercial usage, which includes the contentious addition of a lift and viewing platform to the tallest of the distillery's original chimneys. In Tullamore, County Offaly, a former distillery bonded store, built in 1897 on the bank of the Grand Canal, has been converted into an excellent local museum, part of whose displays deal with the local distilling industry. The only nineteenth-century distillery in the North of Ireland open to the public is at Bushmills, County Antrim.

(4) Grain Milling

In Ireland, the large-scale mechanisation of grain milling began in the mid-eighteenth century, when a government bounty, offered between 1758 and 1797 on flour brought to Dublin, provided the impetus for widespread structural and technological changes in the Irish grain-milling industry.[88] Unlike many other industries in either Britain or Ireland, virtually all the processes involved in grain milling had already been mechanised, which encouraged the concentration of production in increasingly larger units of production. The Irish flour mill was one of the first in Europe to expand vertically, with extra storeys being provided both for more processing plant and additional storage. This development pre-dates Arkwright's multi-storey textile mills of the later eighteenth century. However, there was an earlier but wholly unrelated precedent in the British silk industry, where Thomas Cotchett had built a three-storey silk-throwing mill on the River Derwent in Derby. Cotchett was followed by John and Sir Thomas Lombe in 1721, who built a five-storey silk mill near Cotchett's.[89] Nonetheless, Irish merchants were already building what were effectively multi-storey flour factories well before Arkwright's innovations in the English cotton industry of the 1770s.[90] The adoption of steam power in Irish grain mills also greatly reduced the traditional reliance on water power. Large-scale milling could now be undertaken on the quaysides of Ireland's ports, where grain could be unloaded into adjacent granaries, reduced to flour in nearby mills and conveyed directly from the latter to outgoing ships. Around 2,500 grain mills were at work in Ireland in the period 1835-50, which made the milling industry the most geographically dispersed on the island. This figure was reduced to about 1,100 in 1916, but as late as 1907 milling still accounted for some 10 per cent of

Ireland's recorded industrial output.[91]

The Development of the Multi-Storey Flour Mill in Ireland

(i) *c.* 1738-1800

From the second half of the eighteenth century onwards, the means by which cereal grains were cleaned prior to milling became increasingly more sophisticated, beginning with the introduction of hand- or mechanically-operated winnowing fans. Most of the large later eighteenth-century flour mills and all the nineteenth-century examples were also equipped with mechanically driven flour-dressing machinery, which was used to sieve and grade the flour. The mechanical bolter was the first of a series of power-driven devices employed in mills for more efficient flour dressing, and it is from its widespread application in early Irish industrial mills that the contemporary eighteenth- and nineteenth-century term 'bolting mill' originates. In a typical bolting screen, a textile mesh was drawn over a cylindrical wooden framework, which was rotated by an auxiliary drive from the water-wheel. The meal, which was fed in at one end of the drum thus formed, was graded by being forced through the mesh from which only flour of the desired grade could emerge. A 'bolting' mill was in existence at Islandbridge on the River Liffey near Dublin in 1738, while according to Charles Smith, Samuel Pike of Cork ran a 'curious' bolting mill near the town around 1750.[92] From the late eighteenth century onwards, *wire machines*, which enabled different grades of flour to be separated simultaneously, were also in use in the larger Irish mills. By 1796, there was at least one specialist machine maker in Cork at Fishamble Lane, William Mozly, who manufactured bolting machines, wheat cylinders, winnowing and screening machines, which he supplied to mills in the locality.[93]

The additional grain-cleaning and flour-dressing machinery required that at least a third storey be added to the mill building, largely to accommodate grain storage. Indeed, most of the early bolting mills are likely to have been three storeys high, and to have operated up to three pairs of stones. William Colles' flour and oat mill at Abbeyvale on the River Nore near Kilkenny town, completed in 1762, is described as being 'three stories high', and, if we assume that the early mills at Cork and Dublin were similar in layout, then these were built at least 30 years before Arkwright's integrated cotton mills.

Andrew Mervyn's mill at Naul, County Meath, had three pairs of French burr stones in 1761 and three flour bolters (all powered by a single water-wheel), along with a weighing room, the latter probably being on the ground floor.[94] The drive to three pairs of stones could only have been achieved through either a layshaft or spur gearing, and the introduction of the bolting mill presumably marks the introduction of both of these forms of power transmission into Ireland. Auxiliary drives, extending through two floors, would also have been required for the bolters, grain elevators, a winnowing fan and a sack hoist, in other words, altogether more sophisticated gear linkages than would have been in existence elsewhere in Ireland. The importance of these new forms of power transmission to the development of large-scale milling in this country has been completely ignored.[95] As we have already seen, flour and meal mills with two or more pairs of millstones, powered by the same water-wheel, were by no means universal when the original Valuation Survey was conducted in the late 1840s, while in a number of midland and western counties these were still in a minority. The machinery of the bolting mill, it is clear, could only have been operated with either layshaft or spur gearing. As to the introduction of this technology, it seems likely to have been via English millwrights and machine workers brought over to Ireland. Indeed, the machinery of Richard Bonner's mill at Oldtown near Naas, County Kildare, was claimed by Bonner to have been erected by the 'most skilful English artists', some time before 1763.[96] In England, spur-wheel gearing in water mills (which may have been derived from that of windmills) was in existence by the seventeenth century, and was certainly more widespread in English water mills by the 1730s. Layshaft gearing was also in use in England by the 1720s.[97] The likelihood is, therefore, that both means of power transmission were first introduced to Ireland, from England, with the development of bolting mills.

All of the early mills, although large by contemporary standards, were soon to be overshadowed by developments in Limerick and at Slane, County Meath. Between 1762 and 1764, Andrew Welsh and Edward Uzold built what was then the largest industrial structure in Ireland on the bank of the Limerick Canal near the lock to the Abbey River. The mill, designed by Uzold, cost £6,000, and powered six millstones, four bolting machines and four sets of fulling stocks, all actuated by two water-wheels turned by water from the canal. In addition, the mills straddled an inlet from the adjacent Abbey River, which enabled barges and 'boats of considerable burden' to gain direct access to its granaries. The Lock Mills are depicted on Christopher Colles' map of the city of Limerick of 1769, where they are shown as a 'U'-shaped range of buildings with a rectangular central block. An early twentieth-century photograph of the mills shows the main six-storey mill block, which has a half-hipped roof and a decorative parapet facing the canal bank; it is flanked by what appears to be a grain store.[98]

Two years after the Lock Mills were completed in 1766, the largest water-powered flour mill in Europe was designed and built by the engineer, David Jebb, near the village of Slane, County Meath, using capital mainly supplied by Townley Balfour of Townley Hall, County Louth. Ten years later, in 1776, in his capacity of mill manager, Jebb showed Arthur Young around the mills, which he described as 'a large and handsome edifice such as no mill I have seen in England can be compared with'. The five-storey mill was then the largest industrial building in Ireland, being 138 ft long, 54 ft wide and 42 ft high (42.06 m by 16.45 m by 12.8 m). It consisted of a gabled block, 'T'-shaped in plan, with a central bay which projected forward with an eaves pediment. In Young's famous description, the grain was lifted to the fifth-storey grain loft, which had a capacity of 5,000 barrels, by means of a water-powered bucket elevator. It was then dried in two large kilns, which could process 80 barrels in a 24 hour period. No fewer than seven pairs of millstones – the largest number ever operated in an Irish flour mill up to that date – ground some 120 barrels of flour per day.[99] In his capacity as engineer to the Commissioners of Inland Navigation on the Boyne Navigation works, Jebb had overseen the construction of the Boyne Navigation to Slane, which had probably been completed before the mill opened, giving it a waterway to the Irish Sea via the Boyne and thence to Dublin.[100] The mill-race of the Slane mills was also the most impressive in Ireland, consisting of an 800 ft (243.84 m) long walled canal with mooring wharves and dry dock for boats. In the 1830s, the mills had three undershot water-wheels, each 38 ft (11.58 m) in diameter. The company which ran the mills also owned large granaries in Drogheda, Dundalk and Balbriggan, along with a fleet of

9.11 *Henry's Mills, Millbrook, near Oldcastle, County Meath, constructed in 1777.*

lighters and ships which plied the River Boyne and the Irish Sea. In the early nineteenth century, the Slane Mills, which still stand, were converted to a flax mill later and into a cotton mill early in the twentieth century.[101]

The 1758 bounty energised the Irish flour milling industry to the extent that some 166 mills were opened throughout Ireland between 1758 and 1785, even in western counties such as Galway.[102] Large multi-storey mills continued to be built, as at Millbrook, near Oldcastle, County Meath, in 1777 (figure 9.11), which survives and has a 'T'-shaped ground plan like the Slane mill, Milford, County Carlow, constructed between 1786 and 1790, which was originally 125 ft long by 45 ft wide (38.1 m by 13.71 m) a seven-storey mill at Ballyduggan, County Down, completed in the 1790s and recently restored, and the Lee Mills complex at Cork established by Atwell Hayes in 1787. In the 1840s, the Milford complex, which now comprised the original six-storey flour mill (since demolished) and a six-storey oatmeal mills (which survives), was powered by a 120 hp Fairbairn suspension wheel which worked 22 pairs of millstones.[103] The spread of these mills also ensured increased familiarity with new forms of power transmission, which was not infrequently designed by English millwrights. In the final decade of the eighteenth century, two further technological innovations were introduced into Irish milling. The first was the use of cast-iron gearing, an early example of which was installed in a mill near Youghal, County Cork in 1792.[104] The second was the steam engine. By 1798, Henry Jackson had established a steam-powered flour mill

9.12 *Glynn's stores, Kilrush, County Clare, built c. 1837, with distinctive castellated gables facing the quay front.*

at Phoenix Street, Dublin, while in 1800, Isaac Morgan of Cork had imported a 12 hp Boulton and Watt engine for his flour mill near George's Quay.[105] The flour mill, at once, became independent of its traditional source of power, and the existing water-powered mills soon found that that they had to install steam engines to compete with the new generation of mills being erected on Ireland's quaysides.

Grain storage in multi-storey mills was clearly a priority from the outset but, as their capacity increased, their storage requirements alone necessitated larger kilning facilities and separate warehousing. The construction of corn and flour stores was an important, although often neglected, aspect of the infrastructural development of the Irish flour-milling industry, although the grain stores of Cork city's quayside have recently been studied. From the late eighteenth century onwards, multi-storey 'corn stores' or granaries became an increasingly common feature of Ireland's quaysides. The majority of the Cork granaries, for example, were situated either on the city's quaysides or on the side streets leading to them, and were equipped with large drying kilns and coal storage yards. An important feature of all grain storage buildings in Cork was proper ventilation, which took the form of either closely spaced windows on each floor, or louvred vents. The more typical nineteenth-century Cork grain stores had three to four storeys, with central or near central loading bays on each storey facing the quayside or the street frontage. In most cases, the loading doors were situated on the gable end of the building, with a projecting overhead sack hoist (complete with a ridge canopy or *lucam*) positioned at the gable's peak. During the second half of the nineteenth century, direct access to the quaysides of Ireland's ports became an important locational consideration, and increasingly so when the Irish flour-milling industry came to rely on imported grain. One of the most interesting surviving structures of the period is the six-storey grain store at Kilcarberry Mills, County Wexford, completed in 1826. This was positioned directly across the wheel pit from the mill's main eighteenth-century block. This curious structure has semi-circular arched windows on all elevations, complete with their original cast-iron frames, a rare survival. At Kilrush, County Clare, two rather imposing, six-storey grain stores of *c.* 1837, with castellated gables facing the quayside, have survived in excellent condition (figure 9.12). These latter were owned by the Glynn family, who later converted them into roller mills in the early 1880s. The ancillary buildings associated with the stores, such as workshops and stables, also survive. Large grain stores do, of course, also survive at other inland sites such as Ballymahon, County Longford (figure 9.13), completed *c.* 1837. In 1873, James Bannatyne and Sons erected a six-storey grain store, flanked by two large service towers at each end, within the Limerick floating docks complex (see Chapter 15). This structure is one of the largest and best-preserved examples of its type and general date range in Ireland. In the main,

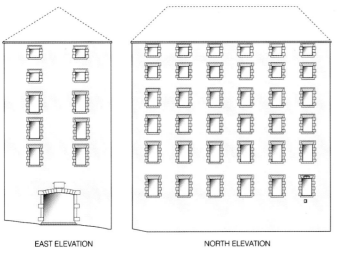

EAST ELEVATION   NORTH ELEVATION

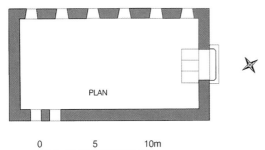

PLAN

0   5   10m

9.13 *Elevation and plan of multi-storey grain store at Ballymahon, County Longford, c. 1837, before conversion to apartments (left);*
9.14 *Birr Mills, County Offaly, c. 1820. The water-wheels and mill-races are reconstructed (below).*

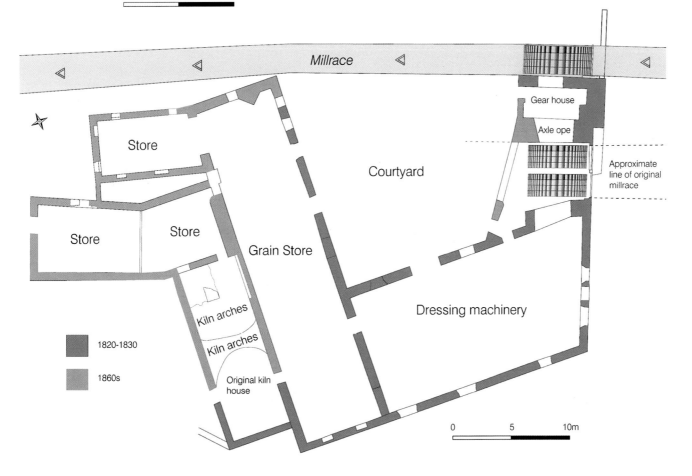

Millrace

Gear house

Axle ope

Approximate line of original millrace

Store

Store

Store

Courtyard

Grain Store

Kiln arches

Kiln arches

Original kiln house

Dressing machinery

1820-1830

1860s

0   5   10m

Irish grain stores do not display this level of architectural ornamentation.

(ii) 1800 – c. 1874

The period 1800-75 is characterised by two major developments, the introduction of steam engines as energy supplements to Irish flour mills and the increase in the number of new steam-powered mills at Irish ports. At mill sites where the steam engine was intended as a back-up for water-powered plant, the engine was usually housed in a separate building and linked independently to its own set of millstones. The period 1830-50, in particular, witnessed the installation of steam engines at many of the larger Irish mills. By the 1820s, Irish machine foundries were already manufacturing steam engines for Irish flour mills, although when compound engines were introduced, Irish mill owners tended to order new engines from reputable English foundries. Other technological developments included the introduction of new mechanical grain-cleaning plant, principally *rotary cleaners* and *cockle cylinders*. Rotary cleaners consisted of a wire mesh drum, equipped with internal rotating brushes, into which grain was fed. The grain in the drum was forced up against its wire mesh by the brushes, which forced out any smaller particles of dirt. Cockle cylinders separated foreign seeds from the grain, while a further device called *rubble reels* removed dirt and stones.[106]

Nonetheless, in the period 1800-30, water-powered sites remained at a premium, and large-scale water-powered flour mills continued to be built when conditions allowed. Good examples can still be seen at the Santa Cruse Mills, Carigahorrig, County Tipperary (1805), the Birr Mills, County Offaly (*c.* 1820) (figure 9.14), and Plassy Mills, County Limerick (1824). Laurence Corban's Maryville Mills, County Cork, built in 1818 and demolished in 1995, were very typical of the new flour mills of the period, working six pairs of millstones pow-

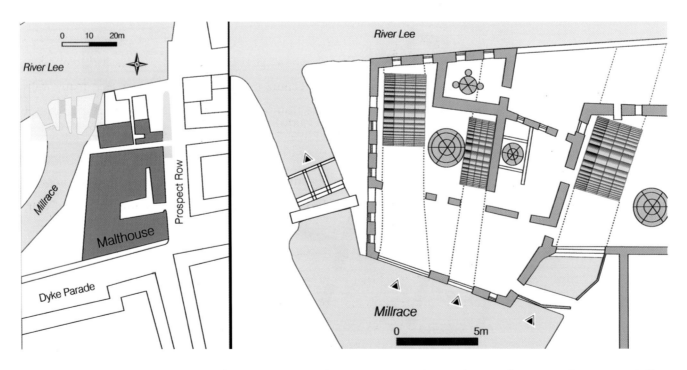

9.15 *The Lee Mills, Cork city, built in the years 1825-31, as they were in 1870. The complex now forms part of University College Cork. Three large watermills originally powered by 15 pairs of millstones.*

ered by a 20 ft (6.09 m) diameter water-wheel. The Birr Mills comprise an original roughly 'U'-shaped block of buildings, which had internally housed water-wheels, set at one end of the main range of three-storey buildings. Spital Mills near Timoleague, County Cork, built *c.* 1829 and demolished in 1992, mirrored the 'T'-shaped ground plan of the Slane mill, its five-storey projecting gable in this instance serving as a grain store. Plassy Mills, which drew water from the Shannon by means of a mill-race almost one mile long, was a six-storey structure set on the bank of the River Shannon, facing the entrance to the Killaloe Canal. It is a unique industrial building of this period, having a seven-storey tower at one end with a stone spiral staircase running all the way to top. The tower, which still stands (although most of the rest of the mill survives at ground floor level only), is built with ornate ogee-headed windows with hood mouldings, along with ornamental gunloops. When leased by Reuben Harvey in the 1830s, Harvey, who had a granary and store at Limerick a few miles distant, actually used carrier pigeons to send messages between each site.[107]

The largest water-powered flour mills to be built in this period were the Lee Mills at Cork, which comprised of a series of six- and seven-storey mill buildings, which were entirely rebuilt on the site of Hayes's Mills by Beamish and Crawford in the period 1825-31. Henry Inglis, who visited Cork in the early 1830s, was taken aback at the scale of operations involved and what he considered to be the 'perfection of everything connected with them'.[108] Significantly, the original cast-iron water-wheels were supplied by the local Vulcan ironworks, but the machinery driven by these was erected by Peele, Williams and Peele of Manchester. By the late 1840s, this was one of the largest water-powered flour mills in Ireland, with three 20 ft (6.09 m) diameter undershot water-wheels powering fifteen pairs of stones (figure 9.15).[109] However, there was an earlier precedent for the use of English mill work when, in 1820, John Rennie designed the machinery for Thomas Walker's flour mill at Crosse's Green, Cork. Indeed, this was a common practice in Ireland during the late eighteenth century and early decades of the nineteenth, until such time as English millwrights and machine makers had established foundries at Ireland's principal ports. As Walker explained to Rennie in April 1814, '... having seen many mills in this neighbourhood [i.e., north County Cork] ineffective from any errors in the calculations, we do not like to depend on the engineers here. I will most cheerfully pay the [extra] expense'.[110]

From the 1820s onwards, the number of steam-powered flour mills in Ireland was beginning to increase but, by and large, these tended to be within the environs of ports or near navigable rivers, where coal could be easily obtained. However, while most flour mills continued to rely on water power for the greater part of year, by the 1830s, the larger mills within the vicinity of towns were obliged to install steam-powered plant in order to be able to compete with those established on the quaysides. By the 1850s even the larger mills in market towns had to follow suit. As we have seen, the first moves towards the establishment of steam-powered port mills were made in Dublin and Cork in the period 1798-1800. In 1810, John Norris Russell, a wealthy Limerick city merchant, established what was to become, for many years, the largest port mill in Ireland on Limerick's Dock Road. By the second half of the nineteenth century, it was the largest producer of ground maize in the former United Kingdom and, in 1837, a nine-storey grain store (which remained the largest in Ireland for many years) was added to it.[111] In Cork, the establishment of a new Corn Exchange on the city's Albert Quay in 1833 hastened the creation of new corn stores and mills on the city's quaysides. In 1834, William Dunbar obtained the lease to a steam mill on George's Quay, which had ready access to both the river and the Cornmarket which, by 1844, employed a 35 hp engine to work eight pairs of stones in one mill and three pairs in an adjacent one, which processed oats. The mill also had a corn store capable of storing 10,000 barrels.[112] John Furlong's Lapp's Quay Flour Mill, Cork, built in 1852, is the best surviving example of a mid-nineteenth-century purpose-built Irish steam mill of the period, which retained it original smokestack until 1998. The five-storey, gabled 'Rock' flour mill, Derry, built on the Foyle wharfs in the early 1850s is similar to Furlong's mill, in terms of its location and in certain architectural details such as its windows, but is altogether a much larger structure.[113] However, we should not forget that the overall numbers of steam-powered mills in Ireland were always small compared to the number of mills which used water power only. In 1891, only 68 of the 1,482 mills in the country, were powered by steam only, while a total of 75 used a combination of water and steam: ten years later, 99 of the 1,351 mills in operation were wholly steam-powered.[114]

(iii) 1875–1920

The scale of operations in Dublin and Belfast flour mills had increased exponentially by the early 1870s. Patrick Boland's Ringsend mill in Dublin was operating no fewer than 63 pairs of millstones by the end of the decade, while in 1873, the Dublin North City Milling Company at Glasnevin employed both steam and water power to drive some 34 millstone sets. By the beginning of the 1870s, however, a series of circumstances had combined to seriously undermine the very foundations of the Irish flour milling industry. The post-famine depopulation of Ireland and the consequent decline in the Irish grain acreage, coupled with the arrival of cheaper American flour in Britain, had a catastrophic effect on Irish flour mills; so much so that by 1885, about two-thirds of Irish flour mills had gone out of business.[115] The same period corresponds to the adoption of new roller milling technology by American firms, which enabled them to sell their surplus output cheaply to Britain and Ireland. Only by adopting this technology could Irish and English mills hope to compete, and so in the period 1875-80, a number of Irish mills rose to the challenge, but not all were successful. American wheats were harder than those grown in the UK, and traditional millstones tended not only to abrade them but also to produce poor-quality flour.[116] The mills already established at Ireland's ports had an important locational advantage, as imported American wheat was now the mainstay of the trade. Those which had not done so were compelled to make this move.

In the roller process, the wheat grains are gradually reduced by being passed between pairs of metal rollers. The grain passes, successively, between three main types of rollers, each set of which has individual rollers which revolve at a different speed: one roll to hold the stock for another roll rotating at a faster speed, whose function it is to cut the grain. The grain is first passed through *break rolls*, whose fluted surfaces help to tear it open, while scraping the endosperm from the bran skin. It is then passed through *scratch rolls*, which reduce the size of the semolina granules and remove any residual bran skin. Finally, it is passed through reduction rolls with smooth surfaces, reducing the granules to flour.[117]

The new roller milling system had many positive advantages in terms both of an improved product and

9.16 *Ebenezer Shackleton's mills, Carlow c. 1900 (far left). In 1879, a Henry Simon of Manchester roller system was installed, which was the first successful use of roller mills in Ireland;* **9.17** *Bernard Hughes' Model Mill on Divis Street, Belfast, built between 1877 and 1882 (left);* **9.18** *Boland's Mills, on the Grand Canal Docks, Dublin (below).*

increased production. In traditional flour mills, the use of millstones for manufacturing flour tended to produce more coarse household grades than fine white flour. This affected its keeping quality and, in consequence, even the larger steam mills within the immediate hinterlands of Irish and British ports tended to supply local rather than national markets. The roller milling system, in which the different components of the wheat were carefully reduced and separated between sets of rollers, was developed in Hungary and improved upon in the USA and Europe.[118] As early as 1845, three Irish mills at Lucan and Chapelizod, County Dublin, and Tandaragee, were already partially employing early forms of roller to bruise wheat.[119] No further attempts appear to have been made in Ireland to experiment with roller milling until Russell and Sons of Limerick had a Buchholz system installed in 1863-4, to be followed by S.S. Allen of Midleton, County Cork in 1872, although in the latter case this was reported as being unsuccessful.[120] What appears to have been the first successful use of roller miller plant in Ireland, however, began in 1879 when a Henry Simon of Manchester roller system was set up in Ebenezer Shackleton's mill at Carlow (figure 9.16). During the installation of this system, Simon met a talented young Irish mill manager called William Stringer, who was later to join Simon's staff as a milling expert.

The spread of roller milling technology in Ireland was itself part of an information revolution created by William

265

Dunham, founder of the influential industry journal, *Milling*, in 1875. Dunham kept his readers up-to-date with news of all the latest developments in Hungary. His readership, to be sure, was by no means content to learn about the new technology in the comfort of their mill offices, and the UK millers' association arranged visits for its members to Hungary. On one such occasion, in 1877, when 40 millers from the UK went to Budapest to investigate, at first hand, gradual reduction milling, the party included eight Irishmen, notably R. Shackleton of Dublin and J.R. Furlong of Fermoy, County Cork. Between 1879 and 1885, Henry Simon of Manchester supplied 26 complete roller plants to Irish customers.[121] Simon was, of course, not the only supplier to the Irish industry, and while he was the largest, rival systems such as Harrison Carter's (which was similar) also enjoyed some favour in Ireland, Boland's Ringsend Mill in 1880 being a notable success.[122]

Nevertheless, stone-grinding flour mills were still being built, such as Sand's Mill, completed in 1876 on the banks of the former Newry Canal, which is an impressive six-storey structure, with Venetian-arched windows and a denticulated cornice.[123] Between 1877 and 1882, Bernard Hughes of Belfast had completed his Model Mill on Divis Street, a seven-storey structure which was to become one of the largest of its type in the UK (figure 9.17).[124] A Simon roller plant was installed in 1882. This massive brick-built structure was the first of its type in Ireland, and in 1882, a further storey was added to create a building eight storeys high, 170 ft long and 75 ft wide (51.81 m by 22.86 m). It was demolished in 1966, but in its day was the only Irish roller mill which could compare in terms of scale to many of the larger mills in England.[125]

The more imposing late nineteenth-century roller mills, such as the Model Mill in Belfast, have not survived, and those which have, such as Boland's Mills (figure 9.18) on the Grand Canal Dock, along with the adjacent former Dock Mill, Dublin, are exceptional. Shackleton's former Anna Liffey Mills, near Lucan, County Dublin, retain the best-preserved roller milling plant and associated machinery, installed by Miag of Germany in the early 1930s (figure 9.19). This machinery was powered by a series of water turbines (see Chapter 1); the mill was recently taken into care by Fingal County Council, and is undergoing restoration. Russell's Newtown Pery Mill on Limerick's Dock Road, was one of the largest roller mills in Ireland by the end of the nineteenth century, whose plant was powered by a 350 hp engine in 1880s, the largest ever installed in a nineteenth-century Irish roller mill.[126] In Cork, the first

9.19 *Roller milling plant and associated machinery, installed by Miag of Germany in the early 1930s in Shackleton's mills, Lucan, County Dublin.*

10
Engineering Industries and Shipbuilding

As in the rest of the former United Kingdom, iron foundries and engineering works were relatively common in Ireland's ports and market towns by the early decades of the nineteenth century. The fact that iron, steel and coal had to be imported does not appear to have actively discouraged their establishment, as the creation of new industries and the expansion of existing ones had increased the demand for machinery. The spread of railways and of utility industries such as gas, along with the beginning of steamship navigation and the transition from wooden to iron shipbuilding, all provided new customers for Irish iron foundries. Even in rural localities, spade and shovel mills had come into existence in the later eighteenth century to cater for the needs of a largely unmechanised and labour-intensive Irish agriculture (see Chapter 7). As in other Irish industries, the key contrast with the rest of the United Kingdom was that of scale where in Ireland, as we have seen, there were some noteworthy exceptions which exceeded all expectations. Out of Ireland's native engineering industries in the second half of the nineteenth-century, however, there emerged an industrial giant, which was to become not only the principal innovator in its field but the largest business of its type anywhere. The Belfast shipbuilding firm of Harland and Wolff grew to become the largest shipyard in the world. In 1920, the firm bought the west-of-Scotland steelmakers, David Colville and Sons, a move which enabled them to control and gain access to something which no Irish industrial enterprise, then or now, has been able to achieve: 800,000 steel ingots and 9 million tons of coal *per annum*.[1] However, despite their success and their demand for steel, Harland and Wolff never established a steel mill in Ireland (see Chapter 4). Even they, it seems, had to bow to the inevitable.

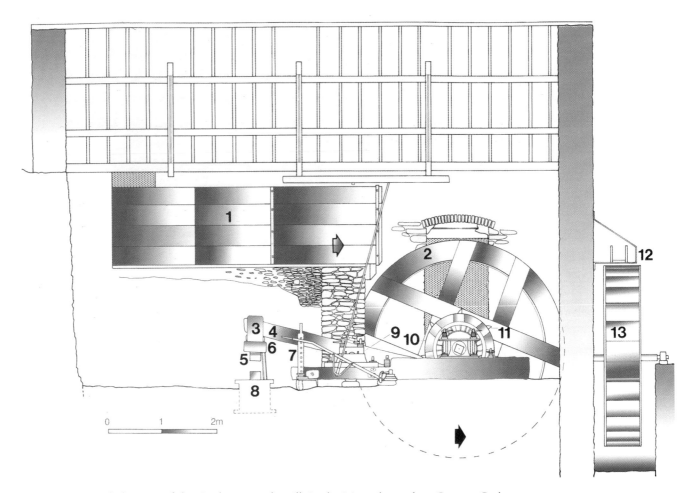

10.1 *Sectional elevation of the Coolowen spade mill, in the Monard complex, County Cork.*

(1) Spade Mills

Between *c.* 1750 and 1960, over 70 water-powered spade and shovel mills are known to have been at work throughout Ireland, with a notable concentration in the Ulster counties. The mechanisation of Irish agriculture, in relative terms, was a painfully slow process, hampered, for the most part, by the small size of land holdings. In northern and western Ireland, particularly in areas of marginal land, the spade was an almost universal tillage implement, while in certain areas, ploughs could not be used. Moreover, even in areas where ploughs could be employed, the availability of cheap labour tended to encourage the use of the spadesman.[2] Thus, spade cultivation survived in many areas, but for many smallholders and migrant *spailpíní* (agricultural labourers), not just any type of spade would do. Each locality usually had its own preferred design of spade, and the often bewildering regional variation of Irish spade types – there are in excess of 1,100 varieties and sizes of the one-sided spade alone – attests to the doggedness with which people adhered to their individual preferences.[3] In consequence, when water-powered spade mills became established in the eighteenth century, they were obliged to keep patterns for the different types of spade used within their intended catchment areas.[4]

The Irish spade mill was essentially a water-powered forge which, in its most basic form, comsisted of a water-powered tilt hammer and forge, the forge itself often being serviced by a water-powered bellows (figure 10.1). Some spade mills, particularly in the Ulster counties, were quite large, although in most instances, the *modus operandi* of these small rural, spade mills throughout the island was generally similar.[5] Outside Ireland, in areas such as the environs of Sheffield and in Devon, batteries of tilt hammers, operated by a single water-wheel, were employed, although it is not clear how widespread this practice was in England.[6] In Ireland, however, the latter arrangement was practically unknown and, indeed, there

10.2 *Matt Porteous using Coolowen trip hammer in the early 1940s.*

is only site at Edenreagh, County Derry, where this may have been employed.[7] Almost invariably, a breast shot water-wheel was employed to actuate a single trip hammer and often a grinding wheel for dressing the hammer bits, connected to the main drive shaft through a simple clutch mechanism and bevel gearing. However, the English sites were often employed in edging tools, i.e., the hammer welding of steel edges to a wide variety of tools such as sickles and scythes, a practice for which there is little evidence in Irish spade mills after the 1850s.

In some of the County Cork spade mills (the largest concentration outside Ulster), the water-wheel was used to power three mechanisms, the trip hammer (figure 10.2), the grindstone and a guillotine via an eccentric connected to a fly wheel on the water-wheel's drive shaft. In addition, a separate overshot water-wheel was employed to power the forge bellows, a rare practice in the Ulster spade mills. Nonetheless, the County Cork mills do have some interesting parallels with those of northern areas of the country. Both the Doolargy spade mills near Ravensdale, County Louth, and the Monard spade mills near Cork have revetment walls constructed with large lumps of slag and iron waste. The latter are the residues of scrapping – the heating and fusing of scrap metal - which were cleaned from the base of the hearth. In the main, only the larger spade mills such as Doolargy, County Louth (figure 10.3), Coalisland, County Tyrone and Monard, County Cork, were involved in scrapping, but in county Cork at least two further sites, including a small mill at Curraheen, near Cork city, are also known to have undertaken it.[8] Of the larger and older Irish spade mill complexes, the best surviving example is the Monard and Coolowen Ironworks, near Cork, which operated between *c.* 1790 and 1960. It

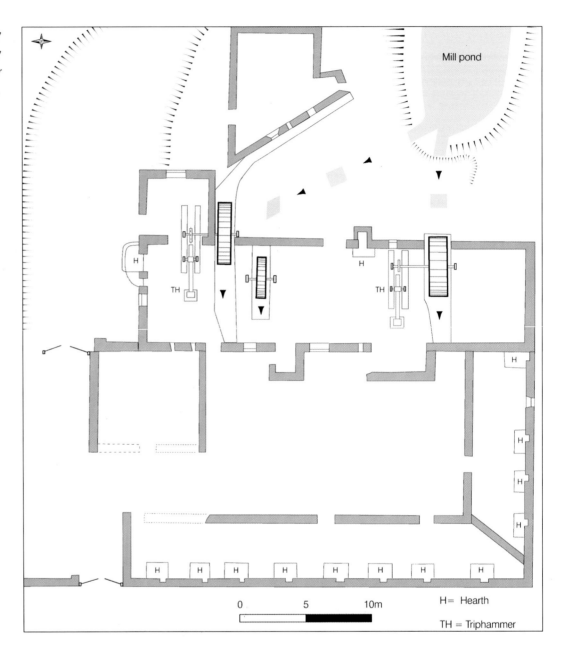

10.3 *The Doolargy spade mills, County Louth (after Gailey 1982).*

Mill pond

0   5   10m

H= Hearth

TH = Triphammer

occupies a small, picturesque glacial valley on the headwaters of the Blarney River, which discharges in torrents through a series of narrow, sandstone gorges, upon which four spade mills were built between 1790 and 1863.[9] The layout of the site is similar to Derby's ironworks at Coalbrookdale in Shropshire, and there is some evidence to suggest that the Derby family and the Beales, who established Monard, had some connections through their involvement with the Society of Friends.[10] A series of workers' houses, some dating from the late eighteenth century, are also in evidence at Monard, all of which, at the time of writing, are occupied. Patterson's mills, near Templepatrick, County Antrim, the last commercially operated spade mill in Ireland, was acquired by the National Trust for Northern Ireland in 1992. It was established some time after 1917, and its main prime mover was an American- made Leffel water turbine.[11] The former spademill complex at Coalisland, County Tyrone, has been removed and rebuilt at the Ulster Folk and Transport Museum at Cultra, County Down.

(2) Iron Foundries and Engineering Works

As we have seen, the charcoal-fired blast furnaces established in Ireland during the seventeenth and eighteenth centuries could only last as long as the forests they consumed. Moreover, the types of metal casting which were undertaken at them were, in any case, somewhat limited. By the end of the eighteenth century, however, iron smelting and foundry work had, in many instances, already become separate processes. Foundry work no longer necessitated the smelting of iron directly from its ores, as the development of new types of furnace now enabled both pig and bar iron to be re-melted and cast into increasingly more complicated forms, such as machine parts. This processed iron could now be imported from England, Scotland and Wales, where both iron ore and the coal used to smelt them were much cheaper, to be re-melted in Irish foundries with locally acquired scrap iron, and used to manufacture a wide range of implements and machines.

During the eighteenth century two new varieties of iron furnace were introduced. The first of these was the *air furnace*, which was essentially a reverberatory furnace, a form of which had already been introduced into Ireland as early as the late seventeenth century for lead smelting (see Chapter 5). Early iron foundries required a much larger output of molten metal for casting purposes, which could be achieved considerably quicker and cheaper in an air furnace. In Ireland, the iron works established at Leixlip, County Kildare, in 1742, seems likely to have used such a furnace for casting purposes. The works had a warehouse for it products at Leixlip, and in the period 1806-13, some 4,000 tons of iron was transported along the Royal Canal for its use.[12] In 1763, the Englishman, John Wynn Baker, set up an agricultural implement works at Loughlinstown, near Celbridge, County Kildare, which also seems likely to have employed an air furnace.[13] Neither of the latter are explicitly called foundries, but as the work they were involved in would have required castings, we can reasonably infer that reverberatory furnaces were in use. Likewise, all other Irish foundries must also have employed them before the development of the cupola furnace in the 1790s. These include Stewart Hadskis' iron foundry in Belfast, established in 1760, a second Belfast foundry set up in 1783, the Beechmount Iron Works, Woodside near Healy's Bridge, County Cork (1788), and Seymour and Bell's foundry on Lapp's Quay, Cork (1789).[14] Most of these early foundries were already beginning to be established near ports or navigable waterways, by means of which they could obtain cargoes of imported iron and coal. There are no known examples of air furnaces in Ireland and, indeed, there is only surviving instance in the United Kingdom at Abersychan Ironworks in Gwent.[15]

The second form of furnace to be introduced into Ireland in the late eighteenth century was the *cupola*, which had been developed by John Wilkinson in his Welsh iron works, and patented by him in 1794.[16] In the cupola furnace, a mixture of pig-iron, scrap cast-iron and coke as fuel, were fed into the top of a stack-like structure made of cast-iron staves bound together with wrought iron hoops and lined internally with refractory bricks. The temperature was maintained by a blast of air from a steam-powered blowing engine, and the molten metal was drawn off through a tap hole at the base of the stack. The molten metal was often run off into green-sand moulds (formed with a mixture of sand and some clay) on the foundry floor. Its introduction into Ireland seems likely to have been in the late 1790s, and the large iron foundry set up in Belfast 1799 may well have been the first in Ireland to employ a cupola furnace.[17] However, if this was not the case, then it seems certain that Thomas Barnes' Hive Iron Works on Hanover Street, Cork, had one upon its establishment in 1800.

The spread of iron foundries throughout Ireland's major ports and county towns was a direct response to the rapidly changing technological climate of the late eighteenth century. Technological changes in the iron industry had made cast-iron a much cheaper commodity, and it was beginning to replace wood in the basic components of water-powered wheels, power transmission systems and machinery. The increased use of cast-iron framing and beams in building design, and the emergence of steam-driven prime movers, also encouraged the creation of new foundries. Beginning with the substitution of oak axles with cast-iron ones, power transmission using cast-iron components became possible through the efforts of British engineers such as John Smeaton (1724-92) and John Rennie, the latter successfully introducing cast-iron shafting and gearing into his Albion Mill, on the River Thames by Blackfriars Bridge, in 1784.[18] The development of the suspension water-wheel by Hewes and Fairbairn (see Chapter 1) also led to the construction of cast-iron water-wheels.

The introduction of cast-iron frames for industrial buildings in Ireland during the early nineteenth-century, and later of cast-iron roof trusses, provided additional work for Irish foundries, while cast-iron also came to be used decoratively from the early decades of the nineteenth century onwards. The development of public utilities such as gas and water supply provided further outlets for Irish foundries and engineering works, as did the railway boom of the late 1840s, in which local foundries made an important contribution to the development of Ireland's railway infrastructure. The introduction of iron shipbuilding in the 1840s provided an additional fillip to the heavy-engineering industry of Ireland's ports.

In Chapter 8, we saw how James Kerchoffer had established a manufactory for cotton machinery in the early 1780s. The development of specialist machine makers in Ireland was, however, somewhat slower than in England, and English manufacturers continued to find a ready market here. By the first decade of the nineteenth century, a Yorkshireman was making cotton machinery in the Belfast area, but as late as the 1820s, the larger Belfast cotton mill owners such as Boomer were acquiring their machinery and gearing from specialist Manchester foundries.[19]

A similar pattern is evident in other branches of Irish industry. J.B. Sullivan's paper mill near Dripsey, County Cork, bought a Fourdrinier brothers' paper making machine in 1807 from Bryan Donkin's Fort Place works at Bermondsey, near London.[20] These same mills were visited in 1824 by George and Robert Stephenson, after which the firm of Robert Stephenson and Co. supplied them with a boiler and paper making machinery.[21] Nonetheless, the repertoire of Irish foundries did expand in the first half of the nineteenth century, and a handful of specialist machine makers (mostly in Belfast) did emerge to supply both national and international demand. For the most part, however, Irish foundries supplied local markets.

Comparatively speaking, little is known about the physical development of late eighteenth- and nineteenth-century Irish iron foundries. In Cork city, all of the principal early nineteenth-century iron foundries and engineering works, such as the Hive Iron Works on Hanover Street (figure 10.4) and the nearby Vulcan Works, the

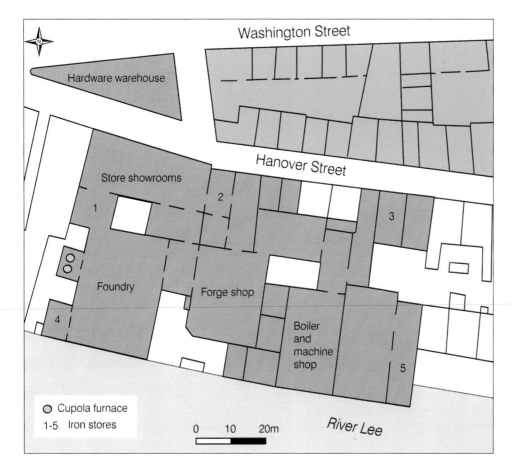

Washington Street

Hardware warehouse

Hanover Street

Store showrooms

1

2

3

Foundry

Forge shop

4

Boiler and machine shop

5

○ Cupola furnace

1-5 Iron stores

0 10 20m

River Lee

10.4 *Plan of the Hive Iron Works, Cork, in 1898. This foundry was originally established on this site in 1800 by Thomas Barnes.*

Union Iron Works (Lapp's Island) and the Eagle Foundry (Kyrl's Quay), were built adjacent to the quays. This was certainly not the case in either Dublin or Belfast, but all Irish iron foundries, by the middle of the nineteenth century, would have shared certain features. The manufacture of large castings and the assembly of both prime movers (such as water-wheels and steam engines) and machines required an extensive covered area in which bulky components could be lifted into position in the course of their assembly. This was commonly known as the *erecting shop*, and was generally provided with a tall, wide doorway (often with an elaborate stone or brick arch) which facilitated the dispatch of large castings or machines from the building. A travelling crane, which would have run on rollers laid along main longitudinal walls of the machine hall or erecting shop, was also a common feature of most Irish foundries, and enabled larger castings to be carried from one end of the shop to the other. In Cork city, the King Street works were equipped with a travelling gantry crane, which in 1829 was used in the manufacture of a large cast-iron water-wheel for a County Kildare flour mill.[22] The erecting shop was also generally sub-divided into two bays, one of which catered for the assembly of new machines, the other for the dis-assembly, overhaul and repair of existing machinery. Jib cranes, often attached to the side walls, and capable of moving through 180 degrees, would also have been on hand for the more localised movement of components. The machine hall or erecting shop was often connected to a multi-storeyed building which housed pattern-makers shops, finishing shops and model-makers' shops, all of which would have adjoined a foundry and forge shops. A single steam engine normally powered the furnace bellows, along with the

273

10.5 *Swivel section of Shannonbridge, manufactured by Robert Mallet's foundry in 1843 (top left);* **10.6** *Advertisement for Manisty's Dundalk foundry of 1886, (from G.H. Bassett's* Louth County guide and directory *(London, 1886) (above right);* **10.7** *Surviving Hanover Street façade of the former Hive Iron Foundry, Cork (above centre);* **10.8** *Hanover Street warehouse (completed in 1829) of the former of the Hive Iron Foundry, Cork (above left).*

ancillary machinery such as grinders and drills, although a smaller, portable engine may also have been employed for this latter purpose.

Many of Ireland's nineteenth-century iron foundries were established in the 1820s and 1830s, usually to serve expanding local markets for machinery and general millwork in the food-processing industries. These include the King Street Iron Works (1816) and the Vulcan Iron Works (early 1820s) in Cork, Shekleton's Foundry, Dundalk (1821), Mallet's Foundry, Dublin (1820s), and MacAdam's Soho Foundry, Belfast (1834). All of the latter produced a wide range of items and tended not to specialise in any particular area. The railway boom of the 1840s provided further room for growth, and at least one Irish foundry, the Falls Foundry in Belfast, was established by James Combe and William Dunville in 1845, to cater for it.[23] In the first half of the nineteenth century, a number of iron foundries also manufactured copper and brass (e.g., Cooke's foundry in Derry, set up in 1821), while some were also bell foundries (e.g., the Hive Iron Works and the King Street Iron Works, Cork).[24] Cooke's foundry and copper works, indeed, would have been very typical of the period. In 1835, it consumed 326 tons of pig and bar iron and 14 tons of copper in the manufacture of milling plant, metal pipes, pillars and grates. Its markets extended throughout Ulster and into southern counties such as Roscommon, which it supplied with flour, scutching mill machinery as well as plough parts.[25]

A number of the larger foundries began to supply machines and prime movers on a national and international basis from about the middle of the nineteenth century onwards. Robert Mallet's foundry manufactured the swivel sections for the Shannon bridges at Athlone and Portumna (1841), Banagher (1842), Lanesborough (1844) and Shannonbridge (1845, figure 10.5). It also made the roofs for the railway stations at Armagh, Belfast, Cork and Portadown. Indeed, Mallet also won and completed railway contracts in England, most noticeably the engine shed at Miles Platting (1849), near Manchester, for the Lancashire and Yorkshire Railway Company, which became known as the 'Irish shed', and the Wakefield passenger shed for the Wakefield-Barnsley branch line, completed in 1850.[26] In Belfast, the Falls Foundry, on Howard Street North, became the main manufacturer of flax spinning machinery in the UK after 1860, and by the turn of the twentieth century was supplying steam engines to English concerns.[27] Edward Manisty's foundry in Dundalk (figure 10.6) fabricated railway footbridges for lines in Counties Tipperary and Cork, and made the tobacco processing machinery for the local firm of P. J. Carroll.[28] Others, such as the Millroad/Distillery Road ironworks, established by James Pierce (1813-68), specialised in the manufacture of agricultural machinery.[29] The plant of R. & F. Keane's foundry, originally established at Cappoquin, County Waterford, was moved to a site near Wexford (which was reclaimed in the years 1897-99), where it became the Wexford Engineering Company. The Company's Star Ironworks (named after the five-pointed star used a trademark by the Cappoquin foundry) developed into an important manufacturer of agricultural machinery.[30]

The larger Irish foundries and engineering works also proved to be technological innovators, and a number made important contributions to nineteenth-century industrial technology. Robert Mallet developed and patented 'buckled plates', whereby a series of metal plates could be riveted together to form a rigid composite plate. He had begun experimenting with these in 1840, patenting the idea in 1852, and thereafter his buckled plates (which enabled the required thickness of iron and steel plates used in bridge construction to be reduced) began to be used in the construction of metal bridges throughout the world. In 1853, these were used in the construction of the 70 ft (24.36 m)-wide entrance gates on the newly-opened floating docks at Limerick, in Westminster Bridge in London in 1859, in St Pancras Station, London (1867) and in a road bridge over the River Trent at Nottingham in 1870. Bindon Stoney also employed them in the rebuilding of Essex Bridge in Dublin in 1870.[31] James and Robert MacAdam's Soho Foundry in Belfast manufactured the first Fourneyron-type reaction turbines in either Britain or Ireland in the late 1840s, while the Hive Iron Foundry made the first Jonval-type turbine in these islands.[32] In 1889, the Falls Foundry erected the first example of what was to become known as rope driving, which revolutionised multi-storey power transmission in textile mills.[33]

Unfortunately, only a handful of nineteenth-century Irish foundries have survived, and these are all in a fragmentary state. The façade of the Hive Iron Works survives on the north side of Hanover Street in Cork (figure 10.7), the greater part of surviving buildings being demolished in the late 1980s. However, the three-storey warehouse, a formal structure with elaborate pilasters and moulded parapets, completed in 1829 by Thomas Barnes survives at the time of writing (figure 10.8).[34]

(3) Tractor and Automobile Manufacture

In the early years of Irish motoring, the skills of the traditional coach maker were required to build car bodies, and by this means, coach-making firms, in a surprising number of Ireland's towns, began to diversify into motor engineering. Dr John Colohan who, around 1896, became the first documented Irish motorist (see Chapter 2), was a controlling partner of John Hutton and Sons' long established coach-making firm of Summerhill, near Mountjoy Square in Dublin.[35] Under Colohan's management, Suttons became a fully-fledged motor engineering works. On present evidence, however, the first commercial motor works appears to be that created by W.F. Peare (1869-1948) and William Davis Goff at Catherine Street, Waterford, in *c.* 1908.[36] O'Gorman Brothers of Clonmel, originally coach makers, had also become motor engineers by 1918. Clonmel, indeed, owing to the circumstance by which Bianconi's principal coaching routes tended to cross through it, rapidly became a centre for the early Irish industry, and had more motor firms than Cork, Dublin and Belfast in the industry's early years.[37] Motor vehicle registration became compulsory in Ireland in 1903 and, by 1904, *The Irish Times* estimated that upwards of 213 motor cars and some 286 motor cycles were owned on the island. In 1909, the number of vehicles registered would suggest that these figures had increased fifteen fold.[38] The increased use of motor cars brought with it other needs – everything from special clothing to chauffeurs. But, of course, cars also required refined oil in the form of petroleum, which had to be imported from the USA, and, in 1898, Ireland's first oil terminal was opened at the East Wall in Dublin by the Anglo-American Oil Company.[39]

By 1912, Henry Ford had decided that Cork was to become the location for his first manufacturing presence outside the USA. There seems to be little doubt that Cork had no special economic attractions for any branch of American industry, and it appears that Ford's motives were wholly philanthropic. Cork, it is clear, was chosen largely for social and political reasons: Henry Ford's ancestral home was near Clonakilty in County Cork and Ford himself had visited there in 1912.[40] The raw materials needed for the mass production of tractors were non-existent at any Irish location, while the demand for tractors in Ireland could only be optimistically described as negligible.[41] The decision to locate a large tractor factory at Cork was given the full backing of the British government which passed an act of parliament to enable Ford to purchase the tractor works site at the City Park.[42] For his part, Henry Ford gave the British government an assurance that his company would not profit on the sale of tractors to the government, while Ford did not even charge for the use of his patents.[43]

Wharves were built to the east of Cork, on the City Park side of the River Lee to accommodate the new tractor factory (figure 10.9), followed by an enormous machine shop and a mobile crane to facilitate the production of pig-iron from the factory's furnace. At its opening, in 1919, the Cork plant covered over 330,000 sq ft.[44] In July 1919, the first Fordson tractor, a 22 hp, four-cylinder model which could work with either kerosene or paraffin, rolled off the Cork assembly line, and by the end of that year, some 300 tractors were completed.[45] However,

10.9 *The remains of the Ford factory at Cork, probably designed by Henry Ford's architect Albert Kahn and completed in 1919.*

it soon became evident that the production of the Fordson tractor was not enough to keep the Cork plant going. Cork had been intended to function as an assembly and production plant for Britain and Europe, but when tractor production reached a peak of 3,626 in 1920, the demand for tractors in post-First World War Europe slumped alarmingly. It became abundantly clear that the Cork plant could not produce tractors economically, and so Ford decided that the Cork works should begin to manufacture Model T components for the new Ford plant at Manchester.[46] Nonetheless, in the early months of 1920, the company invested a further £327,000 on the expansion of its foundry and a machine shop, which was fitted out with new equipment, whilst the existing wharfage was also expanded. The foundation of the Irish Free State, however, brought further burdens for the Cork plant. New duties by the British government were now placed on the cost of Model T parts manufactured at Cork and exported to Manchester, the net result of which was that it was no longer viable to produce parts for the British market in Ireland. The future of the plant was assured, however, by its transformation into an assembly plant for Ford Model T cars for the Irish market, the production of which, at Cork, ended in 1927, by which time over 10,000 cars had been assembled.[47]

In 1928, the parent company made the momentous decision to transfer the production of its tractors from its Dearborn, Michigan plant in the USA to Cork, and in the winter of 1928-9, all the machinery of the Dearborn plant was shipped there.[48] Cork was now the largest tractor factory in the world, a position it held up until 1932 when Henry Ford and Son decided to shift tractor production from Cork to its plant at Dagenham in England.[49] The Ford Motor Works in Cork remained one of the largest employers in the Cork region up until its closure in the early 1980s. Extensive remains of the original tractor factory, which was clearly designed by Ford's architect Albert Kahn (a brother of Julius Kahn, who had invented the reinforced concrete

277

system that bears his name; see Chapter 6), along with warehouses and custom-built wharfage are in evidence, most of which are now used as storage facilities.[50]

(4) Railway Works

In Ireland from the late 1840s onwards, in line with contemporary English practice, the main railway companies began to establish their own locomotive and carriage works. By the late 1830s, the Dublin and Kingstown Railway (D&KR, see Chapter 14) had already decided to manufacture its own locomotives when, in 1836, it purchased the former Dock Distillery of Coffey and Co. on Grand Canal Street, which it proceeded to convert into repair shops and an engine depot. In 1839, the company's existing engine depot was transferred to the Grand Canal Street works. From the outset, it is clear that the company regarded the repair shops and the engine depot as a single unit. Throughout its entire working life, the Grand Canal Street works wrestled with space constraints, which purpose-built locomotive works such as the Great Southern and Western works at Inchicore and the Great Northern works at Dundalk had avoided.[51]

The former Dock Distillery (demolished in the late 1990s) adjacent to the main terminus at Westland Row (Pearse) Station was duly fitted out as a locomotive construction shop, and, in 1839, Richard Pim superintended the construction of *Princess*: this was the first locomotive to be constructed by an Irish railway company in its own works, and the third known to have been so constructed by a railway company in the former United Kingdom. To place Pim's achievement in perspective, the Liverpool and Manchester Railway did not construct its first locomotive until 1841. In 1834, the D&KR had, in any case, already entered world railway history when it became the first company in the world to use locomotives with accessible outside cylinders, placed horizontally at the leading end.[52] This basic design was applied to almost all steam locomotives built over the subsequent 150 years or so of steam (see Chapter 14).

Almost one-third of the 2,300 steam locomotives used by Ireland's 78 railway companies – a total of 690 – were manufactured here, mostly by the larger railway companies.[53] Of these, some 406 were manufactured in the Great Southern and Western Railway Company's works at Inchicore on the outskirts of Dublin, and 132 at the Midland and Great Western Railway (MGWR) Company's works at Broadstone, Dublin. Two independent Irish foundries, Grendon's of Drogheda and Spence of Dublin, were also responsible for 106 of the locomotives supplied to Irish companies.[54] Further railway works were established by, amongst others, the Belfast and Northern Counties Railway at their York Road terminus in Belfast, which made its first locomotive in 1870, the Cork, Bandon and South Coast Railway, which set up a small works near its Albert Quay terminus, and the Waterford and Limerick Railway, which established a locomotive works at Limerick.[55]

The Great Southern and Western Railway (GS&WR) Company's works at Inchichore, near Dublin, was built on a green-field site a few kilometres to the north of Kingsbridge (Heuston) Station in 1846, and, by 1851, it had become a small industrial village, complete with about 96 workers' houses and a population of 656. In 1896, the works covered some 52 acres and came to employ 2,000 in its heyday.[56] Between 1852 and 1957, the

Inchichore works was the largest in Ireland, and, by 1863, 44 of the 103 locomotives in use on the GS&WR network had been made there. As in English railway works, self-sufficiency was the order of the day, and almost every component of the locomotive, save specialist items such as air brakes, would have been manufactured within the works. Inchichore was thus provided with a boiler shop, foundries and a wheel shop, which dispatched fabricated sections to an erecting shop, complete with an overhead traverser crane that was used to assemble the various components on the engine's frame. The Inchichore complex is still in use for engine and carriage repairs, but has long since ceased to manufacture either railway engines or rolling stock.

Extensive remains of the Great Northern Railway Company's works, designed by its chief engineer, W.H. Mills, and completed in 1881, survive on the outskirts of Dundalk, County Louth. Its erecting shop could accommodate twelve locomotives at a time and was equipped with a 40-ton traverser crane, built by a Manchester company. The works also had a large fitting shop, a smithy, which had twelve smith's hearths and two steam hammers, and three large workshops for carriage construction and repair. As at Inchichore, the Dundalk works took on the appearance of an industrial village, where the railway company built 40 workers' houses. The works turned out its first locomotive in 1887.[57]

(5) Shipbuilding

(i) Wooden Sailing Ships

In the second half of the eighteenth century, many Irish ports were engaged in shipbuilding and repairing where, in the main, the smaller ports were engaged in the manufacture of vessels for fishing, while larger shipyards such as those at Dublin, Cork, and Waterford built ocean-going ships.[58] Between 1788 and 1800, around 515 ships were built in Ireland, but in the 1770s, Cork and Dublin were already emerging as the principal Irish shipbuilding ports.[59] By 1776, some 40 per cent of the Irish vessels in Lloyd's Register were built at Cork.[60] In 1814, around 49 per cent of the ship's tonnage built in Ireland originated in three Irish ports, and although Dublin was the main shipbuilding port by 1815, by 1826 it was surpassed by Cork.[61]

The principal types of timber sailing ships built in Ireland during the nineteenth century – barques, West Indiamen, brigantines, and schooners – reflected the needs of its international ocean-going trade. West Indiamen, by the early nineteenth century, were around 300 tons, and were preferred for their speed and high performance under sail (rather than cargo-carrying capacity) during Atlantic voyages. They also imitated the American practice of using light canvas sails, which allowed them to carry a high suit of sails.[62] All sailing vessels were, however, custom built. The opening up of the opium trade in the 1830s, for example, led to a demand for fast schooners that could negotiate the shallower waters of China's coastline.[63] Yet, for the most part, merchant ships in use up to the early part of the nineteenth century in the Atlantic trade were seldom more than 200 tons, while the average size of such vessels was determined by the length of the voyage, the goods carried by them and navigational considerations.[64] The late eighteenth century also saw the introduction of improved rigging in ships, which led not only to enhanced sailing conditions but also to smaller crews. Other eighteenth-century

10.10 *Grid iron (c. 1870) at the former Cork Harbour Commissioners dockyard, Cork.*

developments included the development of the round-headed rudder (which reduced the tendency for the ships to be swamped by following seas), the introduction of the ship's wheel and the sheathing of ship's hulls with copper. This latter innovation protected the hull from the *teredo navalis*, a wood-boring worm which attacked ship's timbers in tropical seas.[65]

At the end of the eighteenth and during the opening decades of the nineteenth century proper shipbuilding facilities were rare in Irish ports. At Cork, indeed, in the early years of the nineteenth century, shipwrights often worked on stages erected in the River Lee.[66] Gridirons – large wooden frames constructed on estuarine mud flats – were also used for repairs, the ship being floated onto the framework when the tide was in, upon which it came to rest when the tide went out, but in such a way that it was raised off the mud. A rare late nineteenth-century example, built by the Cork Harbour Commissioners adjacent to their Water Street boatyard, survives *in situ* (figure 10.10). However, while ships under 75 tons could be constructed in the open air either on beaches or tidal slobs, the increase in size in vessels brought on by the expansion of international trade required purpose-built yards.[67] The 'large and commodious and well built dry dock with sufficient flood gates and every convenience for the reception of all vessels' at Waterford in 1746 would have been by no means common.[68] Waterford, indeed, had at least one drydock in 1735, while a Dublin yard began to operate one on the south side of the River Liffey by around 1794.[69] In 1790, Michael Cardiff's and Michael Kehoe's yard on Dublin's City Quay launched a vessel of 500 tons, which was then the largest vessel of any type to be built in Ireland.[70] A second Irish yard, William Ritchie's at Belfast, was also building vessels up to 450 tons by 1811. Ritchie had transferred his business from Saltcoats in Ayrshire to Belfast, in 1791, and, in 1792, he launched his first vessel, *Hibernia*, of 300 tons.[71] Ritchie's contribution to the Belfast port infrastructure was duly recognised by the Belfast Ballast Board, which commissioned him to build a graving dock in 1796, completed in 1800.[72] The latter, known as the Clarendon No. 1 graving dock, still survives. By the middle of the nineteenth century, most Irish ports would

have had a graving dock, in which a ship's hull could be 'graved', i.e., cleaned of accretions and re-tarred. The sides of the dock would normally be formed with cut stone steps, which could be used to wedge wooden props around the vessel once the dock had been drained (figure 10.11). At its riverside end, the dock would be equipped with flood gates, which would enable a vessel to be floated in, and, once closed, facilitate the pumping out of water in the dock. Well-preserved examples of Irish graving docks, in addition to Clarendon No. 1 dock, include the Clarendon No. 2 graving dock of 1826 and the Limerick dock, completed in 1873 (figure 10.12).[73]

In the early nineteenth century, wooden shipbuilding in Ireland was by no means a capital-intensive enterprise, as the workshops employed were no bigger than those employed in other trades. Morton's shipyard in Dublin,

10.11 *Drydock in use in Dublin shipyard in 1927 (top);* **10.12** *Limerick drydock, completed in 1873 (above).*

10.13 *Patent slip, originally built for Knight's shipbuilding yard at Cork, of c. 1828 (left);*

for example, which included the proprietor's own house, was set out in 1812 at a cost of £5,000.[74] However, such yards were compelled to stockpile large amounts of timber of different sizes so as to be prepared to meet any requirement, at any time and, as a direct consequence, individual yards had to order their timber well in advance.[75] To a certain extent, the size of ships was restricted by that of the harbours able to receive them, and up to 1850 few could accommodate ships in excess of 500 tons.[76] Nonetheless, by the 1820s, the larger Irish yards were obliged to install mechanical means of pulling ships out of the water for repairs. In 1828, Cork became, along with Dublin and Waterford, one of the first Irish ports to have a dockyard equipped with a patent slip, when John Knight had one constructed at his Brickfields yard. This general trend was followed by Derry in 1830, when a patent slip which could accommodate vessels up to 300 tons was completed.[77] White's yard at Waterford had a Morton's patent slip around the same time, while even a relatively insignificant landing place such as Kilrush, County Clare, had a steam-powered slip in 1837.[78] Patent slipways enabled ships to be mechanically hoisted out of the water, using either a man-powered capstan or a steam hoist, which made it possible for repairs to be carried out without the use of a dry or graving dock. Knight's patent slip had a manually operated 120 ft (43.5 m) carriage, with which a handful of men could haul a vessel of up to 500 tons from the River Lee in around one hour.[79] This latter survives in the present-day Cork Harbour Commissioner's boatyard, complete with the remains of the metal track for its carriage, along with the remains of its later steam-powered hoist shed (figure 10.13).[80]

By the early 1830s, Cork harbour became the principal centre of the Irish shipbuilding trade, by which time the increasing size and sophistication of its shipyard facilities were already beginning to reflect its new status. In 1834, the largest drydock built up to that time in Ireland, being some 350 ft long and 80 ft 6in wide (121.8 m by 27.99 m), with the capacity to accommodate a 1,200 ton vessel, was completed at Passage West by William and Henry Browne.[81] The yard was almost immediately expanded when, in 1835, it became equipped with a forge, rigging and sail lofts. In 1840, the drydock was renamed the *Victoria*, during the Queen's visit of that year, and a second large drydock, the *Albert* Dock, which was 50 ft (17.4 m) wide, was completed in the early 1850s (figure 10.14).[82] As shown on a map of *c.* 1855 the shipyard buildings were laid out in a 'U'-shaped plan around the docks, complete with a mast house, rigging and sail loft, forges and an engine house and foundry at the waterside. The Victoria and Albert Docks were filled in the late 1980s to accommodate quayside development at Passage West. Joseph Wheeler, the Cork city shipbuilder, transferred his operations to Rushbrooke, almost immediately across the river from the Passage shipyard, in the 1850s. The centre-piece of his yard was a large

10.14 *Browne's shipyard at Passage West, Cork harbour, c. 1855 (right).*

drydock designed by Sir John Rennie (1794-1874), which was 400 ft long and 58 ft wide (139.2 m by 20.18 m), the first part of which was completed, after two years' work, in 1856.[83] In 1859, what was then believed to have been the largest vessel ever to have docked in Ireland, the 347 ft (120.75 m) *Weser*, entered Wheeler's dry-dock for repairs.[84] The largest wooden ship ever to have been built in Ireland seems to have been the *Merrie England* (201.5 ft long or 70.12 m), which was launched at White's yard at Waterford in 1856.[85] Wooden sailing ships also needed extensive repairs and re-fits to meet Lloyd's classification, an 'A1' classification requiring that this be renewed after twelve years. A renewal of the latter was only valid for a further eight years, and a third classification for four years.[86]

(ii) Steam Ships and the Beginnings of Iron Shipbuilding

In 1815, Andrew and Michael Hennessy's yard at Passage West in Cork harbour completed the first steam boat hull to be manufactured in Ireland, for which Boulton and Watt of the Soho Foundry in Birmingham supplied a 12 hp side lever model, with spur wheel drive to the paddle shaft.[87] As in the case of the majority of early paddle engines, the engine of Hennessy's *City Of Cork* worked on the second motion, in which spur gearing was used to gear the motion of the crankshaft either up or down to that of the paddle shaft.[88] The Hennessy's second foray into paddle steamer manufacture, in 1816, led to the first completely Irish manufactured steamship, the *Waterloo*, the engines of which were built at Thomas A. Barnes' Hive Iron Works by James Atkinson. The response of other Irish shipyards to this new technology was somewhat slower. Indeed, the first steamship launched from a Belfast yard, the 200-ton *Belfast*, whose 70 hp engines had been manufactured at Coates and Young's Lagan Foundry, did not leave the stocks until 1820, while in Dublin, the first attempt to manufacture marine steam engines was at the Ringsend Foundry in 1829 for the *Marchioness Wellesley*.[89]

The advent of the paddle steamer influenced two important developments. The first involved the creation of more efficient sea communications between Britain and Ireland, beginning with the Greenock-Belfast service in 1818, which became the first regular passenger service by steamship in open waters, to be followed by a

283

Liverpool-Belfast service (1819) and a Cork-Bristol route in 1821.[90] But, more importantly perhaps, the evolution of steam navigation also accelerated the transition from wooden to iron ships. The steamship, it is clear, was totally unsuited to traditional wooden ship construction, as the vibration of large marine steam engines was ill-suited to what was essentially a flexible structure, made from thousands of separate pieces of timber. In addition, larger timber ships required particular care in port, especially before the introduction of floating or wet docks (see Chapter 15), when they were obliged to lay on the bottom in tidal berths. Such an arrangement would clearly not have suited vessels with propeller shafts.[91] This essential incompatibility between wooden construction and steam propulsion became even more pronounced when the screw propeller was introduced. Moreover, the large oak timbers, which were traditionally preferred for shipbuilding, were becoming scarcer by the middle of the nineteenth century, presenting an acute dilemma for the British Admiralty.[92] Yet despite these difficulties, the sailing ship continued until the end of the nineteenth century to be more economically viable for carrying bulk cargoes on long voyages. Nonetheless, while the paddle steamer proved to be an excellent dispatch boat and tug and general purpose passenger boat in both inland waters and the Irish Sea, it was not without its problems. Its paddles suffered from variable immersion which limited their effectiveness, particularly in rougher seas, while their essential design characteristics invariably produced a shape which was long and narrow and wholly unsuited for the carriage of bulk cargoes.[93]

Initially, the substitution of iron for wood in shipbuilding faced a number of technical difficulties. In the early years, iron construction tended to be expensive, while the skills involved were often scarce. Furthermore, both iron plate and girders of a consistent quality proved difficult to source.[94] Additional problems included corrosion, the absence of anti-fouling measures before the 1850s, and the alarming fact that early iron ships proved to be a hindrance to compass navigation. A magnetic deviation was created by the hammering and general vibration experienced by the ship while under construction, which created a permanent magnetic field. This, in turn, interfered with the readings of the ship's compass and made navigation extremely hazardous.[95] A further problem involved the creation of condensation and bilge water in iron hulls, which tended to contaminate cargoes such as tea and coffee, but this was quickly solved by improving ventilation and by rinsing the cargo decks from time to time.[96] Ireland and an Irish-owned steamship played an important role in the earliest attempts to combat compass deviation. A River Shannon steamer, *Garryowen*, owned by the Dublin Steamship Company and built by Laird's of Birkenhead in 1834, was used in experiments into the phenomenon of compass deviation in iron ships, conducted in Tarbert Bay, in 1835, by the British Admiralty. *Garryowen*, when it left Laird's yard, was the largest iron ship in the world, and was the world's first steam ship to be fitted with iron bulkheads.[97] However, while the results of these experiments were deemed to be a success, they were, in fact, seriously flawed.[98] Nonetheless, the considerable advantages of iron construction – lower construction and maintenance costs, increased stowage, and greater strength – could not be ignored.[99] The durability of iron ships was amply demonstrated in Dundrum Bay in 1846-7, when the Bristol-built *Great Britain* (which had foundered in 1846) was towed off, having survived the winter storms unscathed.[100]

In 1838, the Lagan Foundry of Coates and Young of Belfast, which by this period, had become the main manufacturer of marine steam engines in Ireland, built the *Countess of Caledon*, the first iron ship to be made in Ireland, for the Ulster Steam Navigation Company.[101] Kinsale-born William Coppin's shipyard at Derry launched the iron-paddle steamer *Maiden City* in 1841. Earlier, in 1840, Coppin had added a foundry and engineering works to his shipyard, and had begun to manufacture marine steam engines.[102] He was followed in 1844 by the Cork firm of R.J. Lecky, which launched a small iron ship for river navigation.[103] Lecky would later form a partnership with his brother-in-law, James Beale, and together they would bring English workers experienced in the manufacture of iron ships to Cork.[104] In 1847, Joseph Malcomson's Neptune Ironworks in Waterford also began to make iron ships, producing some 40 steam ships in the period 1847-82.[105] Malcomson had earlier persuaded John Horn (1814-93), who had trained in Robert Napier's marine engineering firm on the River Clyde, to run the Neptune works.[106] During his management of the yard (1849-70), he introduced a number of important innovations, which included the use of Portland cement in the SS *Cuba* in 1858, where it was applied to the inside bottom of the ship's hull as an anti-corrosive measure. Earlier, in 1856, in the construction of the *Aboena* he became the first to dispense with the bowsprit and figurehead – two of the most distinctive features of traditional sailing ships – which he replaced with the straight prow. This latter innovation was not employed by Harland and Wolff until 1861.[107] By the 1840s, Cork's declining transatlantic trade was undermining its markets for shipbuilding and repairs, while its concentration on traditional wooden ships effectively yielded the initiative to the Ulster shipyards. Belfast, in particular, was better positioned to take advantage of its proximity to Scottish coal and iron.[108]

The next main phase in the development of the iron steamship was the introduction of the screw propeller, in which the principle of the Archimedian screw was used as a means of propulsion. This latter principle was patented in Britain by Francis Petit Smith and, in 1838, experiments with his patent led to the construction of the screw propeller ship *Archimedes*, which quickly demonstrated the superiority of the new means of propulsion over the paddle steamer. Not only was the screw propeller much more efficient than paddle steamer, it was also easier to steer. However, for ocean-going ships, it soon became apparent that more powerful and efficient marine steam engines would be required, along with direct drive machinery, to produce the revolutions required by the screw propeller.[109] William Coppin, the Derry shipbuilder, was an early convert to screw propulsion, and, in 1842, F.P. Smith travelled to Derry to supervise the installation of a screw propeller in the *Great Northern* which, upon its launch in 1842, was the largest screw vessel built up to that time.[110] The first iron screw propeller steamer to be built in Cork was launched in 1846, at Lecky and Beale's yard, while in 1849, Joseph Malcomson had the specifications for paddles changed to a screw propeller for the SS *Mars* when it was still in the stocks.[111] The screw propeller, as a means of propulsion, was a significant improvement upon the paddle steamer, but with inefficient marine steam engines, the sailing ship still had the edge in low-cost carriage. But by the 1850s, the British engineer, John Elder, had taken out a patent for triple and quadruple expansion marine engines, while in 1862 Alfred Holt had developed a tandem compound marine steam engine for cargo liners.[112] The introduction of compounding to marine engines, which required less fuel and consequently less coal bunker capacity on ships equipped with such engines, effectively marked the beginning of the end of the sail-

10.15 *Panorama of Harland and Wolff's Queen's Island shipyard, Belfast, in 1891.*

ing ship as the principal form of ocean-going carrier.[113]

This new era of the iron ship with compound and triple expansion engines came to be almost wholly dominated in Ireland by Edward Harland and Gustav Wolff's yard in Belfast which, in its heyday, was to become the world's largest shipyard (figure 10.15). In 1858, Harland acquired a lease to Joseph Hickson's former yard on Queen's Island, and quickly became the principal innovator in the British shipbuilding industry, when he advocated a high length : beam ratio for his ships. These new vessels could carry more passengers and cargo by virtue of their increased length, while heavy lifts upon such vessels were now undertaken with steam-powered winches and braces, which required smaller crews. Furthermore, Harland's new design of ships had flat bottoms (nicknamed 'Belfast bottoms'), and their extraordinary length relative to other ships of the period gave rise to the epithet 'Bibby coffins', after the Liverpool company to whom Harland initially supplied ships. In 1861, Harland entered his famous partnership with Wolff, and together they proceeded to revolutionise the design of the transatlantic passenger liner.[114] One of their main innovations was to increase the comfort of transatlantic liners by building a saloon which now extended across the entire width of the ship, and by providing passenger cabins which corresponded to those of luxury hotels.[115] The first ship of this type was the *Oceanic*, a 3,707-ton iron liner, built in 1871 for the White Star Line, whose vertical tandem compound engines were manufactured by Maudslay and Field of London, the Belfast company having no engine foundry of their own until 1880. This London firm also built engines for Harland and Wolff's larger ships *Britannic* (1874) and *Germanic* (1875).[116] Harland and Wolff were amongst the first shipyards to experiment with steel hulls in the 1860s, but it was not until the introduction of the open hearth steel process that this became a viable proposition. In 1879, *Rotomahana*, the world's first large steel-hulled vessel, was launched by William Denny of Dumbarton, which was followed two years later by Harland and Wolff's *Arabic* and *Coptic*.[117] The changeover to steel construction necessitated new machinery, and so in the period 1880-81, the Belfast yard invested in new plant; by 1885 it had nine large slipways, a large iron foundry, a boiler shop and fitting, turning and erecting shops (figure 10.16).

In 1874, the ocean steamer *Propontis*, owned by W.H. Dixon of Liverpool, became the first ship of its type to be equipped with triple expansion engines, thus beginning an age of faster and more economical steamships.[118] These engines were compact, fuel efficient and could operate with only simple maintenance and under a wide range of speeds. The age of the sailing ship was effectively over. Nonetheless, well into the 1880s, all ocean-going steamships continued to be fitted out with rigging and sails, which was a throwback to the days when marine steam engines were liable to breakdown and also, to a certain extent, a means of reassuring passengers. Indeed, Harland and Wolff's first ocean-going liner to be fitted with triple expansion engines, *Teutonic* (1889), along with its White Star Line sister ship *Majestic*, were the first ships entirely to abandon sails.[119] During the first decade of the twentieth century, the yard embarked upon the construction of what were, in their day, the world's largest ocean liners, the *Olympic* (launched in 1910) and the *Titanic*, which famously sank on her first ocean voyage with a loss of 1,513 lives in 1912. In 1914, Harland and Wolff employed a staggering 24,425 people.[120] The 1,742nd and last ship to be launched from Harland and Wolff's yard, on 18 June 2003, was the *Anvil Point*. The international significance of the site has been duly recognised by the Environment and Heritage Service in Northern Ireland, which has scheduled the slipways used in the construction of *Titanic* and her sister ships *Olympic* and *Britannic*. The Hamilton, Alexandra and Thompson drydocks (of which the Thompson was inaugurated by the *Titanic* in 1911), along with the former Harland and Wolff administrative and drawing office buildings, are also protected structures.

Belfast also had two other large shipyards, up to 1893, namely Workman and Clarke's, set up by two former Harland and Wolff managers in 1879, and

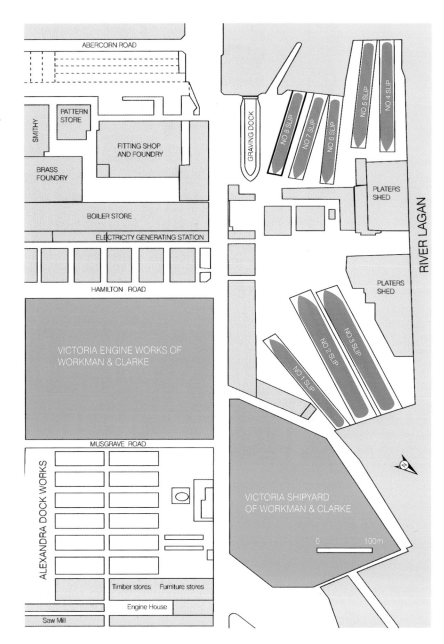

10.16 *Plan of Harland and Wolff's shipyard in 1912 (after, Moss and Hume 1986).*

10.17 *Workman and Clarke engine for SS* Divis *now a working exhibit at the Steam Museum, Straffan, County Kildare (above);* **10.18** *Dublin ship-yard crane and engine in 1927 (right).*

McIllwain and Lewis (established in 1863). McIllwain's was subsumed by Workman and Clarke in 1893. Indeed, although Belfast is normally associated with Harland and Wolff, Workman and Clarke were also a yard of international importance and in the period 1900-23 actually produced more ships than their principal Belfast rival (figure 10.17). By the early decades of the twentieth century, Harland and Wolff and Workman and Clarke were responsible for some 8 per cent of the world's output. But, despite Workman and Clarke's relative degree of success and its pioneering role in the UK in development of turbo-diesel propulsion, the firm went out of business in 1935.[121] Outside Belfast, only a few Irish ports, most notably Dublin, were involved in the construction and repair of ships (figure 10.18).

11

Chemical and Miscellaneous Industries

(Tanning and Paper Making)

Although Irish-born scientists, such as Ferguson, Higgins, Muspratt and Gamble, had each made important contributions to the development of industrial chemistry in the eighteenth and nineteenth centuries, for the most part, with some notable exceptions, the Irish chemical industry in the same period consisted of a series of small-scale enterprises. These ranged in size from the enormous gunpowder manufactory at Ballincollig, County Cork, and the Goulding fertiliser works in Ireland's main ports, to the small soap factories situated in the larger towns. Very few works in Ireland did, in fact, manufacture fine chemicals, while there was only one paint factory of note (at Cork) on the entire island. Ireland's tanneries and paper mills did at one time, however, bear favorable comparison with similar works elsewhere in the former UK. In the case of the tanning industry, despite the international reputation of certain Irish leathers, technological stagnation brought about its rapid decline in the second half of the nineteenth century.

(1) Chemical Industries

(i) Bleaching Chemicals

From the mid-1750s onwards, scientists such as Francis Home, William Cullen and Joseph Black in Scotland, and James Ferguson, Richard Kirwan and William Higgins in Ireland, had been experimenting with the replacement of dilute vitriol (sulphuric acid), and later hydrochloric acid, for buttermilk in the traditional souring process employed in the bleaching of linen cloth. Home had used vitriol in bleaching trials as early as 1756, and had been followed by Ferguson in this regard in 1770.[1] The use of vitriol effectively reduced the bleaching process from upwards of seven to four months, and Ulster bleachers were quick to appreciate the time-saving factor involved. The success of Home's experiments, and their implications for the Irish linen industry, encouraged Thomas Grey and Waddell Cunningham to set up a vitriol works at Lisburn, County Antrim, by 1761. A further vitriol plant was established by James Christy at Moyallon, County Down, in 1786.[2]

Pioneering work in 1786, conducted by the French chemist, Claude Louis Berthollet, established that 'oxygenate muriate of potash' (chlorine) could be used as an effective bleaching agent. It seems likely that the Irish chemist, Dr Richard Kirwan (1733-1812), was the first to introduce the idea of chlorine bleaching to Ireland, upon his return from London scientific circles in 1787, either from his knowledge of Berthollet's published work or through his contacts with the Swedish scientist, Carl Wilhelm Scheele. A further Irish scientist, Dr William Higgins, also appears to have been familiar with the process from at least 1788 onwards.[3] The Irish Linen Board announced its interest in such improvements to the bleaching process through the offer of a bounty, and, in 1791, published a report on its progress to that date. In 1795, it appointed William Higgins, by then Professor of Chemistry to the Dublin Society, as its chemist, and Higgins set about conducting experiments at John Duffy's bleach green at Ballsbridge, near Dublin.[4] However, the expense of the potash solution used in Berthollet's process threatened its long-term viability as an alternative to the traditional sour, and it was not until its replacement with lime that it became more widely adopted.

The key breakthrough was made by Charles Tennant, a Scottish bleacher at Darnly near Glasgow, who in 1798 patented a new process in which a suspension of lime replaced the existing solution of potash. The slaked lime used in the manufacture of Tennant's bleaching powder was not only cheaper than potash but also more reliable as a bleaching agent. Within a short period of time, Tennant and his partner, Charles McIntosh, set up the St Rollox chemical works at Glasgow to manufacture bleaching powder. In 1798, Tennant's younger brother, Robert, and James Fox toured Ireland to promote the new bleaching powder, and were followed by Charles Tennant himself later in the same year, who set out to demonstrate to Irish bleachers the benefits of his invention. Tennant established the Bleaching Salt Company at Malahide, County Dublin, which eventually closed in 1806 but, according to William Higgins, some 30 plants had been created in Ulster alone by 1799.[5]

(ii) Explosives

Gunpowder had been manufactured in Ireland on an *ad hoc* basis, within the environs of Dublin, around the end of the sixteenth century and the beginning of the seventeenth. On present evidence, this activity was conducted on a small scale, and it was not until *c.* 1717 that a more permanent gunpowder mills, with up to seven mills, was established at Corkagh on the River Camac, between Baldonnell and Clondalkin, by one Nicholas Grueber. A second powder mill was erected in the Camac Valley, by William Caldbeck, near the latter-day Clondalkin paper mills site, which operated until the end of the eighteenth century. The original mill pond

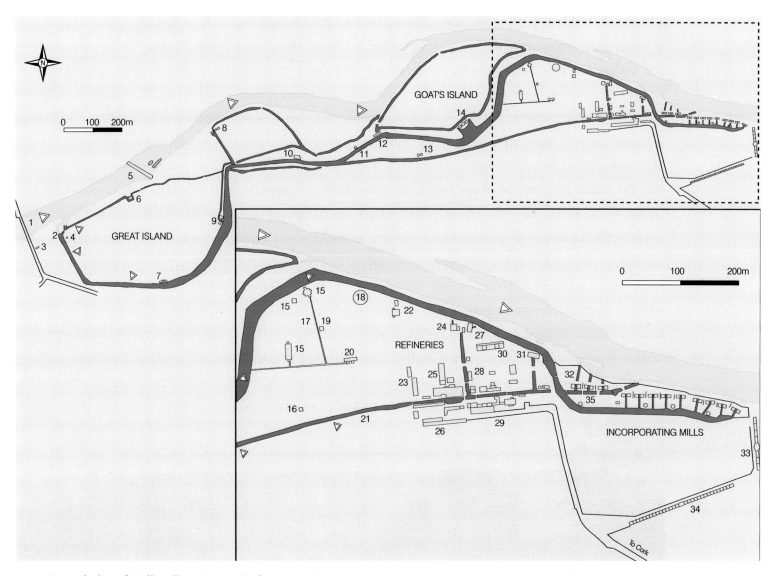

11.1 *General plan of, Ballincollig, County Cork, 1794–1903.*

still survives, along with the foundations of a number of the original buildings, near Clondalkin. The last phase of the Dublin industry is marked by the establishment of Henry Arabin's mill, somewhere near Dublin around 1796, which had ceased to function some time before 1822.[6]

Until the establishment of the Ballincollig Gunpowder Mills, near Cork, therefore, the Irish explosives industry had been centred within the environs of Dublin. Within a relatively short period of time, however, the Ballincollig mills had become the centre of this industry. Between 1794 and 1815, the mills were the largest in Ireland and amongst the most extensive in the former United Kingdom. Moreover, in the second main period of their use, between 1833 and 1903, during which they were the only gunpowder mills in Ireland, the Ballincollig mills appears to have been second in size only to Waltham Abbey in England.

The Ballincollig Gunpowder Mills were established by Charles Henry Leslie, a Cork banker, and John Travers, in 1794. Access to the port of Cork, some six miles to the east, was a critical factor in the choice of

291

site, as production was clearly aimed at supplying the needs of the government. Nonetheless, further important criteria specific to the manufacture of gunpowder also had to be taken into consideration. In the first instance the site needed to be sufficiently large and isolated to enable a notoriously hazardous series of processes to be carried out. Furthermore, as nearly all the latter were mechanised, access to a water source which could be readily converted into energy was essential while, at the same time, in order to minimise the danger of chain-reaction type explosions, the buildings within the complex had to be well spaced out. In consequence, the main feeder channel within the complex (particularly in the period after 1804) had to cover a distance of almost 2.5 km. The latter did, however, also facilitate the water-borne transportation of materials around the entire site (figure 11.1). In the post-1804 period, this system of hydro-power/transportation canals became one of the unique features of the complex. Leslie and Travers' manufactory occupied an area of just over 90 acres (compared to an area of over 431 acres when it came under Board of Ordnance control), situated in the eastern sector of the present complex. The only surviving features of Leslie and Travers' manufactory which can be identified with any certainty are the original hydro-power/navigation channel (running west-east through the complex), incorporating mill units 1 and 2, and the canal bridge immediately to the east of the incorporating mills.[7]

Black gunpowder has three principal constituents: saltpetre (potassium nitrate), charcoal and sulphur, which were mixed in the proportions 75:15:10. Saltpetre was imported into Cork from India and sulphur from Sicily.

11.2 *Reconstructed incorporating mill Ballincollig Gunpowder Mills, County Cork. The original mill at this location dates to 1794.*

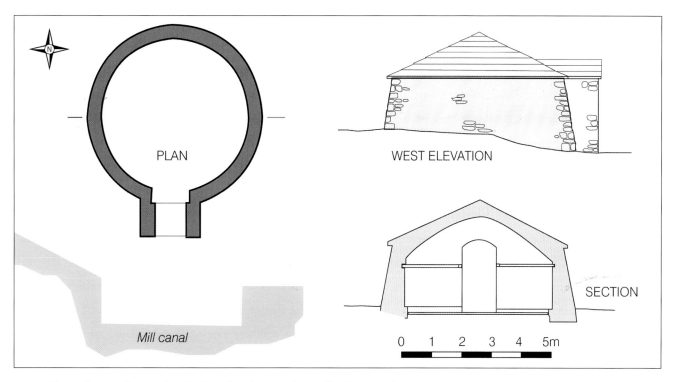

11.3 *Charge house of c. 1806 at Ballincollig Gunpowder Mills, County Cork.*

The only locally acquired ingredient was charcoal which was provided by plantations of the appropriate woods, such as willow and alder, within the complex. By reference to fig. 11.1, it will be seen that most of the buildings within the complex are concentrated around the refineries. This was a necessary precaution, as the ingredients were not yet mixed and were thus, relatively speaking, not as volatile. But in processes that involved the finishing of the powder after its initial mixing, the plant and buildings involved had to be widely spaced apart. In the *incorporating* or *composition* mills section of the complex, in which the ingredients were mechanically ground together, the double mill units were separated by substantial free-standing blast walls, which were supposed to deflect any flying debris resulting from an explosion away from the adjacent mill units. The incorporating mill buildings themselves were invariably of light wooden construction (figure 11.2), which tended to reduce the risk of injury to millworkers in the event of an explosion and to enable the mill to be recommissioned as soon as possible. By the 1850s, there were 24 individual incorporating mill units, which consisted of twelve double mills. In each mill, two pairs of edge runner stones were driven by a single breast-fed water-wheel.[8] There were, in addition, three circular charge houses, with corbelled roofs, situated directly upon the mill canal, in which the ingredients were temporarily stored prior to incorporation (figure 11.3).

After incorporation, the *mill cake*, as it was then termed, was transferred by canal to the press houses in the west of the complex, where the density of the cake was increased by the action of a hydraulic press to remove excess moisture. The product resulting from this was called *press cake*, which was then broken up with a large mallet to produce fragments which could be safely introduced into the *corning house*. In the corning house, the press cake was mechanically forced through sieves, the action of which broke the powder fragments into finer pieces. However, the corning process produced dust which tended to attract moisture to the powder if not removed. The powder was, therefore, transported by canal to the *dusting house*, where the dust was removed by tumbling it in gauze-covered rollers.[9]

The powder was then transferred to the *glazing house*, where it was tumbled in a slowly rotating reel or drum, the action of which rounded the powder grains and imparted to them a slight gloss (hence 'glazing'). A small amount of graphite was also added to render the powder more resistant to moisture, and it was this which gave the powder it distinctive black appearance. In the next process, the powder was removed to the *stove house*, which, at Ballincollig, took the form of a distinctive oval boiler house with drying houses on either side. The powder was stored in wooden casks varying in size from 5 to 100 lbs, and at least 50 coopers were employed on site to manufacture these.[10] Two magazines to the east of the refinery buildings were used to store the powder before its collection by customers or its transportation to the docks at Cork.

The effective area of the mills, including administration buildings, a network of canals and the new cavalry barracks, was greatly expanded in the period 1806-15, when the complex was under the control of the British Board of Ordnance, and the greater part of the 431 acres involved was enclosed behind a high stone wall. Accommodation was also provided for 30 labourers and a foreman at Faversham Square, near the junction of the Cork-Macroom road and the Inishcarra Bridge road, and in two rows of mill workers cottages – Waltham Abbey Row and Coopers Row - at the eastern extremity of the complex. Waltham Abbey Row and Cooper's Row are still extant, although the workers' housing built by Leslie and Travers has long since been demolished.[11] In 1833, the Board of Ordnance sold the mills to the Liverpool firm of Tobin and Horsefall for £15,000 and, within a short period of time, work on the recommissioning of the mill canals was underway. Under Tobin's management the mills were transformed into one of the most up-to-date manufactories in Europe. Tobin built an additional eight incorporating mill units, four in the 1840s and four in the 1850s, to supplement the operation of the pre-1815 mills.[12]

The decline of the gunpowder industry was brought about by the introduction of chemically manufactured explosives such as nitrocellulose (gun-cotton) and nitroglycerine, and, ultimately, by Alfred Nobel's dynamite.[13] From the second half of the nineteenth century onwards, gunpowder manufacturers found it increasingly difficult to compete with manufacturers of the 'new explosives', and were all but powerless to arrest the decline in demand for gunpowder. In its heyday, the Ballincollig factory's markets included most of Ireland, the Lancashire, Yorkshire, Staffordshire and south Wales coalfields, Africa, South America and the West Indies.[14] In 1898, Ballincollig formed part of an amalgamation of eight gunpowder mills (mostly English) under the management of the English firm of Curtis and Harvey, and only the onset of the Boer War seems to have prevented its immediate closure, which followed almost immediately afterwards in 1903.[15]

In the period after 1850, up to 30 water-powered installations were at work within the Ballincollig complex, an arrangement which was unparalleled in Ireland during the nineteenth century. Over 90 per cent of the original buildings within the complex survive, in various states of preservation, and were formerly the focus of a comprehensive programme of conservation by Cork County Council. To date, one of the charge houses has been entirely restored, as has a gunpowder incorporating mill, which is in working order. To facilitate the operation of this mill, large sections of the canal were also repaired. Two gunpowder incorporating mills survive at Corkagh, near Clondalkin, one of which is 6.75 m square but, unlike the Ballincollig examples, these are single units. However, at Kilmateed, which formed part of the original Corkagh complex, the remains of a two-unit incorporating mill, served by a central water-wheel, have survived.

The decline of the Irish gunpowder industry in the 1890s contrasted sharply with the rise of a newly created chemical explosives industry at Arklow, County Wicklow. In 1890, Sir James Dewar and Sir Frederick Dewar had patented *cordite*, a compound of 58 per cent nitroglycerine, 37 per cent gun-cotton and 5 per cent vaseline, which was to become the principal gun propellant of the twentieth century. G. Kynoch and Company, a Birmingham munitions manufacturer, decided to establish a cordite factory in Ireland, opting for a pre-existing chemical works at Arklow. This latter had been set up around 1872, to the design of John Morrison of Walter Morrison and Company, and had been equipped with plant for producing sulphuric acid, sodium sulphate, acetone, artificial fertilisers and soap.[16] The chemical works had been created for the use of the Wicklow Copper Mining Company, which had employed sulphur and pyrites from the Ballymurtagh mines to manufacture sulphuric acid. Kynoch's plant began operations in 1896, using coal-fired gas-producer plant to power electrical generators, with further additions in quick succession, which included a gun-cotton works (1896), a new acetone plant (1898), a pricric acid plant (1899) and a sulphuric acid plant (1900).[17] The company also purchased the Drimnagh Paper Mills in 1901 and the Clondalkin Paper Mills in 1906, thereby acquiring complete control over the paper it required for cartridges and wrappings.[18]

Elaborate measures were taken to minimise explosions, and, wherever possible, buildings were constructed with wood, while each structure was provided with double doors and a thermometer that could be seen from the outside. Individual buildings had sheet lead floors, turned up at the walls, while the walls were rendered dust proof by means of a smooth covering. Tramlines were laid to provide a means of safe transportation of volatile materials to buildings within the complex, the trucks being pulled by horses, donkeys or mules or, indeed, pushed by workers. A short stretch of canal was also constructed, on which a barge made by local boat builders, John Tyrell and Sons of Arklow, was pulled by horses. The plant flourished during the First World War, but was unable to survive the contraction in the explosives industry which followed in its wake, closing for the last time in 1918. Unfortunately, very little survives of this remarkable complex.

(iii) Superphosphates, Alkalis, Soda, Iodine, Salt and Fine Chemicals

In the first half of the nineteenth century, Sir James Murray (1788-1871) had already begun to manufacture artificial manures in the Belfast area, but later transferred his works to Dublin in 1841. Murray was subsequently to apply for, and be granted, a patent for the manufacture of a dry superphosphate, which in turn was acquired by J.B. Lawes in England.[19] In 1856, William and Humphrey Manders Goulding laid the foundation of what was to become an international artificial fertiliser empire, when they purchased the Glen Distillery at Blackpool, Cork, establishing a factory there in 1857. The latter, which became the Gouldings Glen Chemical Works (later

II.4 *Drogheda manure works in 1892, from Stratten and Stratten 1892.*

W. & H.M. Goulding Ltd.), covered an area of approximately eight acres. Gouldings manufactured superphosphates, using bones collected throughout Ireland and phosphates imported from the US and Africa. The imported bones were reduced to powder in crushing mills within the complex, prior to being dissolved in sulphuric acid. In the 1850s, Gouldings imported sulphuric acid, but from 1860 onwards installed their own sulphuric acid manufacturing plant, which originally had one lead chamber and increased to five in 1868. The acid itself was produced using sulphur extracted from imported Spanish pyrites, and later using pyrites mined at Avoca, County Wicklow. By 1917, some 70 kilns were operated on a 24 hour basis to produce around 500 tons of sulphuric acid per week. The residues resulting from this process, after the sulphur had been burnt off, were sent to England, where copper was extracted from the cinders.[20]

In the late 1860s, the advance of the Goulding's empire continued apace with the creation of a Dublin manure works in 1869, complete with acid plant, a bone mill, grinding machinery and a tramway which connected the complex with the Liffey wharves.[21] In the period 1872-92, a further plant operated at Limerick, followed by a manure works at Gracedieu, Waterford, which was opened in 1878 but closed in 1898. By the early 1870s, mineral phosphates were beginning to replace bones in the manufacturing process, and in 1873, the company took the step of buying phosphate beds near Cahors in France. Further plants were created in Shetland and Florida in the 1890s, and, by 1902, Goulding had six Irish factories: Derry, Belfast, Dublin(2), Waterford and Cork, by which time phosphates from north Africa had replaced those previously sourced from elsewhere. All the Irish plants, indeed, with the exception of Gouldings Glen in Cork, had quayside locations, in response to the importation of phosphates. Gouldings acquired a controlling interest in the Drogheda Chemical Manure Company and the Dublin and Wicklow Manure Company in 1919 (figure 11.4), the former originally established in 1870 on the Drogheda Docks, the latter at Murrough, County Wicklow, in 1868, after buying out the Dublin Vitriol Works, at Ballybough, County Dublin, originally set up in 1806.[22]

Two Irish industrial chemists, James Muspratt (1793-1886) and Josias Christopher Gamble (1776-1848), became pioneers of the British alkali industry, Muspratt, indeed, becoming the principal figure in the development of synthetic alkali production in the UK. Muspratt set up a chemical factory in Dublin to produce hydrochloric acid and prussiate of polish, moving his business to Vauxhall Road in Liverpool in 1822-3, where he commenced the manufacture of soda using the Leblanc process.[23] Gamble, on the other hand, had originally been an Ulster Presbyterian minister, who had gained a good knowledge of Tennant's bleaching powder

process, and left the ministry to set up a chlorine bleach factory in County Monaghan, which he later moved to a site near Dublin. Gamble emigrated to England in 1828, where he became involved with Muspratt, but later, in 1836, he entered a partnership with William Proctor, thus laying the foundations for the multi-national Proctor and Gamble.[24]

Apart from its widespread use as a fertiliser, kelp was also an important source of potash and soda. Yet, before the advent of the Leblanc process for the manufacture of soda by chemical means in the 1790s, coastal seaweeds were the only accessible source of soda. The latter was, of course, required for the manufacture of both glass and soap, but the importance of the linen industry in Ireland meant that its main application was for the finishing of linen cloth. Kelp was essentially the residues produced by burning seaweed which, when mixed with water, caused the soda to dissolve to form washing soda. The highly alkaline lye, thus formed, was

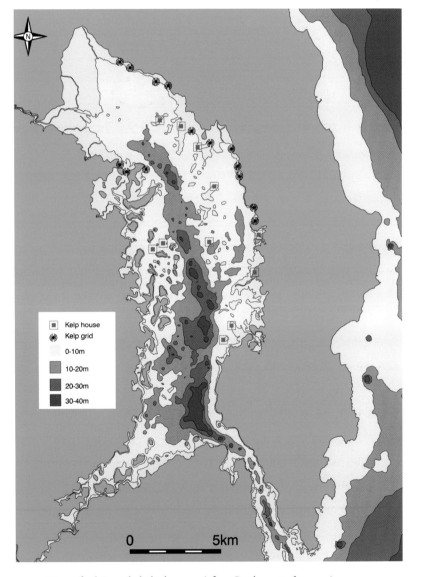

11.5 *Strangford Lough kelp houses, (after Conkey et al. 2002).*

297

used to bleach linen cloth, but by mixing this lye with slaked lime (calcium hydroxide), the bleacher created caustic soda (sodium hydroxide), a powerful and effective bleaching agent.[25]

Kelp kilns were often simple rectangular structures, consisting of a rubblestone enclosing wall, which supported a metal grate for burning. The kiln itself was generally 12-15 ft (3.65 m-4.57 m) long 2-3 ft (0.60 m-0.91 m) wide and around 3 ft high, and was built in such a way as to enable the draught rising to the grate to be regulated. On the Inishkea Islands, off the coast of Mullet peninsula, County Mayo, a well preserved kelp kiln survives at Porteen na Laghta on the South Island.[26] In normal circumstances, five tons of dried weed were needed to manufacture one ton of kelp, from which some three hundredweight of soda could be extracted, if the kelp were properly burnt. However, because of the high solubility of soda, it was necessary to protect the drying seaweed from rain while it was being dried. Apart from the remnants of kelp kilns, other buildings associated with the industry, such as kelp storehouses, have survived at Church Bay and Carnlough, County Antrim.[27] Up to 21 kelp kiln sites, were identified during the Strangford Lough Survey, most of which were located on islands, along with a number of kelp storehouses (figure 11.5).[28]

Yet kelp was by no means the sole source of soda, and it was to face firm and ultimately overwhelming competition from saltwort (*salsola*). The latter grew in coastal areas, where it absorbed soda from saltwater, particularly in the Mediterranean regions such as the Spanish coastline. Here, it was burned to form an ash called *barilla*, which was exported both to England and Ireland, yet it was for a time more expensive than kelp and also ran the risk of interruption of supply during wartime. However, after the defeat of Napoleon early in the nineteenth century, its supply to the United Kingdom was recommenced, whilst duties on the importation of barilla to Ireland were ended in 1823, developments which caused the price of kelp to collapse. The final blow for the kelp industry, however, came with the end of the salt tax in 1825, where the decrease in the price of salt encouraged the increased use of Nicholas Leblanc's process, patented in 1791, in which soda could be manufactured synthetically from a chemical reaction involving salt, sulphuric acid, coal and limestone.[29]

Nonetheless, the fortunes of the industry were revived somewhat in the wake of Bernard Courtois' accidental discovery, in 1811, of iodine in kelp residues. Throughout the nineteenth century, iodine began increasingly to be employed in medicines, dyes and even photography. A further discovery by Ure, in 1817, demonstrated that manganese dioxide and sulphuric acid could be used to extract iodine from the spent lye (itself obtained from kelp) by soap boilers. Ure's discovery led to the establishment of an industry which extracted iodine from seaweed in the mid-nineteenth century, beginning in France and spreading to Scotland. In 1845, an iodine factory was set up at Ramelton, County Donegal, by John Ward, which was demolished in the 1960s. Indeed, most of the kelp manufactured along the coast of County Antrim was exported to Glasgow, which became the hub of Britain's iodine industry by the middle of the nineteenth century.[30] In the early 1850s, an iodine factory was set up at Long Walk in Galway city, which went on to find markets for its product in Britain, Europe and the United States. One of its owners, the chemist James Smith McArdle, experimented with the extraction of compounds from seaweed in the 1850s, and went on to secure a new patent for iodine. In 1863, the Long Walk manufactory became the Irish Iodine and Marine Salts Co., which went on to erect a kelp-drying shed and a kiln on Aran, but was to close in the early 1870s.[31] This latter enterprise fell victim to improved means of extracting iodine from seaweed and the importation of cheaper iodine derived from the Chilean nitrate beds, towards the end of the nineteenth century, which created a serious decline in the Irish kelp industry prior to 1914. Nonetheless, kelp burning for iodine continued in Ireland as late as 1953.

Although fertiliser manufacture was Ireland's main chemical industry during the nineteenth century, both paint and various fine chemicals used for analytical purposes were also manufactured here. From the early 1880s onwards, the Shandon Chemical Works, on the Commons Road, Cork, produced both in a plant which extended over some two acres by the end of the nineteenth century. The company concerned, Harringtons Ltd (later Harrington & Goodlass Wall) was at one time the sole manufacturers of 'fire red' colour in Britain and Ireland, and was also the only firm in Ireland making distempers (powder-based colours painted onto plaster or chalk) and varnishes around this time, in addition to the manufacture of printing inks.[32] Harringtons also exported fine chemicals to the universities of Oxford, Cambridge, Owen's College, Manchester and Canterbury College, New Zealand, and, in the 1890s, became the first Irish firm to manufacture both paint and varnish. The GS&WR bought all its paint from Harringtons in the late nineteenth and early twentieth centuries. Harrington & Goodlass Wall is the only chemical works of its type in Ireland that is still in operation, and remains the largest manufacturer of paints on the island. Small sections of the original complex, including a series of single-storey buildings, are still in use (figure 11.6).[33]

The growth of the textile industry in Ireland in the eighteenth and nineteenth centuries brought with it an increased demand for soap for use in textile processing. With the introduction of the Leblanc process in

11.6 *Shandon chemical works, Cork. The main block of buildings shown here were erected in the 1880s.*

which, as we have seen, common salt could be converted into soda, the manufacture of soap could now be organised on a sounder industrial footing. Three types of soap were made in Ireland, each of which was essentially a mixture of oils and fats with mild alkalis. These were classified as hard soaps, soda soaps (which utilised soda, or sodium carbonate), and soft or potash soaps, which used potassium carbonate.[34] The latter type, as at McClinton's candle and soap factory, at Donaghmore, near Dungannon, County Tyrone, was preferred for fine toilet soap.[35] In addition, the main types of fats employed in the manufacture of hard soaps were tallow, lard, palm oil and coconut oil, while linseed oil, castor oil and fish oils were commonly used for soft soaps.[36]

Indeed, in nineteenth-century Ireland, the organisation of soap manufacture generally tended to betray its traditional relationship with the craft of chandlery and candle-making. In both trades, access to animal fat from the urban slaughterhouses was an important locational factor, while each trade was often practiced under the same roof.[37] Comparatively speaking, little is currently known about the layout and organisation of nineteenth-century soap manufactories in Ireland, but more recent work on the Cork industry has shed some light on these matters, while there are also surviving accounts of county Tyrone and Dublin soap works from the turn of the twentieth century. The largest concentration of soap works in Cork city was in an area known as the Marsh, where up to 30 or so soap works were in operation during the nineteenth century. The combined output of these soap works was quite small, but in Duncan Street in the late 1860s there was one soap factory which was producing up to 60 tons of soap per week.[38] Smiddy and Company's Soap Works on Watercourse Road, which was established in the 1890s, used an 80 hp engine to power all its machinery, and consisted of a soap house, which had several large boiling pans, and a cleansing room in which the ingredients were mechanically cleaned. The soap was conveyed from the cleansing pans to a series of iron frames or boxes, where it was allowed to stand until it hardened into large square blocks. These blocks were later cut up into individual bars of soap, which were then removed to the packing room, where the boxes used for the dispatch of the goods were made up. The *eyes* or waste matter, resulting from the manufacturing process, were a valuable source of glycerine, which was later distilled for use in the manufacture of nitroglycerine and ultimately dynamite, whilst the salt employed in the process could be continually reused.[39] In Dublin, Belfast and Cork soap works, toilet soaps were generally cut into shavings, to which colouring and perfuming mixes were

11.7 *Soap factory at Donaghmore, near Dungannon, County Tyrone in 1902.*

added and compressed between stone rollers. In the main, soaps manufactured with caustic soda and tallow tended to be hard and opaque, whilst those formed from potash and linseed oil tended to be soft and clear. At the turn of the twentieth century, most of Ireland's soap works were concentrated in Ulster, which included six in Belfast, three in Derry and one at Donaghmore, County Tyrone (figure 11.7). Dublin also had six factories in the same period, while Cork had two.[40]

The manufacture of salt from brine, using artificial heat in salt pans, is recorded at Dundrum on the coast of County Down as early as 1212.[41] In the period before mechanical refrigeration, salt was a vital commodity, particularly as a preservative for the products of Ireland's agricultural and fishing industries, but it was not until the seventeenth century that larger salt works began to be developed on the Antrim coastline. Needless to say, the climate of Ireland militated against the solar evaporation of brine and, as between six and eight tons of coal were required to produce one ton of salt, any potential salt works in Ireland required access to cheap fuel. Only in County Antrim, indeed, where there are coal outcrops on a two-mile stretch of coast between Ballycastle and Fairhead, did it prove really viable to site salt pans, and it is here that we find the earliest surviving sites in Ireland. A salt works is recorded here in 1629, and, from this period onwards, salt pans were in operation in the Ballycastle area into the early nineteenth century.[42] Saltpans are also shown on Greenville Collins' map of Dublin of 1686, about 2 km east of Clontarf Head, while salt houses are also shown near Booterstown and Dollymount. However, English legislation of 1702, under which rock salt could now be exported to Ireland tax free, actively encouraged the development of an Irish salt industry. By 1750, some 10,000 tons of rock salt were imported in Ireland, which had increased to 30,000 tons at the height of the Napoleonic Wars, during which the Irish provision trade reached its peak.[43]

With notable exceptions such as Slade in County Wexford, all the surviving coastal salt pans in Ireland are located on the Antrim coast. The Slade saltworks on the Hook peninsula used imported rock salt from Cheshire, and Welsh coal to boil it. The site was founded in either the late seventeenth or early eighteenth centuries, in all likelihood by William Mansell, to profit from the Newfoundland fisheries, but was out of use by 1746. Remnants of a series of curious corbelled structures associated with the salt works are still in evidence on the quayside at Slade.[44] An oblong stone salt pan, 12 by 20 ft (6.09 m) in extent, and around 5 ft (1.52 m) deep, survives near Ballycastle, while at Slade a series of subdivided salt pans (5 by 3.5 m) extend over an area 60 m long.[45] A further site nearby at Broughanlea, near Ballycastle, has a salt pan constructed with wrought iron plates, to form a metal tank 20 ft (6.09 m) by 16 ft (4.87 m) in extent. This latter would have had a capacity of about 2,000 gallons of brine, from which around 500 lbs of salt could have been extracted.[46] The eighteenth-century salt works on the Castle Ward Estate, at Killough, County Down, required 1 ton of Ballycastle coal to produce 1 ton of salt.[47]

Elsewhere in Ireland, the processing of imported rock salt, particularly in the larger ports associated with the provisions trade, such as Cork, was normally combined with lime burning, the expedient being to economise on the use of coal by using the heat of the lime kiln in the purification of imported rock salt.[48] Cork was unquestionably the centre of the salt and lime trade, with upwards of eleven manufactories at work within its environs throughout the nineteenth century, although the proportion of these that continued to produce quicklime was reduced to four by 1893.[49]

The combination of salt and lime manufacture appears to be unique to Ireland, but as the only area in Ireland with deposits of rock salt is situated in the Carrickfergus area of County Antrim (which were only discovered in the 1850s), nearly all the rock salt refined in Ireland was imported.[50] Salt was, of course, one of the principal ingredients of butter, a commodity in which Cork had a premier international profile, but both the rock salt and the culm used in its manufacture had to be imported. For the greater part of the eighteenth and the early decades of the nineteenth centuries, salt manufacture in Ireland received special treatment under English legislation. But in 1825, salt duties which had hitherto favoured the Irish salt industry, were abolished, and the industry went into decline.[51]

The importance of the provision trade in Cork city created the largest urban salt processing industry on the island. The earliest known salt and lime works established in Cork date to the 1760s, and in all instances the availability of running water appears to have been a primary locational consideration. As in the case of the John Street salt and lime works, metal salt pans and water reservoirs were needed for refining the salt, using the heat from the lime kilns, whilst force pumps were also necessary for filling the reservoirs. The Maylor Street works in 1801, for example, had three kilns and three pans along with 'rocking cisterns', the kilns being presumably built in a continuous block with a salt pan to each. The output from the Cork works could also be substantial, as at Shine's at Windmill Road/Summerhill South, which, in 1848, had the capacity to produce 25,000 barrels of lime *per annum* along with 200 tons of salt.[52]

By the end of the nineteenth century, at least two Cork city salt manufacturers, McCauliffe's of Watercourse Road and Spillane's of Leitrim Street, were buying salt from the Earl of Downshire's estate at Carrickfergus.[53] In 1903, Spillane's works kept two large lime kilns constantly working, burning limestone transported by horse and cart from limestone quarries in the Douglas Road area of Cork, and refining salt from Carrickfergus rock salt in 1½ ton lumps. The salt was reduced to brine in three large cisterns, 40-50 ft (12.19 m-15.24 m) in diameter, made of stout planks bound together with iron bands. The rock salt was laid on top of perforated platforms surmounting the cisterns, upon which the rock salt was dissolved into brine using spring water. The perforated floor served as a filter for the removal of impurities and, once the brine had passed into the cisterns, it was conveyed via pipes to one or other of four large boiling vats. The final quality and texture of the refined salt was largely determined by the duration and extent of the heat applied to the boiling vats. If a coarse salt was required – the type generally used for curing meat – a slow heat was applied to the vat. But if salt of a finer texture was required a more moderate heating was employed. The salt collected after the boiling process was ready for immediate use, and was removed from the cisterns by shovel.[54] Unfortunately, there are no substantial remains of an Irish lime and salt works, but at Muddy Hill lime and salt works, near Mallow, County Cork, the remnants of what is likely to have been a salt pan, in the form of a corroded iron lining, survive on top of a battery of two lime kilns built into a rock face (see Chapter 6).[55]

(2)Tanning

Where, as in England, tanning and currying were nearly always conducted by separate, specialist concerns, in Ireland, both activities were generally carried out by the same firm.[56] The contrast between Irish and English practice is also marked by the tendency in Ireland for the manufacture of 'uppers' and harness leather, and that used for the soles of shoes, to be undertaken by individual Irish firms. In England, in direct contrast to Irish custom, these activities were usually carried out by separate firms.[57] During the nineteenth century, the tannery was a commonplace in many Irish market towns, supplying local needs, although on a national level the number of working tanneries declined rapidly in the second half of that century. English revenue legislation, indeed, took a steady toll on Irish tanneries. In 1796, there were a total of 876 licensed tanners in Ireland, falling to 574 in 1818 and to 476 in 1823.[58]

As the hub of Ireland's provision trade, and with an enormous cattle market, Cork became the most important centre of the Irish tanning industry, with no fewer than 44 tanneries in 1822, reaching a peak in 1842 when some 48 tanneries were at work, mostly in the Blackpool area of the city.[59] Dublin, indeed, despite its larger population, had some 36 tanneries in 1768, which rose to 45 in 1800, located, for the most part in the James' Street, Cork Street, Mill Street, Dolphin's Barn and Kilmainham areas.[60] According to Wakefield, in 1812, the leather produced in Irish tanneries was of poor quality, but later in the same century the reputation of Irish leather in general had achieved an international standing. Yet, despite the undisputed quality of the product, this was not enough to ensure the long-term survival of Ireland's tanning and currying industries. Faster methods of producing lower-quality but usable leather (ultimately with the use of chromic acid) led to the rapid decline of the industry in Cork and elsewhere. In 1853, there were only sixteen tanneries within the city of Cork, and by the turn of the century only four.[61] Technological stagnation within the industry, competition from cheaper American leather goods, a fall-off in the quality of South American hides and the importation of ready-made boots from England also exacted a heavy toll on the industry.[62] By 1924, there were only four tanneries working on the entire island, producing sole and harness leather.[63] Thus tanning had already become a passing phase of industrial activity by the early years of the twentieth century, and this, as we shall see, has had a serious effect on the surviving remains of this industry in Ireland. But before we turn to the archaeology of tanning, let us first consider the various processes involved.

The manufacture of leather involves two processes: *tanning*, in which a raw skin or hide is rendered imputrescible through impregnation with tannic acid, and *currying*, in which a skilled worker finishes the leather by converting it into a material which can be used by leather workers such as shoemakers and harness makers. Before tanning proper could begin, the hides were first soaked in a *limepit*, which was filled with an alkaline liquor made out of milk of lime, the effect of which was to loosen the hairs on the skin so that the tanner could scrape them off, without damaging the grain of the leather. The hide was then removed from the pit and spread over a wooden beam, and then scraped on both sides with tanners' knives. In most cases, the hide would then be returned to the lime pit for a short period and then scraped again with a *scudding knife*. The hide was then divided into several parts – a process called *rounding* – the thickest and most prized section, the *butt*, being

303

divided into two sections called *bends*, after which the hide was then ready for tanning.[64]

Even the smallest tannery in a country town would have had at least one bark mill for grinding the vegetable matter used in mixing the tanning liquor. Bark houses and a bark mill are recorded at Kells, County Kilkenny, in 1763, while at Waterford in 1765 there was a 'fine bark kiln [and] two bark mills'. In 1794 the Dublin Society offered a premium to a Chester tanner called Paul Pantin, to produce a new type of bark grinding machine, and to James Lambic in 1802, the latter producing a bark grinding machine which received 'the entire approbation of the principal tanners of Dublin'.[65] Nonetheless, well into the nineteenth century, the bark continued to be finely ground by the traditional method under horse-powered, edge-runner stones, water power being used much less frequently for this purpose in urban areas, and generally in country districts only. Edge-runner mills were replaced, later in the nineteenth century, by special cutting blades powered by small steam engines. A rare surviving example of an edge-runner millstone used in an Irish bark mill, at Gortin, County Tyrone, has been recorded by Alan McCutcheon.[66]

Native oak bark and imported barks from Algeria and Spain were used in the tanning of upper and harness leather, whilst oak, cork and valonia were used for tanning sole leather.[67] Valonia, or acorn cups from Mediterranean oaks, were imported from eastern Mediterranean locations such as Smyrna in Turkey.[68] The tannin in the bark was originally extracted by immersion in cold water in *leaching pits*, where it was left to stand for a number of weeks, but, by the late 1840s, most tanyards would have been equipped with steam boilers. These latter were now used for boiling the water required for *steam leaches*, hot water being used to draw out the tannin and thus create a tanning liquor. Steam from these boilers was also employed for heating the drying lofts. By the second half of the nineteenth century, Irish tanneries began to be equipped with steam engines which, in addition to powering bark mills, also appear to have been used for working pumps. Hackett's tannery on Fitton Street in Cork, indeed, was reputedly the first tannery in Ireland to have a steam engine installed.[69]

In the traditional process of vegetable tanning, each hide was progressively exposed to a succession of liquors of increasing strength in order to fix more tan. As the stronger liquors became divested of their ability to fix tan, they were pumped down the yard to the earlier stages of the process, which ensured that this process was not only continuous but more economic in terms of the materials used. The hides were first placed in a series of eight to twelve pits called *suspenders*, in which they were suspended from poles laid across the top of a pit containing the weakest tanning solution, a process which ensured that absorption of the tanning liquor would be uniform when they were moved on to stronger solutions.

The hides were than transferred to *handling* pits, which contained progressively stronger tanning liquors, in which they were laid flat and moved from pit to pit, at regular intervals, being turned over in the liquor on a daily basis. Upon the satisfactory completion of this process, the hides were then smoothened out before being conveyed to the *layer* pits. A layer of ground bark about 6 in deep was laid on the bottom of this pit and the hide was subsequently laid flat on top of it, the hide itself being then covered with about half an inch of the same material, and a second hide was later spread out on top of it. The pit continued to be layered in this fashion until it was almost full, whereupon a layer of tanning material about 1 ft (0.30 m) thick was spread on top of the final layer. A mixture of tanning material and cold water was then added, after which the hides were left in the pits for between nine and eighteen months, or longer, depending on their thickness and the quality required. When this process had been completed, the hides were rinsed and smoothened out before being removed to the drying lofts. The type of leather preferred for the soles of shoes, which needed an abrasion-resistant surface, would be removed from the drying loft part way through the drying process, either to be hammered or compressed by a roller, after which it was returned to the loft.[70]

In the *currying*, or finishing, process, the leather was first dampened in a vat of warm water or weak tannin before being softened by the pummelling action of heavy mallets. The leather was then scoured on both faces with scrubbing brushes before being smoothened out. The next process, in which the currier pared down the leather to the required thickness on a near vertical *curriers' beam*, required great skill. Then, after further cleaning to remove loose tanning materials, the leather was partially dried, before being 'stuffed' (i.e., impregnated) with a warm dubbin made from tallow and fish oils. The skins were permeated with fat for about one week prior to being hung up to dry in a warm room, after which unwanted grease was removed.

The main considerations affecting the siting of tanneries were direct access to raw hides and a reliable water supply. In the cities and the rural market towns, tanneries were often located near a shambles or a cattle market, where hides could be procured from butchers, but, towards the end of the nineteenth century, the Argentinian cattle industry became a principal source of supply for Irish tanners. For urban tanneries, a source of running water was by no means easily acquired, and so artesian wells were sunk to guarantee a regular supply. Ryan's tannery, originally established in 1785 at Thomastown, County Kilkenny, closing in 1931, derived water from the nearby rectory well, while a stave-lined well was excavated at Wise's tannery on Blarney Street, Cork, in 1988.[71] In most cases, the tannery buildings were built around a central yard, the centre of which was taken up with the various handling pits, tanning pits, leaching pits and lime pits. A network of wooden pipes connected the various pits, in which a combination of gravity and force or double-acting pumps was used to direct water or tanning liquors through the pipe network. A large section of a set of nineteenth century tannery pipes were investigated at Blarney Street, Cork, which consisted of two parallel rows of bored wooden pipes, spigot-jointed at either extremity and bound with wrought iron collars. Holes had been bored on their upper faces, presumably to provide vertical tappings for wood-lined tanning pits. A series of wood-lined tanning pits, associated with O'Donnell's tannery in the Athlunkard Street area of the King's Island at Limerick, were excavated in 1996, where a row of up to seven pits, each connected by a series of octagonal wooden pipes, *c.* 40 cm wide, were investigated.[72]

The buildings of the tannery complex generally consisted either of an enclosed courtyard or a courtyard open on one side, which included the bark stores, bark mills, the drying lofts (usually situated over the boiler house) and offices, and, if currying was undertaken by the same firm, currying sheds and beam houses. The layer pits and handler pits were commonly situated in rows along the side walls, under the cover of lean-to structures. Russell's tannery, at Clonmel, County Tipperary, which was flanked on one side by the River Suir, had an enclosed courtyard, one side of which, as depicted in an illustration of late 1889, included a three-storey

11.8 *Russell's Tannery, Clonmel, County Tipperary in 1889.*

building equipped with louvred vents for drying tanned hides. The same illustration also shows lean-to struc-tures along the side walls, which presumably covered layer and handler pits (figure 11.8).[73] Lime, leaching and suspender pits, however, were located in the open air. Nonetheless, although the area covered by tannery buildings was often modest, that taken up by the various preparatory and tanning pits could frequently be considerable. In medium-sized tanneries with up to 60 pits, such as Ryan's at Thomastown, the courtyard and buildings could cover up to one acre; but at larger tanneries with in excess of 100 pits, such as Hegarty's tannery on Blarney Street, Cork, the premises commonly extended over 3-4 acres.[74]

In the period *c.* 1750-1900, upwards on 900 tanneries had, at various periods, been in operation throughout Ireland, but very little survives of these sites, save for the occasional boundary wall or storage shed, as at Dunne's Tannery on Watercourse Road, Cork, and at John Street, Drogheda.[75] In the main, the poor preservation of Irish tanneries – there is nothing comparable to the Rhaeadr Tannery in the Welsh Folk Museum – is because so many urban sites have either been completely built over, or adapted for an alternative use. In either case, the preparatory and tanning pits are generally filled in, and only come to light subsequently during archaeological excavation. Tannery (suspender?) pits, of seventeenth- or eighteenth-century date, have been excavated at Winetavern Street, Coleraine, each of which was constructed with plank walls and plank floors, around 1 m wide.[76] Two layer pits, of likely nineteenth-century date, have also been investigated at Mount Brown in the former

Kilmainham tannery district of Dublin. These latter were plank-lined, the planks themselves being of planed timber, and each contained a 0.4 m thick layer of mulch made up of tree bark, which would seem to indicate that they were layer pits.[77] A series of five plank and post-construction tannery pits were excavated at the site of the former Dunne's Tannery on Watercourse Road, Cork, each of which was around 1 m square in extent. One of these pits retained a layer of oily debris, which could suggest that it was a suspender pit.[78] The excavation of a likely nineteenth-century tannery at College Street/Lonsdale Road, Armagh, also revealed a large number of plank-lined tanning pits, laid together in parallel rows. A number of these yielded bark mulch, which would suggest that they were layer pits.[79] At the time of writing, the only systematic field survey of Irish urban tanneries has been conducted for Cork city, which revealed sections of the drying lofts of the Allinett's Lane tannery off Watercourse Road, the storage sheds of the Corkeran's Quay tannery and the

11.9 *Watercourse Road tannery, Cork.*

tannery drying sheds of Dunne's Tannery on Watercourse Road. However, these were demolished shortly before this book went to print in 2006 (figure 11.9).[80]

(3) Paper Making

The creation of a parliament in Dublin was, perhaps, the main stimulus for the establishment of an Irish paper industry. Beginning with William Lake's paper mill at Rathfarnham, County Dublin, in 1719, no fewer than 26 paper mills were at work within the environs of the capital during the eighteenth century, mostly on the rivers Liffey, Camac and Dodder.[81] Similarly, in Cork, which was the centre of the Munster paper trade, there were at least eleven mills in operation, chiefly on the Butlerstown, Brooklodge and Glashaboy rivers to the northeast of the city by 1841, the first recorded example being at Glanmire in 1713.[82] In all, some 50 paper mills seem to have been at work in Ireland by the 1780s, the main concentrations being in Dublin and Cork, with outliers in County Antrim and in Galway.[83] The most important factors of location for Irish paper mills, in both the eighteenth and nineteenth centuries, were threefold: access to a large urban market, a plentiful supply of rags for making pulp, and clear running water (figure 11.10).

Up to the middle of the eighteenth century, cotton and linen rags were first introduced into a water-powered stamping mill, which reduced them to a pulp. This latter was then diluted in water in a wooden vat, into which

307

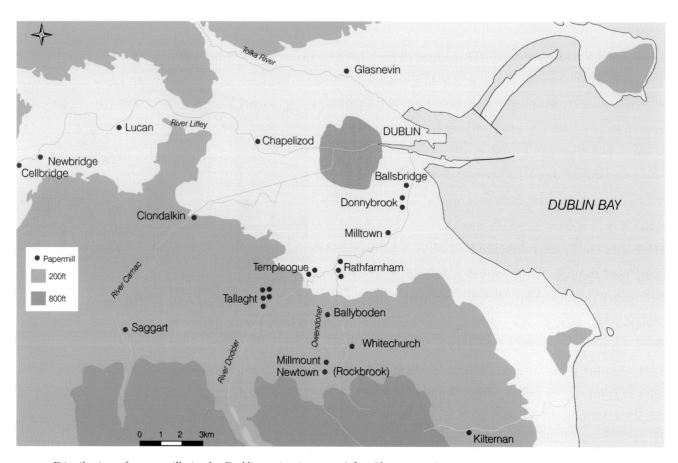

11.10 *Distribution of paper mills in the Dublin region in 1800, (after Shorter 1971).*

a *deckle* frame (a wire screen held in a wooden surround) was dipped by a skilled operative, to form a web of fibres on the mesh. The water was then drained off and the web, thus formed, was carefully removed, stacked on felts and pressed on a screw press to expel excess moisture. After being removed from the felts, the paper webs were then hung in a loft fitted with special louvred vents, which admitted air to the loft but excluded direct sunlight.[84] Nonetheless, despite the use of water-powered rag pulping machinery, paper was still essentially a hand-made process up to the early nineteenth century. There was, however, a further important innovation in the pulping process, with the introduction of the *Hollander*. The latter was, as the name suggests, originally a Dutch development of the late seventeenth century, which was introduced by the 1720s into England. In its essentials, the Hollander consisted of an oblong wooden tub, in which a wooden roller, manufactured from a tree trunk, rotated horizontally. A series of about 30 to 60 knives were slotted into this trunk and their combined action more efficiently macerated the linen and cotton rags, while at the same time requiring less motive power than stamping mills. Indeed, the introduction of the Hollander actually led to the increase in size of paper mills, which could now more easily accommodate Hollanders than stamps.[85] The earliest recorded use of Hollanders in Ireland is by Thomas Slater, at Templeogue in 1737, and, by the 1750s, these appear to have replaced stamps in Irish paper mills.[86]

Two descriptions of eighteenth-century Irish paper mills have come down to us, one for Jenkins' mill at Blarney, County Cork, in the 1780s, the other courtesy of the American paper manufacturer, Josiah Gilpin

(1765-1841), who visited the Rathfarnham paper mills of Nun, Taylor and Graham in 1796. At the Blarney mills, a large water-wheel powered two beating engines for preparing pulp for the vats, which were located on the ground floor, the loft above this being used to store rags. The mills were also equipped with wheelwrights' and carpenters' workshops, along with terraced houses for some of the workforce, which numbered up to 140 in 1780.[87] Gilpin tells us that the main mill building at the Rathfarnham mills had a brick-built lower storey with a wooden-framed drying loft above, which was painted white. There were four mills in total, the fourth of which had been recently built, and the interiors of the various rooms, he observed, had all been neatly plastered and whitewashed. Gilpin also prepared a careful sketch plan of one of these mills, which shows a single water-wheel powering what appear to be two Hollander beating engines and a duster via rim gearing.[88]

The products of Irish paper mills in the eighteenth century include fine writing and printing papers, the latter being used to produce the *Journals of the Irish House of Commons*, which exhibit the watermarks of about twelve Irish paper manufacturers. Wall hangings, and ordinary packing papers were also made.[89] The use of vats and deckles in the manufacture of paper, however, in what was essentially a batch process, necessarily set limits on the amount of paper that could be produced at any one time. The increased demand for print, and the consequent increase in the need for paper, provided a stimulus for new paper-making technology. In 1798, Nicholas Louis Robert (1761-1828), a clerk inspector of workmen in a French paper mill at Essonnes, completed work on a revolutionary continuous paper making machine. Its basic principle was further developed, in England, by Henry and Sealy Fourdrinier, and their partner, John Gamble, who, by 1807, had designed a reasonably effective paper-making machine.[90] In what became known as the Fourdrinier machine, the pulp was now directed continuously on to a moving gauze belt. Excess water and moisture were drained through the gauze, while additional pressure was applied to expel any remaining water from the pulp, up to the point at which the web was sufficiently strong to support itself. In the same principle, which is used in modern paper making machinery, the web was then passed between steam-heated rollers to remove any residual moisture. The first Fourdrinier machine was installed in a paper mill, actually owned by the Fourdriniers, at St Noets, Huntingdonshire, in 1807. By this period, the Cork paper manufacturer, J.B. Sullivan, who had established paper mills at Dripsey, Blarney, Beechmount, Towerbridge and Springhill, all within the immediate hinterland of the port of Cork, had become personally acquainted with the Fourdriniers and had persuaded them to supply him with a new machine for his mill at Dripsey in 1807. This latter was the first of its type to be installed in a paper mill outside England, and provided employment to about 400 workers, using three water-wheels, six vats and six presses. Sullivan has also acquired licenses to equip his mills near, Blarney, but bankruptcy appears to have prevented this. Nonetheless, by 1824, Fourdrinier machines had been installed at three mills within the environs of Cork, and in at least one Dublin mill.[91]

The first three decades of the nineteenth century witnessed considerable expansion within the Irish paper making industry, and, by 1824, some 54 mills were in operation throughout the country, rising to 60 in 1838. However, by the early 1850s, this figure had declined to 28, and in Cork, where fifteen mills were at work in 1837, there were only three in 1852.[92] By the end of the nineteenth century, the industry was largely concentrated in the Dublin area, in the large mills at Saggart, Clondalkin. Early in the nineteenth century, wood pulp

11.11 *Early nineteenth-century illustration of paper mill at Beechmount, County Cork.*

began to replace the traditional linen and cotton rags in paper manufacture, but by this period experiments with pulp made from straw had already been undertaken in the Cork district, and by the 1850s a number of mills in Dublin and Cork had bought a patent to manufacture paper in this way.[93] In 1920, there were only six paper mills operating in Ireland, the John McDonnell and Co.'s Swiftbrook Mills, Saggart, County Dublin, established in 1795, the Newbrook mill, Rathfarnham, County Dublin, established *c.* 1819, the Drimnagh mill at Inchicore, Dublin, and the Ballyclare mills and the Inver mills at Larne, County Antrim.[94]

For the most part, the surviving remains of Ireland's nineteenth-century paper mills are fragmentary, and thus far no machinery dating to this period has been identified. The wood-framed drying lofts, of the type referred to by Josiah Gilpin, were a standard feature of Irish paper mills. These are shown in what appears to be the earliest known illustration of an Irish mill at Beechmount, County Cork (figure 11.11), in a Dublin mill illustrated by Wakeman in 1837, and in a watercolour of Joy's paper mill near Belfast, by Ernest Hamford around 1882.[95] This wooden shuttering has, indeed, survived in former Ulster paper mills at Leckpatrick, near Strabane, County Tyrone, at Tartlaghan, near Dungannon, County Tyrone.[96] A small section of a late eighteenth-century paper mill survives at Annacotty, County Limerick, while substantial remains of the Saggart mills, including two water-wheel pits, can still be seen.

12

Roads
and Bridges

nglish travellers in Ireland in the late eighteenth and the early nineteenth centuries were amazed at the relatively high quality of Irish roads. English roads, they agreed, could in no way compare with those of Ireland. Yet, in a curious way, the high standard of Irish roads was a symptom of under-development. Ireland, it is clear, could have good roads, but only because the volume of traffic which had run down English roads did not exist there. Irish roads, indeed, were more attuned to the needs of small-wheeled vehicles carrying light loads, and were not likely to have been worn out by heavy goods traffic. For the most part, a county-based administrative system was is no small way responsible for the relatively high quality of Irish roads. However, throughout Ireland, there were no fewer than three principal ways in which both intra- and inter-county roads were constructed and maintained from the second half of the eighteenth century onwards: (1) *by Grand Jury presentment*, (2) *by turnpike trust* and (3) *by the Irish Board of Public Works*.

(1) Roads

(i) Presentment Roads

From the early seventeenth century onwards, a remarkable system for road construction and repair evolved out of local government in Ireland, under which Irish Grand Juries of assize were empowered to levy direct taxes for the repair and construction of roads, causeways, toghers and bridges that were 'broken or decayed'. The membership of the Grand Jury was chosen by the high sheriff, usually from the county's influential property owners, and thus it became, for the most part, an instrument of the wealthy protestant ascendancy.[1] There were originally 40 Grand Juries in Ireland, one for each county and eight for the urban counties, with a

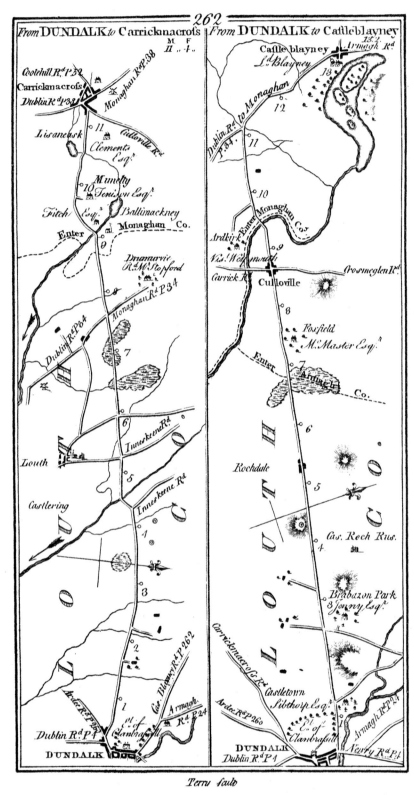

12.1 *Direct alignment road, between Dundalk and Castleblayney, from Taylor and Skinner 1778.*

further Grand Jury being created when County Tipperary was divided into two Ridings in 1838.[2] From 1710 onwards, Grand Juries were empowered to undertake the construction and repair of roads by presentment, a system under which almost anybody could make a proposal to the Grand Jury to build or repair a road. If the Grand Jury accepted this proposal, it could make a presentment that monies be allocated from the county *cess* (rates) to pay a contractor to build the road. Further legislation followed, beginning with an act of 1720, aimed at preventing abuses in the system, under which every presentment henceforth had to be accompanied by a sworn affidavit, to the effect that the works involved were actually necessary, while an act of 1727 obliged Grand Juries to appoint surveyors to oversee individual projects.[3]

Under a further act of 1739, the Grand Juries were empowered to buy land on which to build new roads, but were now required to 'facilitate the laying out of roads in straight lines from market town to market town'.[4] In the years 1759 and 1765, additional legislation transferred road charges from the counties to the baronies; the 1765 act, indeed, transferred the initiative in road building to Irish landlords by transferring the task of building and repairing main roads from parishes to the Grand Juries. During the period 1775-1800, the annual income of Ireland's Grand Juries effectively trebled, and upwards of 75 per cent of these funds were employed on road schemes.[5] An act of 1777-8 further allowed the Grand Jury to grant contracts for the repair of roads, by which time the repair and general maintenance of most of the county roads had become its complete responsibility. In this way, Irish Grand Juries became responsible for the bulk of the roads constructed in the eighteenth and nineteenth centuries. The Grand Jury system of road management had no real analogue in Britain, and its origin and structure owed much to social and economic conditions peculiar to Ireland. Most contemporary commentators complained about their financial mismanagement and, indeed, their priorities with regard to road construction were by no means always intended to benefit the entire population. Nevertheless, despite the idiosyncrasies of Grand Jury roads and the questionable utility of some of them, the system was efficient enough to ensure that the quality of Irish roads by the early nineteenth century often exceeded those of contemporary Britain.

So what was the nature of these roads? The 1727 act specified that all roads built by presentment had to be gravelled to a width of 12 ft (3.65 m), and be at least 21 ft (9.14 m) wide, later widened to 30 ft between the fences (of which 14 ft was to be gravelled) in the 1759 act. Increased attention was also given to proper foundations, surfacing and adequate drainage. In 1780, Arthur Young commented on the parliamentary stipulations for Grand Jury roads, noting that some '14 feet of it [was] formed with stone and gravel'.[6] According to Carr, writing in 1806, presentment roads were normally formed by 'throwing up a foundation of earth in the middle, from the outsides, by placing a layer of limestone on this, broken to about the size of an egg, by scattering earth on the stones to make them bind and by throwing over the whole a coat of gravel when it can be had.'[7]

The use of gravel for road surfacing was widespread in Ireland, largely because it could be acquired cheaply in most districts. However, Irish conditions markedly differed from those of England, both in terms of the poor load-bearing capacities of Ireland's peaty sub-soils, and in regard to the much smaller traffic densities, particularly where the use of wheeled vehicles was concerned. A light surfacing material, such as gravel, which would assist in spreading the load, was thus frequently employed, although rendering this sufficiently compact was a common problem in the era before the steam roller.[8]

The 1739 act also encouraged the construction of long straight roads, such as that between Ballynahinch and Hillsborough, County Down, arising from the stipulation that these should link market towns, in an attempt to stop landlords from proposing presentments for roads to suit their own ends.[9] These so-called *direct-alignment* roads were also cheaper to construct, and, until the 1760s, Grand Juries showed a marked preference for laying out 'geometrical' roads that were laid in straight lines, without proper reference to the difficulty of the terrain they happened to traverse (figure 12.1).[10] Many roads of this type also tended to have steep gradients unsuited to wheeled vehicles, and were also prone to becoming impassable on certain stretches during the winter months. Compared to the roads built by the Board of Works, from the early 1820s onwards, the surfacing of early eighteenth-century presentment roads may have often left much to be desired. Nonetheless, the general lightness of the wheeled traffic using them was such that they fared tolerably well during the winter months, whilst many appear to have been able to dry out quickly after wet spells. The steep gradients of many presentment roads, however, became a major problem in the second half of the eighteenth century, with an expansion in the volume of wheeled traffic on Irish roads, and the increased length of journeys. The necessity of reducing road gradients, indeed, was manifest in the new turnpike road legislation of the 1760s and

1770s, which encouraged the construction of level roads, practices that were eventually to be followed by presentment roads.[11]

The increased volume of vehicular traffic was itself an index of Ireland's burgeoning domestic economy, in which important land trade routes were becoming established to carry linen from Ulster to Dublin, flour from all over Ireland (encouraged by government bounties) to Dublin and butter from the Munster counties to Cork. In Ulster, linen carriers were among the first to recognise the superior qualities of the 'scotch cart' over the Irish, or common car, which had solid wheels. As Wakefield noted, in 1812, the scotch cart could carry at least 700 weights more than the common car, and its use spread to the rest of Ireland by the 1830s.[12] Nonetheless, the increased employment of these new cars required not only improved road gradients, but also better road surfaces, while at the same time roads were now required to be wider, as were bridges.

The creation of an Irish Post Office in 1784 focused welcome attention on the amelioration of existing road gradients, particularly where mail coach roads were concerned. There could, indeed, be no other option, as the increased use of wheeled vehicles in Ireland necessitated this. Under an Act of 1805, both turnpike and presentment roads in Ireland used by Post Office mails now had to meet a series of new standards designed to improve their general upkeep. In accordance with the provisions of this act, some 2,068 miles of road throughout Ireland were surveyed and planned between 1805 and 1826. All such roads were henceforth required to be at least 42 ft (12.20 m) wide between fences and have a gradient of less than 1 in 35, although only a few roads planned by the Post Office, such as the mail coach road from Belfast to Lisburn, were ever laid out.[13]

The increased technical appreciation by Grand Juries of modern road engineering requirements could not in itself improve existing roads. This realisation found legal expression in an act of 1817, under which all Irish Grand Juries were now obliged, by statute, to have any works conducted by presentment certified by County Surveyors, a measure calculated to prevent waste of public funds. The latter, in addition to passing a Board of Engineers examination, were also required to prepare maps, plans and all other necessary documentation needed for tenders, to attend all presentment sessions and to supervise the work of contractors. The Grand Juries' responsibility for county road networks increased steadily throughout the nineteenth century, as also did the road mileage created by them. In County Down, for example, Grand Jury road mileage expanded from 550 miles in 1739, to 1,600 miles in 1810, while in Ireland's largest county, Cork, the length of road under contract in the East Riding increased from 1,599 miles in 1834 to 2,300 miles by 1844.[14] According to Edmund Leahy, who had been appointed Cork's first County Surveyor in 1834, the Cork Grand Jury was responsible for a total mileage of 3,365 in 1843.[15] Irish Grand Juries were also responsible for the erection of mile-posts and, when new roads were constructed, for the erection of fences. Further reform was attempted under an act of 1836, which allowed cess payers to attend Grand Jury sessions dealing with roads, while, henceforth, all related financial business was to be conducted in public. The effect of this act appears to have been limited, as the Royal Commission which sat in the period 1840-2 to investigate the affairs of Grand Juries was less than flattering in its conclusions.[16] Nonetheless, the Grand Jury system survived until the 1898 Local Government Act, which

created the current system of county councils.

(ii) Turnpikes

The system under which roads were built by turnpike trust, one that had been in existence in England since 1663, was not introduced into Ireland until 1729. For the Irish parliament, the turnpike system was a means of obviating a long-running oversight of the presentment system, whereby individual counties tended to neglect roads on their administrative borders. The development of regional capitals, indeed, early in the eighteenth century, created further pressure on inter-county roads, which were already poorly maintained. However, by introducing turnpiked roads, it was hoped to alleviate this problem while simultaneously easing pressure on the public purse.[17]

In many instances, turnpike roads, like presentment roads, were a product of local initiative. A turnpike road was built and maintained by a turnpike trust, usually run by local landowners who could raise the finance necessary to obtain an act of parliament. The turnpike act invested powers in named trustees to erect gates and toll houses at which to collect tolls, but most importantly of all advanced a loan with which to build the road. These tolls were collected from most road users, save pedestrians and local farmers who had to use the road on a daily basis, and these monies were employed for the upkeep of the road and to repay the parliamentary loan. Toll houses were built near large towns or important crossroads, and a gate (*turnpike*) was built across the road. On payment of the requisite toll, which varied in accordance to the size of the vehicle and the type of wheel it employed, the toll house keeper would open the gate.

The first turnpike in Ireland, created under an act of 1729, was built between the capital and Kilcullen in County Kildare, quickly followed by a toll road between Dublin and Navan in the same year. In 1731, a further eight turnpike acts provided additional toll roads, amongst others, between Kilkenny and Clonmel, and Cork and Dublin via Kilworth Mountain.[18] By 1758, there were 29 turnpike trusts operating in Ireland, responsible for some 1,216 statute miles (or 955.5 Irish miles), and, by 1786, five of the fifteen roads leading to Dublin had been turnpiked, along with the four main roads emanating from Cork.[19] In the early years, the standard of surfacing was generally good, but began to decline soon after owing to the poor return of tolls. The Irish Grand Jury system of road construction and repair, as we have seen, saw to it that there was no shortage of good, toll-free roads in Ireland by the end of the eighteenth century. The steady decline in the quality of Irish turnpikes ensured that, by the 1770s, they had become a key target for the criticism of English visitors to Ireland, and, in 1778, Dublin Corporation actually petitioned parliament to terminate all turnpikes servicing the capital. In many instances, indeed, turnpike acts were even allowed to expire, which effectively decreased the total mileage of turnpike roads in Ireland to 780 by 1831 (figure 12.2).[20]

However, in the wake of the legislation of 1784, which established an independent Irish Post Office, mail-coach services were established to serve the principal Irish towns, beginning with the Cork-Dublin line in 1789. The tolls paid by mail coaches using turnpikes were a welcome and often lucrative source of income for the turnpike trusts, and the early decades of the nineteenth century saw an upturn in their fortunes. In consequence, the finances of many Irish turnpikes improved substantially in the first half of the nineteenth century, when the condition of many of them began to compare favourably to that of the presentment roads. By 1837, it is clear that many were accommodating high traffic densities. Nonetheless, the existence of so many good toll-free

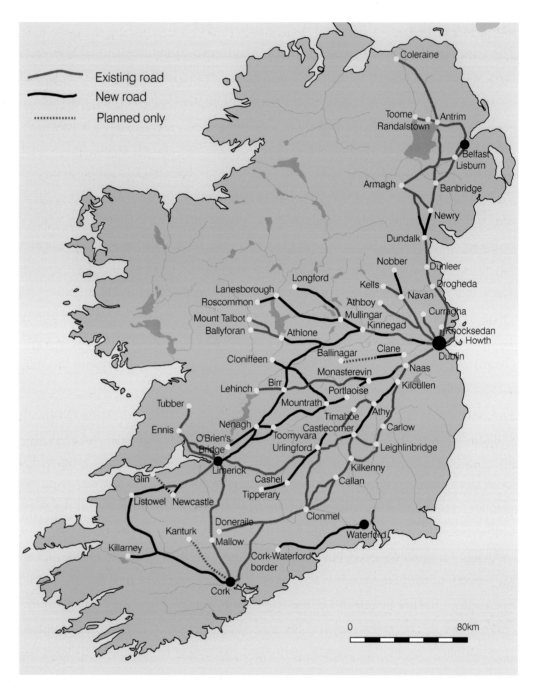

12.2 *Irish turnpike acts passed before 1805 (after Andrews 1964).*

roads and the advent of the railways brought a terminal decline in the fortunes of the Irish turnpike roads, the extent of which had fallen from approximately 1,500 miles in 1820 to 300 in 1856. By the 1820s, England had some 40,000 km of turnpiked roads.[21] In 1857, all Irish turnpikes were abolished, and the roads themselves were transferred to the authority of local Grand Juries, whilst in 1861, mail coach routes (which now covered only 238 miles) had been discontinued.[22]

The turnpike trust was at once a road administration and management entity, responsible for removing obstructions such as snow and fallen trees, for back filling quarries and other features which could be potential hiding places for highwaymen and, of course, for road maintenance. It was a general practice to employ contractors to undertake repairs; they acquired stone and sand locally, the stone being reduced with hammers to the requisite sizes by labourers sitting on straw-filled sacks at the roadside.[23] The frequency of this practice led to the construction of small niches in roadside walls, in which the men could break stones and the finished product could be stored and inspected by the road engineer, without interruption to traffic. A number of these stone breakers' niches have survived in Counties Waterford, Tipperary and Galway.

In the 1750s, turnpike roads were made using one of two construction techniques, the first of which involved the excavation of side drains, 40 ft (12.19 m) apart. The material won from the drainage ditches was then spread along the centre of the road to form the foundation of a carriageway, 12-18 ft (3.65 m-5.58 m) wide, which was covered with over 1 ft of clay and gravel. Such a road was built between Mountrath and Cloneshin in 1753, 40 ft wide, with a carriageway 18 ft wide, covered with a layer of clay and gravel 15 in thick.[24] The second method of turnpike road construction involved cutting a trench for the carriageway, 5 in deep, which was filled with gravel raised to a height of 3 in above the edge of the trench in the middle, falling to a height of 1 in at the sides to form a camber. Contemporary Irish accounts, indeed, stress the importance of proper drainage and the provision of a camber, each important components of MacAdam's later roads.[25]

Although Irish turnpiked roads brought about improved engineering standards, particularly where gradients were concerned, Irish turnpike trusts, for the most part, did not engage the services of civil engineers. However, the trustees of the Dublin and Dunleer turnpike did employ William Dargan in 1831 to undertake an important realignment of the Ballough to Balrothery section of its route, and one suspects that engineering advice would also have been necessary for the widening of bridge carriageways. The increased use of cutting and filling, in which roads were cut directly through obstacles to maintain a gradient, and where the waste material resulting from this process was employed to build an embanked section of road in a low-lying area would, of course, have required engineering expertise. Deep cuttings could significantly improve gradients, as on the Dublin and Dunleer turnpike on its southern approach to Drogheda, County Louth, in 1794, and on the deep cut made through the town of Banbridge, County Down, between 1831 and 1832.[26]

Turnpikes which covered long cross-country routes were invariably major undertakings. The undertaker of the Cork-Tralee turnpike (completed in 1748), John Murphy of Castleisland, undertook to build 56 miles of road, nine large bridges, 15 smaller ones, along with toll houses and turnpike gates. The road was, in addition, required to be 30 ft (9.14 m) wide with parallel drainage ditches and was to have a gravelled surface 15 ft (4.57 m) wide. This was to become the principal route for farmers from Kerry and western County Cork, transporting butter to the Cork Butter Exchange. Large stretches of this direct alignment road still survive, complete with original boundary walls and side drains.[27]

(iii) Roads Built by the Board of Public Works

Towards the end of the eighteenth century, it was becoming increasingly clear to government interests that the development of Ireland's road network was fundamental to future economic prosperity. To be sure, this came with the realisation that local initiative could not be fully relied upon to advance this cause, and that the

12.3 *Roads built by Richard Griffith in Munster (after O'Keeffe 1980).*

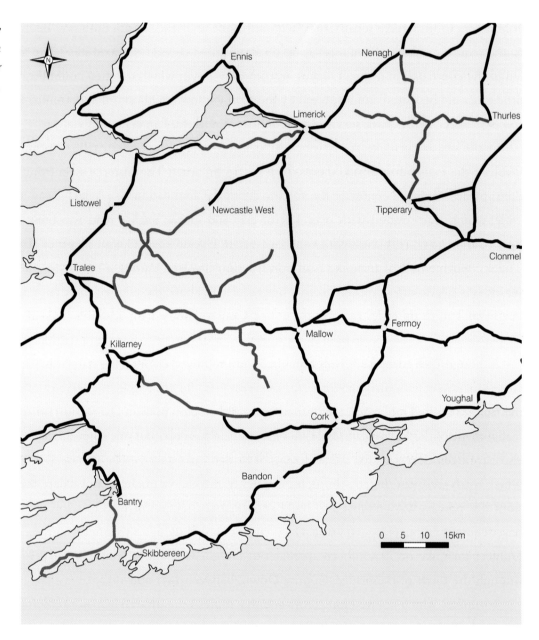

government would henceforth, to some extent, have to directly finance such developments. From the outset, Major Alexander Taylor played a key role in the government's plans and, in the period 1780-1827, Taylor made an enormous contribution to the development of Ireland's road network. Both Taylor and his brother, George, had been trained in Scotland, and George went on to survey some 8,000 miles of Irish roads with his partner, Andrew Skinner, with a £300 grant from the Irish parliament. This was later published in an atlas format as *Maps of the roads of Ireland* in 1778.[28]

However, the government's and Taylor's first direct intervention into road building in Ireland involved a military road in the Wicklow Mountains. The rationale behind the Wicklow military road was the continuing operations of rebels of the 1798 rebellion, led by Michael Dwyer, who continued to hold out in the Wicklow Mountains, to the alarm of the local gentry. The line of the new road was laid out by Taylor in 1799, work beginning in August 1800, with a workforce of 200 soldiers. In total, some 30 miles of road were eventually opened between Rathfarnham, near Dublin, and Aghavannagh in County Wicklow. In essence, the military function of the road was to enable troops to be moved quickly into the hitherto inaccessible areas of the Wicklow Mountains, in much the same way as military roads had previously been constructed in the Scottish highlands. And, to this end, a series of barracks were also built along its length, principally at Glencree, Laragh, Drumgoff and Aghavannagh.[29] As originally constructed, the Wicklow military road was 12 ft (3.65 m) wide and cost, on average, about £1,280 per mile to build. Surviving features, such as 'sewers' or road culverts, are in evidence on the Owendoher River on the Massy estate, where the culvert takes the form of unmortared abutments surmounted by massive granite slabs. This latter, along with five others on the section of road to Laragh, are similar to those constructed by General Wade on the Scottish military roads.[30]

Nevertheless, direct government intervention in Ireland's road infrastructure remained mostly notional until around 1817, when bad harvests and an economic downturn were brought on, in the main, by the agricultural depression which followed in the wake of the Napoleonic Wars. In Munster, this culminated in the Whiteboy insurrection of 1821, whose aftermath finally convinced the British government to undertake essential public works as a form of relief, under which public funds were to be expended on such works in the Munster counties most affected by the disturbances. In 1822, a 38 year-old Dublin engineer and geologist called Richard Griffith was dispatched to survey the area and direct the necessary works.[31]

Griffith was well aware of the shortcomings of the county Grand Juries where inter-county border roads were concerned. By the early 1820s, indeed, large areas of Kerry, Cork and Limerick were served by extremely bad roads or, at worst, by no roads at all. The fact that inter-county link roads between Cork, Kerry and Limerick were non-existent in many border areas, and that the roads linking these areas with the port of Cork followed unnecessarily indirect routes, did not help matters. Griffith's immediate concern, therefore, was to improve these vital arteries of commerce between the principal towns of Kerry and Limerick and the port of Cork. Furthermore, as Griffith quickly realised, the route taken by Kerry farmers to convey their butter to the Cork Butter Exchange should be as direct as possible. In 1822, this road was 78 Irish miles or 99 English miles (1 Irish mile = 2,240 yards, 1 English mile = 1,760 yards, thus 11 Irish miles was the equivalent of approximately 14 English or statute miles) from Listowel in County Kerry to Cork. The distance between both towns, after Griffith's new road between Newmarket and Listowel was completed in 1829, was reduced from 102 to 66 statute miles. In building this road, Griffith sought to improve the transport of butter to the exchange at Cork.

Between 1822 and 1836 Griffith was responsible for the construction of some 243 miles of road in Counties Cork, Kerry, Tipperary and Limerick. In most cases, the design of his roads matched those of principal British road engineers of his day (figure 12.3). When conditions allowed, the main roads were generally 32 ft (9.75 m) wide between fences, with cross, back and guard drains provided, where appropriate. The main difference between Griffith's specifications and those of Thomas Telford (1757-1834) and John Loudon MacAdam (1756-1836), however, lay in Griffith's insistence on the addition of a layer of either clay or loam immediately above the road's pavement. Both Telford and MacAdam expressly advised against this, simply because the pavement could be more

319

easily damaged by ground water and frost.[32] Nonetheless, Griffith's achievement in both engineering and humanitarian terms was immense. New roads enabled farmers to haul stone from limestone quarries to lime kilns, the quicklime of which was used to improve agricultural yields. Greater yields meant increased prosperity and, within a decade, there was a marked improvement in the well-being of formerly isolated and impoverished rural communities.

Further and more extensive government intervention in road building in Ireland was made possible under the provisions of the Public Works (Ireland) Act of 1831. The most important civil engineering project ever attempted in Ireland up to that time, the Antrim coast road, was begun one year after this act was passed. Financed by presentment and the Board of Works, some 33 miles of road were built between 1832 and 1842, mostly under the direction of the Scottish engineer and surveyor, William Bald.[33] The Antrim coast road was designed to provide more accessible road links between the coastal towns of the Antrim glens, which hitherto had had to rely on steep mountain roads, often impassable during the winter months. Along the shoreline to Cushendun, sections of the overhang of the cliffs were blasted onto the foreshore, and the rock thus won used to create a berm, upon which the road was built. To build one section of the road, Bald also progressively drained a deep peat bog, using a technique that was to be later employed in the construction of the Midland and Great Western Railway in the Irish midlands. One of the most impressive surviving features of the Antrim coast Road, the three-span Glendun Viaduct (which carries the road at a height of over 80 ft (24.38 m) above the Glendun river), was designed by the Antrim County Surveyor, Charles Lanyon, and completed in 1839.[34]

(iv) The Beginnings of Modern Road Design: Innovation in Ireland *c.* 1813-50

By the early decades of the nineteenth century, road engineering in Ireland was very much in line with that of contemporary England. William Dargan had also employed Thomas Telford's specifications on the Howth to Dublin road in 1824, which essentially completed the connection between London and Dublin via the Holyhead to Howth steam packet.[35] Apart from the marked reduction in road gradients, effected by contouring and cutting and filling, there was also a vast improvement in road surfacing through the use of binding or metalling of roads. This is commonly referred to as 'MacAdamising', after John MacAdam, with whom it became associated, but it was actually specified by Telford for a Scottish highland road as early as 1802. In its essentials, MacAdamising involves the breaking of stones to a uniform size which, when incorporated into the road, physically bind together in a homogenous mass. This latter, to vehicular traffic passing over it, formed a firm and unyielding surface, and offered only the smallest resistance to carriage wheels.

In 1813, Richard Lovell Edgeworth (1744-1817), of Edgeworthstown, County Longford (better known as the father of the novelist, Maria Edgeworth) published his *Essay on the construction of roads and carriages*, in which he outlined what are essentially the modern principles of road construction, the thrust of which was similar to those espoused by his better-known contemporaries, MacAdam and Telford. Up to quite recently, it was generally held that Lovell Edgeworth's treatise antedates MacAdam's influential work *Remarks on the present system of road making* of 1816. However, this was clearly not the case, for Edgeworth did not experiment with layers of broken stone (as propounded by MacAdam) but with rounded gravel.[36] Lovell Edgeworth's ideas, it must be said, did little to influence contemporary engineering practice, and he was not the first to propose the metalling or MacAdamising of road surfaces. Yet his ideas, although essentially different to those of MacAdam, were both sound in principle and in practice, as he demonstrated by building and maintaining metalled roads at Edgeworthstown. Lovell Edgeworth argued that the upper road surface should be made with broken, pounded stone, 8-10 in deep for main roads and around two-thirds of this depth for minor or country roads. But, unlike MacAdam, he proposed that a blinding, or surface, layer (as in modern practice) be employed to further compact the road surface. Furthermore, whereas MacAdam insisted upon a flat surface, Lovell Edgeworth argued for a camber, again a feature of modern metalled roads.[37]

Nonetheless, significant improvements to the basic design of Irish roads, as we have seen, were already being proposed by engineers, such as Alexander Taylor, who went on to supervise the survey of Ireland's post roads, under the provisions of the 1805 act, which included what may have been the world's first traffic engineering standard for road gradients.[38] And, while Richard Griffith was not engaged by Taylor for his surveys, he implemented, very closely, a mixture of the main tenets proposed by Telford and MacAdam on his major road works in Cork and Kerry. However, he did not agree with the increased road widths of 42-50 ft (12.80 m-15.24 m), which the 1805 act proposed, and in this he was echoing Lovell Edgeworth's earlier belief that this would be impractical in mountain areas, where a width of some 20 ft (6.09 m) would be sufficient. The majority of road engineers of the period, it is clear, did not agree, as an inventory of 1,600 miles of Ireland's primary roads suggests. From the latter, it appears that the average width between the fences was 42 ft.[39] During the era of the Great Famine, many presentment roads were built to a width of only 24 ft (7.31 m), with a drainage ditch along one side.[40] As a young engineer, the future Sir John Macneill appears to have introduced the innovation employing of iron-shod wooden rollers for compacting road surfaces into Ireland, a practice of which the chairman of the Irish Board of Works and first president of the Institution of Civil Engineers of Ireland, John Burgoyne, was to become an important advocate in the 1820s.[41] Macneill also developed a device he called a 'pirameter' that was, in essence, a dynanometer which could be used to measure the amount of tractive force needed to draw loads along a road, an instrument praised by his mentor, Thomas Telford.[42]

Despite the efforts of Grand Juries and the Board of Works, the construction of long lines of new road was effectively over by the middle of the nineteenth century, and, in 1854, all the roads previously administered by the Board of Works became the responsibility of the regional Grand Juries. Yet, while the construction of new roads had all but ceased by this period, the expenditure of the Grand Juries on roads actually increased, as they now tended to concentrate on repairs and improvements to existing roads. However, apart from the burden of maintenance, post-Famine depopulation appears to have substantially reduced the need for more road mileage, as also did the creation of a national railway network, which increasingly became the principal means of long-distance transportation.[43]

(v) Road Archaeology in Ireland

Apart from bridges, which are discussed in the next section, the principal surviving vestiges of Ireland's eighteenth-

and nineteenth-century network of presentment and turnpike roads are mileposts, toll houses and coaching houses. Of the latter, mileposts are clearly the most common survival. The earliest Irish mileposts were erected by Grand Juries, and generally consisted of a roughly cut, triangular section, stone slabs with the distance between major towns, in Irish miles, incised on one face. A rare variant of this, installed at an intersection near Rostellan, County Cork, is inscribed with the date 1734, and indicates the distances to various locations in the area both in Irish and English miles. Some 30 milestones, mostly of eighteenth-century date, have been identified in County Galway, most of which are flat stones, up to 1m high, with a number indicating the distance incised on the outward face.[44]

Mileposts were later erected by the first turnpiked roads and, as early as 1753, surveyors employed by the Dublin and Navan turnpike were instructed to 'provide proper flagg stones to be affixed in the ground at the distance of 320 perches each (the same being one mile) and have the number cut in each stone'.[45] The locations of turnpike mileposts are, indeed, depicted in Taylor and Skinner's Irish road atlas of 1778, a good example of which survives near Julianstown, County Meath, on the Dublin and Dunleer turnpike. For the most part, however, early mileposts within the environs of urban areas, as in the case of the re-erected eighteenth-century example on the former Limerick-Dublin turnpike on the present day Castletroy road in Limerick, are very rare. A series of stone mileposts on the Cork to Limerick road, which survived *in situ* up to the early 1990s until, that is, Cork County Council made the ill-considered decision to remove them to decorate the new line of road between Cork and Mallow, was perhaps the longest section of Irish road to retain its original mile markers. In 1826, the Irish mile was officially abolished, and soon afterwards existing mileposts tended to be moved to represent the shorter, 1,760 yard, intervals of English or statute miles, which initially caused confusion.[46] In at least one instance, the trustees of the Dublin and Dunleer turnpike, in the 1830s, found occasion to complain that its competitor, the Ashbourne, Drogheda and Dublin turnpike, had actually deliberately misrepresented the mileage of its road to give the impression that Drogheda was only 22 miles from Dublin.[47]

From around the first decade of the nineteenth century, following English practice, cast-iron mileposts began to be erected by Irish Grand Juries and turnpike trusts. Early forms consisted of a triangular stone slab with a cast-iron plaque, indicating the distance to the nearest market town attached to it, as on an example of *c.* 1810, near Lisburn, County Antrim.[48] However, what were essentially cast-iron copies of the eighteenth-century, 'v'-sectioned, milepost, appear to have been much more common. Rare urban examples of the latter, cast by the Hive Iron Works, Cork, in 1829, and erected for the Cork to Skibbereen mail coach road, survive at two locations in Cork city.[49] Similar mileposts, cast by a London foundry in 1831, can still be seen on the Dungarvan to Waterford road and on the N72 to Lismore, County Waterford (figure 12.4).[50]

Compared to England, Scotland and Wales, surviving eighteenth- and nineteenth-century turnpike toll houses in Ireland are quite rare. There are two likely reasons for this: firstly because turnpiked roads were less common than in the rest of the former United Kingdom, and secondly because many of the English trusts were not dissolved until the 1870s and 1880s. In Ireland, as we have seen, all turnpike trusts were dissolved in the 1850s. Road widening schemes and the modification of important road junctions are also likely to have led

12.4 *Iron milepost, cast by the London foundry in 1831, on the Dungarvan to Waterford road, County Waterford (left);*
12.5 *Backnamullagh turnpike house, between Hillsborough and Dromore, County Down (right).*

to the removal of many toll house buildings, to the extent that, at the time of writing, only five or six surviving structures have been identified in Ireland. However, a number of these, such as the toll houses at Backnamullagh, between Hillsborough and Dromore (figure 12.5), County Down and Blessington, County Wicklow, were clearly modelled on English prototypes. At least three of the surviving sites, at Backnamullagh, which probably dates to the 1740s, the toll cottage at Rushin Gate in the Slieve Bloom district and the now ruinous toll house at Glenduff on the Cork-Tipperary border, are eighteenth-century.[51]

The surviving sites are generally rectangular in plan, with hipped roofs and a half hexagonal projection facing the road, as at Backnamullagh. The latter had large windows on each face, which enabled the toll house keeper to view the road from each direction. A similar toll house formerly existed at Dromore, on the Belfast to Banbridge turnpike, while a further example, outside Blessington, County Wicklow, also has a roadside projection for viewing road users, but in this instance it is rectangular in plan.[52] The internal space was often simply divided into two rooms, that at the front for collecting tolls and that at the rear providing living accommodation. Indeed, the rectangular ground plan and half hexagonal roadside projection is a common feature of one of the five known types of English turnpike toll house.[53] Our knowledge of the forms of toll gates employed in Ireland is wholly based on contemporary illustrations. The most informative of these is a sketch by G.A. Montgomery of the early 1820s, which shows both a toll house and a toll gate (figure 12.6). In this illustration the toll house is depicted as a small single-storey cottage with a hipped roof, with a doorway and single window to one side of it on the roadside elevation. However, a further window is shown in the side of this structure, which presumably would have provided a view of the road in that direction, and one might reasonably infer that a similar window existed on the opposite wall. The toll gate consisted of a central wooden gate for

12.6 *Rare contemporary illustration of Irish turnpike gate and toll house, dating to the early 1820s, by G. A. Montgomery.*

wheeled traffic, with single or half gates at each of its extremities for pedestrians. Of course, it is impossible to say how representative this arrangement was for other Irish turnpikes. A surviving drawing of a toll gate on the Dublin-Dunleer turnpike of the 1830s shows an arrangement of two swivelling half gates.

(2) Bridges

(i) Wooden Bridges

The earliest Irish bridges were built of wood, which generally consisted of a series of trestles or frames erected in the bed of the river, on top of which a deck or wooden walkway was constructed. On present evidence, the oldest bridge of this type to have come to light in Ireland spanned a 150 m section of the River Shannon, near the early monastic site of Clonmacnoise, County Offaly. This latter bridge has been dated by dendrochronology to AD 804, and doubtless similar bridges were also built at the most important river crossings in Ireland through-out the medieval period.[54] However, the expense of bridge construction ensured that ferries continued to be an important means of crossing wide rivers well into the eighteenth century. In Cork city, indeed, three ferries were still in operation on the north channel of the River Lee in the early decades of the nineteenth century.[55]

Nonetheless, although masonry bridges began to be built in Ireland from the late medieval period onwards, both early bridges of this type and those constructed with timber tended to be susceptible to damage during winter floods. Furthermore, bridges built on tidal sections of rivers were also subject to tidal scour, and this proved especially problematical when wide rivers such as the Foyle at Derry and the Slaney at Wexford had to be spanned. As we shall see, timber was generally replaced with stone as the principal building material for bridges throughout the eighteenth century, but in the period 1789-96, an ingenious American builder called Lemuel Cox built no fewer than seven substantial timber bridges in Ireland.

Cox's first successful wide-span timber bridge, built between Boston and Charleston, opened in 1786, and shortly afterwards he was invited by Derry Corporation to present proposals for a similar bridge over the River Foyle. The Foyle bridge, which was constructed with lengths of Quebec oak up to 80 ft (24.38 m) long, opened to pedestrians in 1790 and for wheeled traffic in 1791, and remained in service until its replacement with Carlisle Bridge in 1863. As built, Cox's Foyle bridge was his second longest in Ireland at 1,068 ft (325.52 m) and 40 ft (12.19 m) wide, his third Irish bridge across the Slaney, at Wexford, was 1,556 ft (474.26 m) long. After the completion of the Foyle bridge, he went on to build wide-span timber bridges at Waterford (1792, replaced in 1912), Wexford (1794-5, replaced in 1872), Ferrycarrig (1794, replaced in 1912) and New Ross, in County Wexford (1794) and Mountgarret (1794) and Portumna, County Galway (1796). Of these, the only visible surviving remnants of Cox's Irish bridges are the abutments of the Ferrycarrig bridge over the River Slaney.[56] One of the last examples to remain in use, spanning the River Suir at Waterford, which was 832 ft long and 40 ft wide (253.59 m by 12.19 m), had no fewer than 40 sets of oaken piers.[57] Timber viaducts were also built during the early period of railway development in Ireland (see Chapter 14), but as late 1829, Alexander Nimmo (1783-1832) had commenced work on a timber trestle bridge, 490 m long, to connect the road to the north of Youghal, County Cork, with County Waterford.[58]

(ii) Masonry Bridges

A small number of Irish masonry bridges, such as Leighlin Bridge over the River Barrow and the bridge at Slane, County Meath, are traditionally held to be medieval. However, none of the latter have been positively dated, nor has their fabric been analysed in detail, and until such time as this occurs, it seems unlikely that these are earlier than the sixteenth or seventeenth centuries. There are, however, at least three likely later medieval examples at Cadamstown, County Offaly, Trim, County Meath and Waterford. The difficulties involved in dating early masonry bridges in Ireland are highlighted by the bridge of Finnea, County Westmeath, which, on documentary evidence, probably dates to the period 1620-30 (figure 12.7), even though its arches are formed by wattle centring, a technique commonly employed in the construction of vaulted floors in Irish sixteenth- and seventeenth-century tower houses.[59]

There are, nonetheless, at least two varieties of what might be termed 'vernacular' bridges in Ireland, the

325

12.7 *Seventeenth-century bridge at Finnea, County Westmeath. The flood arches, shown here, have wickerwork centring.*

so-called *clapper* and the arched *packhorse* bridges, which survive in more remote areas, where they mark earlier and long defunct communication routes. Clapper bridges consist of narrow, rough masonry piers, surmounted by stone slabs that form a deck or walkway. A number of these survive in Munster, but their known distribution is by no means exclusively located there. One of the better surviving examples spans the Awbeg river at Ballybeg, near Buttevant, County Cork, although there are two examples which span the River Lee, within 150 m of each other, at Dromanallig, south of Ballingeary, County Cork.[60] Other impressive examples of clapper bridges survive near Louisburgh, County Mayo and on the Camoge river, at Knockainey, County Limerick.[61]

Packhorse bridges are a feature of upland areas of both Ireland and Britain, in the era before the road improvements of the eighteenth century enabled wheeled vehicles to traverse most areas. In this period, carts and carriages were rare, and the transportation of goods across country was undertaken by packhorses. Indeed, most of the butter brought by Munster farmers to the Butter Exchange at Cork, in the second half of the eighteenth century and prior to the improvements carried out by Griffith to the road networks in Cork, Kerry and Limerick, was carried by packhorses.[62] In certain parts of Ireland, such as the Cork and Kerry mountains, the lines of original packhorse tracks can still be traced, but their existence can also be inferred from the survival of small packhorse bridges. Heavily laden packhorses could not safely ford most streams without getting into difficulties and, indeed, endangering their loads, and so at key crossing points along the route, these distinctive narrow, 'hump-back' bridges were constructed. In most cases, packhorse bridges do not have parapets so as not to obstruct the loads slung on either side of the horse.[63] They are found throughout Ireland, and good examples survive at Gortamullin near Kenmare, County Kerry and at Garraman in the Connemara region of County Galway.[64]

Packhorse bridges were constructed with a single rudimentary, semi-circular masonry arch. But throughout the eighteenth century, as road networks for wheeled vehicles expanded, more elaborate bridges, with wider carriageways and spans and more sophisticated arch forms, began to be more extensively employed. Early eighteenth-century road bridges generally had a series of semi-circular arches, built of undressed stone, with a distinctive 'hump-backed' profile. The voussoirs, or stones used to construct the ring of the arch, were almost invariably formed with rubblestone and, indeed, the use of cut stone for these is nearly always a feature of bridges constructed towards the end of the eighteenth century and later. Carriageways of early bridges are also extremely narrow – in certain instances only 12-14 ft (3.65 m-4.26 m) wide – as at Glanworth bridge, County Cork, and the Ennisgag toll bridge in County Kilkenny. The narrowness of the carriageway often necessitated the construction of 'V'-shaped pedestrian refuges along the bridge parapet (figure 12.8), which were usually created by extending the cutwaters up to the parapet. With the increase in wheeled traffic, however, bridges with narrow carriageways became a liability, and, in the period 1729-1856, various turnpike acts began to stipulate that bridges on these roads should be widened.[65] Evidence for bridge widening can often be clearly seen under surviving bridge arches as, for example, on the Kells Bridge over the Kings River and the mid-seventeenth-century Tower Bridge, in county Kilkenny. Southgate Bridge in Cork, whose west-facing or upriver section was originally constructed by Coltsman in 1713, was widened on the downriver section by Alexander Deane in 1824 (figure 12.9).[66]

The arches of the bridge are carried on a series of stone piers which are constructed on the riverbed, with abutments (lateral supports)

12.8 *Eighteenth pedestrian 'vee' on the Ennisgag toll bridge, County Kilkenny.*

327

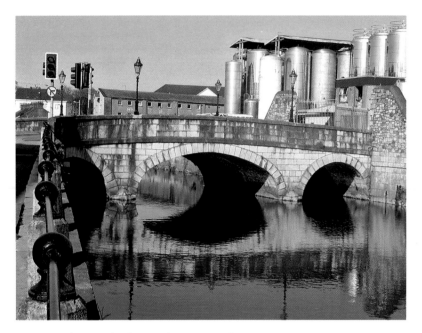

12.9 *South Gate bridge, Cork, constructed in 1713.*

built into the opposing banks of the river. Both the piers and the abutments are constructed with coursed masonry, with an infill of mortared rubble packed behind this, which made them susceptible to scouring. This was generally the most common reason for bridge failure, and to counteract this, cutwaters or wedge-shaped projections, were added to the downriver section of the bridge piers. In the early decades of the nineteenth century it also became a frequent practice for the foundations of bridge piers to be built upon a stone pavement, which significantly diminished the risk of their being undermined, particularly during winter floods. Cutwaters did, in addition, provide protection for the bridge piers from the potential damage of large floating objects such as tree trunks carried in floodwaters, while the streamlining of piers also eventually contributed to the minimisation of scour. The construction of bridge piers, with prepared foundations, was made easier with the introduction of coffer dams. These latter were created by driving vertical wooden piles into the bed of the river, to form a tight fitting box that could be pumped free of water to facilitate building work within the dam. The earliest recorded use of coffer dams in Ireland was during the construction of the five-arch Grattan Bridge, on the River Liffey in Dublin, designed by George Semple and built between 1753 and 1755 (figure 12.10).[67] Bridge piers for St John's Bridge in Kilkenny of *c.* 1763 have recently been excavated under controlled conditions and also revealed the remains of a coffer dam consisting of vertical grooved timbers.[68]

During the eighteenth century, when masonry bridges were increasingly required to span wider rivers, larger arch spans began to be employed as a means of reducing the number of piers erected in the bed of the river, and thus minimise the risk that these might be undermined by the scouring action of river currents. Semi-circular arches were now replaced with segmental and elliptical arches, which produced a flatter bridge profile that significantly reduced the gradient required of the approach roads. Wider bridge spans, indeed, where the bridge itself was now built outwards instead of upwards, also brought down the cost of bridge construction. Nonetheless, the erection of these more elaborate arch forms required both a skilled stonemason to shape the voussoirs and a master carpenter to build the wooden-framed centring around which the ring of the arch was formed.

A series of elaborate, multi-span elliptical arched bridges, which include Graiguenamanagh Bridge (on the River Barrow), Inistiogue Bridge (on the Nore) and Green's Bridge and St John's Bridge on the Nore in Kilkenny, were built in the 1760s. George Smith, a pupil of George Semple, designed Graiguenamanagh Bridge, Green's

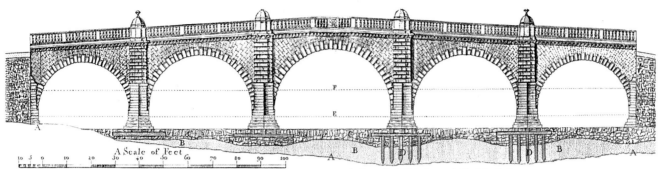

The East Elevation and Section of the Foundation of *ESSEX BRIDGE,*

Bridge (1765) and St John's Bridge, each of which have classical embellishments, two (Graiguenamanagh and Greens) in the Palladian style. The downstream face of Inistiogue Bridge, indeed, is based on the design of Blackfriars Bridge in London, and it is clear that, from the 1760s onwards, the design of Irish bridges was very much in the mainstream of developments elsewhere.[69] At Shannonbridge, the nearest crossing of the Shannon to Galway Bay, and some six miles to the northwest of Shannon Harbour, a mid-eighteenth-century bridge was provided with bridge defences, unique in either Britain or Ireland. These latter features, collectively termed

12.10 *Grattan Bridge, on the River Liffey in Dublin, designed by George Semple and built between 1753 and 1755 (top);*
12.11 *The Lucan Bridge, the longest single arch masonry bridge to be built in Ireland, designed by the architect and builder, George Knowles and completed c. 1814 (above).*

329

12.12 *Alexander Nimmo's Wellesley (Sarsfield) Bridge, completed in 1835, which spans the River Shannon at Limerick.*

a *tête-de-pont* (i.e., a bridgehead), were built after 1810 and completed before 1817.[70]

In the closing decades of the eighteenth century, wide, single span, masonry bridges were beginning to be constructed in Ireland. The architect, Thomas Ivory (1732-86), designed a bridge and causeway over the River Blackwater at Lismore, County Waterford, built between 1774 and 1779, which had a single span of 100 ft (30.48 m), the largest ever constructed in Ireland up to that time.[71] In 1793, the span of Ivory's bridge was exceeded by a design attributed to the Scottish architect, Alexander Stevens, which spans the River Liffey at Islandbridge, outside Dublin. This is called Sarah Bridge, after Sarah, Countess of Westmoreland, who laid its foundation stone in 1791. Sarah Bridge has a span of 104 ft 5 in (*c.* 32 m) and is still the second largest masonry arch bridge in Ireland. The longest single arch masonry bridge to be built here is the Lucan Bridge, designed by the architect and builder, George Knowles (figure 12.11). It has a single arch span of 110 ft (33.52 m) and its parapet has cast-iron railings, manufactured in the Phoenix Iron Works at Islandbridge, date-stamped 1814.[72]

The period 1820–*c.* 1865 witnessed the construction of many new multi-span, masonry bridges, with both segmental and elliptical arches. These latter served two main purposes: to provide additional nodes of communication on wider rivers such as the Shannon, and new crossing points across rivers in Ireland's main cities. Richard Griffith, alone, was responsible for the construction of some 128 new single- and multi-span bridges in Counties Cork, Kerry and Limerick, the most imposing of which is his Listowel Bridge, completed in 1829, which is 320 ft (97.53 m) long and has five segmental arches. Other surviving examples include the Feale Bridge and the Goldbourne Bridge on the Newcastle to Castleisland road.[73] Griffith also designed Wellington Bridge, which spans the north channel of the River Lee at Cork, completed in 1830. This latter bridge, which was built by the Pain brothers, James and George Richard, was intended to improve cross-river communications by facilitating more direct access for butter traffic from the west of the county and Kerry to the Butter Exchange at Shandon. Wellington Bridge is constructed with cut limestone, and has three arches, with two side arches of 45 ft (13.71 m) span and a centre arch of 50 ft (15.24 m): the bridge piers were sunk in caissons.[74] The Pain brothers were themselves responsible for the design of two of the bridges on the River Shannon at Limerick, Athlunkard Bridge, which has five 67 ft (20.42 m) span segmental arches, and Thomond Bridge, built between 1838 and 1840 by the Board of Works.[75] However, by far the most elaborate bridge spanning the Shannon at

Limerick is Alexander Nimmo's Wellesley (Sarsfield) Bridge, which was completed in 1835 (figure 12.12). Nimmo, who had worked under Thomas Telford in Scotland, and who had first come to Ireland in 1825, based his design on that of Jean Adolphe Perronet's famous Pont Neuilly near Paris, of which it is a half-scale replica. In Nimmo's design, the arches are constructed using Perronet's 'bell-mouthing' technique, in which the external flat segmental arches on the front elevation change into an elliptical form on the arch interior.[76]

During the 1840s, significant improvements to the Shannon Navigation, which were intended to accommodate river steamer traffic between the port of Limerick, the town of Athlone in County Westmeath and the Grand Canal and Royal Canal harbours (each of which linked Dublin by water to the Shannon), resulted in major changes to the existing Shannon bridges. In most cases, the principal modification involved the addition of an opening span, through which steamers could navigate the river. At Shannonbridge, for example, Thomas Rhodes, chief engineer to the Shannon Commissioners, designed an opening span which was manufactured by J. and R. Mallet of Dublin and installed in 1843. However, in some instances, completely new bridges were built, as at Athlone (1841-44), Lanesborough, County Longford (1843), and at Tarmonbarry, each of which had swivel sections. Further multi-span masonry bridges were erected on the Shannon in County Leitrim, at Drumsna and Jamestown in the late 1840s, at Banagher, County Offaly (figure 12.13), and at Carrick on Shannon in 1847.[77] An important improvement to the navigation of the River Bann was effected in the 1850s, when a swing section

12.13 *Masonry-arched bridge on the Shannon at Banagher, County Offaly, built for the Shannon Commissioners in 1847.*

was added to the existing bridge at Portglenone, which had been opened in 1847.[78] Other masonry bridges of note, erected within the same period, include Queen's Bridge on the River Lagan at Belfast, designed by Thomas Woodhouse and John Frazer and completed in 1843, and the bridge on lower Bann at Coleraine, County Derry, built with Scottish granite in the years 1841-40.[79] By the 1860s, however, new wide-span bridges were beginning to be built with iron girders, although a few impressive masonry bridges, such as St Patrick's Bridge, Cork, designed by Sir John Benson (1861), on the north channel of the River Lee, continued to be built. This latter had three semi-elliptical arches, with a centre span of 60 ft (18.28 m) and two side arches with 54 ft (16.45 m) spans, and was, in its day, the second widest bridge (after Westminster Bridge on the River Thames) in the former United Kingdom.[80]

From the later medieval period in Ireland, a number of bridges, especially those in urban areas, could only be used upon payment of a toll, a custom that is continued in the latter-day East Link Toll Bridge in Dublin. In certain instances, indeed, the toll was discontinued after the cost of the bridge's construction was recouped from collected tolls or, as in the case of Studdert's Bridge, at Bunratty, County Clare, in 1884, when the local Grand Jury bought out the right to do so.[81] The village of Castlebridge, seven miles north of Wexford town, even developed a thriving milling and malting trade, when merchants diverted trade there as a means of avoiding bridge tolls at Wexford.[82] One of the most impressive bridge toll houses to survive in Ireland is the Leixlip, County Kildare, bridge toll house, which could date to the middle of the eighteenth century.[83] Rossmanagher bridge, on the Ratty river near Sixmilebridge, County Clare, built by Henry D'Esterre in 1784, has two of the most curious bridge toll houses in either Ireland or Britain. These latter, positioned on opposing sides of the bridge parapets, resemble defensive towers which almost dwarf the bridge itself. Some few miles distant from Rossmanagher, there is a further toll bridge on the Ratty river, built by the Studdert family early in the nineteenth century, whose original toll house became the present public house called 'Durty Nelly's'.[84] Lemuel Cox's bridges at Waterford and Derry also had small toll houses, which are shown in early nineteenth-century photographs. Perhaps the best surviving example of an early nineteenth-century bridge toll house in Ireland is that at Athlunkard Bridge, at Corbally, near Limerick. The latter, which dates to 1826, with its half-hexagonal projection facing the bridge toll gates, closely resembles Irish turnpike toll houses such as Backnamullagh. Original toll tokens for the Athlunkard bridge, which depict the toll gates, are held in the collections of Limerick City Museum.[85]

(iii) Iron and Suspension Bridges

Cast-iron arch bridges had been built in England from the late 1770s onwards, and by 1815, both Thomas Telford and John Rennie were already designing iron-framed bridges with wide spans. But in Ireland, bridges of this type, prior to 1820, were extremely rare.[86] Ireland's first metal bridge is the Liffey or 'Ha' penny' Bridge of 1816, which provided pedestrian access from Merchant's Arch to the north quays in Dublin (figure 12.14). It has an elliptical profile, formed by three parallel cast-iron ribs, which span a distance of 139 ft 9 in (*c.* 43 m) between angled, cut stone masonry abutments. The bridge was probably designed by John Windsor, of the Abraham Darby III foundry at Coalbrookdale in Shropshire, where the bridge itself was cast.[87] In December

12.14 *The Ha'penny bridge, Ireland's first metal bridge on the Liffey at Dublin, completed in 1816 (top left);* **12.15** *Oakpark bridge built by the Coalbrookdale foundry for the Oakpark estate, in County Carlow, in 1817–18 (top right);* **12.16** *King George IV's visit to Ireland, in 1821, was commemorated by the construction of a single-span iron bridge (Kingsbridge, latterly Seán Heuston Bridge) across the River Liffey, near the present-day Heuston Station, in 1828 (above).*

2001, the Liffey Bridge was re-opened after a €1.9 m refurbishment, in which upwards of 98 per cent of the original ironwork was retained. A further cast-iron bridge was supplied by the Coalbrookdale foundry to the Oakpark estate, in County Carlow, in 1817–18, which was recently recorded by Ron Cox (figure 12.15).

In 1818, J. Doyle's foundry at Limerick cast a 53 ft 9 in (16.22 m) span iron-arched bridge for Sir Matthew Barrington's estate to the southwest of Limerick: the first iron road bridge in Ireland to be manufactured by an Irish foundry.[88] King George IV's visit to Ireland, in 1821, was commemorated by the construction of a single-span iron bridge (Kingsbridge, latterly Seán Heuston Bridge) across the River Liffey, near the present-day Heuston Station, in 1828. Kingsbridge, which has a span of 98 ft (29.87 m), was designed by the architect,

12.17 *The Birr Castle suspension bridge, built shortly before 1816. This is the oldest surviving example in Europe.*

George Papworth, and was cast in the nearby Phoenix Ironworks on Parkgate Street (figure 12.16).[89] A further single-span iron bridge, with a 95 ft (28.95 m) span, which was constructed by Robert Daglish Jnr of the St Helen's Foundry in Lancashire in 1858, was erected further downstream, opening as Victoria (latterly Rory O'More) Bridge in 1861.[90] The second largest single-span iron bridge of this type to be erected in Ireland, however, was Sir John Benson's North Gate Bridge at Cork, which opened in 1864. North Gate Bridge was fabricated by the Liverpool firm of Rankin and Company, and consisted of eight cast-iron ribs, which formed a cast-iron arch. It was replaced by the present-day Griffith's Bridge in 1961.[91]

The basic principle of the suspension bridge involves suspending a bridge deck or roadway from either wrought iron cables or chains, which are slung between uprights on either side of the span. Generally these were of lightweight construction, but, at the same time, the suspension principle permitted wide spans, which became particularly important when the limits of cast-iron spans were reached in the 1820s. In Ireland, however, only a small number of suspension bridges were built during the nineteenth century which, with the exception of the Kenmare bridge, had relatively short spans varying between 26-73 ft (7.92 m-22.25 m). On present evidence, the first Irish suspension bridge was a footbridge commissioned by William Parsons, the 2nd Earl of Rosse, to span the Camcor River inside Birr Castle demesne in County Offaly. The Birr Castle suspension bridge (figure 12.17), which appears to have been built shortly before 1826, has a relatively short span of 44 ft (13.41 m), but some parts of its structure are clearly original, which makes it the oldest surviving wire suspension bridge in Europe. A second bridge, of similar construction (and perhaps also in date), also survives about 12 miles upstream from the Birr Castle example, at Kinnity Castle.[92]

The first suspension road bridge to be built in Ireland was designed by William Bald in 1840, to carry the Glengariff to Killarney road over the estuary of the Roughty river, at Kenmare, County Kerry. A central tower was erected on an island in the middle of the estuary, from which were suspended two half catenaries (pairs of chains), which supported the roadway. In the period 1931-32, the Kenmare suspension bridge was replaced with the existing ferro-concrete bridge, designed by

12.18 *St John's Bridge, Kilkenny. When completed, in 1912, this had the longest span of any reinforced concrete arch road bridge (43 m) in either Britain or Ireland.*

Mouchel and Partners of London.[93] An early surviving example of a suspension bridge manufactured by an Irish foundry spans an artificial channel led from the River Liffey on the former Barton estate at Straffan, County Kildare. The Straffan footbridge has a span of 45 ft (13.71 m), and was made by Courtney and Stephens' Dublin foundry in 1849.[94]

In 1836, James Dredge of Bath patented his 'taper principle', in which he proposed that both suspension chains of reducing thickness and inclined wedges be used in the construction of suspension bridges. The advantages of Dredge's system were threefold. The decreasing thickness of the chain links reduced, in turn, the weight of the bridge, the amount of wrought iron required to erect it and the time required for its construction. Dredge went on to build some 50 such bridges, five of which were erected in Ulster in the period 1843-8 but, while many of these are no longer extant in Britain, three of the Irish examples survive.[95] These latter include the 71 ft (21.64 m) span suspension bridge at Caledon, manufactured by the Armagh Foundry in 1845, the 66 ft (20.11 m) span Moyola Bridge (1846) at Castledawson and the Ballievig Bridge at Banbridge (1845).[96]

(iv) Concrete Bridges

As we shall see, most of Ireland's early ferro-concrete bridges were designed by Mouchel and Partners, using the Hennebique system (see Chapter 6), but the earliest known concrete bridge to be built in Ireland, completed in 1909, to provide access to the Mizen Head lighthouse station in County Cork, was the first of its type anywhere. The Mizen Head bridge spans 172 ft (52.42 m) which was, in its day, the longest span of any reinforced concrete arch bridge in either Britain or Ireland. It was designed by M. Ridley of Westminster, and employed the Ridley-Cammel system, in which an indented steel bar was used as reinforcement. On present evidence, this bridge is likely to be the first Irish example to use precast concrete components.[97] Mouchel and Partners designed the Drumlone Bridge, near Lisnaskea, county Fermanagh (1909), and the Cruit Island footbridge, County Donegal (1912), both using the Hennebique system, while both the Drumlone Bridge and St

John's Bridge, County Kilkenny (1912), were built by J. and R. Thompson of Belfast, the Irish licensees of the Hennebique system (figure 12.18).[98] St John's Bridge, upon completion, also had the distinction of having the longest span of any reinforced concrete arch road bridge (43 m) in either Britain or Ireland.[99] Other varieties of reinforced concrete were also introduced here for bridge construction, most notably the Kahn system (see Chapter 6). Indeed, its earliest recorded use in Ireland was in the construction of the King's Bridge, Belfast, completed in 1912, the first multiple-span Kahn bridge known in these islands.[100] In 1915, 'The Deeps' Bridge, which spans the River Slaney between Enniscorthy and Ferrycarrig, County Wexford, was completed using British Reinforced Concrete as the primary building material.[101]

Both 'The Deeps' Bridge and the John Redmond Bridge at Waterford, the latter designed by Mouchel and Partners and built using the Hennebique system (opening in 1913), had electrically-powered opening spans which employed Scherzer's 'Rolling Lift Bridge' principle. This lifting mechanism was first used to effect on the Chicago River Bridge, and had been patented by William Scherzer in 1893. It was first adopted in Ireland in Cork and Dublin, where the needs of busy traffic on bridges, upon which lifting spans were necessary to facilitate the movement of ships or barges, required a mechanism which could be lowered and raised within minutes. Thus in Cork, the Cork City Railway Company built two bridges: Brian Boru Bridge (237 ft or 72.23 m long) on the north channel of the River Lee and Clontarf Bridge, 197 ft or 60.04 m long), on the river's south channel, each with lifting spans of 62 ft (18.89 m), which opened in 1912.[102] Similarly, in 1912, Sir John Purser Griffith, the Chief Engineer of Dublin Port, designed two bridges with Scherzer lifting sections to carry traffic over the Royal Canal as it enters the River Liffey on Dublin's North Wall.[103]

13

Inland Navigation: Canals and Rivers

Perhaps the supreme irony of the industrialisation of the former United Kingdom is that its least industrialised region, Ireland, was to construct its first summit level canal almost twenty years before the
Duke of Bridgewater's privately-financed waterway in England. As we shall presently see, this was
because of direct government funding for Irish inland waterways, but we should not forget that those involved
shared what were essentially the same motives for developing water-borne transport. That the means by which
they were financed were quite different alters little the desire, in both jurisdictions, for a means of improving
communications for industry. The early development of inland navigations in Ireland, mostly under the auspices
of the Irish parliament in the eighteenth century, was initially spurred by the realisation that the future economic prosperity of the country could be impeded by an under-developed road network.

In 1715, the Irish parliament had already introduced an act to encourage the drainage of Ireland's bogs and
to create inland navigations and, by this means, foster industry on the island. This was immediately followed
by small-scale works on an eight-mile stretch of the River Maigue in County Limerick, from Adare to the
Shannon estuary, and on a section of the River Liffey between Lucan, County Dublin, and Leixlip, County
Kildare, in the 1720s.[1] However, the 1715 act did little to attract privately funded canal ventures which were, in
any case, discouraged by the failure of the Liffey scheme. Thus, in 1729, the Irish parliament passed a further

13.1 *The Irish canal network (after Delany 1988).*

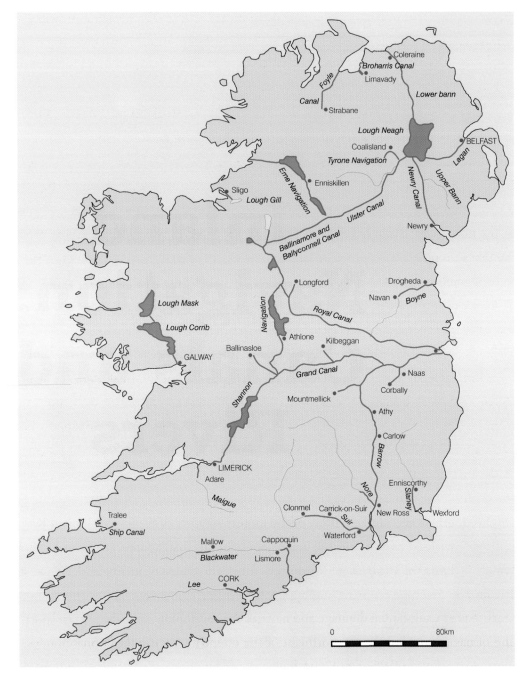

act which introduced two important measures. The first of these involved the raising of levies on certain luxury goods, called 'tillage duties', which could be used to promote economic development. The second established four provisional bodies called 'Commissioners of Inland Navigation', who were empowered to spend these monies on navigation works.[2] However, the main financial impetus behind the development of Ireland's canal network came directly from the Irish parliament, which had from the 1750s and largely for political reasons, allocated enormous amounts of surplus public funding towards the development of existing navigable rivers and the creation of a canal network. In the period 1730–87, considerable financial resources – in all some Ir£800,000 – were allocated to canal development by the Irish parliament.[3] Indeed, the funding of canals in the post-Famine period was also politically motivated as their construction provided a convenient form of relief works. Thus, whereas in England early canals were almost exclusively a product of private enterprise, in Ireland parliament was the prime mover, where direct government intervention ensured that Ireland's canal age got underway before that of any other region of these islands.

Ireland's canal-building era begins with construction work on the Newry canal in 1731 which, upon completion in 1742, linked Newry with the inland basin around Lough Neagh, via a canal between Carlingford Lough with the Upper Bann near the County Armagh town of Portadown, and ended with the opening of the Ballinamore and Ballyconnell Canal in 1859 (figure 13.1). The rational behind the 18½ mile-long Newry Canal was to exploit the coal deposits in County Tyrone, between Dungannon and Coalisland, for which a bounty of Ir£1,000 had been offered (as early as 1717) for the delivery of the first 500 tons to Dublin.[4] This was also the first summit canal in either Britain or Ireland, completed some years before the Sankey Brook at St Helen's in Lancashire (which was not authorised until 1755), and the Bridgewater Canal at Manchester.[5] A second Irish colliery canal, originally intended to carry coal from the Dromagh coal mines in County Cork via the River Blackwater to the port of Youghal, County Cork, began construction in 1755, under the supervision of William Ockenden. A short 2½ mile stretch of the canal was built between Mallow and Lombardstown, which was completed in 1761, the same year, incidentally, as the opening of the Bridgewater Canal.[6]

In 1733 work began on the Tyrone Navigation, followed in the 1750s by the Lagan Navigation (1756), the main line of the Grand Canal (1756), the Boyne Navigation (1748), the Shannon Navigation (1755), the Nore Navigation (1755) and the Barrow Navigation (1759).[7] Canal construction continued apace with the completion of the Newry Ship Canal in 1769, the Lagan Navigation, linking Belfast Lough with Lough Neagh in 1794, the Tyrone Navigation (1787) and the Strabane Canal (1796). In 1804, the main line of the Grand Canal, from Dublin to the River Shannon, was completed, followed by that of the Royal Canal in 1817. Important lake navigations were also constructed, which included the Lough Allen Canal (1818-20), the Ulster Canal (a link between Lough Neagh and Upper Lough Erne), constructed between 1825 and 1842, the Lough Corrib Navigation, which linked it with the sea at Galway (1848-52) and the Lough Erne scheme (1881-90). Furthermore, in the years 1839-50, substantial drainage and navigational improvements were effected on the River Shannon. A third line of navigation, linking the northeast of the country with the River Shannon, got underway in 1846, when work began on the Ballinamore and Ballyconnell Canal, which provided a link between the Ulster Canal and the Shannon. By 1906, despite long years of direct government funding, there were only some 848 miles of canal in Ireland, compared to some 3,747 miles for England and Wales.[8]

The standard of Irish roads, as outlined in the preceding chapter, had significantly improved by the middle of the eighteenth century. But by this period, road haulage costs still averaged around one shilling per mile, whereas the cost of water-borne transport, around 1800, could be as little as two pence per ton per mile. Nonetheless, while the development of a canal network in Ireland impacted significantly on the cost of bulk transport, in the long term, the lack of industrial development here greatly reduced their economic impact. Indeed, in England canal construction was intended to serve existing trade, by linking regions that were already industrially developed. In Ireland, in direct contrast, the two main canal networks linking Dublin with the Irish midlands, traversed mainly agricultural areas, while Ireland's coal mines delivered nothing near their promised wealth.[9] The lack of significant industrial concentration throughout most of the island, therefore, meant that the Irish canal infrastructure was destined to become an extravagant failure. In 1906, Irish canals carried on average some 946 tons per mile: in England and Wales, the equivalent tonnage was 10,989.[10]

(1) Canals

Well before construction work got underway, a principal engineer was appointed to survey the proposed canal route and thereafter to prepare plans and details of the route, together with the main features to be constructed along it, such as locks, bridges and aqueducts. In his *Treatise on inland navigation* of 1763, Charles Vallancey (1725-1812), who had surveyed part of the Grand Canal route, recommended that boring should be taken as often as possible along the proposed line of canal, and that cross sections be dug along it order to evaluate local soils and geology.[11] Once the route had been set out, and the main constructional details had been agreed and finalised, the day-to-day work involved in the canal's construction would commonly be placed under the supervision of a resident engineer. The latter, and his assistants, would then peg out the line of the cut, allotting sections to a number of canal contractors who would be commissioned to carry out the construction work.[12] However, as the work involved often took many years to complete, canals were usually a collaborative effort, often between many engineers and consultants over a long period. Thus, on the Newry Canal, the initial construction works, undertaken between 1731-6, were overseen by Richard Castle (later Cassels), a German-born engineer who was responsible for the construction of the first stone canal lock in either Britain or Ireland on the Newry route.[13] Castle was, however, dismissed in 1736 and was replaced by the English engineer, Thomas Steers, who went on to complete the canal in 1741 with the assistance of A. Gilbert.[14] Similarly, Thomas Omer was appointed principal engineer of the Grand Canal by the Commissioners of Inland Navigation and carried out the surveys for the route, work on which began in 1756. By 1763, he had completed 12 miles of canal, but later works were supervised by John Trail and, later still, by Charles Tarrant. English engineers such as William Jessop, who acted as a consultant on the Grand Canal in the years 1773-1802, as did John Smeaton, were also heavily involved in Irish canal projects. Robert Whitworth, indeed, James Brindley's assistant, was responsible for surveying the line of the Belfast-Lough Neagh waterway.[15]

As mechanical excavators were not used in general Irish construction work until the late nineteenth century, a considerable amount of human muscle power was required to build canals. For the most part, this was marshalled by private contractors, although it was not until the early nineteenth century that large-scale contracting got underway. In the early years of the Grand Canal's construction, most of the work was carried out by many small-scale, local contractors, to whom the Grand Canal Company supplied all the building materials and workmen's tools, and transported these materials by boat to the works in hand. However, two smaller contractors on the Grand Canal, David Henry and Bernard Mullins, eventually amalgamated their efforts with John

McMahon in 1808, to form the most successful Irish canal contracting company, Henry, Mullins and McMahon, who went on to win the contract for extension to the Royal Canal.[16] William Dargan was also involved in Irish canal construction work, and was contractor both for the Kilbeggan, County Westmeath, line of the Grand Canal in 1830, and for the Ulster Canal, where he replaced Henry, Mullins and McMahon, who had fallen out with Thomas Telford.[17] The workforce involved on the larger canal schemes was truly massive. No fewer than 3,944 men participated in construction work on the Grand Canal in 1790, while in the same year, 2,000 men began work on the Royal Canal. Enormous amounts of earth and rock were excavated by hand, the Grand Canal system alone, which eventually extended over 154 miles, was, on average, 30 ft (9.14 m) wide and 5 ft (1.52 m) deep at the centre.[18]

When the lie of the land was uneven, the level of the canal was maintained either by cutting directly through an obstacle or by raising it up on an artificial embankment, but as the canal moved away from its summit, sudden changes in slope were negotiated by means of locks. For the most part, deep cuttings were not required in Ireland, among the more notable being Clonlara cut on the Limerick-Killaloe Navigation and the two-mile-long 'Deep Sinking' which carries the Royal Canal through the Carpenterstown Quarries, near Clonsilla, County Dublin. On the same stretch of this canal, an enormous embanked aqueduct, about 30.5 m high, was also built to carry it over the Rye Water, which flowed beneath it in a semi-circular tunnel, 30 ft (9.14 m) wide and 230 ft (70.10 m) long.[19] The bogs of the Irish midlands, indeed, also posed acute engineering difficulties. It proved necessary, for example, to carry long stretches of the Grand Canal on artificial embankments. Thomas Omer had, in fact, originally planned that it traverse the Bog of Allen by means of a cutting, but it was John Smeaton's proposal, to direct it northwards to Edenderry, that was eventually adopted. However, Smeaton's scheme did not allow any time for the underlying bog to drain and, as a direct consequence, the bog on either side of the canal embankments subsided, creating major problems later on.[20] The section of the Royal Canal between the River Boyne and Blackshade Bridge was also embanked, the embankments themselves being staunched with a large quantity of puddled clay.[21] A stretch of the Ulster Canal near Benburb, County Tyrone, which flowed through a natural gorge cut by the River Blackwater, was formed by cutting a rock cut ledge or bench on one side of the gorge, and using the material thus won to build an embankment to retain the opposite bank of the canal.[22]

Irish canal engineers and contractors quickly learnt from Smeaton's essential mistake, that of not only failing to provide proper drainage but of not allowing a number years for the bog to subside, before construction work could commence. Henry, Mullins and McMahon did, however, put their experience in constructing canals through deep bogs to profitable use. In the early 1820s, while building the Ballinasloe extension of the Grand Canal, the partners had already developed a tried and tested technique for building canals through bogs (figure 13.2). Some 12 of the 14½ miles of this canal were to be constructed through a bog, which varied in depth from 26-46 ft (7.92 m-14.02 m). They began by excavating a channel along the centre line of the canal and by cutting channels on either side of this that were to form the canal's outer edges. Additional drainage ditches were cut at set distances from the centre of the canal, which were themselves cut by cross drains, with the

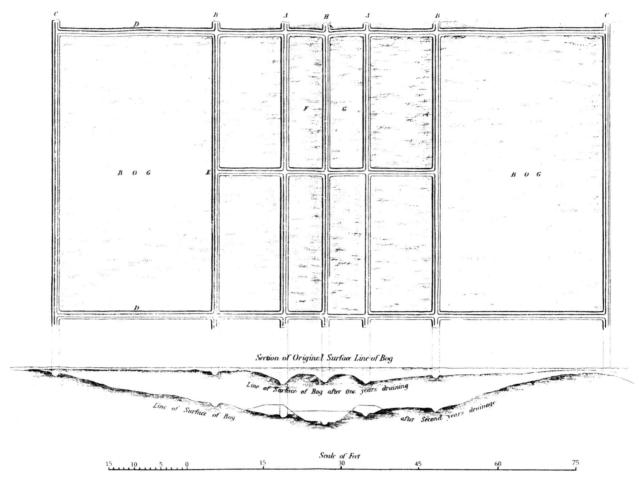

13.2 *Bernard Mullins' scheme for bog drainage to facilitate the extension of the Grand Canal from Shannon Harbour, from Mullins 1846.*

matrix of drainage channels combining to effect uniformity of bog subsidence within the immediate environs of the canal, which would not require high embankments.[23]

Cuttings and embankments could each be employed to lead canals through most terrain, but in order to keep the canal level when it was directed across a river valley, it became necessary to build an aqueduct. In England long canal tunnels were also constructed, when high country made a cutting impractical, but in Ireland canal tunnels were exceptionally rare. Davis Ducart (see below) suggested that an underground canal be executed at the Drumglass collieries in County Tyrone, which were to be equipped with ventilating shafts, while in 1802 Israel Rhodes, an engineer for the Grand Canal Company, had proposed that a small drainage tunnel be built at the Company's collieries at Doonane, County Laois, which could later be widened to accommodate small boats.[24] However, nothing came of these schemes, and the only canal tunnel to survive in Ireland, on the Ulster Canal, is extremely short, and passes beneath Old Cross Square in Monaghan.[25]

Canal aqueducts are essentially single-or multi-span arched bridges which carry the canal across the gorge or ravine in a masonry-lined trough, sealed with large quantities of puddled clay. On the Rye Water aqueduct, for example, a short section of the Royal Canal was carried along its extent within a 3 ft (0.91 m) thick brick trough.[26] The Grand Canal and the Barrow Navigation have a total of eight aqueducts, which include those crossing the River Liffey, near Sallins, County Kildare (the Leinster aqueduct), and that crossing the River Barrow at Monasterevin, County Kildare (the Barrow aqueduct).[27] Work on the Leinster aqueduct, which has five arches of 25 ft (7.62 m) span, designed by Richard Evans, began in 1780 (figure 13.3 and 13.4). The Barrow aqueduct, designed by Hamilton Killaly and built between 1827 and 1831, has three segmental arches of 41 ft 6 in (12.64 m) span.[28] The most impressive examples on the Royal Canal are the Boyne aqueduct, which crosses the River Boyne near Logwood, County Meath, designed by Richard Evans and completed in 1804, and the Whitworth aqueduct. The latter was designed by the Irish canal engineer, John Killaly, whose son, Hamilton, designed the Barrow aqueduct, and carries the Royal Canal over the River Inny near Abbeyshrule, County Longford.[29] In Ulster, eighteenth-century aqueducts associated with the Newry Canal and Ducart's Canal also survive there. The ten-arch aqueduct at Terryhogan, near Scarva, County Armagh, which carries the feeder of the Newry Canal, is probably the oldest surviving example in Ireland. The aqueduct at Newmills, County Tyrone, which carries Ducart's 'tub-boat' canal over the River Torrent, and which was completed in the 1760s, is also extant.[30]

In a summit level canal, water is distributed to the various sections from the highest level stretch of the canal, or summit level. A constant and reliable water supply was critical to the long-term operation of a canal, and great care was always taken to ensure that the summit level was supplied by a dependable source, though

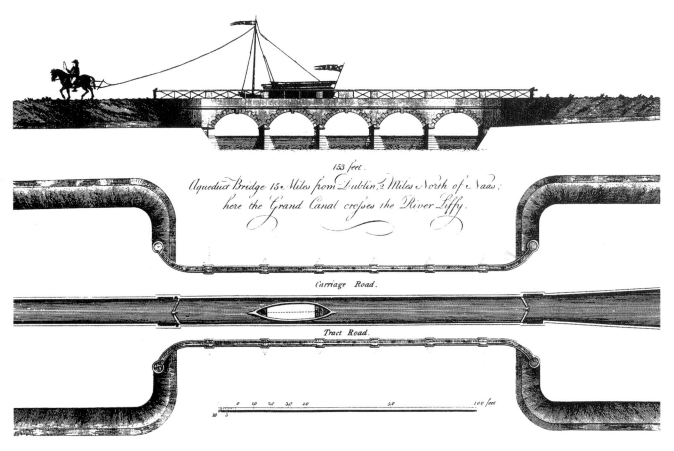

13.3 *The Leinster aqueduct, designed by Richard Evans, from cartouche of* Taylor's Map of County Kildare *(1783).*

13.4 *The Leinster aqueduct in 2004 (left);* **13.5** *The first lock of the Limerick-Killaloe Canal, completed in the early 1760s, at Limerick (left).*

this could not always be guaranteed. Even canals built in the nineteenth century, such as the Ulster Canal, completed in 1841, could experience severe difficulties with its water supply, when it was forced to close between 1865 and 1873 until the problem could be remedied.[31] The summit level of the Grand Canal, near Lowtown, County Kildare, originally received its water from two feeders, the Milltown feeder or 'Grand Supply' and the Blackwood feeder. The Milltown feeder, which is fed by several springs originating in Pollardstown Fen, County Kildare, is almost 8 miles long, while the Blackwood feeder (which was closed in 1952) was designed as a reserve supply and had a reservoir at Foranfan.[32] The River Morell, a tributary of the River Liffey in County Kildare, was the first supply of water used by Thomas Omer for the Grand Canal, as it extended outwards from Dublin towards Robertstown, County Kildare. A series of dams and a sluice house were employed to direct the river water into the canal cut, which was to become the principal supply of water to the city of Dublin up to the opening of the Vartry Reservoir in the 1860s.[33] Lough Owel, near Mullingar, County Westmeath, is the main source for the Royal Canal, while a further natural lake, Lough Quigg near Monaghan town, supplied the summit level for the Ulster Canal.[34]

In its essentials, a canal along any given section consists of a series of stretches or *pounds* (commonly referred to as *levels* in Ireland), in which the same water level was maintained. However, as the canal descended from its summit, the levels between one pound and that immediately next to it would inevitably vary. Thus, in practice, boats ascending to or descending from the summit level had to negotiate rises and falls in slope by means of pound locks. A pound lock is a rectangular chamber, the sides of which were formed by massive ashlar masonry walls, finished on top by flat coping stones. The chamber, thus formed, was provided with heavy wooden gates at each end, balanced by wooden beams, by means of which they could levered open. A boat descending to a lower level or pound entered the lock from the higher level, and the upper lock gates were closed behind it. Each lock gate generally had two sluice gates or *paddles*, which could be lifted upwards by rack and pinion gears (*paddle gears*), and by opening the paddles on the lower gates the lock chamber could be emptied into the lower level. As the chamber emptied the boat descended, and when the reduced water level in the lock equalled that of the lower level, the lower gates were opened.

The first pound locks to be built in Ireland were designed in the 1730s for the Newry Canal by Richard Castle who, in his *Essay on artificial navigation* of 1730, demonstrated a good knowledge of contemporary Dutch and French canals.[35] Not surprisingly, his early pound locks, and those subsequently constructed by his successor, Thomas Steers, were based on French prototypes. Indeed, the two locks built by Steers were fed by means of pipes in the side walls rather than by sluices, whilst the tail sections were built of brick.[36] However, while the foundations of the lock chambers were piled, their floors were timbered. In later Irish pound locks this feature was to be replaced with a more durable stone pavement. Considerable effort was also expended in rendering the lock chamber as watertight as possible, the sides and base being packed with puddled clay, while *terras* mortar (a form of hydraulic mortar imported from Holland, consisting of ground basaltic rock mixed with lime) was also used for the masonry.[37] The first lock of the Limerick-Killaloe Canal, indeed, completed in the early 1760s, even has a decorative cut stone scroll carved on the outer faces of the opposing lock chamber walls (figure 13.5).[38]

Lock chambers on the early canals and river navigations of the 1750s, following European practice, tended to be both wide and long. The lock at Longueville, completed in 1759 by William Ockenden, on the Mallow-Lombardstown Canal, was 154½ ft long and 21 ft 8 in wide (47.1 by 66.6 m), over twice the length and considerably wider than the typical Grand Canal lock of the 1770s. The ashlar masonry in the lock chamber walls of this rare survival of a continental-type lock survive *in situ* at Longueville, just outside Mallow, despite being damaged by Cork County Council road works during the 1980s. Omer's early locks on the Grand Canal at Clondalkin (the 11th), Lucan Road (12th) and Lyons (13th), were actually built to the dimensions 137 ft by 20 ft (41.75 m-6.09 m), but were later reduced after deliberations by John Trail and, later still, by John Smeaton. The primary considerations were twofold: the large amount of water required to fill such locks, and the size of the boats suitable for the Irish canal trade. Smeaton argued that, as boats carrying upwards of 40 tons would be most suited to the volume of trade that could be expected on Irish canals, locks 60 ft by 14 ft (18.28 m by 4.26 m) would suffice.[39] These became the standard dimensions of Grand Canal locks, although the ones at Shannon Harbour were built to a larger size to conform to those of the early Shannon works.[40] However, although the key factors determining the size of boats using a canal were the length and width of the lock chamber, canal engineers in Ireland, as late as the middle of the nineteenth century, gave little thought to standardisation. The smallest lock on the Grand Canal was actually 0.4 m narrower than its equivalent on the Newry, Tyrone and Lagan navigations. Boats plying the Royal Canal could not navigate the Grand Canal, and boats from either of these networks were unable to use the Shannon Navigation. The narrowest of the 26 locks on the Ulster Canal was only, in fact, 11 ft 8½ in (3.1 m) wide, which effectively precluded lighters from other inland navigations in Ulster from using it.[41]

On English canals, in order to facilitate the passage of a canal through a particularly sharp gradient, pound locks were often spaced quite close together to form what are collectively known as a *flight* of locks. Very steep inclines required that locks be built, in quick succession, one above the other, to form what are termed *risers* or *staircase* pairs, although multiple flights of closely spaced locks do not occur in Ireland where, at best, only *double locks* were built. The constant movement of boats 'locking up' and down a canal made heavy demands

on the canal feeders supplying the summit level. Water shortages were by no means uncommon during dry summers, especially if trade was heavy, and so to reduce the risk of insufficiencies of supply on the Grand Canal, side ponds were provided, first for the 20th lock at Ticknevin in 1838, followed later by the 16th and 17th locks.[42]

As a canal could not discharge directly into a tidal river, tidal or sea locks were built to enable vessels to lock up and down between the still water environment of the canal and the fluctuating tidal levels of the river. Sea locks were constructed to connect both the Grand and Royal Canals to the River Liffey, while the Newry Canal was provided with a tidal lock at Newry. The three most impressive surviving sea locks in Ireland, however, were designed by William Jessop for the entrance to the Grand Canal Docks at Ringsend, during the early

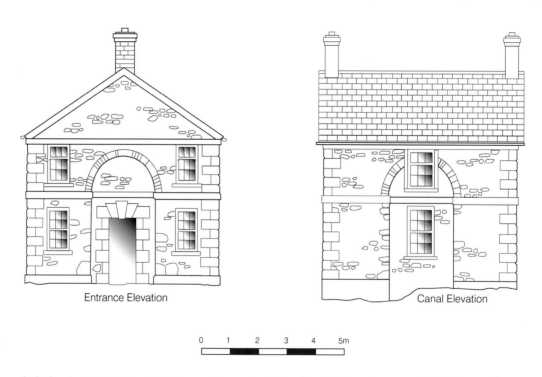

Entrance Elevation

Canal Elevation

0 1 2 3 4 5m

13.6 *The sea lock for the Grand Canal Docks at Ringsend, designed by William Jessop, and which opened in 1796 (top left);* **13.7** *Omer's lockhouse at Shannonbridge, c. 1756 (top right);* **13.8** *Omer's lockhouse on the Lagan navigation for the Drum Bridge lock, Upper Malone, near Belfast, (after McCutcheon 1980), (above).*

1790s (figure 13.6).[43] Two of these, including Camden Lock, 149 ft long by 28 ft wide (45.41 m by 8.53 m), and Buckingham Lock, were built to accommodate the passage of ocean-going vessels into the Grand Canal Docks. The third and smallest, Westmoreland Lock, which, like the others, was named after English viceroys, was intended for canal boats. However, by the late 1830s the largest of these, Camden Lock, had become too narrow for the newer varieties of paddle steamer of that period.[44] Of three surviving sea locks, only the Buckingham and Westmoreland locks are currently in working order.

Most canal and river navigation locks required full-time operators, who might even be called upon to open a lock during the night, and so lock keepers were provided with accommodation at the lock itself, very often in a small, single-storey cottage. Thomas Omer designed a distinctive lock-keeper's house in the 1750s, which was used on the Shannon works at Shannonbridge in *c.* 1756 (figure 13.7), at Banagher (which survives), Lanesborough and Roosky (both demolished in the 1840s), on the Grand Canal for the 12th lock near the Lucan road bridge in the mid-1750s, on the Lagan Navigation for the Drum Bridge lock, Upper Malone, near Belfast (figure 13.8) and on the 7th lock near Seymour Hill in the 1760s. Nonetheless, John Brownrigg, engineer to the Grand Canal Company, reported in 1801 that Omer's lock-keeper's house at Clondara on the

13.9 *The 26th ('Boland's') lock on the Grand Canal near Tullamore, County Offaly, with its distinctive lock keeper's house, completed in 1799.*

Shannon navigation, like his others, 'smoaks so dreadfully as to be scarcely habitable at some Times'.[45] A further mid-eighteenth-century lockhouse, built by William Ockenden in 1759, is now in a ruinous state at the Longueville lock of the Mallow-Lombardstown canal. The surviving lock-keeper's house at the first lock of the Limerick-Killaloe Canal, at Limerick, also dates to the late 1750s, but was, somewhat unusually, also used as a venue for meetings of the Limerick Navigation Company in its early years.[46] The recently restored lock keeper's house on the 26th lock ('Boland's') of the Grand Canal, near Tullamore, County Offaly, an elaborate two-storey structure with a castellated tower, completed in 1799, is unique amongst Irish buildings of this type (figure 13.9). However, the canal company certainly did not appreciate the builder's efforts, refusing to pay the extra cost of its construction.[47] Nevertheless, the design of lock-keepers' houses varied considerably, even on separate stretches of the same canal. One of the early examples on the Royal Canal, at the 10th lock at Ashtown, has a half-hexagonal projection on its front elevation, similar to those found on turnpike toll houses (see Chapter 12). John Killaly designed different lock-keeper's houses for the extension of the Royal Canal to the Shannon in 1814, good examples of which can still be seen at the 35th and 36th locks at Ballynacarrigy. Despite poor wages, the position of lock keeper, with its free house and small garden, was considered a secure one, and canal locks were commonly operated by the same family for many generations.[48]

On Irish canals, the ascent and descent of boats between the intervening levels to the summit, was almost exclusively effected by the use of pound locks. However, on the extension of the Newry Canal to the Drumglass collieries in County Tyrone in the late 1770s, a wholly novel approach was applied, though not with any lasting success. The Drumglass Canal was designed by Davis Ducart (Daviso de Arcort), an architect of Franco-Italian descent who, during his career in Ireland, became a fashionable exponent of Palladianism.[49] Apparently influenced by contemporary developments on the Bridgewater Canal, Ducart eschewed the use of pound locks on the Coalisland waterway opting, instead, for stone-arched ramps (*dry hurries*), by means of which special canal boats could be hauled up to the next level.[50] These latter were, in essence, an early form of inclined plane, various forms of which were later used on certain English canals as a means of minimising the delays encountered by heavy traffic at flights of locks, and of conserving water. Yet these were by no means considered important concerns by Ducart's contemporaries in Irish canal engineering, and one can only presume that his interest in inclined planes may have stemmed from his inexperience in this field.

Work on Ducart's canal appears to have been completed by 1773, save for the inclined planes, where some doubts remained as to how these were to be operated. A water-wheel appears to have been the original choice of prime mover but, on John Smeaton's advice, the dry hurries became counterbalanced to enable a loaded boat descending the ramp to pull an empty boat upwards in the opposite direction. To facilitate this self-acting mechanism, the ramps were doubled in width, upon which the boats were chained together in pairs, while a horse gin (see Chapter 1) was set up at each dry hurry to pull the boats out of the upper pound. However, this arrangement created problems from the outset, and so Ducart built parallel railways, upon which ran a four-wheeled carriage or cradle, that the tub boat sat upon. Ducart's inclined planes, completed in 1777, although ultimately unsuccessful, were the first of their type to be employed in either Britain or Ireland. The remains of two of the original three dry hurries survive at Drumreagh Etra, near Coalisland and Farlough Lake, County Tyrone. Counterbalanced inclined planes were later used on the Ketley Canal in Shropshire, in 1788, on the Shropshire and Shrewsbury Canals, and inside the Worsley coal mine near Manchester in the 1790s.[51] The Ketley Canal also had double-railed tracks and this, along with the three Shropshire examples, were made by the Coalbrookdale Ironworks.[52]

Apart from the difficulties created by the all too obvious lack of standardisation of canal locks in Ireland, canal boats pulled by horses could not navigate either rivers or lakes. Thus, canal boats plying the Grand and Royal canals, upon reaching the Shannon, were commonly towed by steamboats or forced to tranship their cargoes to small sailing vessels or steamboats. Nonetheless, while Irish canals were originally intended to facilitate cheap bulk transport, from a relatively early period, passenger services were also provided. In 1780, passenger boats were introduced on the Grand Canal, serving Osberstown, near Sallins in County Kildare, and Dublin. This service was extended to Robertstown in 1784 and Athy, County Kildare, in 1791, with boats leaving Dublin at 3am in the morning and arriving at Athy by 6pm. Early passenger boats were 52 ft long by 9 ft 10 in (15.25 m by 2.99 m) wide and also, somewhat surprisingly, pioneered features of modern transportation, such as carefully measured punctuality and on-board catering. Indeed, these became the first public transport vessels to be equipped with clocks. The only public clock in Athy in 1798 was at the Grand Canal Company's passenger depot. Passenger boats were also equipped with a galley, which cooked a variety of hot food for customers, and even carried live fowl.[53]

The growing importance of canal passenger traffic led to the construction of a total of seven canal hotels, five on the Grand Canal, including the first at Sallins, County Kildare, in 1784, and two on the Royal Canal. The other four Grand Canal hotels were built at Robertstown, County Kildare (figure 13.10), Tullamore, County Offaly, Portobello, near Dublin, and Shannon Harbour, of which only three survive: Robertstown (1801), Portobello (1807) and Shannon Harbour (1806), this latter in ruins.[54] The Royal Canal Company hotels were established at Broadstone Harbour in Dublin (part of which survives) and at Moyvalley, County Meath. Of these, only the Moyvalley hotel, as in the case of the Grand Canal examples, was purpose built, opening in 1807.[55] Although they cost almost Ir £30, 000 to construct, the Grand Canal hotels quickly became another victim of improved road passenger services. The best surviving examples are at Robertstown (recently restored) and Portobello, designed by company engineer Thomas Colbourne, currently used as a third-level college.[56]

In order to augment its passenger services, the Grand Canal Company attempted to persuade coaching services to link up with its own boats, but by the early years of the nineteenth century, competition from more efficient road travel encouraged the Grand Canal Company to investigate new means of propelling its boats. The paddle steamer, *City of Cork*, built at Cork in 1815 (see Chapter 10) aroused the company's interest in the potential of steamships, and in 1816 it seized the opportunity of experimenting with the towing capabilities of such vessels, using the paddle steamer *Princess Charlotte*. James Scott carried out further experiments on the company's behalf at the Ringsend basin in 1822, while Robert Mallet was approached in the late 1820s to design steam-powered canal boats.[57] In the late 1820s, unsuccessful attempts were made by the Grand Canal Company to improve the design of the existing passenger boats, to make them speedier.[58] In the face of stiff

13.10 *Grand Canal hotel at Robertstown, County Kildare, completed in 1801 (left);* **13.11** *Flyboat on the Royal Canal near Dublin, from Hall's Ireland (1841) (right).*

competition from coaching companies, such as Bianconi's in the early 1830s, the Royal Canal Company looked outside Ireland for inspiration. On the Paisley Canal, in Glasgow, lightweight passenger boats capable of speeds of up to ten miles an hour, while carrying up to 110 passengers, had been in existence for some time. These were known as 'Scotch' or 'fly boats' and, in 1833, the Royal Canal Company became the first in Ireland to introduce them for canal passenger services, reducing the trip from Dublin to Mullingar by some four hours (figure 13.11).[59] Fly boats were first used on the Grand Canal in the following year, but this was not enough to stem the declining demand for canal passenger services in general, which were ended in 1852, a victim of the advent of railways. Further attempts had been made in the 1840s to introduce steam boats on to the Grand Canal, but the two twin-screw passage boats, built by Barrington of Ringsend, were not a success and ended up as towing steamers. Indeed, a further experiment with steam-towing tugs in the 1860s also failed because of the delays created in forming trains of canal boats and, in 1873, horse traction was re-introduced. Nonetheless, in 1911, Ireland became the first region within the former United Kingdom to introduce motorised canal boats, when a Bolinder diesel engine was installed in an Irish vessel.[60]

The construction of Ireland's canal network required an elaborate infrastructure of ancillary buildings and services, which ultimately led to the development of what became inland ports, providing everything from industrial wharfage and warehousing to drydocks and stabling. Canal basins, or 'harbours' as they were known in Ireland, were sited at seaports and at important inland locations. At seaports, canal harbours facilitated the transhipment of cargoes from ocean-going ships to either lighters or barges, which could navigate natural or artificial waterways. Inland canal basins, on the other hand, served as nodal points for the transportation of bulk cargoes such as grain, turf and building materials. To be sure, the creation of canal harbours not only augmented inland trade at existing towns such as Mullingar and Tullamore, but also led to the creation of new canal villages such as Robertstown and Monasterevin in County Kildare, and Shannon Harbour.

The first canal basin to be constructed in Ireland was completed in the 1760s at Coalisland for the Tyrone Navigation. Unfortunately, the canal feeder from the River Torrent was directed in to the basin, carrying with it silt and other water-borne debris, which not only impaired the use of the basin itself but also of several lock chambers and levels downstream from it.[61] James' Street Harbour (near the latter day Guinness's Brewery), completed by the 1780s, was the original Dublin terminus of the Grand Canal. By the 1830s, an extensive range of buildings (now mostly demolished) had grown up around the canal basin, which included houses for company officials and key tradesmen, stores, stables, dry docks and fitting and harness-makers' shops. The harbour was sited next to the City Basin, the municipal water storage reservoir of Dublin Corporation (see Chapter 16), which the canal company had agreed to supply with water in 1772, commencing service in 1777. A similar rationale, indeed, also influenced the construction of a further city basin, in 1806, next to and contemporaneous with the canal harbour at Portobello, on the Grand Canal's Circular Line.

Irish canal harbours, therefore, performed a number of essential functions, principally storage, administration, maintenance and accommodation for either officials or passengers. Stores and warehouses were almost a universal feature. Canal warehouses were commonly two to three storeys high, often with projecting canopies on the canal side elevation as, for example, at James' Street, Athy, Naas and Tullamore, which provided cover for boats tied up alongside. However, warehouses which enabled the entry of canal boats via an arched opening into an indoor dock were unknown in Irish canal harbours, although at least two examples have been documented for eighteenth-century mills at Slane, County Meath, and Limerick, which were associated with river navigations (see Chapter 9). Good examples of nineteenth-century Grand Canal warehouses survive at Kilbeggan harbour, County Westmeath, which has been recently restored, at Daingean (formerly Philipstown), County Offaly (figure 13.12), and at Monasterevin, County Kildare, recently converted to apartments. A fine late nineteenth-century bonded warehouse, restored for use as a local museum, survives on the Grand Canal at Tullamore. Other specialist buildings include the butter market, established at the Royal Canal harbour at Longford by the Earl of

Longford, and Daly's malt house, built in 1871, at Monasterevin harbour on the Barrow line of the Grand Canal. In 1808, the Grand Canal Company completed a coal yard at Lowtown, County Kildare, to store the output from its recently acquired collieries at Doonane, County Laois. Further coal yards were later provided at Ringsend and James' Street harbours.[62] Nearly all canal harbours would have been equipped with stabling for both canal and cart horses, along with hay stores and a smithy. Larger harbours, such as James'

13.12 *Nineteenth-century canal warehouse at Daingean, County Offaly.*

Street, Portobello and Tullamore on the Grand Canal, and Mullingar and Richmond on the Royal Canal, were equipped with dry docks and other boat maintenance facilities. Of these, the best surviving examples are the canal boat dry docks at Richmond and Mullingar harbours on the Royal Canal.

Accommodation for key personnel and administrative buildings was also provided, a good example of which is the surviving harbour-master's house at Kilbeggan harbour. Other important survivals of the former canal haulage trade are quayside cranes, usually of the swivelling derrick variety. The winch was generally activated by metal gear wheels, set on the crane post, whose winding mechanism commonly had a ratchet, which prevented it from accidentally slipping when carrying a load. A distinctive variety of cast-iron swivelling crane was installed by the Shannon Commissioners during the mid-nineteenth century, at various locations on the Shannon Navigation, good examples of which are still in evidence, at Shannonbridge and at Lock Quay on the Shannon canal at Limerick. Swivelling canal wharf cranes also survive on the Killaloe Canal at Killaloe, County Clare, and at Tullamore harbour.

The Grand Canal Docks at Ringsend in Dublin, completed in 1796 to the design of William Jessop, were the largest of two canal wet or floating docks to be built in Ireland. They form the terminus of the Circular Line of the Grand Canal, linking the main line of the canal (which originally terminated at James' Street harbour) from the 1st lock on Suir Road, with the River Liffey at Ringsend. The canal harbour at Portobello is also situated on the Circular Line which, as we have seen, became the terminus for passenger boats. The Grand Canal Docks, completed between 1790 and 1796, is 'L'-shaped in plan and covers an area of 24.5 acres (9.9 ha) adjacent to the south bank of the River Liffey, where it is joined by the River Dodder.[63] Sea locks facilitated access to the Liffey, while it was also originally equipped with graving docks. The docks were designed to accommodate 150 sea-going ships, but the limited size of the locks eventually rendered them unsuitable for the increasing width of steamships. Nevertheless, at their greatest extent the docks provided some 5, 300 ft (1,615 m) of wharfage. William Jessop's construction work on the docks are, nonetheless, significant in that they involve the earliest recorded use of steam engines in Ireland for draining civil engineering works (see Chapter 2), while upon completion these docks were the largest of their type anywhere in Britain or Ireland before 1800. The Royal Canal Docks were much smaller and comprised little more than a widened stretch of canal with quays on each side, with a large sea lock providing access to the River Liffey. By extending this area up to the 1st lock on the Royal Canal the Midland Great Western Railway Company created the Spencer Dock, which was opened in 1873.

The line of a canal, through both open countryside and urban areas, inevitably intersected many roads, while occasionally it could cut entire farms in half. Thus, the construction of a canal required the erection of many bridges in order, on the one hand, that existing roads could be carried over it, and on the other to accommodate landowners whose land was bisected by it. On the Grand Canal and the Barrow Navigation, for example, a total of 168 bridges were built between the late 1750s and the mid 1830s.[64] For the most part, the vast majority of the surviving eighteenth- and early-nineteenth century Irish canal bridges are single-span, masonry arched structures. However, a number of Omer's early bridges on the Grand Canal near Clondalkin in County

Dublin were constructed with timber, although these were removed when passenger services were first introduced, owing to their restricted headroom.[65] Nevertheless, wooden accommodation bridges were built as late as 1855, on the Ballinamore and Ballyconnell Canal, at Derrinhip and Cloncooly.

Two basic varieties of masonry arched bridge were built on eighteenth and early nineteenth-century Irish canals. The first, and more common, is the distinctive hump-backed, narrow-waisted bridge, which spanned both the canal and the towpath (figure 13.13). The second variety was used to span the tail of a lock chamber, where the fall of the ground was used to obviate the need for a steep approach ramp. In most cases, particularly on early bridges, three-centred arches were employed, which afforded extra head room for both canal and towpath, as on the road bridge over the Newry Canal at Jerrettspass, County Armagh, which was designed by John Brownrigg and completed in 1808. Early nineteenth-century bridges, however, were increasingly built with elliptical arches, such as those designed in the 1830s by John Killaly for the Ulster Canal (figure 13.14), while on occasion segmental arches were built for tail bridges over canal locks. On the majority of bridges, the rise

of the parapet describes a graceful curve, but on a small number of bridges the rise forms an apex, as on Mack's Bridge (1808), on the Coalisland Canal, and at Lock Quay bridge at the first lock of the Limerick-Killaloe Canal at Limerick, which was built in the early 1760s.[66] The arch of the latter bridge has brick voussoirs, which are very rare in Ireland, almost all canal bridges, indeed, being constructed exclusively with stone. Ornamentation on Irish

13.13 *Griffith Bridge, a typical early nineteenth-century Grand Canal humpback bridge, at Shannon Harbour, County Offaly (top);* Above: **13.14** *Humpback bridge of the 1830s on Ulster Canal, designed John Killaly, at Benburb, County Tyrone (above).*

13.15 *Campbell's Bridge on the Grand Canal, County Offaly (far left);* **13.16** *Early nineteenth-century canal mile-post Killaloe Canal, near Clonlara, County Clare (left).*

canal bridges is usually quite spartan (figure 13.15), being confined to a string course above the arch and, frequently, on early bridges, a plaque bearing the date of construction along with the name of the canal engineer responsible. One of the Limerick-Killaloe Canal bridges, at Clonlara, County Clare, completed in 1769, even had a Sheela-na-gig (a later medieval exhibitionist sculpture) built into its north parapet.[67] *Roving* or *turn-over* bridges which, on English canals, enabled a barge horse to pass over a bridge to a towpath on the opposite side without being untethered, are unknown in Ireland. There are, however, a few Irish examples of canal bridges that have a separate horse archway on the towpath, most notably at the 'High Bridge', at Ballyskeagh, near Lambeg, County Down, the Goudy Bridge, near Aghagullon, County Antrim, and the Ballyconnell Bridge on the Ballinamore Canal. Furthermore, whereas iron bridges were being built to span English canals, by the early decades of the nineteenth century in Ireland, canal bridges continued to be built with masonry, despite the existence of good iron foundries.

Nonetheless, Irish conditions created what is arguably one of the most significant technological developments in the evolution of masonry arched bridges when, in 1787, William Chapman (1749-1832), a Northumberland engineer, who had originally come to Ireland as a representative of Boulton and Watt, solved the long-standing difficulty of aligning roads with either canal or river bridges.[68] The essential problem with pre-existing masonry bridges was that they were built 'square on', or at right angles to the banks of the river or canal and that, in consequence, the road had to be realigned to accommodate the bridge. However, the directors of the Kildare Canal asked Chapman to try to maintain the existing road alignments as they crossed over the canal. This was Chapman's first ever appointment as a canal engineer, a circumstance that may well have influenced his decision to investigate new possibilities. In the event, he decided that 'the joints in the voussoirs should be rectangular with the face of the oblique arch in place of parallel with its abutment', in other words, that the arch should be built skew-wise between its abutments, which enabled the axial alignment of the bridge to more closely match that of the road.[69] Chapman built three skew bridges on the Kildare Canal between 1787 and 1789, at Osberstown, Oldtown and Naas but, as these did not have towpaths and were lower than those on the Grand Canal, they were replaced with more conventional bridges in 1808, when this canal was taken over by the Grand Canal Company.[70] Nevertheless, Chapman's technique became known as the helicoidal or 'English' method of skew arch construction, and became the standard means of building masonry skew arches.[71] Surviving canal skew bridges are both rare and late in Ireland, the Newbrook Road Bridge, built in 1849-50 to carry the Carrick-on-Shannon to Ballinamore Road over the Ballinamore-Ballyconnell Canal, being one of the more noteworthy. Nineteenth-century iron canal bridges are also a rarity in this country. Indeed, most of the surviving examples are lift bridges, with overhead or 'Dutch' frames, as at Monasterevin, County Kildare and the Liffey Bridge, at Bagenalstown, County Carlow. A rare guillotine bridge, with a vertical drawbridge-type action, also survives on the Barrow Navigation at Levitstown, County Carlow. On later canals, as one might expect, newer forms of bridge, influenced by the railway era, were employed, a good example of which is the wrought-iron lattice girder bridge at Drumanary on the Ballinamore-Ballyconnell Canal.

In the era when all canal boats were pulled by horses, the towpath was an extremely important component of the canal. It was invariably built with a rubble foundation, and very often was constructed with upcast spoil from the excavation of the canal bed. On sections of canal that were built through bogs, indeed, the towpath was generally formed with clay.[72] A camber was also commonly formed at the water's edge, while additional reinforcement was provided on sections leading into locks, which were built with masonry. On the Ballinamore-Ballyconnell Canal, the towpath in marshy areas was laid with split railway sleepers.[73] As on roads of the period, most Irish canals were equipped with mileposts, good examples of which survive on the Royal Canal (showing the distance in Irish miles) and on the Limerick-Killaloe Canal near Clonlara (figure 13.16).

(2) River Navigations

In Ireland, all the major river and lake systems, with the exception of the River Suir, required substantial civil engineering works to accommodate the free movement of most forms of inland cargo vessel. From the middle of the eighteenth century onwards, when large-scale works were begun on the improvement of the rivers Boyne, Shannon, Barrow, Nore, Suir and the Blackwater in Munster, the principal means by which such obstacles as shoals, shallows and falls were avoided involved the construction of bypass canals. The typical Irish river navigation of the eighteenth and nineteenth centuries, therefore, comprised a mixture of natural watercourse and artificial cut. However, the canals used to bypass natural obstacles on the larger rivers differed from more conventional still-water canals in two key respects. First and foremost, the level of water in the canal was maintained by a weir constructed upstream from it, while a single set of lock gates, called a *guard lock*, was often built at the upstream end to prevent damage by winter floods.

Two varieties of lock were constructed on Irish river navigations in the middle of the eighteenth century, *flash locks* and *pound* locks. The flash lock is the earliest type of lock used in either Britain or Ireland, to facilitate the passage of boats through either shallows or weirs but could not, unlike the pound variety, assist river craft in the negotiation of rises in slope. Furthermore, as their essential action involved the release of a rush or 'flash' of water, which carried the boat over the crest of a weir or through the shallows, they could not be used on summit level canals owing to the wastage of water. Boats passing upstream, indeed, had to be manually hauled through the lock. Thomas Omer built flash locks in the 1750s on the Shannon Navigation at Banagher, Shannonbridge and Lanesborough, on short stretches of canal that bypassed shallows. In each case, the opening of a single set of gates (*half locks*) was sufficient to create a flash of water.[74] However, while Thomas Ockenden also built two examples on the Nore Navigation, during the 1750s, no further flash locks were ever constructed on an Irish river navigation, while Omer's bypass canals on the Shannon Navigation were rendered defunct by the introduction of steam bucket dredging in the 1840s.

Owing to the larger size of the types of vessel employed on rivers, pound locks were invariably larger on river navigations than those built for summit level canals. William Ockenden's early locks on the disastrous and uncompleted Nore Navigation of the late 1750s, were a massive 200 ft by 21 ft (60.96 m by 6.4 m), although river navigation locks in Ireland were generally less than half this size.[75] The 23 locks on the late eighteenth-century Barrow Navigation, which made the River Barrow navigable from its tidal reaches at St Mullins, County Carlow, to Monasterevin, County Kildare, where it linked up the Grand Canal network, were 80 ft by 30 ft (24.38 m by 9.14 m) in extent. Yet the locks on the Limerick-Killaloe Navigation (105 ft by 19 ft or 32 m by 5.79 m) were, from the outset, too narrow to admit sea-going vessels to the middle and upper Shannon.[76] Guard locks were also provided on early navigations, as at Athlone on the Shannon Navigation in the late 1750s and on the Boyne Navigation at Slane, County Meath, in the 1760s.[77] On Irish river navigations, however, flights of locks are only found at the Union locks at Sprucefield on the Lagan Navigation, where a flight of four locks over a distance of about 100 yds lifts the water level through 26 ft (7.92 m).[78] As on still-water canals, a full-time presence was required at locks, and their operators were provided with houses, fine examples of which, as we have seen, were designed by Omer for the Lagan and Shannon navigations. On the Lagan, eighteen lock keepers were responsible for the care of 27 locks, where the lock-keeper's duties included guiding the boats through in the order at which they arrived at the lock as well as conserving water.[79] Good examples of lock keepers' houses have recently been restored at Moneypenny's Lock on the Newry Navigation and at Carricklead Lock on the Barrow Navigation.

Canal feeder weirs are an often neglected feature of river navigations, despite the fact that on the Barrow Navigation alone no fewer than 22 were built to service 23 of the locks. In the main, two basic types of weir were employed to regulate the height of water in a bypass canal. The first variety was built directly across the river, upstream of the bypass canal, and commonly described as an arc in plan, as at the tidal lock on the Barrow Navigation at St Mullins. The second was 'L'-shaped in plan, the main section of which ran along the long axis of the river itself, leading into the rear of the lock chamber, with the crest of the weir serving as a lead in to the lock. Similar weirs were also built on the Barrow Navigation at Milford, County Carlow, and at Carlow town.

The advent of the steam dredger to Ireland's inland waterways in 1817 enabled shallows and shoals to be physically removed from river channels. In that year, John Hughes of Poplar, who had been involved earlier

13.17 *Ballycurran lighthouse on Upper Lough Corrib, Ireland's only known lake navigation light tower. This was probably built in 1775 by Henry Lynch as a beacon for a dangerous section of the waters leading into Ballycurran Bay (Courtesy, Paul Duffy).*

with dredging operations on the River Thames at Blackhall, began work on the River Suir to facilitate the passage of sea-going vessels to Waterford. Hughes' dredging machinery appears to have been powered by a table top engine, manufactured by the Neath Abbey Iron Works in Wales.[80] On the River Shannon in the 1840s, steam bucket dredging was begun on the main channel, while at Meelick, Omer's bypass canal was superseded by a large lock (Victoria Lock), capable of accommodating river steamers. The channel was also bucket-dredged at Athlone, where a new lock and extensive weir were constructed.

Lighthouses (see Chapter 15) are invariably associated with the coastline, but at Ballycurran, on Upper Lough Corrib, Ireland's only known lake navigation light tower survives (figure 13.17). This appears to have been built in 1775 by Henry Lynch (who had earlier erected the adjacent boathouse in 1772) as a beacon for a dangerous section of the waters leading into Ballycurran Bay. The lighthouse formed part of a system of navigation markers (one of which survives to the south of it). A stone spiral staircase facilitated access to the lantern portion at the top, the roof of which is formed with, of all things, a millstone.[81]

(3) Lake Navigations and Inland Steamships

The River Shannon, at 224 miles the longest river system in either Britain or Ireland, is technically both a river and lake navigation, passing through some fifteen lakes, including three of Ireland's most extensive, Lough Allen, Lough Ree and Lough Derg, on its course from County Cavan to Limerick. The ultimate ambition of the Irish parliament was to create links between all Ireland's main natural waterways, by connecting Lough Neagh with the Upper and Lower Lough Erne system and with the Shannon, and by this means provide multiple outlets to the sea at Limerick, Ballyshannon (on Donegal Bay), Belfast, Coleraine and Newry.[82] Yet before the development of river navigations, no large vessels could operate on either Lough Neagh, the largest natural lake in these islands, or on Lough Corrib, Ireland's second-largest lake. Paddle steamers were introduced to Irish inland waters in the early 1820s, first as tugs and later as passenger vessels. James McCleery of the Lagan Navigation Company commissioned a wooden paddle steamer, the *Marchioness of Donegall*, in 1821, to operate as a towing vessel for Lough Neagh lighters, which was later followed by William Dargan's *Countess of Caledon*, the first passenger steamer to operate on the lake.[83]

As early as 1817, a paddle steamer called *The Lady of the Shannon* had operated on the lower Shannon, but it was not until 1826, when John Grantham introduced the *Marquis Wellesley*, via the Grand Canal to the middle Shannon, that a steam vessel operated on the main section of the river.[84] Grantham sold his ship to Charles Wye Williams of the City of Dublin Steam Packet Co. in 1828, and Williams set up the Irish Inland Navigation Company, with a headquarters established in the 1830s on the Shannon at Killaloe, County Clare, where a small steamboat quay still survives.[85] Williams also experimented with curious retractable vessels, specifically designed to obviate the very real problem of the narrow locks on the Shannon Navigation. His first attempt to get around this was the *Gazelle*, whose bow section could be hoisted into a perpendicular position, thus shortening the length of the vessel and enabling it to pass into a lock. The second was his own ingenious idea, an 80 ft (24.38 m) long horse-drawn ship called the *Nonsuch*, which could be reduced to 60 ft (18.28 m) by raising the bow and stern sections. Williams was also responsible for bringing the *Lady Lansdowne* to the Shannon in 1833, which was built by Lairds of Birkenhead and shipped in sections to Killaloe, where it was reassembled, and for commissioning the *Garryowen*, which began plying the Shannon estuary in 1834 (see Chapter 10). The hulk of the *Lady Lansdowne* was discovered by the Lakeside Hotel, Killaloe, in 1957, and subsequent investigations by the Merseyside Sub-Aqua Club in 1967 revealed that the main frame and bulkheads were still intact.[86]

The survival and regeneration of Ireland's inland waterways have come about through a wider appreciation of their amenity value. In the Republic of Ireland, the Canals Act was passed in 1986 under whose provisions the ownership of the Grand and Royal Canals, and the Barrow Navigation, was transferred from Córas Iompair Éireann (CIÉ) to the Office of Public Works. With the creation of Dúchas in 1997, responsibility for these waterways was ceded to this new heritage agency.[87] In the Operational Programme for Tourism 1994-99, EC structural funding of £19.55 m was allocated to waterway projects. Under the terms of the Good Friday Agreement, the regeneration of Ireland's inland waterways received an even greater boost when it was decided that they were to become one of the proposed six North/South Implementation Bodies. As early as 1906, a British government commission had recommended that these waterways should be placed under government control; in April 2000, this became a reality with the creation of a cross-border body called Waterways Ireland, with a head office in Enniskillen. In the late 1980s and 1990s, the conservation and restoration of inland waterways in Ireland had continued apace. Extensive restoration works have been successfully carried out on large sections of the Royal Canal network, and it is expected that its entire length will be re-opened to the Shannon in 2007. Large-scale works have also been undertaken on the Shannon Navigation, while the navigation into Lough Allen was re-opened in 1996. The Ballinamore and Ballyconnell Canal was restored as the Shannon-Erne Waterway, and the Shannon is once again linked with Lough Erne.[88]

14

Railways

As in Great Britain, the first railed roads or *waggon ways* used in Ireland's extractive industries were effectively horse-drawn tramways, on which wheeled carts or trucks were pulled by horses, on wooden and later iron tram lines (*plateways*). On present evidence, the earliest reference to this practice in Ireland dates to the period 1740-41, when Hugh Boyd employed a 310 yard (283.46 m) long timber waggon way at Ballycastle, County Antrim, to transport stone quarried from local cliffs to his harbour improvement works. Oak and fir were used to construct rails with a gauge of 3 ft (0.91 m), while a passage cut through a rock outcrop to maintain the level of the track bed must surely rank as the first railway cutting in Ireland.[1] A further wooden waggon way was in use for the surface transport of coal at the Ballycastle collieries in the period 1752-80, while a colliery at Drumglass, County Tyrone also had a waggon way as early as 1754. This latter was apparently defunct by 1758, although John Smeaton suggested that Ducart's tub boat canal (which itself employed rails on its inclined planes, see Chapter 13) serving these coal mines be replaced by a waggon way in 1774, part of which seems to have been built, but was never completed.[2] By the final decades of the eighteenth century, the use of wooden waggon ways is likely to have been widespread in Ireland's extractive industries, and even Richard Lovell Edgeworth, no mean innovator in his own right (see Chapter 12), used portable wooden tram lines in bog reclamation work on his estates in County Westmeath and Longford in the years 1786-9.[3] As late as the 1920s, indeed, both trams and rails made of wood were employed at the Rossmore Colliery, County Kilkenny. A railway with either wooden or iron tracks seems likely to have been laid to convey stone for the construction of Howth harbour, from *c.* 1807 or no later than 1809 when John Rennie became chief engineer of the works. By 1814, limestone from the Earl of Howth's quarry at Kilrock was certainly being hauled on what may have been a plateway to the Howth harbour works, in rail trucks with flanged wheels, a rare example of which forms part of the collections of the Transport Museum in Howth.[4] The basic form of this wagon suggests that it could have operated on iron rails; however, as none are extent from this site, the first documented example of iron plateways in Ireland are the 'metal railed ways' that George Halpin (see Chapter 16), inspector of works to Dublin Ballast Board, was ordered to construct in 1816 through the quarries at Bullock and Sandycove.

On present evidence, the first archaeologically documented plateway in Ireland was built to serve the Valentia Island slate quarries in the period 1816-30. This tramway system is very similar to those known from Welsh quarries of the 1820s (see Chapter 6) and, although these were usually built to a gauge of 2 ft, there are a number such as that at Nantlle, completed in 1828, that were built to a 3 ft 6 in gauge. Two lengths of cast-iron rectangular section rail are preserved in the Valentia Island Heritage Centre, along with a *sleeper chair*, a combination of chair and sleeper. The sleeper, which, like the tram rails, also echoes Welsh practices of the same period, was cast by McSwiney's King Street Iron Works in Cork, established in 1816.[5]

In 1819, perhaps on the initiative of John Rennie who became Chief Engineer on the construction of the new Kingstown (Dún Laoghaire) harbour, iron plateways were laid to connect these works with the granite quarries at Dalkey and Glasthule. By the early 1820s, a *funicular* railway, consisting of six trucks on an endless chain, had been constructed, where the weight of the trucks making the descent pulled the empties back up to the quarries. Each of the trucks was capable of carrying loads of up to 25 tons of stone and, in 1826, about 250 tons a day were being brought to the site on the tramway. A railway embankment and tunnel built to accommodate this line must surely be the first examples of their kind to be built in Ireland; some remains of the railed incline are still in evidence at the Dalkey quarry.[6] Sir John Rennie, John Rennie's son, is also known to have supplied railways, in 1835, to the Newry Navigation Co. for use in dredging works.[7]

Tramways were also employed at a number of Irish metal mines by the early years of the nineteenth century. At the Arigna ironworks (see Chapter 4) a 500 yard long tramway was at work in the period *c.* 1805-8, while around 1826 a tramway 5500 yards (over 3 miles) long was built to connect Aughybehy colliery to Arigna iron works upon which a single horse could haul some nine to ten tons in single wagon.[8] The tramway was listed amongst the assets of the mining company in 1831, and its track bed was actually reused by the Arigna coal mines extension of the Cavan and Leitrim Railway, completed in 1920.[9] A 2 ft or 2 ft 6 in gauge horse tramway, some 1.5 miles long, was also built at the Creevelea Iron Works, County Leitrim (see Chapter 4), in 1852.

In the main, the use of horse tramways in nineteenth-century Ireland was confined to quarries, brickworks and coalmines. Within the environs of Belfast alone, indeed, no fewer than fourteen brickworks were equipped with tramways. However, unlike waggon ways in Britain, the Irish examples almost invariably had few associated features such as bridges and tunnels. The four-mile-long tramway connecting the Cavehill Quarries to the northwest of Belfast with the city's quaysides, which was provided with tunnels at the Cavehill and Antrim Road junction, at Alexandra Road and York Road, is unusual in this respect. Furthermore, it also holds the distinction of being the first rail line to be incorporated in Ulster in 1832 (and the third on the whole island). Nonetheless, most early nineteenth-century tramways were much less ambitious, such as the short stretch built to convey coal from the quay at Dunmore East, County Waterford, in 1832, to adjacent lime kilns, along with limestone from a nearby quarry.[10] In the early 1850s, Henry Hodgson built a horse-drawn mineral tramway to carry ore from his mines at Ballygahan in County Wicklow to Arklow, of which a tramway arch at Ballygahan and a tunnel near Avoca survive.[11]

(1) The Development of the Railway Network

Although a railway between Limerick and Waterford had been authorised as early as 1826 (the same year as Britain's first locomotive-drawn line, the Liverpool and Manchester Railway), Ireland's railway age begins some six years after that of England when, in 1834, a 5.5 mile line was opened between Dublin and Kingstown (Dún Laoghaire).[12] Dublin became one of the first European capitals to have a suburban railway (figure 14.1), but thereafter railway development was, in relative terms, rather slow, with the national railway mileage increasing to only 31¼ miles by 1842. Nonetheless, it continued apace during the 1840s, reaching 400 miles (640 km) in 1850, increasing to 865 miles (1,400 km) by the mid-1850s and, within a further decade, more than doubling to 1,900 miles (3,057 km) by 1866.[13]

As with its road and inland navigation infrastructure, Ireland's railway network was hardly justified by its underdeveloped economy. The greater part of the island's foreign trade scarcely touched the railways, as most of the country's centres of production and consumption were on the east coast, while railways were not required for the conveyance of imported coal, some four-fifths of which were directly consumed in the eastern cities.[14] Nevertheless, as events were to prove, the construction of railways in Ireland, where costs per mile were three times lower than contemporary Britain, had significant advantages.[15] First and foremost, labour was much cheaper here, as was the cost of land, while railways, once established, were not threatened by aggressive competition from other forms of transport. Indeed, the relatively flat nature of the interior also made railway construction significantly cheaper, requiring fewer tunnels or expensive viaducts.[16] Thus, while the volume of traffic on Irish railways was considerably smaller than that of Britain, Irish railway companies could still pay attractive dividends.

In the period 1834-1900, no fewer than 75 separate railway companies had operated in Ireland, of which the three largest, the Great Southern and Western Railway (GS & WR), the Great Northern Railway (Ireland) or (GNR(I)), and the Midland and Great Western Railway (MGWR), controlled around 75 per cent of goods and passenger traffic.[17] Of these, the GS & WR, with a route mileage of 1,150

14.1 *The Dublin and Kingstown line in 1835, from a contemporary print.*

miles, was by far the largest, linking Dublin with Cork in the extreme south and Limerick in the west.[18] The total Irish rail mileage was 3,412 in 1906, which was controlled by no fewer than 29 railway companies. This figure had increased by just over 66 by 1922 but, by the early 1930s, the smaller lines were already beginning to close in the face of stiff competition from motorised road transport. In 1924, the GS &WR, the MGWR and the Cork, Bandon and South Coast Railway (CB & SCR) were merged to create the Great Southern Railway and in the following year went on to acquire the remaining companies within the Irish Free State, to form the Great Southern Railway (GSR). The final amalgamation involved over 2,000 route miles, most of which was unnecessary and overstaffed. From the outset, the new company faced many problems, not least of which was a declining population and an underdeveloped economy and, by the onset of the Second World War, its long-term viability without direct government aid could no longer be assured. It was dissolved by Dáil Éireann in 1944, and its assets merged with those of the Dublin United Transport Company to form Córas Iompair Éireann (CIÉ), which came into being in 1945.[19] Initially this was a private-sector company with a government subsidy, but it was nationalised in 1950 along with the Grand Canal, which now formed part of CIÉ. In the north of Ireland, the Stormont government established the Ulster Transport Authority (UTA) in the aftermath of the Second World War, which absorbed the Belfast and County Down Railway (B & CDR) in 1958, and the northern lines of the GNR, many of whose lines it quickly closed. The UTA was dissolved in 1968 and its rail services taken over by the present Northern Ireland Railways (NIR) company. In the south, CIÉ also brought about many line closures, particularly in the 1950s and early 1960s, to the extent that, by the early 1990s, with the combined closures north and south of the border, Ireland's total railway mileage had been eroded to some 1,432 miles, controlled by three railway authorities: Iarnród Éireann, NIR, and the Fishguard & Rosslare Railways and Harbours Company, jointly run by British Rail and CIÉ.

(2) Railway Construction

During the early years of canal construction in Ireland, European, British and Irish engineers had tackled a wide range of technical challenges, ranging from bog drainage to the evolution of skew bridges. The advent of railways brought its own problems, but by the early 1830s there was already a growing number of Irish engineers who had learnt their profession in Britain. Ireland's main railway contractor, William Dargan (1799-1867), along with his contemporary, Sir John Macneill (1793-1880), the most important nineteenth-century Irish railway engineer, had both worked for Thomas Telford. Beginning with the Dublin and Kingstown Railway in 1831, Dargan had already completed some 600 miles of railway in Ireland by 1853.[20] In August 1825, the brothers George and John Rennie Jnr, the sons of John Rennie, appointed the young Wexford-born engineer Charles Blacker Vignoles (1793-1875), to survey the route of the Liverpool and Manchester Railway. Vignoles was to become engineer for the western end of the line until a disagreement with George Stephenson led to his resignation in 1826.[21] He went on to engineer Ireland's first railway along with the English Midland Counties Railway, and to design the flat-bottomed, 'I'-sectioned rails which bear his name. Macneill, whose railway career began in

Scotland, became one of the leading 'railway mania' engineers in Ireland, and had already achieved acclaim for his work on the Dublin and Drogheda railway, completed in 1844, and was knighted for it. He was also responsible for surveying many of the northern railway routes and for laying out the GS & WR.[22]

Joseph Philip Ronayne (1822-76) acquired his earliest railway engineering experience in the office of John Macneill, working first on Irish arterial lines and then on the Cork and Bandon line, where he had assisted Charles Nixon, who himself had worked under I.K. Brunel. Ronayne became a railway contractor upon his return to Ireland from a stint on the Californian goldfields, and was responsible for the construction of the Queenstown branch of the Cork-Youghal line, for the Cork to Macroom railway and, shortly before his death, winning the contract for the Thurles-Clonmel line.

Most of Ireland's railways were thus designed and built by Irish-born engineers who had garnered experience in England and, in consequence, there was, unlike during the canal era, considerably less input from English consultants. Indeed, although former assistants of I.K. Brunel, such as Nixon and O.E. Edwardes (who became engineer for the Cork-Youghal line), did work in Ireland, Brunel's involvement in Irish railway development was largely confined to promoting the English Great Western Railway's abortive scheme to build an east-coast line, linking Dublin, Wicklow, Wexford, Waterford and Cork, and as consultant to the Dublin and South Eastern Railway (1845-59).[23] Nonetheless, as we shall presently see, there was no shortage of innovation in Irish railway engineering in areas as diverse as the design of the masonry arch and steel bridges and the laying of track.

On early railways, the *ruling gradient*, or the steepest climb which steam locomotives were permitted on any section of the route, was kept as near level as possible, owing to the more limited haulage capacities of early steam locomotives. The pursuit of a near-level track bed necessitated large scale and expensive civil engineering works, which included deep cuttings and high embankments to maintain the level through high and low ground, along with bridges and viaducts to carry the line over steep river valleys and existing routeways.[24] On the Dublin and Drogheda Railway, as laid out by the English engineer, William Cubitt in the late 1830s, the ruling gradient was 1 in 160, which required the excavation of a cutting at both Malahide and Skerries in County Dublin and the construction of an embankment at Clontarf.[25] However, when many of Ireland's main-line routes were under construction in the 1840s and 1850s, newer and more powerful varieties of locomotive enabled ruling gradients to be increased, which in turn saved on the expense of large earthworks. Material excavated from cuttings would be carried on a temporary track to a section of the route where embankments were to be formed, while both cuttings and embankments were provided with stone- or brick-lined drains to facilitate the run off of water. The deep bogs of the Irish midlands also created problems for railway construction and, while Irish canal contractors had provided practical solutions to leading inland navigations through them (see Chapter 13), previous experience of building railways through such terrain was largely confined to the Liverpool and Manchester Railway's works at Chat Moss in Lancashire. However, George Willoughby Hemans, the engineer of the MGWR, effectively de-watered the 8-mile stretch of the line through these bogs by excavating side drains along the proposed line for the permanent way. Furthermore, as the Royal Canal (which the

MGWR Company had purchased, and had originally planned to drain and run a track along its bed!) ran for about 20 miles through the bogs and acted as an obstruction to natural drainage, in order to lead water away from the railway drains, it became necessary to construct culverts underneath the canal. These latter were made of pine planks, held together with metal hoops, and at least one example was 120 ft (36.57 m) long.[26]

(i) Permanent Way and Gauges

Rail track is usually referred to as *permanent way*, a term originating in a distinction made between the finished track and the temporary one laid by contractors to facilitate railway construction. By the 1840s, permanent way was being laid on a solid bed of broken stones and gravel called *ballast*, which distributed the load of the train and also prevented the build-up of water underneath the track. The universal use of ballast led to the creation of special quarries near most lines. On the MGWR, for example, most of the track ballast was sourced from a quarry at Lecarrow, although at least seven pits were opened along its course over the Esker Riada, a rich source of glacially deposited gravels.[27] The set distance between the inner faces of each rail is called the *gauge*, the determination of which in Ireland has a colourful history. Ireland's first railway, the D & KR, was built to British standard gauge of 4 ft 8½ ins (1435mm), but in 1836, the government-appointed Drummond Commission on Railway Communications in Ireland recommended a gauge of 6 ft 2 ins for the entire island. The Ulster Railway Company was the first to comply with this recommendation, on its first completed section of line between Belfast and Portadown in 1842. However, the prospects of an eventual rail link between Dublin and Belfast were severely dented when the Dublin and Drogheda Railway decided to use the gauge of 5 ft 2 in, which was recommended in the second report of the railway commission of 1838. Major General Pasley was dispatched by the Board of Trade to settle this dispute and thus averting a potential Irish 'gauge war', but in so doing could not, it was clear, avoid controversy. In contemporary England, the makings of what later became known as the 'gauge war' of the 1840s, between George and Robert Stephenson's 4 ft 8½ in gauge (adopted from Tyneside waggon way practice) and Brunel's 7 ft 'broad' gauge, were already brewing. Both gauges had powerful advocates, but Pasley chose to ignore these as commercial, sectoral interests favouring, instead, two gauges of 5 ft and 5 ft 6 in. By mathematically 'splitting the difference' between each of these, Pasley arrived at a compromise of 5 ft 3 in. This later became the Irish standard gauge (figure 14.2), and was confirmed as such in the *Gauges Act (Ireland)* of 1846, the same year that 4 ft 8½ in became the English standard gauge.[28]

In Ireland, some 535 miles, or around 15 per cent of the Irish rail network consisted of narrow gauge lines – more than double the total mileage for the remainder of the former United Kingdom. The Irish narrow gauge of 3 ft (in all likelihood adopted from that of the Isle of Man railways) largely comprised rural services, built to meet the needs of often remote communities, by acting as feeder lines to the standard gauge network (figure 14.3). Nonetheless, the first 16½ miles of such line to be built in Ireland, the Ballymena, Cushendall and Redbay Railway, which opened in 1875, was essentially an industrial railway, conveying iron ore to the Antrim coast. The first Irish narrow gauge passenger and goods line, indeed, was the Ballymena and Larne Railway, County Antrim, which opened in 1878.[29] Further lines, all in the south and west of Ireland, were built under

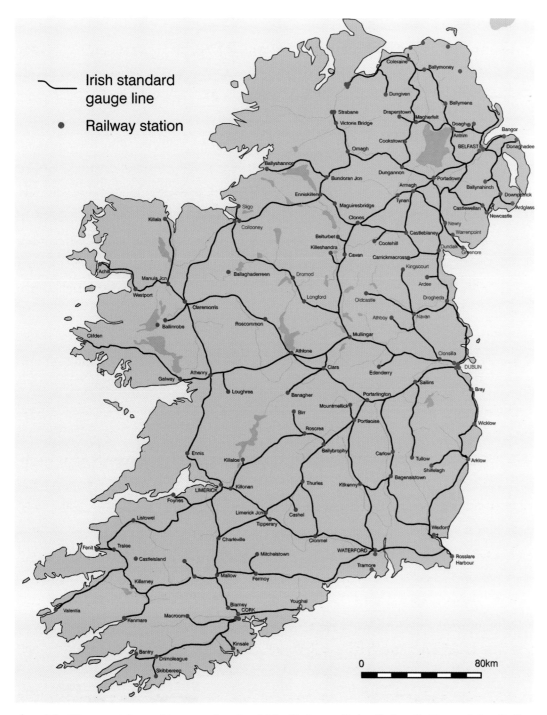

the 1883 *Tramways Act* and later under the *Light Railways (Ireland) Act* of 1889 and the *Railways (Ireland) Act* of 1896. The 1883 act enabled railway promoters to obtain finance from local Grand Juries (whose functions are described in Chapter 12), and by this means encouraged the development of a railway transport network in rural areas.[30] But it also allowed such lines to run along existing public highways, and thus, with the exception of the West and South Clare Railways (1884-1961), the Schull and Skibbereen Railway (1886-1946), the Cork and Muskerry line (1887-1934) and the Tralee and Dingle Railway, each ran along public roads on sections of their individual routes.[31] The Clogher Valley Railway in County Tyrone, did, in fact, follow the public roads for most of its route.[32]

14.3 *Ireland's narrow gauge network at its greatest extent (after Prideaux 1981).*

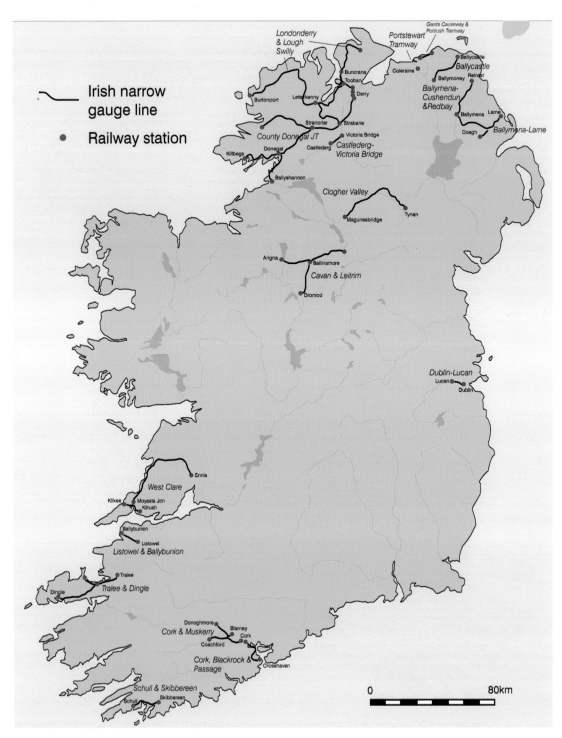

The essential rational for narrow gauge lines in Ireland was that the cost of their construction would be significantly less than standard gauge railways. Indeed, less land was required for their track, while lighter permanent way, and smaller locomotives and rolling stock, did actually reduce establishment costs. Furthermore, additional railway infrastructure such as railway stations was also cheaper. Three lines which began operation as standard gauge, the Cork, Blackrock and Passage Railway, sections of the County Donegal Railways and the Londonderry and Lough Swilly Railway, were actually re-gauged to 3 ft.[33] Yet, upon the completion of most lines, it soon became clear that these required the same number of personnel to operate as a standard gauge line, and from the outset many proved to be uneconomic. To be sure, there was an enormous variation in the loading gauges (i.e., the size limit of vehicles allowed for a particular stretch of line, relative to the height of tunnels and platforms) on each line and the means by which vehicles were coupled together, while nearly all companies bought different locomotives and rolling stock. The Irish narrow gauge peaked during the First World War, but were among the first Irish railways to be closed in the 1920s and 1950s under pressure from road haulage.[34] The last Irish narrow gauge railway, the West Clare line, closed in 1961. Today, Bord na Móna operates the largest network of narrow gauge lines in Europe in the bogs of the Irish midlands.

On Ireland's first railway, the Dublin and Kingstown, Vignoles used an early form of his flat bottom, inverted 'T' section rail with a button top, in 15 ft (4.57 m) lengths.[35] However, following contemporary English practice (as, for example, on Stockton and Darlington Railway), the D & KR track was originally secured on granite blocks set 3 ft (0.9 m) apart. Each block had two rebates, with perforations to receive the fixings for the iron chairs, in which the individual rails were laid. The gauge was maintained by a cross sleeper set every five yards. But, from the outset, the granite sleepers created enormous problems, which prompted Vignoles to conduct what turned out to be ground-breaking experiments with both sleepers and rails on the line in the late 1830s. Hitherto, railway engineers had tended to stress the importance of non-elastic permanent way, but Vignoles, seeking to minimise the damage to both rails and vehicles on the line, successfully replaced the granite sleepers with longitudinal wooden ones, upon which the rails were directly fixed. The use of longitudinal sleepers was later recommended by the Irish Railway Commissions of 1836-8, and the practice was adopted by both the Ulster Railway (1839) and the Dublin and Wicklow Railway (1854-7).[36] Vignoles flat-bottom rail, which was introduced into England in 1837, was stable enough to rest on the sleeper without being wedged upright, whilst as chairs were not required, track construction became at once cheaper and simplified. However, as the spikes used to hold the rail in position did not protect against longitudinal movement with the same effectiveness as the keys used to secure rail in chair, British engineers preferred rails with chairs.[37]

On the D & KR, all the original granite sleepers had been removed by the end of 1839 and, as early as 1837, it became one of the first in either Britain or Ireland to employ bridge rails, although they were not widely adopted on all sections of the line. Bridge rails, so-called because of their hump-backed cross section, which were formed into flanges at their outer edges, were fixed to longitudinal wooden sleepers by means of fang spikes, obviating the need for track chairs. Original bridge rails from the D & KR, along with sections of the line's early granite sleepers, were later re-used in the construction of a running shed at Barrow Street, Dublin, in 1879, which was demolished in 2000, as well as in the embankment between Merrion Gates and Blackrock, where they are still in evidence. Bridge rail did, nonetheless, become the most widely adopted variety of track in nineteenth-century Ireland. The original permanent way on the GS & WR consisted of iron bridge rails, which weighed 90 lbs per yard, while the MG WR used 75 lbs per yard bridge rails in its early years, fastened to longitudinal sleepers, which were kept to the gauge by cross sleepers.[38] There was, indeed, considerable variation in track weights, the Cork, Blackrock and Passage line, which opened in 1850, had 84 lbs per yard bridge rails.[39]

However, both the GS & WR and the MGWR found that bridge rail tended to break under the weight of traffic, and eventually replaced them with flat-bottom rails in the mid 1860s.

By the 1870s, the increased availability of cheaper steel, made possible with the introduction of the Bessemer process, enabled railway companies to substitute iron permanent way with steel rails. The latter were in use from at least 1867 on the Belfast and Ballymena line, but was by no means common on that route for many years after its introduction.[40] The principal advantage of steel permanent way was that it could be manufactured in longer lengths which, in turn, reduced the number of railway joints required, the jolts created by them, and the associated wear and tear on springs of locomotives and rolling stock. Steel rails were used from the late 1870s onwards on the GS & WR and the MGWR. A further refinement to improved rail design was the introduction of fish-eyed joints, which were employed on the Belfast and Ballymena line as early as 1857.[41] Fish plates are steel or wrought-iron plates, used to fix lengths of rail together at either side on their extremities, to produce a solid joint with a smooth running surface. Modern track, which has continuously welded rail and concrete sleepers, does not require these, although sections with fish plates still survive throughout Ireland, most notably on the Waterford-Limerick line. Towards the turn of the nineteenth century, bull-headed rails (which were already becoming common in England by the 1870s) were beginning to be used on major networks such as the GS & WR, and these were to become almost standard in Ireland in the twentieth century.[42] Bull-headed rails are fixed to sleepers in cast-iron track chairs or seats, whose slot was wider than the rail itself, which allowed the rail to be wedged into position.

On standard gauge lines, the weight per yard of track gradually expanded throughout the nineteenth century as loads increased. By way of contrast, narrow gauge track, where loads and speeds were lower, was generally much lighter. On the Schull and Skibbereen Railway, the track was originally 45 lbs per yard, while that on the Finn Valley railway was 65 lbs per yard. CIÉ, indeed, recommended 60 lbs per yard for Irish narrow gauge lines after 1945, with a maximum speed of 25 mph.[43] Narrow gauge track was typically flat-bottomed and, as most lines were built from the 1880s onwards, invariably made of steel. Of course, almost all the light railways built in Ireland had permanent way with two rails, but locomotives on one remarkable 9¼ mile-long line, which operated between Listowel and Ballybunion, in County Kerry, between 1888 and 1924, ran on a single elevated rail or monorail. This was the only line of its type built in either Britain or Ireland using Alphonse Lartigue's system, designed specifically for rough terrain in underdeveloped regions, in which a single rail was elevated on iron trestles.[44]

Ireland was also one of the first regions of the world to employ mechanical track-laying machinery. As early as 1904, a track-laying machine had undergone short trials in the construction of the Rosslare line, but had been judged a failure. But by the mid-1920s, Arthur White Bretland, the Chief Engineer of the MGWR, had developed what became known as the 'Bretland tracklayer', a device with an electrically powered gantry crane for lifting and relaying sections of track. In Bretland's system, the contractors conveyed all the materials required for building the permanent way to a central depot, where sections of track were assembled. These latter were then transported to the section of line under repair and placed in position by the tracklayer which, in its first sixteen months of operation, re-laid some 45 miles of track.[45]

(ii) Bridges, Viaducts and Tunnels

Even local lines were required to pass through or over either natural obstacles or existing roads, and so, at the design stage, railway engineers entered into their calculations the number of bridges, viaducts or tunnels needed on a particular route. Three main types of bridging structures were employed on railways, *underbridges*, which carried the line over a road, canal or narrow river, *overbridges*, which normally carried a road over the railway, and *viaducts*, usually either a wide-span or multi-span bridge. Tunnels, on cost grounds, were generally preferred to deep cuttings, although in certain instances tunnelling through a particularly high relief feature, as at Cork, was the only available option. A number of Ireland's first railway bridges survive on the former Dublin and Kingstown route, which include the fine masonry arch underbridge at Barrow Street, near the Westland Row terminus since rebuilt, although good examples survive at Sandwich Street and Erne Street, which have pedestrian archways (figure 14.4), a stipulation laid down by the Wide Street Commissioners.

The vast majority of masonry-arched railway bridges built between 1833 and 1850 were single-span structures with steep approach ramps at either end. However, arched bridges carrying permanent way could not, owing to the nature of railways, be 'dog-legged' over an obstacle such as a road or small river. The bridge had to carry the line over any feature, at whatever angle was required, and so in many instances skew arches had to be constructed, a good example of which is the three-arched example, on the Dublin and Kingstown line, built to span the Grand Canal dock in 1833-4. Yet the building of such bridges involved a lot of time-consuming work in cutting the voussoirs to the correct angles, in order to create the helical form of the arch ring. Nevertheless, Edward Townsend, Professor of Civil Engineering at University College, Galway (1860-1910), developed a system which simplified the cutting of voussoirs for skew arches, and made the construction of such bridges cheaper.[46] On single-span bridges, the most common arch forms are segmental and elliptical, although semi-circular types were generally preferred for multi-span viaducts. Nearly all the nineteenth-century overbridges on the Dublin and Belfast line had elliptical arches of either brick or cut limestone.[47] Nonetheless, ornamental bridges, such as Macneill's scenic Egyptian arch adopted for the overbridge crossing the Newry-Camlough Road, completed in 1851, or the Gothic arch bridge probably designed by Cork architect, Sir Thomas Deane, for the Cork, Blackrock and Passage Railway in 1848, are rare.[48] In the 1990s, railway

14.4 *Dublin and Kingstown underbridge of 1834 at Erne Street, Dublin.*

14.5 *The Kilnap viaduct, near Cork, designed by Sir John Macneill and built by William Dargan, shown here under construction in a watercolour by R.L Stopford of 1849.*

upgrading works on lines north and south of the border, particularly on the cross-border link, have led to the removal of many existing masonry arches and their replacement with concrete ones.

Timber- and masonry-arched spans were used for viaducts in the early years of railway construction, but all the timber examples were replaced before the end of the nineteenth century. The wooden viaduct at Thomastown, County Kilkenny, on the Waterford-Kilkenny line, completed in 1850 by Robert Mallet, the central span of which, at 200 ft (60.96 m) was, in its day, the longest timber span in the former United Kingdom. This was taken down and an iron viaduct constructed to take its place between 1876-7, while that at Malahide, County Dublin, was replaced in 1860 with a wrought iron bridge manufactured by Courtney and Stephens of Dublin.[49] Further examples on the Dublin and Drogheda line, spanning river estuaries at Rogerstown, Gormanstown and Laytown, were also dismantled and substituted with iron viaducts in the 1880s.[50] Brunel, indeed, also elected to construct an enormous timber viaduct, carried on wooden 'V'-shaped trestles (similar, in many respect to those used on Great Western Railway in Devon and Cornwall) on the Bray Head line in the 1850s.

Several massive, masonry-arched railway viaducts were built in nineteenth-century Ireland, the largest of which, the Craigmore viaduct, near Newry, County Armagh, is also one of the earliest. Built between 1851 and 1852 to span Camlough River valley near Newry, it was designed by Macneill and built by William Dargan. It has eighteen arches of 59 ft 6 in (18.13 m) span, and remains the tallest railway bridge in Ireland. The Borris

Viaduct, completed in 1862, which carried the Dublin, Wicklow and Wexford Railway over the Mountain River valley, to the south of Borris station had sixteen semi-circular arches.[51] Nonetheless, while iron railway bridges were being built contemporaneously, they did not wholly supplant masonry-arched viaducts. A twelve-arch masonry viaduct was built to carry the Schull and Skibbereen line over an inlet of Roaringwater Bay, near Ballydehob, County Cork, in 1884-6, while as late 1892, a viaduct with seven segmental arched spans was built at Newport on the line from Westport to Mallaranny in County Mayo. A series of watercolours by R.L. Stopford depicts the construction of the masonry viaducts at Mallow, Monard and Kilnap on the Mallow–Cork section of the GS & WR in 1849 (figure 14.5). Stopford captures the enormous scale of construction, including the massive wooden centring used to form the arches and the rail-mounted gantry cranes, employed to lower the huge stone blocks into position.

The first iron lattice rail bridge to be built in Ireland is the ornamental footbridge with towers, built at Maritimo for Baron Cloncurry in 1833-4 at Blackrock on the D & KR, although the wider adoption of this principle, for all varieties of railway bridge, can be attributed to Sir John Macneill. In bridge construction, the lattice effect was created by building a matrix of small diameter, wrought-iron bars. The main advantage of the latter was that they could be easily transported and, once on site, could be cut and riveted and then easily assembled to form a large lattice web. Macneill's earliest venture, in 1842, was an 84 ft (25.6 m) span light iron-lattice overbridge for the Dublin and Drogheda line at Raheny in Dublin, built by Pery of Dublin. Macneill's bridge was based on Ithiel Town's American patents, which had originally been obtained in 1820 and 1835 for wooden bridges but, at Raheny, a wrought-iron lattice was employed instead of timber trellis work.[52] This was followed in 1843-5 by a 140 ft (42.67 m) span wrought-iron lattice underbridge over the Royal Canal, built by Grendon of Drogheda which is the first of its type in the world.[53] Francis Bell, an assistant of Macneill's, also designed a wrought-iron box-lattice bridge, the Douglas Viaduct, for the Cork Blackrock and Passage Railway, which was completed in 1847, and went on to design others for the Great Southern and Western and Killarney Junction Railway.[54]

Thus far most of the pioneering iron bridge design work had been undertaken on northern railways, but in the mid-1840s, American innovations in design were brought to Ireland by the English-born but Irish educated engineer, Richard Osborne (1815-99). Osborne was the prime mover in the introduction of a new form of truss, invented by the American engineer, William Howe (1803-52), which used timber chords and diagonals in conjunction with wrought-iron vertical rods. The vertical rods had the advantage of being tightened up as required, and the principle was widely employed in the United States. However, Osborne went on to develop an all-iron Howe truss in the period 1834-45, and had applied his innovation on a number of American bridges. In 1845, he left the United States for Ireland, where he registered his Irish patent in the same year, and began work as one of Vignoles' assistants on the Limerick and Waterford Railway. The first bridge built with Osborne's truss in these islands was an underbridge over the Roxborough Road in Limerick, which was completed in February 1847. A second underbridge was built over the main Limerick–Waterford road at Ballysimon, near Limerick, later in the same year.[55] Neither bridge, unfortunately, survives.

By the late 1840s, iron railway bridges were becoming more common. Iron underbridges were built over the old Dublin road near Cork by a local foundry for the GS & WR in 1847, while in 1851, Fairbairn of Manchester manufactured a bridge to span the River Dodder for a section of the D & KR.[56] They were also, by this period, becoming longer and more elaborate. In 1847, work began on the massive abutments and supporting pillars of the Chetwynd Viaduct, designed by Charles Nixon, on the Cork and Bandon Railway (figure 14.6). The superstructure, which consisted of 1,000 tons of wrought- and cast-iron, and spanned the main Cork to Bandon road and the valley of the Glasheen River, was completed in 1851. The bridge was manufactured by Sir Charles Fox and John Henderson and Company of London, better known for their work on the Crystal Palace, and was made up of lattice girders formed into four eliptical arches, each of 110 ft (33.52 m) span.[57] The viaduct was strengthened in 1901, during which most of the original ironwork was replaced.[58] Fox Henderson and Company was simultaneously working on a viaduct spanning the River Shannon at Athlone, for the MGWR, which they completed in 1851 (figure 14.7). This consisted of wrought-iron lattice 'bowstring' girders with a central cantilevered opening span of 117 ft (37 m) to facilitate navigation on the river.[59] In the same year, work commenced on one of the most technically advanced iron bridges of its day, Macneill's viaduct across the River Boyne at Drogheda, County Louth. Completed in 1853, the Boyne Viaduct was a lattice girder structure 1,760 ft (536.44 m) long, consisting of three river spans and fifteen semi-circular masonry arches, on either side of the river. This was the largest bridge of its type in the world, and the first in which the principle of multiple lattice construction had been employed on such a scale. Yet it was also the first iron bridge to be designed in accordance with stress calculations, whereby the strength of each part, relative to the stress it was expected to withstand, was carefully worked out. This made the bridge lighter and economised on materials, while at the same time eliminating the additional stresses which had bedevilled earlier viaducts.[60]

In 1851-53, a wrought-iron box girder bridge, designed by William Le Fanu and fabricated by Willliam Fairbairn of Manchester to his patent, was built to span the River Suir, near Cahir, County Tipperary, on the Limerick and Waterford line. The significance of the Cahir viaduct – which still carries the Limerick to Waterford railway – is that it is the only surviving example of a bridge built to Fairbairn's patent in these islands which is substantially unaltered.[61] Other important surviving nineteenth-century iron viaducts include the Thomastown Viaduct, spanning the River Nore, near Thomastown, County Kilkenny (figure 14.8), completed in 1877, and the Glensk Viaduct, spanning the valley of the Glensk River between Glenbeigh and Cahirciveen, County Kerry, which opened in 1893.[62]

Although both mass and reinforced concrete were being used in other railway buildings, towards the end of the nineteenth century (see Chapter 6), their employment in bridges was somewhat later. The earliest recorded use of mass concrete in railway bridge construction is in an accommodation bridge on the Rosslare-Waterford line, built for the Fishguard and Rosslare Railways and Harbour Company, which was completed in 1906.[63] Indeed, the first reinforced concrete railway underbridge, which opened in 1918, carried the Athy-Wolfhill colliery branch line across the River Barrow at Athy, County Kildare.[64] However, the 'Horseshoe Bridge' near Carrickfergus, which was designed by the Belfast Office of the London, Midland and Scottish Railway and completed in 1928, was the first of its type to be built in either Britain or Ireland.[65]

14.6 *The Chetwynd Viaduct designed by Charles Nixon, on the Cork and Bandon Railway and completed in 1851. The bridge was manufactured by Sir Charles Fox and John Henderson and Company of London (top);* **14.7** *Railway viaduct on the MGWR, spanning the River Shannon at Athlone, built by Fox Henderson and Company and completed in 1851, (from Measom 1866) (above right);* **14.8** *The Thomastown Viaduct, spanning the River Nore, near Thomastown, County Kilkenny, completed in 1877 (above left).*

Long railways tunnels are a rarity in Ireland, largely because the island's topography was by no means as demanding as that of Britain. Most of the longer Irish tunnels, indeed, were constructed during the early years of the railway boom and, with the exception of the Cork and Bandon line, are generally associated with national rail links. Once the line of the tunnel had been decided upon, the first step involved the sinking of a series of vertical shafts along it, to the depth of the eventual track bed. These latter enabled pilot headings to be excavated in opposing directions, eventually linking up with headings driven from the other shafts, while the shafts themselves, upon completion of the tunnel, would serve as ventilation or air shafts. On two County Cork tunnels,

373

indeed, at Kilpatrick (the first railway tunnel in Ireland used for passenger traffic) on the Cork and Bandon line, and on the tunnel leading into the GS & WR terminus at Cork, miners from the West Carbery mines were employed in the blasting of the tunnel headings.[66] While the pilot headings were underway, tunnelling operations were begun at the opposing tunnel entrances. By this means, several tunnel faces were at work simultaneously and, when these were all joined together, the interior of the tunnel was then opened up to its full size. Drainage channels were then laid in the floor of the tunnel, while the roof was lined with bricks. Some three million bricks from Youghal, County Cork, were used to line the Cork tunnel, whilst those of the Castlerock and Downhill tunnels, on the Londonderry and Coleraine line, were lined with Artliclave brick.[67] Large cut stone portals were also built at the opposing tunnel entrances, that at the station end of the Cork tunnel having a large date stone, bearing the date of its completion in 1855. Yet, despite the use of multiple headings, the construction of long tunnels was a time-consuming process: the 1,355 yard tunnel at Cork took some seven years to complete, from the sinking of the ventilation shafts in 1847 to the completion of the portals in 1855.

The first railway tunnels in Ireland were completed on the Cork and Bandon railway, beginning with the Kilpatrick tunnel, completed in a little over a year using day and night shifts. The tunnel was 170 yards (155.44 m) long, too short for a ventilation shaft, but in the second tunnel at Gogginshill, which was to be 900 yards (1.097 km), three air shafts were sunk in 1847. Upon its completion in 1850, this was, for a short period, the longest in Ireland.[68] The sinking of the four airshafts for the Cork railway tunnel also commenced in 1847, the deepest of which, the Barrackton shaft, was sunk to a depth of 207 ft (63.09 m).[69] Again, this was briefly the longest in Ireland, until its length was exceeded in the 1850s by the Lisummon tunnel on the Great Northern Railway (Ireland) on the Goraghwood-Markethill-Hamilton's Bawn Armagh branch line, which was 1,759 yards (1.798 km) long.[70] I.K. Brunel also designed three tunnels to carry the Dublin and Wicklow line around Bray Head, the longest of which was 300 yards (274. 32 m) long: tunnels 2 and 3 remain in use, although these were eventually bypassed by the last long railway tunnel to built in Ireland. Bray Head 1 was later bypassed by Bray Head 4, some 1,084 yards (0.991 km) long, completed in 1917.[71]

(iii) Locomotives

From the introduction of the steam locomotive into Ireland in 1834 to 1970, when the last examples were taken out of service by the Ulster Transport Authority, some 2,300 engines had operated here. Nonetheless, the appointment of English Chief Mechanical Engineers by the larger Irish railway companies not only ensured that locomotive development in Ireland was kept well within the mainstream of that of the United Kingdom, but also that Irish companies could innovate on their own behalf.

The first six steam locomotives used in Ireland, by the D & KR when it opened in 1834, represented, at once, both the past and the future of British locomotive design. On the three engines supplied by Sharp Bros of Manchester, the cylinders connected to the driving wheels were set vertically alongside the engine's boiler, a common but by no means universal arrangement on existing railway locomotives. However, those built by George Forrester of Liverpool were revolutionary in that they had cylinders set outside and horizontal to the leading end of the locomotive.[72] One of these locomotives, *Vauxhall*, was in fact the first to run on an Irish railway and, while initially this arrangement was not a success, it was to become virtually standard on all steam locomotives at work up to recent times.[73] We have already seen how the D & KR became one of the first in the world to build a locomotive in its own works (see Chapter 10), yet it was also, as will be seen shortly, responsible for two further important innovations.

Steam locomotives use high pressure steam and are non-condensing engines, in other words, the steam is not condensed in the cylinder as part of the cycle but is, instead, exhausted through a funnel or smoke stack (except on certain tramway engines where the steam is condensed, see Chapter 17). On early locomotives, their weight was sufficient to maintain the adhesive force (the frictional grip between a locomotive's driving wheels and the rail track) but as engines became more powerful and heavier, the load on a single pair of driving wheels exposed the permanent way to increased stress. And so additional driving wheels were fitted, both to prevent the wheels from slipping and to spread the weight more evenly on the rails, while coupling rods were now used to connect the driving wheels together on the outside and by this means more effectively combine their driving power. The early engines manufactured by Edward Bury had four wheels; those intended for goods haulage had wheels on each side of engine coupled together to apply the full adhesive force of wheels to the track, while those on passenger engines were uncoupled, but with driving wheels of larger diameter at the rear that allowed them to turn with more freedom at the higher speeds needed for passenger services.[74] An extremely rare surviving 2-2-2 locomotive (no. 36), built in 1847 by Bury Curtis and Kennedy of Liverpool for the GS & WR, is on display at the present Glanmire Road (Kent) Station in Cork (figure 14.9). It has 6 ft (1.82 m) driving wheels and had covered over 350,000 miles when it was withdrawn from service in 1875. The engine is displayed upon original GS & WR 92 lb per yard cast-iron bridge rails.[75]

The designation of railway locomotive types as 2-2-2, 2-4-0T and so forth, is based on the wheel arrangements of individual engines, a system developed by Frederic M. White (1865-1941), a New York Central Railroad official. In White's system, the wheel arrangement is viewed on the engine with its fore end facing to the left of the observer, beginning with the wheels on the leading axle, and followed by the driving wheels and the trailing wheels. An engine with wheels arranged thus **oOo** is designated 2-2-2, **oOO** as 2-4-0, **OO** as 0-4-0 and so on where **O** designates the driving wheels. In the designation 2-4-0T, the 'T' indicates that it is a tank engine (i.e., where the locomotive's fuel and water are carried on its own frame), 'ST' indicates saddle tanks.

The earliest steam locomotives carried their fuel and water in a tender, a small wagon that followed immediately behind it (or, as on a number of early locomotives *preceded* it). However, when passenger services began on the D & KR, it soon became clear that delays were inevitable owing to the necessity of separating the engine from the tender in order that the locomotive could be turned around to make the return journey. As the turntable could only accommodate either the engine or the tender at one time, these had to be uncoupled and turned separately, whereupon they were re-coupled to each other and then to the passenger vehicles. In order to avoid such delays, the D & KR, in 1835, just a year after opening, insisted that Forrester and Company

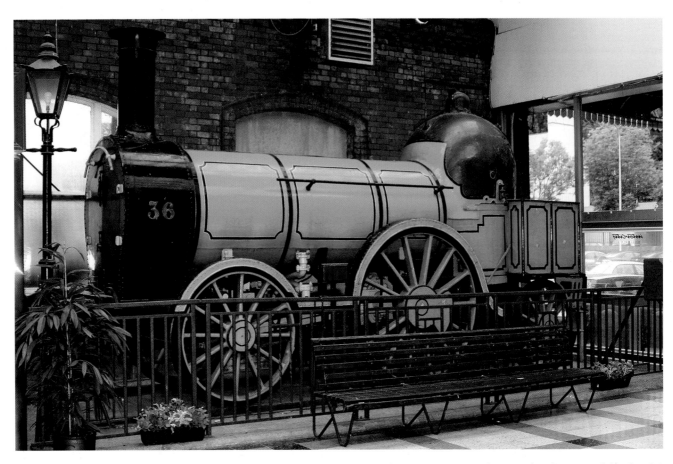

14.9 *An extremely rare surviving 2-2-2 locomotive (no. 36), built in 1847, by Bury Curtis and Kennedy of Liverpool for the GS & WR, on display at the present Glanmire Road (Kent) Station Cork.*

supply them two locomotives that could carry their fuel and water on their own frames and not in a separate tender. The new locomotives, *Victoria* and *Comet*, were the first of the type later known as *tank engines*, to run on a public railway.[76] Nonetheless, tank engines were not widely adopted elsewhere in Ireland until the mid-1840s, when C. Tayleur and Company supplied a number to the Waterford and Kilkenny Railway. Tank engines, however, were to prove invaluable for short distance traffic, as they could be driven in either direction without the use of a turntable, and were also ideally suited to lines with steep gradients, as the added weight of their fuel and water increased the adhesive force of their wheels. Further varieties were to evolve, which included *saddle* tanks, where the tanks were mounted astride the boiler, *well* tanks (mounted between the frames) and *pannier* tanks (cantilevered outwards from the side of the boiler).

In the period 1860-1900, the basic principles and features of locomotive design underwent little change. Engines used for passenger service were four-coupled, while goods engines were six-coupled, the Gorton foundry of Beyer, Peacock and Company becoming the main supplier of locomotives to Irish railway companies.[77] On the GS & WR, there were three main periods of locomotive development, which began with engines purchased from specialist foundries, followed by a stage during which a number of engines were designed and built in its own workshops. The company then went on to standardise its locomotives by building all new engines itself. Between 1852 and 1924, around 90 per cent of its locomotives were made at its Inchicore works, although not surprisingly, its own purpose-built engines were based on English prototypes, given the pedigree of the Chief Mechanical Engineers, as was the case elsewhere in Ireland. The motive power of the GS & WR, for example, followed the same lines as that of Crewe, and in later years of Beyer Peacock, while the Waterford, Limerick and Western Railway emulated the British Great Western Railway.[78] Dublin-born Alexander McDonnell (1829-1904), Locomotive Superintendent of the GS & WR in the period 1864-1882, built the first standard gauge 0-6-4Ts in these islands for shunting and banking duties while also supplying two 0-4-4Ts in 1869-70 for a number of branch lines. These were even more remarkable in that they were the first ever single boiler, Fairlie articulated engines ('Kerry bogies'), based on Robert Fairlie's patent of the 1860s, which usually had a double boiler.[79] This type of locomotive was spread to England via McDonnell, and his successors at Inchicore, the English engineers John Aspinall (1882-1886) and Henry Ivatt (1886-96), each of whom, in turn, went on to work for English railway companies.[80] A bogie is essentially a pivoted undercarriage with two wheels used to support the ends of a carriage or a locomotive and enable it to swivel through a small angle and thus turn through tight curves. Fairlie's first successful bogie engine was used in 1869 on the Ffestiniog Railway in Wales.

After 1900, the introduction of rolling stock with bogies, along with extra passenger vehicles such as dining cars, added substantially to the weight of trains, which led to an increase in the size and haulage capacity of locomotives. As early as 1912, superheating was introduced for narrow gauge engines on the County Donegal system, by Nasmyth, Wilson and Company, and was later provided for larger locomotives on standard gauge lines, in the years 1913-16. In an ordinary boiler, the steam vapours created within it carried moisture which, when they came into contact with metallic surfaces, tended to form droplets of water. These latter interfered with the movement of the pistons, with a consequent reduction in the efficiency of the engine. Steam vapours formed in this way are called *saturated steam*, and the object of superheating is to convert this residual moisture into more steam by converting the saturated component into gas. Superheating thus eliminated the creation of condensation in steam boilers – which reduced the power and effectiveness of the engine – and increased its thermal efficiency with significant savings in fuel economy.

On narrow gauge lines, the vast majority of the locomotives were tank engines, which tended to be smaller than those employed on standard gauge railways. In all some 144 locomotives (built to 66 classes and twenty different wheel arrangements!) were used on Irish narrow gauge lines, the most common class being 0-4-0Ts weighing 7-18 tons, followed by 4-4-Ts, which were the mainstay of the Cork and Muskerry, Cavan and Leitrim and the Schull and Skibbereen lines. The largest narrow gauge engines, not surprisingly, were employed on the longest systems, which were the County Donegal and the Lough Swilly lines.[81]

As early as 1857, the Inchicore works had built a vehicle called a *railcar*, a combined engine and saloon, named *Sprite*, which was used for inspections on the line.[82] Indeed, up to the early years of the twentieth century, this was to be the primary use of railcars, with the MG WR bringing a petrol railcar into service on its Achill line in 1911, which could be driven from either end, with a four cylinder 27 hp engine.[83] However, on the

14.10 *Atmospheric engine at Kingstown Station on the D & KR in 1844.*

County Donegal Railway, the first motor railcar (also originally used as an inspection car) brought into service in 1907, had a Ford engine installed in 1920. This enabled it to carry up to ten passengers, and its success prompted the purchase of further petrol rail cars in 1926.[84] The principal advantage of railcars was that they were much cheaper to run than steam trains, while at the same time they could pick up and set down passengers with the same ease as a motorised bus. Their relatively cheap running costs led to their introduction on to other narrow gauge lines, such as the West Clare line, where they were in use from 1927 onwards.[85]

Thus far we have considered the use of steam and other forms of traction on Irish railways, but on the extension of the D & KR to Dalkey, one of the most remarkable (but ultimately unsuccessful) experiments in locomotive traction was carried out between 1844 and 1854. During this period the Kingstown to Dalkey line employed Samuda and Clegg's 'Atmospheric system', in which the train was propelled by creating a vacuum in a large pipe laid between the rails. Steam pumps were used to extract air from the pipe and create a vacuum, which caused a piston, attached to the underside of a small carriage, to be propelled along the pipe, and with it the entire train. The pipe itself was 15 in in diameter and had a self-sealing slot along its entire length, in which travelled the train's piston. The atmospheric railway created enormous excitement amongst contemporaries, notably C.F. Mallet, who proposed to the French government that all French railways should adopt the system, while Brunel and William Cubitt recommended its adoption by the English Great Western Railway's line between Gravesend and Chatham and the London and Croydon line, respectively. Its principal advantages were that it created no smoke or noise nuisance, while at the same time requiring no expensive locomotives (figure 14.10). However, it also exhibited considerable disadvantages in operation, necessitating, on the one hand, a higher fuel consumption to operate the boilers for its steam pumps at Dalkey, while on the other proving more expensive to build than a conventional railway. Furthermore, important activities such as shunting could not be undertaken on a system that employed a single power source. Continuing difficulties with the system came to a head when a rail link from Dublin to Wexford was proposed, and the likely problems that might be encountered with an atmospheric railway forming part of the Dublin end of the route. With this in mind, the railway company finally decided to convert the Dublin and Kingstown line to conventional steam traction in 1854.[86]

(iv) Rolling Stock

The rolling stock consisted of a wide range of vehicles, for passenger and goods service, that were drawn by the locomotive and which, like the latter, evolved through time to fulfil the changing needs of railway services. The earliest passenger vehicles used in Ireland, on the D & KR, were based on existing road passenger carriages and had four wheels. Early carriages were equipped with the same form of primary suspension as road passenger vehicles, but they also had an almost rigid wheelbase which restricted the types of curves they could traverse, a problem which was only satisfactorily solved with the introduction of bogies or pivoting undercarriages.[87] Nonetheless, the early D & KR vehicles had a wider wheelbase than the carriages employed by its contemporary, the Liverpool and Manchester Railway, which added considerably to the comfort of the passengers.[88] Their earliest railway carriages were also painted in bright colours which, in an era of widespread illiteracy, were used to signify 'first class', 'second class' and so forth, the same colours being used for ticket classes.[89] From around 1839 onwards, the Grand Canal Street locomotive works began to build the company's coaching stock. The earliest surviving railway carriage in Ireland, indeed, is an 'open green' D & KR carriage no. 48, dating from the 1830s, preserved in the Ulster Folk and Transport Museum.[90]

The D & KR was also responsible for a revolutionary type of railway buffer designed by its company secretary, Thomas F. Bergin. Bergin found fault with the double buffers employed on English railway vehicles of the 1830s (and still widely used on working railways today), where although the height of a carriage could vary considerably, according to its load, ordinary buffers could not be adjusted to compensate for this. On early rail carriages, this could result in much jolting and additional discomfort for passengers, and so Bergin developed a 'spring buffer' which minimised the stresses created by carriages buffing together. However, despite its efficacy, it was not adopted elsewhere, largely because it was almost unknown outside the Dublin area.[91]

On later Irish railways such as the GS & WR and the Belfast and County Down Railway, carriage stock, in the early years, was supplied by English coachmakers but, by the late 1840s, established Irish manufacturers of road carriages, such as J.S. Dawson and Hutton of Dublin, were beginning to build passenger vehicles for Irish railway companies.[92] The earliest carriages on the GS &WR were six-wheeled and were manufactured to a standard length of 26 ft (7.92 m), with four to six compartments, but by 1850, the expanding needs of the company led to its decision to open separate carriage and wagon departments. First-class coaches were, as one might expect, upholstered, but no heating was provided until the mid-1860s, while the heating of trains with steam from the locomotive did not become widespread until the 1890s. In third-class carriages, no night lighting was supplied until 1852, and although by 1857 the company was beginning to experiment with gas lighting, no attempt was made to convert all the coaching stock to this form of lighting until 1892.[93] Experimental electric lighting was used on the MGWR in the early 1890s, while in 1892, the Northern Counties Railway introduced oil gas as an illuminant, but was conducting experiments with electric lighting as early 1896.[94] The latter, however, did not come into use on the GS & WR until 1916.[95]

Dawson of Dublin appear to have built the first composite (i.e., a carriage built with separate compartments for different classes) six-wheel saloon in 1847, while on the GS & WR in the early 1860s, composite carriages were introduced for use on branch lines.[96] The first bogie coaches to be brought into service in Ireland appear to have been those acquired for the Waterford and Limerick Railway by Richard Osborne in 1847. Osborne seems to have brought his American experience to bear as the coaches themselves were similar to a type employed on contemporary US railways.[97] Sleeping accommodation was never really necessary for rail travel in Ireland, although the GS & WR introduced a short-lived service in 1879-80. In 1882, the company brought lavatory carriages into service, a service that was not provided on the MGWR until 1893 and on the Dublin and South Eastern Railway until 1895.[98] Basic kitchen facilities were added to two saloons on the B & NCR in 1894, followed by its first dining car in 1899. In 1898, restaurant cars, in which both lighting and cooking were gas powered, were introduced onto GS & WR services.[99] By way of contrast, passenger comforts on narrow gauge lines were few and far between, and although many journeys would have been relatively short, nearly all would have been undertaken in uncomfortable conditions. The Londonderry and Lough Swilly Railway, for example, was one of many never to provide steam heating. Lighting on narrow gauge services was provided first by oil lamps, and later with acetylene gas burners.[100]

Braking on trains, before automatic continuous brakes became compulsory in 1889, was usually achieved by fitting brake levers on either the tender or the guard's van. On mainline trains, indeed, it became standard practice to position brake vans at both the front and the rear of the train. However, the inadequacies of such braking systems were self-evident, and became even more so as both the weights and speeds of trains increased. Thus, from the mid-1840s onwards, systems in which the brakes could be applied to all the carriages simultaneously, or 'continuous brakes', began to be developed in England.[101] As early as 1860, the B & CDR was conducting experiments with continuous brakes, during which three carriages on the Holywood line were fitted with Newall's patent brake.[102] James Young Smith's non-automatic vacuum brake was adopted by the GS & WR company after trials in 1876, to which modifications were made by Aspinall to create a method of automatic operation, which were added to a number of the company's vehicles.[103] The problem with non-automatic braking systems such as Smith's was that, if train carriage became divided, then the brake became ineffective, whereas automatic systems gave simultaneous control of the brakes of vehicles forming the train to either the driver or the guard, whilst if, in the event of carriages becoming divided, the brakes were self-applying. The Board of

Trade had recommended the use of automatic brakes as early as 1877, and the Northern Counties Railway decided to install continuous automatic vacuum brakes in 1882, when two engines and nine carriages were fitted with these in that year.[104] In the wake of the Armagh accident of June 1889, in which 88 passengers died as a result of a train collision at Killuney, on the line from Armagh to Goraghwood, an act of the same year (the *Regulation of Railways Act*) made it compulsory for all railway companies to employ automatic braking systems.[105]

The wagon stock of the GS & WR for its goods services increased from 700 in the mid-1850s to around 8,400 by 1914. This also included about 700 service vehicles such as hopper wagons and gas tanks, the former being used both to transport coal and ballast, the latter to carry a gas supply around the network for lighting trains. Originally, the wagon bodies were constructed with well-seasoned Irish oak, but steel became more commonly used for this purpose by the end of the nineteenth century.[106] All Irish railway companies also had a stock of covered goods wagons, horse boxes, cattle wagons and open box wagons.

(v) Signalling

In the early years of Irish railways, 'policemen' were employed to control the movement of trains using hand signals, but larger companies such as the GS & WR soon began to use semaphore signals. At first, the signals were individually worked by hand levers, but it soon became common practice for a series of levers to be grouped together at one point, under the control of a single policeman. An elementary cabin was provided for the signal points and their operator, and these shelters became the precursors of later signal cabins. Towards the end of the 1850s, the first basic forms of mechanical *interlocking*, or systems in which a signal instructing a train to proceed, once activated, could not be countermanded by a contrary signal, began to be introduced. In other words, the system ensured this signal was given precedence and, indeed, that all the others which were mechanically locked together agreed with it. One of the first locking frames on the GS & WR was installed at Mallow, County Cork, in 1860.[107]

Early signalling systems operated on a time interval, during which a train was supposed to pass between two points. But from the 1860s onwards, the Board of Trade attempted to convince all railway companies in the United Kingdom to adopt block signalling, a system in which only one train, at any given time, was allowed on a fixed section of line. Only when it had passed on was a further train allowed onto that section of line. Yet by 1871, only 36 miles of Ireland's railways used block signalling – largely because of the relative lightness of rail traffic – compared to 3,700 miles in England. In 1869, the GS & WR adopted block signalling between its Dublin terminus at Kingsbridge (Heuston) Station and Inchicore, but initially resisted its widespread introduction on the grounds that its cost was unjustified, relative to the low volume of traffic it was expected to serve. Nonetheless, block signalling was at work on the North Wall branch, on the Kingsbridge-Kildare section and on the line between Blarney and Myrtlehill Junction in County Cork by 1877. In 1878, the Carrickfergus Junction-Ballymena section of the B & NCR, became controlled by block signalling.[108] However, when the *Railway Regulations Act* passed into law in 1889, Irish railway companies were obliged to use block signalling, and by 1892, almost the entire network of the GS & WR was protected by it.[109] Ireland, indeed, made its own

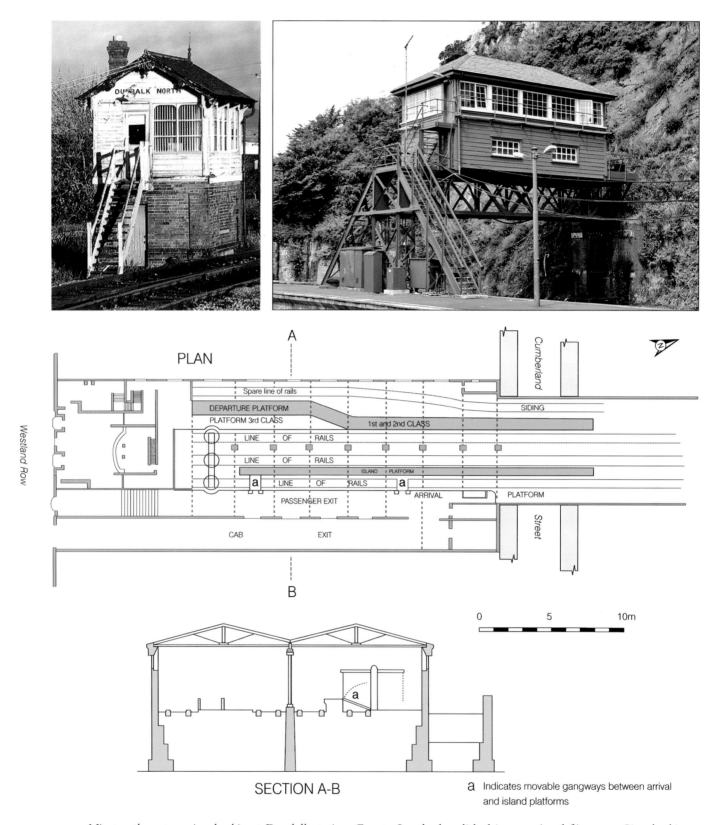

PLAN

Westland Row

Spare line of rails

DEPARTURE PLATFORM

PLATFORM 3rd CLASS

1st and 2nd CLASS

LINE OF RAILS

LINE OF RAILS

ISLAND PLATFORM

a LINE OF RAILS **a**

PASSENGER EXIT

ARRIVAL PLATFORM

CAB EXIT

Cumberland

SIDING

Street

0   5   10m

SECTION A-B

a Indicates movable gangways between arrival and island platforms

I4.II *Nineteenth-century signal cabin at Dundalk station, County Louth, demolished in 2002 (top left);* **I4.I2** *Signal cabin at Waterford North station erected in 1906 for new work on the South Wexford line (top right);* **I4.I3** *Plan of Westland Row Station in 1835, (after Murray 1981) (above).*

unique contribution to the design of signal semaphores, when John Challoner Smith of the Dublin and South Eastern, in 1874, devised the practice of cutting a 'V' or a 'fishtail' at the end of the signal arm, as a means of distinguishing distant signals.[110] Courtney and Stephens was the main Irish supplier of lever frames, although a number of Irish lines actually developed their own lever frames. The Great Northern Railway (Ireland) even went on to produce a version which was adopted, from the 1930s, by the London and North Eastern Railway, which was still being produced by British railways up to 1964.[111]

The design of signal cabins on Irish railways was heavily influenced by English practice, from the 1860s onwards, during which time the typical two-storey signal cabin evolved. This latter development resulted from the introduction of interlocking lever frames, which required additional headroom above the operating floor level. Typical signal boxes of the period *c.* 1870-*c.* 1920 were built of either timber panelling or combinations of timber and brick, the brick being used for the lower storey. The upper section was invariably glazed on all of the elevations, while the roof was commonly gabled (though hipped forms were also used), with decorative barge boards and finials at each end. Up to recently two late nineteenth-century examples of this type survived at Dundalk station (figure 14.11), where one nineteenth-century signal cabin, complete with lever frames (formerly Dundalk Central Cabin), has been dismantled and re-assembled on the current the station platform. The Rush and Lusk signal cabin, on the Malahide-Drogheda line, which has a McKenzie and Holland frame dating from the 1880s, is also of this type.[112] At Waterford North station (figure 14.12), the signal cabin straddles the line on a steel gantry frame, erected in 1906 for new work on the South Wexford line.

(vi) Railway Stations

Early railway stations in Britain and Ireland strove to assume the mantle of permanent public buildings by adopting existing architectural fashions to reassure the travelling public and shareholders alike. The prevailing style for public buildings in the 1830s was of course Classical, and, for the most part, mainline passenger termini of the early 1830s and 1840s tended to reflect this preference, although rural stations in the same period were frequently built in the Gothic Revival style.[113] Ireland's first railway terminus for the D & KR, at Westland Row (figure 14.13), was designed by the line's engineer, Charles Blacker Vignoles. The remaining early stations on the line, at Salthill, Blackrock and Kingstown (figure 14.14), are the work of John Skipton Mulvany (1813-1870), who later became

14.14 *Kingstown Station on the D & KR line, designed by John Skipton Mulvany.*

14.15 *Kingsbridge Station, which opened in 1846 as the Dublin terminus of the GS & WR, designed by the English architect, Sancton Wood (1814-86).*

architect to the MGWR. Of these, the Salthill station (1837) is in a Gothic 'Swiss cottage' style (since demolished), while the Blackrock (1841) and Kingstown stations (1839-42) were very much in the Classical idiom, with Mulvany's trademark porticos *in antis* (i.e., where the portico columns are in the same plane as the front walls).[114] The Blackrock station is the oldest surviving station building in the Republic of Ireland.

Mulvany went on to design the MGWR terminus at Broadstone in a neo-Egyptian style, work upon which began in 1846. However, even at this earlier period, there were clear lines of demarcation in the design of the formal office buildings – the essential frontages of railway stations – and the multi-span, cast-iron framed passenger sheds, the former being architect-designed, the latter usually by the line's principal engineer. Thus while Mulvany designed the frontage to Broadstone Station, the line's engineer, George Willoughby Hemans, a pupil of Sir John Macneill, designed the passenger shed, whose cast-iron roof was manufactured by Richard Turner of Ballsbridge. Similarly, the elaborate neo-Classical frontage of the mainline terminus for the GS & WR at Kingsbridge (Heuston) Station is the work of the English architect, Sancton Wood (1814-86), which opened in 1846 (figure 14.15). However, the passenger shed, which covers some 2.5 acres and is supported on 72 cast-iron columns, was designed by Macneill. With the exception of Ireland's first railway terminus at Westland Row, therefore, early mainline, formal railway station buildings were designed by architects. Nonetheless, while this was invariably true of the termini, smaller stations and ancillary buildings on line itself could often be designed by the principal engineer. Macneill, for example, designed all the GS & WR stations between Dublin and Carlow, along with the mainline stations from Dublin to Kildare. However, the GS & WR stations from Monasterevin to Limerick Junction are nearly all designed by Wood, while after his departure from the company in the early 1850s, later GS & WR station designs can be attributed to a variety of architects such as George Wilkinson (Clara and Athlone stations), Joshua Hargreave Jnr (Gothic structure at Geasehill), as can the stations, goods stores and railway cottages on the Mallow to Killarney line in the 1850s. Indeed, Mulvany's work for the MGWR also involved designs for stations at Killucan, Moate and Athlone (all in Classical style), and the Galway terminus and hotel.[115] The architect George Wilkinson (*c.* 1814-90), however, who designed several railway stations for the MGWR along with the Harcourt Street terminus of the Dublin, Wicklow and Wexford Railway (1859), preferred much simpler architectural forms.[116]

With the exception of the GS & WR terminus at Penrose Quay in Cork, designed by Sir John Benson and completed in 1856, all the early mainline termini in Ireland such as Kingsbridge, Broadstone, along with those of provincial lines, were of the *head* type. In stations of this basic form, passenger arrivals and departures were accommodated in a single building that formed head section of the 'T'-plan layout with the train shed. Arrival and departure platforms, along with their intermediate carriage sidings, were effectively linked by a transverse platform, which formed a concourse at the station head. This latter eventually developed into a circulating area, which is still in use in modern railway stations.[117]

Indeed, by the time Benson set about designing the GS & WR Cork terminus, the railway architect's problems were beginning to become further complicated by the fact that through freight traffic was no longer being accommodated in a common building shared with passenger traffic. Thus, by the mid-1850s, the changing complexion and intensity of rail traffic required specialised building forms for both passenger and goods traffic at mainline termini. The passenger shed was essentially a multi-span canopy, covering the platforms and lines of track that serviced them, along with a number of sidings. The cast-iron framed passenger shed roof at Kingsbridge terminus, for example, originally covered six lines of track. The main 'head' buildings which, as we have seen, were designed by Wood, consisted mainly of administrative buildings, such as a company boardroom and the general manager and traffic manager's offices.[118] Broadstone, however, as at Penrose Quay, had a station hall and only two platforms.[119] But in all instances, the passenger shed was equipped with a cast-iron-framed roof, to counteract the effects of the soot and sparks of locomotives. Separate goods sheds or depots were to become standard in large termini, where the expedient became not to interfere with the movement of passengers. In early station designs, the buildings were either at the end or beside the tracks, to ensure the segregation of arriving and departing trains, and later passenger and freight traffic. For a short

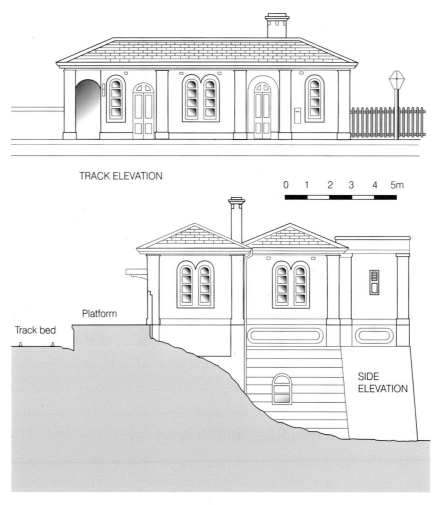

14.16 *Moira station, completed in 1841, on the Great Northern Railway, one of the oldest surviving through stations in Ireland, (after McCutcheon 1980).*

time long, single-platformed stations were in vogue, the best surviving example from this period in Ireland is Limerick Junction.

Stations between the main termini were called 'through' stations, and consisted of opposing 'up' and 'down' passenger platforms, almost always linked by a cast-iron footbridge. Associated structures commonly included a water-tower, or a water column set directly on the platform (examples of which survive at Ballybrophy and Ennis stations), a goods store, cattle pens, coal stores, a signal cabin and a turntable. Moira station, completed in 1841, on the Great Northern Railway, is one of the oldest surviving through stations in Ireland (figure 14.16). It presents a single-storey elevation to the track, but was actually a two-storey building with a basement extending to the base of the embankment upon which it was built. Indeed, through stations built in the first half of the nineteenth century often cleverly exploited high embankments, as at Monasterevin and Portlaoise on the GS & WR line. Such stations were also generally constructed close to existing roads, and almost all have an adjacent over-bridge carrying the road over the line, although the line was also carried over the road if the station nestled upon the side of the embankment.

The passenger buildings usually included offices for the station master, for ticket purchases and parcels, along with waiting rooms for both sexes, often in an 'N'-shaped ground plan, with an intervening covered way supported on wooden or cast-iron columns. A section of the platform immediately in front of the passenger buildings was generally covered by an awning, as at Mallow, County Cork, Dundalk, County Louth, and Malahide, County Dublin. After the early years of railway construction, a wider variety of styles becomes evident, as at Bagenalstown, County Carlow, built in Baroque style (1848), and Helen's Bay, County Down (1864), built in Scottish Baronial style, designed by Charles Lanyon, Chief Engineer to Belfast and County Down Railway. By the 1870s, the design of new railway stations in Ireland is more functional, as the railway was now part of everyday life. As an architectural form, indeed, it no longer craves acceptance. Brick is increasingly used instead of cut-stone, while the actual design of both termini and through stations was more likely to fall within the dictates of a company engineer rather than an architect.

As has been seen (see Chapter 6), concrete had been used in railway buildings as early as the 1880s. Ferroconcrete, indeed, was used in Waterford North station in 1909, the main platform of which, at 1,210ft (368.80 m) long, was the longest in Ireland.[120] Yet the use of pre-cast concrete on Irish railways was pioneered by the Northern Counties Committee of the Midland Railway, whose Chief Engineer was B.D. Wise, for bridges, culverts and fencing posts, among other items. In 1913, a goods shed at Ballymena was constructed with pre-cast concrete slabs.[121]

(vii) Ancillary Buildings and Features

The day-to-day operation of a railway required a large number of ancillary buildings, such as hotels, carriage sheds, running sheds, goods stores, water-towers and accommodation for railway employees. Railway traffic generally consisted of both passengers and freight, each of which had different needs. In the larger mainline termini, for example, freight traffic was eventually separated from passengers, where carriages were shunted into large goods depots and warehouses, as at Cork, where Sir John Benson built a large cut stone depot for the GS & WR terminus in 1856. A further large GS & WR rail depot, completed in 1878 on the North Wall Quays in Dublin, was converted into the present Point Depot (an entertainment venue) in 1988.[122] The smaller through stations, however, generally had a number of sidings (and often a cattle pen) leading to a small goods store, that had either one or two tall semi-circular arched doorways on one gable, through which freight vans and trucks could be shunted. The interior of the goods store also had a raised platform, built to the same level as the loading doors of the freight cars. A series of arched loading doors were usually provided on the opposing long elevation of the goods stores, through which goods could be loaded onto or from horse-drawn vehicles. This loading area was, in addition, usually sheltered from the elements by an overhanging timber awning or canopy, a good example of which survives at the former goods store at Birr station, County Offaly. Small, hand-operated swivelling cranes and weighbridges were also a common feature of these stores. For the most part, Irish nineteenth-century goods stores were built with cut stone, rough ashlar or snecked ashlar masonry, with cut stone or brick door and window dressings. Doagh Station, however, on Belfast and Northern Counties Railway had a freight store built of precast concrete slabs in 1916. Indeed, early goods stores, such as those designed by Hemans at Ballinasloe and Woodlawn, were built in the Gothic style, that at Ballinasloe, County Galway having lancet windows and buttresses.

Locomotive sheds in Britain and Ireland were either rectangular or polygonal (round houses) in plan. Round houses or polygonal sheds were designed to save ground place, but as these were served by a single central turntable this could lead to delays, while circular sheds were more expensive to build. There are only three recorded uses of a roundhouse in Ireland, at the Broadstone terminus of the MGWR, Portadown, County Armagh, and Clones, County Monaghan. The Broadstone example was a ten-road round house, originally constructed in the early 1850s but which, by 1864, had been reduced (by the removal of a number of roads) to a semi-circular structure. In 1873, a new semi-circular roundhouse and an engine shed was built, neither of which survive.[123] The Portadown roundhouse was demolished in 1965 and only the Clones example still survives.[124] Irish locomotive sheds were, therefore, predominantly rectangular 'running sheds', which provided both overnight shelter for locomotives, while simultaneously accommodating important requirements such as coaling, watering and the emptying of ash from the locomotive. Running sheds at the larger termini had slated and glazed roofs, set out in bays, with ventilators built along the ridges, as at Inchicore, and were also commonly provided with basic repair facilities.[125] Between 1908 and 1910, at Clonmel Station, County Tipperary, a reinforced concrete locomotive shed was constructed under the supervision of Robert Booth, who later built the concrete running shed and depot at Limerick station in 1911.

In the 1830s, the Dublin and Kingstown Railway had acquired a pre-existing hotel at Salthill. The first purpose-built railway hotels in Ireland, however, were the MGWR hotel at Eyre Square in Galway (which fronted the railway terminus), completed in 1851, and the GS & WR hotel at Killarney, which opened in 1854.[126] The GS & WR went on to build small hotels at Limerick Junction (1856) and Cork (Glanmire Road, 1894). Additional MGWR hotels, however, at Recess, County Galway (1895), and Mallaranny, County Mayo (1896), both designed by Sir Thomas Deane and Son, were not built until the closing decade of the nineteenth century. Northern railways were also relatively slow in providing passenger hotels. The Belfast and Northern Counties Railway acquired what became the 100-room Northern Counties Hotel at Portrush, while the Station Hotel (later the Midland) was opened at York Road Station in 1898. The London and North Western Railway also opened hotels at Greenore, to service its Irish Sea ferry, and on the North Wall Quay (1890) in Dublin for its Holyhead–Dublin ferry.[127]

Almost all mainline and provincial stations had a water-tower, which normally consisted of a cut stone or brick wide based column, surmounted by a cast-iron tank, to which water was pumped via a manual or steam pump. Frequently these were treated as ornamental features, good examples of which survive at Portarlington Station on the Dublin–Cork line, and at provincial stations such as Tuam, County Galway (cast by a Waterford foundry) and Lismore, County Waterford. The water supply for the Dublin terminus of the Dublin and Drogheda was originally extracted from the third lock of the Royal Canal, by means of a hydraulic ram manufactured by Mallet's foundry of Dublin.[128]

Along the course of the line, railway companies, under an act of 1845, were required to erect mile, half-mile and quarter-mileposts, only on lines carrying passengers, to indicate distances along the line, plus separate stone (and later cast-iron) posts providing the gradient at that point. Other important features include level crossings which, as we have seen, tend to be more common on Irish lines, owing to the relative cheapness of labour. Three basic varieties of level crossing are to be found throughout Ireland: foot crossings, accommodation crossings (where a property was cut by the line) and crossings on public highways, where the line intersected a road. These latter required a permanent, supervised presence by a level crossing keeper, who was accommodated in a small house by the crossing gates.[129] Many such crossing keepers' houses survive throughout Ireland, but only a small number have retained their original form.

14.17 *Nineteenth-century permanent way men's houses at Limerick Junction, County Tipperary.*

In addition to level crossing keepers' accommodation, Irish railway companies also provided cottages for many other employees, such as permanent way men (who well into the twentieth century still had to hammer in the wooden keys twice a day during hot summers), porters, firemen and signalmen. There were eighteen railway houses at Limerick Junction in 1857, where accommodation had been provided from 1848 onwards, which increased to 21 in 1867 and to 35 in 1895 (figure 14.17).[130] The London and North Western Railway also built workers' housing on New Wapping Street, Dublin, near the North Wall.[131]

15

Ports and Harbours

Early Port and Harbour Development in Ireland

From the earliest times, the two most important factors affecting the evolution of ports and harbours have been natural advantage and economic opportunity. Within this scheme of things, a favourable coastal location could be exploited to service the commercial potential of a rich hinterland. However, once a trading settlement has been established, its continuing success was by no means guaranteed, as its original advantages could be quickly undermined by natural processes such as estuarine silting or by human factors as diverse as changing market conditions or the increased size of ships. Three main evolutionary phases governing the physical development of ports may be identified from the medieval period to the eighteenth century. The first of these involves the initial exploitation of a natural coastal feature such as a haven or the head of a river estuary, where ships could be conveniently beached. In the second phase, natural advantage is augmented by the provision of features such as waterfront revetments, wharfs, harbour walls, breakwaters and by the beginning of dredging operations. The third evolutionary stage – which began in Ireland towards the end of the eighteenth century – involved the construction of enclosed docks, in which loading operations could be conducted without interference from the tides.[1] By the second half of the nineteenth century, the larger Irish ports were already providing deep-water berths at existing and new quaysides.

The rapid expansion of Ireland's maritime trade in the eighteenth century, and the commercial and economic development associated with it, brought increased political pressure for improvements to existing port facilities. No Irish port, indeed, was so favourably circumstanced that it could hope expand without major improvements to its approaches. Dublin harbour was naturally disadvantaged by a sand bar at its mouth, formed by the silt

389

discharged from the mouths of the rivers Dodder, Liffey and Tolka into Dublin Bay, whilst its quaysides were quite shallow. The many natural advantages that Cork harbour offered to international shipping, from the earliest times, were largely confined to its lower regions for the greater part of the eighteenth and nineteenth centuries. The location of the city of Cork and the approaches to it along the river from Passage West were entirely unsuited to the types of overseas vessels in use during the eighteenth century, while from the second half of the eighteenth century until the second half of the nineteenth, berthing facilities for overseas vessels at the city's quaysides were entirely inadequate.[2] Similarly, at the port of Belfast, extensive mudflats prevented large vessels from discharging cargoes at the city's quaysides where, as at Cork, they were transhipped to lighters that could negotiate the shallows at its quaysides.

While individuals such as Hugh Boyd at Ballycastle, County Antrim in the late 1730s could continue to develop port facilities on their own initiative, the eighteenth century witnessed the growth of the direct involvement of civic authorities in the improvement of Ireland's ports and harbours.[3] In Dublin, a Ballast Office was created in 1708 which, by 1710, had extended its activities to port reclamation.[4] Between 1786 and 1867, a Corporation for the Improvement of Dublin (replaced by Dublin Port and Docks Board in 1867) was the principal institutional framework responsible for the development of the port of Dublin. Belfast established a Ballast Board in 1787, while Cork had its own Harbour Commissioners from 1813, and Waterford Chamber of Commerce, created in 1815, was empowered in the following year to improve Waterford harbour.[5] During the nineteenth century, the development of steam packet ferries in the Irish Sea area also led to the creation of new port facilities, as did direct government intervention (through the Board of Public Works) in western fishing harbours. Nonetheless, the construction of entirely new ports, as at Greenore at the entrance to Carlingford Lough, between 1869 and 1873, was a rare phenomenon in nineteenth-century Ireland, where large-scale harbour works outside the principal ports were, in the main, by no means a frequent occurrence.

Port and Harbour Improvements

(1) Dredging

Shallow shipping channels and the silting up of harbours presented the single biggest problem to port development in the eighteenth and early nineteenth centuries, and invariably required both an institutional response and a considerable cash outlay. Before the advent of the steam dredger, little could be profitably achieved by spoon dredging (see Chapter 1). In 1815, the Dublin Ballast Board began work with a steam dredger, purchased on the advice of their engineer, George Halpin, who had familiarised himself with recent developments in other countries. The dredger, *Patrick*, was built by Anthony Hill's Dublin yard and its engine which, after contemporary English practice, powered an endless chain of buckets, was supplied by Fenton, Murray and Wood of Leeds.[6] However, although *Patrick* had to be towed into position, it could manoeuvre in a limited fashion by pulling against its front anchors. The material or *dredge stuff* excavated by it was carried out to sea in four newly commissioned lighters of 35 tons each. In 1830, *Patrick* was replaced by a new dredger, a self-propelled vessel built by a Scottish firm at Leith, which was capable of excavating some 1,500 tons of dredge stuff each week.[7] Around 1816, the Waterford Chamber of Commerce also purchased a dredger, which was later sold on to the Cork Harbour Commissioners in 1826.[8] Manual dredging, by private contract, of the shipping channel linking the upper and lower harbours at Cork commenced in 1822, on the shoal near Tivoli, and the 12 hp dredger acquired from Waterford, was followed by a second, 20 hp dredger in 1839.[9] In 1830, the port of Belfast followed suit when a steam dredger began work on the shipping channel. At Belfast, the completion of the first cut into the tidal channel by William Dargan, in 1841, created a 17-acre site that became known as 'Queen's Island', upon which the city's internationally successful shipbuilding industry became established.[10] Large amounts of estuarine deposits were removed from shipping channels during dredging operations, but not all of it was dumped at sea. Dredge stuff was, in fact, also used in harbour reclamation works, as at Cork in the 1850s, where it was brought ashore behind the Navigation Wall to form what eventually became the Marina embankment, and later to fill in slobland near the city.[11] By the middle of the nineteenth century, large-scale dredging had become routine in most Irish ports, but by now the larger size of vessels required increased dredging capacity to ensure not only that existing channels could be deepened but also be continuously maintained at these depths.

In Cork harbour, two new dredgers were at work in the late 1850s in the creation of a vitally needed, new deepwater channel, and in the deepening of the berths at the city's quaysides. Six, 120-ton barges were purchased to remove dredge stuff from the harbour in 1865 but, in the same year, Cork Harbour Commissioners became the first in Ireland to explore the use of hopper barges, whose successful employment on the River Clyde had aroused their interest. Thus, in 1865, they dispatched their mechanical engineer to assess their usefulness for the ongoing dredging operation in the upper harbour.[12] In the hopper float or barge, the vessel was equipped with bottom-opening doors. Once the vessel had been filled by the dredger, it could be towed out to sea where, by opening the bottom doors, the load could be emptied at a location where it would be washed away by tidal currents.[13] The obvious advantages of this system were not lost on the Commissioners, who went on to order four steam hopper barges from Robinson's shipyard at Cork between 1867 and 1871.[14] Hopper barges were used in conjunction with the bucket dredger, *Greenore*, in 1867, during the removal of the sand bar at Carlingford, County Louth, while the new technology was quickly adopted in Dublin port where, between 1869 and 1871, over £500,000 was expended on new dredging plant, which included a new dredger and three steam hopper barges. These latter were designed by the Dublin port engineer, Bindon Blood Stoney, each of which had a capacity of 850-1,000 tons of dredge stuff.[15] For the greater part of the nineteenth century, steam-powered bucket dredgers operated in Irish ports but, in 1895, the Port of Dublin contracted a Dutch firm to provide it with suction dredging plant. This innovation had first been employed by Libby in the American port of Charleston in 1855, and was adopted and further developed in Europe, in Holland and France during the 1870s. Suction dredgers were used at Liverpool in 1893 and were first operated in Ireland, at Dublin, in 1896, where they demonstrated their superiority in the removal of sand and mud.[16]

(2) Breakwaters and Quaysides

The accumulation of river-borne debris and sea sand within shipping channels, it was clear, required constant attention. Yet dredging alone could not, in the long term, be relied upon to remove or even check natural obstructions created by riverine deposition at estuaries. Such problems were particularly severe within the environs of Dublin Bay and its notorious sand bar, whose improvement John Rennie remarked was 'perhaps one of the most difficult subjects which has ever come under the consideration of the civil engineer'.[17] The material deposited by the Liffey, Tolka and Dodder rivers formed two large sand banks, known as the North and South Bulls, which formed constantly shifting and consequently dangerous channels for shipping. Works to remedy

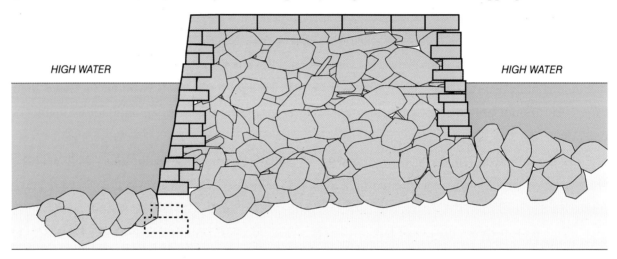

Cross section between Half-Moon Battery and Poolbeg Lighthouse

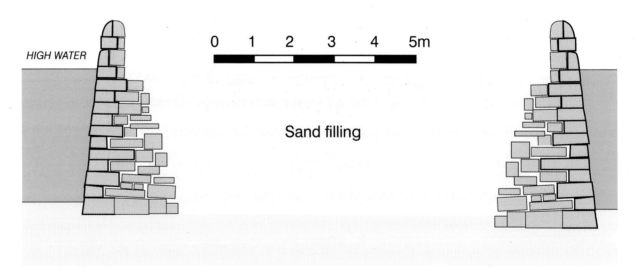

Cross section between Pigeonhouse precinct and Ringsend

15.1 *Section through the South Bull wall, (after de Courcy 1996).*

this problem were begun at a relatively early period, in 1711, commencing with the construction of a timber jetty that was to form the northern side of a straight channel leading from Dublin Bay to the city quaysides. The northern arm of the new channel extended for a distance of 7,938 ft (2.419 km) from Ringsend to the Pigeon House Fort, and from the latter for a distance of 9,816 ft (2.991 km) to the eastern spit of the South Bull. The jetty was constructed with timber caissons, which were assembled at Ringsend and floated to the site where, after being filled with rubble, they were sunk into position. In 1748, the first section between Ringsend and the Pigeon House Fort was rebuilt as a double line of masonry retaining walls with a sand-filled

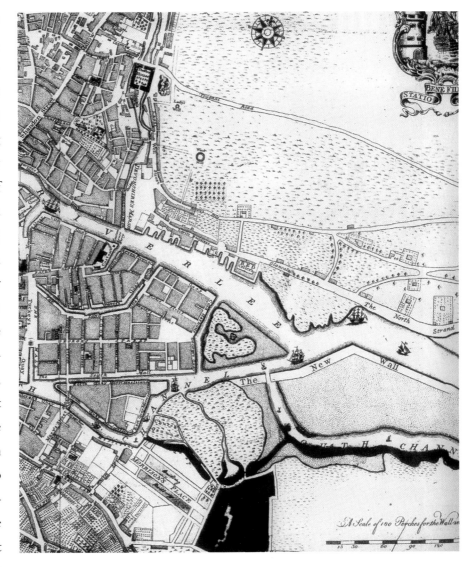

15.2 *The eighteenth-century Navigation Wall at Cork, shown here in 1774 as 'The New Wall'.*

core (figure 15.1). Prior to the construction of the channel, navigation to the Dublin quaysides could often be difficult, obliging larger ships to transfer their cargoes to lighters near Dalkey.[18]

In the long term, however, the sand bar in Dublin Bay would, if not properly dealt with, continue to create problems for shipping. Captain William Bligh, of HMS *Bounty* fame, was commissioned in 1800 to make a detailed survey of Dublin Bay with a view to its improvement, and in his recommendations became one of the first to suggest that a breakwater be constructed on the north side. This, he argued, would create a scouring action in which sand would be washed away from the harbour mouth, by augmenting the flow of the river. This same concept was later proposed by Chapman, Cornielle and John Rennie, but came nowhere near realisation until Francis Giles and George Halpin suggested, in 1819, that a masonry breakwater be constructed from the north shore at Clontarf to a point opposite Poolbeg lighthouse. This latter, the North Bull Wall, some 5,500 ft (1.676 km) long, was completed between 1820 and 1825. It was built with limestone and granite rubblestone

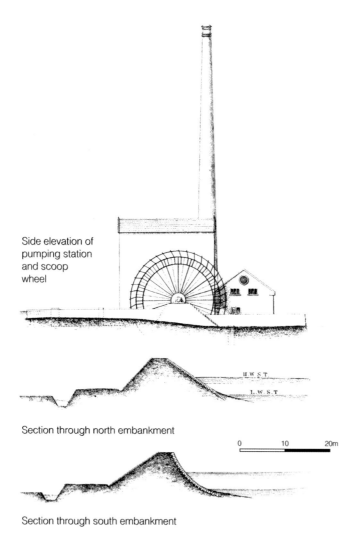

Side elevation of
pumping station
and scoop
wheel

H.W.S.T.

L.W.S.T.

Section through north embankment

0   10   20m

Section through south embankment

15.3 *Drinagh pumping station, County Wexford, completed in the 1850s (top);* **15.4** *The Drinagh scoop wheel, (after Anderson 1866) (above).*

masonry, and effectively formed an artificial mouth for the River Liffey. The scouring effect created by the wall dramatically reduced the level of the sand bar, while at the same preventing sand from the North Bull from being deposited in the river channel. Before the construction of the North Bull breakwater, the depth at low water during the spring tides was only 6 ft (1.82 m); by 1873, it was over 16 ft (4.87 m).[19]

At Cork, until the 1760s, the confluence of north and south channels of the River Lee was bounded at the south by a large tidal marsh created, in the main, by material deposited by the south channel. In this period, work was begun on a masonry breakwater that became known as the 'Navigation Wall' the purpose of which to regularise the current in the north channel of the river, by directing the flow of the south channel into it at a point nearer to the city quays. It also served as a 'tracking' wall, to enable ships facing contrary winds to be pulled by horses up to the city quays (figure 15.2).[20] By 1769, the Navigation Wall extended over 800 yards eastwards, and a parliamentary committee recommended that it be extended further for a distance of 1,160 yards to Lotabeg. Additional grants were made available in the period 1773-84 to enable these works to be completed, and by 1783 some 1,529 yards of tracking wall (the 'New Wall') had been completed. By 1837, the New Wall had been extended for a distance of some 3,000 ft (0.914 km), by which time it was possible for vessels drawing up to 16 ft (4.87 m) of water to proceed directly to the city quays on the high spring tides. In the early 1850s, the Navigation Wall was 7,000 ft (2.133 km) long, with cut stone foundations laid 2 ft (0.60 m) below the low water level of the ordinary spring tides, 3,300 ft (1.005 km) of which were built with dry rubblestone. From the 1850s onwards, dredge stuff from the River Lee was systematically dumped behind the Navigation Wall to form what is now a large area of reclaimed land, known as the Marina embankment. Part of the former New Wall survives as facing wall for this embankment. It is constructed with bonded rubble masonry, and is over 2.3 km long, with an average height of 4.5 m and around 2 m in overall thickness.[21]

At Wexford harbour, shifting sands in the estuary of the River Slaney and a shallow harbour entrance created problems for shipping well into the twentieth century. In the late 1840s, however, an ambitious commercial enterprise was inaugurated by John Redmond who, in association with, amongst others, William Dargan, sought to improve the harbour by reclaiming the large mud banks on either side of it. Redmond's Wexford Harbour Improvement Company received parliamentary sanction in 1846 to erect five large embankments around the northern and southern edges of Wexford harbour, the areas enclosed by which would eventually be pumped dry and reclaimed for agricultural use. It was also hoped that these works would help to confine the River Slaney to a narrower channel, and that both the increased tidal scour and dredging might eventually create a safer deep-water approach to the Wexford quays.[22] In 1847, work began on the construction of the embankment for the North Slob, which was constructed with clay and marl. A pumping station was established at Breast Island, at which a side-lever marine steam engine was used to power a 30 ft (9.14 m) diameter and 6 ft (1.82 m) wide scoop wheel, but the arrangement proved unsatisfactory, and was replaced by a steam-powered Appold centrifugal pump in the 1850s. By this period, the North Slobs had been completely reclaimed and, in 1852, the company turned its attention to the south slobs, obtaining an act in the same year that sanctioned their enclosure with embankments.[23] A pumping station was constructed at Drinagh (figure 15.3), which consisted of a 40 ft (12.19 m) diameter scoop wheel, 10 ft (3.04 m) wide, powered by a condensing engine, designed by the Irish Engineering Company's Seville works at Dublin (figure 15.4). The axle of the scoop wheel, indeed, was also remarkable in that it was manufactured with cast-iron from Creevelea, County Leitrim (see Chapter 4).[24] The remains of the Drinagh pumphouse and its original stack were recently restored by Dúchas, the Heritage Service, and are currently used to interpret the natural history of the Wexford harbour sloblands.

Such large-scale improvements to the approaches of Ireland's ports and harbours would have been of little use without a corresponding expansion of existing quaysides. Surprisingly, the development of the latter managed, for the most part, to keep in step with harbour improvements, particularly in the early decades of the nineteenth century. From the 1730s onwards, timber quaysides and waterfront revetments were gradually replaced with substantial masonry quays. At Ballycastle, County Antrim, Hugh Boyd (see Chapter 14) opened up new limestone quarries for harbour works in 1737, for which he constructed a timber waggon way. Timber for the piling of the Ballycastle quays was even sought as far south as Lismore in County Waterford and from Acton Wood in County Armagh. By the 1730s, the construction of the 'New Quay Wall', which was 5 ft (1.52 m) wide at its foundation and some 18 ft (5.48 m) high, was already well underway at Waterford. In the 1760s, this was admired by Arthur Young, who asserted that it was 'the finest object in this city … unrivalled by any I have seen'. It was, according to his estimate, 'an English mile long'.[25] Nonetheless, timber jetties, piers and quays

395

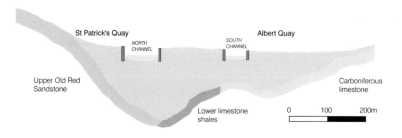

SECTION THROUGH THE RIVER LEE AT CORK

SECTION THROUGH THE SOUTH CHANNEL

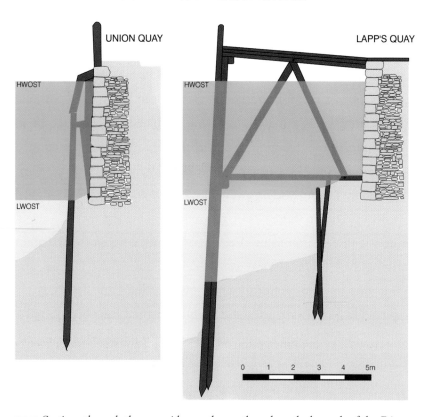

15.5 *Sections through the quaysides on the south and north channels of the River Lee at Cork.*

continued to be built well into the nineteenth century but, by the middle of the eighteenth, the vast majority of the quaysides in Ireland's ports were already being constructed with bonded rubble masonry faced with large cut facing stones. Such walls were also capped with large cut stone copings, secured with iron keys, which helped to prevent their being dislodged by ships knocking against them.

The first parapet walls along the Liffey quays were built in the late eighteenth and early nineteenth centuries, and were generally of bonded rubble with cut stone granite façades. In 1815, the Scottish engineer, Alexander Nimmo (1783-1832), reported that Cork's rubblestone quays were poorly founded, being constructed on the strand at high water level. Fortunately, the city's newly established Harbour Commissioners also considered the maintenance and repair of the city's quay walls to be within its remit and, in the period 1820-33, it undertook a large-scale programme of quay repairs. According to an Admiralty inquiry into Cork docks and harbour improvements, in 1850, there were 26,359 ft (8.034 km) of quay walls at Cork, which had cut limestone foundations that were set 2-4 ft (0.60 m-1.21 m) below the low water of the ordinary spring tides (figure 15.5).[26] At Waterford, by 1817, new quays now extended as far as Lemuel Cox's timber bridge (see Chapter 12). Throughout Ireland, these magnificent stone quaysides still survive, although in more recent years, particularly in Cork city, collapsed cut stone masonry is seldom, if ever, replaced.

The costs of preparing quay walls below water could be prohibitive, and as early as 1863, the engineer of Dublin port, Bindon Blood Stoney, had begun to evaluate the relative costs of both masonry and concrete for this purpose. Stoney undertook a series of tests which established that concrete was actually some 50 per cent cheaper, and he proposed to manufacture monolithic blocks of concrete, up to 350 tons in weight, which would be laid on the river bed as the foundations of quay walls. He was not, however, the first to carry out such a scheme in Ireland.[27] In 1870 James Barton (whom we have encountered earlier in relation to the Boyne Viaduct, see Chapter 14), had already begun to lay 100-ton concrete blocks for the below water section of an 800 yard (731.52 m) quay wall at Greenore harbour, at the entrance to Carlingford Lough, constructed to serve the new Dundalk, Newry and Greenore Railway.[28] Yet for all that, Stoney's scheme to provide new quay walls on the north side of the estuary of the River Liffey was novel in its execution. The conventional method of laying the foundations of quay walls involved the construction of expensive coffer dams, which were continually pumped dry to facilitate building work. However, in Stoney's scheme, the foundations for the concrete monoliths were first excavated by a dredger, while the final levelling off work was carried out on the river bed by men working within a massive diving bell, supplied with compressed air. This latter, which was some 20 ft (6.09 m) square and had a vertical access shaft protected by an airlock, was manufactured by Grendons of Drogheda in 1869. The enormous concrete blocks, which were fabricated nearby, were lifted by a floating crane built by Harland and Wolff in 1866 (the lifting machinery was supplied by Courtney and Stephens of Dublin), and the first of these was lowered into position in 1871. Stoney's method proved to be both expeditious and cheap, and by 1882, over 2,000 ft (609.6 m) of new quay wall, with a depth of 22 ft (6.70 m), had been laid by this means. The exterior face of the wall below water was then faced with Dublin calp limestone, that above water was finished in the usual way with granite ashlar coped with granite blocks.[29]

(3) Artificial Harbours

In 1626, Viscount Montgomery had completed an artificial harbour at Donaghadee, the rebuilding of which took place between 1775 and 1785. By the early decades of the nineteenth century, indeed, entirely new harbours were being created on Ireland's east coast both to accommodate the mails and to provide additional berths near existing ports. These normally took the form of two projecting masonry piers, which almost converged at their outer extremities to form a partially enclosed, artificial harbour. At Howth, to the south of Dublin Bay, an act of parliament of 1807 enabled the construction of what was originally intended as an alternative harbour to Dublin, where the shallow water at the Pigeon House and the shortage of berths within the existing port were beginning to interfere with the delivery of the London mails. Work began on the east pier at Howth in 1808 and by 1809, the work in progress was under the direction of John Rennie, who was to play an important part in the development of Ireland's new harbours. On his recommendation, a west pier was added and, in 1812, a diving bell was used for the first time in Ireland to complete the construction of the pier heads. In 1813, most of the work had been completed, to form an enclosed harbour of around 52 acres, with a 350 ft (106.68 m) wide harbour entrance. Howth was formally established as the mail packet station in 1818, a function in which it ultimately failed owing to a tendency for silting to occur at its harbour mouth, and the mails were eventually transferred to Kingstown harbour.[30]

Rennie had already recommended Dún Laoghaire (renamed Kingstown after 1821) as a prime candidate for harbour development as early as 1802. Parliament authorised an 'asylum harbour' in 1815 and work began, in 1816, on what was originally intended as a single masonry pier, but after consultation with Rennie, in 1817, two embracing piers were eventually constructed to form a partially enclosed area of some 250 acres, with a harbour entrance of 750 ft or 228.6 m in width. A funicular railway (see Chapter 6) was constructed to transport granite from the quarries at Dalkey to the harbour works, at which some 1,000 workers were employed in 1823. After Rennie's death, in 1821, his son, John Rennie Jnr, took over as consultant, but work on the rounded pier heads (which were built with sandstone from Runcorn, on the River Mersey) was still underway in the late 1840s. Nonetheless, mail packet steamers that had originally plied the route between Holyhead and Howth were transferred to Kingstown in 1826. The east pier at Kingstown harbour, in 1853, became the site for the world's first anenometer for measuring the strength of the wind, designed by Professor Robinson of Trinity College, Dublin.[31] This latter feature survives, *in situ*.

John Rennie Snr also designed the new harbour at Donaghadee, whose construction was supervised by John Rennie Jnr between 1821 and 1836. The two piers defining the northern and southern extents of the harbour were 820 ft (249.93 m) and 900 ft (274.32 m) respectively, and their pier heads were constructed with Anglesey limestone. Rennie's harbour, with its lighthouse (built to his own design, and completed in 1832), survives relatively unchanged. Donaghadee harbour was, nonetheless, a commercial failure, despite being built to service the mails, this latter service being transferred to Belfast in 1849, after it was found to be subject frequently to bad local weather conditions. John Rennie Jnr also built an important harbour at Portrush between 1827 and 1836.[32] A further mail packet harbour was built by Alexander Nimmo at Dunmore East, County Waterford, in 1823-25, to service the mail packet steamers from Milford Haven in south Wales.[33]

The construction of entirely new harbours, during the second half of the nineteenth century, was somewhat rarer, and the only two of note – Greenore and Rosslare – were built to accommodate railway links. Between 1869 and 1873, James Barton was responsible for the construction of a new harbour at Greenore for the Dundalk, Newry and Greenore Railway. Barton's purpose-built harbour complex was unique in nineteenth-century Ireland. It was provided with berths, rail sidings, a railway station and hotel as well as goods stores, while its gangways for cattle and passengers were hydraulically operated, and could be raised or lowered with the tides. Barton also built a two-mile long piped water supply, eighteen workers' houses, along with buildings for educational and religious instruction.[34] Rosslare Harbour Commissioners erected a 480 ft (146.30 m) long timber jetty near Greenore Point, County Wexford, in 1873, along with two berths for steamers from Fishguard in south Wales. In 1882, the Dublin, Wicklow and Wexford Railway was extended to Rosslare, and a new jetty was erected, which was replaced by a new harbour in the period 1904-06, after the creation of the

Fishguard and Rosslare Railways and Harbour Company by the English GWR and the Irish GS &WR. This latter harbour was entirely remodelled in the 1960s and 1990s.[35]

(4) Enclosed Docks

Two forms of enclosed docks were constructed in eighteenth- and nineteenth-century Ireland, *dry* or *graving* docks which facilitated repairs and the cleaning of ships, and *wet* or *floating* docks which allowed vessels to be unloaded without interruption from the tides. The port of Belfast was somewhat unique in Ireland in that its low tidal ranges enabled ships to be unloaded at all times, without the inconvenience of waiting for high water. Belfast docks, indeed, owing to this remarkable circumstance, did not have to be enclosed by gates.[36] When John Beresford brought James Gandon over to Ireland in 1781 to build the new Dublin Custom House, his brief also included the provision of enclosed floating docks and warehouses. However, work on the East Dock (for which John Rennie became consultant) did not commence until 1791, and it was only opened in 1796.[37] Rennie was also involved in the design and construction of George's Dock (named after George IV) which was completed in 1821, and in that of the tobacco store ('Stack A'), built to the west of it. This was later followed, in the 1820s, by a further dock leading in from George's Dock, which became known as the 'Inner Dock'. These docks could easily handle most ships using the port up to the 1840s. But, thereafter, the inability of larger vessels to lock in and out of the docks, owing to the expense involved in widening their lock gates, effectively rendered them obsolete. Henceforth, Dublin's port authorities focused increased attention on the provision of deepwater berths upstream from the Custom House.[38] In the 1990s these docks became part of the government-sponsored Irish Financial Services Centre, of which they form a central feature.

The provision of floating docks occurred in only two other Irish ports in the 1850s. The Limerick docks were constructed between 1849 and 1853, under the overall supervision of the Limerick Harbour Commissioner's engineer, John Long. As originally constructed, they consisted of a basin some 7.66 acres in extent, internally faced with massive cut limestone blocks. The original 70 ft (21.33 m) wide eastern entrance was positioned on the downstream side of the dock, and the lock gates were constructed by Robert Mallet's Dublin foundry using his patented 'buckled plates' (see Chapter 10). The present dock entrance, at the west, was added in 1956 when the original one was filled in.[39] Floating docks were also built at Galway in the 1850s, enclosing an area of some six statute acres. However, the deep water offered by the River Suir at Waterford rendered such docks unnecessary, but at Cork the development of wet docks never took place, owing to the lobbying of vested interests. The main channel of the River Lee from Passage West in the upper harbour to the city quaysides was only 3 ft (0.91 m) deep in many places, and vessels of over 80 tons could only reach the city quays safely on the spring tides. In consequence, as late as the early 1870s, large vessels were obliged to tranship at least part of their cargoes to lighters at Passage West. The construction of floating docks, given the size and relative importance of the port of Cork, would appear to have been vital to its long-term interests, yet shipowners and those involved in the transhipment trade (such as warehouse owners at Passage West) successfully combined to prevent this. In

399

the 1870s, the problem was partially solved by the provision of deep-water berths, and subsequently by extending the available wharfage downstream.[40]

(5) Warehouses and Ancillary Features

The industrialisation of the Irish milling industry in the closing decades of the eighteenth century led to the creation of multi-storey grain stores on Ireland's quaysides (see Chapter 9). But before the 1770s, a merchant's house, more often than not, simply faced onto an adjacent street or quayside, with an arched opening on one side to facilitate vehicular access to a small two-storey warehouse and cellar at the rear. A similar pattern can also, indeed, be discerned in early nineteenth-century canal towns such as Edenderry and Tullamore in County Offaly. Yet it is not until the early years of the nineteenth century that large multi-storey port warehousing (other than those used to store grain) began to be constructed in Ireland's ports. In the main, these buildings were substantial structures and, in a number of instances, employed early forms of fireproofing. On Haulbowline Island in Cork harbour, three former British naval victualling stores (which formed part of a complex of six similar structures), completed in 1816-22, were provided with what appears to be an early form of transitional fireproofing, unique in Ireland (figure 15.6). These early three-story and loft warehouses form the east wing of the former navy victualling yard, the buildings in question along with a third, almost identical warehouse, being aligned on a north-south axis. Originally, these were provided with wharfage along their eastern elevations, which was subsequently filled in when the adjacent section of open dock was removed to

15.6 *One of three British Navy victualling stores, constructed on Haulbowline Island in Cork harbour in 1816-22 (top);* **15.7** *Cork bonded warehouses, designed by Abraham Hargreaves and opened in 1818 (above). The interiors are fire-proofed by means of brick vaults.*

accommodate Irish Steel's mill, during the late 1930s. In form, they are essentially Georgian, although, unlike other industrial buildings of the period, they do not have eaves pediments and, while the central warehouse in the naval section has an elaborate campanile with a four-faced clock which are not untypical of late eighteenth-early nineteenth-century British industrial buildings, the Haulbowline warehouses have a much wider roof span. Multi-storey industrial buildings of the period in Ireland almost invariably do not have roof spans in excess of about 20 ft (6.09 m). Two of the three aligned storehouses have two sets of loading doors, one at each storey. The arrangement of the loading doors is common to all six warehouses, and in each case the upper storey was provided with a cast-iron, pivoted crane. These are the earliest surviving examples of their type in Ireland.

Internally, the wooden pine floors are supported on a unique cast-iron framework. Each floor is divided by a stone, spiral staircase, which is cantilevered outwards from the inner face of a sub-rectangular rubblestone stairwell. The cast-iron columns on each floor form a three-bay interior division, set around a square grid. The cast-iron beams which rest upon these columns have an inverted 'T'-section, and their extremities are formed into a semi-circular terminal, which forms an end-to-end joint with a further beam at right angles to it. However, the arrangement of the cast-iron framing in the Haulbowline storehouses differs significantly from industrial buildings of the period in both Britain and Ireland. For while the Haulbowline supporting beams have a hogsback profile similar to those of English fire-proofed buildings of the period, in contemporary British buildings, these beams are used to support a matrix of brick segmental jack arches. Jack-arched floors (see Chapter 8) were the principal means by which textile mills of this period were rendered fireproof. Yet at Haulbowline, flanged sockets set into the upper edges of the girders were used to support wooden joists. This latter arrangement was clearly not fireproof, and would appear to defeat the purpose of installing cast-iron framing. However, the architects of these storehouses may well have had a different rationale in mind. In other industrial buildings in which machinery was employed, the risk of fire was much greater, on account of oil dripping from machinery. But, in this instance, the expedient in employing cast-iron framing may well have been to counteract the stresses incurred from additional loading, where the usual fire risks may well have not been present.

The Cork bonded warehouses, at the rear of the Cork Custom House, designed by Abraham Hargreaves and opened in 1818, are a rare survival of an earlier form of fireproofing (figure 15.7). The ground plan of the bonded warehouses was designed to match the footprint of the newly constructed quayside, being trapezoidal in outline and tapering inwards on a west-east long axis. It is a two-storey and loft structure constructed with random rubble, local green sandstone, cut limestone being employed for both window and door dressings and, of course, for the distinctive fireproof stairwell towers which have a circular ground plan and house stone spiral staircases. On the north-facing elevation, the original hoist mechanisms survive *in situ*. In the interior, the first and second floors are constructed with a matrix of brick rib vaults, built with Youghal brick, similar to that used in Cork harbour Martello towers constructed in the period 1812-14. The vaults are laid on an east-west axis, and spring from a series of square brick columns. Stone flag floors are employed throughout and these, along with the brick vaulting, provided an elementary form of fireproofing. Given the high value nature of the

15.8 *The former tobacco warehouse known as 'Stack A', built by John Rennie to the east of the George IV Dock in Dublin in the early 1820s (left). This is the first completely cast-iron framed warehouse in Ireland;* **15.9** *Section of the façade of the Cork Custom House of 1724, now part of the Crawford Art Gallery (right).*

goods store here (both spirits and tobacco), this was essential, and in the era before cast-iron construction, vaulting provided both protection from fire and a means of ensuring constant temperatures. The wooden-framed and slate awning (which now survives mostly on the west-facing and south-facing elevations) is one of the most interesting extant features of the building. The main timber frame is suspended from the outer face of the building by wrought-iron tensioning rods. These latter are affixed to wrought-iron hoops, affixed to either the flat facing stones decorating the outer ends of the window arches (at first floor level) or into limestone blocks set into the original masonry.

The Cork bonded warehouses and the Haulbowline stores represent, respectively, early and transitional forms of fireproofing. However, the former tobacco warehouse known as 'Stack A', built by John Rennie to the east of the George IV Dock in Dublin in the early 1820s, is the first completely cast-iron framed warehouse in Ireland (figure 15.8). Externally, it is constructed with local brick, and internally it is divided into four 15 ft (4.47 m) wide bays and is 476 ft (145.08 m) long, with roof trusses formed with a wrought-iron tension member and cast-iron compression members, supported on cast-iron columns.[41]

Cranes and hoists, both manually operated and steam-powered, were a relatively common feature of Ireland's ports during the later nineteenth century. Unfortunately, none of Ireland's nineteenth-century steam cranes have survived, but a small number of the cast-iron rotating boom cranes, such as that at George's Dock in Dublin (which is similar to those erected by the Shannon Commissioners at Banagher and Shannonbridge) are still extant. The availability of electricity at Poolbeg during the late nineteenth century led to the erection of electric cranes, which included a 100 ton example, completed in 1903 and dismantled in 1987. A further four,

four-ton examples were built on the North Wall extension, along with electric capstans for hauling wagons.[42] Electric cranes were employed in Belfast in 1918, where electricity also became a vital part of the late nineteenth-century infrastructure of the port when, in 1892, a generating station was opened at the Abercorn basin. This station, by 1894, was supplying current for all the docks, quays and sheds at Belfast.[43]

(6) Custom Houses

In the eighteenth century, no single public building form came to symbolise Ireland's growing international trade more than the custom house. Port revenues steadily increased towards the middle of the century, but until the completion of Ducart's Limerick Custom House in 1769, very few of the provincial examples were distinguished in architectural terms, and the Revenue Commissioners often chose to rent premises rather than invest in permanent buildings.[44] The Cork Custom House of 1724 is the oldest surviving example in Ireland, and now houses a section of the city's Crawford Art Gallery (figure 15.9). According to Charles Smith, in 1750, the building contained an apartment for the Collector of Revenue, and had storehouses on one side which formed two piazzas. Its river frontage to the north, he added, had a crane, while a new canal was cut almost entirely around the main block to provide additional wharfage.

Davis Ducart's Limerick Custom House, begun in 1765 and completed in 1769, was, in its day, the most imposing building of its type ever to have been built in Ireland (figure 15.10). Christopher Colles, whose uncle had developed stone cutting and boring machinery for his Kilkenny quarries (see Chapter 6), served as Ducart's assistant and was the site architect during construction.[45] The original Dublin house, designed by Thomas Burgh, Surveyor General between 1700 and 1730, was completed *c.* 1710, but by the 1770s it was already in an advanced

state of decay. Work began on James Gandon's new Dublin Custom House (an outstanding piece of European neo-Classicism) in 1781, a building which Henry Grattan was to describe as 'bombastic vanity' in 1790, one year before its completion. The walls are of brickwork faced with granite and imported Portland Stone, although the present structure is the product of extensive rebuilding and restoration, subsequent to its burning by the IRA in 1921. The original open arches, set between the pavilions at the east and west, once provided access to the warehouse buildings at the rear.[46] Nineteenth-century customs house are a somewhat rarer feature of Ireland's ports, the two most notable examples

15.10 *The Limerick Customs House, designed by Davis Ducart, and completed in 1769. This is now the permanent home of the Hunt Museum.*

403

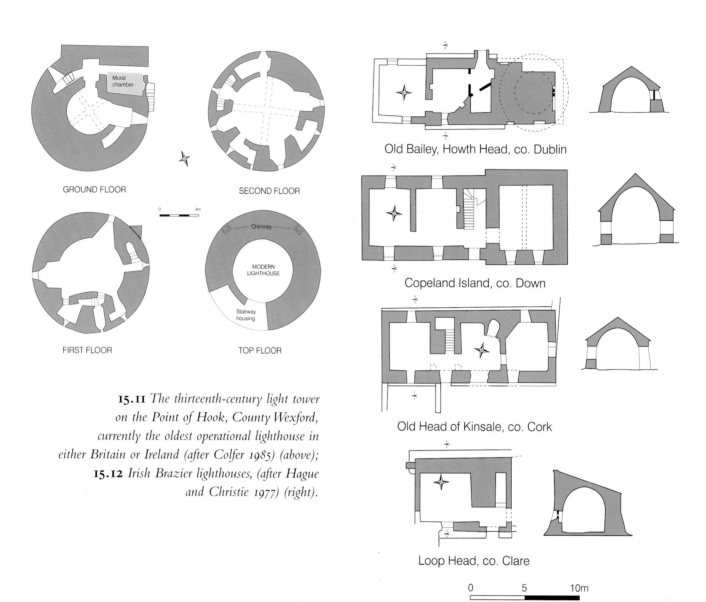

15.11 *The thirteenth-century light tower on the Point of Hook, County Wexford, currently the oldest operational lighthouse in either Britain or Ireland (after Colfer 1985) (above);* **15.12** *Irish Brazier lighthouses, (after Hague and Christie 1977) (right).*

being Abraham Hargreaves building at Cork, completed *c.* 1814 (which also housed the Cork Harbour Commisioners and for which the impressive bonded stores, described above, were built), and Charles Langan's Belfast Custom House (1854-57). This latter which, unlike that at Cork, is no longer extant, also accommodated other Belfast public offices (including a post office).[47]

(7) Lighthouses

From the later medieval period onwards, there is evidence for the use of signalling towers on Ireland's east coast where, as one might expect, it had already become necessary to indicate particularly dangerous areas of the coastline to regular shipping. In the thirteenth century, a vaulted masonry light tower was in operation on the Point of Hook in County Wexford, the greater part of which still survives. The Hook lighthouse is circular in ground plan, with a 12.3 m diameter at its base, while the main body of the tower extends upwards to some 24.7 m. Its walls are 3.7 m thick and its internal height is divided into three vaulted chambers (figure 15.11).[48] In 1863 the present, centrally placed turret was added to the tower, and the lighthouse is currently the oldest operational lighthouse in Britain or Ireland. The Hook tower is likely to have been a *brazier* lighthouse, in which an open fire was lit on an elevated platform, the remainder of the tower providing accommodation for, perhaps, either a tower keeper's family or a small complement of soldiers. Sea marks were also used from at least the sixteenth century onwards, good examples of which, such as the Maiden Tower and the Lady's finger, survive at Mornington where the River Boyne enters the Irish Sea.[49]

Up to 1717, when the Trustees of the Barracks took over responsibility for the maintenance of both Irish barracks and lighthouses, the latter were commonly built under letters patent from the crown, by private individuals, who were empowered to collect tolls from shipping. Thus Sir Thomas Reading, in 1665, acquired patents to erect lighthouses in Ireland, which included two brazier lights on the Hill of Howth, and that on the Old Head of Kinsale.[50] A number of early eighteenth-century Irish cottage lighthouses, principally at the Old Head of Kinsale, County Cork, and at Loop Head on the Shannon estuary, have survived, and it is clear from these that they differ in certain key respects from their contemporary British counterparts (figure 15.12). In its essentials, the Irish cottage lighthouse comprises a stone or brick-vaulted cottage, which has an internal

15.13 *Early eighteenth-century brazier lighthouse on the Old Head of Kinsale, County Cork.*

15.14 *Poolbeg lighthouse on the South Bull wall in Dublin Bay (left);* **15.15** *J.R. Wigham (1829-1906), (right).*

masonry staircase that facilitates access from the interior to a brazier platform on the roof. The internal vault, it is clear, was a fire-prevention measure. However, unlike British examples, where the living quarters were positioned in a tower, in Ireland, such accommodation was provided in what was essentially a modified form of vernacular cottage.[51] Many of these early lighthouses, as in the case of that on the Old Head of Kinsale, were erected on high headlands, but where this was not possible, as on Lighthouse Island in Belfast Lough (*c.* 1717), the brazier was elevated in a 70 ft (21.33 m) high masonry tower.[52] The Old Head of Kinsale (figure 15.13) cottage lighthouse was converted to candle light as early as 1703, and continued in this form until 1714, by which time it was found that the original fire provided a better light. A fire was reinstated from 1714 to 1803 and, indeed, brazier lights continued in use at Howth Head up to 1790 and in Belfast Lough until the beginning of the nineteenth century.[53]

During the second half of the eighteenth century tower lighthouses fired first by candle power and later by oil began to become more common on Ireland's coastal headlands and islands. Lighthouse towers were also beginning to be surmounted by a glazed lantern and assume the distinctive tapering profiles, more familiar to modern observers. Poolbeg lighthouse, on the seaward extremity of the South Bull in Dublin Bay, erected under the supervision of John Smyth and completed in 1767, was the first wave-swept lighthouse to be constructed on the Irish coast (figure 15.14). It also has the distinction of being one of the first lighthouses in either Britain or Ireland to be converted from candle power to oil lamps.[54] John Trail, while architect to the Commissioners of Revenue, built an interesting six-storey, tapering octagonal lighthouse tower at Wicklow Head in 1778, which still survives. This originally had an octagonal lantern which was glazed on five sides, and in its day was one of the most elaborate of its type in either Britain or Ireland.[55]

The transition from candle power to oil lamps in Ireland largely came about after the responsibility for Irish lighthouses became vested in the Commissioners of Revenue in 1796. New building works and renovations were initially carried out for the Commissioners by Thomas Rodgers, who erected three new lighthouses and was responsible for the conversion of candle to oil lamps in five existing ones.[56] The South Rock (Kilwarlin) lighthouse, which lies off the Ards Peninsula in County Down, is of Rodgers' design. It was built with massive granite blocks and work began on it in 1793. Responsibility for Irish lighthouses became vested in the Corporation for Preserving and Improving the Port of Dublin in 1810, which immediately embarked upon the most prolific era of lighthouse building in Ireland's history. In 1810, when the Corporation assumed control, some fourteen lighthouses were at work around Ireland's coastline; by 1867 there were 72, some 58 of which were built under the supervision of George Halpin, Snr, and George Halpin Jnr.[57] These include the Tuskar Rock lighthouse (begun in 1812), which lies five miles to the southeast of Greenore Point in County Wexford, 111 ft (33.83 m) high and 36 ft (10.97 m) in diameter, and the original Fastnet lighthouse, some four and a half miles off the coast of Cape Clear in County Cork.[58]

Fastnet lighthouse is one of two magnificent rock lights built on the Irish coastline, which also includes the South Rock off County Down, referred to in passing above. John Rodgers' light was similar to John Rudyard's original Eddystone lighthouse of 1706 (which was replaced by John Smeaton's famous light in 1756). The South Rock lighthouse is 16.74 m high and was eventually replaced by a lightship in 1877.[59] Halpin Snr's Fastnet lighthouse, constructed between 1848 and 1853, with flanged cast-iron plates supplied by J. and R. Mallet of Dublin, was 28 m high. It had five cast-iron floors, although the keepers were housed in a unique single-storey cast-iron, brick-lined shelter. However, the tower tended to sway in extreme conditions, and its foundations (which were bolted into the rock face) were modified in 1867. In 1896, work began on its eventual replacement, the present-day tower (completed in 1904), constructed with Cornish granite to a height of over 179 ft (54.55 m).[60]

In the early 1860s, a Scottish Quaker gaslight engineer, John R. Wigham (1829-1906) (figure 15.15), who had settled in Dublin, was developing a revolutionary form of gas illumination for lighthouses. Existing oil lamps employed chimneys of poor-quality glass which dimmed the light, while the glass itself was often shattered by the heat of the flame. Wigham's gas lamp, however, was surmounted by a mica flue and did not require a glass chimney. This startling innovation, when installed in the Bailey light beneath Howth Head in 1865 (figure 15.16), provided 3,000 candle power, compared to the 240 hitherto available from oil lamps. Yet, despite its self-evident success, Wigham's patent became embroiled in a scientific controversy involving the Commissioners for Irish Lights and his competitors, although ultimately he prevailed, and thousands of his lights (manufactured in a Dublin foundry) were eventually exported all around the world (figure 15.17). The intermittent or flashing light, with which the modern reader will be most familiar, is also a John R. Wigham innovation. The first such light was installed in the Wicklow Head lighthouse in 1870, in which he added a clockwork valve that turned the gas on and off to produce the world's first intermittent lighthouse beam. A few years later, in 1872, he trebled the candle power of his gas light at the Bailey to 9,000, by which time he had already installed another innovatory light in the Rockabil lighthouse, the first ever to generate regular flashs in groups.[61]

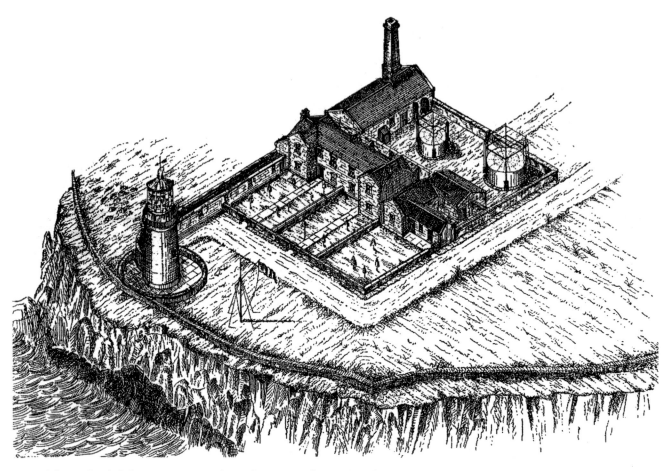

15.16 *The Bailey lighthouse in 1897 as drawn by J.R. Wigham.*

A high degree of self-reliance was required of all lighthouse installations, and not just those in inaccessible locations. Very often, more than one jetty was provided in order to ensure, as near as was possible, that at least one would be always sheltered from changing weather conditions. Other important features included cranes and derricks, steps, paths and an enclosing wall, which provided vital protection (especially on cliff tops) for lighthouse personnel on windy days. In the late 1990s, all remaining manned Irish lighthouses became automated but, up to that time, accommodation had to be provided for lighthouse keepers and, in earlier periods, for their families. The lighthouse was thus required to have a reliable water supply and even vegetable gardens. For the most part, living accommodation was provided in the main body of the tower, but at Blackrock, County Sligo, where a stone beacon had been converted into a lighthouse in 1835, two bedrooms were cantilevred outwards from the body of the tower on cast-iron brackets in 1863. With the widespread adoption of Wigham's patent, producer gas plant became a common feature of Irish lighthouse installations, many of which had small gasholders. In later periods, when acetylene and later still electricity was used to power the light source, additional buildings were added to house generating plant.[62]

In 1833 a self-taught Belfast engineer, Alexander Mitchell (1780-1868), who had been blind from the age of 23, patented a new fixing device for moorings, commonly referred to as the 'screw pile'. Mitchell's invention, which was said to have derived the idea from the domestic corkscrew, generally consisted of a wrought-iron pile up to 20 ft (6.09 m) in length and around 6 in in diameter, while the functional end was equipped with a cast-iron helical screw, which terminated in an open drill bit. By this means, the pile could be 'screwed' into position into most varieties of seabed, save solid rock, and its advantages for fixing permanent structures on shifting sand banks, such as light beacons, were quickly realised. In 1838, screw pile experiments were conducted for a lighthouse on the Maplin sands in the estuary of the River Thames, which were ultimately successful, while in 1834-40, Mitchell erected a pile light at Fleetwood on Wyre in Morecambe Bay. Experiencing one rare failure, on the uncompromising Kish Bank in Dublin Bay, he then went on to successfully install pile lights on the Holywood Bank in Belfast harbour (1844), at Dundalk (1849) and on the Spit Bank at Cobh (1852): these latter two still survive. The new pier at Courtown harbour, County Wexford, was anchored with screw piles in 1847, as later was the seaside pier at Margate (1853-56) and the pier extension at Ryde on the Isle of Wight in 1859. In all, some nineteen of the 42 surviving British Victorian seaside piers were anchored with Mitchell's screw piles. By the end of the nineteenth century, they had been adopted worldwide. Upward of 150 pile lights were erected in North America in the period 1848-1910.[63]

15.17 *Wigham's workshop models of Irish lighthouses.*

Another interesting form of fixed beacon, the so-called 'metal men', were employed at Tramore, County Waterford, and at Perch Rock in Sligo Bay. At Tramore, a total of five towers, each around 3.65 m high, were completed in 1835, the centre tower of which was finished with a cast-iron figure wearing a sailor's uniform with his right arm pointing outwards to the sea. Of course, not all beacons were fixed, and as early as 1735, Ireland's first recorded light ship had been positioned at the entrance to the River Liffey, roughly where the Poolbeg lighthouse now stands. In 1811, a Dutch ship (which was renamed *Redmond* after the Lord Lieutenant who had requested that it be set in place) was brought to Dublin where it was fitted out with a light, before being floated out to position on the Kish bank.[64] There is, indeed, at least one recorded instance at Drogheda, County Louth, of a wooden lighthouse that could be moved on wooden rails to accommodate shifts in the channel.

(7) Coastguard Stations

The Irish coastguard service – whose original duties included monitoring the movements of foreign warships and patrolling the Irish coastline to prevent smuggling – was founded in 1831. It initially formed part of the customs service, but its functions were later transferred to the Admiralty in 1857. In 1858-67, the Irish coastguard, which now comprised of some 230 individual coastguard stations, was reformed into three districts.[65] Throughout the years of the Great Famine, the Board of Works had upgraded 170 existing stations and built a further 60 new ones during the 1850s.[66] In their essentials, these were intended as permanent lookout points on the Irish coastline, a status which was to be reaffirmed in the 1850s when the Board of Works began to build two-storey rectangular accommodation blocks, usually with a watch tower at one end. These were also intended to be defensive buildings, as the coastguard was an armed body and were thus a potential source of weapons for an insurrectionary force. The Ringsend coastguard station of 1874, and the Greystones, County Wicklow, station each have musketry loopholes at first-floor level, while some County Cork examples also had machicolations.[67] That at Tor Head, County Antrim, also functioned as a Lloyd's signal station, which communicated information on each passing ship back to the company, and in the pre-ship-to-shore radio days these stations also reported the safe arrival of transatlantic vessels. Nevertheless, the decline in smuggling activity in the nineteenth century led to the closure of many of these stations, while the increasing provision of lifeboat services also rendered them obsolete.[68]

16

Utility Industries: Water, Sanitation, Gas and Electricity

The origin of utility industries in European cities arose from the need to regularise and control the basic amenities required for urban life beginning, in antiquity, with the provision of water supplies and sanitary services. As the fundamental nature and extent of these services expanded and evolved, the consumer-producer relationships associated with them became more direct. By the eighteenth century this already required intricate planning on the part of municipal authorities. Ideally, essential services such as water supply were kept under public control, but this was by no means always possible, while gas and electricity companies invariably began their operational lives in private hands. Yet regardless of ownership these industries, more than most others, owing to the fact that their product was supplied directly to the consumer, were obliged to keep pace with technological change. This was a consequence of their expanding customer bases and, as long-term demand for water, gas and electricity could nearly always be expected to increase (both for industrial and domestic customers), the networks designed for their operation also had to cater for daily peaks in demand.

(1) Water Supply

Before the establishment of municipal water supplies, the provision of cisterns, wells and pumps, generally to exploit groundwater supplies, was almost always a matter of individual initiative. In the 1770s, Edmund Pery, MP for Limerick, provided a water supply for the citizens at his own expense, establishing a pump at King's Island. He also financed a two-mile-long channel to provide water for the population of the city's Irish Town, while in 1775, in association with the city's other parliamentary representative, he presented a fire engine to each of the town's five parishes.[1] For those who could afford to construct them, artesian wells were the most common means of procuring a regular supply of water in both urban and rural locations. The well shaft was provided either with a winch or capped and fitted with a wooden force pump. An eighteenth-century, stone-lined well depicted on John Rocque's map of 1773 near Smith Street in Cork was excavated in the early 1980s and produced the remains of a two- or possibly three-piece wooden double-acting pump. The lower pump block was 2.7 m long and had a 0.13 m bore which was plugged at its lower extremity, whilst some 20 cm from the base four water intake holes had been bored. The upper cylinder, which could have been an intermediate pump block or a piston chamber, was connected to the lower block by means of a crude spigot joint, which was reinforced with a wrought-iron collar.[2] Its mode of manufacture is similar to those which have survived up to recent times, although the variety of wood preferred for these was larch – the Smith Street pump blocks were of elm: both varieties of wood were extremely resistant to rot. The pump mechanism of the Smith Street example is also similar to more recent instances, in which the water was raised upwards through the piston chamber, to be ejected through a spout at right angles to the pump lever.[3] Indeed, the development of early piped water supplies did little to discourage the continued construction and use of artesian wells. In truth, early piped water was often expensive, unreliable and generally characterised by extremely limited networks. During the late eighteenth century, piped water in Belfast had such a bad name that those who could afford to do so bought water from 'Cromac carts'. These latter were two-wheeled carts that carried a 20-gallon water barrel, which transported water from springs at Cromac near Belfast and sold it to households at a ha'penny a half gallon.[4] Water carts were also, it is clear, a common feature of eighteenth-century Dublin.[5]

Until the development of more sophisticated distribution networks, employing cast-iron mains, water-supply networks in Dublin, Cork and Belfast operated with wooden water mains serving cisterns and public fountains. The earliest recorded piped supply is at Belfast where, in 1678, George McCarthey and Captain Robert Leathes directed water from the Tuck Mill dam to the city in 'wooden pipes bound with iron'. From 1682, this supply was maintained by Grand Jury presentment and, in 1733, the waterworks were leased by William 'pipe water' Johnston, who constructed additional pipe branches.[6] During the eighteenth century, open storage reservoirs or 'basins' had been constructed in both Dublin and Cork to supply new networks of wooden water mains. In their essentials, these were simple storage tanks, probably built with stone-lined revetment walls and sealed along the bottom with puddled clay. Freshwater was directed into them either from adjacent streams, springs or abstracted from the non-tidal sections of a major river, as was the case in Cork, Limerick and, also, for a period, in the city of Dublin. In Dublin, Cork and Waterford, city basins were constructed on modest elevations, in order to facilitate the fall of water, by gravity, through the wooden mains. In 1722, the 'City Basin' south of St James' Street in Dublin was completed, and this latter, which was long, narrow and almost trapezoidal in plan, covered around 1.5 hectares in 1741. It is illustrated by Charles Brooking in the 'prospects' or sketches accompanying his *A map of the city and suburbs of Dublin* of 1728 (figure 16.1), where it is shown as having an irregular outline, and appears to have been constructed by excavation rather than embankment.[7] This was later to receive a supply from the adjacent Grand Canal harbour at James' Street and continued to do so until it was closed in 1869. A second city basin was constructed at Portobello, next to the canal harbour on the Circular Line of the Grand Canal, in 1806, to supplement the city's water supply until its closure in 1870.[8] At Cork, the first 'city basin' was built on the adjacent hillside, at a height of *c.* 60 ft (1.82 m) Ordnance Datum, into which untreated river water was pumped. Its capacity is not known, but it appears that one of the expectations of its builders was that it could, to some extent, serve as a settling tank for turbid water.[9] A second reservoir was completed alongside this in 1774, but their lack of elevation restricted the number of areas within the city that they could supply, whilst the reservoir itself was only about 5 ft (1.52 m) deep.[10]

In the late 1730s in Dublin and in the early 1760s in Cork, the respective municipal authorities opted for supplies pumped from the rivers Liffey and Lee. Dublin Corporation appointed an English engineer, James Scanlon, in 1739 to report on the feasibility of abstracting a new water supply from the Liffey at Islandbridge. Scanlon recommended that water be pumped from the head race of the existing Islandbridge mills (using the motive power of two of the five existing water-wheels) to supply sections of the city on the north bank of the Liffey, thereby reducing the pressure on the city basin. Plans were also made to pump water from this source to the city basin, but

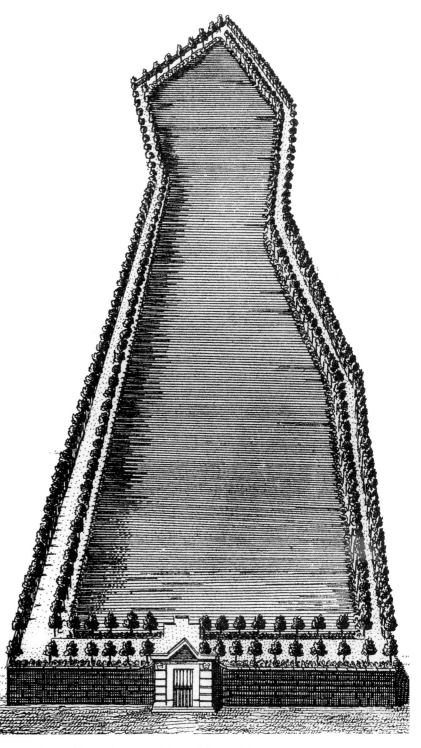

16.1 *The Dublin city basin as depicted by Brooking in 1728.*

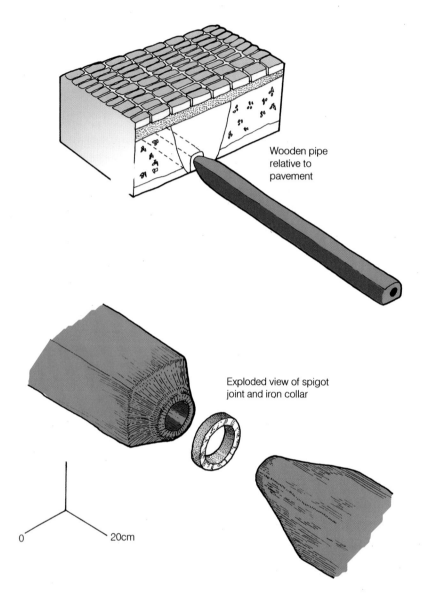

Wooden pipe relative to pavement

Exploded view of spigot joint and iron collar

0   20cm

16.2 *Eighteenth-century wooden water mains from Cork city.*

these were abandoned in 1765 when the decision was made to use the Grand Canal for this purpose.[11] In the early 1760s, the common council of Cork was empowered to establish a Pipe Water Company and, by 1762, the architect/engineer, Davis Ducart, had completed a set of plans for its proposed waterworks.[12] Six years later, in 1768, the Pipe Water Company's works was completed on the north bank of the River Lee, on the site now occupied by the turbine house, erected in 1888. The original foundation stone of the 1768 pumping station, which bears the inscription 'Cork Pipe Water Company Established 1768', along with the municipal crest, has been incorporated into east wall of the 1888 structure.

For the greater part of the eighteenth century and into the first half of the nineteenth, wooden water mains were used in Dublin, Cork, Belfast and Waterford (figure 16.2). Lead pipes had been employed in Waterford from at least 1758 onwards, while bored stone water pipes had been supplied by Christopher Colles' Kilkenny works (see Chapter 6) to Cork in the first half of the eighteenth century, but do not seem to have been widely used.[13] English elm appears to have been the preferred variety of wood selected for water mains, but both larch and fir were also employed. The water main from Islandbridge to the city of Dublin was constructed, in 1746, of Norwegian fir cut from lengths 10 -14 ft (3–4.2 m) long, but other mains in the city were made from elm, which was regularly imported during the eighteenth century for this purpose.[14] Early in the twentieth century, a probable eighteenth-century pine water main, 14 ft long, of 8 inches square section and with a 5 in bore, was unearthed in Dublin, while in Cork, in 1970 an 18 m section of the Pipe Water Company's original wooden water mains were exposed during road works on South Terrace.[15] Two complete sections of the latter, 5.6 m and 5.7 m respectively, were investigated *in situ*. These had been adze-dressed externally to a roughly square section of 25 cm, and formed at their extremities to create crude spigots. In this way, the tapered end of one pipe could be forced into the end of another, with wrought-iron straps fitted onto the collars to reinforce the joint. Each of these pipes was of larch, and had been bored from both ends to a thickness of 9 cm. The South Terrace pipes did not have side tappings, simply because the material used in their construction was unsuited to bearing substantial internal pressures.[16] In consequence, wooden water mains could only be used to feed cisterns and fountains and functioned with insufficient pressure to operate upstairs plumbing. Only with the introduction of cast-iron water pipes did proper forcing mains (i.e., where the water was pumped through the pipe under constant pressure) become possible. In the late eighteenth century, Andrew Coffey (father of Aeneas, the inventor of the first practical patent still, see Chapter 9), an engineer at the Islandbridge waterworks, began to investigate the advantages of cast-iron mains. In 1809, the *Metal Mains Act* came into force in Dublin, and thereafter cast-iron pipes quickly came to replace wooden mains in the capital.[17] In Cork and Belfast, however, the introduction of cast-iron mains was somewhat slower where, in both cases, the first iron water pipes were not laid until the late 1850s.[18]

Technical improvements aside, expanding the capacity of existing water supplies was the single biggest difficulty facing all of Ireland's city authorities in the first half of the nineteenth century. Nor, as we shall presently see, was there a single engineering solution to the problem of expanding urban water networks. The water supply of the capital is a case in point where, for several decades, the Grand and Royal Canals were used to fill the main city basins. In 1772, Dublin Corporation entered into an agreement with the Grand Canal Company to supply water to the city basin, an arrangement that began in 1777 and ended in 1869.[19] John Rennie, when called upon to report on the water supply of Dublin in 1803, was also convinced of the utility of the city's canals as a means of providing an ample supply of water, and concluded that the Royal Canal could supply most of the capital's needs. By 1805, the Corporation appears to have concurred in this view, and began to favour the Grand and Royal Canals as more practical, long-term sources than either the Dodder or the Liffey. A Boulton and Watt rotative beam engine originally purchased for the Islandbridge waterworks was eventually sold on to a Dublin distiller, without ever being used (see Chapter 9).[20] Portobello basin was opened in 1806 and, in 1814, a new city basin at Blessington Street on the north side of the Liffey, some 0.7 hectares in extent, was opened to abstract a supply from the Royal Canal.[21] The Blessington Street reservoir is the only Dublin city basin to survive.

Elsewhere in Ireland, two principal means were employed to supply water to municipal water reservoirs. The first of these, used from the early eighteenth century onwards in Dublin, and later in Cork, was to use water and steam-powered force pumps to supply either mains or elevated reservoirs. The second, called a *constant supply* – which was by far the most commonly employed in Ireland's cities and country towns – involved the impounding of streams or rivers in an elevated, artificial reservoir. In the latter case, especially in the two largest nineteenth-century cities, Dublin and Belfast, this eventually necessitated the abstraction of water from sources several miles outside their municipal boundaries.

The Cork Corporation Waterworks was the oldest, continuously used municipal water supply installation in Ireland. From its origins in the 1760s until the early 1990s, an uninterrupted supply of water from the River

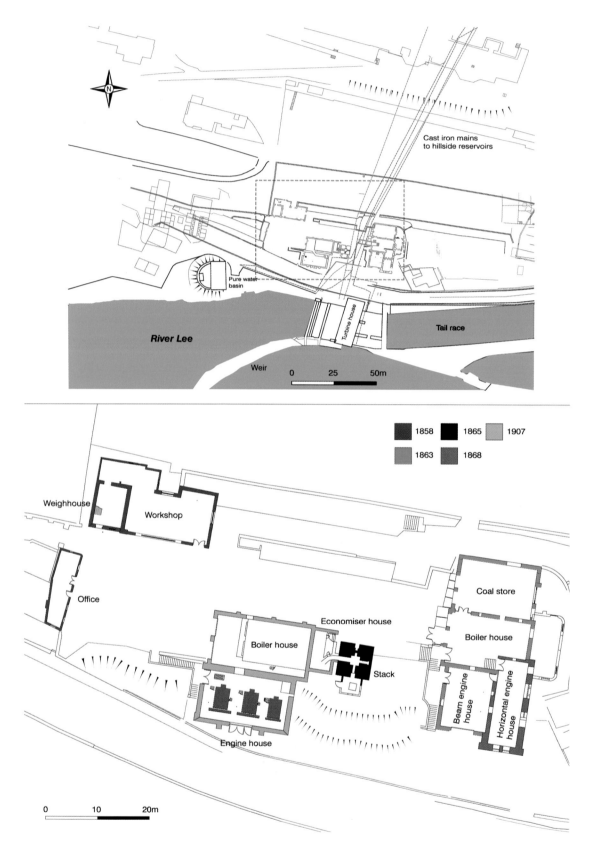

Labels within the figure:
Cast iron mains to hillside reservoirs

Pure water basin

River Lee

Turbine house

Tail race

Weir

0   25   50m

1858   1865   1907

1863   1868

Weighhouse

Workshop

Office

Coal store

Economiser house

Boiler house

Boiler house

Stack

Beam engine house

Horizontal engine house

Engine house

0   10   20m

16.3 *Cork Corporation Waterworks, general plan. The steam engines, their houses and associated plant were restored by Cork City Council in 2004-5.*

Lee has been pumped into storage reservoirs on the adjacent hillside. As in other expanding Irish cities in the first half of the nineteenth century, the ability of existing wooden pipe networks to supply the future needs of the city had become a matter of concern. Thus, in 1842 and 1843, the Corporation commissioned Thomas Wicksteed, the engineer of the East London Waterworks and one of the most important water engineers of his day, to report on the city of Cork's existing services. But it was not until 1858 that a new pumping station, the largest of its type ever to be built in Ireland, was completed by John Benson, the Cork City Architect. Benson built two new reservoirs, a low-level reservoir, extending over an acre and capable of holding up to 3.5 million gallons for the supply of the low-lying areas of the city, along with a second, high-level reservoir, with a capacity of 0.75 million gallons designed to supply the higher districts. The new pumping plant consisted of a 90 hp Cornish beam engine, by MacAdam Brothers of Belfast, which was the first engine of its type to be employed in Ireland for pumping a municipal water supply. MacAdam Brothers also supplied two Fourneyron turbines (110 hp in total), the first of their type to be used in these islands for this purpose. The turbines and an existing metal water-wheel were designed to fill the reservoirs for all but the summer months, when the steam plant was used for this task. During the 1860s auxiliary beam engines were acquired, the engine and boiler houses of which survive *in situ*. In 1888, a new turbine house was built on the site the original one of 1858, to which two new turbines, supplied by the American firm of Stout, Mills & Temple of Ohio, were added. Between 1902 and 1907, the water-works was significantly modified with the removal of the Cornish engine of 1858 and its replacement with three inverted vertical triple expansion engines by Combe and Barbour of Belfast (see Chapter 2).[22]

Cork Corporation Waterworks is the best-preserved Victorian water pumping station in Ireland (figure 16.3). Most of the surviving buildings date to the second half of the nineteenth century and to the early years of the last century – these include the beam engine house of 1863, the main stack, 1865, and the turbine house of 1888. The turbine shafts drive a flywheel through a large bevel gear, which in turn powers a reciprocating pump; four of those connected to individual turbine sets are twin double acting (figure 16.4), the other is single double acting. The high- and low-level reservoirs were phased out in the mid-1980s but, remarkably, the turbines continued to perform the function for which they were originally installed, and it was only in 1938 that the steam plant was initially decommissioned after the installation of electrically powered centrifugal pumps.[23]

16.4 *The interior of the turbine pumping house of 1888, at Cork Corporation Waterworks. One of the turbine sets is currently used to generate electricity.*

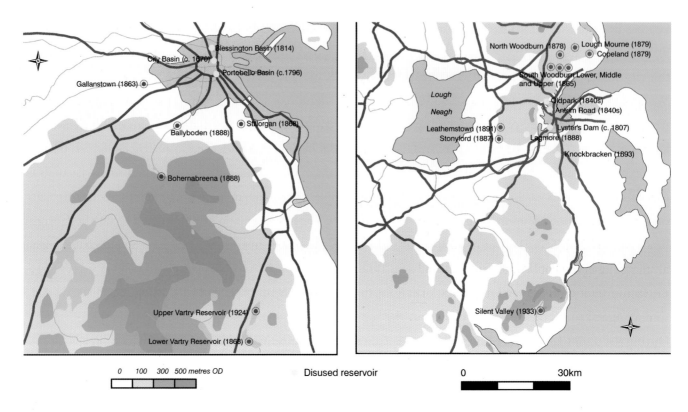

16.5 *The development of the Dublin and Belfast water supply networks, (after Hamond 1997).*

From at least the 1820s onwards at Limerick, a 40 hp beam engine was used to pump water from the River Shannon to fill two masonry reservoirs, on the northern outskirts of the city, near a seventeenth-century fortification known locally as Cromwell's Fort.[24] On present evidence, this is the earliest Irish reference to steam power being used to pump a municipal water supply. The main Galway city works at Terryland, designed by Samuel Roberts and completed in 1867, used two iron water-wheels to actuate its pumping machinery. In 1895, a steam engine was added as an auxiliary and in 1906, the water-wheels were replaced by water turbines.[25] However, this supply proved to be insufficient for the MGWR terminus at Galway which, in 1892, were obliged to obtain parliamentary permission to lay a water main from a former distillery at Newcastle, near the city, using its 36 hp cast-iron suspension water-wheel of 1851 to pump the supply.[26] A cast-iron water-wheel (which survives *in situ*) was also originally used to power pumps, from the late 1890s onwards, at the Bermingham waterworks near Tuam, County Galway. A similar arrangement also formerly existed at the Roscommon town waterworks.[27] In west County Galway, in the 1920s and 1930s, Maurice McSweeny, an assistant County Surveyor in the county's western division, had actually introduced wind-powered public water supplies, some of which remained operational in the 1950s.[28]

In Dublin and Belfast, the first moves to establish constant water supplies took place in the second half of the nineteenth century, beginning with Belfast where, in both instances, prominent English water engineers were employed as consultants. In 1851, John Frederick La Trobe Bateman (1810-89), who had first worked in Ireland conducting surveys for William Fairbairn (and eventually became his son-in-law) was called in by the

Belfast Water Commissioners to investigate how the city might source additional supplies of water.[29] Bateman recommended the construction of surface impounding reservoirs, but the Commissioners seemed unable to follow through. In the Belfast area this inertia proved to have ramifications beyond the desire to provide water for human consumption. The years 1851-65, when there were water shortages within the city, actually trebled insurance premiums. Water was, of course, also increasingly required for fire-fighting, and its scarcity in any built-up area could have serious consequences. However, an act of 1865 finally enabled the Commissioners to implement Bateman's recommendations to use streams and rivers in the Woodburn district, near Carrickfergus, County Antrim. A surface impounding reservoir, formed by earthen embankments with a clay puddle core, was built at Woodburn, which Bateman believed would provide about 6 million gallons per day (but which delivered just over half this). A further act of 1874 sought to remedy the situation through the creation of three addition-al storage reservoirs at Woodburn, a measure followed, some five years later, by the construction of reservoirs at Loughmore (600 million gallons) and Copeland (133.5 million gallons).[30] In all, between 1878 and 1891, a total of nine reservoirs were constructed to service a phenomenal expansion in both domestic and industrial demand (figure 16.5).[31] In 1881, the population of Belfast was about 200,000; by 1890, this had grown to 270,000, with a total daily consumption of 9.5 million gallons. An act of 1884 enabled the Belfast Commissioners to obtain control of the Stoneyford area near Lisburn, some ten miles to the south of the city, where the largest single reservoir to date was built, with a capacity of 810 million gallons.[32]

The Belfast Commissioners' search for new sources of water was extended to the Silent Valley in the Mourne Mountains in 1893. This necessitated the boring of a 2.25 mile long tunnel through the Donard and Thomas Mountain, which was completed in 1899. Water was then directed through a seven-mile stretch known as the 'Newcastle siphon' and then into a three-mile long tunnel, eventually ending up in the Knockreckan basin, some four miles from it. The initial work was completed in 1901, but in the years 1923-33, an enormous embankment was built across the Silent Valley, forming behind an artificial lake, two miles long, 240 acres in extent and with a capacity of around 3,000 million gallons. An entire railway system, upon which full-size locomotives ran on the English standard gauge of 4 ft 8½ in, was built to service the construction works.[33]

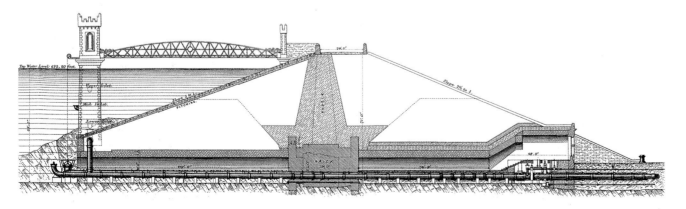

16.6 *The embankment for the Vartry reservoir, from Neville 1874.*

16.7 *Entrance to valve house, at the Vartry reservoir, County Wicklow.*

Dublin, as we have seen, was unique in Ireland in its reliance on water from inland navigations. But by the late 1850s, as in Belfast and Cork, existing demand for water for domestic and industrial purposes was already outstripping the available supply. The Dublin city engineer, Parke Neville, in consultation with Thomas Hawksley (1807-93), one of Britain's most respected waterworks engineers who was, by his own account, responsible for the design and erection of around 150 water-works in Britain, formulated plans for drawing water from Lough Vartry in County Wicklow, over 30 miles to the south of the capital (see figure 16. 5).[34] An impounding dam 1,640 ft (499.87 m) long was built by throwing up an earthen embankment with a clay puddle core, the crest of which was used to carry the road from Roundwood to Wicklow (figure 16.6). The dam, thus formed, created a 410-acre reservoir with a capacity of some 23 million gallons. The works, which were completed between 1862 and 1867, also included a draw-off tunnel, built underneath the embankment. This latter accommodated a series of outlet pipes leading from the masonry draw-off tower (figure 16.7) from which reservoir water was drawn to the adjacent treatment works. In the period 1908-25 a further reservoir, designed by John George O'Sullivan, was created to the north of Lough Vartry.[35] The conveyance of the Lough Vartry water to the capital required the construction of an aque-duct 33 miles long, which involved boring a tunnel some 2.5 miles long, 6 ft (1.82 m) high and 5 ft (1.52 m) wide through solid rock. Part of this work was undertaken with the use of a boring machine that was later used by its inventor, Colonel Beaumont, in exploratory work on an early channel tunnel scheme in England. The aqueduct supplied service reservoirs at Stillorgan, which provided a supply for the southern suburbs of the capital.[36]

Outside of major conurbations and their satellite towns, special initiatives were required for large military barracks such as at Ballincollig, County Cork, were a breastshot water-wheel (backed up by a horse wheel in the summer months) was installed sometime before 1834, to pump water to an artillery barracks from a mill-race in the adjacent gunpowder mills (see Chapter 11). From the outset, the planners of Ireland's largest army barracks on the Curragh of Kildare provided a purpose-built waterworks to supply the needs of some 10,000 infantry and auxiliary personnel. A Liverpool company was contracted to sink a well in 1855, over which was built a brick engine house (supplied by two Lancashire boilers). A vertical engine pumped water to hexagonal cast-iron water tanks, located in the centre of each of the ten original barrack squares, each tank with a capacity of 10,000 gallons.[37]

In Ireland's urban townships and rural towns, the provision of a centralised water supply (usually of the constant variety) is a phenomenon closely associated with the second half of the nineteenth century. Rathmines township, for example, on the outskirts of Dublin, failed to reach agreement with Dublin Corporation on a supply from Vartry network and, instead, entered into an arrangement with the Grand Canal Company. Bateman was consulted on the matter, and a waterworks was completed at Gallanstown in 1863 (some 4½ miles from Rathmines), extracting water from the 8th lock of the Grand Canal. However, from an early stage, it appears that the filter beds constructed near the lock produced water of indifferent and frequently inconsistent quality, while the original water pressure proved insufficient to service the needs of nearby Rathgar. A substantial masonry water-tower – one of the first of any type to be built in Ireland – was constructed to increase water pressure, and filtered water was pumped up to this by two steam engines.[38] On the initiative of Dalkey township engineer, Richard Walsh, residents of the higher areas of Dalkey, County Dublin, were supplied by a 22 ft (6.70 m) diameter, American-made Hammond's Standard Windmill, erected in 1886 but out of use by around 1900.[39]

The village of Ballyvaghan, County Clare, was supplied by a reservoir, lined with puddle clay and with a capacity of 350,000 gallons, constructed on the initiative of Lord Annaly in 1872. Under the *Public Health Act* of 1874, the village was provided with water via cast-iron mains, and a fountain, (which still survives) was erected in 1875.[40] The Ballyvaghan supply was abstracted from springs, as was that of Letterkenny, County Donegal, where a one-month supply stored in a reservoir, for a population of around 2,000, came into existence in 1876, along with hydrants and public fountains.[41] Other county towns to secure modern water supplies in the late nineteenth century included Ennis, County Clare (1880), Rostrevor (1881) and Bangor (1883) in County Down. and Dundalk, County Louth (1891).[42] The closing decades of the nineteenth century and the early decades of the twentieth also witnessed the increasing use of water-towers in the supply of Ireland's country towns, with notable examples surviving at Downpatrick (*c.* 1910) and Hunts Park, Donaghadee, completed in concrete in 1912 by J. and R. Thompson for Donaghadee Urban District Council. The castellated water-tower and fire station at the Curragh Camp in County Kildare, which had a capacity of upwards of 42,000 gallons, and which was completed *c.* 1900, is a further early survival of note.[43]

(2) Sanitation

As with water supply, the provision of improved sanitation and, in particular, the disposal of sewerage, came to be firmly linked with the improvement of public health in nineteenth-century Ireland. In 1866, the *Sanitary Act* was passed which effectively applied the main provisions of the English statutes of 1855 to Ireland, although, from the outset, the expense of their implementation saw to it that they had little initial effect.[44] In all of the main cities and towns, sewers were emptied directly into the nearest source of running water, the disposal of sewerage relying solely on the efficiency with which natural drainage could carry it away from its origin and preferably to the sea. The efficacy of this solution proved to be less than satisfactory on tidal rivers such as the

Lee and Liffey, where tidal movements not only caused sewerage and other effluvia to adhere to the base of quay walls, but also impeded the flow within sewers. In the city of Cork, for example, tidal movements caused the backing up of sewer gases into both houses and streets.[45]

By the middle of the nineteenth century, existing urban networks could no longer cope with expanding populations. The architect, Thomas Deane, had been commissioned to design and construct a main sewer through the city of Cork in 1826 but, by mid century, this was already expected to operate well beyond its intended capacity. In Dublin, in 1853, Parke Neville, the city engineer, drew up plans by which the city's sewerage services might be improved and, although a new system of main drainage was to be legislated for in 1870, it was temporarily abandoned owing to the burden it would impose on the capital's finances. Indeed, the independently-minded townships of Rathmines and Pembroke were already, by 1879, proceeding with their own drainage works. Not until 1892 could Dublin Corporation find the necessary funds to proceed with its main drainage scheme, which was completed in 1900: its implementation relieved the lower reaches of the River Liffey.[46] At Cork, new sewers were provided in some 260 lanes and streets in the period 1854-77, with main sewers laid along the Blackrock Road and York Street during 1865-66. Nonetheless, by the end of 1876, upwards of 5,000 houses did not have connecting sewers, while by the end of 1885, around 2,000 houses still remained unconnected to the main drainage network.[47] The sewer network was extended in 1895-6 but, by the early 1900s, culverted sections of former channels of the River Lee, which had long acted as *de facto* sewers, were beginning to silt up. These latter were shored up and cleaned during the same period, while new ceramic sewerage pipes were laid.[48]

Under an act of 1877, the Dublin townships of Rathmines and Pembroke established a joint drainage board, under which a scheme was developed to carry sewerage from each area to the estuary of the River Liffey, where it discharged near the South Bull Wall. For drainage purposes, the surrounding areas were divided into two sections, one 2, 400 acres in extent which comprised the higher regions and a lower lying area of some 900 acres. The higher area was drained by gravitation, but that at the lower level required a pumping station – the first of its kind in Ireland (and which now survives as a ruin) – built on the banks of the River Dodder, whereby sewerage was pumped to a high level sewer. The Rathmines and Pembroke scheme was completed in 1879 and dealt with an estimated 150 million gallons of sewerage per day.[49]

(3) Gas

Early Town Gas Manufacture in Ireland

In 1795, James Watt's assistant, William Murdoch, set up an experimental form of coal gas lighting at the Old Crummoch factory at Ayrshire, whose success enabled him to install a similar system in Boulton and Watt's Soho Foundry in Birmingham in 1798. However, it was the French scientist, Philippe Lebon, who, in 1786, devised the first practical means of employing gas for lighting, which he called the 'thermolamp'. Lebon manufactured gas by heating wood in a closed retort, but died before he could successfully market his idea.

However, in 1804, Friedrich Winzler (who later changed his name to the more English-sounding Frederick Winsor) a German part con man, part entrepreneur, introduced the London public to a form of gas lighting based on Lebon's design. In 1807, the first London streets were lit by gaslight and six years later, in 1816, Preston in Lancashire became the first town outside London to have gas street lighting.[50]

As has been seen in Chapter 8, Laurence Atkinson was already considering the use of gas lighting in his Celbridge woollen mills as early as 1809. The earliest recorded instance of the use of gas lighting in Ireland, however, is at the home of Waterford iron founder Benjamin Graham, in 1815, who later provided gas lighting to a number of other public and private premises in the city.[51] In February 1816, a Cork newspaper reported that a 'Gas apparatus fitted up by Mr James O'Brien of Tuckey Street draws every night a crowded assembly of the citizens to witness its effects'.[52] O'Brien was using gas to illuminate his shop and its associated workshops in what is clearly the earliest recorded industrial application of a private gas supply in Ireland. By this period, the potential of this new technology seems likely to have been widely known in Ireland and we should, perhaps, not be too surprised that its adoption in Waterford and Cork could be contemporaneous with that of Preston. The Crowe Street Theatre in Dublin installed its own gas plant in 1818 and, in the period 1824-6, three gas companies had been established in Dublin, each operating it own separate mains.[53] In 1825, the Wide-Street Commissioners entered into an arrangement with the United Gas Company of London to provide the city of Cork with gas lighting, commencing operations in 1826 and here, as in other Irish towns, English companies quickly established monopolies of coal gas manufacture and supply.[54] Gas works were later established in all Irish cities and the majority of the larger Irish country towns, most notably Waterford (1830), Kilkenny (1838) and Limerick (1841).[55] By the late 1850s, many of Ireland's county towns were lit by gas lighting.[56]

Coal gas was manufactured in a process called *carbonisation*, whereby bituminous coal with a low ash content was distilled in a refractory vessel called a *retort*. The gas itself was also cleaned in a series of processes that facilitated the extraction of important by-products such as tar and ammonia. Gas retorts were typically 'D'-sectioned tubes, originally made with cast-iron and later (after 1853) with refractory clay and, from the 1920s onwards, with silica. Early retorts were, in addition, heated from a furnace set immediately beneath them in an arrangement called a *direct fire setting*. However, as most of the coke manufactured in the retorts was needed to stoke the furnace, only a small proportion of it was available for sale. A new gas producer furnace invented by Siemens in 1861 largely overcame this problem, and was in turn superseded by the Klonne recuperator after 1885, when even more efficient coke firing became possible.[57] The coal was heated in the retorts at temperatures in excess of $1,000°C$, the effect of which was to drive off the gas and other substances, some of which were later collected and sold.

The crude gas was conducted through a series of cast-iron pipes set in a metal box known as a *condenser*, in which the gas was cooled. As the gas began to cool, the tar began to condense, and was then led to an underground storage tank. A series of rotary pumps, called *exhausters*, set in motion by a steam engine, were employed to move the gas from the retorts to the condenser through the remaining cleaning processes (called *purification*) which removed tar, ammonia and hydrogen sulphide, and finally to the gasholder for distribution. The spent

16.8 *Gasholder dating from the 1880s at the former Barrow Street gasworks at Ringsend, Dublin.*

iron oxide was often sold to manufacturers of sulphuric acid or even used as a weed killer, which in Ireland was called *meather*.[58]

The gas was stored in *gasholders* (commonly known as gasometers), large composite metal tanks manufactured with rolled iron plates. The lower part of the bell rested upon a water-filled tank, the water acting as a seal preventing gas from seeping out. In 2002, the pit of a gasholder associated with a mid-nineteenth century linen spinning mill at Chapelizod, County Dublin was excavated and was found to consist of a 'well' feature, a deep masonry lined pit. The supporting frame for the bell would have rested on the four projecting brick walls built inside the holder well. On present evidence, this feature cannot be older than the mid-1840s. It seems likely that a gasholder of this type could only store one day's supply, but could, nonetheless, enable peak demand to be met on the site without employing additional retorts.

The admission of gas into the bell caused it to rise upwards, and the addition of telescoped sections to the bell from 1824 onwards, which rose and sank telescopically, allowed larger quantities of gas to be stored. Telescopic gasholders appear to have been relatively common in larger Irish gasworks by the late 1860s and, by 1867, the Cork gasworks had a telescopic gasholder 156 ft (47.54 m) in diameter, the largest of its type to have been built in Ireland up to that time.[59] The 'Clayton' (1871) and 'Alliance' (1885) gasholders at Dublin's Barrow Street gasworks were also of the telescopic variety (figure 16.8). These latter are characterised by elaborate wrought-iron frameworks, which were used to guide the upward movement of the telescoped sections of the gasholder. Spiral guided gasholders came into use in Ireland in the 1890s and early years of the twentieth century, and dispensed with the iron guide framework by rotating on spiral rails as the holder filled and emptied. The 'Dickens' gasholder in the Barrow Street works, completed in 1925, was one of the largest of this type to be built in Ireland.[60] Up to the 1920s, however, nearly all forms of gasholder relied on water tanks at their bases and water seals on the individual telescopic sections which, in freezing weather conditions, tended to impede their movement. By this period, waterless gasholders had been developed, the most notable Irish example being that erected by a German company on Sir John Rogerson Quay in 1934.[61] This latter – the largest of its type to have been built in Ireland – had a capacity of 3 million cubic feet, and was dismantled in the late 1990s.

Early gasworks in Ireland were generally sited in low-lying areas of cities and towns, to take advantage of the tendency of gas to rise. These generally had direct access to a navigable waterway (as in the case of Belfast,

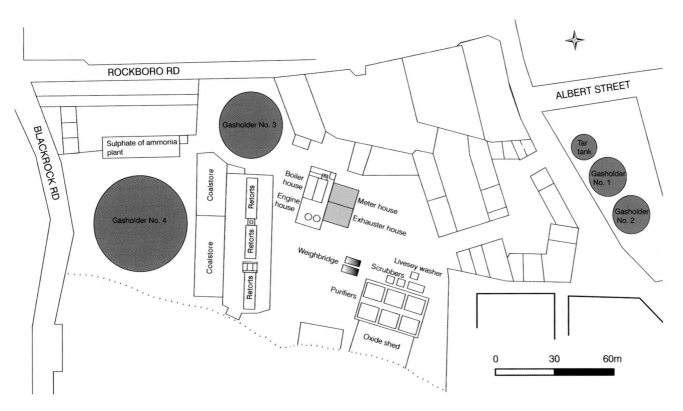

16.9 *The Cork gas works in 1920.*

Cork, Limerick and Clonmel) to accommodate cheap transport of coal and limestone (originally used for cleaning the gas). The Cork gasworks (figure 16.9), on Monerea marsh, also had the valuable advantage of being sited on a source of high-quality limestone that could be directly quarried on the site. Although perhaps not originally intentional, the siting of early gasworks on the margins of towns also enabled them to more readily expand as demand for their product increased. In the second half of the nineteenth century, it also became very common for large industrial installations such as textile mills and institutional buildings like hospitals and universities (and even some large country estates) to build their own private gasworks, particularly if they lay outside existing supply networks.

From the outset, gas companies in Ireland became responsible for complex networks of piping and gas lamps. The Cork gasworks in 1858 was capable of producing up to 1,415,000 cubic metres of gas per annum, distributed through about 35 miles of mains.[62] The greater Dublin area had 3,750 gas lamps in 1884, maintained, on a daily basis, by 23 full-time gas lighters.[63] Gas lighting was normally operated on a regular schedule, that changed only with the seasons: 8pm–4am in spring and summer time and 5pm–7am during the winter months. Gas companies (as in the case of waterworks) were also obliged to introduce metering systems to keep track of consumption by individual consumers, and these had regularly to be inspected to guard against tampering. In Cork alone, the demand for the local gaswork's product was such that, in the period 1858-60, the number of gas meters installed by the company increased from 1,370 to 3,244.[64] Early piping systems did, nevertheless, have a tendency to leak, and considerable quantities were consequently lost in the passage from the gasworks to the

425

consumer. Early metal gas burners were also inefficient, owing to their liability to rust and thus eventually dim the flame, but the development of a non-corrosive burner by William Sugg in 1858 helped to alleviate this defect considerably.[65] Sugg's invention aside, the pace of technological change within the industry and, in particular, with regard to the development of gas for cooking and heating, only speeded up when electricity began to threaten its traditional dominance in the 1880s. The introduction of the Welsbach incandescent mantle (named after its inventor, the Austrian Dr Carl Auer von Welsbach) in 1887 effectively revolutionised the gas industry, by producing a gaslight much brighter (and cheaper) than its predecessors although it was not developed for street lighting until 1895.[66]

The development of acetylene gas – created in a chemical reaction between calcium carbide and water – in the late nineteenth century produced a cleaner, cheaper and less dangerous alternative to traditional coal gas and, by 1902, it was already being used by a number of small firms in Nenagh, Hillsborough, Ballymena and Dundalk.[67] In the early years of the twentieth century Irish gas companies faced an increasingly hostile commercial environment. Extra duties on imported goods necessary for their operation and an independent Irish government, anxious to reap the rewards of its hydro-electric scheme on the River Shannon at Ardnacrusha near Limerick, militated against their future development. While coal gas works held their own in many Irish towns up to the Second World War, the street lighting in Cork had been converted to electricity in 1898.[68] Many had closed by the 1950s, while in Northern Ireland, rapid increases in the price of coal had rendered coal gas manufacture uneconomic. Free State government policy on the development of electricity, after the formation of the ESB and the national implications of a direct supply from Ardnacrusha after 1929 for most Irish county towns, proved to be heavy burdens. With the advent of natural gas from the Kinsale field in the early 1980s, the remaining Irish gasworks (which by this stage had already converted to producing oil gas) were finally closed, followed by gasworks in the Northern Ireland industry in 1988.

In Ireland north and south, nineteenth-century gasworks almost invariably survive in the

16.10 *Retorts at Carrickfergus gas works (left). These are the only surviving examples in Ireland and currently form part of an innovative gasworks museum;* **16.11** *Detail of the Carrickfergus retorts (right).*

most fragmentary form, while the larger city works, such as the Cork and Belfast examples, have recently fallen victim to redevelopment. At Cork, only the original gatehouse of *c.* 1826 (now the oldest surviving gasworks building in Ireland) survives as a façade, the entire mid- to late-nineteenth-century works being demolished in 1999 to accommodate a new headquarters for Bord Gáis Éireann. In many country towns, only the original boundary wall of the gasworks tends to survive, although in some instances the occasional storage building (as at Youghal, County Cork) or engine stack (as at Naas, County Kildare) remain extant. At Limerick, there are substantial remains of original store buildings and an early twentieth-century retort house. However, at Carrickfergus, County Antrim, important remains of a coal-fired gas works survive *in situ*, the only example of its type, indeed, to survive in Ireland and one of three such sites to survive in either Britain or Ireland (figure 16.10 and 16.11). The Carrickfergus works was opened in 1855, originally creating a supply for street lighting but later for heating and cooking for domestic consumers. The 0.6 hectare site has three surviving retort houses that contain five benches of 36 horizontal retorts, along with a variety of purification and distribution plants dating from the 1850s to the 1960s. The works, which closed in 1964, has been carefully restored and opened to the public by the Carrickfergus Gasworks Preservation Society.

(4) Electricity Supply

For many smaller towns and villages throughout Ireland, street lighting by coal gas was simply unaffordable, especially for inland settlements, where the transportation of coal generally proved to be too costly. The advent of electricity generation in the 1880s, however, while it did not necessarily guarantee cheaper energy, certainly enabled smaller communities and isolated industrial units to create electricity for lighting from an existing, renewable source of energy. Yet by 1926, the annual Irish consumption of electricity per head was 23kWh (16kWh in the Free State and 43kWh in Northern Ireland) which was, after Portugal, the second-lowest level in Europe.[69] From the outset, therefore, and in the period leading up to the harnessing of the River Shannon in the late 1920s and the creation of Ireland's revolutionary national electricity grid, hydro-electricity supplies were by no means readily or widely exploited in Ireland. The German authors of the 1924 report on the viability of the hydro-power Shannon scheme were somewhat surprised that a country such as Ireland, with enormous potential for hydro-electricity generation, had long been reliant on imported coal to meet its basic energy requirements.[70]

Up to the development of the incandescent electric light bulb, first by Joseph Swan in 1879 and slightly later by Thomas Edison, the use of electric lighting involved arc lights which were only suitable, owing to their acute brightness, for illuminating large public buildings. The incandescent light bulb, however which, unlike gas lighting, gave off neither heat nor fumes, could now be used in offices and in the home. Furthermore, the development of the electric motor enabled electricity to be employed for transportation, which in turn created additional demand for electricity for tram cars. Although Ireland provided ideal conditions for hydro-electric supplies, the earliest recorded uses of electric lighting here involved current generated by steam. A pattern of employment developed early on where larger urban centres (with ready access to seaborne coal supplies) generated electricity by steam, whilst rural communities developed hydro-electric sources. The first recorded industrial use of electric lighting in Ireland, as was seen in Chapter 9, was during construction work on Guinness' Brewery at Victoria Quay between 1877 and 1879. In 1880, a single electrically powered arc light was erected outside the offices of the *Freeman's Journal* on Princes Street in Dublin.[71] This is the earliest recorded use of electric street lighting in Ireland and was followed, in 1881, by the second documented case of portable electric lighting in Ireland. In February of that year, a contractor called John Delaney employed electric arc lights, powered by a portable generator, to facilitate night-time work on a bridge under construction on the River Lee at Cork.[72] In the same year, the newly formed Dublin Electric Light Company set up a generating station

16.12 *Giant's Causeway generating station at Bushmills, County Antrim.*

at Schoolhouse Lane in Dublin, which provided current for seventeen arc lamps erected on wooden posts on Kildare Street, Dawson Street and St Stephen's Green. In the following year, the number of lampposts had been increased to 114, by which time at least two large companies, Pim's and Jacob's biscuit factory, had been connected up.[73]

Thus far, Irish developments, as in contemporary Britain, involved electric lighting exclusively, until 1883, when the Giant's Causeway, Portrush and Bush Valley Railway and Tramway Company became the third in the world to use electricity for traction on a commercial basis, opening only one month after Volk's Electric Railway at Brighton.[74] The Giant's Causeway Tramway was, nonetheless, the first public electric railway in the world to be powered by hydro-electricity. The Salmon Leap generating station was built, and still survives, on the River Bush in 1882-3, originally powered by two water turbines by Alcott and Company of New York, each generating 45 hp under a head of 8 m (figure 16.12), these latter powered, via belting, a bi-polar Siemens generator. In 1900, the Alcott turbines were replaced by more powerful units manufactured by John Turnbull's Edinburgh foundry, and the station continued in operation up to 1949.[75] A further hydro-electricity electric tramway, and the second of its type in the world, the Bessbrook and Newry, opened in 1885. This was set up by the Richardson family, owners of the local Bessbrook linen mills, and was powered by current generated at Millvale up to its closure in 1948.[76]

In 1882, the Westminster parliament introduced the *Electric Lighting Act* in an attempt to prevent the new electrical companies from creating the type of monopolies gas companies had formally enjoyed. Under the terms of the act, electrical companies were granted licenses to supply current in specified areas for 21 years (later extended to 42 years in amending legislation of 1888), after which time local authorities had the option to buy them out.[77] By this period, the pace of industrial development was more favourable to the adoption of electrical lighting. To a certain extent, private industry was beginning to take the initiative in

16.13 *Dublin Corporation's Fleet Street generating station, early in the twentieth century.*

acquiring dedicated supplies as at the Phoenix Park Distillery in Dublin, where Elwell Parker dynamos were, by 1887, powered using a traditional water-wheel to generate electricity for incandescent lighting.[78] Galway also had a hydro-electric scheme in 1889 which powered lighting on part of the docks and in a number of nearby premises, while at Morrough's woollen mill near Douglas, County Cork, the mill's 250 hp engine was also used to power a generator set for lighting in 1890.[79] In 1891, Carlow became the first Irish provincial town to install public electric lighting using a supply generated at the former Milford flour mills (see Chapter 9).[80] Some time before 1892, Murphy's brewery in Cork installed a Parsons steam turbine with two sets of accumulators, which provided enough current to electrically light the entire Lady's Well complex.[81] This is the earliest recorded use of a steam turbine for electricity generation in Ireland.

By the 1890s, however, the main demand for current was in the larger cities and towns. In 1890, the Alliance and Dublin Gas Company set up a generating station in Dublin's Hawkins Street that supplied current for Grafton Street, Henry Street and George's Street. As early as 1888, Dublin Corporation had already decided to create a municipal electricity service, under its direct control, and to dispense with the services of gas for public lighting purposes. To this end, it opened its own power station on Fleet Street in 1892. The Fleet Street station was powered by six horizontal engines supplied by John Fowler and Company of Leeds, fed by Babcock and Wilcox boilers, actuating dynamos by the British Electrical Engineering Company (figure 16.13). Some 15 miles of high-tension cable supplied current to an area within a radius of Fleet Street, within which many former cast-iron gas lampposts were used to support arc lights. Individual customers were provided outside their premises with transformers which reduced the 2,000 volt current to 100 volts, and enabled incandescent lamps to be used.[82] Demand for the station's product steadily increased to the extent that not only were the premises expanded but by the turn of the twentieth century an entirely new power station site was being considered. The Rathmines and Pembroke townships had already, by this period, decided to go it alone with their own independent power station, which opened in 1900 and provided a DC supply through a three-wire cable, even though the Dublin Corporation network operated with an AC supply.[83] Somewhat controversially, the site of the former packet station between Britain and Ireland at the Pigeon House was chosen for the new Dublin Corporation generating station. Nevertheless, with hindsight, this decision proved not to be as disastrous as some contemporaries may have believed because, as the site was sufficiently removed from the load centre, this necessitated the use of high tension transmission. The Corporation was obliged to employ the most up-to-date three-phase, four-wire system of distribution, and hence Dublin became one of the first cities in the world to adopt this system – later to become an international standard.[84] Extensive remains of the tall, brick-built Pigeon House power station still survive, which includes a large section of the original control panels and switch boards installed by Ferranti in 1903.

Outside Dublin in the 1890s, both hydro- and coal-powered plants developed in a piecemeal fashion. In 1897, a hydro-electric generating station was built on the River Roe at the Dog Leap, near Limavady, County Derry. This originally employed an American-made turbine to generate electricity for both public and domestic use, but in 1897, three MacAdam turbines were added to meet an anticipated increase in demand for its product.

It was operated by the privately owned Limavady Electricity Supply Company, created in 1897, until being taken over by the Electricity Supply Board for Northern Ireland in 1946.[85] The mill-race of a flour mill at Bealick, near Macroom, County Cork, was used, from 1898, to power a generator set for public lighting in the town of Macroom.[86]

At the end of the 1890s, all the main urban centres in Ireland, with the exception of Limerick, had electricity-generating stations and, of these, only Cork and Galway were outside municipal control.[87] Coal-fired generating stations had, in addition, been established at Belfast, Derry, Ballymena and Bangor.[88] In 1896, Cork Corporation obtained a provisional order for an electricity supply both for a series of electric tramways and for public lighting, and was to arrange for a private company to provide the city with a network of electric tramways and public lighting. This was common practice throughout Britain where small power stations often supplied current for tramways and public lighting.[89] The recently formed Cork Electric Tramways and Lighting Company Ltd built its electricity-generating station – a twin-gabled brick structure 100 ft (30.48 m) long – at Albert Road. Its chimney was a self-supporting steel structure 130 ft (39.63 m) high. The station's generating plant was powered by three McIntosh and Seymour side-crank tandem compound condensing engines, supplied with steam from three Babcock and Wilcox boilers. This type of boiler had the advantage of maintaining a good water circulation while at the same time occupying a relatively small floor area. They were commonly used in power stations of the period, and were also employed in the Fleet Street power station in Dublin.[90] In many contemporary generating stations, power transmission was normally by means of a belt drive from the engine to the generator. This was certainly the case at Dublin's Fleet Street Power Station, opened in 1892, and in the majority of the English generating stations. But at Albert Road, the engine crankshafts were directly coupled to six-pole, 200 kW compound wound generators, which yielded 500 volts at 135 rpm. A direct current (DC), three-wire cable system with 460 volts between the outers and the mains, was used for lighting distribution, most of the insulated cables were sheathed in lead.[91] The main brick building of the former Albert Road generating station in Cork survives and is now the headquarters of the National Sculpture Factory. Elsewhere in Ireland, the Dublin United Tramway Company built its own power station in 1906 beside the Grand Canal Docks. This included two steel chimneys over 60 m (demolished in 1943), which became known as the 'Tramway Twins'.[92]

The Shannon Scheme

One year after Independence, in 1923, there were around 300 electrical producers within the new Free State, creating current using coal, oil, gas and water-powered generators. A year later there were some 91 generating stations, of which only four created alternating current. The remainder produced direct current which could not be viably transmitted over distances that exceeded a few hundred yards.[93] Yet before the end of the 1920s, Ireland, one of the least industrialised areas of Europe, and previously one of the lowest consumers of electricity became the first country in the world to have a state-controlled national electricity grid. What became known as the 'Shannon Scheme' was the brainchild of the Irish engineer, Thomas McLaughlin (1896-1957), who had

16.14 *Mechanical excavator at work on mill-race for Ardnacrusha power station (Courtesy of Paul Duffy).*

joined the German electrical engineering giant, Siemens-Schuckert, in 1922. McLaughlin was able to study German power plant design and electrical machinery at first hand, and was particularly impressed with the electrical network established in the Bavarian province of Pomerania (which was in many ways similar to Ireland) that supplied some 60 towns, 1,500 villages and upwards on 3,000 farms.[94] In 1844, Sir Robert Kane had estimated that upwards of 34,000 hp could be created using the waters of the lower Shannon, utilising the fall from Killaloe to Limerick. But, unlike earlier proposals to put this to good use, McLaughlin had fully considered the technical difficulties and had devised practical solutions, with the help of his colleagues at Siemens. Upon his return to Ireland in 1923, he was able to use his close contacts with a number of ministers in the first Free State government to have his proposals presented to the fledgling nation's new power brokers. Bold as it was in conception, McLaughlin's technical vision for the Shannon Scheme further involved the creation of a state-run company to control the production and distribution of electricity generated by the project. This led to the establishment, by legislation, of the Electricity Supply Board (ESB) in 1927, Ireland's first semi-state body with, rather fittingly, McLaughlin as its first managing director.[95]

The contract for the Shannon Scheme was awarded to Siemens-Schuckert in 1925, the largest foreign engineering project to be won by a German firm since the construction of the Baghdad railway. In addition to building the hydro-power station and its associated works at Ardnacrusha, they were also responsible for erecting some 3,400 km of overhead cable in the period 1926-29.[96] At its height in 1928, some 5,000 labourers were employed.[97] The non-existent road network necessitated the construction of a purpose-built railway network some 100 km long, running on two narrow gauges, one of 900 mm (*c.* 2 ft 11½ in) the other 600 mm. This was built by Siemens-Schuckert's sister company, Siemens-Bauunion, and accommodated up to 130 steam loco-motives and as many as 3,000 wagons and other rolling stock. This network was vital during the construction works, and it has been estimated that it was used to carry 7.5 million cubic metres of earth and 1.25 million cubic metres of rock (figure 16.14).[98]

Ideally, the supply for the power station at Ardnacrusha, near Limerick, would have been created by the construction of a large dam across the River Shannon, which would have impounded a supply behind it. However, as local topography precluded this, the waters of the Shannon were brought to the generating station site by what was, in effect, a giant mill-race (figure 16.15). At Parteen Villa, near the village of O'Briensbridge,

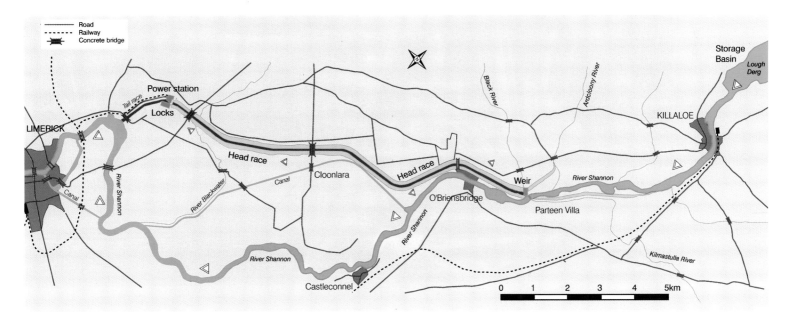

16.15 *General plan of mill-race, weir and power station at Ardnacrusha, (after Duffy 1987).*

some 5 km to the south of the town of Killaloe, a weir was constructed on the Shannon which was designed to raise the water level by 7.55 m, the same as that of Lough Derg. The weir intake has six sluice gates and a fish pass some 190 m long, this latter the largest of its type in the world to have been constructed up to that time. From Parteen Villa, a head race channel 12.6 km long led the water to the hydro-electricity generating station at Ardnacrusha. This latter comprises an intake sluice house, penstocks (figure 16.16), a generating build-ing, a waste channel and navigation locks. The head race channel terminates in a 30 m high dam which sup-plies three 41 m long, 6 m diameter penstocks, each inclined at a slope of 31° and delivering 100 tons of water per second. Ardnacrusha began operations using three Francis turbines in 1929, to which a Kaplan turbine was added in 1934, this latter being the first of its type to utilise a head in excess of 30 m. The tail race is 2.4 km

433

long and returns the waste water to the Shannon further upstream. Three concrete road bridges, all of which survive, were built over the head race, while a further example was constructed over the tail race at Parteen.[99] The Pigeon House generating station was synchronised with Ardnacrusha in 1930 and was finally shut down in the same year; thereafter, the city of Dublin and the greater part of its environs were supplied with current from the Ardnacrusha station. In that same year, the Ford factory at Cork was in receipt of a supply from the Shannon Scheme which, in 1931, generated some 96 per cent of the current used in the Free State.

16.16 *Volute casing for turbines under construction at Ardnacrusha (Courtesy of Paul Duffy).*

17

Aspects of Industrial Settlement: Housing, Urban Transport and Telecommunications

The commercial and industrial development of Ireland's principal cities and towns, in the eighteenth and nineteenth centuries, led to the creation of an extensive and, by the 1850s, increasingly complex urban infrastructure. The growth of Ireland's utility industries, as we have seen in the previous chapter, generally occurred in tandem with the expansion of cities and towns. However, with the establishment of industry within cities, it proved necessary to provide additional infrastructure such as urban transport networks and later telecommunications, yet there were other pressing needs. In industries created on the outskirts of towns and in more remote areas, skilled workers could only be attracted by the provision of housing. This led to the establishment of what were often specially designed workers' settlements, either as adjuncts to pre-existing ones or on greenfield sites some distance from urban areas. A number of Irish industrialists, by the middle of the nineteenth century, were even beginning to exhibit paternalist traits and were providing workers' housing and social infrastructure through a heightened sense of social responsibility.

(1) Industrial Workers' Housing

During the seventeenth century, Irish ironmasters had been obliged to provide, in varying degrees, accommodation, land and a basic social infrastructure for their skilled workers. These latter measures were largely an inducement to attract the requisite personnel from English – and even European – ironworking regions to settle in this country, and by this means relatively large immigrant communities were to become temporarily settled throughout the island (see Chapter 4). This same settlement pattern was to be continued in the nineteenth century in key Irish extractive industries, where again English and Welsh mining specialists were to be housed in what were often self-sufficient industrial communities (see Chapter 5). Mining settlements, of course, tended to be sited away from existing settlements, but so also were early factories and other industrial installations in the eighteenth and nineteenth centuries, in order to harness a reliable supply of water power. In this way, whole new villages were created in which housing and other amenities were provided by companies, anxious that their workforce be close at hand and also, to certain extent, be easier to control. Workers' housing in nineteenth-century Ireland could also be built under the auspices of philanthropic societies or local authorities, although the accommodation provided was intended to improve the living conditions of the working classes in general and was not specific to any factory or, indeed, industry. This is generally referred to as *social housing* to distinguish it from *industrial housing* where the aim, while not always entirely philanthropic, was generally to attract skilled workers to a particular site.[1]

In eighteenth-century Ireland the earliest form of purpose-built (as opposed to vernacular-style) industrial housing was constructed to accommodate lock keepers (see Chapter 13) and turnpike toll house keepers (see Chapter 12). These latter were designed by canal, river navigation and turnpike company engineers and would have crossed the 'vernacular threshold' insofar as they were specially designed and intended as permanent structures.[2] Level crossing keepers' houses, built for the railways in the nineteenth century fall into the same general category. In Ireland, however, early village-type industrial settlement is almost exclusively associated with the development of textile industries. As early as 1750, Charles Smith noted that, at the large sailcloth factory at Donnybrook near Cork, there were 'houses and gardens for the master-workmen, for which they do not pay rent'.[3] The damask weavers, Coulsons of Lisburn, County Antrim, were also providing workers' housing in 1764, followed by John Barbour in 1784, who also created a village for his workers near Lisburn.[4] Thus far, the common theme is the industrialising linen industry and, as we have already seen, Thomas Adderley provided workers' housing for his Ulster weavers at Innishannon, while landlord-sponsored bleach textile villages were already in existence at Blarney, Doneraile, Clonakilty and Macroom in County Cork before the 1770s (see Chapter 8). Robert Brooke had also attempted to build a model industrial village for his cotton mill workers at his short-lived enterprise at Prosperous, County Kildare, in 1782 (see Chapter 8).

In comparative terms, little is currently known about the morphology of eighteenth-century Irish workers' housing, although it seems likely that both single- and two-storey dwellings would have been constructed. Some of the best examples of two-storey, terraced workers' housing of the mid-1780s survive at William Burton

17.1 *Workers' houses at Ballincollig Gunpowder Mills, County Cork, completed in 1806.*

Conyngham's Rutland Island fishing settlement in County Donegal, which were originally provided with back gardens. In the early 1790s, the Monard Iron Works near Cork (see Chapter 10), was laid out both as an industrial unit and a workers' community, strongly rooted in the Quaker ideals of plain dealing, simplicity, equality and self-help of its founder, Thomas Beale. The surviving workers' houses, many of which date to the 1790s, were well-built, two-storey structures and each had access to a garden and fresh water. In 1806, the British Board of Ordnance built housing for its skilled workers at the Ballincollig Gunpowder Mills, County Cork (figure 17.1). The two rows of terraced workers' cottages – Waltham Abbey (or 'long range) Row and Coopers Row (or 'short range') – were constructed around a central green adjacent to the complex's incorporating mills. These were originally one-up one-down houses, constructed with random rubblestone, built in pairs but sharing a common entrance with a yard at the back. Terraced one- and two-storey houses, indeed, appear to have been the almost universal form of industrial workers' housing to have been built in nineteenth-century Ireland.

Most of Ireland's nineteenth-century industrial villages are associated with the Ulster linen industry, many of which were built between 1813 and 1870.[5] As we have seen, the initial impetus was to attract a suitable workforce but, by the 1840s, an emerging paternalism can be discerned in the development of planned or 'model' villages, which also provided a social infrastructure for company employees. As the majority of the workforce was made up of women and children, an increasing number of socially aware mill owners were beginning to

17.2 *Workers' houses at Portlaw model village, County Waterford (left);* **17.3** *A corner of the Portlaw polyvium, extending into an open street space (right).*

believe that such employees needed protection.[6] Dunbar, McMaster and Co. built the village of Dunbarton (named after Hugh Barton, its owner) near Gilford, County Down, where rows of terraced houses were built in the period 1830-40 and, by 1862, the company had erected some 200 houses at a total cost of £10,000. Each house received a monthly inspection from the company, which also executed all repairs and maintenance free of charge.[7] The company's willingness to take responsibility for its employee's lives even extended to the provision of schools, churches, shops and voluntary organisations.[8] Other companies, as we shall now see, were also prepared to take a keen interest in the welfare of their workforce.

In 1847, the Quaker industrialist, John Grubb Richardson, began work on his model village at Bessbrook, County Armagh, a development which was to influence the creation of further Quaker-inspired settlements at Portlaw, County Waterford, and reputedly Cadbury's village of Bourneville. The layout of Bessbrook had been carefully planned (it was to have no pawn shop or public house) and the workers' houses were built to a relatively high standard, with individual privies and yards being provided for many of them.[9] The company was also to build a convalescent home and an orphanage for their new settlement.[10] The Richardsons were related by marriage to the Malcomsons of Waterford and the Bessbrook example was clearly the main influence behind their new village development (which replaced earlier workers' housing for their cotton mill) at Portlaw (figure 17.2). The street pattern was laid out in a *polyvium*, that is, as a series of triangular blocks in which the apex of each triangle converges upon a new open space (figure 17.3). The first houses built in the new village were of two storeys, but these were later replaced with a distinctive single-storey form which had four rooms, a range in the kitchen and the means of providing hot water. At the rear of each dwelling was a privy equipped with a dry closet. The Portlaw houses have a distinctive roof in which fabric was stretched over curved Belfast-type wooden, latticed trusses, the fabric being commonly coated with tar, in this instance a by-product of the company's gasworks in the village. By the 1860s, the company had already built over 300 of this variety of house, large numbers of which survive. The Portlaw roof was also later employed in housing at Bessbrook, Harold's Cross, Dublin, Carrick-on-Suir, County Tipperary, Clara, County Offaly and at Mahony's woollen mill at Blarney, County Cork. The Malcomsons also used the same house design at their coalmines at Gelsenkirchen, in the Westphalia region of Germany.[11]

In the second half of the nineteenth century, nearly all the new workers' housing provided by employers free of charge or for rent was built with brick and was commonly two-storey in form. Textile firms continued to be the main housing providers, such as new textile mills at Donnybrook and Millfield, County Cork, in the mid-1860s, and at Blarney, County Cork, and Lucan, County Dublin, all of whom provided accommodation for their skilled workers. These houses were, however, built near established communities where the workforce could enjoy the benefit of existing amenities. In Ulster, indeed, new workers' housing continued to be erected into the twentieth century, where cheaper building costs and the absence of the stricter building regulations introduced into England continued to make them a viable proposition.[12] Outside the textile industries, the main providers of housing for their workforces were the transport companies and, to a lesser extent, a small number of the larger breweries and distilleries. We have already seen how Irish railway companies constructed single-storey dwellings for their permanent way men (see Chapter 14) but, in Dublin alone, the main transport companies, such as the GS & WR (142 cottages), the MGWR (83 cottages) and the Dublin United Tramways Company (104) were firm believers in providing accommodation for their skilled workers. Guinness, beginning in 1872, were also to build upwards of 180 houses for their employees.[13] The idea of the model village also enjoyed a brief but curious revival on the banks of the River Nore, at Greenvale, near Kilkenny, where the Irish architect, William A. Scott (1871-1921), designed a village of two-storey concrete houses for English woollen mill workers. By 1910, 22 of these cottages, built in the arts and crafts style and originally thatched and lime-washed, had been constructed at Talbot's Inch, County Kilkenny.[14]

(2) Urban Transport Systems

The arrival of suburban railways in the 1830s facilitated the direct transit of people living in smaller towns and villages to Ireland's principal urban centres. However there were no rail links between the main city termini in either Dublin or Cork until the close of the nineteenth century and the early decades of the twentieth, and most urban dwellers made their way around the city streets on foot or, if they could afford to do so, in horse-drawn cars. In the early 1870s, however, early forms of horse-drawn trams were beginning to appear on the city streets of Dublin, Cork and Belfast. Many of these were electrified in the 1890s and the routes lengthened to service not only the expanding suburbs but neighbouring towns and villages.

As we have seen, the first railways were operated with horse traction, but in Ireland these were almost exclusively employed for drawing goods wagons. In 1853, Ireland's first horse-drawn passenger tram began operating on a three-quarter mile track of conventional rails and sleepers, linking the Great Northern Railway's (Ireland) Fintona Junction, on the Omagh-Enniskillen branch, with Fintona, County Tyrone. A single horse was required to pull what was locally called the 'van' over light gradients. The original tram had to accommodate three classes of passenger, and appears to have been more like a stage coach on rails, but more conventional tram forms were later employed. The line continued in operation up to 1957 (the longest continually employed of its type anywhere) and one of the last trams in use, no. 381, is preserved in the Ulster Folk and Transport Museum.[15]

17.4 *Cork horse tram in the early 1870s.*

As the track of conventional permanent way surmounted wooden sleepers, it could not be employed on public roads where it would interfere with other forms of wheeled transport. In urban areas, therefore, tram track had a groove to position the wheel flange, where the upper face of the track was flush with the road surface. Tram lines did, nonetheless, have the important advantages of increasing the load a single horse could pull from about 17 cwts to approximately 40 cwts, while passengers could now enjoy a smoother ride through the streets.

Horse-drawn trams were, in addition, much easier to brake (and thus safer) than a horse-drawn omnibus. For normal operation, up to eleven horses were required for a single tram, where each pair of horses worked for two hours – pulling for a distance of around six miles – after which fresh horses were used, the eleventh horse (at least in theory) acting as a standby. For urban networks, ancillary structures included stabling, granaries and haysheds, blacksmith's forges and occasionally workers' housing were also provided.[16]

Dublin had the first horse trams, from 1872 and, by 1878, no fewer than three separate companies were in operation. These latter amalgamated in 1881, when the Dublin United Tramway Company was formed.[17] The total Dublin mileage of horse trams was 33, the last trams running in 1896. Further networks were established in Cork (figure 17.4) and Belfast in 1872 and in Derry, Galway, Loughgilly and Rostrevor, the last horse trams in Ireland operating in Derry up to 1919 (figure 17.5).[18] Of these, the Cork system lasted for only three years, while all but the Derry trams were later electrified. The Belfast and Derry tram lines were built to the English standard gauge of 4 ft 8½ in, Galway to the 3 ft gauge, and fewer than half were constructed to the Irish standard gauge of 5 ft 3 in.[19]

Although steam locomotives had been employed on conventional Irish railways since the 1830s, their use to pull trams on city streets had been prevented by existing laws and by the legislation under which the horse tramway companies were formed. They were certainly too cumbersome to negotiate tight bends, while their noise and emissions, in addition to having an unsettling effect on horses, were objected to by local residents. By the late 1870s, however, all such objections appear to have faded and in 1877 successful experiments were conducted on the Donnybrook line between Donnybrook and Morehampton Road with the locomotive *Pioneer*.[20] The new locomotives were carefully modified for operation in urban areas. The basic engine frame was much smaller and narrower than that of a conventional railway locomotive and used vertical instead of horizontal

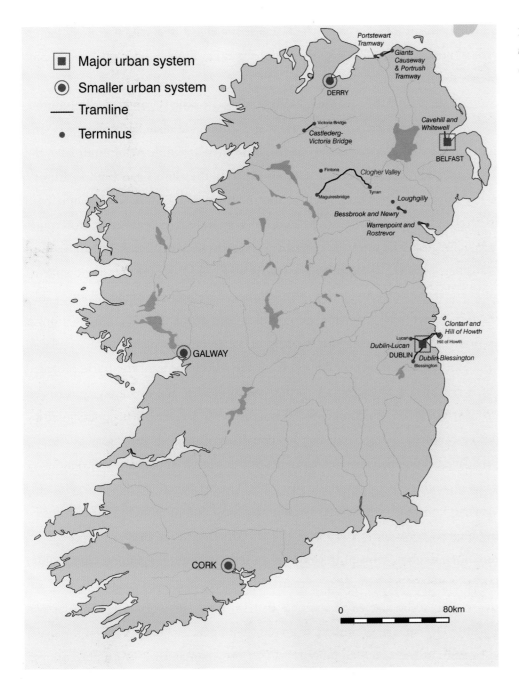

17.5 *Distribution of Irish urban tramway systems, (after Kilroy 1996).*

boilers (powered by one of the earliest recorded uses of smokeless fuel in Ireland) to accommodate this. Superheated steam was also employed to minimise steam emissions, and the provision of taller chimneys ensured that smoke was discharged above the roof level of the tram cars. The locomotives' wheels could also be smaller, as they were not required to move at great speed, while the law required that these also be covered over with side shirtings which reduced noise and splashing.[21] In all, no fewer than six steam tramways were built in Ireland, beginning with the Dublin and Lucan (1881-1900), the Dublin and Blessington (1888-1932), the Portstewart tramway (1882-1926), the Cavehill and Whitwell (1882-1911), Castlederg and Victoria Bridge (1884-1933) and the Clogher Valley line (1887-1942).[22] Many of these steam tramways ran on standard gauge track, although the lines in the Dublin area were built to the Irish standard gauge. Others, such as the Clogher Valley railway, traversed public roads along a large section of their routes, yet ran on a conventional permanent way when cutting across the countryside.

In 1879, Werner von Siemens built the world's first working electric railway for the Berlin Trades Exhibition, which was followed by the first ever public electric railway, in 1881, at Lichterfelde near Berlin. Magnus Volk constructed the United Kingdom's first public electric railway at Brighton in 1883, while one month later, the Portrush-Giant's Causeway Tramway (1883-1949) opened in County Antrim, the third of its kind in Europe but the first hydro-electric powered railway in the world. The line was the brainchild of William Acheson Traill (1844-1933), who had worked with the Geological Survey of Ireland and was anxious to develop the iron mines and limestone quarries of the general region. The tramway company's directors included Sir William Thomson (later Lord Kelvin and brother of James, who had developed the vortex turbine, see Chapter 1), a noted authority on electrical power who had been prominently involved in the technical development of the Atlantic cable, and Werner von Siemens himself.[23] Power was generated using water turbines at Salmon Leap station at Walkmills (see Chapter 16) and, from 1919, at Portrush, with the help of a gas engine which was later replaced with a steam engine. A side conductor rail, raised on wooden posts on the seaward side of the track, provided current for the electric car which ran on a 3 ft gauge.[24] A further hydro-electric tramway was constructed between Bessbrook and Newry (1885-1948), on which ran special wagons with flangeless wheels, designed by Henry Barcroft, a director of the Bessbrook Spinning Company, that could negotiate both rails and public roads. On the Bessbrook system, a central, live rail supplied current, but on its Millvale level, employed a pick-up device on the roof of the car, which came in contact with an overhead live cable. This appears to be the earliest recorded attempt to produce a 'bow current collector', which later became the most commonly used means of supplying current to electric trams. The Bessbrook and Newry tram was also the first to use bogies.[25]

The electrification of existing horse-tram systems in Ireland was somewhat slower, beginning with Dublin in 1896 and followed by Cork in 1898, where an entirely new tramway network had been created. Belfast was the last pre-existing horse-drawn system to be electrified in 1906. In Irish urban networks, the tram car was powered by an overhead cable with a DC voltage of around 500 volts. *Outreaches* or booms carried the overhead cable and were supported by tram poles, which commonly had an ornamental finial or capping on top. In the early years, manually operated points were used at corners but, in 1903, Dublin became the first city in the world to employ automatic points. Dublin, indeed, had the seventh largest electric tramway network in the world and in its day was seen as the most efficient of its type in Europe.[26] Tramway gauges throughout Ireland, however, varied considerably. The Belfast trams ran on the British standard gauge, while Dublin trams, with the exception of the Dublin and Lucan line, on the Irish standard gauge, only this was actually thirteen-sixteenths of an inch narrower than 5 ft 3 in to enable the flanged wheels of conventional standard gauge rolling stock to run on tram rails.[27] The track of the Cork system was laid at a gauge of 2 ft 11½ in (i.e., a half inch narrower than the Irish narrow gauge) for this same reason, although none of the narrow gauge lines operating out of the city are known to have availed of this facility.[28]

Electrification required that the tramway companies construct purpose-built electricity generating stations, the first of which was completed at Shelbourne Road, Ballbridge, for the Dublin Southern Districts Tramway in 1895. The Shelbourne Road station appears to have been the first three-phase plant in Europe and could daily power 50 trams, each weighing ten tons and running at eight miles per hour. The Dublin United Tramways Company opened a new generating station at its Clontarf depot in 1897, which was followed by the Albert Road station of the Cork Electric Lighting and Tramways Company in 1898. This latter, as we have seen (see Chapter 16), was also contractually obliged to supply current for public lighting and domestic use. The Shelbourne and Clontarf plants were replaced by a new electricity generating station on Ringsend Road early in 1901.[29]

The demise of the Irish tramway system began before the Second World War, beginning with Cork in 1931, the increasing importance of motor transport and the humble bicycle being among the principal causes.[30] Only the Belfast and Dublin networks had sufficiently large populations to sustain electric tramways, although these also were eventually to close because of competition from other forms of transport, Dublin trams closing in 1949 followed by Belfast in 1954. The last trams to run in Ireland ceased operations on the Hill of Howth line in 1959.[31] In the greater Dublin area, the main survivals of the tramway era are the former tram depots at Sandymount, Dartry, Clonskea, Terenure and Blackrock, while tram poles can still be seen on the old route between Phoenix Park and Lucan. The Gaint's Causeway tramway depot at Portrush is still extant, while at Cork the original tramway and its electricity generating station still survive at Albert Road.

(3) Telecommunications

The words *telegraph* and *semaphore* are both derived from the Greek, the former meaning to 'write (or describe) at a distance', the latter 'to bear a sign'. A telegraph is, therefore, a device which enables someone to read a 'written' message at some distance, whilst a semaphore merely allows the reading of a pre-determined signal. Before the development of the electric telegraph, the various forms of elementary visual telegraphs required an unobstructed line of sight. However, even when this was possible over relatively long distances, the vagaries of the weather could quickly obscure it, particularly if the signalling station was at a fixed location. The French Revolutionary Wars provided an important stimulus to the technical development of telegraphy systems in both Britain and France, beginning with Claude Chappe's *télégraphe aérien* in 1793 (Chappe was the first to coin the word 'telegraph'), a 'T'-type telegraph. In Chappe's device, the 'T' –frame was formed with a vertical wooden mast 5 m high, with a cross piece at the top, on to which two centre-pivotted rotating arms or indicators were affixed at each end. By turning these arms at different angles, it was possible to indicate more than 25,000 different significations.[32] Nevertheless, even though the Admiralty was fully acquainted with the workings of Chappe's telegraph, as early as 1794, they decided to adopt a much simpler shutter telegraph, effectively ignoring all British attempts to emulate it, including an ingenious device invented by Richard Lovell Edgeworth.[33]

Edgeworth had begun to experiment with telegraphs in the 1760s during a sojourn at Hare Hatch in England,

17.6 *Napoleonic War period signal tower at the entrance to the Old Head of Kinsale, County Cork, with slate cladding.*

but it was not until his return to Ireland to manage the family estate at Edgeworthstown (and only in 1794 when there was a threat of invasion from revolutionary France) that he resumed his efforts. He developed a device in which four separate pointers, with pivotting triangular arms, were aligned in a row. The arms were rotated at set angles each to a maximum of eight different positions. Of these, seven were used to denote figures and, when viewed from left to right, they could represent thousands, hundreds, tens and units. Edgeworth's telegraphic vocabulary consisted of 48 double pages, which included eight classes: common words, less common words, technical terms, persons, officers, places, ships, phrases and sentences. In 1794, he conducted a successful test of his device (which he now called a *tellograph*) over a 12 mile distance between Edgeworthstown and his friend, Lord Longford's, residence, Pakenham Hall, County Longford. He went on to collaborate on its further development with another colleague, John Foster, Speaker of the Irish House of Commons, who helped draw up a vocabulary for the telegraph. Foster lived at Mount Oriel, Collon, County Louth, and from here, Edgeworth set up a line to Dublin, over 40 miles away. Both men conducted a trial of the device over a distance of 15 miles, between Collon and Skryne, County Meath. Yet despite several attempts to encourage the adoption of his device, at the highest levels in Ireland and in England, a permanent 'tellograph' system was never established here. However, in 1804, when another French invasion scare surfaced, he was eventually requested to set up a line between Dublin and Galway – a distance of 120 miles – assisted by his brother-in-law, the Royal Navy captain and later famous hydrographer, Francis Beaufort. In a trial conducted before Lord Hardwicke, messages were said to have passed along the line in eight minutes. Furthermore, as the device could either be set up or dismantled in minutes, it was possible for a commander in the field to vary the line in accordance with his needs, while the components of one station could be carried by two men.[34]

The failure to adopt Edgeworth's invention must surely rank as one of the great lost opportunities in the development of British military technology, and even more so if one considers the official response to the likelihood of a French attack. In the aftermath of the failed French invasion of 1796 and in the years leading up to the Napoleonic Wars, a network of signalling stations was established around the Irish coast. The main period of activity occurred in the years 1804-6, with many of the towers being, for the most part, 'defensible guardhouses' or signal towers. The first of these were constructed in west Cork in 1804, and generally took the form of a square, two-storey masonry tower, with an entrance at first-floor level, and a machicolation over the door. Many of the Cork towers were also weather slated and had an enclosing wall of either masonry or a turf bank (figure 17.6). Good access roads were provided for them and that at Bray Head on Valentia Island still has its original masonry culverts, which carried the road over hillside streams. The signalling system consisted of a mast (usually an old topmast) up to 50 ft (15.24 m) high, surmounted by a cap that helped to secure the flagstaff and a 30 ft (9.14 m) spar set at an angle from the main mast. From this were hung a rectangular flag, a blue pendant and four black balls, all of which were arranged in various combinations to form different signals. A total of 81 signalling stations were established in Ireland, of which the Pigeon House Fort in Dublin was the first post in the chain, but, by 1809, most of these had been abandoned, although some were re-used during the American War of 1812-14.[35]

In the early years, the electric telegraph had been very much a land-based technology, but Samuel Morse soon began to experiment with a submarine cable, laying one across the East River in New York in 1841.[36] Britain was connected to Europe in 1851 when a cable was laid in the English channel to link Dover and Calais and, in the same year, the English and Irish Magnetic Telegraph Company was formed to create cable links between Ireland and Britain. A series of cables were laid across the Irish Sea in the early 1850s, linking Portpatrick in Scotland with Donaghadee in County Down, Holyhead with Howth, and Fishguard with Blackwater in County Wexford.[37] The next great challenge – considered in its day on a par with human flight – was to link the continents of Europe and America with a transatlantic submarine cable. In 1853, using data obtained from a voyage of the US brig *Dolphin*, Lt Matthew Fontaine Maury, head of the US National Observatory, was able to produce the first accurate maps of the floor of the Atlantic Ocean. The results of Maury's survey demonstrated that there was an extensive plateau, without any strong currents, running from Newfoundland to Ireland, a distance of some 1,600 nautical miles.[38] Ireland was thus the ideal location for the European end of the cable, and early on in the planning stages Valentia, with its deep, sheltered port, was chosen as the site for the cable station.

The technical problems facing the transatlantic cable company were enormous. The cable itself had to be heavily insulated from sea water which, owing to its salt content, could also act as a conductor. Gutta percha, a natural latex (of which the Britain had a monopoly through its control of Singapore) proved to be the best available insulator, while the cable itself was heavily armoured with galvanised iron wire. This made it very heavy relative to its length, weighing 1-2 tons per kilometre, and its sheer bulk meant that no single ocean-going vessel then available was able to carry the entire 2,500 miles of cable needed to bridge the Atlantic. In the first attempt to lay the cable in 1857 (which failed), the cable-laying ships had to meet in mid-Atlantic (figure 17.7). The second

17.7 *The* Niagara *laying the Atlantic telegraph cable in 1857, in what proved to be an unsuccessful attempt to link the two continents.* Illustrated London News, *22 August 1857 (top);* **17.8** *The landing of the Atlantic cable at Foilhommerum, Valentia Island in 1865,* Illustrated London News, *5 August 1865 (above).*

attempt, in 1858, did succeed and the instrumentation at the Valentia end was first set up in the slate yard at Knightstown. However, the cable only ever transmitted signals across the Atlantic for three months before being rendered useless by the high currents passed through it. These were believed, by the Atlantic Company's chief electrician, to strengthen the signal but had the effect of wearing down the cable's gutta percha insulator. The cable failed in deep water and had to be abandoned.[39]

Further attempts to lay a working cable were interrupted by the American Civil War but, in 1865, Brunel's *Great Eastern* (the only ship then existing that could carry the entire length) became available for cable laying. However, owing to the size of the cable-laying vessel, the landing points for the cable had to be changed at both ends, whereupon Foilhommerum Bay, opposite Port Magee on Valentia Island, became the official cable station at the Irish end. The 1865 attempt to lay cable was unsuccessful, the cable breaking about 600 miles from Newfoundland, but in 1866, the *Great Eastern* was able not only to complete the laying of the cable but also to raise the 1865 cable from 15,000 ft (4.572 km) off the ocean floor (figure 17.8).[40] In 1865, the First Officer of the *Great Eastern* was the Irishman, Robert Halpin (1836-94), who went on to become its captain in 1867. As master of the vessel, Halpin later oversaw the laying of cables between Brest and Newfoundland and Portugal and Brazil.[41] A relay station was constructed at Foilhommerum Bay, the main walls of which still survive (figure 17.9), while to one side of it can be seen a circular depression which originally housed a reel for the cable. The houses built for the cable station staff, along with the main office, also survive at Knightstown.

A further Ireland-Newfoundland cable was laid by Siemens of London, in 1874, for the Direct United States Telegraph Company, which linked Trinity Bay, Newfoundland, with Ballinskelligs in County Kerry. The German Union Telegraph Company, which had been pressurised by the Imperial German Post Office about the delays in transmissions from Valentia, laid its own cable linking Emden in Germany with Valentia in 1882, which remained in operation up to 1904. However, while additional cables were laid in 1920 linking Valentia with Le Havre and with Sennen in 1923, the introduction of teleprinters towards the end of the First World War removed the need for skilled telegraph operators. The Valentia station became more involved with mechanical relaying, while the Azores became the main focus for transatlantic telegraphic communications. Nonetheless, the Western Union cable station on Valentia remained open up to 1965.[42]

Inland telegraphic services in Ireland, under the *Telegraph Act* of 1868, became a government monopoly controlled by the Post Master General. The Irish Post Office now undertook to provide telegraphic services throughout the island and, by 1870, it had 21 wires linking Ireland with Britain. Ireland's first telephone exchange opened on the top floor of the Commercial Buildings in Dublin's Dame Street in 1880. It was the creation of the United Telephone Company and began operations with just five subscribers. Telephones services expanded slowly in the greater Dublin area but, by 1893, Belfast, Cork, Limerick, Dundalk and Drogheda had functioning exchanges and increasing lists of subscribers and, by 1900, there some 56 telephone exchanges in Ireland. The former state monopoly of telephone services began in 1911, when the Irish Post Office took over the license of the National Telephone Company.[43]

Ireland was also to figure prominently in Guglielmo Marconi's early experiments with wireless telegraphy.

447

Marconi (1874-1937) was the son of an Irish mother, Anna Jameson (of the wealthy distilling family), and an Italian businessman.[44] In 1896, he was granted the first ever patent for wireless telegraphy, gradually improving his apparatus through a series of experiments in both Britain and Ireland, culminating in the famous transmissions between Poldhu in Cornwall and stations in Newfoundland and Nova Scotia in 1901. Earlier, in 1898, he had been commissioned by Lloyds of London to create a link between Rathlin Island and Ballycastle, County Antrim, which became the world's first commercial wireless service. In 1907, Marconi's wireless station near Clifden, County Galway, became the location for the first ever point-to-point fixed wireless station, which provided a wireless link from Ireland to Glace Bay Station on Cape Breton Island, off Nova Scotia. At Clifden, Marconi installed eight enormous radio masts, each over 200 ft (60.96 m) high, the entire system being powered by a turf-powered generator in the years 1907-22, which was later burned down by irregulars during the Irish Civil War.[45]

17.9 *The remains of the original Atlantic cable relay station at Foilhommerum, Valentia Island.*

Epilogue

'Some persons despair of this country ...'

Up to 1922, the island of Ireland formed an important part of the United Kingdom. The extent to which it became a colonial entity is still hotly debated, but economic and social relations with Britain did, nevertheless, have a pervasive and domineering influence on the development of industry in Ireland. The economy of the island had already become closely integrated with that of Britain, before the earliest phase of British industrialisation, and Ireland's subsequent industrial development was not only a direct consequence of her own resource constraints but also of the colonial association with the United Kingdom. Ireland's partial and largely incomplete industrialisation was truly one of bold contradictions. Her shipbuilding, linen, brewing and milling industries were all, during certain periods, of international significance. But in other sectors industrial growth was extremely limited, a circumstance which was not to significantly change after Independence.

The landscapes of industrial and industrialising Ireland have remained as much undiscovered as they have been unimagined. Up to very recently, they had barely been acknowledged by legislation in the Republic of Ireland, where all buildings of post AD 1700 date had long been seen as 'colonial' and thus iconic of British rule. This misplaced, some would say warped, sense of national identity has long since ceased to influence most peoples' perception of Ireland's built environment in the period of European industrialisation. While historic industrial sites and monuments are still 'undervalued', in the sense that have been subject to much less scrutiny, relative to sites of earlier periods, within the last two decades both local and national government has begun to act more favourably towards them.

This survey has dealt, thematically, with Irish industry in the period 1750-1930 as a necessary first step in attempting to understand the nature and extent of Ireland's partial industrialisation. Our next goal, it is clear, should be to develop an archaeological perspective of the society that brought this about. But industry was, of course, only part of that society. The Irish Grand Juries which built and maintained an extraordinary road infra-structure in Ireland in the eighteenth and nineteenth centuries were also, through the provision of courthouses, hospitals, asylums and so forth, to provide part of a vital social infrastructure for the island. A large number of new building forms appear on the Irish landscape in the same period, such estate farm buildings, police and fire stations, schools, banks, post offices, town halls, market houses and theatres. Yet thus far these have almost exclusively been considered purely as architectural forms, rather than as archaeology. These were important physical expressions of Irish society in the eighteenth and nineteenth centuries. They represented, at once, its aspirations and values, but also its urban, rural and colonial identities. This is, no less, the material culture of Ireland in the period of European industrialisation. In Ireland, North and South, it still awaits a more thorough archaeological evaluation.

Notes

Introduction

1 L.A. Clarkson 1996 'Ireland 1841: pre-industrial or proto-industrial; industrialising or de-industrialising' in S.C. Ogilvie and Markus German (ed) *European proto-industrialisation*. (Cambridge), p. 77.

2 D. Dickson 2000 *New foundations. Ireland 1660-1800*. (Dublin), pp. 139-40.

3 W.H. Crawford 1980 'Drapers and bleachers in the early Ulster linen industry' in L.M. Cullen and P. Butel (ed) *Négoce et industrie en France et en Irlande aux XVIIIe et XIXe siécle*. (Paris), pp. 113-20; Dickson *ibid*. p. 140.

4 Dickson 2000, pp. 115-16.

5 Clarkson 1996, p. 77

6 C. O'Grada 1994 *Ireland. A new economic history 1780-1939*. (Oxford), pp. 213ff.

7 M. Rix 1955 'Industrial Archaeology', *The Amateur Historian* **2** (8), pp. 225-9. For contrasting perspectives on the origins of the discipline in the UK see R.A. Buchanan 2000 'The origins of industrial archaeology' in N. Cossons (ed) *Perspectives on industrial archaeology*. (London), pp. 18-35, and J. Walker, M. Nevell and E. Casella 2003 'Introduction: models, methodology and industrial archaeology' in M. Nevell (ed) 2003 *From farmer to factory owner: models, methodology and industrialisation. The archaeology of the industrial revolution in North-West England, Archaeology North West* **6** (16), for 2001-3, pp. 11-16. See also J. Symonds 2005 'Experiencing industry. Beyond machines and the history of technology' in E. Conlin Casella and J. Symonds (ed) 2005 *Industrial archaeology future directions*. (New York) pp. 33-57.

8 For an excellent and concise introduction to recent archaeological theory and the post-medieval period see S. West 1999 'Introduction' in S. Tarlow and S. West (ed) 1999 *The familiar past? Archaeologies of later historical Britain*. (London). pp. 1-15.

9 M. Palmer 1990 'Industrial archaeology: a thematic or period discipline', *Antiquity* **64**, no. 243, pp. 275-85 at 281.

10 R. Newman, R.D. Cranstone, and C. Howard Davis 2001 *The historical archaeology of Britain c. 1540-1900*. (Stroud), p. 8.

11 J. Walker and M. Nevell 2003 'The origins of industrialisation and the Manchester methodology: the roles of landlord, freeholder and tenant in Tameside during industrialization, 1600-1900' in M. Nevell (ed) 2003 *From farmer to factory owner: models, methodology and industrialisation. The archaeology of the industrial revolution in North-West England, Archaeology North West* **6** (16), for 2001-3, pp. 17-26.

12 D. Gwyn 2005 'The landscape archaeology of the Vale of Ffestiniog', *IAR* **XXVII**, 1, pp. 129-36.

13 This survey was commissioned by Dr David Gwyn and Dr Michael Nevell, using a research grant from the Heritage Council of Ireland, and was conducted by the present author and Flor Hurley in 2004.

14 D. Cranstone 2001 'Industrial archaeology – manufacturing a new society' in Newman, R. Cranstone, D. and C. Howard Davis, *The historical archaeology of Britain c. 1540-1900*. (Stroud), p. 183.

15 M. Johnson 1999 'Rethinking historical archaeology' in P. Paulo, M. Hall and S. Jones (ed) *Historical archaeology. Back from the edge*. (London), pp. 23-36.

16 Cranstone 2001, p. 183.

17 C. Rynne 2005 'Technological innovation in the early nineteenth century Irish cotton industry – Overton Cotton mills, County Cork, Thomas Cheek Hewes and the origins of the suspension waterwheel' in E.C. Casella and J. Symonds (ed) *Industrial archaeology. Future Directions*. (New York), pp. 205-16.

18 An earlier version of this section appeared in C. Rynne 2000 (c) 'Industrial archaeology' in N. Buttimer, C. Rynne and H. Guerin (ed) *The Heritage of Ireland*. (Cork), pp. 50-7.

19 E.R.R. Green 1963 *The industrial archaeology of County Down*. (Belfast).

20 M. Palmer and P. Neaverson. 1998 *Industrial archaeology: principles and practice*. (London).

21 W.A. McCutcheon 1966 (b) 'The use of documentary source material in the Northern Ireland survey of industrial archaeology', *EHR* **19**, no. 2, pp. 401-12; see also N. Cunningham 1995 'The McCutcheon archive – a survey of industrial archaeology', *ULS* **15**, no. 1, pp. 62-71.

22 C. Scally, and M. Yates 1985 'The industrial archaeology record for Northern Ireland', *ULS* **9**, no. 21, pp. 178-80.

23 F. Hamond 1998 (a) 'Introduction' in F. Hamond (ed) *Taking stock of Ireland's industrial heritage*. (IHAI: Dublin), pp. 1-3.

24 F. Hamond 1991 *Antrim coast and glens industrial heritage*. (Belfast).

25 R. Delany, 1988 *Ireland's inland waterways*. (Belfast), p. 134.

26 F. Hamond and M. McMahon 2002 *Recording and conserving Ireland's industrial heritage*. (The Heritage Council, Kilkenny), pp. 36-7.

27 Hamond *ibid*. p. 37. For the establishment and functions of the Heritage Council see M. Starrett 2000 'The Heritage Council/An Chomhairle Oidhreachta' in N. Buttimer, C. Rynne and H. Guerin (ed) *The heritage of Ireland*. (Cork), pp. 534-9.

28 Hamond 1998, pp. 1-3.

29 D. Power *et al*. 1992 *Archaeological inventory of County Cork. vol. 1 - West Cork*. (Dublin);
D. Power *et al*. 1994 *Archaeological inventory of County Cork, vol. 2 - East and South Cork*. (Dublin);
D. Power *et al*. 1997 *Archaeological inventory of County Cork, vol. 3 - Mid Cork*. (Dublin).

30   M. Moore 1996 *Archaeological inventory of County Wexford.* (Dublin); G. Scally 1998 'Industrial archaeology survey of county Dublin' in F. Hamond (ed) *Taking stock of Ireland's industrial heritage.* (Dublin), pp. 4-7; C. Rynne 1998 (d) 'The industrial archaeology of Cork city and its environs' in F. Hamond (ed) *Taking stock of Ireland's industrial heritage.* (Dublin), pp. 16-19; C. Rynne 1999 (b) *The industrial archaeology of Cork city and its environs.* (Dublin); M. McMahon 1998 (b) 'Recording the industrial heritage of Dublin's docklands' in F. Hamond (ed) *Taking stock of Ireland's industrial heritage.* (Dublin), pp. 8-11.

31   The most recently published are Anon. 2004 *An introduction to the architectural heritage of county Roscommon.* (Dublin); Anon 2004 *An introduction to the architectural heritage of county Waterford.* (Dublin); Anon 2004 *An introduction to the architectural heritage of county Wicklow.* (Dublin); Anon 2004 *An introduction to the architectural heritage of county Leitrim.* (Dublin).

32   R. Cox 2000 'Civil engineering heritage' in N. Buttimer, C. Rynne and H. Guerin (ed) *The heritage of Ireland.* (Cork), pp. 58-61; R. Lohan 1994 *Guide to the archives of the Office of Public Works.* (Dublin).

33   G.A.J. Cole 1922 *Memoir of localities of minerals of economic importance and metalliferous mines in Ireland.* (Repr. Dublin 1998).

34   I.B. McQuiston 'The National Trust in Northern Ireland' in N. Buttimer, C. Rynne and H. Guerin (ed) *The heritage of Ireland.* (Cork), pp. 554-61.

35   F. Hamond 2000 'Conservation and industrial archaeology' in N. Buttimer, C. Rynne and H. Guerin (ed) *The heritage of Ireland.* (Cork), pp. 358-74.

36   B. Kelleher 2000 'Local authority perspectives' in N. Buttimer, C. Rynne and H. Guerin (ed) *The heritage of Ireland.* (Cork), pp. 506-21; P. Carlton 2000 'The role of FÁS' in N. Buttimer, C. Rynne and H. Guerin (ed) *The heritage of Ireland.* (Cork), pp. 544-53.

37   J. Alfry and T. Putnam 1992 *The industrial heritage: managing resources and uses.* (London).

38   A. Sharpe, 1995 'Development under derelict land grants' in M. Palmer and P. Neaverson (ed) *Managing the industrial heritage: its identification, recording and management.* (Leicester), pp. 133-36.

39   C. Stephen Briggs 1995 'The conservation of non-ferrous mines' in C. Stephen Briggs (ed) *Welsh industrial heritage: a review.*

Chapter 1

1   T. J. Westropp 1918 'Dog wheel at Fortanne, Co. Clare', *JRSAI* **xlviii**, pp. 78-9. Westropp reports that these were termed 'turnspit dogs' and were noted for their 'intelligence and patience'. So much so, indeed, that 'when one of these dogs saw an unusual stir in the kitchen and recognized the beginning of preparations for a large party, he waited till all was well advanced and then absconded', *ibid.* p. 78. A well-preserved dog spit survived, *in situ*, at Walton Court, near Kinsale, County Cork in 1953 (see *Cork Holly Bough* 1953, p. 9).

2   J.K. Major 1985 *Animal powered machines.* (Princes Risborough), p. 1.

3   *Ibid.* p. 15.

4   W. Tighe 1802 *Statistical survey of County Kilkenny.* (Dublin), p. 57; W.A. McCutcheon 1980 *The industrial archaeology of Northern Ireland.* (Belfast), p. 336.

5   W. Dick 1972 (c) 'The Kilalloe slate quarries', *TI* May 1972, p. 42.

6   R.A. Williams 1991 *The Berehaven copper mines Allihies, Co. Cork, S.W. Ireland.* (Worsop), p. 62.

7   G. A. J. Cole 1922 *Memoir and map of localities of minerals of economic importance and metalliferous mines in Ireland.* Memoir of the Geological Survey of Ireland. Mineral Resources, 2 vols. (Dublin).

8   W. A. McCutcheon *The canals of the north of Ireland.* (Newton Abbot), p. 71.

9   A. Gailey 1982 (a) 'Bricks and brick making in Ulster in the 1830s', *UFL* **28**, pp. 61-64; J. Cunningham 1994 'Arney brick and the Florencecourt Tile Brick and Pottery Works', *UFL* **40**, pp. 68-73.

10   T. Breslin 2002 *Claymen of Youghal.* (Youghal), p. 45; C. Rynne 1999 (b) *The industrial archaeology of Cork city and its environs.* (Dublin), pp. 34-5.

11   A. Bielenberg 1991 *Cork's Industrial Revolution 1780-1880: Development or decline?* (Cork), p. 32.

12   J. Dubourdieu 1812 *Statistical survey of the county of Antrim.* (Dublin), p. 465.

13   Rynne 1999 (b), p. 49.

14   P. Lynch and J. Vaizey 1960 *Guinness's Brewery in the Irish economy, 1759-1886.* (Cambridge), p. 154 n.

15   Rynne 1999 (b), p. 68.

16   Paul Duffy, pers. comm.

17   Rynne 1999 (b), p. 156.

18   H. A. Gilligan 1988 *A history of the port of Dublin.* (Dublin), pp. 21-2.

19   McCutcheon 1980, p. 224.

20   D. A. Cronin 1995 *A Galway gentleman in the age of improvement. Robert French of Monivea, 1716-7.* (Dublin), p. 29; Rynne 1999 (b), p. 97.

21   Rynne 1999 (b), p. 164.

22   M. Conry 2001 *Dancing the culm. Burning culm as a domestic and industrial fuel in Ireland.* (Chapelstown, Carlow), pp. 99-100.

23   J. Feehan 1983 *Laois: an environmental history.* (Stradbally), p. 273; A. Gailey 1984 (b) 'Introduction and spread of the horse-powered threshing machine to Ulster's farms in the nineteenth century: some aspects', *UFL* **30**, pp. 37-54 at 40.

24   Gailey 1984 (b), p. 41.

25   Conry 2001, p. 96.

26   T. O'Neill 1982 'Tools and things: machinery on Irish farms 1700-1981', in A. Gailey and D. Ó Hogáin, (ed), *Gold under the furze. Studies in folk life tradition presented to Caoimhín Ó Danachair.* (Dublin), pp. 101-14; Gailey 1984 (b), p. 47.

27   Gailey *ibid.* p. 45.

28   D. Power *et al.* 1994 *Archaeological inventory of County Cork. Vol. 11, East and South Cork.* (Dublin), p. 331.

29   See, for example, Conry 2001, pp. 96ff.

30   P. Duffy, 1986 'Aspects of the engineering history of the west region', *The Engineers' Journal* **40**, September, no. 8, pp. 33-5.

31   Rynne 1999 (b), p. 129.

32   Rynne 1999 (b), p. 118-19.

33   Gilligan 1988, p. 129.

34   R.C. Cox 1982 'Robert Mallet: engineering work in Ireland', in R.C. Cox (ed), *Robert Mallet 1810-1881*. (Dublin), pp. 71-118.

35   For the use and manufacture of traditional wooden pumps in Ireland see J. C. O'Sullivan 1969 'Wooden pumps', *Folk Life* **7**, pp. 101-16. For eighteenth fire-fighting pumps in St Werburgh's church in Dublin see P. Pearson 2000 *The heart of Dublin. Resurgence of a city*. (Dublin), p. 183.

36   C. Rynne 1998 (e) *Technological change in Anglo-Norman Munster*. The Barryscourt Lectures III. (Kinsale) p. 79, re-issued as the J. Ludlow and N. Jameson (ed) 2004 *The Barryscourt Lectures I-X*. (Kinsale), pp. 67-95.

37   M. Moore 1987 *Archaeological inventory of County Meath*. (Dublin), pp. 34, 121, 122, 125 and 164.

38   G. Bowie 1978 'Some notes on tower mills in Ireland', *Trans International Molinological Society* **4**, pp. 65-67; F. Hamond 1989 'The north wind doth blow: windmill evolution in Ulster', in R.B. Schofield (ed) 1989 *The history of technology, science and society 1750-1914* (Jordanstown), unpublished papers; F. Hamond 1997 'Power generation', in F. H. A. Aalen, K. Whelan and M. Stout (eds) 1997 *Atlas of the Irish rural landscape*. (Cork), pp. 225-33.

39   See B. Colfer 2004 *The Hook Peninsula County Wexford*. (Cork), p. 57.

40   Bowie 1978, p. 65.

41   J.A. Claffey, 1980 'Rindoon windmill tower', in H. Murtagh (ed) *Irish Midland studies. Essays in Commemoration of N. W. English*. (Athlone), pp. 84-8.

42   M. Moore 1996 *Archaeological inventory of County Wexford*. (Dublin), p. 193.

43   For the Conlig and Whitespots windmill see A. Woodrow 1978 *A history of the Conlig and Whitespots Lead Mines*. British Mining no. 7, Northern Mine Research Society. (Sheffield), p. 21.

44   For inter-provincial comparisons see Moore's archaeological inventory for Wexford (1996, pp. 193-5), which provides dimensions for the 26 surviving tower mill sites in that county, and the Dúchas inventory for north Galway, which provides similar data for four extant windmill towers; O. Alcock, K. D hÓra and P. Gosling 1999 *Archaeological inventory of County Galway Vol II: North Galway*. (Dublin), pp. 429, 431, 432 and 434.

45   A. O'Sullivan 1984 'Tacumshin windmill – its history and mode of operation', *JWHS* no. 9, pp. 66-73, at p. 67.

46   This is clearly shown on a photograph of the Dundalk windmill at Seatown in *c*. 1860 which is, incidentally, the earliest known photographic image of an Irish windmill. See C. McCall 'The tallest windmill in Ireland', *Jnl Geneaological Soc. Ireland* **4**, Autumn, pp. 34-40.

47   Dr Fred Hamond pers comm. The tallest to survive in Europe is, incidentally, near Brabant in Holland, at 125ft high.

48   F.E. Dickson 1975 (a) 'Dublin Windmills', TI **7**, no. 2, May, p. 46.

49   Hamond 1997, pp. 225-33.

50   McCutcheon 1980, p. 230.

51   J. Kelly 1986 'Prosperous and Irish industrialisation in the late eighteenth century', *JKAS*. no. 3, pp. 441-67, at p. 447.

52   F.E. Dickson 1975 (b) 'Rathgar Quarry', *TI* **7**, no. 3, June, p. 42; Woodrow 1978, p. 22.

53   J. Feehan, 1983 *Laois an environmental history*. (Stradbally), p. 341.

54   Feehan 1983, p. 341.

55   Hamond 1989. The Ballinherly windmill overlooking Strangford Lough was actually rebuilt in *c*. 1796 as a navigation marker, and became such an important feature of navigation on the lough that the British Admiralty effectively banned its demolition early in the twentieth century, see F. Duff 1977 'Windmills around Portaferry and district', *Jnl Upper Ards Hist. Soc.* **1**, pp. 13-15.

56   O'Neill 1984, p. 57.

57   C. Rynne 1998 (b) 'The craft of the millwright in early medieval Munster', in M. Monk and J. Sheehan (ed) *Early Medieval Munster*. (Cork), pp. 87-101.

58   C. Rynne, 2000 (a) 'Water-power in medieval Ireland', in P. Squatriti (ed) *Working with water in medieval Europe: technology and resource use*. (Brill: Leiden-Köln-Boston), pp. 1-50; C. Rynne 2003 'The development of milling technology in Ireland, *c*. 600-1875', in A. Bielenberg (ed) *Irish flour milling – a history 600-2000*. (Dublin), pp. 1-38.

59   C. Rynne 2000 (b) 'The early medieval monastic watermill', in J. White Marshall and G.D. Rourke *High Island an Irish monastery in the Atlantic*. (Dublin), pp. 185-213.

60   Rynne 2000 (a), pp. 47-50.

61   T. McErlean and N. Crothers 2002 'The early medieval tide mills at Nendrum: an interim statement', in T. McErlean, R. McConkey and W. Forsythe *Strangford Lough. An archaeological survey of a maritime landscape*. (Belfast), pp. 200-11.

62   C. Rynne 1989 'The introduction of the vertical water-wheel into Ireland: some recent archaeological evidence', *Medieval Archaeology* **33**, pp. 21-31.

63   C. Rynne 1999 (a) 'Discussion', in R. Cleary 'A vertical-wheeled water-mill at Ardcloyne, Co. Cork', *JCHAS* **104**, pp. 51-6.

64   See M. McMahon, 1998 (a) 'Ireland's industrial heritage', *AI* **12**, no. 2, 44, pp. 11-13.

65   M.B. Mullins 1863 'An historical sketch of engineering in Ireland', *TICEI* **6**, p. 160.

66   Mullins *op. cit*.

67   Rynne 1999 (b), pp. 124-6.

68   C. Rynne 2002 'The industrial archaeology of the textile mill in County Cork, Ireland c. 1780-1930', *III Jornadas de Arqueologia Industrial*, pp. 409-22; C. Rynne 2005 'Technological innovation in the early 19th century Irish cotton industry- Overton cotton mills, county Cork, Thomas Cheek Hewes and the origin of the suspension water-wheel', in E.C. Casella and J. Symonds (ed) 2004 *Industrial archaeology. Future directions*. (New York), pp. 205-16.

69 T.S. Reynolds 1983 *Stronger than a hundred men. A history of the vertical water-wheel.* (London), pp. 297-300.

70 Mr and Mrs S.C. Hall 1841 *Ireland its scenery, character etc.* (London).

71 H.D. Gribbon 1969 *The history of water power in Ulster.* (New York), pp. 20-21.

72 C. Donnelly and F. Hamond 'Investigations at Mullycovet Mill, Belcoo, County Fermanagh', *AI* **13**, no. 2, 48, Summer, pp. 12-14; T. Mulligan 1993 'Cornmills of Leitrim', *Breifne* 8, no. 3, pp. 359-83.

73 Rynne 1999 (b), p. 83.

74 Arthur Young reported that Irish iron foundries were already exporting cast-iron water-wheel components to America in the 1770s, and so it is by no means unreasonable to infer that these and metal gearing were being manufactured for the home market by the end of the eighteenth century. A corn mill near Youghal, County Cork, is recorded as having cast-iron gearing installed in 1792 (see Bielenberg 1991, p. 43).

75 A. Monahan 1963 'An eighteenth-century family linen business: the Faulkners of Wellbrook, Cookstown, Co. Tyrone', *UFL* **9**, pp.30-45, at 32.

76 Decie 1980 'Life and work in an Irish Mining Camp c. 1840; Knockmahon copper mines, co. Waterford', *Decies* **14**, May, pp. 29-42.

77 Williams 1991, p. 40.

78 Monahan 1963, p. 33.

79 P. Stephens 2002 'Fennessy's Weir, Archersgrove, Kilkenny', in I. Bennett (ed) *Excavations 2000: Summary accounts of archaeological excavations in Ireland.* (Bray), pp. 175-6.

80 P. Stephens 2003 'Mill Island and Green's Bridge Weir, Kilkenny', in I. Bennett (ed) *Excavations 2001: Summary accounts of archaeological excavations in Ireland.* (Bray), pp. 215-18; P. Stephens 2003 'Ormond Weir', *ibid.* pp. 218-19.

81 P. Duffy 1994 (b) 'Cloon Weir', *Guaire*, Christmas, pp. 44-5.

82 Rynne 1999 (b), p. 236.

83 B. Wigham and C. Rynne 2001 *A life of usefulness: Abraham Beale and the Monard Ironworks.* (Blarney), pp. 40-45.

84 C. Rynne 2000 (b) 'The early medieval monastic watermill', in J. White Marshall and G.D. Rourke *High Island an Irish monastery in the Atlantic.* (Dublin), pp. 185-213.

85 J.F. la Trobe Bateman 1841 'Description of the Bann reservoirs, County Down, Ireland', *Min. Proc. Inst. Civ. Engrs.* **1**, pp. 168-70.

86 T. McErlean and N. Crothers 2002, pp 200-11; C. Rynne, 1992 'Milling in the 7th-century-Europe's earliest tide mills', *AI* **6**, no.2, Summer, pp. 22-4.

87 G. Bowie 1977 'Tide mills in Ireland', *Irish Engineers Jnl* **30**, 10 November, pp. 9-10.

88 Moore 1990, p. 194.

89 Bowie 1977, p. 9; J. de Courcy 1996 *The Liffey in Dublin.* (Dublin), p. 240.

90 M. Moore 1999 *Archaeological inventory of County Waterford.* (Dublin), pp. 246-7.

91 E.R.R. Green 1963 *The industrial archaeology of County Down.* (Belfast), p. 47.

92 Bowie 1977, p. 10.

93 Reynolds 1983, p. 343.

94 Gribbon 1969, p. 28.

95 Mullins 1863, p. 162.

96 C. Rynne 1989 (a) 'Early water turbines – An Irish history', *TI* **21**, no. 3, p. 19.

97 McCutcheon 1980, p. 261.

98 A. Crocker 2000 'Early water turbines in the British Isles', *IAR* **22**, pp. 83-102, at 95.

99 Rynne 1999 (b), p. 98.

100 Crocker 2000, p. 87.

101 Rynne 1999 (b), p. 231.

102 Mullins 1863, p. 161.

103 Gribbon 1969, pp. 33-5.

104 *Southern Industry*, 1889.

105 Reynolds 1983, pp. 353-8.

106 Cox 1982, p. 85; K. Murray 1981 *Ireland's first railway.* (Dublin), p. 221

107 N. Carter 1994 'Hydraulic rams – reviving a lost technology', *TI* **25**, no. 8, January, pp. 39-42.

Chapter 2

1 A. Bielenberg 1991 *Cork's Industrial Revolution 1780-1880: Development or decline?* (Cork), p. 102.

2 C. Rynne and W. Dick 1998 'The heritage of the stationary steam engine in Ireland, a chronological overview and the prospects for a national inventory', in R. Cox (ed) *Power from Steam.* (Dublin), pp. 29-42.

3 Boulton and Watt Archive, Birmingham City Libraries, main index.

4 H.D. Gribbon 1969 *The history of water power in Ulster.* (New York), p. 183.

5 Gribbon *loc. cit.*

6 G. Lewis Smith 1849 *Ireland, historical and statistical.* Vol III (London), pp. 306-8.

7 Gribbon *ibid.* 180; W. A. McCutcheon 1976, 'The stationary steam engine in Ulster', in C. Ó Danachair (ed) *Folk and Farm, Essays in honour of A. T. Lucas.* (Dublin), pp. 126-50; G. Bowie 1978 (a) 'Early stationary steam engines in Ireland', *IAR* **2**, no. 1, pp. 168-74.

8 L.T.C. Rolt and J.S. Allen 1997 *The steam engine of Thomas Newcomen.* (Ashbourne), pp. 44ff.

9 Bowie *ibid.* p. 168.

10 Gribbon *ibid*. pp. 180-1.

11 Bowie *ibid*. p. 171.

12 Gribbon *ibid*. 180, Bowie 1978 (a), p. 171.

13 R.L. Hills 1989 *Power from steam. A history of the stationary steam engine.* (Cambridge), pp. 31-7.

14 Gribbon *ibid*. 181; Bowie *ibid*. p. 171.

15 Bowie *ibid*. p. 171.

16 Bowie *ibid*. p. 173; Rynne 1999 (b), p. 89.

17 Bowie *ibid*. p. 168; Rynne and Dick 1998, p. 30.

18 Rynne and Dick *loc. cit.*

19 Pers. comm. Fred Hamond.

20 G. Bowie 1972 'The Millhouse Engine in Jameson's Distillery, Bow Street, Dublin', *IA* **9**, no. 3, pp. 265-77.

21 W. Dick 1972 (a) 'The Dublin Corporation steam engine', *TI*, February, p. 46.

22 Bowie 1978 (a), p. 173.

23 Bowie *loc. cit.*

24 G. Bowie 1980 'Surviving stationary steam engines in the Republic of Ireland', *IAR* **4**, no. 1, (1979-80), pp. 81-90. See Bielenberg (1991, p. 101), however, for the correct dating and provenance of this engine.

25 Rynne and Dick 1998, p. 32.

26 L. Ince 1984 *The Neath Abbey iron company.* (Eindhoven), p. 103.

27 Rynne 1999 (b), p. 69.

28 Boulton and Watt Archive, Birmingham City Libraries, main index.

29 M.B. Mullins 1863 'An historical sketch of engineering in Ireland', *TICEI* **6**, pp. 1-181, at 165.

30 For the technical development of Cornish engines see D. B. Barton 1965 *The Cornish beam engine.* (Truro).

31 A. Woodrow 1978 *A history of the Conlig and Whitespots Lead Mines.* (Sheffield), p. 2.

32 Bielenberg 1991, p. 100.

33 K. Murray 1981 *Ireland's first railway.* (Dublin), p. 50; Rynne 1999 (b), p. 231.

34 R.A. Williams 1991 *The Berehaven copper mines Allihies, Co. Cork, S.W. Ireland.* (Worsop), pp. 73-4. A fuller treatment of the development of the Cornish engine in Ireland's mining regions follows in Chapters 3 and 5.

35 Hills 1989, p. 106.

36 G. Bowie 1974 'Two stationary steam engines in Power's Distillery, John's Lane, Dublin', *IA* **II**, no. 3, pp. 209-24.

37 Rynne 1999 (b), p. 91.

38 Mullins 1863, p. 165.

39 Bowie 1980, p. 85.

40 McCutcheon 1976, pp. 141-2.

41 McCutcheon *ibid*. pp. 145-6; Bowie 1980, p. 85.

42 Bowie *loc. cit.*

43 McCutcheon 1976, pp. 138-9.

44 McCutcheon *ibid*. p. 145.

45 J.L. Wood 1981 'The introduction of the Corliss engine to Britain', *TNS* **52**, pp. 1-13; Hills 1989, p. 184.

46 Rynne 1999 (b), p. 103.

47 Rynne *ibid*. p. 241.

48 G. Watkins 2001 *Stationary steam engines of Great Britain, the national photographic collections vol. 3.1: Lancashire.* (Ashbourne), p. 72. Coates' Lagan Foundry was the only Irish firm to supply engines to Lancashire cotton mills. Earlier, in 1891, it had built a horizontal cross compound engine for Lawrence Cotton Ltd's mill at Whitte-le-Woods in Lancashire, see G. Watkins 2002 *Stationary steam engines of Great Britain, the national photographic collections vol. 3.2: Lancashire.* (Ashbourne), p. 196.

49 Rynne and Dick 1998, p. 42.

50 Hills *ibid*. p. 219.

51 McCutcheon *ibid*. pp. 146-7; Rynne and Dick *ibid*. p. 42.

52 Rynne 1999 (b), p. 251.

53 McCutcheon *ibid*. pp. 142-3.

54 J.F. Clarke 1985 'Charles Parsons – the man', *TNS* **58**, pp. 48-51.

55 W.G. Scaife 2000 *From galaxies to turbines. Science, technology and the Parsons family.* (Bristol and Philadelphia), p. 177.

56 N.C. Parsons 1985 'The origins of the steam turbine and the importance of 1884', *TNS* **58**, pp. 21-6; Scaife *ibid*. p. 190.

57 J.M. Mitchell 1985 'The development of the steam turbine generator and the ultimate eclipse of the reciprocating steam engine', *TNS* **58**, pp. 26-31.

58 Scaife *ibid*. p. 438.

59 J.L. Wood 1985 'Rival forms of steam turbine', *TNS* **58**, pp. 33-8; Rynne 1999 (b), p. 251. For the development of the Curtis turbine see E.F.C. Somerscales 1992 'The vertical Curtis steam turbine', *TNS* **63**, pp. 1-52.

60 Rynne 1999 (b), p. 241.

61 Rynne *ibid*. p. 245.

62 P. Knight 1997 *Stationary engine review.* (Ipswich), pp. 3-4.

63 C.F. Smith 1994 *The history of the Royal Irish Automobile Club, 1901-1991.* (Dublin), p. 14.

64   Knight *ibid.* pp. 7-8.

65   G. Fletcher 1915 'Peat as a source of power', *Dept. Agric. and Technical Instruction Jnl.* **xvi**, no. 1, October, pp. 33-8.

66   Anon. 1907 'Utilisation of power for small industries', in *Irish rural life and industry, Irish International Exhibition, 1907*. (Dublin), pp. 121-7.

67   W. Tatlow 1902 'Irish waterpower and its development', *The Irish Builder*, 13 March 1902, no. 1018, **xliiii**, pp. 1063-65.

68   Fletcher 1915, pp. 33-8.

69   Anon. 1907, pp. 121-2.

70   Smith 1994, p. 14; J. O'Donovan 1983 *Wheels and deals. People and places in Irish motoring*. (Dublin), p. 6.

71   T. O'Neill 1982 'Tools and things: machinery on Irish farms 1700-1981', in A. Gailey and D. Ó Hógáin (ed), *Gold under the furze. Studies in folk life tradition presented to Caoimhín Ó Danachair*. (Dublin), pp. 101-14.

Chapter 3

1   T. Farmar 1996 *Heitons – a managed transition. Heitons in the Irish coal, iron and building markets 1818-1996*. (Dublin), p. 6.

2   Farmar *ibid.* p. 6; C. O'Mahony 1997 *In the shadows. Life in Cork 1750-1930*. (Cork), p. 13.

3   M.W. Flinn 1984 *The history of the British coal industry*. (Oxford), p. 222; T.C. Smout 2003 'Energy rich, energy poor: Scotland, Ireland and Iceland', in D. Dickson and C. Ó Gráda (ed) *Refiguring Ireland. Essays in honour of L.M. Cullen*. (Dublin), pp. 19-36 at 27. There were also Irish-controlled mines near Gelsenkirchen, in the coal mining region of the Ruhr, initially financed by James Perry, a director of the Midland and Great Western Railway (see Chapter 14) and Joseph Malcomson, owner of the Portlaw, county Waterford cotton mill (see Chapter 8) and the Neptune Shipyard in Waterford (see Chapter 10). The mines were called *Hibernia* and *Shamrock* and were managed, up to 1864, by William Thomas Mulvany, brother of architect, John Skipton Mulvany, who designed some of Ireland's earliest railway stations (see Chapter 14). For a recent and authoritative account see O. Schmidt-Rutsch 2004 'Hibernia, Shamrock, Erin: William Thomas Mulvany and the "Irish mines", in the Ruhr' *Decies* **59**, 2003, pp. 199-224 (also reproduced in *JMHTI* **4**, pp. 3-10).

4   S. Ni Chinnéide 1974 'A view of Kilkenny city and county in 1790', *JRSAI* **104**, pp. 29-38 at p. 30.

5   Anon. 1921 *Memoir of the coalfields of Ireland, vol 1*. (Dublin) pp. 1-2.

6   Coal workings are listed in the Civil Surveys of 1654-56.

7   W. Nolan 1979 *Fassadinin: Land settlement and society in south east Ireland 1600-1850*. (Dublin) p. 92.

8   M. Dillon 1968 'Coalisland: the evolution of an industrial landscape', *Studia Hibernica* **8**, pp. 79-85 at 81; McCutcheon 1980, pp. 328-9; A Stewart 2002 *Coalisland, County Tyrone in the industrial revolution, 1800-1901*. (Dublin), p. 8.

9   T.P. Power 1993 *Land, politics and society in eighteenth-century Tipperary*. (Oxford), p. 51.

10   F. Hamond 1991 *Antrim coast and glens industrial heritage*. (Belfast), p. 12.

11   C. Smith 1750 *The ancient and present state of the county and city of Cork vol 1*. (Cork repr. 1815), p. 294. For the early development of the north Cork coalfield see Rynne 1999 (b), pp. 23-4.

12   Hamond 1991, p. 14.

13   D.D.C. Pochin Mould 1993 *Discovering Cork*. (Dingle), p. 173; *Cork Examiner* 4 November 1882.

14   McCutcheon 1980, p. 339.

15   J.J. Hassett (ed) 1993 *The history and folklore of Killenaule-Moyglass*. (Midleton), p. 178. For a list of mines operating in County Tipperary in the late 1880s see G.H. Bassett 1889 *County Tipperary 100 years ago. A guide and directory*. (repr. 1991, Belfast), pp. 23, 389, 398-9. According to Bassett, in 1889, all mining operations were by now confined to the Killenaule district.

16   L.J. Kettle 1920 *Irish coal and coalfields*. (Dublin), p. 5.

17   E.J. Riordan 1920 *Modern Irish trade and industry*. (London), p. 144-7; R. Thomas 1994 *Images of industry, coal*. (Over Wallop), p. 1.

18   R.J. Kelly 1902 'The coalfields of Connaught', *Irish Builder* **XLIII**, 17 July, pp. 1324-5; Kettle 1920, p. 22.

19   M. Conry 1999 *Culm crushers*. (Carlow), pp. 11-14.

20   M. Conry 2001 *Dancing the culm. Burning culm as a domestic and industrial fuel in Ireland*. (Chapelstown, Carlow), p. 94.

21   For interesting and informative accounts of the operation of the Castlecomer mines in the twentieth century see T. Lyng 1984 *Castlecomer connections*. (Castlecomer) and J. Walsh and S. Walsh 1999 *In the shadow of the mines*. (Freshford).

22   D. Gilmour 1985 *Economic activities in the Republic of Ireland: a geographical perspective*. (Dublin), pp. 51-2.

23   See, for example, Sir Robert Kane's account in his *Industrial resources of Ireland*. (1845) pp. 10-12.

24   W. Tighe 1802 *Statistical observations relative to the county of Kilkenny*. (Dublin), pp. 48-9; Whelan 1979, p. 145.

25   McCutcheon 1980, p. 338; Feehan 1983, p. 348.

26   McCutcheon *loc. cit.*

27   Anon. 1921, p. 134-5.

28   McCutcheon *ibid.* p. 338.

29   J Dubourdieu 1812 *Statistical survey of the county of Antrim*. (Dublin), pp 74ff; Hamond 1991, p. 13.

30   Lyng 1984, p. 220.

31   Tighe 1802, p. 70.

32   B. Neary 1998 *The candle factory. Five hundred years of Rathborne's, master chandlers*. (Dublin), p. 42.

33   D. Cowman 2002 'The mining boom of 1824-5: Part 2 – Aftermath', *JMHTI* **2**, pp. 28-34, at p. 32; I. Weld 1832 *Statistical survey of County Roscommon*. (Dublin), pp. 44ff.

34   A. Coughlan and F.D. O'Reilly 1992 'The North Cork Coalfields', *Mallow Field Club Jnl.* **10**, pp. 44-53, at p. 47.

35   Tighe 1802, p. 68.

36   Gribbon 1969, pp. 134-5.

37 H. Townsend 1810 *A general and statistical survey of the county of Cork.* (Cork), vol. 1, p. 419.

38 W. Nolan 2004 ' A public benefit: Vere Hunt, Bart and the town of New Birmingham, Co. Tipperary, 1800-18', in H. B. Clarke, J. Prunty and M. Hennessy (ed) *Surveying Ireland's past. Multidisciplinary essays in honour of Anngret Simms.* (Dublin), pp. 415-453, at 437.

39 Weld 1832, p. 44ff; G. Neely 1983 *Kilcooley – land and people in Tipperary.* (Belfast), p. 99-100; Hassett 1993, p. 179.

40 S. Lewis 1837 *A topographical dictionary of Ireland.* (London) Vol. 1, p. 632; McCutcheon *ibid.* 352.

41 K. Brown 1996 'Notes on Cornish engine houses in Ireland 1: Ulster and Leinster', *MHSIN* **14**, September, pp. 5-6.

42 Brown 1996, pp. 5-6; R. Clutterbuck 1996 'Industrial archaeology of an engine house in Slieveardagh, Co. Tipperary', *Trowel, Jnl of the Archaeological Soc. UCD* **vii**, pp. 46-9.

43 Conry 2001, p. 20.

44 Conry *ibid.* 18.

45 Lyng 1984, p. 218.

46 R.A. Jarrell 1997 (a) 'James Ryan and the problem of Irish new technology in British mines in the early nineteenth century', in P. J. Bowler and N. Whyte (ed) *Science and society in Ireland. The social context of science and technology in Ireland 1800-1950.* (Belfast), pp. 67-83, at pp. 67-8.

47 Jarrell *ibid.* p. 76.

48 Jarrell *ibid.* p. 78.

49 D. Cowman 2004 'Documents on mining history', *JMHTI* **4**, pp. 41-7.

50 Weld 1832, 67ff; Stewart 2002, p. 15.

51 Lyng 1984, p. 220.

52 Lyng *ibid.* p. 223.

53 Kettle 1920, p. 21.

54 Stewart 2002, pp. 7ff; B.M.S. Campbell 2003 'Economic progress in the canal age: a case study from Counties Armagh and Down', in D. Dickson and C. Ó Gráda (ed) *Refiguring Ireland. Essays in honour of L.M. Cullen.* (Dublin), pp. 63-93.

55 Mullins 1863, p. 111.

56 Kettle 1920, p. 23.

57 T. Ferris and P. Flanagan 1997 *The Cavan and Leitrim Railway – the last decade – an Irish railway pictorial.* (Leicester), p. 4.

58 Nolan 1979, pp. 92-5.

59 Conry 2001, p. 20.

60 Power 1993, p. 51.

61 Kettle 1920, pp. 18, 21.

62 R.F. Hammond 1979 *The peatlands of Ireland.* (Dublin), p. 1; J. Feehan and G. O'Donovan 1996 *The bogs of Ireland. An introduction to the natural, cultural and industrial heritage of Irish peatlands.* (Dublin) p. 195.

63 Feehan and O'Donovan *loc. cit.*

64 Feehan and O'Donovan *ibid.* pp. 22-4.

65 P. Duffy 1994 (b) 'Turf steam and the Stein Brown Distillery', *NMAJ* **35**, pp. 107-8.

66 L. J. Kettle 1922 'Ireland's sources of power supply III', *Studies* **xi**, no. 43, September, pp. 447–56.

67 Feehan and O'Donovan 1996, pp. 76-7.

68 D. Pochin Mould 1996 'The archaeology of the peat briquette. The Sliabh Each peat works', *AI* **10**, no. 3, Autumn, pp. 17-19.

69 Feehan and O'Donovan 1996, p. 88.

70 Anon. 1864 *Irish Builder* **vi**, no. 109, July pp. 130-31.

71 Kane 1845, p. 55; C.H. Oldham, 1909 *The woollen industry of Ireland.* (Dublin), p. 22.

72 Kane *ibid.* p. 57.

73 R. H. Scott 1863 'On the reduction of iron by the use of condensed peat at Creevelea, county of Leitrim', *Royal Dublin Soc. Jnl.* **iv**, pp. 43-48; A. McDonnell 1863 'On the use of peat in steam engines and Siemens furnaces', *TICEI* **10**, 155-64.

74 G. Fletcher 1915 'Peat as a source of power', *Dept. of Agriculture and Technical Instruction Jnl.* **xvi**, October, pp. 33-38.

75 C. Ó Grada 1994 *Ireland: A new economic history 1780-1939.* (Oxford), p. 324.

76 Feehan and O'Donovan 1996, p. 140

77 Feehan and O'Donovan *ibid.* p. 22

78 Gribbon 1969, p. 75.

79 Feehan and O'Donovan *ibid.* p. 94.

80 *Ibid.* pp. 96-8.

81 *Ibid.* p. 88.

82 L. McNeill 1980 'The Sulphate of Ammonia Co. Ltd – Carnlough', *The Glynns* **8**, pp. 37-40, Hamond 1991, p. 57.

83 Feehan and O'Donovan *ibid.* p. 90.

84 J. Purser Griffith 1933 'Peat in Ireland', *TICEI* **59**, pp. 246-72; Feehan and O'Donovan *ibid.* pp. 107-8.

85 L. Boylan 1975 'The mills of Kildrought', *JKAS* **xv**, pp. 359-75.

Chapter 4

1 J.H. Andrews 1956 'Notes on the historical geography of the Irish iron industry', *Irish Geography* **3**, pp. 139-49; E. McCracken 1971 *The Irish woods since Tudor times. Their distribution and exploitation.* (Newton Abbot); T.C. Barnard, 1985 'Anglo-Irish industrial enterprise: Iron-making at Enniscorthy, Co. Wexford, 1657-92', *PRIA* **85C**, no. 4, pp. 101-44.

2   A. Young 1780 *A tour in Ireland with general observations on the present state of that kingdom.* (London: repr. 1970. A.W. Hutton ed) vol. 2, p. 235.

3   G.H. Kinahan 1889 'Economic geology of Ireland', *Jour. Geological Society Ireland* **8**, p. 90; B.G. Scott 1991 *Early Irish ironworking.* (Belfast), p. 153.

4   G.A.J. Cole 1922 *Memoir and map of localities of minerals of economic importance and metalliferous mines in Ireland.* Memoir of the Geological Survey of Ireland. Mineral Resources (Dublin, repr. 1998) pp. 77-8.

5   Cole 1922, pp. 74, 76 and 86.

6   Cole 1922, p. 70; Hamond 1991, pp. 15-17.

7   H.F. Kearney 1953 'Robert Boyle, ironmaster', *JRSAI* **83**, pp. 156-62; H.R. Schubert 1957 *History of the British iron and steel industry.* (London), p. 407, App. xi.

8   K.J. O'Hagan 1980 'The iron mines of Glenravel', *The Glynns* **8**, pp. 5-10, at 10; D.P. McCracken 1984 'The management of a mid-Victorian Irish iron ore mine: Glenravel, County Antrim, 1866-1887', *IESH* **xi**, pp. 60-72, at 62.

9   Hamond 1991, pp. 17-19.

10   Anon 1915 *Report on the sources and production of iron and other metalliferous ores used in the iron and steel industry.* (London), p. 37; Riordan 1920, p. 148.

11   Kinahan 1889, pp. 64, 81, 90 and 105.

12   Andrews 1956, p. 145.

13   G. Madden 1997 'The iron works of Sliabh Aughty', *Sliabh Aughty, East Clare Heritage Jnl*, no. 7, pp. 48-51; K.H. Hoppen and P. de Brún 1970 'Samuel Molyneux's tour of Kerry, 1709', *JKAHS* **3**, pp. 59-80, at 74.

14   D.B. McNeill 1953 'The little railway mania in Co. Antrim (1872-1882)', *UJA* **16**, 3rd series, pp. 85-92; Hamond 1991, p. 20.

15   B.G. Scott 1985 'The blast furnace in Ireland: a failed industry', *Medieval Iron in Society* **1**, pp. 286-96.

16   T.C. Barnard 1982 'Sir William as Kerry ironmaster', *PRIA* **82C**, pp. 1-32; Barnard 1985, pp. 101-144.

17   See P. Riden 1993 *A gazetteer of charcoal-fired blast furnaces in Great Britain in use since 1660.* (Cardiff).

18   See, for example, Schubert 1957, p. 186 and Kearney 1953, pp. 156ff.

19   G.F. Hammersly 1973 'The charcoal industry and its fuel 1540-1750', *EHR* 2nd series **26**, pp. 593-616.

20   H. Cleere and D. Crossley 1995 *The iron industry of the Weald.* (Cardiff), p. 168.

21   See A. Smith 1841 (ed) *Robert Payne: A brief description of Ireland.* (Dublin); M. MacCarthy-Morrogh, 1986 *The Munster plantation: English emigration to southern Ireland 1583-1641.* (Oxford), p. 231.

22   Barnard 1985, pp. 102-3

23   MacCarthy-Murrogh, 1986, p. 225; E. McCracken 1965 'Supplementary list of Irish charcoal burning ironworks', *UJA* **28**, pp. 132-35, at 132.

24   A.B. Grossart (ed) 1886 *The Lismore papers.* Vol. 6 (London), pp. 51-3.

25   McCracken 1965, pp. 132ff; Riden 1993.

26   Andrews 1956, p. 142.

27   Gribbon 1969, p. 73; Hammersly 1973, p. 595.

28   E. McCracken 1957 'Charcoal burning ironworks in seventeenth and eighteenth Ireland', *UJA* **20**, pp. 123-38; T. Power 1977 'Richard Boyle's ironworks in County Waterford, part 1', *Decies* **5**, pp. 24-30.

29   Acts of Privy Council 1615-6, 491, 1619-21, 305.

30   Barnard 1985, pp. 5ff.

31   McCracken 1971, p. 93.

32   Barnard 1982, p. 10; Barnard 1985, p. 102.

33   Nolan 1979, p. 54; Madden 1997, p. 50.

34   McCracken 1957, p. 124.

35   C. Rynne 2001 'Towards an archaeology of the post-medieval Irish iron industry: the blast furnace in south Munster', *JCHAS* **106**, pp. 101-20.

36   E. Grogan and A. Kilfeather 1997 *Archaeological inventory of county Wicklow.* (Dublin), p. 203.

37   Hammersly 1973, p. 604.

38   M. Kelly Quin 1994 'The evolution of forestry in County Wicklow from prehistory to the present', in K. Hannigan and W. Nolan (ed) *Wicklow history and society. Interdisciplinary essays on the history of an Irish county.* (Dublin), pp. 823-54.

39   McCracken 1971, p. 92.

40   K. Nicholls 2001 'Woodland cover in pre-modern Ireland', in P.J. Duffy, D. Edwards and E. Fitzpatrick (ed) *Gaelic Ireland. Land, lordship and settlement, c. 1250-c. 1650.* (Dublin), pp. 181-206, at 204.

41   See Madden 1997 and Rynne 2001, p. 106.

42   P. O'Sullivan 1988 'The English East India Company at Dundaniel', *Bandon Hist. Jnl.* **4**, pp. 3-14; D. Power *1992 Archaeological inventory of County Cork. Vol. 1 West Cork.* (Dublin), pp. 384-5; E. Cotter 1999 'Adrigole' in I. Bennett (ed) *Excavations 1998, summary accounts of archaeological excavations in Ireland.* (Bray), p. 13.

43   See Riden 1993.

44   Cotter 1999, p. 13; Rynne 2001, p. 106.

45   Rynne 2001, p. 106.

46   J. Meehan 1907 'The arms of the O'Rourkes: a metal casting from county Leitrim seventeenth-century foundries', *JRSAI* **36**, 2, pp. 123-141, at 126, McCracken 1957, pp. 131-2.

47 D. Crossley 1990 *Post medieval archaeology in Britain*. (Leicester), p. 156.

48 Rynne 2001, p. 108.

49 Crossley 1990, p. 158; Cleere and Crossley 1994, p. 244.

50 D. Cranstone 1997 *Derwentcote steel furnace. An industrial monument in County Durham*. (Lancaster), pp. 29, 32-3.

51 Rynne 2001, p. 110.

52 Rynne *ibid*. p. 109.

53 Crossley 1990, p. 159

54 Cleere and Crossley 1994, p. 246.

55 Barnard 1985, pp. 115-16.

56 Nolan 1979, pp. 54-5.

57 Hoppen and De Brún 1970, p. 76.

58 Kearney 1953, p. 157.

59 Kearney *ibid*. p. 158.

60 G. Hay and G.P. Stell 1986 *Monuments of industry an illustrated historical record*. (Glasgow), pp. 108–14; for the Dyfi furnace see Riden 1993, pp. 69-70 and for the Rockley furnace see Crossley 1990, fig. 7.6.

61 J.H. Lewis 1984 'The charcoal-fired blast furnaces of Scotland: a review', *Proc. Soc. Antiq. Scotland* **114**, pp. 433-479.

62 J.M. Lindsay 1977 'The iron industry in the Highlands, charcoal blast furnaces', *Scottish Hist. Rev.* **56**, pp. 49-63, at 56-7.

63 Crossley 1990, p. 158.

64 Crossley *ibid*. p. 160.

65 O.R. Bedwin 1980 'The excavation of a late 16th-century blast furnace at Batsford, Herstmonceux, East Sussex, 1978', *PMA* **14**, pp. 89-112; J. Dinn 1988 'Dyfi furnace excavation 1982-7', *PMA* **22**, pp.111-42.

66 Nolan 1979, pp. 54-5.

67 Rynne 2001, p. 112.

68 See Lewis 1984 and Crossley 1990.

69 Cleere and Crossley 1994, pp. 249-50; Rynne 2001, p. 113.

70 Hoppen and De Brún 1970, p. 76.

71 Hoppen and De Brún *loc. cit.*

72 Barnard 1985, p. 124.

73 Cleere and Crossley 1994, pp. 266-7.

74 A. Gailey 1982 (b) *Spademaking in Ireland*. (Ulster Folk and Transport Museum, Cultra), p. 9.

75 R. Loeber 1994 'Settlers' utilisation of the natural resources', in K. Hannigan and W. Nolan (ed) *Wicklow history and society. Interdisciplinary essays on the history of an Irish county*. (Dublin) pp. 267-304, at 288.

76 Rynne 2001, p. 115-16. In County Wicklow, some seventeenth-century accounts indicate that the earlier forges were circular in plan and were enclosed in buildings from 18-20 ft high, see Loeber 1994, p. 289.

77 C. Smith 1746 *The history of the county and city of Waterford*. (Dublin), p. 62.

78 Rynne 2001, p. 115

79 Andrews 1956, p. 144; Kearney 1953, p. 160.

80 R. Loeber 1991 *The geography and practice of English colonisation in Ireland*. (Athlone), p. 20; Nolan 1979, pp. 53ff.

81 Barnard 1985, pp. 102-3.

82 Kearney 1953, p. 158.

83 Young 1780, vol II, p. 325.

84 E. Neeson 1991 *A history of Irish forestry*. (Dublin), pp. 63, 67 and 91; Kelly Quin 1994, p. 832.

85 Nicholls 2001, p. 188.

86 A. O'Sullivan, and J. Sheehan 1996 *The Iveragh peninsula; an archaeological survey of south Kerry*. (Cork), p. 424.

87 Marquis of Landsdowne 1937 *Glanerought and the Petty Fitzmaurices*. (Oxford), pp. 16-18. See also W.A. Watts 1984 'Contemporary accounts of the Killarney woods, 1580-1870', *Irish Geography* **xvii**, pp. 1-13.

88 C. Smith 1756 *The antient and present state of the county of Kerry*. (repr. 1969, Cork), pp. 94-5.

89 McCracken 1965, p. 132.

90 A. Bell 1908 *The early iron industry of Furness and district*. (Ulverston), pp. 130-4, 222-8, and 287; McCracken 1984, p. 61.

91 Rynne 2001, pp. 116-18.

92 See A. Raistrick 1970 *Dynasty of iron founders. The Darby's and Coalbrookdale*. (Newton Abbot), pp. 25ff, and E. Thomas 1999 *Coalbrookdale and the Darby family. The story of the world's first industrial dynasty*. (York), pp. 12ff.

93 Weld 1832, pp. 36-7.

94 Weld *ibid*. p. 47.

95 *Op. cit* pp. 47 and 60.

96 J.F. Maguire 1853 *The industrial movement in Ireland as illustrated by the national exhibition of 1852*. (Cork), pp. 414-15.

97 Kinahan 1889, p. 74.

98 Maguire *ibid*. p. 144.

99 W. Anderson 1862 'On the reclaimed lands at Wexford harbour, and the machinery employed in draining them', *TICEI* **7**, pp. 102-23.

100 R.H. Scott 1863 'On the reduction of iron by the use of condensed peat at Creevelea, county of Leitrim', *Royal Dublin Soc. Jnl.* **iv**, (1862-3), pp. 43-48.

101   Hamond 1991, p. 81.

102   R.J. Kelly 1902 'The coalfields of Connaught', *Irish Builder* **XLIII**, 17 July, pp. 1324-5.

103   M. Moore 2003 *Archaeological inventory of county Leitrim.* (Dublin) p. 230.

104   See B. Hogan 1980 *A history of Irish steel.* (Dublin).

Chapter 5

1   J.H. Morris, 2001 'A catalogue of mines and mineral occurrences in Ireland', *JMHTI* **1**, pp. 25-37.

2   J.H. Morris and D. Cowman 2001 'An index of listings of Irish mining companies, or mining companies which operated in Ireland, in the Catalogue of the Board of Trade records held in the Public Record Office, Kew, London', *JMHTI* **1**, pp. 9-18.

3   D. Cowman 2001 (a) 'The mining boom of 1824-25, part 1', *JMHTI* **1**, pp. 49-54.

4   Anon 1996 *MHSIN*, Autumn, p. 11.

5   D. Cowman 1978 'The Royal Silver Mines of Bannon', *Decies* **9**, pp. 28-42; D. Cowman 1987 'The German mining experiment at Bannow Bay 1551-52', *JWHS* **11**, pp. 67-82; D. Cowman 1988 'Silvermines – sporadic working:1289-1874', *THJ*, pp. 96-115; D. Cowman 1992 (a) 'The metal mines of Tipperary', *THJ*, pp. 106-115; D. Cowman and J.H. Morris 2003 'A history of quarrying and mining in Ireland', *JMHTI* **3**, pp. 25-32.

6   Decie 1980 'Life and work in an Irish Mining Camp *c.* 1840; Knockmahon copper mines, Co. Waterford', *Decies* **14**, May, pp. 29-42.

7   D. Cowman and T.A. Reilly 1988 *The abandoned mines of West Carbery – Promoters adventurers and miners.* (Dublin), pp. 1-4.

8   W. O'Brien 1994 (a) *Our mining past – the metal mining heritage of Cork.* (Cork), p. 20.

9   Wakefield 1817 *An account of Ireland.* (London), p. 133; G.A.J. Cole 1922 *Memoir and map of localities of minerals of economic importance and metalliferous mines in Ireland.* (Dublin; repr. 1998), p. 41.

10   R.A. Williams 1991 *The Berehaven copper mines Allihies, Co. Cork, S.W. Ireland.* (Worsop), p. 145.

11   J.H. Morris and K. Brown 2001 'The man engine house, Mountain Mine, Allihies, Co. Cork', *JMHTI* **1**, pp. 39-48. For conservation work to date see J.H. Morris 2003 'The man engine house, Mountain Mine, Allihies, Co. Cork: A pictorial record of conservation works', *JMHTI* **3**, pp. 33-40.

12   Williams 1991, p. 169.

13   D. Cowman, 1994 'The mining community at Avoca 1780-1880', in K. Hannigan and W. Nolan (ed) *Wicklow history and society. Interdisciplinary essays on the history of an Irish county.* (Dublin), pp. 761-88.

14   Cowman 1988, p. 103.

15   D. Cowman 1990 'Two Kerry lead-silver mines: Kenmare and Castlemaine', *JKAHS* **23**, pp. 197-219.

16   Decie 1980, p. 36.

17   Cole 1922, p. 39. A further site, a lead mine at Wheatfield, County Kildare, employed a large diameter water-wheel to power drainage pumps in the 1820s, supplied by a two mile-long mill-race, see R. Griffith 1829 *The metallic mines of Leinster.* (Dublin), pp. 27-9 and D. Cowman 2002 'The mining boom of 1824-5: Part 2 – Aftermath', *JMHTI* **2**, pp. 28-34 at 31.

18   K. Brown 2003 'Silvermines engine houses', *JMHTI* **3**, pp. 63-4.

19   W. O'Brien 2004 *Ross Island. Mining, metal and society in Ireland.* (Galway), pp. 82ff, 101-2.

20   Birmingham City Libraries, Boulton and Watt archive, Pf. 631; Wakefield 1817, pp. 131ff; Williams 1991, p. 85, W O'Brien 2000 *Ross Island and the mining heritage of Killarney.* (Galway), p. 27. For the most recent technical evaluation of this engine see K. Brown 2004 'Appendix 5: The steam engines of Ross Island Mine', in W. O'Brien 2004 *Ross Island. Mining, metal and society in Ireland.* (Galway), pp. 625-29.

21   The Neath Abbey company is known to have manufactured at least two pumping engines for the Allihies mines, see L. Ince 1984 *The Neath Abbey iron company.* (Eindhoven), pp 103-4. Harvey's of Hale, on the other hand, supplied steam engines and plant to almost every Irish mining region, including water-wheels for the Luganure mines and for Ballycummisk in the Allihies complex, see R. Cundick 2002 'Harvey's of Hale: sales to Irish mines 1823-1884', *JMHTI*, pp. 15-20.

22   K. Brown 1996 'Notes on Cornish engine houses in Ireland 1: Ulster and Leinster', *MHSIN* **14**, September, pp. 5-6.

23   K. Brown 1997 'The Cornish engine houses of Ireland 2: Avoca, Co. Wicklow', *MHSIN* **14**, December, pp. 6-11 at 6.

24   A. Woodrow 1978 *A history of the Conlig and Whitespots Lead Mines.* (Sheffield), p. 4.

25   N. Coy 1996 'Avoca's industrial age', *TI*, June, pp. 25-27; K. Brown 2002 'A unique Cornish engine house – Williams' in Avoca', *JMHTI* **2**, pp. 21-4.

26   Williams 1991, p. 125; K. Brown 1998 (a) 'Cornish engine houses in Ireland V. Knockmahon/Tankardstown', *MHSIN* **11**, July, pp. 11-12. Further good surviving Cornish engine houses associated with metal mines can also be seen at Cappagh (T. Reilly, 1998 'Cappagh mine, an endangered heritage', *Mizen Jnl.* **6**, pp. 163-75, K. Brown 1998 (b) 'The Cornish engine houses of Ireland III, West Carbery', *MHSIN* **8**, September, pp. 9-12, at 9) and Glandore (P. O'Sullivan, 2002 'Glandore mines, County Cork: history and survey', *JMHTI* **2**, pp. 51-9) in western County Cork.

27   O'Brien 2004, p. 71.

28   Williams 1991, p. 101.

29   Decie 1980, p. 36.

30   Williams 1991, p. 101.

31   O'Brien 1994 (a), p. 22.

32   Cowman and O'Reilly 1988, p. 3; Williams 1991, p. 139; L. Willies 1991 'Lead: ore preparation and smelting', in J. Day and R.F. Tylecote (ed) *The industrial revolution in metals.* (London), pp. 84-130.

33 W. Dick 1972 (b) 'Dressing ore at Wicklow Gap', *TI*, May, p. 36.

34 Williams 1991, p. 59, Decie 1980, p. 36.

35 Woodrow 1978, pp. 11-12.

36 *Cork Constitution* 11 August 1859.

37 S. Chester and N. Burns 2001 'The mines of Barravore, Glenmalure, Co. Wicklow', *JMHTI* **1**, pp. 67-76.

38 N. Coy 1999 'Clement's Mine' *MHSIN* **12**, December, pp. 3-4; Anon. 1996 'Restoring the old Glengowla East lead mine, Oughterard, county Galway', *JMHTI* **1**, Spring, p. 4.

39 Williams 1991, p. 87-9; R. Kane 1845 *The industrial resources of Ireland*. (Dublin repr. 1971) p. 207; Brown 2003, p. 63, Cole 1922, p. 107 .

40 Williams *ibid*. p. 168.

41 Willies 1991, p. 39.

42 *Cork Constitution* 11 August 1859.

43 O'Brien 1994 (a), p. 22.

44 J.H. Morris, P. Lally, and D. Cowman 2002 'A history and survey of mine buildings at the Tassan mine, Co. Monaghan', *JMHTI* **2**, pp. 41-9.

45 Anon. (Spring) 1996, p. 4; Chester and Burns 2001, p. 70ff.

46 O'Brien 1994 (b), p. 22; Chester and Burns 2001, p. 70.

47 C. Callaghan, and W. Forsythe 2000 'The Berehaven copper-mining industry – a maritime perspective', *A I* **14**, 1, 51, pp. 16-19, O'Brien *ibid*. p. 22.

48 E. Duffy 2003 'In search of Hodgson's tramway', *JMHTI* **3**, pp. 21-4.

49 Cowman 1994, p. 773; Williams 1991, p. 142; C. O'Mahony 1987 'Copper mining at Aillihies, Co. Cork', *JCHAS* **xlii**, pp. 71-85.

50 O'Brien 1994 (a), p. 22.

51 D. Cowman 1992 (b) 'Survival, structures and statistics: Knockmahon Copper Mines, 1850-78', *Decies Jnl. of the Old Waterford Soc.* **46**, Autumn, pp. 10-20.

52 Cowman 1994, p. 775.

53 O'Brien 1994 (a), p. 21; O'Sullivan 2002, p. 51.

54 O'Brien 1994 (a), p. 21.

55 W. O'Brien 1994 (b) *Mount Gabriel Bronze Age mining in Ireland*. (Galway), pp. 47ff.

56 R. Burt 1984 *The British lead mining industry*. (Redruth), pp. 254-7.

57 Cowman 1988, p. 99-100; Rynne 1999 (b), p. 23.

58 D. Cowman 2001 (b) 'The metal mines of Dublin city and county, *c.* 1740-1825', *JMHTI* **1**, pp. 61-66, at 61-2.

59 Cole 1922, pp. 109ff.

60 Morris *et al*. 2002, p. 41.

61 Woodrow 1978, p. 9.

62 D. Crossley 1990 *Post-medieval archaeology in Britain*. (Leicester), pp. 188-9.

63 T. Hoppen and P. de Brún (ed) 1970 'Samuel Molyneux's tour of Kerry, 1709', *JKAHS* , pp. 78-9.

64 Cole 1922, p. 113.

65 P. H. Hore (ed) 1901 *History of the town and county of Wexford*. vol II. (London), pp. 235-6.

66 G. Boate, 1860 *Ireland's Natural History* (first published London 1652) in *A collection of tracts and treatises illustrative of the natural history of Ireland*, vol. 1. (Dublin), pp. 103 and 105-6.

67 E. Phillips Shirley *et al*. 1865 'Extracts from the journal of Thomas Dineley Esq. giving some account of his visit to Ireland in the reign of Charles II', *Jnl. Kilkenny and South East of Ireland Arch. Soc.* **V**, part II, pp. 268-90, at 273.

68 Cowman 1988, p. 99.

69 Burt 1984, p. 213.

70 By this period the earlier works, which included the mine, smelter and tools set up in the 1680s had been leased to a new company, who were now operating the furnace observed by Molyneux (see Cowman 1988, p. 99).

71 J. N. Rhodes 1970 *The London Lead Company in North Wales, 1692-1792*. (Unpubl. Phd thesis, Univ. of Leicester) pp. 358-68. In view of this, while the London Lead Company may well have, as Rhodes has argued, introduced Wright's patent into Ireland, they could not have been responsible for the introduction of Hodge's design.

72 D. Cowman 2004 'Documents on mining history', *JMHTI* **4**, pp. 41-7, at 47.

73 Cowman 2001 (b), pp. 61-4; Cole 1922, pp. 97 and 112ff.

74 Cowman *ibid*. p. 64.

75 Kane 1845 pp. 214ff.

76 W. Dick 1971 'Ballycorus chimney', *TI*, February, p. 25.

77 P. Pearson, 1998 *Between the mountains and the sea. Dun Laoghaire-Rathdown county*. (Dublin), pp. 315-16.

78 Willies 1991, p. 119ff.

79 Kane 1845, p. 218.

80 Dick 1971, p. 25.

81 W. St John Joyce 1912 The *neighbourhood of Dublin its topography, antiquities and historical associations*. (Dublin, repr. 1988, The Skellig Press, Dublin), p. 72; Pearson 1998, p. 316.

82 E. St John Lyburn 1916 'Irish minerals and raw materials: opportunities for development', *Dept. of Agric. and Technical Instruction Jnl.* **16**, no. 4, pp. 621-8; Cole 1922, pp. 15-22.

83   Cole *ibid*. pp. 17-18.
84   Cowman and Reilly 1988, pp. 133-6.
85   O'Brien 1994 (a), p. 17.
86   Cole 1922, pp. 139-40.
87   F. Hamond, 1991 *Antrim coast and glens industrial heritage*. (Belfast), pp. 24-5.
88   Hamond *ibid*. p. 29.
89   Cole 1922, pp. 143-7.
90   Cowman 1988, p. 107.
91   Cole 1922, p. 143.

Chapter 6

1   D. Edwards 2003 *The Ormond lordship of County Kilkenny, 1515-1642. The rise and fall of Butler feudal power*. (Dublin), p. 47; F.G. Dimes 1999 (c) 'Sedimentary rocks', in J. Ashurst and F.G. Dimes (ed) *Conservation of building and decorative stone*. (Oxford), pp. 61-124, at 94.
2   N.M. Ryan, 1992 *Sparkling granite. The story of the granite working people of the Three Rock region of County Dublin*. (Dublin), p. 36.
3   P. Wyse Jackson 1993 *The building stones of Dublin, a walking guide*. (Dublin), p. 14.
4   E. McParland 1991 *The Custom House Dublin*. (Dublin), pp. 22ff; H. Duffy 1999 *James Gandon and his times*. (Kinsale), p. 195. As late as 1813, structures such as the bridge at Dungarvan, County Waterford (which still survives) were being built with Portland stone.
5   J. Ruch 1970 'Coade stone in Ireland', *Quarterly Bulletin of the Irish Georgian Soc*. 13, pp. 1-12; C. Freestone 1991 'Forgotten but not lost: the secret of Coade Stone', *Proc. of the Geolog. Assoc*. **102**, pp. 135-8; M. Feely, J. Lidwell and D. Monaghan 1996 'Mrs Coade's stone: a late 18th-century addition to Co. Galway architectural heritage', *JGAHS* **48**, pp. 92-7, at 93-4.
6   P. Rockwell 1995 *The art of stoneworking a reference guide*. (Cambridge), p. 15ff.
7   F.G. Dimes 1999 (a) 'The nature of building and decorative stone', in J. Ashurst and F.G. Dimes (ed) *Conservation of building and decorative stone*. (Oxford), pp. 19-36, at 20.
8   P. Robinson 1985 'From thatch to slate: innovation in roof covering materials for traditional houses in Ulster', *UFL* **31**, pp. 21-35, at 27.
9   P.C. Power 1990 *History of Waterford city and county*. (Cork), pp. 140-1; Anon. 1997 'Society News', *MHSIN*, no. 4, spring, p 2.
10   F.E. Dickson 1975 (b) 'Rathgar Quarry', *TI* **7**, no.3, June, p. 42.
11   Anon. 1998 *MHSIN*, no. 9, December, p. 2; Anon. 1997, p. 2; Kinahan 1889, p. 339.
12   See, for example, the Scrabo sandstone quarries near Belfast, as described in Anon. 1986 *Scrabo Country Park*. (Belfast), p. 16, fig. 3, which shows the plug and feathers technique being used during the early twentieth century.
13   Earlier references to rock blasting in Ireland, such as the clearance of rock for a mill weir at Kildrought, county Kildare in 1705, are quite rare (see L. Boylan 1972 'The mills of Kildrought', *JKAS* **15**, no. 2, pp. 141-55).
14   Ryan 1992, pp. 34ff.
15   E. Estyn Evans and B.S. Turner 1977 *Ireland's Eye. The Photographs of John Welsh*. (Belfast), p. 102 .
16   S. Ó Maitiú and B. O'Reilly 1997 *Ballyknockan a Wicklow stonecutters' village*. (Dublin), pp. 82, 84 and 86.
17   The illustration concerned is in G. Wilkinson 1845 *Practical geology and ancient architecture of Ireland*. (London), plate 2; for the Welsh influence of this hoisting technology see D.R. Gwyn 2000 'Hoisting machinery in the Gwynedd slate industry', *TNS* **71**, pp. 183-204, at 184-5. My thanks to Dr Gwyn for discussing this and other Welsh influences on Irish slate quarries.
18   F. O'Dwyer 1997 'Making connections in Georgian Ireland' *Bulletin of the Irish Georgian Soc*. **xxxviii**, pp. 6-23, at 18; J. Hill 1999 'Davis Ducart and Christopher Colles: architects associated with the Custom House at Limerick', *IADS* **II**, pp. 119-45, at 121.
19   Colles quarry was referred to as early as 1640 as an important source for the building stones of Kilkenny, see W.G. Neely 1989 *Kilkenny, an urban history, 1391-1843*. (Belfast), p. 69; Hill 1999, p. 121.
20   H.F. Berry 1915 *A history of the Royal Dublin Society*. (Dublin), pp. 19-20; J.C.J. Murphy 1948 'Kilkenny marble works', *OKR*, no. 11, pp. 14-19.
21   Tighe 1802, pp. 102-4.
22   F. Nixon 1969 *The industrial archaeology of Derbyshire*. (Newton Abbot), pp. 85-7. My thanks to Dr David Gwyn for this reference.
23   S. Kierse 1995 *Portraits of Killaloe*. (Killaloe), p. 5.
24   D. Gwyn 1991 'Valentia slate slab quarry', *JKAHS* **24** (1995 for 1991), pp. 40-57.
25   Anon. 1986 *Industries of the north one hundred years ago* (repr. of *Industries of Ireland*, part 1, London, 1891), p. 189.
26   *Industries of the north*, p. 131.
27   Kinahan 1889, p. 394-5.
28   S. Johnson 1997 *Johnson's atlas and gazetteer of the railways of Ireland*. (Leicester), p. 130.
29   Ó Maitiú and O'Reilly 1997, pp. 82 and 86.
30   Ryan 1992, p. 19.
31   F.G. Dimes 1999 (c) 'Sedimentary rocks', in J. Ashurst and F.G. Dimes (ed) *Conservation of building and decorative stone*. (Oxford), pp. 61-124, at 94.
32   Rynne 1999 (b), p. 26.
33   Hamond 1991, pp. 26-28.
34   Kinahan 1889, pp. 165 and 184.
35   R. Williams 1989 *Limekilns and limeburning*. (Princes Risborough), pp. 11-15; A.D. Cowper 1927 *Lime and lime mortars*. (London, repr. Donhead Publishing, Shaftesbury, 1998), p. 8.

36 M. Sleeman 1990 'A lost tradition – the forgotten kiln', *Mallow Field Club Jnl*, no. 8, pp 95-100; J.T. Quain 1984 'Lime kilns of Ardmore and Grange', *Ardmore Jnl*, no. 1, pp. 14-17; M. O'Sullivan and L. Downey 2005 'Lime kilns', *AI* **19**, no. 2, Summer, pp. 18-22.

37 Furze was uses as a fuel for lime burning in Cork during the nineteenth century, see A.T. Lucas 1960 *Furze: a survey and history of its uses in Ireland.* (Dublin), pp. 64-5. In one account from Donegal, of 1835, '25 black loads of peat will burn a ton weight of limestone, which will produce upwards of 50 barrels of slacklime', see A. Day and P. McWilliams 1997 (ed) *Ordnance Survey Memoirs of Ireland vol 39. Parishes of County Donegal II 1835-6 mid, west and south Donegal.* (Dublin and Belfast), p. 55. For the use of culm in Irish limekilns see Conry 2001, 191ff.

38 O. Davies 1938 'Kilns for flax drying and lime-burning', *UJA* 3rd series, pp. 79-80.

39 Sleeman 1990, pp. 99-100.

40 D.C. Twohig 1990 'Excavation of three ringforts at Lisduggan North, county Cork', *PRIA* **90C**, pp. 1-33.

41 Williams 1989, p. 23.

42 *The Irish Builder*, 1 June 1867, p. 134; F. Maxwell 1995 'A short account of the Castle Espie lime, brick, tile and pottery works', *Lecale Miscellany* **13**, pp. 58-60; L. Ball and D. Rainey 2002 *A taste of old Comber. The town and its history.* (Dundonald), p. 77. The Castle Espie Hoffmann kiln was constructed just a year after that of the Dorking Greystone Lime Company's kiln at Betchworth, Surrey, see D. Johnson 2003 'Friedrich Edouard Hoffmann and the invention of continuous kiln technology: the archaeology of the Hoffmann kiln and 19th-century industrial development (Part 2)', *IAR* **xxv**, 1, pp. 15-29 at 22.

43 *The Irish Builder*, 15 May 1873, p. 134.

44 Hamond 1991, p. 27.

45 F.G. Dimes 1999 (b) 'Igneous rocks', in J. Ashurst and F.G. Dimes (ed) *Conservation of building and decorative stone.* (Oxford), pp. 37-60 at 47.

46 Kinahan 1889, p. 472.

47 Kinahan *ibid.* pp. 472-4; Dimes 1999 (b), p. 47.

48 Dimes *ibid.* p. 47.

49 Rynne 1999 (b), p. 27.

50 Kinahan, *ibid.* p. 273. Waste from the sandstone flag quarries of the Castlecomer Plateau was traditionally used to make the pillars of corn stands, see M. Conry 2004 *Corn stacks on stilts. Corn stands for spring threshing in Ireland.* (Carlow), pp. 45-6.

51 Kinahan *ibid.* p. 253.

52 Moore 1996, p. 193.

53 Day and McWilliams 1997, pp. 98 and 106.

54 Kinahan 1889, p. 249; J. Cunningham 1998 'A rural industry in west Ulster – stoneworking', *UFL* **44**, pp. 110-116 at 112.

55 Kinahan *ibid.* p. 212. Kinahan also reported that the last millstones manufactured at the Drumdowney quarry were completed in 1875 (*loc. cit*).

56 F.C. Dimes 1999 (d) 'Metamorphic rocks', in J. Ashurst and F. G. Dimes (ed) *Conservation of building and decorative stone.* (Oxford), pp. 135-49 at 137.

57 Kinahan 1889, pp. 335-47; Robinson 1985, p. 27; M. Tobin 2001 'The Rosscarberry slate industry 1830-1954', *Rosscarberry Past and Present* **3**, pp. 55-65.

58 Gwyn 1999, pp. 40-57.

59 Gywn *ibid.* pp. 40ff.

60 W. Dick 1972 (c) 'The Killaloe slate quarries', *TI*, May, p. 42.

61 A.C. Davies 1977 'Roofing Belfast and Dublin 1896-98: American penetration of the Irish market for Welsh slate', *IESH* **iv**, pp. 26-35 at 28.

62 Gwyn 1991, p. 47; Tobin 2001, p. 55-6.

63 Gwyn 1991, p. 49; S. de hÓir 1988 'A Welsh quarryman's grave at Castletown Arra, Co. Tipperary', *NMAJ* **xxx**, pp. 35-8; D. Gwyn 2002 'A Welsh quarryman in County Tipperary: further light on Griffith Parry', *NMAJ* **43**, pp. 35-8.

64 Kinahan 1889, pp. 328 and 335.

65 Davies 1977, p. 27.

66 R. McManus 2002 *Dublin 1910-1940. Shaping the city and suburbs.* (Dublin), pp. 112-16.

67 Rynne 1999 (b), p. 25.

68 Kinahan 1889, p. 137-9.

69 H. Meek and E.M. Jope 1958 'The castle at Newtownstewart, Co. Tyrone', *UJA* 3rd series 21, pp. 109-14; Cowman 1987, pp. 67-82.

70 A. Gailey 1984 (a) *Rural houses in the north of Ireland.* (Edinburgh), p. 60.

71 P. Francis 2000 *Irish delftware. An illustrated history.* (London), pp. 13 and 184, n. 12. For the early modern development of brick making in England see J.W.P. Campbell and A. Saint 2002 'The manufacture and dating of English brickwork', *AJ* **159**, pp. 170-93.

72 Rynne 1999 (b), p. 33.

73 J. de Courcy 1996 *The Liffey in Dublin.* (Dublin), pp. 44, 349.

74 de Courcy 1996, p. 44; Rynne 1999 (b), p. 33.

75 Feehan and O'Donovan 1996, p. 65.

76 Gailey 1982 (a), pp. 61-4.

77 J. Cunningham 1994 'Arney brick and the Florencecourt Tile Brick and Pottery Works', *UFL* **40**, pp. 68-73. at 68.

78 J.G. Delaney 1990 'Brick making in Gillen', *Folklife* **28**, 31-62.

79 Anon. 1902 'Ballinphellic brickworks', *The Irish Builder*, 27 March, xliii, no 1014, pp. 1080-1; Anon. 1902 'Brick, tile and earthenware industry in Ireland', *The Irish Builder*, 27 March, xliii, no 1014, pp. 1088-86.

80   Anon. 1902 'Ballinphellic brickworks', pp. 1080-1; D. Power *et al.* 1994 *Archaeological inventory of county Cork. Vol. 2. East and south Cork.* (Dublin), p. 360.

81   D. Dowling 1972 'Glenmore brickyards: a forgotten industry', *OKR*, no. 24, pp. 42-51.

82   T. Breslin 2002 *The claymen of Youghal.* (Youghal), p. 45.

83   Dowling 1972, pp. 42ff; Delaney 1990, pp. 31ff; M. Fitzgerald 1991 'Industry and commerce in Athlone', in M. Heaney and G. O'Brien (ed) *Athlone bridging the centuries.* (Mullingar), pp. 34-46 at 36.

84   D. Murphy 2000 'Portumna sewerage scheme, Portumna', in I. Bennett (ed) *Excavations 1998: Summary accounts of archaeological excavations in Ireland.* (Bray), p. 88; D. Murphy 2003 'Ballynora, county Cork', in I. Bennett (ed) *Excavations 2001: Summary accounts of archaeological excavations in Ireland.* (Bray), p. 30.

85   K. Wiggins 2004 'Conigar, county Limerick', in I. Bennett (ed) *Excavations 2002: Summary accounts of archaeological excavations in Ireland.* (Bray), p. 315; G. Hull 2004 'Dollas Upper, county Limerick', in I. Bennett (ed) *Excavations 2002: Summary accounts of archaeological excavations in Ireland.* (Bray), p. 318; F. Hurley 2004 'Garraun, county Clare', in I. Bennett (ed) *Excavations 2002: Summary accounts of archaeological excavations in Ireland.* (Bray), pp. 43-4.

86   Anon. 1903 'Kingscourt brick and tile works', *Irish Builder and Engineer* 3 Nov., **xliv**, no. 1056, pp. 2066-9.

87   E. O'Brien 1992 *An historical and social diary of Durrow, county Laois 1708-1992.* (Durrow), pp. 105-6.

88   G. Douglas and M. Oglethorpe 1993 *Brick, tile and fireclay industries in Scotland.* (Edinburgh), p. 7.

89   *Ibid.* p. 7.

90   Anon. 1902, pp. 1085-6.

91   M.D.P. Hammond 1977 'Brick kilns: an illustrated survey', *IAR* **1**, no. 2, Spring, pp. 171-92.

92   Cunningham 1994, p. 70.

93   S. Pavía and J. Bolton 2000 *Stone, brick and mortar: historical use, decay and conservation of building materials in Ireland.* (Bray), p. 197; P. G. Lane and W.H. Nolan 1999 *Laois history and society. Interdisciplinary essays on the history of and Irish county.* (Dublin), unnumbered plates between pp. 524-5, one of which shows beehive kilns at Fleming's fireclay works at The Swan.

94   Johnson 2002, p. 125.

95   Anon. 1903, pp. 1085-6.

96   Anon. 1902 'Ballinphellic brickworks', *The Irish Builder*, 27 March, **xliii**, pp. 1080-1; Anon. 1901 'Dundalk brickworks', *The Irish Builder* 27 March 1901, **xliii**, pp. 674-75.

97   Anon 1903, pp. 2066ff, Anon. 1902 'Ballinphellic brickworks', pp. 674ff; D. Tyrell 1984 'Arklow Terracotta, Brick and Clay Company', *Arklow Hist. Soc. Jnl.* **3**, pp. 36-38.

98   Anon. 1903, pp. 2066-69.

99   Anon. 1902, pp. 1080-1.

100   Rynne 1999 (b), p. 27.

101   J. Byrne 2002 'Sir John Macneill, engineer, inventor and architect', in R. Cox (ed) *Some aspects of the industrial heritage of North-East Ireland.* (Dublin), pp. 1-14 at 3; Cox 1982, p. 84.

102   N.V. Torpey 2004 (a) 'Irish railway bridges', *JIRRS* **22**, no. 153, pp. 2-12, at p. 3.

103   R.C. Cox and M.H. Gould 1998 *Civil engineering heritage Ireland.* (London) p. 254; Rynne 1999 (b), p. 195.

104   B. Irish 2001 *Shipbuilding in Waterford 1820-1882. An historical, technical and pictorial study.* (Bray) p. 228.

105   R.C. Cox 1990 *Bindon Blood Stoney. Biography of a port engineer.* (Dublin), p. 19.

106   Rynne 1999 (b), p. 195.

107   P. O. Jennings 1982 'Concrete in railway engineering practice', *JIRRS* **14**, no. 89, pp. 413-21.

108   Cox and Gould 1998, p. 84.

109   J.W. de Courcy 1971 'Reinforced concrete in Ireland', *TI* **4**, no. 9, December, pp. 29-31.

110   N. Gordon Bowe 1999 ' "The wild heath has broken out again in the heather field": philanthropic endeavour and Arts and Crafts achievement in early 20th century Kilkenny', *IADS* **II**, pp. 67-97 at 73.

111   McManus 2002, p. 116.

112   H. Murphy 1977 'The Drinagh Cement Works', *Old Wexford Soc. Jnl.*, no. 6, (1976-77) pp. 38-41.

113   T. McNeill 1993 'Belfast's first industrial revolution', *Current Archaeology* no. 134, **XII**, no. 2, May/July, pp. 56-7.

114   M. Dunlevy 1988 *Ceramics in Ireland.* (Dublin), pp. 16-17; Francis 2000, p. 7.

115   F. Britton 1994 'Carrickfergus clay', *English Ceramic Circle Trans.* **15**, pt. 2, pp. 308-9; Francis 2000, p. 8;

116   M.A. Fraser 1951 'Some early Dublin potters', *DHR* **xii**, pp. 47-58; Dunlevy 1988, pp. 18-19; Francis 2000, pp. 146ff.

117   For the origin and development of these premiums see M. Dunlevy 1992 'Samuel Madden and the scheme for the encouragement of useful manufactures', in A. Bernelle (ed) *Decantations. A tribute to Maurice Craig.* (Dublin), pp. 21-8.

118   Dunlevy 1988, p. 17; Francis 2000, p. 46.

119   Francis *ibid.* p. 143.

120   Dunlevy *ibid.* p. 20

121   J.B. Cunningham 1997 *The story of Belleek.* (Belleek), pp. 11ff.

122   Cunningham *ibid.* pp. 17-21.

123   *ibid.* pp. 67-8.

124   For the origins of the Staffordshire fine ware potteries see L. Weatherill 1971 *The pottery trade and north Staffordshire 1660-1770.* (Manchester) and D. Baker 1991 *Potworks. The industrial architecture of the Staffordshire potteries.* (London).

125   P. Francis 2001 *A pottery by the Lagan. Irish creamware from the Downshire china manufactory, Belfast, 1787- c. 1806.* (Belfast), p. 2.

126 M. Dunlevy 1982 'Wedgwood in Dublin, 1772-77', *Irish Arts Review* **1**, no. 2, pp. 8-14.

127 M. Reynolds (Dunlevy) 1984 'Irish fine-ceramic potteries, 1769-96', *PMA* **18**, pp. 251-61 at 251-2; Francis 2001, pp. 2-4.

128 Francis 2001, pp. 19-20.

129 Dunlevy 1988, p. 124.

130 A. Carey and R. Meehan 2004 'Excavation of a post-medieval pottery kiln, Tuam, county Galway', *JGHAS* **56**, pp. 37-45.

131 M. McManus 1984 'The potteries of Coalisland, Co. Tyrone: some preliminary notes', *UFL* **30**, pp. 67-77.

132 P. Doyle n.d. *Carrigaline Pottery 1928-1979.* (Dublin).

133 Power *et al.* 1994, p. 359.

134 B. Lacey 1979 'The archaeology of clay pipes and local history', *Ulster Local Studies* **4**, no. 2, pp. 17-19.

135 Weld 1832, pp. 404 and 510; J. Comiskey 1997 'An Irishman's diary', *The Irish Times*, 5 September 1997.

136 A. Peacey 1996 *The archaeology of the clay tobacco pipe XIV. The development of the clay tobacco pipe kiln in the British Isles.* (Oxford), pp. 29-30, 98, 108, 139, 215, 228 and 229; A. Peacey 1997 'Clay pipe kilns', in M.F. Hurley, O.M.B. Scully and S.W.J. McCutcheon *Late Viking Age and Medieval Waterford. Excavations 1986-1992.* (Waterford), pp. 375-9.

137 Peacey 1997, pp. 375-6.

138 Rynne 1999 (b), p. 36.

139 C. O'Brien and J. Farrelly 1997 'Forest glass furnaces in county Offaly', *AI* **11**, no. 4, Winter, pp. 21-3. A glass house was also in operation at Birr, County Offaly in 1623, see Anon. 1973 'The glasshouse at Gurteens and glass developments in Ireland before its establishment', *OKR* **25**, pp. 51-60.

140 M.S. Dudley Westropp 1978 *Irish glass. A history of glass-making in Ireland from the sixteenth century.* (revised ed. M. Boydell, Dublin), p. 39.

141 Crossley 1990, p. 235. For the early industrial development of glassworks in Britain see D. Crossley 2003 'The archaeology of the coal-fuelled glass industry in England', *AJ* **160**, pp. 160-97.

142 Francis 2001, p. 6.

143 F. Hamond 1998 'Water and weed: the exploitation of coastal resources', *ULS* **19**, no. 2, pp. 60-75 at 72.

144 Rynne 1999 (b), p. 171.

145 Dudley Westropp 1978, p. 170.

146 N. Roche 1997 'The glazing fraternity in Ireland in the seventeenth and eighteenth centuries', *Irish Georgian Society Bulletin* **38**, pp. 66-94; N. Roche 1998 'Capturing the light: window glasshouses in Georgian Ireland', *IADS* **1**, pp. 195-9 at 197. For the best and most recent account of the manufacture and use of window glass in eighteenth- and nineteenth-century Ireland see N. Roche 1999 *The legacy of light: a history of Irish windows.* (Bray) esp. pp. 63-73.

147 Rynne 1999 (b), p. 171.

148 J.M. Hearne 1998 'Quaker enterprise and the Waterford Glassworks, 1783-1851', *Decies* **54**, pp. 29-40 at 37.

149 M.E. Daly 1985 *Dublin – The deposed capital a social and economic history 1860-1914.* (Cork), p. 21.

150 Riordan 1920, pp. 166-7.

Chapter 7

1 J. Mokyr 1985 *Why Ireland starved: a quantitative and analytical history of the Irish economy, 1800-1850.* (London), pp. 18-19; T. Jones Hughes 1982 'The large farm in nineteenth century Ireland' in A. Gailey and D. Ó hÓgáin (ed) *Gold under the furze. Studies in Folk tradition presented to Caoimhín Ó Danachair.* (Dublin) pp. 93-100, at p. 92.

2 M. Turner 1996 *After the famine. Irish agriculture 1850-1914.* (Cambridge), pp. 72, 92.

3 K. H. Connell 1950 'The colonization of waste land in Ireland, 1780-1845', *EHR* **3**, 7, pp. 44-71.

4 J. Mokyr 1981 'Irish history with the potato', *IESH* **8**, 20, pp. 8-29; Mokyr 1985, p. 22; Turner 1996, p. 2.

5 Turner *ibid.* p. 22.

6 J. S. Donnelly 1976 'The Irish agricultural depression of 1859-64', *IESH* **3**, pp 33-54; Turner *ibid.* pp. 30-36.

7 Turner *ibid.* p. 129.

8 Turner *op. cit.*

9 J. Bell 1987 'The improvement of Irish farming techniques since 1750: theory and practice', in P. O'Flanagan, P. Ferguson and K. Whelan (ed) *Rural Ireland 1600-1900: modernism and change.* (Cork), pp. 24-41; J. Bell and M. Watson 1986 *Irish farming, implements and techniques 1750-1900.* (Edinburgh), pp. 229-39.

10 Bell and Watson 1986, pp. 5-9.

11 *Ibid.* 5-9; J. Feehan 2003 *Farming in Ireland. History, heritage and environment.* (Dublin) pp. 137ff; R. A. Jarrell 1997 (b) ' Some aspects of the evolution of agricultural and technical education in nineteenth-century Ireland', in P. J. Bowler and N. Whyte (ed) *Science and technology in Ireland. The social context of science and technology in Ireland 1800-1950.* (Belfast), pp. 101-17.

12 Connell 1950, pp. 44-71. Mokyr 1985, p. 173 argues that while this is generally true, Connell overstates his case.

13 Bell and Watson 1986, pp. 71-81.

14 For example, the threshing mill in the townland of Blackcare North, county Antrim; see Hamond, F. 1991 *Antrim coast and glens industrial heritage.* (Belfast). For the machinery of water-powered threshing mills see, M. Watts 1991 'Farm and threshing mill at Poltimore Farm, Farway, Devon', *IAR* **XIII**, no. 2, Spring, pp. 182-9; Hogg 1998, p. 257.

15 Hogg *ibid.* p. 209.

16 N. Harvey 1980 *The industrial archaeology of farming in England and Wales.* (London), p. 176; Bell and Watson *ibid.* p. 217.

17 Bell and Watson *op. cit.*

18 T. O'Neill 1982 'Tools and things: machinery on Irish farms 1700-1981', in A. Gailey and D. Ó hÓgáin (ed) 1982 *Gold under the furze. Studies in Folk tradition presented to Caoimhín Ó Danachair.* (Dublin), pp. 101-14 at p. 110.

19 J. Neill-Watson 1993 *A history of farm mechanisation in Ireland 1890-1990.* (Dublin), pp. 61-62.

20 Watson *ibid.* p. 63.

21 O'Neill 1982, p. 101.

22 C. Rynne 1998 (c) *At the sign of the cow. The Cork Butter Market 1769-1924.* (Cork), pp. 37ff.

23 D, Dickson 1993 'Butter comes to market: the origins of commercial dairying in Cork', in P. O'Flanagan and C. G. Buttimer (ed) *Cork History and Society.* (Dublin), pp. 367-90.

24 C. Ó Grádá 1977 'The origins of the Irish creamery system 1886-1914', *EHR* **30**, pp. 284-303.

25 Rynne 1998 (c), p. 96.

26 J. Foley 1993 'The Irish dairy industry: an historical perspective', *Jnl Soc. Dairy Technology* **46**, pp. 124-38.

27 *Irish Builder*, 1 May 1884, vol. xxvi, no. 585, p. 125.

28 *Southern Industry*, September 1889; R. Ryan 2001 'The butter industry in Ireland', *IESH* **28**, pp. 32-46.

29 *Irish Builder*, 1 May 1884, vol. **26**, no. 585, p. 125.

30 Foley 1993, p. 126.

31 P. Bolger 1977 *The Irish co-operative movement its history and development.* (Dublin), pp. 190-1.

32 Ó Grádá 1977, p. 286; Foley 1993, p. 128.

33 Foley 1993, p. 127.

34 P. Doyle and L. P. F. Smith 1989 *Milk to market. History of the Dublin city milk supply.* (Dublin), p. 18.

35 C. Donnelly and F. Hamond 1999 'Investigations at Mullycovet Mill, Belcoo, county Fermanagh', *AI* **13**, no. 2, 48, Summer, pp. 12-14.

36 T. Mulligan 1993 'Cornmills of Leitrim', *Breifne* 8, no. 3, pp. 359-83, at 371.

37 Lecture by W. H. Crawford 2000, Green 1963, p. 39; for Coole and Britway see P. MacCotter and K. Nicholls (ed) 1996 *The Pipe Roll of Cloyne* (Rotulis Pipae Clonensis). (Cork), p. 73

38 A. M. O'Sullivan, A. M. 1985 'Garrylough mill and the general development of water mills in county Wexford', *Jnl Wexford Hist. Soc.* **10** (1984-5), pp. 86-94.

39 W. A. McCutcheon 1966 (a) 'Water-powered corn and flax scutching mills in Ulster', *UFL* **12**, pp. 41-5; W. A. McCutcheon 1970 'The corn mill in Ulster' *UFL* **15/16**, pp. 72-98; Bowie and Jones 1978, p. 260.

40 French burr stones were imported by Reuben Harvey & Sons from Havre de Grace into Cork during the early 1830s (see *Cork Constitution*, 19 February 1831). For the French burr millstone industry see M. W. Ward 1982 'Millstones from la Ferte-sous-Joarre, France', *IAR* **VI**, Spring, pp. 203-10, and G. T. Tucker 1987 'Millstone making in England', *IAR* **IX**, Spring, pp. 167-88 for burrstone manufacturers in Britain.

41 M. F. Hurley and C. M. Sheehan 1997 'Ovens and kilns', in M. F. Hurley, O. M. B. Scully and S. W. J. McCutcheon, *Late Viking age and medieval Waterford. Excavations 1986-1992.* (Dublin), pp. 73-76; H. T. Knox (1907) 'Notes on gig-mills and drying kilns near Ballyhaunis, County Mayo', *PRIA* **26C**, pp. 263-73.

42 G. Bowie 1979 'Corn drying kilns, meal milling and flour in Ireland', *Folklife* **17**. pp. 5-15, at p. 7.

43 Bowie 1979, pp. 7-9.

44 Hogg 1998, p. 240.

45 See Conry 2001 for the use of culm in the drying of grain.

46 Bowie 1979, p. 7.

47 O' Sullivan 1985, p. 88.

48 P. Robinson 2000 'Water power and 'strong' farmers: the Weir family of Straid Mills, county Antrim', in T. M. Owen (ed) *From Corrib to Cultra. Folklife essays in honour of Alan Gailey.* (Belfast) pp. 39-47.

49 V. L. Pollock 1997 'The herring industry in county Down 1840-1940', in L. Proudfoot (ed) *Down history and society.* (Dublin), pp. 405-29, at p. 406.

50 J. De Courcy Ireland 1981 *Ireland's sea fisheries: a history.* (Dublin), pp. 30-5.

51 D. Power *et al.* 1992 *Archaeological inventory of county Cork. Vol. 1 West Cork.* (Dublin), p. 314. For the south coast fisheries in general see A. Went, 1946 'Pilchards in the south of Ireland', *JCHAS* **51**, pp. 137-57.

52 De Courcy Ireland 1981, p. 41.

53 C. O'Mahony 1993 'Fishing in nineteenth-century Kinsale', *JCHAS* **98**, pp. 113-32 at 113.

54 J. Kelly 1983 'William Burton Conyngham and the North West Fishery of the eighteenth century', *JRSAI* **115**, pp. 64-85.

55 De Courcy Ireland 1981, pp. 42-52; M. McCaughan, 1989 'Dandy, luggers, herring and mackerel, a local study in the context of the Irish Sea fishery in the nineteenth century', in M. McCaughan and J. Appleby (ed) *The Irish Sea: aspects of maritime history.* (Antrim), pp. 121-33, at 122.

56 De Courcy Ireland 1981, pp. 62-3.

57 McCaughan 1989, p. 128.

58 O'Mahony 1993, pp. 124-5.

59 McCaughan 1989, p. 123.

60 W. S. Green 1902 'The sea fisheries of Ireland', in W. P. Coyne (ed) *Ireland Industrial and Agricultural.* (Dublin), pp. 369-86, at 376-7.

61 N. Ó Clearigh 1992 *Valentia a different Irish island.* (Dublin), pp. 75-9.

62 Green 1902, pp. 376-7.

63 V. Pollock 1989 'Change in county Down fisheries in the twentieth century', in M. McCaughan and J. Appleby (ed) *The Irish Sea: aspects of maritime history.* (Antrim), pp. 135-44, at 141.

64 McCaughan 1989, p. 131.

65 S. Fitzgerald 1999 *Mackerel and the making of Baltimore, county Cork 1879-1913.* (Dublin), p. 13.

66 McCaughan 1989, pp. 121-31.

67 V. Pollock 1991 'The introduction of engine power in the county Down sea fisheries'. *UFL* **37**, pp. 1-12.

68 Green 1902, pp. 379-80; de Courcy Ireland 1981, p. 87.

69 W. Brabazon 1848 *The deep sea and coast fisheries of Ireland with suggestions for the working of a fishing company.* (Dublin), p. 25; E. Leahy, 1901 'The sea fisheries of Ireland', *The Irish Rosary* **V**, no. 11, pp. 720-32, at 727; Green 1902, p. 377; Fitzgerald 1999, p. 24.

70 Fitzgerald 1999, pp. 11-13.

71 C. Creedon 1986 *The Cork, Bandon and South Coast Railway. I: 1849-1899.* (Cork), pp. 51-2.

72 De Courcy Ireland 1981, p. 83.

Chapter 8

1 H. D. Gribbon 1978 'The Irish Linen Board, 1711-1828', in L. M. Cullen and T. C. Smout (ed) *Comparative aspects of Scottish and Irish economic and social history 1600-1900.* (Edinburgh), pp. 77-87.

2 W. J. Smyth 1988 'Flax cultivation in Ireland: the development and demise of a regional staple', in W. J. Smyth, and K. Whelan (ed) *Common ground. Essays on the historical geography of Ireland.* (Cork), pp. 129-44, at 240, 249.

3 L. A. Clarkson 1996 'Ireland 1841: pre-industrial or proto-industrial; industrialising or de-industrialising', in S. C. Ogilvie and Markus German (ed) *European proto-industrialisation.* (Cambridge), pp. 67-84.

4 M. McCaughan 1968 'Flax scutching in Ulster: techniques and terminology', *UFL* **14**, pp. 6-13; W. A. McCutcheon 1966 (a) 'Water-powered corn and flax scutching mills in Ulster', *UFL* **12**, pp. 41-51.

5 In 1860 there were 1,045 scutch mills in Ireland, of which 1,017 were in Ulster, 15 in Leinster, 8 in Munster and 5 in Connaught, see Smyth 1988, p. 246. For scutch mills in Cork see Rynne 1999 (b), p. 98.

6 B. Browne, 1991 'A forgotten county Wexford industry', *JWHS* No. 13, pp. 130-34.

7 Rynne 1999 (b), p. 98.

8 McCutcheon 1980, p. 224.

9 W. E. Hogg 1998 *The millers and mills of Ireland of about 1850.* (Dublin), p. 291.

10 T. Hunt 2000 (a) 'The Portlaw Cotton Plant: work and workers 1835-46'. *Decies* **56**, pp 134-46. at pp. 135-6.

11 Giles and Goodall 1992, pp. 6-7.

12 D. J. Owen 1823 *The history of the town of Belfast.* (Belfast). p. 100.

13 Pers. comm. Dr Andy Bielenberg.

14 C. H. Oldham 1909 *The woollen industry of Ireland.* (Dublin). p. 22.

15 B. Messenger 1988 *Picking up the linen threads.* (Belfast), p. 83.

16 McCutcheon 1980, pp. 285ff; J. Hoad, 1997 *This is Donegal tweed.* (Inver), pp. 46-50.

17 Gribbon 1969, pp 110-1; Dickson 1978, pp. 101-04.

18 Dickson 1978, p. 102; Beilenberg 1991, p. 22

19 A. K. Longfield 1967 'Prosperous, 1776-1798', *JKAS* **14**, no. 2, pp. 212-31. at p. 226; Dickson *ibid.* p. 103

20   J. Dubordieu 1812 *A statistical survey of the county of Antrim.* (Dublin), p. 432; F. Geary, 1989 'The Belfast cotton industry revisited', *IHS* **25**, 103, pp. 250-67, at 262-3.

21 Bielenberg 1991, pp. 22ff.

22 A. K. Longfield 1967, pp. 212-31; Gribbon *ibid.* p. 112.

23 Bielenberg 1991, p. 22; A. Bielenberg 1992 'The growth and decline of a textile town: Bandon 1770-1840', *JCHAS* **97**, pp. 111-119.

24 Gribbon *ibid.* pp. 112 -113

25 M. Nevell 2005 'The social archaeology of industrialisation. The example of Manchester during the 17th and 18th centuries', in E. Conlin Casella and J. Symonds (ed) *Industrial archaeology. Future directions.* (New York), pp. 177-204.

26 Gribbon *ibid.* p. 106.

27 Bielenberg 1991, p. 35.

28 A. Day and P. McWilliams (ed) 1990 *Ordnance Survey Memoirs of Ireland Vol. 3. Parish of County Down I 1834-6. South Down.* Institute of Irish Studies/ Royal Irish Academy (Dublin-Belfast), p. 58; Hogg 1998, p. 259.

29 W. G. Rimmer 1960 *John Marshall of Leeds: flax spinners 1788-1886.* (Cambridge).

30 Gribbon 1969, p. 90.

31 Gribbon *ibid.* p. 91.

32 A. Takei 1994 'The first Irish linen mills', *IESH* **21**, pp. 28-38, at 28-30.

33 Gribbon *ibid.* p. 92, Takei *op.cit*

34 Takei *ibid.* p. 30.

35 Jones 1996, p. 412.

36 W. H. Crawford 1994 *The hand loom weavers and the Ulster linen industry.* (Belfast), pp. 30-1, also McCutcheon 1980, pp. 286-7.

37 W. H. Crawford 1986 'The introduction of the flying shuttle into weaving of linen in Ulster', *UFL* **32**, pp. 78-80.

38 Hoad 1997, p. 56.

39   E. R. R. Green 1944 'The cotton hand loom weavers in the north east of Ireland', UJA 3rd series **7**, pp. 35-9.

40   D. McCourt 1962 'Weavers' houses around south-west Lough Neagh', *UFL* **8**, pp. 43-56 at 44.

41   A. Young *A tour in Ireland 1776-70.* (Irish University Press), vol i. pp. 312-5; C. O'Mahony 1984 'Bygone industries of Blarney and Dripsey', *JCHAS* **89**, pp. 77-87, at 77.

42   Bielenberg 1991, p. 27,

43   W. H. Crawford 1993 'A hand loom weaving community in county Down', *UFL* **39**, pp. 1-14 at 1; Crawford 1994, pp. 55-7.

44   See Hoad 1997.

45   Gribbon *ibid.* p. 115.

46   D. G. Neil 1992 *Portlaw: a nineteenth century Quaker enterprise based on a model village.* (Dublin), p. 7.

47   Gribbon *ibid.* pp. 99-100.

48   E. Boyle 1988 'Linenopolis: the rise of the textile industry', in J. C. Beckett *et al. Belfast the making of the city.* (Belfast), p. 47-8.

49   McCutcheon 1980, p. 305.

50   Rynne 1999 (b), p. 96.

51   Bielenberg 1991, p. 37.

52   *Industries of the north*, p. 183.

53   A. K. Longfield, 1960 'Harpur's "watering engine" for bleaching linens at Leixlip', *JKAS,* no. 8, pp. 443-48.

54   For details see A. Monahan, 1963 'An eighteenth century family linen business: the Faulkners of Wellbrook, Cookstown, Co. Tyrone', *UFL* **9**, pp. 30-45.

55   Rynne 1999 (b), p. 98.

56   A. Longfield 1937 'History of the Irish linen and cotton printing industry in the eighteenth century', *JRSAI* lxvii, pp 28-56 at 29-32.

57   Longfield *ibid.* p. 40.

58   A. K. Longfield 1981 'Blarney and Cork: printing on linen and cotton and paper in the eighteenth and early nineteenth centuries', *JRSAI* **iii**, pp. 81-101; A. K. Longfield 1945 'Linen and cotton printing at Stratford-on-Slaney Co. Wicklow', *JRSAI* **75**, pp. 24-31; A. K. Longfield 1946 'Printed cotton from Robinsons of Ballsbridge', *JRSAI* **76**, 13-15; A. K. Longfield 1950 'Printing on linen and cotton at Richardstown and at Mosney in the eighteenth century', *CLAHJ*, pp. 131-5; A. K. Longfield 1955 'Notes on the linen and cotton printing industries in Northern Ireland in the eighteenth century', *Proc. Belfast Nat Hist and P. Soc.* **4**, pp. 53-68.

59   Longfield 1950, p. 132; Dickson *ibid.* p. 104.

60   A. T. Lucas 1967 'Some traditional methods of cloth finishing', *The Advancement of Science* **24**, no 120, pp. 181-92; A. T. Lucas 1968 'Cloth finishing in Ireland', *Folk Life* **6**, pp. 18-67.

61   L. Boylan 1975 'The mills of Kildrought', *JKAS* **15** pp. 359-75 at p. 361.

62   Hogg 1998, p. 103.

63   Boylan 1975, p. 367.

64   Rynne 1999 (b), p. 113.

65   Beilenberg 1991, p. 33.

66   Gribbon 1978, p. 78; Crawford 1994, p. 4.

67   McCutcheon 1980, p. 292; Crawford *ibid.* pp. 17-18.

68   J. Fitzgerald 1981 'The Drogheda textile industry, 1780-1820', *CLAHJ* **20**, no. 1, pp. 36-48 at 39; Green 1963, p. 34.

69   Longfield 1967; Bielenberg 1991, pp. 22-5.

70   Bielenberg 1991, p. 33.

71   S. Curran 1985 'The Merino factory at Ennisnay, Co. Kilkenny', *OKR* **3**, no. 2, pp. 105-20 at 105.

72   Beilenberg *ibid.* p. 16; Takei 1994.

73   Giles and Goodall 1992, p. 26.

74   S. Swailes and J. Marsh 1998 *Structural appraisal of iron-framed textile mills.* (London), p.5.

75   Dickson *ibid.* p. 102,

76   Bielenberg 1991, p. 33.

77   British Parl. Papers, *Select Committee on Artizans and Machinery*, 1824, vol V, pp. 347-8.

78   O'Mahony 1984, p. 80.

79   H. Townsend 1815 *Statistical survey of county Cork.* (Cork).

80   Green 1963, pp. 28-9.

81   Boylan, 1975, p. 364; Hogg 1998, p. 269.

82   Hogg 1998, p. 260

83   Hogg 1998, pp. 255, 259.

84   R. Fitzgerald 1988 'The development of the cast-iron frame in textile mills to 1850', *IAR* **10**, pp. 127-45; Swailes and Marsh 1998, pp. 12ff.

85   T. Hunt 1999 'The origin and development of the Portlaw cotton industry 1825-1840', *Decies*, pp. 17-32.

86   Boylan 1975, p. 361

87   L. Ó Donnchadha 1985 'Overton cotton mill', *Bandon Historical Jnl.*, no. 2, 1985, pp. 3-7; C. Elleson, 1983 *The waters of the Boyne and the Blackwater.* (Dublin), p. 44.

88   Fitzgerald 1988, p. 128.

89   Hunt *ibid.* p. 22.

90 Hunt 2000 (a), p. 139.

91 M. Lenihan 1866 *Limerick its history and antiquities.* (repr. 1991, Cork), p. 468 n; A. Bielenberg 1995 'Mechanised linen manufacture in Limerick in 1859; some clues to the external economies of the Belfast industry', *IESH* **XXII**, pp. 64-76.

92 Boylan 1975. p. 65.

93 M. E. Falkus 1967 'The British gas industry before 1850', *EHR*, 2nd Series **20**, pp. 494-508; M.E. Falkus 1982 'The early development of the British gas industry, 1790-1815', *EHR*, 2nd Series **35**, pp. 217-34.

94 Hunt *ibid.* p. 22; T. Hunt 2000 (b) *Portlaw, county Waterford 1825-1876. Portrait of an industrial village and its cotton mill.* (Dublin), p. 46.

95 Hogg 1999, p. 258.

96 Green 1963, p. 67.

97 Elleson 1983, pp. 44-6.

98 Rynne 1999 (b), p. 108.

99 M. Cohen 1997 (a) 'Rural paths of capitalist development: class formation, paternalism and gender in county Down's linen industry', in L. Proudfoot (ed) *Down history and society.* (Dublin), pp. 567-99 at 578.

100 This mill was destroyed by fire in 2003.

101 Hills 1989, p. 209; Rynne 1999, p. 102.

102 Watkins 1971, vol. 2, pp. 102ff.

103 Rynne 1999 (b), p. 106.

104 Dr Andy Bielenberg, pers. comm.

105 *Southern Industry*, no. 6, September 1889, p. 14.

106 As note 105.

107 *Southern Industry*, no. 6, September 1889, p. 14; McCutcheon 1980; *Industries of the North*, p. 190.

108 *Southern Industry*, no. 6, September 1889, p. 14; G. H. Bassett 1991 *County Tipperary 100 years ago a guide and directory.* (Belfast), p. 160.

109 Rynne 1999 (b), p. 109.

110 Bielenberg 1991, p. 39.

111 See P. Murray 1988 'Novels nuns and the revival of Irish industries: the rector of Westport and the Foxford Woollen Mill 1905-1907', *Cathair na Máirt* **8**, no. 1, pp. 86-99; N. Gordon Bowe 1999 ' "The wild heath has broken out again in the heather field"', Philanthropic endeavour and the Arts and Crafts achievement in early 20th-century Kilkenny', IADS **2**, pp. 67-97.

112 O'Mahony 1984, p. 84; 1989, p. 37; Bielenberg 1991, pp. 37-8.

113 D. Power *et al.* 1997 *Archaeological inventory of County Cork, vol. 3 - Mid Cork.* (Dublin), p. 36.

114 *Industries of North*, p. 65; Rynne 1999 (b), p. 113.

115 *Industries of North*, pp. 183-4; M. Fitzgerald 1991 'Industry and commerce in Athlone', in M. Heaney and G. O'Brien (ed) *Athlone bridging the centuries.* (Mullingar), pp. 34-46 at 38.

Chapter 9

1 T. Callan MaCardle and W. Callan 1902 (a) 'The brewing industry in Ireland', in W. P. Coyne (ed) *Ireland Industrial and Agricultural.* (Dublin), pp. 451-93.

2 I. Donnachie 1979 *A history of the brewing industry in Scotland.* (Edinburgh), p. 101.

3 A. Patrick 1996 'Establishing a typology for the buildings of the floor malting industry', *IAR* **18**, no 2, Spring, pp. 180-200, at 182.

4 L. Pearson 1999 *British breweries: an architectural history.* (London and Rio Grande) p. 15.

5 C. Clark 1998 *The British malting industry since 1830.* (London and Rio Grande), p. 8.

6   The type of malt generally preferred by porter brewers and distillers was that which had been dried for a long period of time.

7 Callan MacArdle and Callan 1902 (a), p. 462; Patrick 1996, p. 183.

8 M. Byrne 1980 'The distilling industry in Offaly, 1780-1954', in H. Murtagh (ed) *Irish Midland studies. Essays in commemoration of N. W. English.* (Athlone), pp. 213-28, 218.

9 Rynne 1999 (b), p. 41.

10 Rynne 1999 (b), p. 44.

11 Bielenberg 1991, p. 67.

12 Stratten and Stratten 1892 *Dublin, Cork and the South of Ireland.* (London), p. 148

13 M. Gwinell 1985 'Some aspects of the economic life of county Wexford in the nineteenth century', *JWHS* No. 10, pp. 5-24.

14 A. M. O'Sullivan 1996 ' Castlebridge', in D. Rowe and C. J. Wilson (ed) *High skies – low lands: an anthology of the Wexford slobs and harbour.* (Enniscorthy), p. 53.

15 K. Whelan 1990 'The Catholic community in eighteenth-century county Wexford', in T. Power and K. Whelan (ed) *Endurance and emergence. Catholics in Ireland in the eighteenth century.* (Dublin), pp. 129-70.

16 M. Tóibín 1998 *Enniscorthy history and heritage.* (Dublin), p. 87.

17 B. Culleton 1994 *Treasures of the landscape: County Wexford's rural heritage.* (Dublin), p. 137.

18 N. Brunicardi 1987 *John Anderson, Entrepreneur.* (Fermoy), p. 16.

19 This complex was surveyed by the author before its demolition in 1998.

20 P. Shaffrey and M. Shaffrey 1983 *Buildings of Irish towns: treasures of everyday architecture.* (Dublin), p. 111.

21 T. H. Corran 1975 *A history of brewing.* (Newton Abbot), pp. 253-6. Robert Perry, their father, is a listed as a brewer in Rathdowney, county Laois in the 1850s, see Hogg, 1998, p. 6.

22   Corran 1975, pp. 256-7.

23   Lynch and Vaizey 1960, p. 8 n.

24   MacArdle and Callan 1902 (a), pp. 473ff.

25   For the development of Smithwicks and the county Kilkenny breweries see T. B. Halpin 1989 'A history of brewing in Kilkenny', *OKR* **IV**, no. 1, pp. 583-91and T. Halpin 2000 'The malting and brewing industry in Kilkenny' in J. Bradley, D. Healy and A. Murphy 2000 (ed) *Themes in Kilkenny's history*. (Kilkenny), pp. 81-92.

26   MacArdle and Callan 1902 (a), p. 470, Gribbon 1969, p. 126.

27   Gribbon *ibid*. p. 127; A. Bielenberg 1998 'The Irish brewing industry and the rise of Guinness, 1790-1914' in R. G. Wilson and T. R. Gourvish (ed) *The dynamics of the international brewing industry since 1800*. (London), pp. 105-22.

28   For the origins of porter see O. McDonagh 1964 'The origins of porter', *EHR*, 2nd ser., **16**, no. 3, pp. 530-35, Corran 1975, pp. 110ff.

29   MacArdle and Callan 1902 (a), p. 462.

30   Callan MacArdle and Callan 1902 (a) *op. cit.*; Donnachie 1979, p. 108.

31   M. Lovett, 1988 *Brewing and breweries*. (Princes Risborough), pp. 3-5.

32   Callan MacArdle and Callan 1902 (a), p. 464; Donnachie 1979, p. 110.

33   According to Callan MacArdle and Callan (1902 (a), p. 469) an average sized Irish brewery at the turn of the twentieth century required 20-25 barrels of water for processes such as cooling, washing and so forth, for every barrel of drink produced.

34   T. R. Gourvish, and R. G. Wilson 1994 *The British brewing industry 1830-1980*. (Cambridge), p. 49.

35   G. H. Bassett 1889 *County Tipperary 100 years ago. A guide and directory.* (repr. 1991, Belfast), p. 99.

36   Callan MacArdle and Callan 1902 (a), p. 479.

37   Lynch and Vaizey *ibid*. p. 240; Callan MacArdle and Callan 1902 (a), p. 472.

38   Lynch and Vaizey *ibid*. p. 70.

39   Rynne 1999 (b), p. 49.

40   Pearson 1999, p. 28.

41   Rynne 2004, p. 210.

42   Rynne 1999 (b), pp. 48ff; D. Dickson, 2005 *Old world colony. Cork and south Munster 1630-1830*. (Cork), p. 388.

43   Rynne 1999 (b), p. 53.

44   The *Dublin Directory* of 1800; G. Bowie 1978 (a) 'Early stationary steam engines in Ireland', *IAR* **2**, no. 1, pp. 168-74. The claim that Lane's Brewery, Cork, had a steam engine around the same time has not been properly documented, see Rynne 1999 (b), p. 48.

45   E. McCauley 1999 'Some problems in building on the Fitzwilliam estate during the agency of Barbara Verschoyle', *IADS* **1**, pp. 99-117, at 113.

46   Lynch and Vaizey *ibid*. p. 155n.

47   See Pearson 1999, pp. 32ff.

48   Bassett 1889, pp. 98- 99; S. O'Donnell 1999 *Clonmel 1840-1900: anatomy of an Irish town*. (Dublin), p. 23.

49   See illustration in Bassett *ibid*. p. 98 and nineteenth-century photographs reproduced in O'Donnell *ibid*.

50   Power *et al*. 1992, p. 387.

51   D. Ó Drisceoil, and D. Ó Drisceoil 1997 *The Murphy's story. The history of Lady's Well Brewery, Cork*. (Cork), pp. 29-30, see also p. 31 for ground plan of brewery in 1856.

52   Rynne 1999 (b), p. 51.

53   Pearson *ibid*. 46; C. E. B. Brett, 1985 *The buildings of Belfast, 1700-1914*. (Belfast), p. 54.

54   Lynch and Vaizey *ibid*. pp. 241ff.

55   Barnard 1889, p. 417.

56   S. R. Dennison and O. MacDonagh 1998 *Guinness 1886-1939 from incorporation to the Second World War*. (Cork), p. 10; Pearson *ibid*. p. 73.

57   Callan MacArdle and Callan 1902 (a), p. 472.

58   *ibid*. p. 472.

59   Callan MacArdle and Callan *ibid* p. 473, A. McCutcheon 1970 *Railway history in pictures. Ireland* vol. 2. (Newton Abbot), pp. 9-11.

60   J. Williams, 1994 *A companion guide to architecture in Ireland*. (Dublin), p. 136; Pearson *ibid*. p. 198.

61   Williams 1994, pp. 136-7; Pearson *ibid*. pp. 103-4.

62   Lynch and Vaizey *ibid*. p. 155n.

63   Callan MacArdle and Callan *ibid*. p. 473; *Brewer's Journal* **33**, May 1897, p. 400, Pearson *ibid*. p. 97.

64   E. B. McGuire 1973 *Irish whiskey. A history of distilling, the spirit trade and excise controls in Ireland*. (Dublin), pp. 128-34.

65   C. A. Wilson 1975 'Burnt wine and cordial waters. The early days of distilling', *Folklife* **13**, pp. 54-65 at 56.

66   McGuire 1973, pp. 24-5.

67   A. Bielenberg 2003 (a) 'The Irish distilling industry under the Union', in D. Dickson and C. Ó Gráda (ed) *Refiguring Ireland. Essays in honour of L. M. Cullen*. (Dublin), pp. 290-314 at 295.

68   T. Callan MaCardle, and W. Callan 1902 (b) 'The distilling industry', in W. P. Coyne (ed) *Ireland Industrial and Agricultural*. (Dublin) pp. 494-511 at 501-3.

69   McGuire *ibid*. pp. 376-7.

70   McGuire *ibid*. p. 38.

71   McGuire *ibid*. p. 39.

72   McGuire *ibid* p. 39n. 26; Rynne 1999 (b), p. 66.

73 E. J. Rothery, 1968 'Aeneas Coffey', *Annals of Science* **23**, pp. 53-71; W. Davis, 1985 'Aeneas Coffey, excise man, distiller and inventor', in C. Mollan, , W. Davis, and B. Finucane (ed) *Some people and places in Irish science and technology.* (Dublin) pp. 22-3.

74 Callan MacArdle and Callan 1902 (b), p. 503; W. A. McCutcheon 1977 *Wheel and spindle aspects of Irish industrial history.* (Belfast), pp. 56-9; Davis 1985, pp. 22-3.

75 O Gráda 1994, p. 298.

76 R. B. Weir 1978 'The patent still distillers and the role of competition in nineteenth century Irish economic history', in L. M. Cullen and T. C. Smout (ed) *Comparative aspects of Scottish and Irish economic and social history 1600-1900.* (Edinburgh), pp. 129-44; A. Bielenberg 1994 'The Watt family and the distillery industry in Derry, 1762-1921', *UFL* **40**, pp. 16-26, at 17.

77 Rynne 1999 (b), p. 69.

78 A. Barnard 1887 *The whiskey distilleries of the United Kingdom.* (London), p. 393; A. Bielenberg 1993 *Locke's Distillery: a history.* (Dublin), pp. 7-8.

79 Barnard *ibid.* p. 421.

80 Rynne 1999 (b), pp. 68-9. These were largely destroyed by fire in 1993.

81 Barnard *ibid.* p. 357.

82 Barnard *ibid.* p. 417.

83 Barnard *ibid.* pp. 361, 377.

84 J. Archer 1801 *Statistical survey of County Dublin.* (Dublin), pp. 203-4; Bowie 1978 (a), p. 171; Rynne 1999 (b), p. 69.

85 Rynne *ibid.* p. 69.

86 Rynne *ibid.* pp. 65 and 68.

87 For the development of Hilton and Hay see G. T. Tucker 1987 'Millstone making in England', *IAR* **IX**, Spring, pp. 167-88.

88 L. M. Cullen 1977 'Eighteenth-century flour milling in Ireland', *IESH* **4**, pp. 5-52.

89 A. Calladine, and J. Fricker 1993 *East Cheshire textile mills.* (London); J. Tann 1970 *The development of the factory.* (London).

90 For related developments in the British textile industries see Giles and Goodall 1992, on Yorkshire and M. Williams, and D. A. Farnie *1992 Cotton mills in Greater Manchester.* (Preston).

91 A. Bielenberg 2003 (b) 'A survey of Irish flour milling 1801-1922', in A. Bielenberg (ed) *Irish flour milling – a history 600-2000.* (Dublin), pp. 59-87 at 59 and 63.

92 Smith 1750, vol.1, p. 167; Cullen 1977, p. 10.

93 Rynne 1999 (b), p. 78.

94 Cullen *ibid.* p. 11.

95 See, for example, McCutcheon 1966 (a).

96 Cullen *ibid.* p. 10.

97 M. Watts 2000 *Water and wind power.* (Princes Risborough), pp. 43-4.

98 Cullen *ibid.* 13; J. Hill 1991 *The building of Limerick.* (Cork), p. 83; J. Kemmy and L. Walsh 1997 *Limerick in old picture postcards.* (Zaltbommel), p. 33.

99 Cullen *ibid.* 13; C. Elleson 1993 *The waters of the Boyne and the Blackwater.* (Dublin), p. 42; C. Casey, and A. Rowan, 1993 *The buildings of Ireland. North Leinster: the counties of Longford, Louth, Meath and Westmeath.* (London), pp. 476-7.

100 Delany 1988, p. 41.

101 Elleson *ibid.* p. 42.

102 Cullen *ibid.* p. 14. For the effects in Galway on the Mount Bellew estate and its lucrative flour trade with Dublin see K. Harvey 1998 *The Bellews of Mount Bellew. A Catholic gentry family in eighteenth-century Ireland.* (Dublin), pp. 133-8.

103 Hall's *Ireland,* vol. 1, p. 405; Cullen *ibid.* p. 16.

104 Bielenberg 1991, p. 43.

105 R. B. McDowel 1941 'The personnel of the Dublin Society of United Irishmen, 1791-4' *Irish Historical Studies* **2**, pp. 12-53, at p. 36; Cullen *ibid.* p. 20; Rynne 1999 (b), p. 89.

106 M. Watts 1983 *Corn milling.* (Princes Risborough), pp. 13-15.

107 Kemmy and Walsh 1997, p. 114.

108 H. D. Inglis 1834 *Ireland in 1834. A journey throughout Ireland during the Spring, Summer and Autumn of 1834.* (London), vol. 1, p. 190.

109 Rynne 1999 (b), pp. 82-3.

110 National Library of Scotland Ms 19816, Henry Walker to John Rennie, 22 May 1814. I am indebted to Dr Andy Bielenberg for this reference.

111 Kemmy and Walsh 1997, p. 65.

112 Rynne 1999 (b), p. 89.

113 McCutcheon 1980, pl. 145. 3.

114 T. W. Rolleston 1902 (a) 'The Irish milling industry', in W. P. Coyne (ed) *Ireland Industrial and Agricultural.* (Dublin), pp.402-7 at 407.

115 Rolleston *ibid.* pp. 402-3; Bielenberg 1991, 47; Ó Gráda 1994, p. 305.

116 G. Jones 2003 'The introduction and establishment of roller milling in Ireland, 1875-1925', in A. Bielenberg (ed) *Irish flour milling – a history 600-2000.* (Dublin), pp. 106-32 at 107.

117 J. F. Lockwood 1962 *Flour milling.* (Stockport), p. 277; Watts 1983, p. 22.

118 R. Perren 1990 'Structural change and market growth in the food industry: flour milling in Britain, Europe and America, 1850-1914', *EHR*, 2nd ser., **43**, no. 3, pp. 420-37.

119 Bielenberg 2003 (b), p. 71.

120 Bielenberg *loc. cit.*; G. Jones 2001 *The millers. A story of technological endeavour and industrial success, 1876-2001.* (Lancaster), p. 141; Jones 2003, p.111.

121 Jones *ibid.* p. 116.

122 Jones *ibid.* p. 111.

123 McCutcheon 1980, pl. 54. 7.

124 J. Magee 2001 *Bernard Hughes of Belfast.* (Belfast), pp. 226-31; Bielenberg 2003 (b), p. 67

125 *Industries of North* 1891, p. 67, see also McCutcheon 1980, pl. 138.1.

126 *Report from the select committee on industries* [Ireland]. HC, 1884-5 (288), ix, pp. 401-2.

Chapter 10

1 M. Moss and J. R. Hume 1986 *Shipbuilders to the world: 125 years of Harland and Wolff 1861-1986.* (Belfast), p. 219.

2 C. Ó Danachair 1970 'The use of the spade in Ireland', in R. A. Gailey and A. Fenton (ed) *The Spade in Northern and Atlantic Europe.* (Belfast), pp. 49-56 at 49.

3 R. A. Gailey 1970 'The typology of the Irish spade', in R. A. Gailey and A. Fenton (ed) *The Spade in Northern and Atlantic Europe.* (Belfast), pp. 35-48 at 35.

4 A. Gailey 1982 (b) *Spade-making in Ireland.* (Cultra), p. 2.

5 Gailey *ibid.* p. 2.

6 B. Wigham and C. Rynne 2000 *'A life of usefulness': Abraham Beale and the Monard Ironworks.* (Blarney), p. 28; see also J. K. Major 1967 *Finch Brothers Foundry, Stickelpath.* (Newton Abbot); Gailey 1982 (b), p. 70 n. 4; J. Reynolds 1970 *Windmill and Watermills.* (London), pp 160-5 and I. Richardstown and M. Watts 1995 'Finch foundry, Devon', *IAR* **XVIII**, 1 Autumn, pp. 83-95. For similar mills in the Sheffield area see D. Crossley 1989 (ed) *Water Power and the Sheffield Rivers.* (Sheffield) and J. Peatman 1989 'The Abbeydale Industrial Hamlet: History and restoration', *IAR* **XI**, 2, pp. 141-54.

7 Gailey *ibid.* p. 27.

8 Wigham and Rynne 2000, p. 29

9 Rynne 1999 (b), pp. 139ff.

10 Wigham and Rynne 2000, p. 5.

11 M. Coulter 1995 'Patterson's spade mill, Northern Ireland', *IAR* **XVII**, no. 1, Autumn, pp. 96-105.

12 J. Eiffe 1986 'Leixlip iron works', *JKAS* **xvi**, no 5, pp. 432-6.

13 Bell and Watson 1986, p. 6. Baker's implement works burned down in 1770, see O'Neill 1982, 104.

14 D. Dickson 2005 *Old world colony. Cork and south Munster 1630-1830.* (Cork), pp. 408, 616 n. 234. For Belfast foundries see W. E. Coe 1969 *The engineering industry of Northern Ireland.* (Newton Abbot), for Beechmount see O' Mahony 1984, pp. 80-81; for Cork city see Bielenberg 1991, p. 93

15 M. Strattan and B. Trinder 1997 *Industrial England.* (London), p. 76.

16 For Wilkinson's ironworks see H. W. Dickinson and R. Jenkins 1927 *James Watt and the steam engine.* (Repr. Encore Editions, London 1989), p. 271n and A. Raistrick 1970 *A dynasty of iron founders.* (Newton Abbot), pp. 148ff.; for the development of the cupola furnace see Strattan and Trinder *ibid.* p. 76.

17 Coe 1969, p. 23.

18 P. N. Wilson 1957 'The water-wheels of John Smeaton', *TNS* **30**, pp. 24-48; Reynolds 1983, p. 289; C. T. G. Boucher 1963 *John Rennie, 1761-1821: The life and work of a great engineer.* (Manchester), p. 80; Hills 1989, p. 72.

19 Dubordieu 1812, 432; F. Geary 1981 'The rise and fall of the Belfast cotton industry', *IESH* **VIII**, pp. 30-49.

20 Hills 1988, p. 103.

21 L. T. C. Rolt 1988 *George and Robert Stephenson. The railway revolution.* (London), p. 93; R. Hills 1988 *Paper making in Britain 1488-1988. A short history.* (London), p. 175.

22 Rynne 1999 (b), p. 133.

23 J. Lindsay 1971 'Falls foundry 1900-14: A textile machinery firm in Belfast', *Textile History* **1**, pp. 350-62 at p. 350.

24 Rynne 1999 (b), p. 126.

25 T. Colby 1837 *Ordnance Survey of the county of Londonderry. Vol. 1 Memoir of the City and North Western Liberties of Londonderry. Parish of Templemore.* (Repr. North West Books, Limavady). p. 310.

26 Cox 1982, pp. 80-86.

27 J. Lindsay 1971, pp. 350-62.

28 See C. O'Mahony 1997 'Made in Manisty's', *JIRRS* **19**, October, no. 134, pp. 439-43; and *JIRRS* **20**, 1997, no. 137, pp. 128-31. Also 'Made in Manisty's' *CLHAJ*, no 3, **23**, pp. 318-328.

29 A. M. O' Sullivan 1997 'Pierces of Wexford', *JWHS* no. 16, pp. 126-42; G. H. Bassett 1885 *Wexford county guide and directory.* (Dublin: repr. Hibernian Imprints, Dublin 1991).

30 J. M. Hearne 2003 'The Star Ironworks', *JWHS*, no. 19, pp. 3-37.

31 J. Martin 1982 'Robert Mallet: the engineering innovator', in R. C. Cox (ed) *Robert Mallet 1810-1881.* (Dublin), pp 101-17. For the Limerick floating docks see K. Donnelly, M. Hoctor and D. Walsh 1994 *A rising tide. The story of Limerick harbour.* (Limerick), p. 20.

32 A. J. Hughes 1998 *Robert Shipboy MacAdam (1808-95) his life and Gaelic proverb collection.* (Belfast), for details of foundry pp. 2, 50, 59; see Rynne 1999 (b), pp. 126-31 for the Hive Iron Foundry.

33   Lindsay 1971, p. 351.

34   Rynne 1999 (b), p. 129.

35   J. Cooke 1992 'John Hutton and Sons, Summerhill, Dublin: coachbuilders 1779-1925', *DHR* **xlv**, pp. 11-27.

36   Smith 1994, p. 35.

37   J. Moore 1982 *Motor makers in Ireland*. (Belfast); D. S. Jacobson 1985 'The motor industry in Ireland', *IESH* **xii**, pp. 109-16.

38   Smith 1994, pp. 78-9

39   *Ibid*. p. 109.

40   Anon. 1977 *The first sixty years 1917-1977 Ford in Ireland*. (Cork), p. 10. Ford was not the only early motor car magnate to have an Irish connection. Frederick York Wolseley, of the famous Austin–Wolseley partnership, was born in Dublin in 1837 and left for Australia when he was seventeen years of age, in 1854. Wolseley and the English engineer Herbert Austin made their first motor car at their Sydney Works at Alma Street in Birmingham in 1895; see J. O'Toole 1995 *Frederick York Wolseley, Mount Wolseley, Tullow, county Carlow*. (Carlow), p. 13.

41   M. Williams 1985 *Ford and and Fordson tractors*. (London), p. 37.

42   Anon. 1977, p. 11.

43   Williams 1985, p. 37.

44   B. Montgomery 2000 *Ford manufacture and assembly at Cork 1919-1984*. (Tankardstown), pp. 18ff.

45   Anon. 1977, p. 14; Williams *ibid*. p. 44.

46   Anon. *op.cit*; Williams *op.cit*.

47   Anon. *ibid*. pp. 18, 21.

48   Williams *ibid*. p. 64.

49   Wiiliams *ibid*. p. 70

50   For Albert Kahn's factory design work for Henry Ford see F. Bucci (1991) *Albert Kahn: architect of Ford*. (New York).

51   K. A. Murray 1970 'The Grand Canal Street Works', *JIRRS*. **9**, February, pp. 172-84.

52   K. A. Murray 1981 *Ireland's first railway*. (Dublin), pp 175-77.

53   J. W. P. Rowledge 1993 *Irish steam locomotive register*. (Leicester), p. 3

54   Rowledge *ibid*. p. 6. Thomas Grendon's of Drogheda was the first Irish foundry to supply railway locomotives to an Irish railway company, see E. Shepherd 1994 *The Midland and Great Western Railway of Ireland: an illustrated history*. (Leicester) p. 83.

55   J. R. L. Currie 1973 *The Northern Counties Railway. Vol 1 Beginnings and development 1845-1903*. (Newton Abbot), p. 117; see also M. Kennedy 2000 *The LMS in Ireland. An Irish railway pictorial*. (Leicester), p. 9. For the Limerick works see C. E. J. Fryer 2000 *The Waterford and Limerick Railway*. (Poole), pp. 117ff.

56   G. Ryan 1996 *The works. Celebrating 150 years of Inchicore railway works*. (N.P.), p. 8.

57   J. McQuillan 1993 *The railway town. The story of the Great Northern Works and Dundalk*. (Dundalk), p. 205.

58   E. B. Anderson 1984 *Sailing ships of Ireland*. (Dublin), pp. xivff.

59   E. McCracken 1971 *The Irish woods since Tudor times*. (Newton Abbot), p. 71.

60   J. de Courcy Ireland 1986 *Ireland and the Irish in maritime history*. (Dún Laoghaire), p. 166.

61   Bielenberg 1991, p. 104.

62   G. S. Laird Clowes 1936 *The story of sail*. (London), p. 119.

63   B. Irish 2001 *Shipbuilding in Waterford 1820-1882. An historical, technical and pictorial study*. (Bray), p. 47.

64   C. French 1995 'Merchant shipping in the British Empire', in R. Gardiner and P. Bosscher (ed) 1995 *The heyday of sail*. (London), pp. 10-23, at pp. 25-27.

65   M. Marshall 1989 *Ocean traders from the Portuguese discoverers to the present day*. (London), pp. 108-114.

66   C. O'Mahony 1989 'Shipbuilding and repairing in nineteenth century Cork', *JCHAS* **94**, pp. 74-87.

67   D. R. MacGregor 1993 (a) 'The wooden sailing ship under 500 tons', in *Sail's last century. The merchant sailing ship 1830-1930*. (London), pp. 42-5.

68   McCracken 1971, p. 70.

69   B. Irish 1992 'Shipbuilding in Waterford', *Decies* no. 46, pp. 40-60, at p. 40.

70   de Courcy 1996, p. 130.

71   J. T. Parker 1989 'Aspects of shipbuilding in Belfast, past and present', in M. McCaughan and J. Appleby (ed) 1989 *The Irish Sea: aspects of maritime history*. (Antrim), pp. 157-62; de Courcy Ireland 1986, p. 167; Moss and Hume 1986, pp. 1ff.

72   Moss and Hume 1986, p. 2.

73   D. J. Owen 1823 *Short history of Belfast*. (Belfast), p. 83; C. E. B. Brett 1985 *Buildings of Belfast 1700-1914*. (Belfast), p. 18; K. Donnelly, M. Hocter and D. Walsh 1994 *A rising tide. The story of Limerick harbour*. (Limerick), pp. 23-4; J. Kemmy and L. Walsh 1997 *Limerick in old picture postcards*. (Zaltbommel), p. 75.

74   S. Pollard and P. Robertson 1979 *The British shipbuilding industry 1870-1914*. (Cambridge, Mass.), p. 71.

75   D. R. MacGregor 1993 (b) 'The wooden sailing ship under 300 tons', *Sail's last century. The merchant sailing ship 1830-1930*. (London) pp. 20-41.

76   MacGregor *ibid*. p. 29.

77   G. Hasson 1997 *Thunder and clatter. The history of shipbuilding in Derry*. (Derry), p. 8.

78   Irish 2001, p. 70.

79   Rynne 1999 (b), p. 119.

80   Edward Manisty, of Manisty's foundry in Dundalk, was a co-founder of the Dundalk Patent Slip Company, created in 1881. Its works had a composite ship cradle of wood and iron, which was prefabricated in Scotland, see O'Mahony 1995, p. 321.

81   C. O'Mahony 1986 *The maritime gateway to Cork. A history of the outports of Passage West and Monkstown, 1754-1942.* (Cork), p. 19.
82   O'Mahony 1986, pp. 22-3, O'Mahony 1989, p. 80.
83   O'Mahony 1986, p. 23.
84   O'Mahony 1989, p. 82.
85   Irish 2001, p. 36.
86   *Ibid.* p. 54.
87   W. Barry 1919 *History of the Port of Cork steam navigation.* (Cork), p. 13; Anderson 1984, pp. 235-6.
88   J. Guthrie 1971 *A history of marine engineering.* (London), p. 38.
89   Moss and Hume 1986, pp. 3-4; Mullins 1863, p. 167.
90   B. Greenhill 1993 'Steam before the screw', in B. Greenhill and R. Gardiner (ed) 1993 *The advent of steam.* (London), pp. 11-27 at pp. 13-14. For Irish passenger steamers in general see D. B McNeill 1969 and 1971 *Irish passenger steamers.* 2 vols (Newton Abbot).
91   Greenhill 1993, p. 22.
92   MacGregor 1993 (b), p. 27.
93   Greenhill 1993, p. 22.
94   Greenhill *ibid.* p. 22
95   S.Ville 1993 'The transition to iron and steel', in *Sail's last century. The merchant sailing ship 1830-1930.* (London), pp. 52-72 at 53-57.
96   Ville 1993, p. 54.
97   McNeill 1971, vol 2, pp. 149-50.
98   Greenhill 1993, p. 24.
99   Ville 1993, p. 53.
100 Ville *ibid.* p. 54; Greenhill 1993, p. 24.
101 Moss and Hume 1986, p. 5.
102 Hasson 1997, p. 12.
103 O'Mahony 1989, p. 78.
104 Rynne 1999 (b), p. 120.
105 Irish 1992, p. 49.
106 Irish 2001, pp. 151ff.
107 *Ibid.* p. 228.
108 Bielenberg 1991, p. 112.
109 E. C. B. Corlett 1993 'The screw propeller and merchant shipping 1840-1865', in B. Greenhill and R. Gardiner (ed) 1993 *The advent of steam.* (London), pp. 83-105.
110 Hasson 1997, pp. 13-16.
111 Irish 1992, p. 50; Rynne 1999 (b), p. 120.
112 D. Griffiths 1993 'Marine engineering development in the nineteenth century', in B. Greenhill and R. Gardiner (ed) 1993 *The advent of steam.* (London), pp. 160-78 at 170; Corlett 1993, p. 99.
113 Griffiths 1993, p. 99.
114 Moss and Hune 1986, pp. 31ff.
115 *Ibid.* p. 33.
116 Griffiths 1993, p. 172.
117 D. Starkey 1993 'The industrial background to the development of the steamship', in B. Greenhill and R. Gardiner (ed) 1993 *The advent of steam.* (London), pp. 127-135 at 134.
118 Griffiths 1993, p. 114.
119 *Ibid.* pp. 118, 123.
120 Moss and Hume 1986, p. 175
121   J. Lynch 1995 'Belfast's third shipyard', *UFL* **41**, pp. 19-25; J. Lynch 1997 'The Belfast shipbuilding industry 1919-1933', *UFL* **43**, pp. 18-24; F. Geary, and W. Johnson, 'Shipbuilding in Belfast, 1861-1986', *IESH* **16**, pp. 42-64.

Chapter 11

1   Musson, A. E. and Robinson, E. 1969 *Science and technology in the industrial revolution.* (Manchester), pp. 251-2.
2   Cohen 1997, p. 52; P. E. Childs 1998 'The early chemical industry and industrialization in Ireland', *Irish Chemical News*, pp. 18-25, at p. 19.
3   Musson and Robinson 1969, pp. 320-1.
4   *Ibid.* p. 321
5   Musson and Robinson 1969, pp. 322-7; Childs 1998, p. 19.
6   G. Kelleher 1992 *Gunpowder to guided missiles – Ireland's war industries.* (Belfast), p. 10.
7   Rynne 1999 (b), p. 151.
8   *Ibid.* p. 155.
9   G. Crocker 1986 *The gunpowder industry.* (Princes Risborough), p. 1; Rynne 1999 (b), pp. 155-6.
10 According to Lammot Du Pont, 55 coopers were employed at Ballincollig in 1858 (see N.B. Wilkinson 1976 'An American powder maker in Great Britain: Lammot du Pont's journal, 1858', *TNS* **47**, pp. 85-96 at p. 94.

11   Waltham Abbey was the main Board of Ordnance controlled gunpowder mills in England. The name Cooper's Row presumably reflects the principal occupation of its inhabitants, coopering being an important trade within the mills throughout the nineteenth century.

12   Rynne *ibid.* pp.156-7.

13   For a detailed and authoritative account of these developments see B. Earl 1978 *Cornish explosives.* (Penzance).

14   Kelleher 1992, p. 78

15   Kelleher 1992, p. 87.

16   J. Andrews 1989 'Arklow's early chemical industry *c.* 1770-1853', *Arklow Hist. Soc. Jnl*, pp. 8-12.

17   Kelleher 1992, p. 118

18   *ibid.* p. 125.

19   W. A. L. Allford, and J. W. Parkes 1953 'Sir James Murray: a pioneer in the making of superphosphate', *Chemistry and Industry*, pp. 852-5; Childs 1998, p. 21.

20   Anon 1956 *W & H.M. Goulding Ltd., Dublin, Ireland. 1856-1956.* (Dublin), p. 4.

21   *Irish Times*, 26 January 1869 and Daly 1985, p. 39.

22   Anon. 1956, p. 5.

23   Musson and Robinson 1969, p. 187.

24   *Ibid.* p. 187, Childs 1998, p. 24.

25   F. Hamond, 1998 (b) 'Water and weed: the exploitation of coastal resources', *ULS* **19**, no. 2, pp. 60-75 at 64-5.

26   B. Dornan 2000 *Mayo's lost islands: the Inishkeas.* (Dublin), pp. 143-5, plates 21a and 21b.

27   Hamond 1998 (b), pp. 66-7.

28   T. McErlean, R. McConkey and W. Forsythe 2002 *Strangford Lough. An archaeological survey of a maritime landscape.* (Belfast), p. 348.

29   Hamond *ibid.* p. 70.

30   Childs 1998, p. 22.

31   J. Cunningham 2004 *'A town tormented by the sea'. Galway: 1790-1914.* (Dublin), p. 179-80. For the company's operations on Aran see T. Robinson 1986 *Stones of Aran: pilgrimage.* (Mullingar), pp. 182-5.

32   D. J. Coakley 1919 *Cork its trade and commerce. Official handbook of the Cork Incorporated Chamber of Commerce and Shipping.* (Cork), p. 187.

33   Rynne 1999 (b), p. 160.

34   Anon. 1902 'Irish work and workers. XVI Soap manufacture', *The Irish Rosary* **6**, no. 10, October, pp. 796-801, at 797

35   Anon. 1903 'Irish work and workers. XIX A successful village industry. An example of paternal treatment of workers', *The Irish Rosary* **9**, no. 1, January, pp. 54-66, at 62.

36   Anon. 1902, p. 797.

37   Anon. 1902; for Belfast candle and soap factories see *Industries of the north*, pp. 70, 110, 153. For industrial candle manufacture in Ireland over the centuries see B. Neary 1998 *The candle factory: five hundred years of Rathborne's master chandlers.* (Dublin).

38   Coakley 1919, p. 200.

39   Rynne 1999 (b), p. 160.

40   Anon. 1902, pp. 799-800.

41   T. E. McNeil 1980 *Anglo-Norman Ulster. The history and archaeology of an Irish barony 1177-1400.* (Edinburgh), p. 141.

42   D. McGill, 1988 'Early saltmaking in the Ballycastle district', *The Glyns* **16**, pp. 15-21, at p. 17; Hamond 1998, pp. 60-61.

43   Hamond *ibid.* p. 61.

44   Colfer 2004, pp. 150-1.

45   McGill 1988, p. 18; P. H. Hore 1904 *History of the town and county of Wexford.* Vol. 4 (reprint: Dublin 1979), pp. 420, 426.

46   McGill 1988, pp. 18-19; Hamond 1998, p. 64.

47   G. G. Ludlow 1992 'An eighteenth-century Irish salt works as described in the Castleward papers', *UFL* **38**, pp. 25-33.

48   J. Sproule (ed) 1854 *The industrial exhibition of 1853.* (Dublin), p. 76. J. Dubourdieu in the *Statistical survey of the county of Antrim.* (1812, p. 416) provides one of the earliest references to this practice.

49   See Guy's Cork *Directory* of 1893.

50   C. G. Ludlow 1989 'An outline of the salt industry in Ireland', in *The history of technology, science and society, 1750-1914.* (Jordanstown), unpublished papers.

51   *Ibid.* p. 10.

52   Rynne 1999 (b), pp. 31-2

53   Rynne 1999 (b), p. 33. Spillane was also buying salt from Cheshire, the cost of transportation from England being less than that from Carrickfergus.

54   *Cork Sun,* 24 October 1903.

55   M. Sleeman 1990 'A lost tradition – the forgotten kiln', *Mallow Field Club Jnl*, no. 8, pp. 95-100.

56   In Wales, from the mid-nineteenth century onwards tanning and currying were carried out on the same premises, see J. G. Jenkins 1973 *The Rhaedr Tannery.* (n.p.), p. 4.

57   T. W. Rolleston 1902 (b) 'The Irish leather and boot-making industry' in W. P. Coyne (ed) *Ireland, industrial and agricultural.* (Dublin), pp. 408-12 at, pp. 408-9.

58   R. Barry 1920 'The resources of Ireland', *Catholic Bulletin* **10**, February 1920, pp. 101-7.

59   *Fourth Report on Revenue in Ireland*, HC, 1822 (606) xiii, App. 58, pp. 343-5; Bielenberg 1991, p. 81.

60   E. McCracken 1971 *The Irish woods since Tudor times.* (Newton Abbot), p. 84.

61   L. M. Cullen 1987 *An economic history of Ireland since 1660.* (2nd ed, London), p. 145.

62 *Southern Industry*, September 1888.

63 E. N. Somers 1924 'The industrial situation. Stimulants required for the speedier development of Irish resources. A review of old and new industries', *Milling*, Oct. 25, pp. xvii-xix.

64 Jenkins 1973, p. 11; Thomson 1982 pp. 141ff.

65 McCracken 1971, p. 87.

66 McCutcheon 1980, pl. 45. 3.

67 According to Stratten and Stratten (1892, 183), James L. Lyons of Cork, Leather, Bark and Valonia Merchants (who had been in business since the eighteenth century), imported bark from Algeria and Spain; see also Rynne 1999 (b), p. 161.

68 See *Cork Constitution*, 23 September 1834.

69 J. B. O'Brien 1985 'The Hacketts: Glimpses of entrepreneurial life in Cork 1800-1870', *JCHAS* **90**, pp. 150-57 at 151.

70 R. S. Thomson 1981 'Leather manufacture in the post medieval period with special reference to Northhamptonshire', *PMA* **15**, 161-175 at 166; R. S. Thomson 1982 'Tanning. Man's first manufacturing process', *TNS* **53**, pp. 139-56 at 141-7.

71 M. Silverman and P. H. Gulliver 1986 *In the valley of the Nore. A social history of Thomastown, county Kilkenny*. (Dublin), p. 59-60.

72 Pers. comm. Flor Hurley.

73 G. H. Bassett 1889 *County Tipperary 100 years ago: a guide and directory*. (Reprint: Belfast, 1991) p. 20.

74 Silverman and Gulliver 1986, p. 60; Rynne 1999, p. 168.

75 M. Conway 2001 'John Street, Drogheda', in E. Bennett (ed) 2001 *Excavations 2000: summary accounts of archaeological excavations in Ireland*. (Bray), pp. 195-7.

76 C. Donnelly and N. Brannon 1998 'Trowelling through history: historical archaeology and the study of early modern Ireland', *History Ireland* **6**, no. 3, Autumn, pp. 22-25.

77 E. Gibbons 2001 'Mount Brown, Kilmainham', in E. Bennett, (ed) 2001 *Excavations 2000: summary accounts of archaeological excavations in Ireland*. (Bray), pp. 84-5.

78 C. Power 2000 (a) 'Blackpool, Cork', in E. Bennett (ed) *Excavations 1998: Summary Accounts of archaeological excavations in Ireland*. (Bray), p. 17; C. Power 2000 (b) 'Blackpool, Cork', in E. Bennett (ed) *Excavations 1999: Summary Accounts of archaeological excavations in Ireland*. (Bray), p. 26.

79 M. Conway 2004 'College Street/Lonsdale Road, Armagh', in E. Bennett (ed) *Excavations 2002: Summary Accounts of archaeological excavations in Ireland*. (Bray), pp. 9-10.

80 Rynne 1999 (b), p. 168.

81 D. J. Clarke 1954 'Paper Making in Ireland', *An Leabarlann* **12**, no. 3, pp. 69-73, at 70; A. H. Shorter 1971 *Paper making in the British Isles. An historical and geographical study*. (Newton Abbot), p. 227

82 Bielenberg 1991, p. 77.

83 Shorter *ibid*. p. 227.

84 D. Hunter 1978 *Paper making. The history and technique of an ancient craft*. (New York), p. 188; R. Hills 1988 *Paper making in Britain 1488-1988. A short history*. (London), pp. 26-7.

85 Hunter 1978, pp. 163ff; Hills 1988, p. 57; W. Dick 1975 'A premium on rags', *TI* **6**, no. 11, p. 42.

86 Shorter *ibid*. p. 227.

87 Bielenberg *ibid*. pp. 78-9.

88 H. B. Hancock and N. B. Wilkinson 1962 'An American manufacturer in Ireland, 1796', *JRSAI xliii*, pt. 2, pp. 125-37, at 129-30.

89 A. K. Longfield 1981 'Blarney and Cork: printing on linen and cotton and paper in the eighteenth and early nineteenth centuries' *JRSAI* **iii**, pp. 81-101.

90 Hills 1988, p. 34

91 Shorter *ibid*. pp. 230-1; Hills 1988, p. 103; Bielenberg *ibid*. p. 79.

92 Clarke 1954, p. 73; Shorter *ibid*. p. 234; Bielenberg. *ibid*. p. 79.

93 Clarke *ibid*. p. 73.

94 E. J. O'Riordan, 1920 *Modern Irish trade and industry*. (London), p. 170.

95 A Simms and P. Fagan 1992 'Villages in county Dublin: their origins and inheritance', in F. H. A. Aalen and K. Whelan (ed) *Dublin city and county: from prehistory to the present. Studies in honour of J. H. Andrews*. (Dublin), pp. 79-115, illustration on p. 115.

96 McCutcheon 1980, pl. 61.1, 61.2.

Chapter 12

1 V. Crossman 1994 *Local government in nineteenth century Ireland*. (Belfast), p. 12.

2 P. J. Meghan 1959 'The administrative work of the Grand Jury', *Administration* **6**, no. 3, pp. 247-264.

3 G. O'Connor 1999 *A history of Galway County Council*. (Galway), p. 23.

4 J. H Andrews 1964 'Road planning in Ireland before the railway age', *Irish Geography* **5** (1), pp. 17-41; P. J. O'Keeffe 1975 'The development of Ireland's road network', *TICEI* **98-9,** pp. 33-112.

5 W. H. Crawford 2002 'The creation and evolution of small towns in Ulster in the seventeenth and eighteenth centuries', in P. Borsay and L. Proudfoot (ed) *Provincial towns in early modern England and Ireland: Change convergence and divergence*. (Oxford), pp. 97-120 at 113.

6 Young 1780, vol. 2, p. 66

7 J. Carr 1806 *The stranger in Ireland or a tour in the southern and western parts of that country in 1805*. (London: repr. 1970 with an introduction by L. M. Cullen), p. 211; D. Nolan 1974 *The County Cork Grand Jury 1836-1899*. (Unpubl. MA, University College Cork), p. 11.

8   D. Broderick 2002 *The first toll roads. Ireland's turnpike roads.* (Cork), p. 149.

9   F. Hamond 1997 'Communications in county Down' in L. Proudfoot (ed) 1995 *Down history and society.* (Dublin), pp. 599-628, at p. 601.

10 J. H. Andrews 1985 *Plantation acres. An historical study of the Irish land surveyor and his maps.* (Omagh), pp. 195-6.

11 Hamond 1997, p. 602, Andrews 1964, pp. 33ff.

12 Andrews 1964, p. 32; D. Broderick 1996 *An early toll-road. The Dublin-Dunleer turnpike.* (Dublin).

13 Andrews 1964, p. 26; P. J. O'Keeffe 1980 'Richard Griffith: Planner and builder of roads', in G. L. Herries Davies and C. R. Mollan (ed) *Richard Griffith 1784-1878.* (Dublin), pp. 57-75; at 60.

14 Hamond 1997, p. 602; Rynne 1999 (b), p. 178.

15 E. Leahy 1844 *A practical treatise on making and preparing roads.* (London), pp. 37-8; B. O'Donoghue 1993 'The office of county surveyor – origins and early years', *TICEI* **117**, pp. 127-230.

16 O'Connor 1999, p. 34.

17 Andrews 1964, p. 25; J. Leckey 1983 'The end of the road: the Kilcullen Turnpike 1844-1848 compared with 1787-1792', *JRSAI* **113**, pp. 106-20.

18 Broderick 2002, p. 37.

19 Broderick 1996, p. 19; 2002, p. 79; D. Ó Gráda 1983 'The rocky road to Dublin: Transport modes and urban growth in the Georgian Age, with particular reference to the turnpike roads', *Studia Hibernica*, no. 22/23, pp. 128-48.

20 Andrews 1964, p. 25; Ó Gráda 1983, p. 136.

21 M. G. Lay 1992 *Ways of the world. A history of the world's roads and of the vehicles that used them.* (New Brunswick), p. 108.

22 Andrews 1964, p. 26.

23 Lecky 1983, p. 106; M. O'Donnell 1992 'Road repairing in 18th century Tipperary', *THJ*, pp. 159-62 at 61. See also P. J. Meghan 1986 'Turnpike roads in county Limerick', *Old Limerick Jnl.* **XX** (Winter), pp. 21-5.

24 E. O'Leary 1914 'Turnpike roads of Kildare, Queens County, etc., in the eighteenth century', *JKAS* **viii** , pp. 118-24 at p. 119.

25 Broderick 2002, p. 52.

26 Broderick 1996, p. 53; McCutcheon 1980, pl. 7. 4.

27 Rynne 1998 (c), p. 76ff.

28 P. J. O'Keeffe 1996 *Alexander Taylor's roadworks in Ireland, 1780-1827.* (Dublin) pp. 4ff; also 1998 'Building the Wicklow military road', *TI* **30**, 2, pp. 22-5.

29 P. Kerrigan 1995 *Castles and Fortifications in Ireland 1485-1945.* (Cork), pp. 180ff. The Glencree barracks is currently a centre for peace and reconciliation, the Aghavannagh site now functions as a youth hostel.

30 O'Keeffe 1998, pp. 24-5. Between 1725 and 1736 Wade supervised the construction of 250 miles (400km) of military roads in the Scottish highlands, see W. Taylor 1976 *The military roads in Scotland.* (Newton Abbot) and B. P. Hindle 1993 *Roads, tracks and their interpretation.* (London), pp. 96-7.

31 S. Ó Luing 1976 'Richard Griffith and the roads of Kerry II', *JKAHS* **9**, pp. 92-124 and 1975 'Richard Griffith and the roads of Kerry I', *JKAHS* **8**, pp. 89-113.

32 O'Keeffe 1980, p. 69.

33 M. G. Storrie 1968 'William Bald, surveyor, cartographer and civil engineer', *Trans. Inst. British Geographers* **47**, pp. 205-31.

34 McCutcheon 1980, p. 30; Hamond 1991, pp. 61-2; Cox and Gould 1998, pp. 169-70.

35 M. McMillen 1991 'The first Macadam road', *TI* **23**, 2, May, pp. 30-31. Telford himself has also been involved in the Howth and Dublin road, see L. T. C. Rolt 1985 *Thomas Telford.* (London), pp. 144-5.

36 Lay 1992, p. 79 convincingly argues that D. Clarke in his *The ingenious Mr Edgeworth* (London, 1965) overstates his case.

37 MacMillen 1991, p. 31.

38 Lay 1992, p. 88.

39 O'Keeffe 1980, pp. 70-1.

40 Cox 1980, p. 41.

41 Lay 1992, p. 85. The Irish engineer Sir John Macneill and Thomas Telford used concrete for road surfacing as early as 1828, on a 2.5km length of Telford's Holyhead Road, at Highgate Park in North London (*ibid.* 220). Macneill went on to secure a patent for the technique in 1828. See J .G. Byrne 2002 'Sir John Macneill 1793-1880 engineer, inventor and architect', in *Some aspects of the industrial heritage of North-East Ireland.* (Dublin), pp. 1-14. See also J. Quartermaine, B. Trinder and R. Turner 2003 *Thomas Telford's Holyhead Road: The A5 in North Wales.* (York)

42 See H. Parnell 1833 *A treatise on roads.* (London), where Macneill describes the device in Appendix 1; Byrne 2002, p. 3.

43 Hamond 1997, p. 605.

44 P. O'Dowd 2001 'On roads and milestones in county Galway', *JGAHS* 53, pp. 105-19.

45 Broderick 2002, pp. 54-5.

46 Broderick 2002, p. 171.

47 Broderick 1996, p. 50.

48 McCutcheon 1980, pl. 4.2.

49 Rynne 1999 (b), pp. 180-1.

50 P. C. Power 2000 *A history of Dungarvan and district.* (Dungarvan), p. 136.

51 McCutcheon 1980, pl. 4; J. Feehan 1979 *The landscape of Slieve Bloom: a study of its natural and human heritage.* (Dublin), p. 150.

52 Green 1963, pl. 21; W. Dick 1974 'Turnpikes', *TI* **5**, no. 12, March, p. 54.

53 See J. Butt and I. Donnachie 1979 *Industrial archaeology in the British Isles*. (London), p. 164; N. Cossons 1987 *The B.P. book of industrial archaeology*. (Newton Abbot), p. 241.

54 S. Duke 1996 'An ancient Irish bridge', *TI* **28**, no. 3, September, pp. 31-2; F. Moore 1996 'Ireland's oldest bridge', *AI* **10**, no. 38, pp. 24-7.

55 Rynne 1999 (b), p. 190.

56 P. O'Keeffe and T. Simington 1991 *Irish stone bridges. History and heritage*. (Dublin), pp. 258-68.

57 G. Sutton 1993 'Waterford bridge 1793-1911', *Decies* **48**, pp. 49-53; P. Grogan 1999 'Some aspects of Lemuel Cox's bridge', *Decies* **55**, pp. 27-48.

58 P. C. Power 1990 *History of Waterford city and county*. (Cork), p. 137.

59 C. Manning 1997 'The bridge at Finnea and the man who built it', *AI* **11**, no. 39, pp. 29-33.

60 D. Power *et al.* 1997 *Archaeological inventory of county Cork. Vol.3 Mid-Cork*. (Dublin), pp. 410-1; C. J. F. McCarthy 1999 'An antiquary's notebook 20', *JCHAS* **104**, pp. 147-53 at 149.

61 M. Barry 1985 *Across deep waters. Bridges of Ireland*. (Dublin), p. 110; O'Keeffe and Simmington 1991, p. 73.

62 Rynne 1998 (c), p. 73.

63 Hindle 1993, p. 87.

64 Barry 1985, p. 123; A. O'Sullivan, and J. Sheehan, 1996 *The Iveragh peninsula; an archaeological survey of south Kerry*. (Cork), p. 422.

65 O'Keeffe and Simmington 1991, p. 34.

66 N. Brunicardi 1985 *The bridge at Fermoy*. (Fermoy), p. 11; Rynne 1999 (b), p. 187.

67 Cox and Gould 1998, pp. 42-3. Semple describes his pioneering use of coffer dams in his *A treatise on building in water*. (Dublin, 1776).

68 I. W. Doyle 2003 'The lost bridge of Kilkenny city. John's Bridge, 1765-1910', *AI* 17, Spring, pp. 8-12; C. Cullen 2003 'The history of St John's Bridge, Kilkenny', *OKR*, pp. 126-40.

69 T. Ruddock 1979 *Arch bridges and their builders 1785-1835*. (Cambridge), p. 105; Cox and Gould 1998, p. 95.

70 Kerrigan 1995, p. 225.

71 J. Meridith, 1998 '"No small thing" Thomas Ivory's bridge at Lismore', *Irish Arts Review* **14**, pp. 102-14.

72 O'Keeffe and Simmington 1991, pp. 270-4; Cox and Gould 1998, p. 40.

73 O'Keeffe 1980, p. 64; Cox and Gould 1998, pp 251-2.

74 Rynne 1999 (b), p. 191.

75 Cox and Gould 1998, pp. 246-7 and pp. 252-3.

76 Ruddock 1979, pp. 198-200; Barry 1985, p. 103; Cox and Gould 1998, pp. 247-9.

77 Cox and Gould 1998, pp. 67-8, 215-16.

78 McCutcheon 1980, pl. 2. 6.

79 McCutcheon 1980, p. 38.

80 Cox and Gould 1998, p. 254; Rynne 1999 (b), p. 194.

81 P. Duffy and E. Rynne 1996 'Studdert's Bridge, Bunratty', *NMAJ* **37**, pp. 107-11.

82 Gwinell 1985, p. 11.

83 H. Maguire (ed) 2002 *An introduction to the architectural heritage of county Kildare*. (Dublin), p. 27, fig. 21.

84 Duffy and Rynne 1996, p. 111.

85 S. Spellisey 1998 *The history of Limerick city*. (Limerick), p. 126. The former and current Thomond bridges in Limerick also had toll houses, the latter still extant, see J. Grene Barry 1909 'Old Limerick bridges', *NMAJ* **1**, no. 1, pp. 7-13.

86 B. Trinder 1979 'The first iron bridges', *IAR* **III**, no. 2, Spring, pp. 112-2.

87 De Courcy has recently argued that this was not the case, based on the lack of corroboratory documentation in the Coalbrookdale archive (see J. W. De Courcy 1991 'The Ha'penny bridge in Dublin', *The Structural Engineer* **69**, no. 3 February, pp. 44-7). There is, however, at least one contemporary English source, of 1816, which refers to its manufacture at Coalbrookdale; see M. Craig 1982 *The architecture of Ireland from the earliest times to 1880*. (London), p. 277.

88 Cox and Gould 1998, p. 214-15.

89 Cox and Gould 1998, p. 47.

90 Cox and Gould 1998, p. 45-6; I. Hedley, and I. Scott 1999 'The St Helens Iron Foundry', *IAR* **XXI**, pp. 53-9 at 53.

91 Rynne 1999 (b), p. 195.

92 Cox and Gould 1998, pp. 70-1.

93 Barry 1985, p. 94; Cox and Gould 1998, pp. 269-70

94 Cox and Gould 1998, p. 119.

95 D. McQuillan 1992 'Dredge suspension bridges in Northern Ireland: history and heritage', *The Structural Engineer* **70**, no. 7, April, pp. 119-26 at pp. 119-20.

96 McQuillan 1992, pp. 121ff.

97 Anon. 1910 'Footbridge at Mizen Head Ireland', *Concrete and Construction Engineer* **5**, pp. 847-50; Cox and Gould 1998, pp. 267-8.

98 J. S. E. De Vesian 1910 'Ferroconcrete in road bridge construction', *Proc. of the First Irish Road Congress* (Dublin), p. 137.

99 Anon. 1911 'Reinforced concrete bridge over the Nore, Kilkenny', *Concrete and Construction Engineer* **6**, no. 3, pp. 223-26; Cox and Gould 1998, pp. 121, 188-89.

100 Anon. 1913 'Ferroconcrete bridge over the River Lagan', *The Engineer* **115**, pp. 493-4; Cox and Gould 1998, pp. 137-8.

101 Anon. 1915 'Reinforced concrete roads', *The Irish Builder and Engineer* **57**, no. 19, p. 399; Cox and Gould 1998, p. 122.

102 Rynne 1999 (b), p. 220.

103 Sir J. Purser Griffith 1912 'The twin Scherzer bridges on the North Wall quay, Dublin across the entrance to the Royal Canal and the Spencer Docks', *TICEI* **38**, pp. 176-204; Cox and Gould 1998, pp. 20-1.

Chapter 13

1   R. Delany 1988 *A celebration of 250 years of Ireland's inland waterways*. (Belfast), p. 11.

2   Delany 1988, p. 12; P. Clarke 1992 *The Royal Canal. The complete story*. (Dublin), pp. 13-14.

3   W. A. McCutcheon 1993 'The transport revolution: canals and river navigations' in K. B. Nowlan (ed) *Travel and transport in Ireland*. (Dublin), pp. 64-81.

4   Delany *ibid*. p. 19.

5   McCutcheon 1993, p. 63.

6   J. Jackson 1987 'Mallow-Lombardstown Canal', *Mallow Field Club Journal*, no. 3, pp. 22-9.

7   McCutcheon 1993, pp. 64-5.

8   V. T. H. Delany and D. R. Delany 1966 *The canals of the South of Ireland*. (Newton Abbot), p. 213.

9   Delany and Delany 1966, p. 203.

10   *ibid*. p. 213

11   M. Nevin 1993 'General Charles Vallancey 1725-1812', *JRSAI* **123**, pp. 19-58; Clarke 1992, p. 27.

12   N. Crowe 1994 *English Heritage book of canals*. (London), pp. 25-6.

13   J. Hill 1999 'Davis Ducart and Christopher Colles: architects associated with the Custom House at Limerick', *IADS* **II**, pp. 119-145, at p. 131.

14   W. A. McCutcheon 1963 'The Newry Navigation: the earliest inland canal in the British Isles', *Geographical Jnl*. **129**, pt 4, pp. 446-80; Green 1963, pp. 64-70.

15   Delany 1988, pp. 54-6.

16   R. Delany 1992 *Ireland's Royal Canal 1789-1992*. (Dublin), pp. 63-4.

17   Delany 1988, pp. 152-3.

18   G. D'Arcy 1969 *Portrait of the Grand Canal*. (Dublin), p. 12.

19   Clarke 1992, pp. 42ff; Delany 1992, pp. 7-8; Cox and Gould 1998, p. 65.

20   Delany 1973, pp. 20-2.

21   Delany 1992, p. 53.

22   McCutcheon 1965 p. 53.

23   Delany 1973, pp. 92-3.

24   *ibid*. pp. 143-4

25   McCutcheon 1980, pl. 20.2.

26   Delany 1992, pp. 37-8, 53.

27   D'Arcy 1969, p. 12.

28   Delany 1973, pp. 22-3, 97-8.

29   Delany 1973, 77ff; Cox and Gould 1998, pp. 66-7.

30   McCutcheon 1980, p. 62.

31   McCutcheon *ibid*. p. 110.

32   *ibid*. p. 213

33   Delany 1973, p. 14-15; Delany 1988, p. 76.

34   Delany 1992, p. 13.

35   T. U. Sadlier 1911 'Richard Castle architect', *JRSAI* **xli**, 31, pp. 241-5; R. Cox 2002 'Richard Castle', in A. W. Skempton *et al*. (ed) *A biographical dictionary of civil engineers in Great Britain and Ireland. Vol. 1 1500-1830*. (London), pp. 121-2.

36   McCutcheon 1965, p. 22.

37   Delany 1973, p. 23.

38   This was presumably the 'needless ornament', referred to by Brownrigg is his report on this canal of 1801, see M. Murphy 1980 'The Limerick Navigation Company, 1697-1836', *NMAJ* **xxii**, pp. 43-61, at 49.

39   Delany 1973, p. 20.

40   *ibid*. p. 14-15; Delany 1988, p. 66-7

41   Delany 1988, pp. 150-52; McCutcheon 1980, p. 68.

42   Delany 1995, p. 99.

43   C. Hadfield and A. W. Skempton 1979 *William Jessop, engineer*. (London), pp. 97-8.

44   Delany 1973, pp. 56-9; Anon. 1996 *The Grand Canal Docks*. (Dublin), p. 14.

45   Delany 1988, p. 54

46   Murphy 1980, p. 46.

47   Delany 1995, p. 46.

48   Delany 1973, p. 188.

49   For Ducart's architectural work see The Knight of Glin 1967 'A baroque Palladian in Ireland: the architecture of Davis Ducart – I', *Country Life* **cxlii**, 28 September, pp. 735-9; 1967 'The last Palladian in Ireland: the architecture of Davis Ducart – II', *ibid*. **cxlii**, 5 October, pp. 798-801; F. O'Dwyer 1997 (a) 'Making connections in Georgian Ireland', *Bulletin of the Irish Georgian Soc*. 28. pp. 7-23, at p. 16. For the most recent account of his architectural and engineering work in Ireland, see Hill 1999.

50   W. A. McCutcheon 1965 *The canals of the north of Ireland*. (Newton Abbot), p. 69.

51   McCutcheon 1965, pp. 70-71.

52 C. Hadfield 1986 *World canals, inland navigation past and present*. (London), p. 71.

53 H. Phillips 1922 'The Grand Canal: (2) The passenger boats', *JKAS* **10**, pp. 3-18.

54 R. Delany 1972 'Robertstown Hotel', *Canaliana, Annual Bulletin of the Robertstown Muintir na Tire*, pp. 5-8.

55 Clarke 1992, pp. 81-3.

56 Delany 1995, p. 136.

57 Delany *ibid.* p. 119.

58 Delany 1995, pp. 119-20.

59 Clarke 1992, pp. 80-1.

60 Delany 1995, p. 102

61 McCutcheon 1965, p. 65.

62 Delany 1995, p. 149.

63 Anon. 1986, p. 5-8.

64 Darcy 1969, p. 12.

65 Delany 1995, p. 22.

66 Murphy 1980, p. 46.

67 E. Rynne 1967 'A Sheela-na-Gig at Clonlara, co. Clare', *NMAJ* **x**, pp. 221-2. This bridge was removed in 1964, and replaced with a concrete one, upon which the Sheila-na-gig has been re-mounted.

68 For Chapman's engineering career see R. W. Rennison 2002 'William Chapman', in Skempton *et al.* (ed) 2002, pp. 124-32.

69 See C. A. Rees 1819 *The cyclopaedia, or universal dictionary of arts, sciences and literature*. (London); R. B. Schofield 1989 'Developments in bridge design and construction during the canal era of the late eighteenth century', in R. B. Schofield (ed) 1989 *The history of technology, science and society 1750-1914* (Jordanstown), unpublished papers.

70 R. Delany 1995 *The Grand Canal of Ireland*. (2nd ed.) pp. 58-9.

71 Schofield 1989 *op. cit.*

72 Feehan and O'Donovan 1996, pp. 65-7.

73 P. Flanagan 1972 *The Ballinamore and Ballyconnell Canal*. (Newton Abbot), pp. 65-7.

74 Delany 1988, p. 48.

75 Delany 1988, pp. 68-71.

76 McNeill 1971, p. 165.

77 R. Delany 1980 'Athlone navigation works, 1757-1849', in Murtagh, H. (ed) *Irish midland studies. Essays in commemoration of N.W. English* (Athlone), pp. 193-204; Delany 1988, p. 41.

78 M. Blair 1994 *Once upon the Lagan*. (Belfast), p. 31.

79 Blair 1994, p. 1.

80 Delany 1988, p. 71; A. W. Skempton 1976 'A history of the steam dredger', *TNS* **47**, pp. 97-116; Ince 1984, p. 115.

81 Pers. comm. Paul Duffy.

82 Delany 1988, p. 168.

83 McNeill 1969, p. 174.

84 I. Murphy 1974 'Pre-Famine passenger services on the Lower Shannon', *NMAJ* **XVI**, pp. 70-83, at 71, McNeill 1971, p. 168.

85 Delany 1988, p. 58; S. Kierse 1995 *Portraits of Killaloe*. (Killaloe), p. 33.

86 Kierse 1995, p. 34.

87 R. Delany 2004 *Ireland's inland waterways. Celebrating 300 years*. (Belfast), pp. 185-6.

88 *Ibid.* pp. 188-99.

Chapter 14

1 H. Boyd 1981 'Ballycastle harbour. An account of the progress of Ballycastle Harbour, together with a representation of the present state of the works', (Repr. of 1743 account) *The Glynns* **9**, pp. 5-15.

2 McCutcheon 1965, p. 71; McCutcheon 1980, p. 65. A sale notice of 1793 lists 'a wagon road which leads to the [Tyrone] navigation', see S. Johnson 1997 *Johnson's atlas and gazetteer of the railways of Ireland*. (Leicester), p. 134.

3 J. W. P. Rowledge 1993 *A regional history of Irish railways. Vol. XVI Ireland*. (Trowbridge), p. 21.

4 J. Kilroy 1998 *Trams to the Hill of Howth, a photographic tribute*. (Newtownards), pp. 6-7.

5 D. Gwyn, 1991 'Valentia slate slab quarry', *JKAHS*, no 24, pp. 40-7.

6 P. Pearson 1991 *Dun Laoghaire Kingstown*. (Dublin), p. 24; R. Lohan 1994 *Guide to the archives of the Office of Public Works*. (Dublin), p. 152.

7 A. Day and P. McWilliams (ed) 1990 *Ordnance Survey Memoirs of Ireland. Vol. 3 Parishes of county Down I, 1834-6*. (Dublin and Belfast), p. 88.

8 I. Weld 1832 *Statistical survey of the county of Roscommon*. (Dublin), pp. 67ff.

9 Weld 1832, p. 76; T. Ferris, and P. Flanagan 1997 *The Cavan and Leitrim Railway. The last decade*. (Leicester), pp. 49-50.

10 M. Swift 1999 *Historical maps of Ireland*. (London), pp. 126-7.

11 E. Duffy 2003 'In search of Hodgson's tramway', *JMHTI* **3**, pp. 21-4.

12 C. E. J. Fryer 2000 *The Waterford and Limerick Railway*. (Poole), p. 7.

13 K. B. Nowlan 1993 'The transport revolution: the coming of the railways', in K. B. Nowlan (ed) 1993 *Travel and transport in Ireland*. (Dublin), pp. 96-109.

14 J. Lee 1993 'The golden age of Irish railways', in K. B. Nowlan (ed) 1993 *Travel and transport in Ireland*. (Dublin), pp. 110-19.

15 J. Lee 1969 'The provision of capital for early Irish railways, 1830-53', *Irish Historical Studies* **16**, pp. 33-63.

16 G. W. Hemans 1889 'On the railway system in Ireland', *TICEI* **xviii** (1888-9), pp. 45-54.

17 Lee 1993, p. 17.

18 K. A. Murray and D. B. Macneill 1976 *The Great Southern and Western Railway.* (Wicklow), p. 11.

19 H. C. Casserley 1974 *Outline of Irish railway history.* (Newton Abbot); F. Mulligan 1983 *One hundred and fifty years of Irish railways.* (Dublin), pp. 168ff.

20 K. A. Murray 1950 'William Dargan' *JIRRS* **2**, pp. 94-102, R. Cox 2002 (a) 'William Dargan', in Skempton *et al.* (ed), p. 171.

21 L.T.C. Rolt 1980 *Isambard Kingdom Brunel.* (Harmondsworth). pp. 114-15.

22 McCutcheon 1980, p. 106; C. J. A. Robertson 1983 *The origins of the Scottish railway system 1722-1844.* (Edinburgh), pp. 196-7.

23 For Nixon see C. Creedon 1986 *The Cork, Bandon and South Coast Railway. Vol. 1, 1849-1899.* (Cork), p. 10; for Brunel's Irish involvement see Rolt 1980, p. 196 and A. Buchanan 2002 *Brunel. The life and times of Isambard Kingdom Brunel.* (London and New York), pp. 84-5; for his involvement with the Dublin and South Eastern Railway see E. Shepherd and G. Beesley 1998 *The Dublin & South Eastern Railway. An illustrated history.* (Leicester), pp.10ff.

24 J. Simmons 1991 *The Victorian railway.* (London), p. 19ff ; R. Morris 1999 *The archaeology of railways.* (Stroud), p. 37.

25 N. E. Gamble 1981 (a) 'The Dublin and Drogheda Railway Part I', *JIRRS* **14**, no. 84, pp. 162-70.

26 G. W. Hemans 1850 'An account of the construction of the Midland Great Western Railway of Ireland, over a tract of bogs in the counties of Meath and West Meath', *TICEI* **40**, pt 1, pp. 48-80; Cox and Gould 1998, p. 77.

27 E. Shepherd 1994 *The Midland and Great Western Railway of Ireland. An illustrated history.* (Leicester), p. 108.

28 T. Middlemass 1981 *Irish standard gauge railways.* (Newton Abbot), p. 6; Rowledge 1995, pp. 22-3; Buchanan 2002, pp. 68-9.

29 H. Fayle 1970 *Narrow gauge railways of Ireland.* (East Ardsley), p. 7; J. D. C. A. Prideaux 1981 *The Irish narrow gauge railway.* (Newton Abbot), p. 5; T. Ferris 1993 (a) *The Irish narrow gauge: a pictorial history. Vol. I From Cork to Cavan.* (Belfast), pp. 6-7.

30 M. H. Gould 1991 'The effect of government policy on railway building in Ireland', *TNS* **62**, pp. 81-96.

31 P. Taylor 1994 *The West Clare Railway.* (Brighton), pp. 35ff; J. I. C. Boyd 1999 *The Schull & Skibbereen Railway.* (Usk), pp. 107ff.; D. J. Rowlands 1977 *The Tralee and Dingle Railway.* (Dublin), pp. 6-7.

32 E. M. Patterson 1972 *The Clogher Valley Railway.* (Newton Abbot); T. Ferris 1993 *The Irish narrow gauge: a pictorial history. Vol. 2 The Ulster Lines.* (Belfast), p. 11.

33 E. M. Patterson 1982 *The County Donegal Railways.* (Newton Abbot), p. 40; S. Flanders 1997 *Londonderry & Lough Swilly Railway. An Irish railway pictorial.* (Leicester), p. 2; Rynne 1999, p. 270, n. 124.

34 Prideaux 1981, pp. 8ff.

35 Murray 1981, pp. 149-50.

36 Murray 1981, pp. 152ff.

37 J. Simmons and G. Biddle 1999 *The Oxford companion to British railway history. From 1603 to the 1990s.* (Oxford), pp. 519-20.

38 Murray and Macneill 1976, p. 179; Shepherd 1994, p. 108.

39 S. C. Jenkins 1993 *The Cork, Blackrock and Passage Railway.* (Oxford), p. 15.

40 N. G. L. Currie 1973 *The Northern Counties Railway. Vol. I Beginnings and development 1845-1903.* (Newton Abbot), pp. 56-8.

41 Currie 1973, p. 117.

42 Murray and Macneill 1976, p. 179.

43 Boyd 1999, p. 245, E. M. Patterson 1982 *The County Donegal Railways.* (Newton Abbot), p. 15.

44 M. Guerin 1988 *The Lartigue. The Listowel and Ballybunion Railway. (Listowel); A. T. Newham 1989 The Listowel and Ballybunion Railway.* (Headington).

45 K. A. Murray 1977 'The Bretland tracklayer', *JIRRS* **13**, no. 73, pp. 74-88.

46 P. Duffy 1999 'Engineering', in T. Foley (ed) 1999 *From Queen's College to National University. Essays on the academic history of QCG/UCG/NUI, Galway.* (Dublin), pp. 125-41, at 130-31.

47 O. Doyle 1996 'Bridges – Dublin Border', *JIRRS* **19**, no. 130, pp. 237-40.

48 McCutcheon 1980, p. 160; F. O'Dwyer 1997 (b) *The architecture of Deane and Woodward.* (Cork), pp. 113-14.

49 N. V. Torpey 2004 (b) 'Irish railway bridges – 2', *JIRRS* **22**, no, 154, pp. 122-8 at p. 122.

50 N. E. Gamble 1981 (b) 'The Dublin and Drogheda Railway. Part II', *JIRRS* **14**, no. 85, pp. 228-35.

51 Cox and Gould 1998, pp. 115-6.

52 J. Rapley 2003 *The Brittania and other tubular bridges and the men who built them.* (Stroud), p. 33.

53 J. G. James 1981 'The evolution of iron bridge trusses to 1850', *TNS* **52**, pp. 67-101; 81ff; Rapley *ibid.* p. 33.

54 James 1981, p. 82; Jenkins 1993, p. 15.

55 K. A. Murray 1978 (a) 'Richard Osborne at Limerick – 1', *JIRRS* **13**, no. 77, pp. 294-300; K. A. Murray 1978 (b) 'Richard Osborne at Limerick – 2', *JIRRS* **14**, no. 82, pp. 320-34; James 1981, p. 86.

56 Murray 1981, p. 143. The Dodder bridge was replaced in 1934.

57 W. E. Shepherd 1984 'The Cork, Bandon and South Coast Railway-1', *JIRRS* **15**, no. 14, June, pp. 209-18, p. 210 Creedon 1986, p. 14.

58 C. Creedon 1989 *The Cork, Bandon and South Coast Railway. 2: 1900-1950.* (Cork), p. 8.

59 Shepherd 1994, pp. 16ff; Cox and Gould 1998, p. 78.

60 R. C. Cox 1990 *Bindon Blood Stoney. Biography of a port engineer.* (Dublin), p. 11; G. B. Howden 1934 'Reconstruction of the Boyne viaduct', *TICEI* **60**, pp. 71-111; K. A. Murray 1949 'The Boyne viaduct', *JIRRS*, no. 5, 14-17 (repr. in *Jnl Old Drogheda Soc.*, no. 6, 1989, pp. 5-18). A controversy ensued between Macneill and his assistant James Barton over who actually designed the innovative iron work, credit for which seems to have been largely Barton's. See C. O'Mahony, 1990 'Iron rails and harbour walls: James Barton of Farnderg', *CLAHJ* **22**, pp. 134-49; C. O'Mahony, 1993 'James Barton, engineer', *JIRRS* **18**, no. 122, pp. 262-74; Duffy 1999, p. 129.

61   Cox and Gould 1998, pp. 263-4. Fairbairn supplied three further bridges to Irish railway companies, in 1850-1 to span the R. Suck near Ballinasloe, county Galway and Lough Atalia near Galway, both for the MGWR. Of these, only that on the Suck survives and is still in service, see N.V. Torpey 2004 (a) 'Irish railway bridges – 1', *JIRRS* **22**, no, 153, pp. 2-12, at p. 12.

62   C. R. Galwey 1879 'On the Nore Viaduct at Thomastown', *TICEI* **12**, pp. 133-51; P. J. Flanagan 1970 'The Nore Viaduct', *JIRRS* **9**, no. 52, pp. 236-8; Cox and Gould 1998, pp. 118-19.

63   Barry 1985, p. 20.

64   P. O. Jennings 1982 'Concrete in railway engineering practice', *JIRRS* **14**, no. 89, pp. 413-21.

65   R. L. McIlmoyle 1930 'Reinforced concrete railway bridges', *Concrete and Construction Eng.* **25**, pp. 37-45.

66   Creedon 1986, p. 11; Rynne 1999 (b), p. 209, E. Shepherd 2005 *Cork Bandon & South-Coast Railway.* (Hinckley, Leicester), p. 17.

67   Rynne 1999 (b), *op. cit.* McCutcheon 1980, p. 169.

68   Creedon 1986, p. 11

69   Rynne 1999 (b), p. 209.

70   McCutcheon 1980, p. 163.

71   K. A. Murray 1980 'Bray Head', *JIRRS* **14**, no. 82, pp. 71-84.

72   Murray 1981, p. 174.

73   Murray 1981, pp. 176ff.

74   Simmons 1991, p. 72

75   Murray and Macneill 1976, p. 142; Middlemas 1981, p. 15.

76   Murray 1981, p. 179.

77   McCutcheon 1969, p. 20.

78   Middlemass 1981, p. 26. The English engineer, J. G. Robinson was a formative influence on the engine designs employed by the Waterford and Limerick Railway in the years 1886-1910, see D. Jackson 1996 *J. G. Robinson. A lifetime's work.* (Headington).

79   Murray and Macneill 1976, p. 146; H. Ellis 1954 *British railway history: an outline from the accession of William IV to the nationalisation of railways 1830-1876.* (London), p. 372.

80   Middlemass 1981, p. 29.

81   Prideaux 1981, pp. 58ff. For the work of Ivatt and Aspinall at Inchicore see J. E. Chacksfield 2003 *The Coey/Cowie brothers. All railwaymen.* (Headington) pp. 17-19.

82   Murray and Macneill 1976, p. 166.

83   Shepherd 1994, p. 89.

84   Patterson 1982, pp. 154-5.

85   Taylor 1994, p. 111.

86   Murray 1981, pp. 49ff.

87   D. Jenkinson 1996 *The history of British railway carriages 1900-1955.* (York), pp. 7ff.

88   Murray 1981, p. 195.

89   *ibid.* p. 195.

90   *ibid.* p. 200.

91   *ibid.* p. 191.

92   D. G. Coakham 1986 'BCDR coaches of 80 years – 1', *JIRRS* **16**, no. 101, pp. 120-32 at 120.

93   Murray and Macneill 1976, pp. 158ff.

94   Shepherd 1994, p. 92; Currie 1973, p. 222.

95   Murray and Macneill 1976, pp. 160ff.

96   Murray and Macneill 1976, p. 158; Shepherd 1994, p. 95.

97   Fryer 2000, p. 133.

98   Murray and Macneill 1976, p. 160; Shepherd 1994, p. 93; E. Shepherd and G. Beesley 1998 *Dublin and South Eastern Railway.* (Leicester), p. 95.

99   Currie 1973, p. 222, Murray and Macneill 1976, pp. 160ff.

100   S. Flanders 1997 *The Londonderry and Lough Swilly Railway. An Irish railway pictorial.* (Leicester), p. 4.

101   Simmons and Biddle 1999, p. 41.

102   Coakham 1986, p. 122.

103   Murray and Macneill 1976, p. 164.

104   Currie 1973, p. 223.

105   D. Wood 1989 *The fateful day. A commemorative book of the Armagh Railway disaster June 12th 1889.* (Armagh).

106   Murray and Macneill 1976, p. 168.

107   *ibid.* p. 180.

108   Currie 1973, p. 128.

109   Murray and Macneill 1976, p. 181.

110   Shepherd and Beesley 1998, p. 127.

111   D. Stirling 2005 'The Irish contribution to railway signalling', *JIRRS* **22**, no 156, pp. 194-201 at 194-5.

112   O. Doyle 1993 'Malahide and Drogheda signalling', *JIRRS* **19**, no. 130, pp. 237-40.

113   J. Sheehy 1975 'Railway architecture – its heyday', *JIRRS* **12**, no. 68, pp. 125-138.

114   F. O'Dwyer, 2000 'The architecture of John Skipton Mulvany (1813-1870)', *IADS* **III**, pp. 11-75, at 25.

115   Sheehy 1975, p. 127; O'Dwyer 2000, pp. 32-8.

116　M. Gould and R. Cox 2003 'The railway stations of George Wilkinson', *IADS* **VI**, pp. 183-201.

117　C. L.V. Meeks 1956 *The railway station. An architectural history*. (New Haven and London), pp. 30ff.

118　W. M. Jacob 1944 'Kingsbridge terminus', *DHR* **6**, pp. 107-20.

119　M. Killeen 1981 'Broadstone railway station to bus garage', *DHR* **34**, pp. 140-54.

120　Rowledge 1995, p. 98.

121　McCutcheon 1980, p. 181.

122　D. O'Carroll, and S. Fitzpatrick (ed) 1996 *Hoggers, lords and railwaymen. A history of the Custom House Docks, Dublin*. (Dublin), p. 57.

123　Shepherd 1994, p. 102.

124　E. Duffy 2004 'Railway roundhouse, Clones', *Newsletter Industrial Heritage Association of Ireland*, p. 6.

125　Simmons and Biddle 1999, pp. 146-7.

126　Shepherd 1994, p. 112; Murray and Macneill 1976, p. 183.

127　O'Carroll and Fitzpatrick 1996, p. 99.

128　Gamble 1981 (b) 'The Dublin and Drogheda Railway, 1844-1847 – part 2', *JIRRS* **14**, no. 85, pp. 228-35.

129　Simmons and Biddle 1999, p. 262.

130　P. J. Slattery 1998 *The life and times of a railwayman. Limerick Junction 150 years on*. (Shannon), pp. 172, 196, 232-6.

131　O'Carroll and Fitzpatrick 1996, p. 101.

Chapter 15

1　A. Buchanan 1977 *The industrial archaeology of Britain*. (London), p. 274.

2　Rynne 1999 (b), p. 197

3　H. Boyd 1981 'Ballycastle Harbour. An account of the progress of Ballycastle Harbour, together with a representation of the present state of the works', *The Glynns* **9**, pp. 5-15 (repr. of original of 1743).

4　De Courcy Ireland 1988, p. 139.

5　Rynne 1999 (b), p. 197; Marmion 1855, p. 556.

6　For the early technical development of steam dredgers see Skempton, A. W. 1975 'A history of the steam dredger 1797-1830', *TNS* **47**, pp. 97-116, who omits the Irish evidence.

7　Gilligan 1988, p. 130.

8　A. Marmion 1855 *The ancient and modern history of the maritime ports of Ireland*. (London). For mid-nineteenth-century dredging operations in Waterford see A. Brophy 2004 'Port of Waterford: extracts form the records of Waterford Harbour Commissioners, from their establishment in 1816 to the Report of the Ports and Harbours Tribunal, 1930', *Decies* **60**, pp. 151-69 at pp. 158-60.

9　Marmion 1855, p. 528; O'Mahony 1986, p. 12.

10　E. Jones 1958 'Land reclamation in Belfast Lough', *UJA* **21**, pp. 132-141; R. Sweetman 1988 'The development of the port', in J. C. Beckett, *et al.* 1988 *Belfast, the making of the city 1800-1914*. (Belfast), pp. 57-70; see also R. Sweetman 1989 'The development of Belfast Harbour', in M. McCaughan and J. Appleby (ed) *The Irish Sea: aspects of maritime history*. (Belfast), pp. 101-10.

11　Coakley 1919, p. 85; Rynne 1999 (b), p. 200.

12　Rynne 1999 (b), p. 200.

13　Gilligan 1988, pp. 130-1.

14　Coakley 1919, p. 85; Rynne 1999 (b), p. 200.

15　R. C. Cox 1990 *Bindon Blood Stoney. Biography of a port engineer*. (Dublin), pp. 23-6.

16　Cox 1990, p. 27.

17　de Courcy 1996, p. 24.

18　Cox and Gould 1998, p. 13.

19　Cox and Gould 1998, pp. 13-14; G. O'Flaherty 1988 'Mature and stately, through the city', in E. Healy, C. Moriarty and G. O'Flaherty (ed) *The book of the Liffey from source to the sea*. (Dublin), pp. 117-62; J. Purser Griffith 1879 'The improvement of the bar of Dublin Harbour by artificial scour', *Min. Proc. Instn Civil Engineers* **58** (1878-9), pp. 104-43.

20　Coakley 1919, p. 84; W. O'Sullivan 1937 *The economic history of Cork City from the earliest times to the Act of Union*. (Cork), p. 209.

21　P. Langford and S. Mulherin 1982 *Cork City quay walls*. (Dublin), p. 3-4; Rynne 1999 (b), p. 201.

22　N. Furlong 1996 'The history of land reclamation in Wexford harbour', in D. Row and C. J. Wilson (ed) *High skies-low lands. An anthology of the Wexford slobs and harbour*. (Enniscorthy), pp. 83-96; Cox and Gould 1998, p. 99.

23　Cox and Gould 1998, p. 99.

24　W. Anderson 1862 'On the reclaimed lands at Wexford harbour, and the machinery employed in draining them', *TICEI* **7**, pp. 102-23.

25　See J. Mannion 1988 'The maritime trade of Waterford in the eighteenth century', in W. J. Smyth and K. Whelan (ed) 1988 *Common Ground. Essays on the historical geography of Ireland presented to T. Jones Hughes*. (Cork), pp. 208-33, 224ff.

26　Rynne 1999 (b), p. 199.

27　See Cox 1990, p. 19.

28　Canice O'Mahony 1993 'James Barton, engineer', *JIRRS* **18**, 122, p. 269.

29　Cox 1990, p. 19.

30　J. Rennie 1854 *The theory, formation and construction of British and foreign ports*. (London), pp. 199-200; Cox and Gould 1998, pp. 25-7; J. De Courcy Ireland 2001 *History of Dun Laoghaire Harbour*. (Dublin), pp. 14ff.

31 P. Pearson 1991 *Dun Laoghaire Kingstown.* (Dublin), p. 37.

32 W. A. McCutcheon 1985 'Transport 1820-1914', in L. Kennedy and P. Ollerenshaw (ed) *An economic history of Ulster.* (Manchester), pp. 109-36 at p. 132; Cox and Gould 1998, pp-149-50.

33 Cox and Gould 1998, p. 235.

34 Canice O'Mahony 1993, pp. 269-71.

35 Cox and Gould 1998, p. 104.

36 W. A. Maguire 1995 *Belfast.* (Keele), p. 69.

37 Gilligan 1988, p. 132; H. Duffy 1999 *James Gandon and his times.* (Kinsale), p. 264. The East Dock was closed in 1927 and later filled in.

38 Gilligan *ibid.* p. 133.

39 A. Lenihan 1866 *Limerick its history and antiquities.* (repr. Mercier Press, Cork), p. 471; K. Donnelly, M. Hoctor and D. Walsh 1994 *A rising tide. The story of Limerick harbour.* (Limerick), p. 19; Cox and Gould 1998, p. 239.

40 Marmion *ibid.* pp. 529-31; Rynne 1999 (b), p. 200.

41 Cox and Gould 1998, p. 19.

42 Gilligan 1988, p. 147-8.

43 D. J. Owen 1917 *A short history of the port of Belfast.* (Belfast), p. 37; Maguire 1995, p. 69.

44 E. McParland 2001 *Public architecture in Ireland 1680-1760.* (New Haven and London), p. 119.

45 J. Hill 1999 'Davis Ducart and Christopher Colles: architects associated with the Custom House at Limerick', *IADS* **II**, pp 119-45. The Limerick Custom House is now the permanent home of the Hunt Museum.

46 E. McParland 1991 *The Custom House Dublin.* (Dublin), p. 29.

47 F. O'Dwyer 2002 'Building empires: architecture, politics and the Board of Works 1760-1860', *IADS* **V**, pp. 108-175.

48 W. Colfer 1985 'The tower of Hook', *JWHS* **10**. pp. 69-78 and Colfer 2004, pp. 84ff.

49 Craig 1982, p. 277.

50 Gilligan 1988, p. 71.

51 P. Beaver 1971 *A history of lighthouses.* (London) pp. 86-8; D. B. Hague and R. Christie 1977 *Lighthouses: their architecture, history and archaeology.* (Llandysul), pp. 86ff; D. Power *et al.* 1994 *Archaeological inventory of county Cork. Vol 2. East and South Cork.* (Dublin), p. 295.

52 Hague and Christie 1977, p. 88.

53 Hague and Christie 1977, pp. 87-8; Gilligan 1988, pp. 71ff.

54 Cox and Gould 1998, p. 16.

55 Hague and Christie 1977, p. 91.

56 Gilligan 1988, p. 72.

57 *ibid.* p. 83.

58 Cox and Gould 1998, pp. 105, 236. Both of these were designed by Halpin snr.

59 Hague and Christie 1977, p. 129.

60 C. W. Scott 1906 *History of the Fastnet lighthouse.* (London); Beaver 1971; Cox and Gould 1998, p. 236; J. Morrisey 2004 *A history of the Fastnet lighthouse.* (Dublin), pp. 91-12.

61 De Courcy Ireland 1986, p. 258.

62 M. Coulter 1998 'An introduction to lighthouses. History, technology, architecture and archaeology', *ULS* **19**, Spring/Summer, pp. 27-44.

63 A. Mitchell 1848 'On submarine foundations: particularly the screw-pile and moorings', *Min. Proc. Inst. Civ. Engrs* **7**, pp. 108-46; F. J. Biggar 1907 'Alexander Mitchell, the famous blind engineer of Belfast', *Proc. Belfast Nat. Hist and Phil. Soc.* , pp. 19-29. The best recent account is by R. Cox 2002 (b) 'Alexander Mitchell and the screw pile', in *Some aspects of the industrial heritage of North East Ireland* (Dublin) pp. 15-28.

64 De Courcy Ireland 1986, p. 171; Gilligan 1988, p. 81.

65 P. Kerrigan 1982 'Irish Coastguard stations 1858-67', *The Irish Sword* **14**, pp. 103-05.

66 Lohan 1994, p. 78.

67 Kerrigan 1995, p. 263.

68 Hamond 1991, p. 68.

Chapter 16

1 Hill 1991, pp. 78-9.

2 R. M. Cleary 1985 'Excavation of wall and wooden pump (off Smith Street, Cork City)', *JCHAS* **90**, pp. 120-26.

3 J. C. O'Sullivan 1969 'Wooden pumps', *Folklife* **7**, pp. 101-16.

4 J. Loudan 1940 *In search of water being a history of the Belfast water supply.* (Belfast), p. 16.

5 James Malton's 'The Provost's House, Trinity College, Dublin' shows a Dublin water cart of *c.* 1794, see M. Dunlevy 1994 'Dublin in the early nineteenth century: domestic evidence', in R. Gillespie and B. P. Kennedy (ed) *Ireland. Art into history.* (Dublin and Colorado), pp. 185-206.

6 Loudan *ibid.* pp. 11-12.

7 See C. Brooking 1983 *The City of Dublin 1728.* Reproduced from *A map of the city and suburbs of Dublin …; with an introduction and notes by Maurice Craig.* (Dublin).

8 Delany 1973, pp. 138, 191.

9 M. J. O'Kelly 1970 'Wooden water mains at South Terrace, Cork', *JCHAS* **75**, pp. 125-8.

10 R. Caulfield 1876 *The council book of the Corporation of Cork*. (Guildford), p. 895; Rynne 1999 (b), p. 227.

11 J. de Courcy 1996 *The Liffey in Dublin*. (Dublin), pp. 132-3.

12 Caulfield 1876, pp. 751-2; O'Sullivan 1937, p. 143.

13 S. Carroll 1972 'Waterford's water supply', *Old Waterford Soc. Jnl* **iii**, pp. 116-7; Hill 1999, p. 123.

14 de Courcy Ireland 1996, p. 132.

15 P. Power 1918 'An ancient wooden water pipe', *JRSAI* **xlvii**, pp. 78-9.

16 O'Kelly 1970, pp. 121ff.

17 de Courcy 1996, p. 132.

18 Loudon 1940, p. 46; Rynne 1989, p. 231.

19 Delany 1973, p. 19.

20 de Courcy 1996, p. 133,

21 de Courcy 1996 *op. cit.*

22 Rynne 1999 (b), p. 241.

23 *ibid*. p. 245.

24 Lenihan 1866, pp. 476-7.

25 P. Duffy 1999 'Engineering', in T. Foley (ed) *From Queen's College to National University. Essays on the academic history of QCG/UCG/NUI Galway*. (Dublin) pp. 124-41 at 137-8.

26 Duffy *ibid* p. 138. The iron breastshot wheel was originally installed to power the distillery's plant, see S. Roberts 1851 'An account of an iron breast wheel, 36hp, recently erected at the Newcastle Distillery in Galway', *TICEI* **4**, pp. 53-7.

27 Pers. comm. Paul Duffy.

28 Duffy *ibid*. p. 137.

29 Loudon 1940, pp. 47ff. For details of Bateman's work as a water engineer see P. Russell 1981 'John Frederic La Trobe-Bateman (1810-1889) Water Engineer', *TNS* **52**, pp. 119-38.

30 Loudon 1940, pp. 66-7.

31 Cox and Gould 1998, pp. 143-4.

32 Loudon 1940, pp. 67-9.

33 McCutcheon 1970, p. 9.

34 Hawksley built pumping stations for the Nottingham Waterworks Company and for at least 18 other towns throughout England; see G. M. Binnie 1981 *Early Victorian water engineers*. (London), pp. 131-2. However, after his work on the Liverpool waterworks he tended to concentrate on constant supplies i.e., water supply systems based on forming reservoirs through the construction of dams. His other noteworthy contributions to Irish water engineering were as consultant to Cork Corporation in 1860 and on the Wexford waterworks.

35 P. Neville 1874 'On the water supply of the city of Dublin', *Min. Proc. Inst. Civil Engrs* **38**, pp. 1-149; J. C. O'Sullivan 1908 'Description of the works in connection with the proposed additional storage reservoir at Roundwood, county Wicklow', *TICEI* **34**, pp. 94-120, Cox and Gould 1998, pp. 124-6.

36 Neville 1874, *ibid.*, G. Low 1865 'Description of a rock boring machine', *Proc. Inst. Mech, Engrs.*, pp. 179-200.

37 C. Costello 1996 *A most delightful station: the British army on the Curragh of Kildare, Ireland 1855-1922*. (Cork), pp. 26-7.

38 S. Ó Maitiú 2003 *Dublin's surburban towns 1834-1930. Governing Clontarf, Drumcondra, Dalkey, Killiney, Kilmainham, Pembroke, Kingstown, Blackrock, Rathmines and Rathgar*. (Dublin), pp. 87-89.

39 Ó Maitiú *ibid*. p. 91.

40 J. Andrews 1875 'On Burren waterworks', *TICEI* **11**, pp. 12-23; Cox and Gould 1998, p. 241.

41 Anon. 1876 *Irish Builder*, 1 October 1876, **xviii** no. 403, p. 295.

42 For Ennis see *Irish Builder* 1 Nov 1880, **xxii**, no. 501, p. 307, Rostrevor, *ibid*. 1 Nov 1881, **xxxiii**, no. 525, p. 314; Bangor, *ibid* 15 Sept 1883, **xxv**, no. 570, p. 296-7 and Dundalk, *ibid*. 1 Oct 1891, **xxxiii**, no. 534, pp. 300-3.

43 Cox and Gould 1998, Anon. *Irish Builder* 1 Dec 1899, **xli**, no. 957, p. 198.

44 J. Prunty 1999 *Dublin slums, 1800-1925: a study in urban geography*. (Dublin) p. 70.

45 O'Mahony 1997, p. 242.

46 Prunty *ibid*. pp. 86-8.

47 O'Mahony 1997, pp. 243-5, 258-60.

48 *Ibid*. p. 318.

49 Ó Maitiú 2003, pp. 101-2. M. McMahon 2005 'Zwei Dubliner Vororte bauten Irlands erstes Abwassersytem', *Industrie-Kultur* **6**, 2, p. 16.

50 H. Barty King 1984 *New flame. How gas changed the commercial, domestic and industrial life of Britain between 1813 and 1984*. (Tavistock), pp. 16-20; J. Griffiths 1992 *The third man. The life and times of William Murdoch 1754-1839 the inventor of gas lighting*. (London), pp. 240-1 and 264ff.

51 B. Irish 2001 *Shipbuilding in Waterford 1820-1882. An historical, technical and pictorial study*. (Bray), pp 14-15.

52 C. J. O'Sullivan 1987 *The gasmakers. Historical perspectives on the Irish gas industry*. (Dublin), p. 75; Rynne 1999 (b), p. 246.

53 O'Sullivan 1987, p. 33.

54 Rynne 1999 (b), p. 245.

55 E. J. Law 1997 'The origins and early years of Kilkenny gasworks', *OKR* **49**, pp. 66-73.

56 O'Sullivan 1987, p. 40.

57 G. B. L. Wilson 1974 'The small country gasworks', *TNS* **40**, pp. 33-43.

58 Wilson 1974, p. 39; O'Sullivan 1987, p. 18.

59 Rynne 1999 (b), p. 247.

60 C. McCabe 1992 'History of town gas industry in Ireland', *DHR* **xlv**, no. 1, pp. 28-40.

61 McCabe *ibid*. p. 32.

62 Rynne 1999 (b), p. 246.

63 McCabe 1992, p. 36.

64 Rynne 1999 (b), p. 247.

65 Barty-King 1984, p. 117.

66 *Ibid*. pp. 155-7.

67 O'Sullivan 1987, p. 137.

68 Rynne 1999 (b), p. 247.

69 L. Schoen 2002 'The Irish Free State and the electricity industry', in A. Bielenberg (ed) 2002 *The Shannon Scheme and the electrification of the Irish Free State*. (Dublin), pp. 20-27, at 29.

70 G. O'Beirne and M. O'Connor 2002 'Siemens-Schuckert and the electrification of the Irish Free State', in A. Bielenberg (ed) 2002 *The Shannon Scheme and the electrification of the Irish Free State*. (Dublin), pp. 73-99, at 77.

71 M. Manning and M. McDowell 1984 *Electricity supply in Ireland. The history of the ESB*. (Dublin), p. 1; N. O'Flanagan 1992 'Dublin's current history', *TI* **24**, no. 5, pp. 42-4.

72 Rynne 1999 (b), p. 195.

73 Manning and McDowell 1984, p. 1.

74 J. H. McGuigan 1964 *The Giant's Causeway tramway*. (Oxford), p. 12. The world's first public electric railway opened in 1881 at Lichterfelde near Berlin.

75 McGuigan *ibid*. pp. 84ff; A. McCutcheon 1985 'The Salmon Leap power station, county Antrim', in C. Mollan, W. Davies and B. Finucane (ed) *Some people and places in Irish science and technology*. (Dublin), pp. 106-7.

76 J. Kilroy 1996 *Irish trams*. (Dublin), p. 63-4.

77 Manning and McDowell 1984, pp. 3-5; Ó Maitiú 2003, pp. 163-5.

78 Barnard 1887, pp. 380-1

79 Rynne 1999 (b), p. 250.

80 Manning and McDowell 1984, p. 2; Anon. 1989 'Electricity comes to Carlow' *Carloviana, Jnl of Old Carlow Soc*. 1988-9, no. 36, p. 24.

81 The circuits, alternating switches etc. were installed by Gerald Percival (Stratten and Stratten 1892, pp. 145-6), who established Cork's first firm of electrical contractors. Percival and Brother Dominic Burke made an electric tramcar which ran at the 1889 exhibition at the Corn Exchange on Anglesea Street, W. McGrath 1981 *Tram tracks through Cork*. (Cork), p. 26.

82 Manning and McDowell 1984, p. 7-8; O'Flanagan 1992, p. 43.

83 Ó Maitiú 2003, p. 166.

84 Manning and McDowell 1984, pp. 11-12.

85 Gribbon 1969, p. 143.

86 D. D. C Pochin-Mould 1991 *Discovering Cork*. (Dingle), p. 163-4.

87 Manning and MacDowell 1984, p. 14.

88 Gribbon 1969, p. 143.

89 Cossons 1987, p. 228.

90 Hills 1989, p. 221; O'Flanagan 1992, p. 42.

91 Rynne 1999 (b), p. 251.

92 De Courcy 1996, p. 140.

93 Schoen 2002, p. 29.

94 B. Delany 2002 'McLaughlin, the genesis of the Shannon Scheme and the ESB', in A. Bielenberg (ed) 2002 *The Shannon Scheme and the electrification of the Irish Free State*. (Dublin), pp. 11-27, at 11-12.

95 Delany 2002, pp. 14-17.

96 O'Beirne and O'Connor 2002, pp. 73-99.

97 M. McCarthy 2002 'How the Shannon Scheme workers lived', in A. Bielenberg (ed) 2002 *The Shannon Scheme and the electrification of the Irish Free State*. (Dublin), pp. 48-72, at p. 51. For fuller treatment of the labour force see M. McCarthy 2004 *High tension. Life on the Shannon Scheme*. (Dublin).

98 B. Delany 2002 'The railway system for the Shannon Scheme', in A. Bielenberg (ed) 2002 *The Shannon Scheme and the electrification of the Irish Free State*. (Dublin), pp. 100-13.

99 P. Duffy 1987 'Ardnacrusha –birthplace of the ESB', *NMAJ* **29**, pp. 68-72; B. Cullen 2002 'Some notable features of the design and operational history of Ardnacrusha since 1929', in A. Bielenberg (ed) 2002 *The Shannon Scheme and the electrification of the Irish Free State*. (Dublin), pp. 138-54.

Chapter 17

1 For the origins and development of social housing in Ireland see F. H. A. Aalen 1985 'The working-class housing movement in Dublin, 1850-1920', in M. J. Bannon (ed) *The emergence of Irish planning 1880-1920*. (Dublin), pp. 131-88; F. H. A. Aalen 1990 'Health and housing in Dublin c. 1850-1921', in F. H. A. Aalen and K. Whelan (ed) *Dublin city and county: from prehistory to present. Studies in honour of J. H. Andrews*. (Dublin), pp. 279-304; M. Fraser 1996 *John Bull's other homes. State housing and British policy in Ireland, 1883-1922*. (Liverpool).

2 J. Alfrey and C. Clarke 1993 *The landscape of industry. Patterns of change in the Ironbridge Gorge*. (London and New York), p. 172.

3 C. Smith 1750 *The ancient and present state of the county and city of Cork.* (Cork), vol. 1, p. 358.

4 D. S. Macneice 1981 'Industrial villages of Ulster, 1800-1900', in P. Roebuck (ed) *Plantation to partition. Essays in Ulster history in honour J. L. McCracken.* (Belfast) pp. 172-90.

5 McNeice 1981, p. 173.

6 M. Cohen 1997 (b) *Linen, family and community in Tullylish, Co. Down, 1690-1940.* (Dublin), p. 120-1.

7 Cohen *ibid.* pp. 130-32.

8 *Ibid.* p. 165

9 G. Miley, J. Cronin and M. Sleeman 2003 *Portlaw county Waterford. Conservation Plan.* (Heritage Council, np), p. 18.

10 MacNiece 1981, p. 174.

11 Miley *et al.* 2003, pp. 18-19.

12 MacNeice 1981, p. 189.

13 Fraser 1996, p. 69.

14 N. Gordon Bowe 1999 ' "The wild heath has broken out again in the heather field"' Philanthropic endeavour and the Arts and Crafts achievement in early 20th-century Kilkenny', *IADS* **2**, pp. 67-97.

15 N. Johnston 1992 *The Fintona horse tram. The story of a unique Irish branch line.* (Omagh) pp. 10-15.

16 J. Kilroy 1996 *Irish trams.* (Dublin), p. 11.

17 M. Corcoran 2000 *Through streets broad and narrow. A history of Dublin Trams.* (Leicester), pp. 10-17.

18 W. McGrath 1981 *Tram tracks through Cork.* (Cork), pp. 20-1; M. H. Waller and P. Waller 1992 *British and Irish tramway systems since 1945.* (Runnymede), pp. 15, 60-61.

19 Kilroy *ibid.* pp. 9-13.

20 Corcoran 2000, p. 23.

21 Kilroy *ibid.* p. 12.

22 A. T. Newham 1964 *The Dublin and Lucan Tramway.* (Headington); H. Fayle and A. T. Newham 1963 *The Dublin and Blessington Tramway.* (Repr. 1980 Headington); J. R. L. Currie 1968 *The Portstewart Tramway.* (Headington); E. M. Patterson 1998 *The Castlederg and Victoria Bridge Tramway.* (Newtownards); E. M. Patterson 1972 *The Clogher Valley Railway.* (Newton Abbot).

23 J. H. McGuigan 1964 *The Giant's Causeway Tramway. The pioneer hydro-electric railway.* (Oxford) pp. 6-7.

24 McGuigan 1964, p. 46. The Ulster Folk and Transport Museum has in its collection a open carriage ('toast rack'), built for the line in 1885, while the National Transport Museum at Howth Castle has the body of Electric Car No. 9 from the railway, which would appear to be the oldest surviving example of an electric tramcar in the world, see Kilroy 1996, p. 125

25 Kilroy *ibid.* pp. 10, 63.

26 Kilroy *op. cit.*

27 Corcoran 2000, p. 33.

28 McGrath 1981, pp. 39-40.

29 Corcoran 2000, pp. 33, 37.

30 For early Cork bus services see W. A. Swanton 1992 *Cork's early buses. The story of Southern Motorways and its times.* (Cork); for Ulster see M. L. Kennedy and D. B. McNeill 1997 *Early bus services in Ulster.* (Belfast).

31 J. Kilroy 1999 *Trams to the Hill of Howth. A photographic tribute.* (Newtownards), p. 4.

32 G. Wilson 1976 *The old telegraphs.* (London), pp. 124-6.

33 Wilson 1976, p. 11.

34 Wilson 1976, pp. 103-10.

35 Kerrigan 1993, pp. 156ff.

36 G. Cookson 2003 *The cable. The wire that changed the world.* (Stroud), p. 8.

37 E. G. Hall 1993 *The electric age. Telecommunications in Ireland.* (Dublin), p. 28.

38 P. J. Hughill 1999 *Global communications since 1844. Geopolitics and technology.* (Baltimore and London), pp. 30-3.

39 Hughill 1999, pp. 28-30; Cookson 2000, pp. 81-82.

40 D. D. C. Pochin Mould 1978 *Valentia portrait of an island.* (Dublin), pp. 107-8.

41 J. Rees 1994 'Captain Robert Halpin, cable king', *TI* **25**, March, pp. 34-7. Jim Rees has also written a comprehensive biography of Halpin *The life of Captain Robert Halpin.* (Dublin, 1993).

42 Hall 1993, pp. 30-3

43 Hall *ibid.* p. 36-40.

44 For the most recent account of Marconi's Irish projects see M. Sexton 2005 *Marconi. The Irish connection.* (Dublin).

45 M. Sexton 1995 'Marconi's wireless telegraph station at Crookhaven', *Mizen Jnl,* no. 3, pp. 79-90. See also G. R. Garrat 1994 *The early history of radio: from Faraday to Marconi.* (London).

List of Illustrations

All photographs and illustrations by the author unless otherwise stated.

Chapter 1

Chapter 2

Chapter 3

Chapter 11

Chapter 12

Chapter 13

Chapter 14

14.6   The Chetwynd Viaduct designed by Charles Nixon, on the Cork and Bandon Railway and completed in 1851.

14.7   Railway viaduct on the MGWR, spanning the River Shannon at Athlone viaduct, built by Fox Henderson and Company and completed in 1851, from G. S. Measom *The official illustrated guide to the Midland Great Western and Dublin Drogheda Railway.* (London, 1866).

14.8   The Thomastown viaduct, spanning the River Nore, near Thomastown, County Kilkenny, completed in 1877.

14.9   2-2-2 locomotive (no. 36), built in 1847, by Bury Curtis and Kennedy of Liverpool for the GS & WR, on display at the present Glanmire Road (Kent) station.

14.10   Atmospheric engine at Kingstown Station on the D&KR in 1844. Courtesy of the *Illustrated London News*.

14.11   Nineteenth-century signal cabin at Dundalk station, County Louth, demolished in 2002.

14.12   Signal cabin at Waterford North station erected in 1906 for new work on the South Wexford line.

14.13   Plan of Westland Row Station in 1835 (after Murray 1981).

14.14   Kingstown Station on the D &KR line, designed by John Skipton Mulvany.

14.15   Kingsbridge Station, which opened in 1846 as the Dublin terminus of the GS & WR, designed by the English architect, Sancton Wood (1814-86).

14.16   Moira station, completed in 1841, on the Great Northern Railway, one of the oldest surviving through stations in Ireland (after McCutcheon 1980).

14.17   Nineteenth-century permanent way men's houses at Limerick Junction, County Tipperary.

Chapter 15

15.1   Section through the South Bull wall (after de Courcy 1996).

15.2   The eighteenth-century Navigation Wall at Cork.

15.3   Drinagh pumping station, County Wexford, completed in the 1850s.

15.4   The Drinagh scoop wheel (after Anderson 1866).

15.5   Sections through the quaysides on the south and north channels of the River Lee at Cork.

15.6   One of three British Navy victualling stores, constructed on Haulbowline Island in Cork harbour in 1816-22.

15.7   Cork bonded warehouses, designed by Abraham Hargreaves and opened in 1818.

15.8   The former tobacco warehouse known as 'Stack A', built by John Rennie to the east of the George IV Dock in Dublin in the early 1820s.

15.9   Section of façade of the Cork Custom House of 1724, now part of the Crawford Art Gallery.

15.10   The Limerick Custom House, designed by Davis Ducart, and completed in 1769.

15.11   The thirteenth-century light tower on the Point of Hook, County Wexford (after Colfer 1985).

15.12   Irish Brazier lighthouses (after Hague and Christie 1977).

15.13   Early eighteenth-century brazier lighthouse on the Old Head of Kinsale, County Cork.

15.14   Poolbeg lighthouse on the South Bull wall in Dublin Bay.

15.15   J. R Wigham. Courtesy of Billy Wigham.

15.16   The Bailey lighthouse in 1897 as drawn by J. R. Wigham. Courtesy of Billy Wigham.

15.17   Wigham's workshop models of Irish lighthouses. Courtesy of Billy Wigham.

Chapter 16

16.1   The Dublin city basin as depicted by Brooking in 1728.

16.2   Eighteenth-century wooden water mains from Cork city.

16.3   Cork Corporation Waterworks, general plan.

16.4   The interior of the turbine pumping house of 1888, at Cork Corporation Waterworks.

16.5   The development of the Dublin and Belfast water supply networks (after Hamond 1997).

16.6   The embankment for the Vartry reservoir, from Neville 1874.

16.7   Entrance to valve house at the Vartry reservoir.

16.8   Gasholder dating from the 1880s at the former Barrow Street gasworks at Ringsend, Dublin

16.9   The Cork gas works in 1920.

16.10   Retorts at Carrickfergus gas works. Courtesy of Flame, The Gasworks Museum of Ireland.

16.11   Detail of the Carrickfergus retorts. Courtesy of Flame, The Gasworks Museum of Ireland.

16.12   Giant's Causeway generating station at Bushmills, County Antrim.

16.13   Dublin Corporation's Fleet Street generating station, early in the twentieth century. Courtesy of Dublin City Archives.

16.14   Mechanical excavator at work on millrace for Ardnacrusha power station. Courtesy of Paul Duffy.

16.15   General plan of millrace, weir and power station at Ardnacrusha (after Duffy 1987).

16.16   Volute casing for turbines under construction at Ardnacrusha. Courtesy of Paul Duffy.

Chapter 17

17.1   Workers' houses at Ballincollig Gunpowder Mills, County Cork.

17.2   Workers' houses at Portlaw model village, County Waterford.

17.3   Portlaw *polyvium*, corner extending into open street space.

17.4   Cork horse tram in early 1870s. Day Collection, courtesy of Chris and Amy Ramsden.

17.5   Distribution of Irish urban tramway systems (after Kilroy 1996).

17.6   Napoleonic War period signal tower at entrance to Old Head of Kinsale, County Cork, with slate cladding.

17.7   The *Niagara* laying the Atlantic telegraph cable in 1857. *Illustrated London News*, 22 August 1857 (Courtesy of the *Illustrated London News*).

17.8   The landing of the Atlantic cable at Foilhommerum, Valentia Island in 1865. *Illustrated London News*, 5 August 1865 (Courtesy of the *Illustrated London News*).

17.9   The remains of the original Atlantic cable relay station at Foilhommerum, Valentia Island.

Bibliography

Abbreviations

AI	Archaeology Ireland
AJ	Archaeological Journal
CLAHJ	County Louth Archaeological and Historical Journal
DHR	Dublin Historical Record
EHR	Economic History Review
IA	Industrial Archaeology
IAR	Industrial Archaeology Review
IADS	Irish Architectural and Decorative Studies
IESH	Irish Economic and Social History
JCHAS	Journal of the Cork Historical and Archaeological Society
JGAHS	Journal of the Galway Archaeological and Historical Society
JIRRS	Journal of the Irish Railway Record Society
JKAS	Journal of the Kildare Archaeological Society
JKAHS	Journal of the Kerry Archaeological and Historical Society
JMHTI	Journal of the Mining Heritage Trust of Ireland
JRSAI	Journal of the Royal Society of Antiquaries of Ireland
JWHS	Journal of the Wexford Historical Society
NMAJ	North Munster Antiquarian Journal
MHSIN	Mining History Society of Ireland Newsletter
OKR	Old Kilkenny Review
PMA	Post Medieval Archaeology
PRIA	Proceedings of the Royal Irish Academy
TICEI	Transactions of the Institution of Civil Engineers of Ireland
THJ	Tipperary Historical Journal
TI	Technology Ireland
TNS	Transactions of the Newcomen Society
UFL	Ulster Folklife
UJA	Ulster Journal of Archaeology
ULS	Ulster Local Studies

Aalen, F.H.A. 1985 'The working-class housing movement in Dublin, 1850-1920', in M.J. Bannon (ed) 1985 *The emergence of Irish planning 1880-1920*. (Dublin), pp. 131-88.

Aalen, F.H.A. 1990 'Health and housing in Dublin *c.* 1850-1921', in F.H.A. Aalen and K. Whelan (ed) 1990 *Dublin city and county: from pre-history to present. Studies in honour of J.H. Andrews*. (Dublin), pp. 279-304.

Alcock, O. D hÓra, K. and Gosling, P. 1999 *Archaeological inventory of county Galway Vol II: North Galway*. (Dublin).

Alfrey, J. and Clarke, C. 1993 *The landscape of industry. Patterns of change in the Ironbridge Gorge*. (London and New York).

Alfry, J. and Putnam, T. 1992 *The industrial heritage: managing resources and uses*. (London).

Allford, W.A.L. and Parkes, J.W. 1953 'Sir James Murray: a pioneer in the making of superphosphate', *Chemistry and Industry*, pp. 852-5.

Anderson, E.B. 1984 *Sailing ships of Ireland*. (Dublin).

Anderson, W. 1862 'On the reclaimed lands at Wexford harbour, and the machinery employed in draining them', *TICEI* 7, pp. 102-23.

Andrews, J. 1875 'On Burren waterworks', *TICEI* 11, pp. 12-23.

Andrews, J. 1989 'Arklow's early chemical industry *c.* 1770-1853' *Arklow Hist. Soc. Jnl*, pp. 8-12.

Andrews, J.H. 1956 'Notes on the historical geography of the Irish iron industry', *Irish Geography* 3, pp. 139-49.

Andrews, J.H. 1964 'Road planning in Ireland before the railway age', *Irish Geography* 5 (1), pp. 17-41.

Andrews, J.H. 1985 *Plantation acres. An historical study of the Irish land surveyor and his maps.* (Omagh).

Anon. 1864 *The Irish Builder*, July 1864 **vi,** no. 109, pp. 130-1.

Anon. 1876 *The Irish Builder*, 1 October 1876, **xviii** no. 403, p. 295.

Anon. 1899 *The Irish Builder*, 1 December 1899, **xli,** no. 957, p. 198.

Anon. 1901 'Dundalk brickworks', *The Irish Builder*, 27 March 1901, **xliii,** pp. 674-5.

Anon. 1902 (a) 'Ballinphellic brickworks', *The Irish Builder*, 27 March, **xliii,** no 1014, pp. 1080-1

Anon. 1902 (b) 'Brick, tile and earthenware industry in Ireland', *The Irish Builder*, 27 March, **xliii,** no 1014, pp. 1088-86.

Anon. 1902 (c) 'Irish work and workers. XVI Soap manufacture', *The Irish Rosary* **6**, no. 10, Oct., pp. 796-801.

Anon. 1903 (a) 'Kingscourt brick and tile works', *Irish Builder and Engineer,* 3 November, **xliv,** no. 1056, pp. 2066-9.

Anon. 1903 (b) 'Irish work and workers. XIX, A successful village industry. An example of paternal treatment of workers', *The Irish Rosary* **9**, no. 1, January, pp. 54-66.

Anon. 1907 'Utilisation of power for small industries', in *Irish rural life and industry, Irish International Exhibition, 1907* (Dublin), pp. 121-7.

Anon. 1910 'Footbridge at Mizen Head Ireland', *Concrete and Construction Engineer* **5**, pp. 847-50.

Anon. 1911 'Reinforced concrete bridge over the Nore, Kilkenny', *Concrete and Construction Engineer* **6**, no. 3, pp. 223-6.

Anon. 1913 'Ferroconcrete bridge over the River Lagan', *The Engineer* **115**, pp. 493-4.

Anon. 1915 'Reinforced concrete roads', *The Irish Builder and Engineer* **57**, no. 19, p. 399.

Anon. 1915 *Report on the sources and production of iron and other metalliferous ores used in the iron and steel industry.* (London).

Anon. 1973 'The glasshouse at Gurteens and glass developments in Ireland before its establishment', *OKR* **25**, pp. 51-60.

Anon. 1977 *The first sixty years 1917-1977 Ford in Ireland.* (Cork).

Anon. 1986 *Industries of the north one hundred years ago.* (Repr. of *Industries of Ireland, part 1*, London, 1891).

Anon. 1986 *Scrabo Country Park.* (Belfast).

Anon. 1989 'Electricity comes to Carlow', *Carloviana, Jnl of Old Carlow Soc.* no. 36, p. 24.

Anon. 1996 'Restoring the old Glengowla East lead mine, Oughterard, County Galway', *JMHTI* **1**, Spring, p. 4.

Anon. 1996 *MHSIN,* Autumn, p. 11.

Anon. 1996 *The Grand Canal Docks.* (Dublin).

Anon. 1997 'Society News', *MHSIN*, no. 4, spring, p 2.

Anon. 1998 *MHSIN,* no. 9, December, p. 2.

Anon. 2004 *An introduction to the architectural heritage of county Roscommon.* (Dublin).

Anon. 2004 *An introduction to the architectural heritage of county Waterford.* (Dublin).

Anon. 2004 *An introduction to the architectural heritage of county Wicklow.* (Dublin).

Anon. 2004 *An introduction to the architectural heritage of county Leitrim.* (Dublin).

Archer, J. 1801 *Statistical survey of County Dublin.* (Dublin).

Baker, D. 1991 *Potworks. The industrial architecture of the Staffordshire potteries* (London).

Ball, L. and Rainey, D. 2002 *A taste of old Comber. The town and its history.* (Dundonald).

Barnard, A. 1887 *The whiskey distilleries of the United Kingdom.* (London).

Barnard, T.C. 1982 'Sir William as Kerry ironmaster', *PRIA* **82C**, pp. 1-32.

Barnard, T. C. 1985 'Anglo-Irish industrial enterprise: Iron-making at Enniscorthy, Co. Wexford, 1657-92', *PRIA* **85C**, no. 4, pp. 101-44.

Barry, M. 1985 *Across deep waters. Bridges of Ireland.* (Dublin).

Barry, R. 1920 'The resources of Ireland', *Catholic Bulletin* **10**, February 1920, pp. 101-7.

Barry, W. 1919 *History of the Port of Cork steam navigation.* (Cork).

Barton, D.B. 1965 *The Cornish beam engine.* (Truro).

Barty King, H. 1984 *New flame. How gas changed the commercial, domestic and industrial life of Britain between 1813 and 1984.* (Tavistock).

Bassett, G.H. 1885 *Wexford county guide and directory.* (Repr. Dublin,1991).

Bassett, G.H. 1886 *Louth County guide and directory.* (Repr. Dundalgan Press, Dundalk, 1998).

Bassett, G.H. 1889 *County Tipperary 100 years ago. A guide and directory* (Repr. 1991, Belfast).

Bateman, J.F. la Trobe 1841 'Description of the Bann reservoirs, county Down, Ireland', *Min. Proc. Inst. Civ. Engrs.* **1**, pp. 168-70.

Beaver, P. 1971 *A history of lighthouses.* (London).

Bedwin, O.R. 1980 'The excavation of a late 16th- century blast furnace at Batsford, Herstmonceux, East Sussex, 1978', *PMA* **14**, pp. 89-112.

Bell, A. 1908 *The early iron industry of Furness and district.* (Ulverston).

Bell, J. 1987 'The improvement of Irish farming techniques since 1750: theory and practice', in P. O'Flanagan, P. Ferguson and K. Whelan (ed) 1987 *Rural Ireland 1600-1900: modernism and change.* (Cork), pp. 24-41.

Bell, J. and Watson, M. 1986 *Irish farming, implements and techniques 1750-1900.* (Edinburgh).

Berry, H.F. 1915 *A history of the Royal Dublin Society.* (Dublin).

Bielenberg A. 1991 *Cork's Industrial Revolution 1780-1880: Development or decline?* (Cork).

Bielenberg, A. 1992 'The growth and decline of a textile town: Bandon 1770-1840', *JCHAS* **97**, pp. 111-119.

Bielenberg, A. 1993 *Locke's Distillery: a history.* (Dublin).

Bielenberg, A. 1994 'The Watt family and the distillery industry in Derry, 1762-1921', *UFL* **40**, pp. 16-26.

Bielenberg, A. 1995 'Mechanised linen manufacture in Limerick in 1859; some clues to the external economies of the Belfast industry', *IESH* **XXII**, pp. 64-76.

Bielenberg, A. 1998 'The Irish brewing industry and the rise of Guinness, 1790-1914', in R.G. Wilson and T.R. Gourvish (ed) 1998 *The dynamics of the international brewing industry since 1800*. (London), pp. 105-22.

Bielenberg, A. 2003 (a) 'The Irish distilling industry under the Union', in D. Dickson and C. Ó Gráda (ed) 2003 *Refiguring Ireland. Essays in honour of L.M. Cullen* (Dublin), pp. 290-314.

Bielenberg, A. 2003 (b) '*A survey of Irish flour milling 1801-1922*', in A. Bielenberg (ed) *Irish Flour milling – a history 600-2000* (Dublin), pp. 59-87.

Biggar, F.J. 1907 'Alexander Mitchell, the famous blind engineer of Belfast', *Proc. Belfast Nat. Hist and Phil. Soc.* pp. 19-29.

Binnie, G.M. 1981 *Early Victorian water engineers.* (London).

Blair, M. 1994 *Once upon the Lagan.* (Belfast).

Boate, G. 1860 *Ireland's Natural History* (first published London 1652) in *A collection of tracts and treatises illustrative of the natural history of Ireland*, vol. 1 (Dublin).

Bolger, P. 1977 *The Irish co-operative movement its history and development.* (Dublin).

Boucher, C.T.G. 1963 *John Rennie, 1761-1821: The life and work of a great engineer.* (Manchester).

Bowie, G. 1972 'The Millhouse Engine in Jameson's Distillery. Bow Street, Dublin', *IA* **9**, no. 3, pp. 265-77.

Bowie, G. 1974 'Two stationary steam engines in Power's Distillery, John's Lane, Dublin', *IA* **II**, no. 3, pp. 209-24.

Bowie, G. 1977 'Tide mills in Ireland', *Irish Engineers' Jnl* **30**, 10 November, pp. 9-10.

Bowie, G. 1978 (a) 'Early stationary steam engines in Ireland', *IAR* **2**, no. 1, pp. 168-74.

Bowie, G. 1978 (b) 'Some notes on tower mills in Ireland', *Trans International Molinological Society* **4**, pp. 65-7.

Bowie, G. 1979 'Corn drying kilns, meal milling and flour in Ireland', *Folklife* **17**, pp. 5-15.

Bowie, G. 1980 'Surviving stationary steam engines in the Republic of Ireland', *IAR* **4**, no. 1, (1979-80), pp. 81-90.

Boyd, H. 1981 'Ballycastle harbour. An account of the progress of Ballycastle Harbour, together with a representation of the present state of the works' (Repr. of 1743 account), *The Glynns* **9**, pp. 5-15.

Boyd, J.I.C. 1999 *The Schull & Skibbereen Railway.* (Usk).

Boylan, L. 1972 'The mills of Kildrought', *JKAS* **12**, no. 2, pp. 141-55.

Boylan, L. 1975 'The mills of Kildrought', *JKAS* **15**, pp. 359-75.

Boyle, E. 1988 'Linenopolis: the rise of the textile industry', in J.C. Beckett *et al. Belfast the making of the city*. (Belfast), pp. 41-85.

Brabazon, W. 1848 *The deep sea and coast fisheries of Ireland with suggestions for the working of a fishing company.* (Dublin).

Breslin, T. 2002 *The claymen of Youghal.* (Youghal).

Brett, C.E.B. 1985 *The buildings of Belfast, 1700-1914.* (Belfast).

Britton, F. 1994 'Carrickfergus clay', *English Ceramic Circle Trans.* **15**, pt. 2, pp. 308-9.

Broderick, D. 1996 *An early toll-road. The Dublin-Dunleer turnpike.* (Dublin).

Broderick, D. 2002 *The first toll roads. Ireland's turnpike roads.* (Cork).

Brooking, C. 1983 *The City of Dublin 1728. Reproduced from A map of the city and suburbs of Dublin …; with an introduction and notes by Maurice Craig.* (Dublin).

Brophy, A. 2004 'Port of Waterford: extracts form the records of Waterford Harbour Commissioners, from their establishment in 1816 to the Report of the Ports and Harbours Tribunal, 1930', *Decies* **60**, pp. 151-69.

Brown, K. 1996 'Notes on Cornish engine houses in Ireland 1: Ulster and Leinster', *MHSIN* **14**, September, pp. 5-6.

Brown, K. 1998 (a) 'Cornish engine houses in Ireland V. Knockmahon/Tankardstown', *MHSIN* **11**, July, pp. 11-12.

Brown, K. 1998 (b) 'The Cornish engine houses of Ireland III, West Carbery', *MHSIN* **8**, September, pp. 9-12.

Brown, K. 2002 'A unique Cornish engine house – Williams' in Avoca', *JMHTI* **2**, pp. 21-4.

Brown, K. 2003 'Silvermines engine houses', *JMHTI* **3**, pp. 63-4.

Brown, K. 2004 'Appendix 5: The steam engines of Ross Island Mine', in W. O'Brien 2004 *Ross Island. Mining, metal and society in Ireland.* (Galway), pp. 625-29.

Browne, B. 1991 'A forgotten county Wexford industry', *JWHS* No. 13, pp. 130-4.

Brunicardi, N. 1985 *The bridge at Fermoy.* (Fermoy).

Brunskill, R.W. 1990 *Brick building in Britain.* (London).

Bucci, F. (1991) *Albert Kahn: architect of Ford.* (New York).

Buchanan, R.A. 1977 *The industrial archaeology of Britain.* (London).

Buchanan, R.A. 2000 'The origins of industrial archaeology', in N. Cossons (ed) 2000 *Perspectives on industrial archaeology.* (London), pp. 18-35.

Buchanan, A. 2002 *Brunel. The life and times of Isambard Kingdom Brunel.* (London and New York).

Burt, R. 1984 *The British lead mining industry.* (Redruth).

Butt, J. and Donnachie, I. 1979 *Industrial archaeology in the British Isles.* (London).

Byrne, J. 2002 'Sir John Macneill, engineer, inventor and architect', in R. Cox (ed) 2002 *Some aspects of the industrial heritage of North-East Ireland.* (Dublin), pp. 1-14.

Byrne, M. 1980 'The distilling industry in Offaly, 1780-1954', in H. Murtagh (ed) 1980 *Irish Midland studies. Essays in commemoration of N.W. English.* (Athlone), pp. 213-28.

Calladine, A. and Fricker, J. 1993 *East Cheshire textile mills.* (London).

Callaghan, C. and Forsythe, W. 2000 'The Berehaven copper-mining industry – a maritime perspective', *AI* **14**, 1, 51, pp. 16-19.

Callan MacCardle, T. and Callan, W. 1902 (a) 'The brewing industry in Ireland', in W.P. Coyne, (ed) 1902 *Ireland Industrial and Agricultural.* (Dublin), pp. 451-93.

Callan MaCardle, T. and Callan, W. 1902 (b) 'The distilling industry', in W.P. Coyne (ed) 1902 *Ireland Industrial and Agricultural.* (Dublin), pp. 494-511.

495

Campbell, B.M.S. 2003 'Economic progress in the canal age: a case study from counties Armagh and Down', in D. Dickson and C. Ó Gráda (ed) 2003 *Refiguring Ireland. Essays in honour of L. M. Cullen*. (Dublin), pp. 63-93.

Campbell, J.W.P. and A. Saint 2002 'The manufacture and dating of English brickwork', *AJ* **159**, pp. 170-93.

Carey, A. and Meehan, R. 2004 'Excavation of a post-medieval pottery kiln, Tuam, County Galway', *JGHAS* **56**, pp. 37-45.

Carlton, P. 2000 'The role of FÁS' in N. Buttimer, C. Rynne and H. Guerin (ed) 2000 *The Heritage of Ireland*. (Cork), pp. 544-53.

Carr, J. 1806 *The stranger in Ireland or a tour in the southern and western parts of that country in 1805*. (London: Repr. 1970 with an introduction by L.M. Cullen).

Carroll, S. 1971 'Waterford's water supply', *Old Waterford Soc. Yearbook* **iii**, pp. 116-17.

Carter, N. 1994 'Hydraulic rams – reviving a lost technology', *TI* **25**, no 8, January, pp. 39-42.

Casey, C. and Rowan, A.1993 *The buildings of Ireland. North Leinster: the counties of Longford, Louth, Meath and Westmeath*. (London).

Casserley, H.C. 1974 *Outline of Irish railway history*. (Newton Abbot).

Caulfield, R. 1876 *The council book of the Corporation of Cork*. (Guildford).

Chacksfield, J.E. 2003 *The Coey/Cowie brothers. All railwaymen*. (Headington).

Chester, S. and Burns, N. 2001 'The mines of Barravore, Glenmalure, Co. Wicklow', *JMHTI* **1**, pp. 67-76.

Childs, P.E. 1998 'The early chemical industry and industrialization in Ireland', *Irish Chemical News*, pp. 18-25.

Ni Chinnéide, S. 1974 'A view of Kilkenny city and county in 1790', *JRSAI* **104**, pp. 29-38.

Claffey, J.A. 1980 'Rindoon windmill tower', in H. Murtagh (ed) 1980 *Irish Midland studies. Essays in Commemoration of N. W. English*. (Athlone) pp. 84-8.

Clark, C. 1998 *The British malting industry since 1830*. (London).

Clarke, D. 1965 *The ingenious Mr Edgeworth*. (London).

Clarke, D.J. 1954 'Paper-making in Ireland', *An Leabarlann* **12**, no. 3, pp. 69-73.

Clarke, P. 1992 *The Royal Canal. The complete story*. (Dublin).

Clarkson, L.A. 1996 'Ireland 1841: pre-industrial or proto-industrial; industrializing or de-industrialising', in S.C. Ogilvie and Markus German (ed) 1996 *European proto-industrialisation*. (Cambridge), pp. 67-84.

Cleary, R.M. 1985 'Excavation of wall and wooden pump (off Smith Street, Cork City)', *JCHAS* **90**, pp. 120-26.

Cleere, H. and Crossley, D. 1995 *The iron industry of the Weald*. (Cardiff).

Clutterbuck, R. 1996 'Industrial archaeology of an engine house in Slieveardagh, Co. Tipperary' *Trowel, Jnl of the Archaeological Soc. UCD* **vii**, pp. 46-9.

Coakham, D.G. 1986 'BCDR coaches of 80 years – 1', *JIRRS* **16**, no. 101, pp. 120-32.

Coakley, D.J. 1919 *Cork its trade and commerce. Official handbook of the Cork Incorporated Chamber of Commerce and Shipping*. (Cork).

Cohen, M. 1997 (a) 'Rural paths of capitalist development: class formation, paternalism and gender in county Down's linen industry', in L. Proudfoot (ed) 1997 *Down history and society. Interdisciplinary essays on the history of an Irish county*. (Dublin), pp. 567-99.

Cohen, M. 1997 (b) *Linen, family and community in Tullylish, Co. Down, 1690-1940*. (Dublin).

Cole, G.A.J. 1922 *Memoir and map of localities of minerals of economic importance and metalliferous mines in Ireland*. Survey of Ireland. Mineral Resources, 2 vols. (Dublin. Repr. 1998).

Colfer, W. 1985 'The tower of Hook', *JWHS* **10**, pp. 69-78.

Colfer, B. 2004 *The Hook Peninsula county Wexford*. (Cork).

Comiskey, J. 1997 'An Irishman's diary', *The Irish Times*, 5th September 1997.

Connell, K.H. 1950 'The colonization of waste land in Ireland, 1780-1845', *EHR* **3**, 7, pp. 44-71.

Conry, M. 1999 *Culm crushers*. (Carlow).

Conry, M. 2001 *Dancing the culm. Burning culm as a domestic and industrial fuel in Ireland*. (Chapelstown, Carlow).

Conry, M. 2004 *Corn stacks on stilts. Corn stands for spring threshing in Ireland*. (Carlow).

Conway, M. 2001 'John Street, Drogheda', in E. Bennett (ed) 2001 *Excavations 2000: summary accounts of archaeological excavations in Ireland*. (Bray), pp. 195-7.

Cooke, J. 1992 'John Hutton and Sons, Summerhill, Dublin: coachbuilders 1779-1925', *DHR* **xlv**, pp. 11-27.

Cookson, G. 2003 *The cable. The wire that changed the world*. (Stroud).

Corcoran, M. 2000 *Through streets broad and narrow. A history of Dublin Trams*. (Leicester).

Corlett, E.C.B. 1993 'The screw propeller and merchant shipping 1840-1865', in B. Greenhill and R. Gardiner (ed) 1993 *The advent of steam*. (London), pp. 83-105.

Corran, T.H. 1975 *A history of brewing*. (Newton Abbot).

Cossons, N. 1987 *The B.P. book of industrial archaeology*. (Newton Abbot).

Costello, C. 1996 *A most delightful station: the British army on the Curragh of Kildare, Ireland 1855-1922*. (Cork).

Cotter, E. 1999 'Adrigole', in I. Bennett (ed) 1999 *Excavations 1998, summary accounts of archaeological excavations in Ireland*. (Bray).

Coughlan, A. and O'Reilly, F.D. 1992 'The North Cork Coalfields', *Mallow Field Club Jnl*. **10**, pp. 44-53.

Coulter, M. 1995 'Patterson's spade mill, Northern Ireland', *IAR* **XVII**, no. 1, Autumn, pp. 96-105.

Coulter, M. 1998 'An introduction to lighthouses. History, technology, architecture and archaeology', *ULS* **19**, Spring/Summer, pp. 27-44.

Cowman, D. 1978 'The Royal Silver Mines of Bannow', *Decies* **9**, pp. 28-42.

Cowman, D. 1987 'The German mining experiment at Bannow Bay 1551-52', *JWHS* **11**, pp. 67-82.

Cowman, D. 1988 'The Silvermines – sporadic working: 1289-1874', *THJ*, pp. 96-115.

Cowman, D. 1990 'Two Kerry lead-silver mines: Kenmare and Castlemaine', *JKAHS* **23**, pp. 197-219.

Cowman, D. 1992 (a) 'The metal mines of Tipperary', *THJ*, pp. 106-115.

Cowman, D. 1992 (b) 'Survival, structures and statistics: Knockmahon Copper Mines, 1850-78', *Decies* **46**, Autumn, pp. 10-20.

Cowman, D. 1992 (c) 'Trade and society in Waterford city 1800-1840', in W. Nolan, T.P. Power and D. Cowman (ed) 1992 *Waterford history and society. Interdisciplinary essays on the history of an Irish county*. (Dublin).

Cowman, D. 1994 'The mining community at Avoca 1780-1880', in K. Hannigan and W. Nolan (ed) 1994 *Wicklow history and society. Interdisciplinary essays on the history of an Irish county*. (Dublin) pp. 761-88.

Cowman, D. 2001 (a) 'The mining boom of 1824-25, part 1', *JMHTI* **1**, pp. 49-54.

Cowman, D. 2001 (b) 'The metal mines of Dublin city and county, *c.* 1740-1825', *JMHTI* **1**, pp. 61-66.

Cowman, D. 2002 'The mining boom of 1824-5: Part 2 – Aftermath', *JMHTI* **2**, pp. 28-34.

Cowman, D. 2004 'Documents on mining history', *JMHTI* **4**, pp. 41-7.

Cowman, D. and Morris, J.H. 2003 'A history of quarrying and mining in Ireland', *JMHTI* **3**, pp. 25-32.

Cowman, D. and Reilly, T.A. 1988 *The abandoned mines of West Carbery – Promoters adventurers and miners*. (Worsop).

Cowper, A.D. 1927 *Lime and lime mortars*. (London, Repr. Donhead Publishing, Shaftesbury, 1998).

Cox, R.C. 1982 'Robert Mallet: engineering work in Ireland', in R.C. Cox (ed) 1982 *Robert Mallet 1810-1881*. (Dublin), pp. 71-118.

Cox, R.C. 1990 *Bindon Blood Stoney. Biography of a port engineer*. (Dublin).

Cox, R. 2000 'Civil engineering heritage', in N. Buttimer, C. Rynne and H. Guerin (ed) 2000 *The Heritage of Ireland*. (Cork), pp. 58-61.

Cox, R. 2002 (a) 'William Dargan' in A. Skempton *et al.* (ed) 2002 *A biographical dictionary of civil engineers in Great Britain and Ireland*. (London), p. 171.

Cox, R. 2002 (b) 'Alexander Mitchell and the screw pile', in *Some aspects of the industrial heritage of North East Ireland*. (Dublin), pp. 15-28.

Cox, R.C. and Gould, M.H. 1998 *Civil engineering heritage Ireland*. (London).

Coy, N. 1996 'Avoca's industrial age', *TI*, June, pp. 25-27.

Coy, N. 1999 'Clement's Mine', *MHSIN* **12**, December, pp. 3-4.

Craig, M. 1983 *The architecture of Ireland from the earliest times to 1880*. (London).

Cranstone, D. 1997 *Derwentcote steel furnace. An industrial monument in county Durham*. (Lancaster).

Cranstone, D. 2001 'Industrial archaeology – manufacturing a new society', in R. Newman, D. Cranstone and C. Howard Davis, *The historical archaeology of Britain c. 1540-1900*. (Stroud) pp. 185-210.

Crawford, W.H. 1980 'Drapers and bleachers in the early Ulster linen industry', in L. M. Cullen and P. Butel (ed) 1980 *Négoce et industrie en France et en Irlande aux XVIIIᵉ et XIXᵉ siécle*. (Paris), pp. 113-20.

Crawford, W.H. 1986 'The introduction of the flying shuttle into weaving of linen in Ulster', *UFL* 32, pp. 78-80.

Crawford, W.H. 1993 'A handloom weaving community in county Down', *UFL* **39**, pp. 1-14.

Crawford, W.H. 1994 *The handloom weavers and the Ulster linen industry*. (Belfast).

Crawford, W.H. 2002 'The creation and evolution of small towns in Ulster in the seventeenth and eighteenth centuries', in P. Borsay and L. Proudfoot (ed) 2002 *Provincial towns in early modern England and Ireland: Change convergence and divergence*. (Oxford), pp. 97-120.

Creedon, C. 1986 *The Cork, Bandon and South Coast Railway. I: 1849-1899*. (Cork).

Creedon, C. 1989 *The Cork, Bandon and South Coast Railway. II: 1900-1950*. (Cork).

Crocker, A. 2000 'Early water turbines in the British Isles', *IAR* **22**, pp. 83-102.

Crocker, G. 1986 *The gunpowder industry*. (Princes Risborough).

Cronin, D.A. 1995 *A Galway gentleman in the age of improvement. Robert French of Monivea, 1716-79*. (Dublin).

Crossley, D. 1989 (ed) *Water Power and the Sheffield Rivers*. (Sheffield).

Crossley, D. 1990 *Post-medieval archaeology in Britain*. (Leicester).

Crossley, D. 2003 'The archaeology of the coal-fuelled glass industry in England', *AJ* **160**, pp.160-97.

Crossman, V. 1994 *Local government in nineteenth-century Ireland*. (Belfast).

Crowe, N. 1994 *English Heritage book of canals*. (London).

Cullen, B. 2002 'Some notable features of the design and operational history of Ardnacrusha since 1929', in A. Bielenberg (ed) 2002 *The Shannon Scheme and the electrification of the Irish Free State*. (Dublin), pp. 138-54.

Cullen, C. 2003 'The history of St John's Bridge, Kilkenny', *OKR*, pp. 126-40.

Cullen, L.M. 1977 'Eighteenth-century flour milling in Ireland', *IESH* **4**, pp. 5-52.

Cullen, L.M. 1987 *An economic history of Ireland since 1660*. (2nd ed, London).

Culleton, B. 1994 *Treasures of the landscape: County Wexford's rural heritage*. (Wexford).

Cundick, R. 2002 'Harvey's of Hale: sales to Irish mines 1823-1884', *JMHTI*, pp.15-20.

Cunningham, J. 1994 'Arney brick and the Florencecourt Tile Brick and Pottery Works', *UFL* **40**, pp. 68-73.

Cunningham, J.B. 1997 *The story of Belleek*. (Belleek).

Cunningham, J. 1998 'A rural industry in west Ulster – stoneworking', *UFL* **44**, pp. 110-116.

Cunningham, J. 2004 *'A town tormented by the sea' Galway: 1790-1914*. (Dublin).

Cunningham, N. 1995 'The McCutcheon archive – a survey of industrial archaeology', *ULS* **15**, no. 1, pp. 62-71.

Curran, S. 1985 'The Merino factory at Ennisnay, Co. Kilkenny', *OKR* **3**, no. 2, pp.105-20.

Currie, J.R.L. 1968 *The Portstewart Tramway*. (Headington).

Currie, J.R.L. 1973 *The Northern Counties Railway. Vol 1 Beginnings and development 1845-1903*. (Newton Abbot).

Daly, M.E. 1985 *Dublin – The deposed capital: a social and economic history 1860-1914*. (Cork).

D'Arcy, G. 1969 *Portrait of the Grand Canal*. (Dublin).

Davies, A.C. 1977 'Roofing Belfast and Dublin 1896-98: American penetration of the Irish market for Welsh slate', *IESH* **iv**, pp. 26-35.

Davies, O. 1938 'Kilns for flax drying and lime-burning', *UJA* 3rd series **1**, pp. 79-80.

Davis, W. 1985 'Aeneas Coffey, excise man, distiller and inventor' in C. Mollan, W. Davis and B. Finucane (ed) *Some people and places in Irish science and technology*. (Dublin), pp. 22-3.

Day, A. and McWilliams, P. (ed) 1990 *Ordnance Survey Memoirs of Ireland. Vol. 3 Parishes of County Down I, 1834-6.* (Dublin and Belfast).

Day, A. and McWilliams, P. (ed) 1997 *Ordnance Survey Memoirs of Ireland vol 39. Parishes of County Donegal II 1835-6 mid, west and south Donegal* (Dublin and Belfast).

Decie 1980 'Life and work in an Irish Mining Camp *c.* 1840; Knockmahon copper mines, Co. Waterford', *Decies* **14**, May, pp. 29-42.

de Courcy J.W. 1971 'Reinforced concrete in Ireland', *TI* **4**, no. 9, December, pp. 29-31.

de Courcy, J.W. 1991 'The Ha'penny bridge in Dublin', *The Structural Engineer* **69**, no. 3 February, pp. 44-7.

de Courcy, J.W. 1996 *The Liffey in Dublin*. (Dublin).

de Courcy Ireland, J. 1981 *Ireland's sea fisheries: a history*. (Dublin).

De Courcy Ireland, J. 2001 *History of Dun Laoghaire Harbour*. (Dublin).

De Vesian, J.S.E. 1910 'Ferroconcrete in road bridge construction', *Proc. of the First Irish Road Congress*. (Dublin), p. 137.

de hÓir, S. 1988 'A Welsh quarryman's grave at Castletown Arra, Co. Tipperary', *NMAJ* **xxx**, pp. 35-8.

Delany, B. 2002 (a) 'McLaughlin, the genesis of the Shannon Scheme and the ESB', in A. Bielenberg (ed) 2002 *The Shannon Scheme and the electrification of the Irish Free State*. (Dublin), pp. 11-27.

Delany, B. 2002 (b) 'The railway system for the Shannon Scheme', in A. Bielenberg (ed) 2002 *The Shannon Scheme and the electrification of the Irish Free State* (Dublin), pp. 100-13.

Delany, R. 1972 'Robertstown Hotel', *Canaliana*, Annual Bulletin of the Robertstown Muintir na Tire, pp. 5-8.

Delany, R. 1973 *The Grand Canal of Ireland*. (Newton Abbot).

Delany, R. 1980 'Athlone navigation works, 1757-1849', in H. Murtagh (ed) 1980 *Irish midland studies. Essays in commemoration of N.W. English*. (Athlone), pp. 193-204.

Delany, R. 1988 *Ireland's inland waterways*. (Belfast).

Delany, R. 1992 *Ireland's Royal Canal 1789-1992*. (Dublin).

Delany, V.T.H. and Delany, D.R. 1966 *The canals of the South of Ireland*. (Newton Abbot).

Delaney, J.G. 1990 'Brickmaking in Gillen', *Folklife* **28**, pp. 31-62.

Dennison, S.R. and MacDonagh, O. 1998 *Guinness 1886-1939 from incorporation to the Second World War*. (Cork).

Dick, W. 1971 'Ballycorus chimney', *TI*, February, p. 25.

Dick, W. 1972 (a) 'The Dublin Corporation steam engine', *TI*, February, p. 46.

Dick, W. 1972 (b) 'Dressing ore at Wicklow Gap', *TI*, May, p. 36.

Dick, W. 1972 (c) 'The Killaloe slate quarries', *TI*, May, p. 42.

Dick, W. 1974 'Turnpikes', *TI* **5**, no. 12, March, p. 54.

Dick, W. 1975 'A premium on rags', *TI* **6**, no. 11, p. 42.

Dickinson, H.W. and Jenkins, R. 1927 *James Watt and the steam engine*. (Repr. London 1989).

Dickson, D. 1977 *The economic history of the Cork region in the eighteenth century*. unpubl. PhD thesis, Trinity College, Dublin.

Dickson, D. 1993 'Butter comes to market: the origins of commercial dairying in Cork', in P. O'Flanagan, and C.G. Buttimer, (ed) 1993 *Cork History and Society. Interdisciplinary essays on the history of an Irish county*. (Dublin), pp. 367-90.

Dickson, D. 2000 *New foundations. Ireland 1660-1800*. (Dublin).

Dickson, D. 2005 *Old world colony. Cork and south Munster 1630-1830*. (Cork).

Dickson, F.E. 1975 (a) 'Dublin Windmills', *TI* **7**, no.2, May, p. 46.

Dickson, F.E. 1975 (b) 'Rathgar Quarry', *TI* **7**, no.3, June, p. 42.

Dillon, M. 1968 'Coalisland: the evolution of an industrial landscape', *Studia Hibernica* **8**, pp. 75-95.

Dimes, F.G. 1999 (a) 'The nature of building and decorative stone', in J. Ashurst and F. G. Dimes (ed) 1999 *Conservation of building and decorative stone*. (Oxford), pp. 19-36.

Dimes, F.G. 1999 (b) 'Igneous rocks', in J. Ashurst and F.G. Dimes (ed) 1999 *Conservation of building and decorative stone*. (Oxford), pp. 37-60.

Dimes, F.G. 1999 (c) 'Sedimentary rocks', in J. Ashurst and F.G. Dimes (ed) 1999 *Conservation of building and decorative stone*. (Oxford), pp. 61-124.

Dimes, F.G. 1999 (d) 'Metamorphic rocks', in J. Ashurst and F.G. Dimes (ed) *Conservation of building and decorative stone*. (Oxford), pp. 135-49.

Dinn, J. 1988 'Dyfi furnace excavation 1982-7', *PMA* **22**, pp.111-42.

Donnachie, I. 1979 *A history of the brewing industry in Scotland*. (Edinburgh).

Donnelly, C. and Brannon, N. 1998 'Trowelling through history: historical archaeology and the study of early modern Ireland', *History Ireland* **6**, no. 3, Autumn, pp. 22-25.

Donnelly, C. and Hamond, F 1999 'Investigations at Mullycovet Mill, Belcoo, county Fermanagh', *AI* **13**, no. 2, 48, Summer, pp. 12-14.

Donnelly, K., Hoctor, M. and Walsh, D. 1994 *A rising tide. The story of Limerick harbour*. (Limerick).

Donnelly, J. S. 1976 'The Irish agricultural depression of 1859-64', *IESH* **3**, pp 33-54.

Dornan, B. 2000 *Mayo's lost islands: the Inishkeas*. (Dublin).

Douglas, G. and Oglethorpe, M.1993 *Brick, tile and fireclay industries in Scotland*. (Edinburgh).

Dowling, D. 1972 'Glenmore brickyards: a forgotten industry', *OKR*, no. 24, pp. 42-51.

Doyle, I.W. 2003 'The lost bridge of Kilkenny city. John's Bridge, 1765-1910', *AI* **17**, Spring, pp. 8-12.

Doyle, O. 1993 'Malahide and Drogheda signalling', *JIRRS* **19**, no. 130, pp. 237-40.

Doyle, O. 1996 'Bridges – Dublin Border', *JIRRS* **19**, no. 130, pp. 237-40.

Doyle, P. n.d. *Carrigaline Pottery 1928-1979*. (Dublin).

Doyle, P. and Smith, L. P. F. 1989 *Milk to market. History of the Dublin city milk supply*. (Dublin).

Dubourdieu, J. 1812 *Statistical survey of the county of Antrim*. (Dublin).

Dudley Westropp, M.S. 1978 *Irish glass. A history of glass-making in Ireland from the sixteenth century*. (revised ed. M. Boydell, Dublin).

Duff, F. 1977 'Windmills around Portaferry and district', *Jnl Upper Ards Hist. Soc.* 1, pp. 13-15.

Duffy, E. 2003 'In search of Hodgson's tramway', *JMHTI* **3**, pp. 21-4.

Duffy, E. 2004 'Railway roundhouse, Clones', *Newsletter Industrial Heritage Association of Ireland*, p. 6.

Duffy, H. 1999 *James Gandon and his times*. (Kinsale).

Duffy, P 1986 'Aspects of the engineering history of the west region', *The Engineers' Journal* **40**, September, no. 8, pp. 33-5.

Duffy, P. 1987 'Ardnacrusha –birthplace of the ESB', *NMAJ* **29**, pp. 68-72.

Duffy, P. 1994 (a) 'Cloon Weir', *Guaire*, Christmas, pp. 44-5.

Duffy, P. 1994 (b) 'Turf, steam and the Stein Brown Distillery', *NMAJ* 35, pp. 107-8.

Duffy, P. 2004 'The pre-history of the Shannon Scheme', *History Ireland* **12**, Winter, no. 4, pp. 34-8.

Duffy, P. and Rynne, E. 1996 'Studdert's Bridge, Bunratty', *NMAJ* **37**, pp. 107-11.

Duke, S. 1996 'An ancient Irish bridge' *TI* **28**, no. 3, September, pp. 31-2.

Dunlevy, M. 1982 'Wedgwood in Dublin, 1772-77', *Irish Arts Review* **1**, no. 2, pp. 8-14.

Dunlevy, M. 1988 *Ceramics in Ireland*. (Dublin).

Dunlevy, M. 1992 'Samuel Madden and the scheme for the encouragement of useful manufactures', in A. Bernelle (ed) 1992 *Decantations. A tribute to Maurice Craig Craig*. (Dublin), pp. 21-8.

Earl, B. 1978 *Cornish explosives*. (Penzance).

Edwards, D. 2003 *The Ormond lordship of county Kilkenny, 1515-1642. The rise and fall of Butler feudal power*. (Dublin).

Eiffe, J. 1986 'Leixlip iron works', *JKAS* xvi, no 5, pp. 432-6.

Elleson, C. 1983 *The waters of the Boyne and the Blackwater*. (Dublin).

Ellis, H. 1954 *British railway history: an outline from the accession of William IV to the nationalization of railways 1830-1876*. (London).

Evans, E. Estyn and Turner, B.S. 1977 *Ireland's Eye. The Photographs of John Welsh*. (Belfast).

Falkus, M.E. 1967 'The British gas industry before 1850', *EHR*, 2nd Series **20**, pp. 494-508.

Falkus, M.E. 1982 'The early development of the British gas industry, 1790-1815', *EHR*, 2nd Series **35**, pp. 217-34.

Fairbairn, W. 1871 *Treatise on mills and millwork*. (London), 2 vols, 3rd ed.

Farmar, T. 1996 *Heitons – a managed transition. Heitons in the Irish coal, iron and building markets 1818-1996*. (Dublin).

Fayle, H. 1970 *Narrow gauge railways of Ireland*. (East Ardsley).

Fayle, H. and Newham, A.T. 1963 *The Dublin and Blessington Tramway*. (Repr. 1980, Headington).

Feehan, J. 1979 *The landscape of Slieve Bloom: a study of its natural and human heritage*. (Dublin)

Feehan, J. 1983 *Laois an environmental history*. (Stradbally).

Feehan, J. and O'Donovan, G. 1996 *The bogs of Ireland. An introduction to the natural, cultural and industrial heritage of Irish peatlands*. (Dublin).

Feehan, J. 2003 *Farming in Ireland. History, heritage and environment*. (Dublin).

Feely, M., Lidwell, J. and Monaghan, D. 1996 'Mrs Coade's stone: a late eighteenth century addition to Co. Galway architectural heritage', *JGAHS* **48**, pp. 92-7.

Ferris, T. 1993 (a) *The Irish narrow gauge: a pictorial history. Vol. I From Cork to Cavan*. (Belfast).

Ferris, T. 1993 (b) *The Irish narrow gauge: a pictorial history. Vol. 2 The Ulster Lines*. (Belfast).

Ferris, T. and Flanagan, P. 1997 *The Cavan and Leitrim Railway – the last decade – an Irish railway pictorial*. (Leicester).

Fitzgerald, J. 1981 'The Drogheda textile industry, 1780-1820', *CLHAJ* **20**, no. 1, pp. 36-48.

Fitzgerald, M. 1991 'Industry and commerce in Athlone', in M. Heaney and G. O'Brien (ed) 1991 *Athlone bridging the centuries*. (Mullingar), pp. 34-46.

Fitzgerald, R. 1988 'The development of the cast iron frame in textile mills to 1850', *IAR* **10**, pp. 127-45.

Fitzgerald, S. 1999 *Mackerel and the making of Baltimore, county Cork 1879-1913*. (Dublin).

Flanagan, P.J. 1970 'The Nore Viaduct', *JIRRS* **9**, no. 52, pp. 236-8.

Flanagan, P. 1972 *The Ballinamore and Ballyconnell Canal*. (Newton Abbot).

Flanders, S. 1997 *The Londonderry and Lough Swilly Railway. An Irish railway pictorial*. (Leicester).

Fletcher, G. 1915 'Peat as a source of power', *Dept. Agric. and Technical Instruction Jnl.* **xvi**, no. 1, October, pp. 33-8.

Flinn, M.W. 1984 *The history of the British coal industry*. (Oxford).

Foley, J. 1993 'The Irish dairy industry: an historical perspective', *Jnl Soc. Dairy Technology* **46**, pp. 124-38.

Francis, P. 2000 *Irish delftware. An illustrated history*. (London)

Francis, P. 2001 *A pottery by the Lagan. Irish creamware from the Downshire china manufactory, Belfast, 1787- c. 1806*. (Belfast).

Fraser, M. 1996 *John Bull's other homes. State housing and British policy in Ireland, 1883-1922*. (Liverpool).

Fraser, M.A. 1951 'Some early Dublin potters', *DHR*. **xii**, pp. 47-58.

Fraser, R. 1801 *General view of agriculture … of the county of Wicklow*. (Dublin).

Freestone, C. 1991 'Forgotten but not lost: the secret of Coade Stone', *Proc. of the Geolog. Assoc.* **102**, pp. 135-8.

French, C. 1995 'Merchant shipping in the British Empire', in R. Gardiner and P. Bosscher (ed) 1995 *The heyday of sail*. (London), pp. 10-23.

Fryer, C.E.J. 2000 *The Waterford and Limerick Railway*. (Poole).

Furlong, N. 1996 'The history of land reclamation in Wexford harbour', in D. Row and C. J. Wilson (ed) 1996 *High skies-low lands. An anthology of the Wexford slobs and harbour.* (Enniscorthy), pp. 83-96

Gailey, R.A. 1970 'The typology of the Irish spade', in R.A. Gailey and A. Fenton (ed) 1970 *The Spade in Northern and Atlantic Europe.* (Belfast), pp. 35-48.

Gailey, A. 1982 (a) 'Bricks and brick-making in Ulster in the 1830s', *UFL* **28** pp. 61-64.

Gailey, A. 1982 (b) *Spademaking in Ireland.* (Cultra).

Gailey, A. 1984 (a) *Rural houses in the north of Ireland.* (Edinburgh).

Gailey, A. 1984 (b) 'Introduction and spread of the horse-powered threshing machine to Ulster's farms in the nineteenth century: some aspects', *UFL* **30**, pp. 37-54.

Galwey, C.R. 1879 'On the Nore Viaduct at Thomastown', *TICEI* **12**, pp. 133-51.

Gamble, N.E. 1981 (a) 'The Dublin and Drogheda Railway Part I', *JIRRS* **14**, no. 84, pp. 162-70.

Gamble, N.E. 1981 (b) 'The Dublin and Drogheda Railway. Part II', *JIRRS* **14**, no. 85, pp. 228-35.

Garrat, G.R. 1994 *The early history of radio: from Faraday to Marconi.* (London).

Geary, F. 1981 'The rise and fall of the Belfast cotton industry', *IESH* **VIII**, pp. 30-49.

Geary, F. 1989 'The Belfast cotton industry revisited', *IHS* **25**, 103, pp. 250-67.

Geary, F. and Johnson, W. 1989 'Shipbuilding in Belfast, 1861-1986', *IESH* **16**, pp. 42-64.

Gibbons, E. 2001 Mount Brown, Kilmainham', in E. Bennett (ed) 2001 *Excavations 2000: summary accounts of archaeological excavations in Ireland.* (Bray), pp. 84-5.

Giles, C. and Goodall, I.H. 1992 *Yorkshire textile mills. The buildings of the Yorkshire textile industry 1770-1930.* (London).

Gilligan, H.A. 1988 *A history of the port of Dublin.* (Dublin).

Gilmour, D. 1985 *Economic activities in the Republic of Ireland: a geographical perspective.* (Dublin).

Gordon Bowe, N. 1999 ' "The wild heath has broken out again in the heather field" ' Philanthropic endeavour and the Arts and Crafts achievement in early twentieth-century Kilkenny', *IADS* **2**, pp. 67-97.

Gould, M.H. 1991 'The effect of government policy on railway building in Ireland', *TNS* **62**, pp. 81-96.

Gould, M. and Cox, R. 2003 'The railway stations of George Wilkinson', *IADS* **VI**, pp. 183-201.

Gourvish, T.R. and Wilson, R.G. 1994 *The British brewing industry 1830-1980.* (Cambridge).

Green, E.R.R. 1944 'The cotton handloom weavers in the north east of Ireland', *UJA* 3rd series 7, pp. 35-9.

Green E.R.R. 1963 *The industrial archaeology of County Down.* (Belfast).

Green, W.S. 1902 'The sea fisheries of Ireland', in W.P. Coyne (ed) 1902 *Ireland Industrial and Agricultural.* (Dublin), pp. 369-86.

Greenhill, B. 'Steam before the screw', in B. Greenhill and R. Gardiner (ed) 1993 *The advent of steam.* (London), pp. 11-27.

Grene Barry, J. 1909 'Old Limerick bridges', *NMAJ* **1**, no. 1, pp. 7-13.

Gribbon, H.D. 1969 *The history of water power in Ulster.* (New York).

Gribbon, H.D. 1978 'The Irish Linen Board, 1711-1828', in L.M. Cullen, and T.C. Smout (ed) 1978 *Comparative aspects of Scottish and Irish economic and social history 1600-1900.* (Edinburgh), pp. 77-87.

Griffith, R. 1829 *The metallic mines of Leinster.* (Dublin).

Griffiths, D. 1993 'Marine engineering development in the nineteenth century', in B. Greenhill and R. Gardiner (ed) 1993 *The advent of steam.* (London), pp. 160-78.

Griffiths, J. 1992 *The third man. The life and times of William Murdoch 1754-1839 the inventor of gas lighting.* (London).

Grogan, P. 1999 'Some aspects of Lemuel Cox's bridge', *Decies* **55**, pp. 27-48.

Grogan, E. and Kilfeather, A.1997 *Archaeological inventory of County Wicklow.* (Dublin).

Grossart, A.B. (ed) 1886 *The Lismore papers.* Vol. 6 (London).

Guerin, M. 1988 *The Lartigue. The Listowel and Ballybunion Railway.* (Listowel).

Silverman, M.S. and Gulliver, P.H. 1986 *In the valley of the Nore. A social history of Thomastown, County Kilkenny.* (Dublin).

Guthrie, J. 1971 *A history of marine engineering.* (London).

Gwinell, M. 1985 'Some aspects of the economic life of County Wexford in the nineteenth century', *JWHS* No. 10, pp. 5-24.

Gwyn, D. 1991 'Valentia slate slab quarry', *JKAHS* **24** (1995 for 1991), pp. 40-57.

Gwyn, D. 2000 'Hoisting machinery in the Gwynedd slate industry', *TNS* **71**, pp. 183-204.

Gwyn, D. 2002 'A Welsh quarryman in county Tipperary: further light on Griffith Parry', *NMAJ* **43**, pp. 35-8.

Gwyn, D. 2005 'The landscape archaeology of the Vale of Ffestiniog', *IAR* **XXVII**, 1, pp. 129-36.

Hadfield, C. 1986 *World canals, inland navigation past and present.* (London).

Hadfield, C. and Skempton, A.W. 1979 *William Jessop, engineer.* (London).

Hague, D.B. and Christie, R. 1977 *Lighthouses: their architecture, history and archaeology.* (Llandysul).

Hall, E.G. 1993 *The electric age. Telecommunications in Ireland.* (Dublin).

Hall, Mr and Mrs S.C. 1841 *Ireland its scenery, character etc.* 3 vols. (London).

Halpin, T.B. 1989 'A history of brewing in Kilkenny', *OKR* **IV**, no. 1, pp. 583-91.

Halpin, T. 2000 'The malting and brewing industry in Kilkenny', in J. Bradley, D. Healy and A. Murphy 2000 (ed) *Themes in Kilkenny's history.* (Kilkenny), pp. 81-92.

Hamond, F. 1989 'The north wind doth blow: windmill evolution in Ulster', in R. Schofield (ed) *The history of technology, science and society 1750-1914.* (Jordanstown). Unpubl. Papers.

Hamond, F. 1991 *Antrim coast and glens industrial heritage.* (Belfast).

Hamond, F. 1997 'Power generation', in F.H.A. Aalen, K. Whelan and M. Stout (ed) 1997 *Atlas of the Irish rural landscape*. (Cork), pp. 225–33.

Hamond, F. 1997 'Communications in county Down', in L. Proudfoot (ed) 1995 *Down history and society. Interdisciplinary essays on the history of an Irish county*. (Dublin) pp. 599-628.

Hamond, F. 1998 (a) 'Water and weed: the exploitation of coastal resources', *ULS* **19**, no. 2, pp. 60-75.

Hamond, F. 1998 (b) 'Introduction', in F. Hamond (ed) 1998 *Taking stock of Ireland's industrial heritage*. (Dublin), pp. 1-3.

Hamond, F. 2000 'Conservation and industrial archaeology', in N. Buttimer, C. Rynne and H. Guerin (ed) 2000 *The heritage of Ireland*. (Cork), pp. 358-74.

Hamond, F. and McMahon, M. 2002 *Recording and conserving Ireland's industrial heritage*. (Kilkenny).

Hammersly, G.F. 1973 'The charcoal industry and its fuel 1540-1750', *EHR* 2nd series **26**, pp. 593-616.

Hammond, M.D.P. 1977 'Brick kilns: an illustrated survey', *IAR* **1**, no. 2, Spring, pp. 171-92.

Hammond, R.F. 1979 *The peatlands of Ireland*. (Dublin).

Hancock, H.B. and Wilkinson, N.B. 1962 'An American manufacturer in Ireland, 1796', *JRSAI* **xliii**, pt. 2, pp. 125-37.

Harvey, K. 1998 *The Bellews of Mount Bellew. A Catholic gentry family in eighteenth-century Ireland*. (Dublin).

Harvey, N. 1980 *The industrial archaeology of farming in England and Wales*. (London).

Hassett, J.J. (ed) 1993 *The history and folklore of Killenaule-Moyglass*. (Midleton).

Hasson, G. 1997 *Thunder and clatter. The history of shipbuilding in Derry*. (Derry).

Hay, G. and Stell, G.P. 1986 *Monuments of industry an illustrated historical record*. (Glasgow).

Hearne, J.M. 1998 'Quaker enterprise and the Waterford Glassworks, 1783-1851', *Decies* **54**, pp. 29-40.

Hearne, J.M. 2003 'The Star Ironworks' *JWHS*, no. 19, pp. 3-37.

Hedley, I. and Scott, I. 1999 'The St Helen's Iron Foundry' *IAR* **XXI**, pp. 53-9.

Hemans, G.W 1850 'An account of the construction of the Midland Great Western Railway of Ireland, over a tract of bogs in the counties of Meath and West Meath', *TICEI* **40**, pt 1, pp. 48-80.

Hemans, G.W. 1889 'On the railway system in Ireland', *TICEI* **xviii** (1888-9), pp. 121-57.

Hill, J. 1991 *The building of Limerick*. (Cork).

Hill, J. 1999 'Davis Ducart and Christopher Colles: architects associated with the Custom House at Limerick', *IADS* **II**, pp. 119-45.

Hills, R. 1988 *Papermaking in Britain 1488-1988. A short history*. (London).

Hills, R. 1989 *Power from steam. A history of the stationary steam engine*. (Cambridge).

Hindle, B.P. 1993 *Roads, tracks and their interpretation*. (London).

Hoad, J. 1997 *This is Donegal tweed*. (Inver).

Hogan, B. 1980 *A history of Irish Steel*. (Dublin).

Hogg, W.E. 1998 *The millers and mills of Ireland of about 1850*. (Sandycove, Dublin).

Hoppen, T. and de Brún, P. (ed) 1970 'Samuel Molyneux's tour of Kerry, 1709', *JKAHS* No. 3, pp. 59-80.

Hore, P.H. (ed) 1901 *History of the town and county of Wexford*. vol II. (London).

Howden, G.B. 1934 'Reconstruction of the Boyne viaduct', *TICEI* **60**, pp. 71-111.

Hughes, A.J. 1998 *Robert Shipboy MacAdam (1808-95) his life and Gaelic proverb collection*. (Belfast).

Hughill, P.J. 1999 *Global communications since 1844. Geopolitics and technology*. (Baltimore and London).

Hunt, T. 1999 'The origin and development of the Portlaw cotton industry 1825-1840', *Decies,* pp.17-32.

Hunt, T. 2000 (a) 'The Portlaw Cotton Plant: work and workers 1835-46' *Decies* **56**, pp.134-46.

Hunt, T. 2000 (b) *Portlaw, county Waterford 1825-1876. Portrait of an industrial village and its cotton mill*. (Dublin).

Hunter, D. 1978 *Papermaking. The history and technique of an ancient craft*. (New York).

Hurley, M.F. and Sheehan, C.M. 1997 'Ovens and kilns', in M.F. Hurley, O.M.B. Scully and S.W.J. McCutcheon 1997 *Late Viking age and Medieval Waterford. Excavations 1986-1992*. (Dublin), pp. 273-7.

Ince, L. 1984 *The Neath Abbey iron company*. (Eindhoven).

Inglis, H.D. 1834 *Ireland in 1834. A journey throughout Ireland during the Spring, Summer and Autumn of 1834*. 2 vols (London).

Irish, B. 1992 'Shipbuilding in Waterford', *Decies* no. 46, pp. 40-60.

Irish, B. 2001 *Shipbuilding in Waterford 1820-1882. An historical, technical and pictorial study*. (Bray).

Jackson, D. 1996 *J.G. Robinson. A lifetime's work*. (Headington).

Jackson, J. 1987 'Mallow-Lombardstown Canal', *Mallow Field Club Journal*, no. 3, pp. 22-9.

Jacob, W.M. 1944 'Kingsbridge terminus', *DHR* **6**, pp. 107-20.

James, J.G. 1981 'The evolution of iron bridge trusses to 1850', *TNS* **52**, pp. 67-101.

Jarrell, R.A. 1997 (a) 'James Ryan and the problem of Irish new technology in British mines in the early nineteenth century', in P.J. Bowler and N. Whyte (ed) 1997 *Science and society in Ireland. The social context of science and technology in Ireland 1800-1950*. (Belfast), pp. 67-83.

Jarrell, R.A. 1997 (b) 'Some aspects of the evolution of agricultural and technical education in nineteenth-century Ireland', in P.J. Bowler and N. Whyte (ed) 1997 *Science and technology in Ireland. The social context of science and technology in Ireland 1800-1950*. (Belfast), pp. 101-17.

Jenkins, J.G. 1973 *The Rhaedr Tannery*. (n.p.)

Jenkins, S.C. 1993 *The Cork, Blackrock and Passage Railway*. (Oxford).

Jenkinson, D. 1996 *The history of British railway carriages 1900-1955*. (York).

Jennings, P.O. 1982 'Concrete in railway engineering practice', *JIRRS* **14**, no. 89, pp. 413-21.

Johnson, D. 2002 'Friedrich Edouard Hoffmann and the invention of continuous kiln technology: the archaeology of the Hoffmann kiln and nineteenth century industrial development (Part 1)', *IAR* **xxiv**, 2, pp. 119-32.

Johnson, D. 2003 'Friedrich Edouard Hoffmann and the invention of continuous kiln technology: the archaeology of the Hoffmann kiln and 19th century industrial development (Part 2)', *IAR* **xxv**, 1, pp. 15-29.

Johnson, M. 1999 'Rethinking historical archaeology', in P. Paulo, M. Hall and S. Jones (ed) 1999 *Historical archaeology. Back from the edge.* (London), pp. 23-36.

Johnson, S. 1997 *Johnson's atlas and gazetteer of the railways of Ireland.* (Leicester).

Johnston, N. 1992 *The Fintona horse tram. The story of a unique Irish branch line.* (Omagh).

Jones, E. 1958 'Land reclamation in Belfast Lough', *UJA* **21**, pp. 132-141.

Jones, G. 2001 *The Millers. A story of technological endeavour and industrial success, 1870-2001.* (Lancaster).

Jones, G. 2003 'The introduction and establishment of roller milling in Ireland, 1875-1925', in A. Bielenberg (ed) 2003 *Irish flour milling – a history 600-2000.* (Dublin), pp. 106-32.

Jones Hughes, T. 1982 'The large farm in nineteenth century Ireland', in A. Gailey, and D. Ó hÓgáin (ed) 1982 *Gold under the furze. Studies in Folk tradition presented to Caoimhín Ó Danachair.* (Dublin), pp. 93-100.

Kane, R. 1845 *The industrial resources of Ireland.* (2nd edition, Dublin).

Kearney, H.F. 1953 'Robert Boyle, ironmaster', *JRSAI* **83**, pp. 156-62.

Kelleher, B. 2000 'Local authority perspectives', in N. Buttimer, C. Rynne and H. Guerin (ed) 2000 *The Heritage of Ireland.* (Cork), pp. 506-21.

Kelleher, G. 1992 *Gunpowder to guided missiles –Ireland's war industries.* (Belfast).

Kelly, J. 1983 'William Burton Conyngham and the North West Fishery of the eighteenth century', *JRSAI* **115**, pp. 64-85.

Kelly, J. 1986 'Prosperous and Irish industrialisation in the late eighteenth century', *JKAS* no. 3, pp. 441-67.

Kelly, R.J. 1902 'The coalfields of Connaught', *The Irish Builder* **XLIII**, 17 July, pp. 1324-5.

Kelly Quin, M. 1994 'The evolution of forestry in county Wicklow from prehistory to the present', K. Hannigan and W. Nolan (ed) 1994 *Wicklow history and society. Interdisciplinary essays on the history of an Irish county.* (Dublin), pp. 823-54.

Kemmy, J. and Walsh, L. 1997 *Limerick in old picture postcards.* (Zaltbommel).

Kennedy, M. 2000 *The LMS in Ireland. An Irish railway pictorial.* (Leicester).

Kennedy, M.L. and McNeill, D.B. 1997 *Early bus services in Ulster.* (Belfast).

Kerrigan, P. 1982 'Irish Coastguard stations 1858-67', *The Irish Sword* **14**, pp. 103-5.

Kerrigan, P. 1995 *Castles and Fortifications in Ireland 1485-1945.* (Cork).

Kettle, L.J. 1920 *Irish coal and coalfields.* (Dublin).

Kettle, L.J. 1922 'Ireland's sources of power supply III' *Studies* **xi**, no. 43, September, pp. 447-56.

Kierse, S. 1995 *Portraits of Killaloe.* (Killaloe).

Killeen, M. 1981 'Broadstone railway station to bus garage', *DHR* **34**, pp. 140-54.

Kilroy, J. 1996 *Irish trams.* (Dublin).

Kilroy, J. 1998 *Trams to the Hill of Howth, a photographic tribute.* (Newtownards).

Kinahan, G.H. 1889 'Economic geology of Ireland', *Jour. Geological Society Ireland* **8.**

Knight, P. 1997 *Stationary engine review.* (Ipswich).

Knight of Glin 1967 (a) 'A baroque Palladian in Ireland: the architecture of Davis Ducart – I', *Country Life* **cxlii**, 28 September, pp. 735-9.

Knight of Glin 1967 (b) 'The last Palladian in Ireland: the architecture of Davis Ducart – II', *Country Life* **cxlii**, 5 October, pp. 798-801.

Knox, H.T. 1907 'Notes on gig-mills and drying kilns near Ballyhaunis, County Mayo', *PRIA* **26C** (1906-7) pp. 263-73.

Lacey, B. 1979 'The archaeology of clay pipes and local history', *ULS* **4**, no. 2, pp. 17-19.

Laird Clowes, G.S. 1936 *The story of sail.* (London).

Landsdowne, Marquis of 1937 *Glanerought and the Petty Fitzmaurices.* (Oxford).

Lane, P.G. and Nolan, W.H. 1999 *Laois history and society. Interdisciplinary essays on the history of and Irish county.* (Dublin).

Langford, P. and Mulherin, S. 1982 *Cork City quay walls.* (Dublin).

Law, E.J. 1997 'The origins and early years of Kilkenny gasworks', *OKR* **49**, pp. 66-73.

Lay, M.G. 1992 *Ways of the world. A history of the world's roads and of the vehicles that used them.* (New Brunswick).

Leahy, E. 1844 *A practical treatise on making and preparing roads.* (London).

Leahy, E. 1901 'The sea fisheries of Ireland', *The Irish Rosary* **V**, no. 11, pp. 720-32.

Leckey, J. 1983 'The end of the road: the Kilcullen Turnpike 1844-1848 compared with 1787-1792', *JRSAI* **113**, pp. 106-20.

Lee, J. 1969 'The provision of capital for early Irish railways, 1830-53', *Irish Historical Studies* **16**, pp. 33-63.

Lee, J. 1993 'The golden age of Irish railways', in K.B. Nowlan (ed) 1993 *Travel and transport in Ireland.* (Dublin), pp. 110-19.

Lenihan, A. 1866 *Limerick its history and antiquities.* (Repr. 1991 Cork).

Lewis, J.H. 1984 'The charcoal-fired blast furnaces of Scotland: a review'. *Proc. Soc. Antiq. Scotland* **114**, pp. 433-479.

Lewis, S. 1837 *A topographical dictionary of Ireland.* 2 vols (London).

Lewis Smith, G. 1849 *Ireland, historical and statistical.* Vol III (London).

Lindsay, J. 1971 'Falls foundry 1900-14: A textile machinery firm in Belfast', *Textile History* **1**, pp. 350-62. (Newton Abbot).

Lindsay, J.M. 1977 'The iron industry in the Highlands, charcoal blast furnaces', *Scottish Hist. Rev.* **56**, pp. 49-63.

Loeber, R. 1991 *The geography and practice of English colonization in Ireland.* (Athlone).

Loeber, R. 1994 'Settlers' utilisation of the natural resources', in K. Hannigan and W. Nolan (ed) 1994 *Wicklow history and society. Interdisciplinary essays on the history of an Irish county*. (Dublin), pp. 267-304.

Lohan, R. 1994 *Guide to the archives of the Office of Public Works*. (Dublin).

Longfield, A.K. 1937 'History of the Irish linen and cotton printing industry in the eighteenth century', *JRSAI* **lxvii**, pp. 28-56.

Longfield, A.K. 1945 'Linen and cotton printing at Stratford-on-Slaney Co. Wicklow', *JRSAI* **75**, pp. 24-31.

Longfield, A.K. 1946 'Printed cotton from Robinsons of Ballsbridge', *JRSAI*, **76**, pp. 13-15.

Longfield, A.K. 1950 'Printing on linen and cotton at Richardstown and at Mosney in the eighteenth century', *CLAHJ*, pp. 131-5.

Longfield, A.K. 1955 'Notes on the linen and cotton printing industries in Northern Ireland in the eighteenth century', *Proc. Belfast Nat Hist and P. Soc.* **4**, (1950-55), pp. 53-68.

Longfield, A.K. 1960 'Harpur's "watering engine" for bleaching linens at Leixlip', *JKAS*, no. 8, pp. 443-8.

Longfield, A.K. 1967 'Prosperous, 1776-1798', *JKAS* **14**, no. 2, pp. 212-31.

Longfield, A.K. 1981 'Blarney and Cork: printing on linen and cotton and paper in the eighteenth and early nineteenth centuries', *JRSAI* **iii**, pp. 81-101.

Loudan, J. 1940 *In search of water being a history of the Belfast water supply*. (Belfast).

Lovett, M. 1988 *Brewing and breweries*. (Princes Risborough).

Low, G. 1865 'Description of a rock boring machine', *Proc. Inst. Mech, Engrs.*, pp. 179-200.

Lucas, A.T. 1960 *Furze: a survey and history of its uses in Ireland*. (Dublin).

Lucas, A.T. 1967 'Some traditional methods of cloth finishing', *The Advancement of Science* **24**, no 120, pp. 181-92.

Lucas, A.T. 1968 'Cloth finishing in Ireland', *Folk Life* **6**, pp.18-67.

Ludlow, C.G. 1989 'An outline of the salt industry in Ireland', in R. Scofield (ed) *The history of technology, science and society, 1750-1914*. (Jordanstown) unpubl. papers.

Ludlow, G.G. 1992 'An eighteenth-century Irish salt works as described in the Castleward papers', *UFL* **38**, pp. 25-33.

Lynch, J. 1995 'Belfast's third shipyard', *UFL* **41**, pp. 19-25.

Lynch, J. 1997 'The Belfast shipbuilding industry 1919-1933', *UFL* **43**, pp. 18-24.

Lynch, P. and Vaizey, J. 1960 *Guinness's Brewery in the Irish economy, 1759-1886*. (Cambridge).

Lyng, T. 1984 *Castlecomer connections*. (Castlecomer).

MacCotter, P. and Nicholls, K. (ed) 1996 *The Pipe Roll of Cloyne* (Rotulis Pipae Clonensis), (Cork).

Macneice, D.S. 1981 'Industrial villages of Ulster, 1800-1900', in P. Roebuck (ed) 1981 *Plantation to partition. Essays in Ulster history in honour J.L. McCracken*. (Belfast), pp. 172-90.

Madden, G. 1997 'The iron works of Sliabh Aughty', *Sliabh Aughty, East Clare Heritage Jnl*, no. 7, pp. 48-51.

MacGregor, D. R. 1993 (a) 'The wooden sailing ship under 500 tons', in *Sail's last century. The merchant sailing ship 1830-1930*. (London) pp. 42-5.

MacGregor, D. R. 1993 (b) 'The wooden sailing ship under 300 tons', *Sail's last century. The merchant sailing ship 1830-1930*. (London) pp. 20-41.

Maguire, H. (ed) 2002 *An introduction to the architectural heritage of county Kildare*. (Dublin).

Maguire, J.F. 1853 *The industrial movement in Ireland as illustrated by the national exhibition of 1852*. (Cork).

Maguire, W.A. 1995 *Belfast*. (Keele).

Major, J. K. 1967 *Finch Brothers Foundry, Stickelpath*. (Newton Abbot).

Major, J. K. 1985 *Animal powered machines*. (Princes Risborought).

Manning, C. 1997 'The bridge at Finnea and the man who built it', *AI* **11**, no. 39, pp. 29-33.

Manning, M. and McDowell, M. 1984 *Electricity supply in Ireland. The history of the ESB*. (Dublin).

Mannion, J. 1988 'The maritime trade of Waterford in the eighteenth century', in W. J. Smyth and K. Whelan (ed) 1988 *Common Ground. Essays on the historical geography of Ireland presented to T. Jones Hughes*. (Cork), pp. 208-33.

Marmion, A. 1855 *The ancient and modern history of the maritime ports of Ireland*. (London).

Marshall, M. 1989 *Ocean traders from the Portuguese discoverers to the present day*. (London).

Martin, J. 1982 'Robert Mallet: the engineering innovator', in R.C. Cox (ed) 1982 *Robert Mallet 1810-1881*. (Dublin), pp 101-17.

Maxwell, F. 1995 'A short account of the Castle Espie lime, brick, tile and pottery works', *Lecale Miscellany* **13**, pp. 58-60.

McCabe, C. 1992 'History of town gas industry in Ireland', *DHR* **xlv**, no. 1, pp. 28-40.

McCall, C. 'The tallest windmill in Ireland' *Jnl Geneaological Soc. Ireland* **4**, Autumn, pp. 34-40.

McCarthy, C.J.F. 1999 'An antiquary's notebook 20', *JCHAS* **104**, pp. 147-53.

McCarthy, M. 2002 'How the Shannon Scheme workers lived', in A. Bielenberg (ed) 2002 *The Shannon Scheme and the electrification of the Irish Free State* (Dublin), pp. 48-72.

McCarthy M. 2004 *High tension. Life on the Shannon Scheme*. (Dublin).

MacCarthy-Murrogh, M. 1986 *The Munster plantation: English emigration to southern Ireland 1583-1641*. (Oxford).

McCaughan, M. 1968 'Flax scutching in Ulster: techniques and terminology', *UFL* **14**, pp. 6-13.

McCaughan, M. 1989 'Dandy, luggers, herring and mackerel, a local study in the context of the Irish Sea fishery in the nineteenth century', in M. McCaughan and J. Appleby (ed) 1989 *The Irish Sea: aspects of maritime history*. (Antrim), pp. 121-33.

McCauley, E. 1999 'Some problems in building on the Fitzwilliam estate during the agency of Barbara Verschoyle', *IADS* **1**, pp. 99-117.

McCourt, D. 1962 'Weavers' houses around south-west Lough Neagh', *UFL* **8**, pp. 43-56.

McCracken, D.P. 1984 'The management of a mid-Victorian Irish iron ore mine: Glenravel, county Antrim, 1866-1887', *IESH* **xi**, pp. 60-72.

McCracken, E. 1957 'Charcoal burning ironworks in seventeenth- and eighteenth-century Ireland', *UJA* **20**, 123-38.

McCracken, E. 1965 'Supplementary list of Irish charcoal burning ironworks', *UJA* **28**, pp. 132-5.

McCracken, E. 1971 *The Irish woods since Tudor times. Their distribution and exploitation.* (Newton Abbot).

McCutcheon, W.A. 1963 'The Newry Navigation: the earliest inland canal in the British Isles', *Geographical Jnl.* **129**, pt 4, pp. 446-80.

McCutcheon, W.A. 1965 *The canals of the north of Ireland.* (Newton Abbot).

McCutcheon, W.A. 1966 (a) 'Water-powered corn and flax scutching mills in Ulster', *UFL* **12**, pp. 41-5.

McCutcheon, W.A. 1966 (b) 'The use of documentary source material in the Northern Ireland survey of industrial archaeology', *EHR* **19**, no. 2, 401-12.

McCutcheon, A. 1969 *Railway history in pictures. Ireland vol. 1.* (Newton Abbot).

McCutcheon, A. 1970 *Railway history in pictures. Ireland vol. 2.* (Newton Abbot).

McCutcheon, W.A. 1970 'The corn mill in Ulster', *UFL* **15/16**, pp. 72-98.

McCutcheon, W.A. 1976 'The stationary steam engine in Ulster', in C. Ó Danachair, C. (ed) 1976 *Folk and Farm, Essays in honour of A. T. Lucas.* (Dublin), pp. 26-50.

McCutcheon, W.A. 1977 *Wheel and spindle aspects of Irish industrial history.* (Belfast).

McCutcheon, W.A. 1980 *The industrial archaeology of Northern Ireland.* (Belfast).

McCutcheon (W) A. 1985 'The Salmon Leap power station, county Antrim', in C. Mollan, W. Davies and B. Finucane (ed) 1985 *Some people and places in Irish science and technology.* (Dublin), pp. 106-7.

McCutcheon, W.A. 1993 'The transport revolution: canals and river navigations', in K.B. Nowlan (ed) 1993 *Travel and transport in Ireland* (Dublin), pp. 64-81.

McDonagh, O. 1964 'The origins of porter', *EHR*, 2nd ser., **16**, no. 3, pp. 530-35.

McDonnell. A. 1863 'On the use of peat in steam engines and Siemens furnaces', *TICEI* **10**, pp. 155-64.

McDowell. R.B. 1941 'The personnel of the Dublin Society of United Irishmen, 1791-4' *Irish Historical Studies* **2**, pp. 12-53.

McErlean, T. and Crothers, N. 2002 'The early medieval tide mills at Nendrum: an interim statement', in T. McErlean, R. McConkey and W. Forsythe *Strangford Lough. An archaeological survey of a maritime landscape.* (Belfast), pp. 200-11.

McGill, D. 1988 'Early saltmaking in the Ballycastle district'. *The Glynns* **16**, pp. 15-21.

McGrath. W. 1981 *Tram tracks through Cork.* (Cork).

McGuigan, J.H. 1964 *The Giant's Causeway tramway. The pioneer hydro-electric railway.* (Oxford).

McGuire, E.B. 1973 *Irish whiskey. A history of distilling, the spirit trade and excise controls in Ireland.* (Dublin).

McIlmoyle, R.L. 1930 'Reinforced concrete railway bridges', *Concrete and Construction Eng.* **25**, pp. 37-45.

McMahon, M. 1998 (a) 'Ireland's industrial heritage', *AI* **12**, no. 2, 44, pp.11-13.

McMahon, M. 1998 (b) 'Recording the industrial heritage of Dublin's docklands', in F. Hamond (ed) 1998 *Taking stock of Ireland's industrial heritage.* (Dublin), pp. 8-11.

McMahon, M. 2005 'Zwei Dubliner Vororte bauten Irlands erstes Abwassersytem', *Industrie-Kultur* **6**, 2, p. 16.

McManus, M. 1984 'The potteries of Coalisland, Co. Tyrone: some preliminary notes', *UFL* **30**, pp. 67-77.

McManus, R. 2002 *Dublin 1910-1940. Shaping the city and suburbs.* (Dublin).

McMillen, M. 1991 'The first Macadam road', *TII* **23**, 2, May, pp. 30-31.

McNeill, D.B. 1953 'The little railway mania in Co. Antrim (1872-1882)', *UJA* **16**, 3rd series, pp. 85-92.

McNeill, D.B. 1969-1971 *Irish passenger steamers.* 2 vols (Newton Abbot).

McNeill, L. 1980 'The Sulphate of Ammonia Co. Ltd – Carnlough' *The Glynns* **8**, pp. 37-40.

McNeill, T. 1993 'Belfast's first industrial revolution', *Current Archaeology* no. 134, **XII**, no. 2, May/July, pp. 56-7.

McNeil, T. E. 1980 *Anglo-Norman Ulster. The history and archaeology of an Irish barony 1177-1400.* (Edinburgh).

McParland, E. 1991 *The Custom House Dublin.* (Dublin).

McParland, E. 2001 *Public architecture in Ireland 1680-1760.* (New Haven and London).

McQuillan, D. 1992 'Dredge suspension bridges in Northern Ireland: history and heritage', *The Structural Engineer* **70**, no. 7, April, pp. 19-26.

McQuillan, J. 1993 *The railway town. The story of the Great Northern Works and Dundalk.* (Dundalk).

McQuiston, I.B. 'The National Trust in Northern Ireland', in N. Buttimer, C. Rynne and H. Guerin (ed) 2000 *The Heritage of Ireland.* (Cork), pp. 554-61.

Measom, G.S. 1866 *The official illustrated guide to the Midland Great Western and Dublin Drogheda Railway.* (London).

Meehan, J. 1907 'The arms of the O'Rourkes: a metal casting from county Leitrim seventeenth-century foundries', *JRSAI* **36**, 2, pp. 123-141.

Meek, H. and Jope, E.M. 1958 'The use of brick in the north of Ireland 1580-1640', *UJA* 3rd series **21**, pp.113-14.

Meeks, C.L.V. 1956 *The railway station. An architectural history.* (New Haven and London).

Meghan, P. J. 1959 'The administrative work of the Grand Jury', *Administration* **6**, no. 3, pp. 247-264.

Meghan, P. J. 1986 'Turnpike roads in county Limerick', *Old Limerick Jnl.* **XX** (Winter), pp. 21-5.

Meridith, J. 1998 '"No small thing" Thomas Ivory's bridge at Lismore', *Irish Arts Review* **14**, pp. 102-14.

Messenger, B. 1988 *Picking up the linen threads.* (Belfast).

Middlemass, T. 1981 *Irish standard gauge railways.* (Newton Abbot).

Miley, G. Cronin J. and Sleeman, M. 2003 *Portlaw county Waterford. Conservation Plan.* (Heritage Council, np).

Mitchell, A. 1848 'On submarine foundations: particularly the screw-pile and moorings', *Min. Proc. Inst. Civ. Engrs* **7**, pp. 108-46.

Mitchell, J.M. 1985 'The development of the steam turbine generator and the ultimate eclipse of the reciprocating steam engine', *TNS* **58**, pp. 26-31.

Mokyr, J. 1981 'Irish history with the potato', *IESH* **8**. 20, pp. 8-29.

Mokyr, J. 1985 *Why Ireland starved: a quantitative and analytical history of the Irish economy, 1800-1850.* (London).

Monahan, A. 1963 'An eighteenth-century family linen business: the Faulkners of Wellbrook, Cookstown, Co. Tyrone', *UFL* **9**, pp. 30-45.

Montgomery, B. 2000 *Ford manufacture and assembly at Cork 1919-1984.* (Tankardstown).

Moore, F. 1996 'Ireland's oldest bridge', *AI* **10**, no. 38, pp. 24-7.

Moore, J. 1982 *Motor makers in Ireland.* (Belfast).

Moore, M. 1987 *Archaeological inventory of county Meath.* (Dublin).

Moore, M. 1996 *Archaeological inventory of County Wexford.* (Dublin).

Moore, M. 1999 *Archaeological inventory of County Waterford.* (Dublin).

Moore, M. 2003 *Archaeological inventory of county Leitrim* (Dublin).

Morris, J.H. 2001 'A catalogue of mines and mineral occurrences in Ireland', *JMHT1* **1**, pp. 25-37.

Morris, J.H. 2003 'The man engine house, Mountain Mine, Allihies, Co. Cork: A pictorial record of conservation works', *JMHTI* **3**, pp. 33-40.

Morris, J.H. and Brown, K. 2001 'The man engine house, Mountain Mine, Allihies, Co. Cork', *JMHTI* **1**, pp. 39-48.

Morris, J.H. and Cowman, D. 2001 'An index of listings of Irish mining companies, or mining companies which operated in Ireland, in the Catalogue of the Board of Trade records held in the Public Record Office, Kew, London', *JMHTI* **1**, pp. 9-18.

Morris, J.H., Lally, P. and Cowman, D, 2002 'A history and survey of mine buildings at the Tassan mine, Co. Monaghan', *JMHTI* **2**, pp. 41-9.

Morris, R. 1999 *The archaeology of railways.* (Stroud).

Morrisey, J. 2004 *A history of the Fastnet lighthouse.* (Dublin).

Moss, M. and Hume, J.R. 1986 *Shipbuilders to the world: 125 years of Harland and Wolff 1861-1986.* (Belfast).

Mulligan, F. 1983 *One hundred and fifty years of Irish railways.* (Dublin).

Mulligan, T. 1993 'Cornmills of Leitrim', *Breifne* 8, no. 3, pp. 359-83.

Mullins, M.B. 1863 'An historical sketch of engineering in Ireland', *TICEI* **6**, pp. 1-181.

Mullins, B. and Mullins, M.B. 1846 'On the origin and reclamation of peat bog, with some observations on the construction of roads, rail ways and canals in bog', *TICEI* **2**, pp. 1-48.

Murphy, D. 2000 'Portumna, sewerage works, Portumna' in I. Bennett (ed) 2000 *Excavations 1998: Summary accounts of archaeological excavations in Ireland.* (Bray), p. 88.

Murphy, D. 2003 'Ballynora, county Cork', in I. Bennett (ed) 2003 *Excavations 2001: Summary accounts of archaeological excavations in Ireland.* (Bray), p. 30.

Murphy, H. 1977 'The Drinagh Cement Works', *Old Wexford Soc. Jnl.*, no. 6, (1976-77) pp. 38-41.

Murphy, I. 1974 'Pre-Famine passenger services on the Lower Shannon', *NMAJ* **xvi**, pp. 70-83.

Murphy, J.C.J. 1948 'Kilkenny marble works', *OKR*, no. 11, pp. 14-19.

Murphy, M. 1980 'The Limerick Navigation Company, 1697-1836', *NMAJ* **xxii**, pp. 43-61.

Murray, K.A. 1949 'The Boyne viaduct', *JIRRS*, no. 5, pp. 14-17 (Repr. in *Jnl Old Drogheda Soc*, no. 6, 1989, pp. 5-18).

Murray, K.A. 1950 'William Dargan', *JIRRS* **2**, pp. 94-102.

Murray, K.A. 1970 'The Grand Canal Street Works', *JIRRS.* **9**, February, pp. 172-84.

Murray, K.A. 1977 'The Bretland tracklayer', *JIRRS* **13**, no. 73, pp. 74-88.

Murray, K.A. 1978 (a) 'Richard Osborne at Limerick – 1', *JIRRS* **13**, no. 77, pp. 294-300.

Murray, K.A. 1978 (b) 'Richard Osborne at Limerick – 2', *JIRRS* **14**, no. 82, pp. 320-34.

Murray, K.A. 1980 'Bray Head', *JIRRS* **14**, no. 82, pp. 71-84.

Murray, K.A. 1981 *Ireland's first railway.* (Dublin).

Murray, K.A. and McNeill, D. B. 1976 *The Great Southern and Western Railway.* (Wicklow).

Murray, P. 1988 'Novels nuns and the revival of Irish industries: the rector of Westport and the Foxford Woollen Mill 1905-1907', *Cathair na Máirt* **8**, no. 1, pp. 86-99.

Musson, A.E. and Robinson, E. 1969 *Science and technology in the industrial revolution.* (Manchester).

Neary, B. 1998 *The candle factory. Five hundred years of Rathborne's, master chandlers.* (Dublin).

Neely, W.G. 1983 *Kilcooley – land and people in Tipperary.* (Belfast).

Neely, W.G. 1989 *Kilkenny, an urban history, 1391-1843.* (Belfast).

Neeson, E. 1991 *A history of Irish forestry.* (Dublin).

Neil, D.G. 1992 *Portlaw: a nineteenth century Quaker enterprise based on a model village.* Occasional papers in Irish Quaker history no. 1. (Dublin).

Neill-Watson, J. 1993 *A history of farm mechanisation in Ireland 1890-1990.* (Dublin).

Nevell, M. 2005 'The social archaeology of industrialisation. The example of Manchester during the seventeenth and eighteenth centuries', in E. Conlin Casella and J. Symonds (ed) 2005 *Industrial archaeology. Future directions.* (New York), pp. 177-204.

Nevin, M. 1993 'General Charles Vallancy 1725-1812', *JRSAI* **123**, pp. 19-58.

Neville, P. 1874 'On the water supply of the city of Dublin', *Min. Proc. Inst. Civil Engrs* **38**, pp. 1-149.

Newham, A.T. 1964 *The Dublin and Lucan Tramway.* (Headington).

Newham, A.T. 1989 *The Listowel and Ballybunion Railway.* (Headington).

Newman, R. Cranstone, R.D. and Howard Davis, C. 2001 *The historical archaeology of Britain c. 1540-1900.* (Stroud).

Nicholls, K. 2001 'Woodland cover in pre-modern Ireland', in P.J. Duffy, D. Edwards and E. Fitzpatrick 2001 (ed) *Gaelic Ireland. Land, lordship and settlement, c. 1250- c. 1650.* (Dublin), pp. 181-206.

Nixon, F. 1969 *The industrial archaeology of Derbyshire.* (Newton Abbot).

Nolan, D. 1974 *The County Cork Grand Jury 1836-1899.* (Unpubl. MA, University College Cork).

Nolan, W. 1979 *Fassidinin: Land settlement and society in south east Ireland 1600-1850.* (Dublin).

Nolan, W. 2004 '"A public benefit: Vere Hunt, Bart and the town of New Birmingham, Co. Tipperary, 1800-18', in H.B. Clarke, J. Prunty and M. Hennessy (ed) 2004 *Surveying Ireland's past. Multidisciplinary essays in honour of Anngret Simms*. (Dublin), pp. 415-453.

Nowlan, K.B. 1993 'The transport revolution: the coming of the railways', in K.B. Nowlan (ed) 1993 *Travel and transport in Ireland*. (Dublin), pp. 96-109.

Oldham, C.H. 1909 *The woollen industry of Ireland*. (Dublin).

O'Beirne, G. and O'Connor, M. 2002 'Siemens-Schuckert and the electrification of the Irish Free State', in A. Bielenberg (ed) 2002 *The Shannon Scheme and the electrification of the Irish Free State*. (Dublin), pp. 73-99.

O'Brien, C. and Farrelly, J. 1997 'Forest glass furnaces in county Offaly', *AI* **11**, no. 4, Winter, pp. 21-3.

O'Brien, E. 1992 *An historical and social diary of Durrow, county Laois 1708-1992*. (Durrow).

O'Brien, J.B. 1985 'The Hacketts: Glimpses of entrepreneurial life in Cork 1800-1870', *JCHAS* **90**, pp. 150-57.

O'Brien, W. 1994 (a) *Our mining past – the metal mining heritage of Cork*. (Cork).

O'Brien, W. 1994 (b) *Mount Gabriel. Bronze Age mining in Ireland*. (Galway).

O'Brien, W. 1996 *Bronze Age copper mining in Britain and Ireland*. (Princes Risborough).

O'Brien, W. 2000 *Ross Island and the mining heritage of Killarney*. (Galway).

O'Brien, W. 2004 *Ross Island. Mining, metal and society in Ireland*. (Galway).

O'Carroll, D. and Fitzpatrick, S. (ed) 1996 *Hoggers, lords and railwaymen. A history of the Custom House Docks, Dublin*. (Dublin).

Ó Clearigh, N. 1992 *Valentia a different Irish island*. (Dublin).

O'Connor, G. 1999 *A history of Galway County Council*. (Galway).

Ó Danachair, C. 1970 'The use of the spade in Ireland', in R.A. Gailey and A. Fenton (ed) 1970 *The Spade in Northern and Atlantic Europe*. (Belfast), pp. 49-56.

O' Donnchadha, L. 1985 'Overton cotton mill', *Bandon Historical Jnl* **II**, pp. 3-7.

O'Donnell, M. 1992 'Road repairing in eighteenth century Tipperary', *THJ*, pp. 159-62.

O'Donnell, S. 1999 *Clonmel 1840-1900: anatomy of an Irish town*. (Dublin).

O'Donoghue, B. 1993 'The office of county surveyor – origins and early years', *TICEI* **117**, pp. 127-230.

O'Donovan, J. 1983 *Wheels and deals. People and places in Irish motoring*. (Dublin).

O'Dowd, P. 2001 'On roads and milestones in county Galway', *JGAHS* **53**, pp. 105-19.

Ó Drisceoil, D. and Ó Drisceoil, D. 1997 *The Murphy's story. The history of Lady's Well Brewery, Cork*. (Cork).

O'Dwyer, F. 1997 (a) 'Making connections in Georgian Ireland', *Bulletin of the Irish Georgian Soc.* **xxxviii**, pp. 6-23.

O'Dwyer, F. 1997 (b) *The architecture of Deane and Woodward*. (Cork).

O'Dwyer, F. 2000 'The architecture of John Skipton Mulvany (1813-1870)', *IADS* **III**, pp. 11-75.

O'Dwyer, F. 2002 'Building empires: architecture, politics and the Board of Works', *IADS* **V**, pp. 109-175.

O'Flaherty, G. 1988 'Mature and stately, through the city', in E. Healy, C. Moriarty and G. O'Flaherty (ed) 1988 *The book of the Liffey from source to the sea*. (Dublin), pp. 117-62.

O'Flanagan, N. 1992 'Dublin's current history', *TI* **24**, no. 5, pp. 42-4.

Ó Grádá, C. 1977 'The origins of the Irish creamery system 1886-1914', *EHR* **30**, pp. 284-303.

Ó Gráda, C. 1994 *Ireland: A new economic history 1780-1939*. (Oxford).

Ó Gráda, D. 1983 'The rocky road to Dublin: Transport modes and urban growth in the Georgian Age, with particular reference to the turn pike roads', *Studia Hibernica*, no. 22/23, pp. 128-48.

O'Hagan, K.J. 1980 'The iron mines of Glenravel', *The Glynns* **8**, pp. 5-10.

O'Keeffe, P.J. 1975 'The development of Ireland's road network', *TICEI* **98-9,** pp. 33-112.

O'Keeffe, P.J. 1980 'Richard Griffith: Planner and builder of roads', in G.L. Herries Davies and C.R. Mollan (ed) 1980 *Richard Griffith 1784-1878*. (Dublin), pp. 57-75.

O'Keeffe, P.J. 1996 *Alexander Taylor's roadworks in Ireland, 1780-1827*. (Dublin).

O'Keeffe, P.J. 1998 'Building the Wicklow military road', *TI* **30**, 2, pp. 22-5.

O'Keeffe, P. and Simington, T. 1991 *Irish stone bridges. History and heritage*. (Dublin).

O'Kelly, M.J. 1970 'Wooden water mains at South Terrace, Cork', *JCHAS* **75**, pp. 125-8.

O'Leary, E. 1914 'Turnpike roads of Kildare, Queens County, etc., in the eighteenth century', *JKAS* **viii** , pp. 118-24.

Ó Luing, S. 1975 'Richard Griffith and the roads of Kerry I', *JKAHS* **8**, pp. 89-113.

Ó Luing, S. 1976 'Richard Griffith and the roads of Kerry II', *JKAHS* **9**, pp. 92-124.

O'Mahony, Canice 1990 'Iron rails and harbour walls: James Barton of Farnderg', *CLAHJ* **22**, pp. 134-49.

O'Mahony, Canice 1993 'James Barton, engineer', *JIRRS* **18**, no. 122, pp. 262-74.

O'Mahony, Canice 1997 (a) 'Made in Manisty's', *JIRRS* 19, October, no. 134, pp. 439-43.

O'Mahony, Canice 1997 (b) 'Made in Manisty's', *JIRRS* 20, no. 137, pp. 128-31.

O'Mahony, Canice 1998 **'**Made in Manisty's', *CLHAJ*, no 3, **23**, pp. 318-328.

O'Mahony, Colman 1984 'Bygone industries of Blarney and Dripsey', *JCHAS* **89**, pp. 77-87.

O'Mahony, Colman 1986 *The maritime gateway to Cork. A history of the outports of Passage West and Monkstown, 1754-1942*. (Cork).

O'Mahony, Colman 1987 'Copper mining at Allihies, Co. Cork', *JCHAS* **92**, pp. 71-85.

O'Mahony, Colman 1989 'Shipbuilding and repairing in nineteenth century Cork', *JCHAS* **94**, pp. 74-87.

O'Mahony, Colman 1993 'Fishing in nineteenth-century Kinsale', *JCHAS* **98**, pp. 113-32.

O'Mahony, Colman 1997 *In the shadows. Life in Cork 1750-1930*. (Cork).

Ó Maitiú, S. 2003 *Dublin's surburban towns 1834-1930. Governing Clontarf, Drumcondra, Dalkey, Killiney, Kilmainham, Pembroke, Kingstown, Blackrock, Rathmines and Rathgar.* (Dublin).

Ó Maitiú, S. and O'Reilly, B.1997 *Ballyknockan a Wicklow stonecutters' village.* (Dublin).

O'Neill, T. 1982 'Tools and things: machinery on Irish farms 1700-1981', in A. Gailey and D. Ó hÓgáin (ed) 1982 *Gold under the furze. Studies in folk life tradition presented to Caoimhín O Danachair.* (Dublin), pp. 101-14.

O'Sullivan, A. 1984 'Tacumshin windmill – its history and mode of operation', *JWHS,* no. 9 (1983-4), pp. 66-73.

O'Sullivan, A.M. 1985 'Garrylough mill and the general development of watermills in county Wexford', *JWHS* **10** (1984-5), pp. 86-94.

O'Sullivan, A.M. 1996 'Castlebridge', in D. Rowe and C.J. Wilson (ed) 1996 *High skies – low lands: an anthology of the Wexford slobs and habour.* (Enniscorthy), p. 53.

O'Sullivan, A.M. 1997 'Pierces of Wexford', *JWHS* no. 16, pp. 126-42.

O'Sullivan, C.J. 1987 *The gasmakers. Historical perspectives on the Irish gas industry.* (Dublin).

O'Sullivan, J.C. 1908 'Description of the works in connection with the proposed additional storage reservoir at Roundwood, County Wicklow', *TICEI* **34**, pp. 94-120.

O'Sullivan, J. C. 1969 'Wooden pumps', *Folk Life* **7**, pp. 101-16.

O'Sullivan, M. and Downey, L. 2005 'Lime kilns', *AI* **19**, no. 2, Summer, pp. 18-22.

O'Sullivan, P. 1988 'The English East India Company at Dundaniel', *Bandon Hist. Jnl.* **4**, pp. 3-14.

O'Sullivan, P. 2002 'Glandore mines, county Cork: history and survey', *JMHTI* **2**, pp. 51-9.

O'Sullivan, W. 1937 *The economic history of Cork City from the earliest times to the Act of Union.* (Cork).

O'Sullivan, A. and Sheehan, J. 1996 *The Iveragh peninsula; an archaeological survey of south Kerry.* (Cork).

O'Toole, J. 1995 *Frederick York Wolseley, Mount Wolseley, Tullow, County Carlow.* (Carlow).

Owen, D.J. 1823 *The history of the town of Belfast.* (Belfast).

Owen, D.J. 1917 *A short history of the port of Belfast.* (Belfast).

Palmer, M. 1990 'Industrial archaeology: a thematic or period discipline', *Antiquity* **64**, no. 243, pp. 275-85.

Palmer, M. and Neaverson, P. 1998 *Industrial archaeology: principles and practice.* (London).

Parker, J.T. 1989 'Aspects of shipbuilding in Belfast, past and present' in M. McCaughan and J. Appleby (ed) 1989 *The Irish Sea: aspects of maritime history.* (Antrim), pp. 157-62.

Parsons, N.C. 1985 'The origins of the steam turbine and the importance of 1884', *TNS* **58**, pp. 21-6.

Patrick, A. 1996 'Establishing a typology for the buildings of the floor malting industry', *IAR* **18**, no 2, Spring, pp. 180-200.

Patterson, E.M. 1972 *The Clogher Valley Railway.* (Newton Abbot).

Patterson, E.M. 1982 *The County Donegal Railways.* (Newton Abbot).

Patterson, E.M. 1998 *The Castlederg and Victoria Bridge Tramway.* (Newtownards).

Pavía, S. and Bolton, J. 2000 *Stone, brick and mortar: historical use, decay and conservation of building materials in Ireland.* (Bray).

Peacey, A. 1996 *The archaeology of the clay tobacco pipe XIV. The development of the clay tobacco pipe kiln in the British Isles.* (Oxford).

Peacey, A. 1997 'Clay pipe kilns', in M.F. Hurley, O.M.B. Scully and S.W.J. McCutcheon 1997 *Late Viking Age and Medieval Waterford. Excavations 1986-1992.* (Waterford), pp. 375-9.

Pearson, L. 1999 *British breweries: an architectural history.* (London).

Pearson, P. 1991 *Dun Laoghaire Kingstown.* (Dublin).

Pearson, P. 1998 *Between the mountains and the sea. Dun Laoghaire-Rathdown County.* (Dublin).

Pearson, P. 2000 *The heart of Dublin. Resurgence of a city.* (Dublin).

Peatman, J. 1989 'The Abbeydale Industrial Hamlet: History and restoration', *IAR* **XI**, 2, pp. 141-54.

Perren, R. 1990 'Structural change and market growth in the food industry: flour milling in Britain, Europe and America, 1850-1914', *EHR,* 2nd ser., **43**, no. 3, pp. 420-37.

Phillips, H. 1922 'The Grand Canal: (2) The passenger boats', *JKAS* **10**, pp. 3-18.

Phillips Shirley, E. *et al.* 1865 'Extracts from the journal of Thomas Dineley Esq. giving some account of his visit to Ireland in the reign of Charles II' *Jnl. Kilkenny and South East of Ireland Arch. Soc.* **V**, part II, pp. 268-90.

Pochin Mould, D.D.C. 1978 *Valentia portrait of an island.* (Dublin).

Pochin Mould, D.D.C. 1993 *Discovering Cork.* (Dingle).

Pochin Mould, D. (D.C.) 1996 'The archaeology of the peat briquette. The Sliabh Each peat works', *AI* **10**, no. 3, Autumn, pp. 17-19.

Pollard, S. and Robertson, P. 1979 *The British shipbuilding industry 1870-1914.* (Cambridge, Mass).

Pollock, V. 1989 'Change in county Down fisheries in the twentieth century', in M. McCaughan and J. Appleby (ed) 1989 *The Irish Sea: aspects of maritime history.* (Antrim), pp. 135-44

Pollock, V. 1991 'The introduction of engine power in the county Down sea fisheries', *UFL* **37**, pp. 1-12.

Pollock, V.L. 1997 'The herring industry in County Down 1840-1940', in L. Proudfoot (ed) 1997 *Down history and society. Interdisciplinary essays on the history of an Irish county.* (Dublin), pp. 405-29.

Power, C. 2000 (a) 'Blackpool, Cork', in E. Bennett (ed) 2000 *Excavations 1998: Summary Accounts of archaeological excavations in Ireland.* (Bray), p. 17.

Power, C. 2000 (b) 'Blackpool, Cork', in E. Bennett (ed) *Excavations 1999: Summary Accounts of archaeological excavations in Ireland.* (Bray), p. 26.

Power, D. *et al.* 1992 *Archaeological inventory of County Cork. vol. 1 – West Cork.* (Dublin).

Power, D. *et al.* 1994 *Archaeological inventory of County Cork, vol. 2 – East and South Cork.* (Dublin).

Power, D. *et al.* 1997 *Archaeological inventory of County Cork, vol. 3 – Mid Cork.* (Dublin).

Power, P. 1918 'An ancient wooden water pipe', *JRSAI* **xlvii**, pp. 78-9.

Power, P.C. 1990 *History of Waterford city and county*. (Cork).

Power, P.C. 2000 *A history of Dungarvan and district*. (Dungarvan).

Power, T. 1977 'Richard Boyle's ironworks in county Waterford, part 1', *Decies* **5**, pp. 24-30.

Power, T.P. 1993 *Land, politics and society in eighteenth-century Tipperary*. (Oxford).

Prideaux, J.D.C.A. 1981 *The Irish narrow gauge railway*. (Newton Abbot).

Prunty, J. 1999 *Dublin slums, 1800-1925: a study in urban geography*. (Dublin).

Purser Griffith J. 1879 'The improvement of the bar of Dublin Harbour by artificial scour', *Min. Proc. Instn Civil Engineers* **58** (1878-9), pp. 104-43.

Purser Griffith, Sir J. 1912 'The twin Scherzer bridges on the North Wall quay, Dublin across the entrance to the Royal Canal and the Spencer Docks', *TICEI* **38**, pp. 176-204.

Purser Griffith, Sir J. 1933 'Peat in Ireland', *TICEI* **59**, pp. 246-72.

Quain, J.T. 1984 'Lime kilns of Ardmore and Grange', *Ardmore Jnl*, no. 1, pp. 14–17.

Quartermaine, J., Trinder, B. and Turner, R. 2003 *Thomas Telford's Holyhead Road: The A5 in North Wales*. (York).

Raistrick, A. 1970 *Dynasty of iron founders. The Darby's and Coalbrookdale*. (Newton Abbot).

Rapley, J. 2003 *The Brittania and other tubular bridges and the men who built them*. (Stroud).

Rees, J. 1993 *The life of Captain Robert Halpin*. (Dublin).

Rees, J. 1994 'Captain Robert Halpin, cable king', *TI* **25**, March, pp. 34-7.

Reilly, T. 1998 'Cappagh mine, an endangered heritage', *Mizen Jnl.* **6**, pp. 163-75.

Rennie, J. 1854 *The theory, formation and construction of British and foreign ports*. (London).

Rennison, R.W. 2002 'William Chapman', in A. Skempton *et al.* (ed) 2002 *A biographical dictionary of civil engineers in Great Britain and Ireland*. (London), pp. 124-32.

Reynolds, J. 1970 *Windmill and Watermills*. (London).

Reynolds, M. 1984 'Irish fine-ceramic potteries. 1769-96', *PMA* **18**, pp. 251-61.

Reynolds, T.S. 1983 *Stronger than a hundred men. A history of the vertical waterwheel*. (London).

Rhodes, J.N. 1970 *The London Lead Company in North Wales, 1692-1792*. (Unpubl. Phd thesis, Univ. of Leicester).

Richardstown, I. and Watts, M. 1995 'Finch foundry, Devon', *IAR* XVIII, 1, Autumn, pp. 83-95.

Riden, P. 1993 *A gazetteer of charcoal-fired blast furnaces in Great Britain in use since 1660*. (Cardiff).

Riordan, E.J. 1920 *Modern Irish trade and industry*. (London).

Rimmer, W.G. 1960 *John Marshall of Leeds: flax spinners 1788-1886*. (Cambridge).

Rix, M. 1955 'Industrial Archaeology', *The Amateur Historian* **2** (8), pp. 225-9.

Roberts, S. 1851 'An account of an iron breast wheel, 36hp, recently erected at the Newcastle Distillery in Galway', *TICEI* **4**, pp. 53-7.

Robertson, C.J.A. 1983 *The origins of the Scottish railway system 1722-1844*. (Edinburgh).

Robinson, P. 1985 'From thatch to slate: innovation in roof covering materials for traditional houses in Ulster', *UFL* **31**, pp. 21-35.

Robinson, P. 2000 'Water power and 'strong' farmers: the Weir family of Straid Mills, County Antrim', in T.M. Owen (ed) 2000 *From Corrib to Cultra. Folklife essays in honour of Alan Gailey*. (Belfast), pp. 39-47.

Robinson, T. 1986 *Stones of Aran: pilgrimage*. (Mullingar).

Roche, N. 1997 'The glazing fraternity in Ireland in the seventeenth and eighteenth centuries', *Irish Georgian Society Bulletin* **38**, pp. 66-94.

Roche, N. 1998 'Capturing the light: window glasshouses in Georgian Ireland', *IADS* **1**, pp. 195-9.

Roche, N. 1999 *The legacy of light: a history of Irish windows*. (Bray).

Rockwell, P. 1995 *The art of stoneworking a reference guide*. (Cambridge).

Rolleston, T.W. 1902 (a) 'The Irish milling industry', in W.P. Coyne, (ed) 1902 *Ireland Industrial and Agricultural*. (Dublin), pp.402-7.

Rolleston, T.W. 1902 (b) 'The Irish leather and boot-making industry', in W.P. Coyne (ed) 1902 *Ireland, industrial and agricultural* (Dublin), pp. 408-12.

Rolt, L.T.C. 1980 *Isambard Kingdom Brunel*. (Harmondsworth).

Rolt, L.T.C. 1985 *Thomas Telford*. (London).

Rolt, L.T.C. 1988 *George and Robert Stephenson. The railway revolution*. (London).

Rolt, L.T.C. and Allen, J.S. 1997 *The steam engine of Thomas Newcomen*. (Ashbourne).

Rothery, E.J. 1968 'Aneas Coffey', *Annals of Science* **23**, pp. 53-71.

Rowlands, D.J. 1977 *The Tralee and Dingle Railway*. (Dublin).

Rowledge, J.W.P. 1993 *Irish steam locomotive register*. (Leicester).

Rowledge, J.W.P. 1995 *A regional history of Irish railways. Vol. XVI Ireland*. (Trowbridge).

Ruch, J. 1970 'Coade stone in Ireland', *Quarterly Bulletin of the Irish Georgian Soc.* 13, pp. 1-12.

Ruddock, T. 1979 *Arch bridges and their builders 1785-1835*. (Cambridge).

Russell, P. 1981 'John Frederic La Trobe-Bateman (1810-1889) Water Engineer', *TNS* **52**, pp. 119-38.

Ryan, G. 1996 *The works. Celebrating 150 years of Inchicore railway works*. (n.p.).

Ryan, N.M. 1992 *Sparkling granite. The story of the granite working people of the Three Rock region of County Dublin*. (Dublin).

Ryan, R. 2001 'The butter industry in Ireland', *IESH* **28**, pp. 32-46.

Rynne, C. 1989 (a) 'The introduction of the vertical waterwheel into Ireland: some recent archaeological evidence', *Medieval Archaeology* **33**, pp. 21-31.

Rynne, C. 1989 (b) 'Early water turbines – An Irish history', *TI* 21, no. 3, p. 19.

Rynne, C. 1989 (c) 'The influence of the linen industry in the south of Ireland on the adoption of the water turbine', in R. Schofield (ed) *The history of technology, science and society 1750-1914*. (Jordanstown). Unpubl. Papers.

Rynne, C. 1992 'Milling in the 7th-century-europe's earliest tide mills', *AI* **6**, no.2, Summer, pp. 22-4.

Rynne, C. 1998 (a) *Technological change in Anglo-Norman Munster*. The Barryscourt Lectures III. (Kinsale).

Rynne, C. 1998 (b) 'The craft of the millwright in early medieval Munster', in M. Monk and J. Sheehan (ed) 1998 *Early Medieval Munster*. (Cork), pp. 87-101.

Rynne, C. 1998 (c) *At the sign of the cow. The Cork Butter Market 1769-1924*. (Cork).

Rynne, C. 1998 (d) 'The industrial archaeology of Cork city and its environs', in F. Hamond (ed) 1998 *Taking stock of Ireland's industrial heritage*. (Dublin), pp. 16-19.

Rynne, C. 1999 (a) 'Discussion' in Cleary, R. 'A vertical-wheeled water-mill at Ardcloyne, Co. Cork', *JCHAS* **104**, pp. 51-6.

Rynne, C. 1999 (b) *The industrial archaeology of Cork city and its environs*. (Dublin).

Rynne, C. 2000 (a) 'Water-power in medieval Ireland', in P. Squatriti (ed) 2000 *Working with water in medieval Europe: technology and resource use*. (Leiden-Köln-Boston), pp. 1-50.

Rynne, C. 2000 (b) 'The early medieval monastic watermill' in J. White Marshall and G. D. Rourke *High Island an Irish monastery in the Atlantic*. (Dublin), pp. 185-213.

C. Rynne 2000 (c) 'Industrial archaeology', in N. Buttimer, C. Rynne and H. Guerin (ed) 2000 *The heritage of Ireland*. (Cork), pp. 50-7.

Rynne, C. 2001 'Towards an archaeology of the post-medieval Irish iron industry: the blast furnace in south Munster', *JCHAS* 106, pp. 101-20

Rynne, C. 2002 'The industrial archaeology of the textile mill in county Cork, Ireland *c.* 1780-1930', *III Jornadas de Arqueologia Industrial*, pp. 409-22.

Rynne, C. 2003 'The development of milling technology in Ireland, *c.* 600-1875', in A. Bielenberg (ed) 2003 *Irish flour milling – a history 600-2000*. (Dublin), pp. 1-38.

Rynne, C. 2005 'Technological innovation in the early 19th century Irish cotton industry – Overton cotton mills, county Cork, Thomas Cheek Hewes and the origin of the suspension waterwheel', in E. C. Casella and J. Symonds (ed) 2005 *Industrial archaeology. Future directions*. (New York), pp. 205-16.

Rynne, C. and Dick, W. 1998 'The heritage of the stationary steam engine in Ireland, a chronological overview and the prospects for a national inventory', in R. Cox (ed) 1998 *Power from Steam*. (Dublin), pp. 29-42.

Rynne, E. 1967 'A Sheela-na-Gig at Clonlara, co. Clare', *NMAJ* **10**, pp. 221-2.

Sadlier, T.U. 1911 'Richard Castle architect', *JRSAI* **xli**, 31, pp. 241-5.

Scaife, W.G. 2000 *From galaxies to turbines. Science, technology and the Parsons family*. (Bristol and Philadelphia).

Scally, G. 1998 'Industrial archaeology survey of county Dublin', in F. Hamond (ed) 1998 *Taking stock of Ireland's industrial heritage*. (Dublin), pp. 4-7.

Scally, C. and Yates, M. 1985 'The industrial archaeology record for Northern Ireland', *ULS* **9**, no. 21, pp. 178-80.

Schmidt-Rutsch, O. 2004 '*Hibernia, Shamrock, Erin*: William Thomas Mulvany and the "Irish mines" in the Ruhr', *Decies* **59**, pp. 199-224.

Schofield, R.B. 1989 'Developments in bridge design and construction during the canal era of the late eighteenth century' in in R. Schofield (ed) *The history of technology, science and society 1750-1914*. (Jordanstown). Unpubl. Papers.

Scott, B.G. 1985 'The blast furnace in Ireland: a failed industry', *Medieval Iron in Society* **1**, pp. 286-96.

Scott, B.G. 1991 *Early Irish ironworking*. (Belfast).

Scott, C.W. 1906 *History of the Fastnet lighthouse*. (London).

Scott, R.H. 1863 'On the reduction of iron by the use of condensed peat at Creevelea, county of Leitrim', *Royal Dublin Soc. Jnl.* **iv**, (1862-3), pp. 43-48.

Schoen, L. 2002 'The Irish Free State and the electricity industry', in A. Bielenberg (ed) 2002 *The Shannon Scheme and the electrification of the Irish Free State*. (Dublin), pp. 20-27.

Schubert, H.R. 1957 *History of the British iron and steel industry*. (London).

Semple, G. 1776 *A treatise on building in water*. (Dublin).

Sexton, M. 1995 'Marconi's wireless telegraph station at Crookhaven', *Mizen Jnl*, no. 3, pp. 79-90.

Sexton, M. 2005 *Marconi. The Irish connection*. (Dublin).

Shaffrey, P. and Shaffrey, M. 1983 *Buildings of Irish towns: treasures of everyday architecture*. (Dublin).

Sharpe, A. 1995 'Development under derelict land grants', in M. Palmer and P. Neaverson (ed) 1995 *Managing the industrial heritage: its identification, recording and management*. (Leicester), pp. 133-36.

Sheehy, J. 1975 'Railway architecture – its heyday', *JIRRS* **12**, no. 68, pp. 125-138.

Shepherd, E. 1984 'The Cork, Bandon and South Coast Railway-1', *JIRRS* **15**, no. 14, June, pp. 209-18.

Shepherd, E. 1994 *The Midland and Great Western Railway of Ireland: an illustrated history*. (Leicester).

Shepherd, E. 2005 *Cork Bandon & South-Coast Railway*. (Hinckley, Leicester).

Shepherd, E. and Beesley, G. 1998 *The Dublin & South Eastern Railway. An illustrated history*. (Leicester).

Shorter, A.H. 1971 *Paper making in the British Isles. An historical and geographical study*. (Newton Abbot).

Simms, A. and Fagan, P. 1992 'Villlages in county Dublin: their origins and inheritance', in F.H.A. Aalen and K. Whelan (ed) 1992 *Dublin city and county: from prehistory to the present. Studies in honour of J.H. Andrews*. (Dublin), pp. 79-115.

Simmons, J. 1991 *The Victorian railway*. (London).

Simmons, J. and Biddle, G. 1999 *The Oxford companion to British railway history. From 1603 to the 1990s*. (Oxford).

Skempton, A. W. 1976 'A history of the steam dredger', *TNS* **47**, pp. 97-116.

Slattery, P.J. 1998 *The life and times of a railwayman. Limerick Junction 150 years on.* (Shannon).

Sleeman, M. 1990 'A lost tradition – the forgotten kiln', *Mallow Field Club Jnl*, no. 8, pp. 95-100.

Smith, A. 1841 (ed) *Robert Payne: A brief description of Ireland.* (Dublin).

Smith, C. 1746 *The history of the county and city of Waterford.* (Dublin).

Smith, C. 1750 *The ancient and present state of the county and city of Cork.* 2 vols (Cork Repr. 1815).

Smith, C. 1756 *The antient and present state of the county of Kerry.* (Repr. 1969, Cork).

Smith, C.F. 1994 *The history of the Royal Irish Automobile Club, 1901-1991.* (Dublin).

Smout, T.C. 2003 'Energy rich, energy poor: Scotland, Ireland and Iceland', in D. Dickson and C. Ó Gráda (ed) 2003 *Refiguring Ireland. Essays in honour of L.M. Cullen.* (Dublin), pp. 19-36.

Smyth, W.J. 1988 'Flax cultivation in Ireland: the development and demise of a regional staple', in W.J. Smyth and K. Whelan, (ed) 1988 *Common ground. Essays on the historical geography of Ireland.* (Cork), pp. 129-44.

Somers, E.N. 1924 'The industrial situation. Stimulants required for the speedier development of Irish resources. A review of old and new industries', *Milling*, 25 Oct., pp. xvii-xix.

Somerscales, E.F.C. 1992 'The vertical Curtis steam turbine', *TNS* **63**, pp. 1-52.

Spellisey, S. 1998 *The history of Limerick city.* (Limerick).

Sproule, J. (ed) 1854 *The industrial exhibition of 1853.* (Dublin).

St John Joyce, W. 1912 *The neighbourhood of Dublin its topography, antiquities and historical associations.* (Repr. 1988, Dublin).

St. John Lyburn, E. 1916 'Irish minerals and raw materials: opportunities for development', *Dept. of Agric. and Technical Instruction Jnl.* **16**, no. 4, pp. 621-8.

Starkey, D. 1993 'The industrial background to the development of the steamship', in B. Greenhill and R. Gardiner (ed) 1993 *The advent of steam.* (London), pp. 127-135.

Starrett, M. 2000 'The Heritage Council/An Chomlairle Oidhreachta', in N. Buttimer, C. Rynne and H. Guerin (ed) 2000 *The Heritage of Ireland.* (Cork), pp. 534-9.

Stephens, P. 2002 'Fennessy's Weir, Archersgrove, Kilkenny', in I. Bennett (ed) 2002 *Excavations 2000: Summary accounts of archaeological excavations in Ireland.* (Bray), pp. 175-6.

Stephens, P. 2003 (a) 'Mill Island and Green's Bridge Weir, Kilkenny', in I. Bennett (ed) 2003 *Excavations 2001: Summary accounts of archaeological excavations in Ireland.* (Bray), pp. 215-18.

Stephens, P. 2003 (b) 'Ormond Weir', in I. Bennett (ed) 2003 *Excavations 2001: Summary accounts of archaeological excavations in Ireland.* (Bray), pp. 218-19.

Stephen Briggs, C. 1995 'The conservation of non-ferrous mines', in C. Stephen Briggs (ed) 1995 *Welsh industrial heritage: review.* (London), pp. 32-41.

Stewart, A. 2002 *Coalisland, county Tyrone in the industrial revolution, 1800-1901.* (Dublin).

Stirling, D. 2005 'The Irish contribution to railway signalling', *JIRRS* **22**, no 156, pp. 194-201.

Storrie, M.G. 1968 'William Bald, surveyor, cartographer and civil engineer', *Trans. Inst. British Geographers* **47**, pp. 205-31.

Strattan, M. and Trinder, B. 1997 *Industrial England.* (London).

Stratten and Stratten 1892 *Dublin, Cork and the South of Ireland.* (London).

Sutton, G. 1993 'Waterford bridge 1793-1911', *Decies* **48**, pp. 49-53.

Swailes, S and Marsh, J. 1998 *Structural appraisal of iron-framed textile mills.* (London).

Swanton, W.A. 1992 *Cork's early buses. The story of Southern Motorways and its times.* (Cork).

Sweetman, R. 1988 'The development of the port', in J.C. Beckett, *et al.* 1988 *Belfast, the making of the city 1800-1914.* (Belfast), pp. 57-70.

Sweetman, R. 1989 'The development of Belfast Harbour', in M. McCaughan and J. Appleby (ed) 1989 *The Irish Sea: aspects of maritime history.* (Belfast), pp. 101-10.

Swift, M. 1999 *Historical maps of Ireland.* (London).

Symonds, J. 2005 'Experiencing industry. Beyond machines and the history of technology', in E. Conlin Casella and J. Symonds (ed) 2005 *Industrial archaeology future directions.* (New York) pp. 33-57.

Takei, A. 1994 'The first Irish linen mills', *IESH* **21**, pp. 8-38.

Tann, J. 1970 *The development of the factory.* (London).

Tann J. and Gwyn Jones R. 1996 'Technology and transformation: the diffusion of the roller mill in the British flour milling industry, 1870-1907', *Technology and Culture* **37**, no. 1, pp. 36-69.

Tatlow, W. 1902 'Irish waterpower and its development', *The Irish Builder*, 13 March 1902, no. 1018, **xliiii**, pp. 1063-65.

Taylor, P. 1994 *The West Clare Railway.* (Brighton).

Taylor, W. 1976 *The military roads in Scotland.* (Newton Abbot).

Taylor, G. and Skinner, A. 1778 *Maps of the roads of Ireland.* (1968 Repr. with an introduction by J.H. Andrews, Shannon). 2nd edition, Dublin, 1783.

Tighe, W. 1802 *Statistical observations relative to the County of Kilkenny.* (Dublin).

Thomas, E. 1999 *Coalbrookdale and the Darby family. The story of the world's first industrial dynasty.* (York).

Thomas, R. 1994 *Images of industry, coal.* (Over Wallop).

Thomson, R.S. 1981 'Leather manufacture in the post medieval period with special reference to Northhamptonshire', *PMA* **15**, pp. 161-175.

Thomson, R.S. 1982 'Tanning. Man's first manufacturing process', *TNS* **53**, pp. 139-56.

Tobin, M. 2001 'The Rosscarberry slate industry 1830-1954', *Rosscarberry Past and Present* **3**, pp. 55-65.

Tóibín, M. 1998 *Enniscorthy history and heritage*. (Dublin).

Torpey, N.V. 2004 (a) 'Irish railway bridges – 1', *JIRRS* **22**, no. 153, pp. 2-12.

Torpey, N.V. 2004 (b) 'Irish railway bridges – 2', *JIRRS* **22**, no, 154, pp. 122-8.

Townsend, H. 1810 *A general and statistical survey of the county of Cork*. (Cork) 2 vols.

Trinder, B. 1979 'The first iron bridges', *IAR* **III**, no. 2, Spring, pp. 112-21.

Tucker, G.T. 1987 'Millstone making in England', *IAR* **IX**, Spring, pp. 167–88.

Turner, M. 1996 *After the famine. Irish agriculture 1850-1914*. (Cambridge).

Twohig , D.C. 1990 'Excavation of three ringforts at Lisduggan North, County Cork', *PRIA* **90C**, pp. 1-33.

Tyrell. D. 1984 'Arklow Terracotta, Brick and Clay Company' *Arklow Hist. Soc. Jnl.* **3**, pp. 36-38.

Ville. S. 1993 'The transition to iron and steel' in *Sail's last century. The merchant sailing ship 1830-1930*. (London), pp. 52-72.

Wakefield, E. 1817 *An account of Ireland*. London.

Walker, J. and Nevell, M. 2003 'The origins of industrialisation and the Manchester methodology: the roles of landlord, freeholder and tenant in Tameside during industrialization, 1600-1900', in M. Nevell (ed) 2003 *From farmer to factory owner: models, methodology and industrialisation. The archaeology of the industrial revolution in North-West England*, *Archaeology North West* **6** (16), for 2001-3, pp. 17-26.

Walker, J. Nevell, M. and Casella, E. 2003 'Introduction: models, methodology and industrial archaeology', in M. Nevell (ed) 2003 *From farmer to factory owner: models, methodology and industrialisation. The archaeology of the industrial revolution in North-West England*, *Archaeology North West* **6** (16), for 2001-3, pp. 11-16.

Walsh, J. and Walsh, S. 1999 *In the shadow of the mines*. (Freshford).

Ward, M.W. 1982 'Millstones from la Ferte-sous-Joarre, France', *IAR* **VI**, Spring, pp. 203-10.

Watkins, G. 2001 *Stationary steam engines of Great Britain, the national photographic collections vol. 3.1: Lancashire*. (Ashbourne).

Watkins, G. 2002 *Stationary steam engines of Great Britain, the national photographic collections vol. 3.2: Lancashire*. (Ashbourne).

Watts, M. 1983 *Corn milling*. (Princes Risborough).

Watts, M. 1991 'Farm and threshing mill at Poltimore Farm, Farway, Devon', *IAR* **XIII**, no. 2, Spring, pp. 182-9.

Watts, W. A. 1984 'Contemporary accounts of the Killarney woods, 1580-1870', *Irish Geography* **xvii**, pp. 1-13.

Weatherill, L. 1971 *The pottery trade and north Staffordshire 1660-1770*. (Manchester).

Weir, R.B. 1978 'The patent still distillers and the role of competition in nineteenth century Irish economic history', in L.M. Cullen and T.C. Smout (ed) 1978 *Comparative aspects of Scottish and Irish economic and social history 1600-1900*. (Edinburgh), pp. 129-44.

Weir, R. B. 1995 *The history of the Distillers Company 1877-1939. Diversification and growth in whisky and chemicals*. (Oxford).

Weld, I. 1832 *Statistical survey of County Roscommon*. (Dublin).

Went, A. 1946 'Pilchards in the south of Ireland', *JCHAS* **51**, pp.137-57.

West, S. 1999 'Introduction', in S. Tarlow and S. West (ed) 1999 *The familiar past? Archaeologies of later historical Britain*. (London), pp. 1-15.

Westropp, T.J. 1918 'Dog wheel at Fortanne, Co. Clare', *JRSAI* **xlviii**, pp. 78-9.

Whelan, K. 1990 'The Catholic community in eighteenth-century county Wexford', in T. Power and K. Whelan (ed) 1990 *Endurance and emergence. Catholics in Ireland in the eighteenth century*. (Dublin) pp. 129-70.

Wigham, B. and Rynne, C. 2000 *'A life of usefulness': Abraham Beale and the Monard Ironworks*. (Blarney).

Wilkinson, G. 1845 *Practical geology and ancient architecture of Ireland*. (London).

Wilkinson, N.B. 1976 'An American powdermaker in Great Britain: Lammot du Pont's journal, 1858', *TNS* **47**, pp. 85-96

Williams, J. 1994 *A companion guide to architecture in Ireland*. (Dublin).

Williams, M. 1985 *Ford and and Fordson tractors*. (London).

Williams, R. 1989 *Limekilns and limeburning*. (Princes Risborough).

Williams, R.A. 1991 *The Berehaven copper mines Allihies, Co. Cork, S.W. Ireland*. Northern Mine Research Society. (Worsop).

Williams, M. and. Farnie, D.A 1992 *Cotton mills in Greater Manchester*. (Preston).

Willies, L. 1991 'Lead: ore preparation and smelting' in J. Day and R.F. Tylecote (ed) 1991 *The industrial revolution in metals*. (London), pp. 84-130.

Wilson, C.A. 1975 'Burnt wine and cordial waters. The early days of distilling', *Folklife* **13**, pp. 54-65.

Wilson, G. 1976 *The old telegraphs*. (London).

Wilson, G.B. L. 1974 'The small country gasworks', *TNS* **40**, pp. 33-43.

Wilson, P.N. 1957 'The waterwheels of John Smeaton', *TNS* **30**, pp. 24-48.

Wood, D. 1989 *The fateful day. A commemorative book of the Armagh Railway disaster June 12th 1889*. (Armagh).

Wood, J.L. 1981 'The introduction of the Corliss engine to Britain', *TNS* **52**, (1980-81), pp. 1-13.

Wood, J.L. 1985 'Rival forms of steam turbine', *TNS* **58**, pp. 33-8.

Woodrow, A. 1978 *A history of the Conlig and Whitespots Lead Mines*. (Sheffield).

Wyse Jackson, P. 1993 *The building stones of Dublin, a walking guide*. (Dublin).

Young, A. 1780 *A tour in Ireland with general observations on the present state of that kingdom* 2 vols. (London: Repr. 1970, A. W. Hutton ed).

Index